Tools for Analyzing the World's Languages
Morphology and Syntax

Summer Institute of Linguistics

Volume Editors

Eugene Loos
Laurie Nelson

Production Staff

Eugene Loos, Managing Editor
Laurie Nelson, Production Manager
Hazel Shorey, Graphic Arts

Tools for Analyzing the World's Languages
Morphology and Syntax

J. Albert Bickford

Based on earlier work by
John Daly
Larry Lyman
Mary Rhodes

A Publication of
The Summer Institute of Linguistics
Dallas

Copies of this and other publications of the Summer Institute of Linguistics may be obtained from

International Academic Bookstore
Summer Institute of Linguistics
7500 W Camp Wisdom Road
Dallas, TX 75236-5699 USA

Voice: 972-708-7404
Fax: 972-708-7433
E-mail: academic_books@sil.org
Internet: http://www.sil.org

Contents

Practical Helps

24   Hints for Linguistic Writing 351
25   Guide to Writing a Grammar Sketch 355
26   Grammar Filing 363
27   Lexical Filing 371

      References 381
      Index..389

Preface

Why this book?

I offer this book as a bridge builder.

Its intended audience is people who want to learn how to do basic linguistic analysis, particularly on languages about which little information is available. Such is the task facing many linguists, anthropologists, missionaries, and community development workers who are involved in some way with minority language groups. For such people, an 'Introduction to Linguistics' seldom provides enough concentrated attention to any one subdiscipline to enable them to do significant analysis. Graduate courses, on the other hand, are often too technical and specialized to be helpful for initial descriptive analysis and may incorrectly assume that students can acquire basic analytical skills on their own. At both levels, it is common to find courses that concentrate an inordinate amount of time on a relatively small sample of languages, so that students fail to learn, through personal experience, both the richness of variety that is possible in natural language and the striking similarities among all languages.

So, this is the first gap this book tries to bridge. I have aimed to provide an introduction to morphological and syntactic analysis, at the upper undergraduate level, which covers both general characteristics of language and specific theoretical formulations and does so through rich exposure to diverse data from the whole world. Although originally designed for courses offered by the Summer Institute of Linguistics, I hope it will also prove useful at other institutions.

This book also tries to bridge the gap that often exists between language description and formal linguistic theory. To the extent that a linguistic theory approaches explanatory adequacy, it can help guide a descriptive analyst in fruitful directions. On the other hand, if descriptive linguists are aware of theoretical claims and find conflicts with facts in particular languages, they then have an opportunity to make a theoretical contribution and thus further refine our understanding of universal language structure. It is hoped that this book will contribute to this symbiosis of linguistic description and linguistic theory.

I anticipate that a substantial percentage of readers will choose a career that includes the description of one of the thousands of languages that still remain largely undocumented. Some will spend years living in remote areas among speakers of these languages. They will learn their language and their unique perspective on this world we all share, while at the same time offering their linguistic expertise in such activities as orthography design, language planning, promotion of literacy, and development of a body of literature. This, in turn, will help bridge the gaps that separate language groups from each other and promote the spread of mutual understanding and true peace. My hope is that this book will be used by God to contribute to that end.

Why a new book?

This book developed out of a course offered by the Summer Institute of Linguistics at the University of North Dakota. It began as brief summaries of lectures by John Daly, which Mary Rhodes prepared in the mid-1970s. These summaries were later expanded by them and Larry Lyman into a full textbook (Daly, Lyman, and Rhodes 1981). I assumed responsibility for the course in 1982 and, with the permission of the original authors, began expanding and updating the textbook. When my early revisions began to be used elsewhere, it seemed right to polish and publish the new version separately.

I have organized the chapters according to a sequence of instruction that I have found to work well. It alternates between morphology and syntax, rather than attempting to treat one subject in full before starting the other. This helps keeps students' understanding well-rounded and balanced, which is especially important because there are often subtle ways in which steadily increasing understanding and competence in each area enhances the other. However, the material does lend itself to a certain amount of flexibility in sequencing, at least after the first ten chapters. If you are considering other possible orderings, consult the prerequisites that are included at the beginning of each chapter.

I have included a number of very practical suggestions about how to go about doing descriptive linguistics, especially in chapters 24–27. Although these suggestions may seem fairly obvious (at least to some people), I have found that many students will not figure them out on their own, and indeed some have a learning style that seems to be greatly helped by such 'down-to-earth' advice. I have tried to keep such suggestions genuinely helpful (rather than just recounting arbitrary or outdated traditions) and relevant to the main themes of the book.

Although only a few exercises are included in the current version, I and several colleagues in SIL expect to be able to distribute electronic copies of lesson plans and exercises that we have developed for use with this textbook.[1] In addition, since the structure of the text follows, to some extent, the outline of Daly, Lyman, and Rhodes 1981, the lesson plans and exercises published then should still prove useful. There are also several good collections of exercises produced by others (e.g., Nida 1949, Gleason 1955, Ohio State University Department of Linguistics 1994, Merrifield et. al. 1987, Jensen 1990).

My writing style is fairly personal and informal, at times even colloquial. This has been helpful in keeping my courses relaxed and fun; I believe it enables people to learn more. I hope that it is equally helpful in other cultural contexts, or at least, it will not seriously interfere with learning in countries where higher education is more formal than is typical in the United States.

Why this approach?

The primary aim of this book is to enable students to do linguistic analysis, hence the title *Tools for Analyzing the World's Languages*. These "tools" are theoretical devices drawn from a number of frameworks associated with the generative tradition. At the same time, I've included information about typology and function that is normally not part of a generative course. In both these ways, the book does not fall neatly into any one established theoretical camp, but rather tries to bridge the gaps between them and acquaint students early on with the basic understandings about language that linguists generally share, regardless of their theoretical orientation.

I've avoided teaching linguistic theory without providing a solid understanding of the phenomena that the theory is meant to account for. When this is done (as it too often is, whether deliberately or inadvertently), the result typically appears pointless and overly complex to students and promotes a divisive, cliquish, and uninformed adherence to a particular 'party line'. On the other hand, certain terminology, notation, formal analyses, and other theory-specific understandings can be very helpful in teaching about language. They can serve as an initial concrete conceptual structure on which to hang a person's growing linguistic understanding, and they help develop the habit of thinking about

---

[1] Contact TXSIL (7500 W. Camp Wisdom Rd., Dallas, TX 75236, USA, 972-708-7340) for further information.

language precisely and objectively. And since any understanding about natural language is at some level a theoretical understanding, one can never escape theory.

The goal, then, has been to use enough theory to highlight the characteristics of natural language structure covered in this book, but no more. I have sought to provide a level of theoretical sophistication which, based on my classroom experience, is appropriate for students' first exposure to grammatical analysis and which keeps the focus more on useful concepts than on specific formulations of them. The concern is not to make the text all-inclusive theoretically, but rather to include those linguistic phenomena that an analyst needs to deal with in the first few years of fieldwork. The phenomena may be talked about from some theoretical perspective, but the primary concern is with the phenomena themselves.

The principle frameworks drawn from are Transformational Grammar (starting with the Extended Standard Theory but with some more recent material from Government-binding Theory), A-morphous Morphology, Relational Grammar, Lexical Functional Grammar, Generalized Phrase Structure Grammar, Head-driven Phrase Structure Grammar, as well as the literature on linguistic typology, language universals, and functional approaches to linguistic structure. Since the book is structured around linguistic phenomena, it does not reflect the specialties of any one framework. The result, although somewhat eclectic and certainly in need of refinement at many points, works well pedagogically. It has shown itself effective in helping people learn the basic concepts of morphology and syntax, in equipping them to do grammatical analysis in the field, and in preparing them to move into any of a number of more refined theoretical frameworks.

I have not felt it necessary to incorporate the most recent ideas in linguistic theory. A substantial portion of the book is based on theoretical proposals from the 1970s and 1980s, though some are more recent. Important ideas need time to prove themselves, so I usually wait before incorporating a leading idea, notation, or formalism. Also, it often takes time to figure out an appropriate way to extract an important insight about language from the formalism within which it was first presented and blend it with the rest of the course.

For example, I have not incorporated traces or any other mechanism for dealing with unbounded dependencies (see Wasow 1985:201–2) nor introduced the concept of strict cyclicity, and I have retained stipulative forms of phrase structure rules and transformations, rather than attempt the more abstract approaches of more recent approaches to syntax. Since these devices are covered well in many other textbooks, and since the aim of this book is to prepare people for the first few years of fieldwork (in which theoretically-sophisticated analysis usually takes a back seat to determining the basic facts of morphological and intraclausal structure), I have largely ignored them.

When alternative lines of analysis are available for a particular phenomenon, I have usually presented just one that works reasonably well in most languages, sometimes indicating alternatives in footnotes. Presenting too many analyses would distract from the main goal of learning the phenomenon itself. For example, this is one reason for adopting only the 'silent verb' analysis of nonactive clauses that lack overt copulas (chapter 14 "Nonactive Complements," pp. 194), though other analyses are certainly possible.

Acknowledgments

Although I take full responsibility for these materials in their current form, they are not uniquely my own. They bear the contributions of numerous colleagues and students, far too many to even remember, let alone mention here. But let me try.

First of all, I owe a deep debt of gratitude to Larry Lyman, Mary Rhodes, and most especially John Daly, who graciously allowed me to use their work as the starting point of this book. Though I have made numerous changes, many of their contributions still remain. John especially established the basic organization of the material and provided much valuable counsel to me both as I first began revising his work and later as my version approached final form. Indeed, at one time John and I planned to coauthor this revision. Though still supportive of the project, in the end he felt it best to remove his name as an author. I hope that the way he, Mary, and Larry are listed on the title page adequately expresses the important part they played in developing this book.

Rob Starr successfully urged me to incorporate many significant theoretical ideas during the early 1980s. Erin Hesse prepared the initial draft of chapter 2 "Standard Grammatical Terminology" and Neil Baumgartner did much of the basic research for the first draft of chapter 20 "Word Division and Clitics." More intangible contributions have been made by teaching assistants who have made numerous helpful suggestions in the course of their duties; of these, three stand out for length of service: Betty Brown, Neil Baumgartner, and Jane Speck. Others who have given very useful comments include (in no particular order) Anita Bickford, Tom Phinnemore, Penny Phinnemore, John Roberts, Arto Antilla, Steve Quakenbush, David Payne, David Weber, Mike Maxwell, Doris Bartholomew, Russ Cooper, Carole Jamieson Capen, Shedd Waskosky, Ben Unseth, Rick Thiele, Laura Nelson de Dios, Chuck Speck, Dan Friesen, Beth Merrill, Tom Bogle, Cory Schwepler, Fred Depp, and certainly many others whom I have unfortunately forgotten. Eugene Loos and Laurie Nelson have been very supportive in their roles as editors for this book and have pointed out many places in which the core content of the book (in addition to its appearance) could be improved. Finally, there are the hundreds of students who struggled with rough early versions, who helped refine them by identifying places where improvement was needed, and who did so both enthusiastically and kindly. Thank you, all of you!

Steve Marlett has been a faithful friend for my entire linguistic career and has encouraged and supported me in many ways, as a teacher, boss, and colleague. He is the one who suggested the present title, which so well summarizes the nature and intent of this book. He and many other colleagues in the Mexico Branch of SIL have graciously released me from responsibilities in the branch in order to teach at the University of North Dakota during the summers and to work on this book even at other times.

I have appreciated the opportunity to interact with other scholars about the theoretical foundations of the course. Sandra Chung, Mark Baker, and Jim McCloskey have been especially helpful in this regard.

John Daly's first version of these materials relied heavily on Tagmemics. Though this dependence is no longer apparent, I retain a deep debt of gratitude to my colleagues Ken Pike, Ben Elson, Bob Longacre, Velma Pickett, David Thomas, and others who developed it, demonstrated its practical application in linguistic fieldwork, and helped nurture many young linguistic minds on it. Not only that, they established an environment in which people like John and myself were encouraged to pursue different sets of theoretical assumptions, allowing this book to flower and grow.

I am especially grateful to my wife, Anita, who keyboarded early versions of several chapters, read and commented on the whole book several times, and most important of all, put up with her husband's preoccupation with it over more than fifteen years. (This includes times when she was working on books of her own and would have preferred to concentrate on them more than is possible when there are two simultaneous major projects in one family.) Her encouragement and advice has been invaluable many times and helped make it possible to carry this long project through to completion. My children, too, have been understanding and supportive, especially through the final push to publication.

And, of course, supreme thanks go to my Lord and Savior, without whose help absolutely none of this would have been possible. I belong to him, and so does this book.

Albert Bickford
Summer Institute of Linguistics
P.O. Box 8987
Catalina AZ 85738-0987
U.S.A.

albert_bickford@sil.org

17 October 1998

Preliminaries

1
Introduction

1.1. Goals

As you study this book, I trust that you will gain three main things from it:

◎ increased understanding about language
◎ an introduction to linguistic theory
◎ analytical skills

First, I hope you will gain an understanding of what language is, specifically in the areas of MORPHOLOGY (the study of word structure) and SYNTAX (the study of sentence structure). This includes characteristics that are found in all or most languages as well as ways that languages typically differ from one another (and in particular how they may differ from your native language).

Second, I hope you will become familiar with important terminology and theoretical concepts used by linguists to describe languages. Theoretical concepts are essential for organizing our understanding of language. Most of these are shared in some form by virtually all linguists, although some are unique to one or another theoretical framework. This book is built primarily around a set of linguistic theories called generative grammar, containing many ideas that all generative theories share in common plus some specific ideas from particular theories that are especially useful.[1]

Third, I hope you will come away from this book with more than a head crammed with facts about language—I want you to be able to actively *do* linguistic analysis. When faced with a language which no linguist has ever studied, what can you do to figure out the grammar yourself? Of course, such skills must be learned by doing, not reading, so much of this learning can only take place while working directly with language data yourself. This book is intended to be used with a classroom course, accompanied by suitable exercises; without them you will miss out on developing many important analytical skills. But, the book will at least give you a head start, by giving hints, techniques, and practical suggestions that you can apply to your analytical work.

Finally, beyond these 'official' educational goals, I have an unofficial agenda as well. I hope that many of you will catch the excitement I have experienced in studying languages and linguistics and will seriously consider making a career of it. There are thousands of languages in the world waiting to be studied and so many things yet to learn about who we humans are as linguistic creatures. There are also multitudes of places where linguists can make positive contributions among minority language groups, both by collaborating with them in literacy and education and, through research

---

[1]For details on this, see the Preface.

and publication, helping increase the prestige of one of their most intimate possessions: their language. I hope that you will seriously consider joining me in these endeavors.

Not everyone should be a linguist, of course. Some of you may discover that you would not enjoy or don't have the aptitude for a career involving linguistics. As unpleasant as this discovery may be, it is better to make it sooner than later. If through this book I have provided you with an accurate picture of what linguistics is so you can make good decisions about your future, I will be pleased and feel my work to have been worthwhile, no matter what you decide.

1.2. How to read the book

There are a number of features in each chapter that will help you learn the material in it.

Most chapters begin with a statement of goals. These are stated not in terms of what I have tried to do or what your instructor will do, but in terms of what *you* should be able to do after learning the material in the chapter. (To fully achieve them, you will need to practice using the concepts by analyzing data in class or in homework.) You can use these goals as a checklist to help determine if you have mastered the material in the chapter.

After the list of goals there is a list of the most important chapters that you should have read previously. I've included this because some of the chapters can be read out of order, so this will alert you and your instructors to which ones must be read in a certain order. I also suggest that before you read a chapter, you take five minutes to review the chapters mentioned as prerequisites; this will make the new chapter easier to understand.

From time to time there are short questions for you to answer before continuing reading. The answers to them are in the footnotes. You can use these to check your comprehension of what you've read so far.

At the end of most chapters, there are several sections:

- Review of key terms: a brief synopsis of the important terminology introduced in that chapter
- Questions for analysis: questions to guide your analysis of the topic discussed in the chapter
- Sample descriptions: brief examples of how to describe data like that discussed in the chapter
- For further reading: other things that you might want to read, if you have a particular interest in the topic, taken from more advanced textbooks and some of the more important original literature

There is an extensive system of cross-references and an index which can help you locate material in different parts of the book. The index includes languages, names of most linguists, special symbols, terminology, and important concepts which are mentioned throughout the book. Page numbers in italics indicate places that I expect will provide the most helpful information on an index entry.

I've added footnotes generously, but they are not essential for understanding the text. They are addressed primarily to instructors and other experienced linguists who may be using the book. Some answer questions that would not occur to most people encountering this material for the first time, but may be of interest to some students. Others point out further fine points that would be distracting or confusing if included in the main text. Others give references to the linguistic literature, acknowledging the works on which this textbook is based; compared to what is mentioned in the 'For further reading' sections, these footnotes tend to be more technical. But, you be the judge: read the footnotes if you find them helpful; if not, feel free to ignore any or all of them.

1.3. For further reading

This book assumes a general familiarity with linguistics as a whole, such as you might get in a university course called "Introduction to Linguistics." If you do not have this background, get a good introductory textbook, such as Fromkin and Rodman 1998 or Akmajian, Demers, Farmer, and

Harnish 1990. (It is standard practice in linguistics to give bibliographic citations by author and date; you can look up the complete references in the bibliography.)

In addition, chapter 1 of Radford 1988 provides an excellent introduction to key concepts of modern linguistics, especially generative grammar. I have found it to be essential reading for my own students, as it answers most of the questions that tend to pester them in the first few chapters of this book. Rather than attempt my own (probably inferior) explanation of this material, I simply urge you to read Radford's treatment of it. More generally, his book provides one of the clearest introductions available to Transformational Grammar (the most famous theory in the generative tradition, and one which is very important in this book). You will see several references to it in the 'For further reading' sections.

2
Standard Grammatical Terminology

2.1. Goals and prerequisites

This chapter will help you do the following:

- ◎ review terminology that is commonly used in grammars written for nonlinguists and use it appropriately to describe examples in your native language (whether English or something else) that are similar to those in this chapter
- ◎ relax a bit in spite of what might seem like a terminological blizzard during the first few chapters of this book (or the first few days of any course that uses it)

This chapter provides a brief review of terminology that you probably have encountered in your previous studies of the grammar of English or some other language. If you have not encountered these terms before, it will help you start learning them. It may usefully be read before any of chapters 3, 4, or 5.

Most of these terms are explained with more precision later in the book;[1] the explanations here are only what we need to get started. Even getting started can be awkward, though; some of the early explanations assume at least a vague familiarity with terms explained later in the chapter. (As in all subjects, it is not possible to provide definitions for every term without becoming circular.) So, read the chapter more than once if necessary, and it should become clearer each time.

2.2. Word classes (parts of speech)

Words can be divided into classes or categories, traditionally called PARTS OF SPEECH. The usual classes that are mentioned in traditional grammars are explained below. (See chapter 5 "Introduction to Syntax" for further examples and explanations for most of them.)

---

[1]Most of the definitions and explanations in this chapter are comparable to what students may have encountered in courses about the grammar of their native language or in foreign language classes. Many definitions beg for considerable refinement, and I have attempted to offer better explanations later. For a review, however, I have felt it best to keep the explanations simple and familiar. Further, I have confined the examples almost exclusively to English, under the assumption that most readers are either native English speakers or have sufficient familiarity with traditional approaches to English grammar to follow the examples.

Noun

A NOUN refers to a person, place, thing, idea, or abstract concept. Within a clause, a noun typically functions as any one of the following: subject of the verb, direct object of the verb, indirect object of the verb, or object of a preposition.

Nouns can be subdivided into smaller groups in several ways. One subdivision is into proper and common nouns. A PROPER noun is the name of a particular individual, location, or product, e.g., *Becky, Lyndon Johnson, Canada, New York, Toyota, Nestlé Quik*. A COMMON noun is a generic name for any member of a group that shares certain characteristic properties: e.g., *professor, building, nomination*.

Another subdivision is into count and mass nouns. A COUNT noun refers to items which can be counted (i.e., which can co-occur with a numeral), e.g., *boy, pencil, carrot, car*. A MASS noun refers to items which cannot be counted, because they are conceived of as an undifferentiated mass, e.g., *water, sand, corn, oxygen*. Mass nouns are always singular in form.

Pronoun

PRONOUNS are used as replacements for nouns and noun phrases. Like nouns, pronouns refer to people, places, things, ideas, or concepts. They occur in the same positions in the clause as noun phrases. The basic difference between nouns and pronouns is that pronouns refer to someone/something in terms of their role in the speech situation. For instance, *I* is the designation that a speaker uses for himself, and *you* is the designation the speaker uses for the person(s) being talked to. When someone new starts speaking, these pronouns suddenly refer to a new set of individuals; their interpretation depends on a fact of the speech situation (who is speaking to whom).

English personal pronouns can be classified according to person, number, gender, and how they are used within a sentence.

(1)

		Subject		Object		Possessive		Reflexive	
		Sg.	Pl.	Sg.	Pl.	Sg.	Pl.	Sg.	Pl.
first person		*I*	*we*	*me*	*us*	*my*	*our*	*myself*	*ourselves*
second person		*you*				*your*		*yourself*	*yourselves*
third person	masculine	*he*		*him*		*his*		*himself*	
	feminine	*she*	*they*	*her*	*them*	*her*	*their*	*herself*	*themselves*
	neuter	*it*		*it*		*its*		*itself*	

There are also INDEFINITE PRONOUNS, e.g., *one, ones, some, someone, something,* and what could be called POSSESSED PRONOUNS (referring to the thing possessed), e.g., *mine, ours, yours, his, hers, theirs*.

Verb

A VERB is the core of a clause, the word that links the different parts of the clause together. Verbs generally indicate an action, a relation, or an experience: e.g., *walk, punch, undergird, own, realize*.

Adjective

An ADJECTIVE describes a property or characteristic of a noun, e.g., *beautiful, large, ordinary, overwhelming*. Adjectives in some sentence positions can also modify pronouns, as in 'He was greatly *embarrassed*'. Note that some things traditionally called adjectives really belong in separate classes: quantifiers, articles, or demonstratives (see below).

Quantifier

A QUANTIFIER tells how many or how much there is of an entity, e.g., *one, two, some, all, many.* A NUMERAL is a special type of quantifier which indicates a precise number: e.g., *zero, one, two, three, first, second, third.*

Adverb

According to traditional grammar, an ADVERB modifies an adjective, another adverb, a verb, or a whole clause or sentence. Adverbs are used for a variety of purposes.

(2)   Function   Example

degree	*very, completely*
manner	*quickly, well*
certainty	*possibly, certainly*
circumstance	*early, later, there, then*
negation	*not*

In other words, adverbs are a mixed bag and probably shouldn't be grouped together. (See chapter 9 "Obliques," p. 98, for a more detailed explanation and a better analysis.)

Article

An ARTICLE helps pick out individuals designated by common nouns. In English, the DEFINITE article, *the,* indicates that the speaker assumes that the person spoken to knows which individual the noun refers to. The INDEFINITE article, *a,* indicates that the speaker does not assume that the one spoken to can identify the individual(s) the noun refers to.[2]

Demonstrative

DEMONSTRATIVES point out an object (person or thing) in time or space. Demonstratives may either function in place of or alongside a noun (i.e., either as a pronoun or as a modifier of a noun). English demonstratives can be classified by number and according to whether they locate the object near the speaker (PROXIMAL) or away from the speaker (DISTAL).

(3)

	Singular	Plural
Proximal	*this*	*these*
Distal	*that*	*those*

For further discussion, see chapter 7 "Embedding and Noun Phrase Structure," p. 71.

Preposition

A PREPOSITION indicates the relation of a following noun phrase to the rest of the sentence, e.g., *to, with, from, by, for, of.* The following noun phrase is called the OBJECT of the preposition. (For further discussion, see chapter 9 "Obliques," p. 95.)

---

[2]In this book, the term ARTICLE is seldom used. Articles are usually analyzed as a special type of DETERMINER; see chapter 5 "Introduction to Syntax" (p. 39).

Conjunction

A CONJUNCTION joins two units to make a larger unit. For example, the conjunction *and* can join two noun phrases to form a larger phrase *(John and his brother)* or two verbs to form a compound verb *(jumped and ran)*.

Conjunctions are either coordinate or subordinate. COORDINATING (or COORDINATE) CONJUNCTIONS are used when the two units joined together are alike and of equal importance, e.g., *and, or, but*. SUBORDINATING (or SUBORDINATE) CONJUNCTIONS are used when the units joined have different importance, e.g., *because, since, although, if, before, while, when, so that*. (See below under CLAUSE for further examples.)

2.3. Clauses and other units of speech

Clause

A CLAUSE includes at least a subject (either expressed or implied in a command) and a verb:

(4)   *Birds fly.*
        (You) scram!

The following are not usually considered clauses, because they lack a verb and/or a subject:

(5)   *Oh no!*
        Thank you.
        Wow!

Clauses are classified depending on whether they can stand alone. An INDEPENDENT (or MAIN) clause can stand alone as a sentence.

(6)   *Arthur is handsome.*

An EMBEDDED (or SUBORDINATE or DEPENDENT) clause cannot stand alone as a sentence.

(7)   *After we heard the voice...*
        ...because Harold refused to listen.

There are three main types of embedded clauses: complement, relative, and adverbial.[3] A COMPLEMENT CLAUSE completes an independent clause by functioning as its subject or direct object.

(8)   *[That the world is round] bothers me.*
        They do not know [what they are doing].

A RELATIVE CLAUSE functions like an adjective within a noun phrase, helping to identify what the noun phrase refers to or providing additional information about it.

(9)   *The true light [that gives light to everyone]...*
        The man [who was king]...

An ADVERBIAL CLAUSE functions like an adverb inside a main clause.

---

[3] ADVERBIAL CLAUSE is the traditional label for what this book later calls an OBLIQUE CLAUSE.

(10)   *[When I have time,] I'll sleep.*
       [If you really want to,] go ahead.

The words like *when* and *if* that introduce adverbial clauses are generally called SUBORDINATING CONJUNCTIONS. (For more on embedded clauses, see chapter 22.)
    Two independent clauses can also be joined by a COORDINATING CONJUNCTION.

(11)   *[He spoke to us,]* **and** *[we answered him].*
       [Grammar can be fun,] **but** *[not everyone realizes this].*

Sentence

A SENTENCE is traditionally described as a group of words expressing a complete thought, consisting of one or more clauses. (See examples above, under CLAUSE.)

Phrase

A PHRASE is traditionally considered a group of words acting as a single unit, but which is not a complete clause. Phrases are named after their principal member. For example, a NOUN PHRASE is built around a noun, e.g., *two yellow* **tortillas,** and a PREPOSITIONAL PHRASE is built around a preposition, e.g., **near** *Los Angeles.*

Word

A WORD is traditionally understood to be a stretch of speech that is written with letters surrounded by spaces or punctuation. This is not a very good definition, because it is based on what may be arbitrary conventions in a writing system. For a better characterization of WORD which is based on actual characteristics of speech, see chapter 20 "Word Division and Clitics."

2.4. Grammatical relations and transitivity

Noun phrases can be classified according to their function in the basic sentence, particularly their relationship to the verb. This function is called their GRAMMATICAL RELATION or GRAMMATICAL FUNCTION. The most important grammatical relations are SUBJECT, (DIRECT) OBJECT, and INDIRECT OBJECT. (For further discussion, see chapters 5 "Introduction to Syntax" and 8 "Verbal Valence.")

Subject

The SUBJECT is the noun phrase or pronoun that typically (but not always, e.g., in passives) does the action, has the experience, or has the characteristic described in the rest of the clause. The subject is highlighted in the following sentences:

(12)   **Betty** *tidied her desk before going home.*
       Their ferocious dog *bit the neighbor's child.*
       She *is very popular.*

Direct Object

The DIRECT OBJECT (sometimes called simply OBJECT) is typically the noun phrase or pronoun that is acted on by the verb. The direct object in the example below is highlighted:

(13)   *Betty tidied* **her desk** *before going home.*
       Their ferocious dog bit **the neighbor's child.**

Indirect Object

The INDIRECT OBJECT is a phrase which typically refers to someone who receives an object or a message. It may be helpful to contrast indirect object with direct object.

(14)   Direct object   Indirect object

Mike sent   *the package*   *to his girlfriend.*
Lorraine threw   *the Frisbee*   *to Daniel.*
Manuela said   *many kind things*   *to me.*

In many traditional grammars, INDIRECT OBJECT does not refer to the same class of phrases that it does in this book. In this book, indirect objects in English are always prepositional phrases; elsewhere, you may find *me* in '*Manuela told* **me** *many kind things*' classified as an indirect object, but not here. Even among linguists, there is some disagreement over the analysis of clauses like these, but the analysis adopted here is probably the most widely used. To those familiar with other analyses, I apologize for the potential confusion, but in fact very little in this book depends on the issue. For further discussion and justification, see chapter 8 "Verbal Valence" (p. 77).

Transitivity

Clauses containing a direct object are TRANSITIVE.

(15)   *He appreciated her contribution.*
       She needed our help.
       Repeat the sentence again, please.

Clauses not containing a direct object are INTRANSITIVE.

(16)   *He moved to Arizona permanently.*
       His wife died after a long illness.
       He screamed at the top of his lungs.

2.5. Grammatical categories relevant primarily to nouns and pronouns

GRAMMATICAL CATEGORY refers to a way of classifying nouns, verbs, or other words, based on certain systematic differences between them, such as PERSON, NUMBER, and TENSE. The ones discussed in this section relate most directly to nouns and pronouns; those that relate primarily to verbs are discussed in the next section.

Person

PERSON indicates whether a person or thing is the speaker or the one(s) spoken to.

(17)   FIRST PERSON   the person referred to is the speaker (or a group that includes him/her)
       SECOND PERSON   the person referred to is the one(s) spoken to (or a group that includes the
                       one(s) spoken to but does not include the speaker)
       THIRD PERSON   the person(s) or thing(s) referred to is/are neither the speaker nor the
                       one(s) spoken to

First person and second person are relevant only for pronouns and for prefixes and suffixes with pronoun-like meanings. Nouns in most languages are always third person.

Number

NUMBER indicates whether a noun is SINGULAR (referring to one item) or PLURAL (more than one).

(18)   Singular   Plural

woman   *women*
backhoe   *backhoes*
revival   *revivals*

Gender

GENDER refers to a semi-arbitrary classification of nouns based in part on the sex or animacy of the thing described.

(19)   MASCULINE   males
       FEMININE   females
       NEUTER   things that are neither male nor female
       ANIMATE   animals
       INANIMATE   plants and nonliving things

Note, however, that such classifications in languages are somewhat arbitrary; not all feminine nouns may refer to things that are inherently female and some things that are inherently female may be in some other category. For example, *Mädchen* 'maiden' in German is neuter.

In English, gender is relevant only to third person singular pronouns (*he, she, it*). In many other languages, nouns, too, are divided into different groups based on gender. The gender of the noun may make requirements about the form of its modifiers. For example, in French the definite article (*the*) has different forms (*le* versus *la*) depending on the noun's gender.

(20)   *le roi*   'the king' (masculine)
       la reine   'the queen' (feminine)

For further discussion, see chapter 19 "Case and Agreement" (p. 262).

Case

CASE refers to a way of marking a noun or pronoun to indicate its grammatical relation or other function within a clause. In English, case is relevant only to pronouns (*I, me, my*). In other languages, case is also important for nouns. (For further discussion, see chapter 19 "Case and Agreement," p. 252.)

(21)   NOMINATIVE   used for subjects
       ACCUSATIVE   used for direct objects
       DATIVE   used for indirect objects
       OBJECTIVE   used for more than one type of object
       GENITIVE   used for possessors

In any one language, cases with these names may have more uses than what are listed here.

2.6. Grammatical categories relevant primarily to verbs

Most commonly, the following terms are used to describe the morphology of verbs, but may also be applied to whole clauses.

Tense

TENSE indicates something about the time of a verb with respect to the moment of speech. It includes the categories of past, present, and future, among others.

PAST TENSE: Occurring prior to the moment of speech.

(22)   *He walked to town.*

PRESENT TENSE: Occurring over a span of time that includes the moment of speech.

(23)   *He is walking to town.*
       He walks to town every day.

FUTURE TENSE: Occurring after the moment of speech.

(24)   *He will walk to town.*

For further discussion, see chapter 4 "Introduction to Morphology" (p. 27).

Aspect

ASPECT indicates something about the perspective from which the time span of a situation (event or state) is viewed or its relationship to the time span of other situations. Aspect ignores the location of that time span with respect to the moment of speech. (Only progressive and perfect aspect are relevant to the structure of English, so the examples below for the other terms only illustrate the types of clauses in which they would be used. Don't look for any part of English structure to apply the terms to.)

PERFECTIVE ASPECT: designates an event which is viewed as a complete whole.

(25)   *She ran a marathon last year.*
       She will run another one this spring.

IMPERFECTIVE ASPECT: designates an event which is viewed as consisting of several phases. There are two different types: habitual and progressive.

HABITUAL ASPECT: A subtype of imperfective aspect; typically designates that the action of the verb occurs repeatedly over a period of time.

(26)   *She used to run three miles a day.*
       Now she runs four miles a day.
       (When she starts training seriously,) she will run ten miles a day.

PROGRESSIVE ASPECT: A subtype of imperfective aspect; designates a single event which is viewed as being in progress at a certain time.

(27)   *She was still running at three o'clock.*
       She is running (right now).
       She will still be running at midnight.

PERFECT is sometimes classified as an aspect also, but might better be considered a type of tense (Comrie 1976:52–65, Comrie 1985b:77–82); it designates a past event which has present relevance and is often translated with words like 'have' and 'already'.

(28)   *She had never run so fast before.*
       Already she has passed the 15 mile mark.
       By noon, she will have finished.

For further discussion, see chapter 4 "Introduction to Morphology" (p. 27).

Mood

MOOD indicates something about the relation of the event described by a clause to the real world.

INDICATIVE MOOD: the event described in the clause is stated to occur in the real world.

(29)   *Linguistics books put some people to sleep and fascinate others.*

IMPERATIVE MOOD: the event is commanded, not stated.

(30)   *Stop climbing the wall!*

SUBJUNCTIVE MOOD is a term used mostly in European languages to refer to a form of the verb used for hypothetical or unreal events, as well as a variety of other uses. It exists marginally in English ('If I were king...', 'Long may he live') and is dropping out of use, especially by younger speakers. The term SUBJUNCTIVE is not generally used by linguists for other languages.

EXCLAMATORY is a term that is sometimes used alongside INDICATIVE and IMPERATIVE. It refers to sentences that express surprise or other strong emotion, such as "What a party!"—sentences that are usually punctuated with an exclamation mark. However, it is unlike the other terms above, since it usually does not play a role in word formation, so it is not usually classified as a mood.

For further discussion, see chapters 4 "Introduction to Morphology" (p. 28) and 17 "Commands" (pp. 235ff).

Voice

VOICE indicates something about the semantic relationship between the subject and the verb. In ACTIVE VOICE, the subject typically is performing an action or experiencing some mental event.

(31)   *Mrs. O'Leary's heifer kicked the burning lantern into the hay.*

In PASSIVE VOICE, the subject typically is being acted upon.

(32)   *The burning lantern was kicked into the hay by Mrs. O'Leary's heifer.*

For further discussion, see chapter 21 "Passive and Voice" (p. 298).

2.7. For further reading

If the explanations above are not sufficient, check out Crystal's (1991) *A Dictionary of Linguistics and Phonetics* or Trask's (1993) *A Dictionary of Grammatical Terms in Linguistics*. Many university libraries have dictionaries of linguistic terminology in their reference sections, but these two are probably the most current and readable and are inexpensive enough that I recommend you buy one or both. Another good source is the electronic glossary of linguistic terminology available at http://www.sil.org/linguistics/glossary.

There are several articles in Shopen 1985 that you might find useful if you want more details about these topics, especially as they relate to languages other than English. (Hint: Although written for students, they presume some linguistic background, so it might be good to wait until after you have worked through most of this book before pursuing them.) Schachter (1985) looks at parts of speech. Andrews (1985) touches on grammatical relations. Keenan (1985a) and Foley and van Valin (1985) cover passive. All of Shopen 1985, vol. 2 covers multiclause sentences. Anderson and Keenan (1985) survey grammatical categories relevant to nouns, pronouns, demonstratives, and adverbs, such as person, number, gender, social rank, and spatial and temporal relations. Chung and Timberlake (1985) survey tense, aspect, and mood (three grammatical categories that most people find puzzling at first), with examples from several different languages. (If you want to go deeper on these three topics, for tense see Comrie 1985b, for aspect see Comrie 1976, for mood see Palmer 1986.)

Morphology Group 1

3
Morphemes and Hypotheses

3.1. Goals and prerequisites

This chapter will help you do the following:

- ◎ state the definition of MORPHEME
- ◎ make hypotheses about morphemes and their meanings in simple straightforward data
- ◎ use appropriate technical linguistic terminology to gloss morphemes in nouns

It assumes that you are familiar with the following material:

- ✓ the purpose of the special sections in each chapter of this book and how to use them (chapter 1 "Introduction")

It may also be useful to be familiar with the following:

- ✓ terminology commonly used by traditional school grammars (chapter 2 "Standard Grammatical Terminology")

3.2. Morphemes

In doing linguistic analysis, we first isolate the MINIMAL MEANINGFUL UNITS of the language. By 'minimal meaningful unit', I mean that the unit cannot be further subdivided and still have some meaning assigned to it. Such units are called MORPHEMES.

For example, consider the English word *unreadiness*. As speakers of English, we can divide this word into three parts and assign some meaning to each part.

(1) *un-*   not
     ready   prepared
     -ness   the quality of being _____

We cannot subdivide these into smaller meaningful pieces. In *un-*, we cannot assign a meaning to just the vowel *u* or the consonant *n*. The meaning is carried by the two sounds taken together; this meaningful combination of sounds constitutes a morpheme. Likewise we cannot assign meaning to *dy*, but only to the whole morpheme *ready*.

Notice in (1) that prefixes are written with a hyphen at the end, suffixes with a hyphen at the beginning, and stems with no hyphen. This is a standard convention, and I will follow it throughout the book.[1]

Other examples abound. In English, *cats* consists of two morphemes: *cat* plus the plural suffix *-s; going* consists of *go* plus *-ing*, which means something like 'in the process of'; *faster* consists of *fast* plus *-er*, which means 'more'; *killed* consists of *kill* plus the past tense morpheme *-ed; ability* consists of *abil* (a variant of *able*) plus the morpheme *-ity* which turns an adjective into an abstract noun.

3.3. Making hypotheses about morphemes

Now let's consider some data where the morphemes are unknown to us. We must find them using the approximate English translations (or GLOSSES) provided. Consider the sentences below from Choapan Zapotec (Otomanguean, Mexico).[2]

(2)	ɾao ʒua jeta	John eats tortillas.
	ɾao lipi za	Philemon eats beans.
	ɾao maka bela	Macaria eats fish.
	reʔn ʒua za	John wants beans.
	reʔn lipi bela	Philemon wants fish.
	reʔn maka jeta	Macaria wants tortillas.

One way to start is by looking for items that recur in the data with a corresponding constant meaning somewhere in the glosses. This technique is known as finding RECURRING PARTIALS WITH CORRESPONDING CONSTANT MEANING. In the data above, we see that *ɾao* recurs several times and corresponds with the meaning 'eats', so *ɾao* probably means 'eat'. Likewise, *reʔn* recurs several times and corresponds with the meaning 'wants', so *reʔn* probably means 'want'. In the same manner you can guess the meanings of all the other words. (Try to do so before reading further.)[3]

What we have done is to form a HYPOTHESIS (precise educated guess) about the meanings of each individual word, and then we check that hypothesis against all the data. Whenever we make a hypothesis, it is important to check it out against further data, which may either CONFIRM or CONTRADICT it. We must remain open to the possibility that, although the hypothesis works for the data immediately in front of us, we may find evidence later that will cause us to modify it or completely rework it.

Analyzing morphemes becomes more difficult when a word consists of more than one morpheme, so that we need to identify not only the meaning of each piece, but also the boundaries between them. In this case, the best procedure is to use a different technique, called finding CONTRAST IN A FRAME. For example, consider the additional Choapan Zapotec data below:

(3)	ɾaowaʔ	I eat.	waowaʔ	I will eat.
	ɾaoloʔ	You (singular) eat.	waoloʔ	You (singular) will eat.
	ɾaobiʔ	He/she eats.	waobiʔ	He/she will eat.
	ɾaobaʔ	It (an animal) eats.	waobaʔ	It (an animal) will eat.

---

[1]Some linguists write hyphens on both sides of a prefix or suffix that is not first or last in a word; this, however, makes them look like INFIXES; see chapter 13 "Nonlinear Affixation," p. 168ff.

[2]All information about Choapan Zapotec in this book is from Larry Lyman (personal communication). It is transcribed using standard IPA symbols representing contrastive segments (phonemes). Tone, though contrastive, does not need to be represented in the practical orthography nor is it represented here.

[3]See (4) for one possible answer.

When we compare the first four forms, we see that *-waʔ* apparently means 'I', *-loʔ* apparently means 'you (singular)', *-biʔ* apparently means 'he/she', and *-baʔ* apparently means 'it (animal)'.[4]

By comparing *raowaʔ* with *waowaʔ*, *raoloʔ* with *waoloʔ*, etc., we see that *r-* and *w-* also contrast. A reasonable hypothesis as to their meaning is that *r-* means 'present tense' and *w-* means 'future tense'. But, this means one of our earlier hypotheses needs revision. While examining (2), we hypothesized that *rao* was a morpheme meaning 'eat'. Now, we see that it contains two morphemes; *r-* 'present' and *ao* 'eat'. And, it is reasonable to assume that *reʔn* likewise consists of two morphemes: *r-* 'present' and *eʔn* 'want'.

We can now list our hypothesis about all the morphemes in the data:

(4)
ao	eat	*ʒua*	John	*za*	beans
eʔn	want	*lipi*	Philemon	*bela*	fish
		maka	Macaria	*jɛta*	tortillas

-waʔ	first person singular	*r-*	present tense
-loʔ	second person singular	*w-*	future tense
-biʔ	third person human singular		
-baʔ	third person animal singular		

3.4. Linguistic terminology for glossing morphemes

Notice the specialized linguistic terms that are used to GLOSS (i.e., indicate the meaning of) the verbal suffixes. These terms are not used just for the sake of sounding erudite. They are used because in many languages there are morphemes that don't specify NUMBER (SINGULAR or PLURAL) or GENDER (MASCULINE, FEMININE, or NEUTER); they mean just 'FIRST PERSON (I or we)', 'SECOND PERSON (you, either singular or plural)', or 'THIRD PERSON (he, she, it, or they)'. Meanings of morphemes in many languages may not line up neatly with meanings of morphemes in languages you may be familiar with. But, by using specialized terminology like PERSON, NUMBER, and GENDER, we can zero in on the precise meaning of each.

For instance, consider the way that possession is indicated in Nahuatl (Aztec) of Mecayapan (Uto-Aztecan, Mexico).[5]

(5)
nokal	my house
mokal	your house
ikal	his house

Just looking at these glosses, it would be tempting to analyze *no-* as 'my', *mo-* as 'your', and *i-* as 'his'. But this is not correct, as further examples show. For one thing, *ikal* can also mean 'her house' or 'its house'. So, let's revise our analysis of *i-* to say that it means 'third person singular possessor' (i.e., 'his, her, or its').

But even more revisions are needed; look at the following forms:

---

[4]Further data would show that these hypotheses are only partially correct. Larry and Rosemary Lyman (personal communication) note that the first and second person suffixes are strictly singular, as there are completely different suffixes for plural. However, in third person plural, the same suffixes are used as in the third person singular forms, with an additional morpheme *-yaka* 'third person plural' that appears between the verb and the third person suffixes. Thus, the third person suffixes would be better glossed as 'third person human' or 'third person animal', with no mention of number. The first person singular shown here is only used with certain verbs; the more common form is *-aʔ*. Finally, these 'suffixes' are actually bound words, like the Mixtec pronouns in chapter 20 "Word Division and Clitics," pp. 280ff.

[5]Mecayapan (Isthmus) Nahuatl data from Wolgemuth 1981:47. Transcription based on the practical orthography, but with standard IPA symbols.

(6) *nokalmeh*   our (excluding you) house
     tokal   our (including you) house
     amokal   your (plural) house
     ikalmeh   their house

By contrasting these forms with the others, it is clear that *-meh* means 'plural', but only when second person is not involved (in third person plural and first person plural EXCLUSIVE). When the possessor is first and second person together (i.e., for first person plural INCLUSIVE), the prefix *to-* is used, and when more than one second person is possessor (without the speaker), *amo-* is used. Thus, *amo-* is 'second person plural possessor' and *mo-* in (5) is just 'second person singular possessor'.[6]

We see too that *i-* is not limited to singular possessors, but means simply 'third person possessor'. Similarly, *no-* does not mean 'my' but rather 'first person possessor', and it means that only in first person singular and first person plural exclusive. So, the best gloss is 'first person exclusive possessor'.

Thus, the meanings of this rather complicated set of morphemes can be characterized as follows:

(7) *no-*   first person exclusive possessor
     mo-   second person singular possessor
     i-   third person possessor
     to-   first person plural inclusive possessor
     amo-   second person plural possessor
     -meh   non-second person plural possessor

When we gloss morphemes, we want to zero in on the precise meaning of each. We strive to characterize it in terms of the full range of situations where it is used while not including any situations where it is not used. If possible, we want to avoid making lists of meanings, like 'his, her, its, their'; these tend to be clumsy and imprecise and usually fail to express significant generalizations about the meaning. Technical linguistic terminology like PERSON, NUMBER, and INCLUSIVE makes it possible to state the meaning of morphemes clearly, precisely, and generally.

3.5. Avoiding pitfalls

There are several important cautions to observe when analyzing morphemes.

One, take translations and glosses with a grain of salt. As we saw above, they're usually in the ballpark but it is often difficult to represent the exact meaning of a morpheme in one language by a translation into another. Get used to using specialized linguistic terms, especially for pronouns, prefixes, and suffixes.

Two, don't jump to conclusions about the gloss of a morpheme. Keep aware of alternative possibilities and don't get locked into any conclusion as if it was fact; always be ready to revise your hypothesis in light of new data. As a practical matter, use pencil, not pen, to mark morpheme breaks and other hypotheses on your data, so that you can easily erase the marks when you change your mind.

Three, when you are trying to determine the meaning of prefixes and suffixes, rely on contrast in a frame, not just on recurring meanings. For instance, consider the following data from Swahili (Bantu, East Africa):[7]

---

[6]An alternate hypothesis could be that *amo* is actually two morphemes: *mo-* is 'second person possessor', used in both singular and plural, and *a-* is 'second person plural possessor'. Both analyses posit two distinct morphemes; there seems to be no strong reason to favor one over the other.

[7]Swahili data from Wilson 1985:18–19, 33.

(8) *anataka*   he is wanting
     anajaribu   he is trying
     anakuja   he is coming
     anapiga   he is beating (someone)

Clearly, there is a recurring sequence *ana-*, but it is not clear how many morphemes it contains. Nor is it possible to tell what it means; it could mean any or all of the following: third person, masculine, singular, present tense, incompletive aspect (i.e., an action that is presented as being in progress), or realis mood (something that is true, as opposed to false or conjectural). There are many more possibilities, since languages can vary quite a bit in the sort of information that they include in a verb and frequently include morphemes with meanings which are quite different from what you may be used to from your previous language study. However, just a few forms that show minimal contrast clarify things considerably:

(9) *ninakuja*   I am coming
     alitaka   he wanted

If you contrast these with the other four forms, you will make quite a bit of progress towards a good morphological analysis. (Try it!)

Four, don't expect a morpheme to be a complete syllable. It can for example be a single consonant, like the tense prefixes in Choapan Zapotec (4) or the plural suffix *-s* in English. Although it is often the case that morpheme boundaries and syllable boundaries coincide, it is also often the case that they do not.

3.6. Review of key terms

Linguistic analysis is the process of examining data (consisting of forms in a language plus their GLOSSES), forming HYPOTHESES about the language's structure, and checking those hypotheses against further examples which may either CONFIRM or CONTRADICT them.

The analysis of a language begins with isolating its MINIMAL MEANINGFUL UNITS, that is, its MORPHEMES. This is done by looking for RECURRING PARTIALS WITH CORRESPONDING CONSTANT MEANING and CONTRAST IN A FRAME. Morphemes associated with nouns frequently have abstract meanings, which are best GLOSSED with technical linguistic terms like PERSON (FIRST, SECOND, or THIRD), EXCLUSIVE, INCLUSIVE, GENDER (MASCULINE, FEMININE, or NEUTER), and NUMBER (SINGULAR or PLURAL).

3.7. For further reading

This book assumes at least a basic familiarity with phonetic transcription.[8] I have tried to follow standard usage as described in Pullum and Ladusaw 1996. If you are unsure what a symbol means, you can look it up in that book.

---

[8]Mostly, this book follows the recommendations of the International Phonetic Association, but sometimes uses symbols drawn from the practice of American linguists. Note, however, that data often appears in a language's normal practical orthography or whatever transcription system is found in the source, particularly when the phonological content is irrelevant to the discussion. See the footnotes for clarifications on ambiguous or uncommon symbols. If you want to use data in this book for other purposes, please refer to any original published sources cited.

4
Introduction to Morphology

4.1. Goals and prerequisites

This chapter will help you do the following:

- ◎ state a more precise definition of MORPHEME and explain how it is better than the one given in the previous chapter
- ◎ use appropriate terms for glossing meanings commonly found in verbal morphology
- ◎ use appropriate terms for classifying and describing morphemes and morphological systems
- ◎ construct position class charts to describe data in an agglutinative morphological system
- ◎ write a clear and concise prose description of such a system

It assumes that you are familiar with the following material:

- ✓ traditional terminology which applies to verbal morphology (chapter 2 "Standard Grammatical Terminology")
- ✓ how to isolate morphemes and guess their meanings (chapter 3 "Morphemes and Hypotheses")

You may want to read chapter 24 "Hints for Linguistic Writing" at the same time as this chapter.

4.2. What is a morpheme?

A common definition of MORPHEME is the one given in chapter 3 "Morphemes and Hypotheses" (p. 19), that it is a minimal meaningful unit in a language. As a shorthand memory device, this definition is quite adequate, but it requires some more explanation and also some expansion to make it more precise.

The term MINIMAL does not mean 'smallest' (even though linguists sometimes even say 'smallest' when they really mean 'minimal'). If we take 'smallest' literally, then the smallest meaningful units in English are limited to -s 'plural', -d 'past', a 'indefinite article', and other morphemes that consist only of a single segment. (A SEGMENT is a single sound in spoken language, roughly corresponding to a letter in written form.) Absolute size is not what is important here; a unit does not need to be particularly small to be a morpheme, but it does need to be minimal in the sense of being UNANALYZABLE. Even though the word *category* is fairly long, it is still a single morpheme, because it cannot be further split up (analyzed) into meaningful pieces. (That is, *category* has nothing to do with *cat,* and *egory* is completely meaningless.)

The term MEANINGFUL includes either LEXICAL or GRAMMATICAL meaning. LEXICAL MEANING is the type that we are used to looking up in a dictionary. It includes the meanings of such morphemes as *plum, press, early,* and *tomorrow.* When analyzing another language, you will recognize lexical meanings because they generally translate easily into equivalent ordinary words or phrases in other languages; that is, they can be glossed with TRANSLATION EQUIVALENTS.

Morphemes with GRAMMATICAL MEANINGS, on the other hand, do not usually translate directly from one language to another. Instead, when we gloss them, it is usually necessary to describe their meaning with technical linguistic terminology like 'plural', 'first person', 'perfective', and 'past'. These meanings are called 'grammatical' because they have more to do with the grammar of a language than with its vocabulary. They usually cannot be fully described unless you take into account the larger grammatical context in which they occur. A good example of this is the past tense suffix *-d,* which can occur on verbs in some contexts, but not in others. (The asterisk in front of an example sentence indicates that it is in some way unacceptable.)

(1)   a.   *He arrived two hours ago.*
          b.   **He didn't arrived yet.*

This example also points out another problem with the shorthand definition for MORPHEME given above, since there is more to a morpheme than just its meaning, or SEMANTICS. Part of the analysis of a morpheme includes a statement about its morphological and syntactic properties, that is, how it combines with other morphemes to form words and how these words combine to form sentences. The past tense suffix does not occur just anywhere, but only on verbs in specific contexts.

As another example, consider the two morphemes that are spelled *-s* in English, as in *turtle-s* and *plod-s.* Their meanings are clearly grammatical; the first means 'plural' and the second means 'singular'. But there is more to them than just their meaning. It is also important that both are suffixes and that the first one occurs in nouns while the second occurs in verbs. Further, the verbal suffix *-s* does not tell anything about the meaning of the verb itself, but rather about the meaning of another part of the clause, the subject. (*The turtle plods slowly* does not mean that the turtle plods only once, but that only one turtle plods.) These are not facts so much about the meaning of the morphemes themselves, but about how they combine with other morphemes to form sentences. They are facts about their GRAMMAR.

Further, even morphemes with lexical meaning have grammatical properties. Consider the two homophonous morphemes 'week' and 'weak'. Besides having different (lexical) meanings, they also have different grammatical properties—one is a noun and the other is an adjective.

So, when we say that a morpheme is a minimal meaningful unit, we must understand this to include both lexical and grammatical meaning. And, the definition should not just say that a morpheme is 'meaningful', but that it has grammatical as well as semantic properties.

Finally, a morpheme is pronounced in a certain way; it has PHONOLOGICAL properties. The shorthand definition 'minimal meaningful unit' doesn't mention phonology explicitly, although it hints at it by talking about a morpheme as a UNIT. But, 'unit' must be understood abstractly, not just as a string of segments. For example, the rising intonation that occurs in a question like 'You ate a snake?' should be considered to be a morpheme; yet it is not a segment, but rather spread out over the entire sentence. And, the plural form of *man* is not *man-s* but *men;* there is no way to isolate one string of segments that means 'male adult human' and another that means 'plural'. Rather, the phonological part of the plural morpheme consists of the *change* in the quality of a vowel from 'a' to 'e'; this same vowel is also clearly part of the morpheme meaning 'male adult human'.

In other words, when we are analyzing morphemes, it is not always possible to draw neat morpheme cuts between segments; sometimes two or more morphemes are superimposed in one segment. Thinking of a morpheme as a string of segments works only in the simplest cases. Later (especially in chapter 13 "Nonlinear Affixation"), this book presents some of the complexities which make the process of identifying morphemes more difficult. In these cases, it is most helpful not to think of a morpheme as a 'unit', since this often implies a string of segments.

All this brings us to an improved definition of morpheme. A morpheme is 'a consistent and unanalyzable association of phonological, grammatical, and semantic information'. This definition mentions 'phonological information' without implying that it is a string of segments. And, it explicitly includes mention of grammar as well as semantics.

A key idea behind this definition is that a sentence's structure consists of many associations of phonological, grammatical, and semantic information. This is true at all levels, no matter how large a unit we are working with. Take the sentence 'All people are mortal'. It has phonological properties (it is pronounced approximately as [ɔl pipl̩ aɹ moɹtl̩]), grammatical properties (it consists of a sequence of nouns, a verb, etc., and is itself a sentence), and semantic properties (it means that everyone is going to die). In analyzing a language, we break down these complex units into smaller units like *all* and *people,* each of which has this three-way association of phonology, grammar, and semantics.

But, once we break things down into morphemes, we have to quit, since further analysis would destroy the association. The morpheme [ɔl] 'all' cannot be analyzed further into [ɔ] and [l]; both segments are meaningless, and they do not have any grammatical properties of their own. Morphemes like 'all' are unanalyzable. They are rock-bottom, indivisible pieces of the meaningful structure of a language.

This association of meaning and grammar with sound is what distinguishes the study of morphology and syntax from the study of phonology. Phonology is concerned with sounds alone, in the abstract, and generally ignores any meaning or grammatical properties they may have. Morphology and syntax, on the other hand, are always concerned with units that have meanings and which combine with other such units in specific ways. Thus, the fundamental thing we study in morphology and syntax is the morpheme, not the segment, syllable, or any of the other units that are important in phonology.

4.3. Verbal morphology

Verbal morphology typically involves many more grammatical meanings than noun morphology. Now is the time to discuss TENSE, ASPECT, MOOD, and AGREEMENT in more detail than previously, so you will be able to recognize these meanings when you encounter them in data. Some are covered in even more detail in later chapters.

TENSE refers to the relation between the time of the situation described by the verb and the moment of speech.[1] You are probably already familiar with the distinction between PAST, PRESENT, and FUTURE. (If not, see chapter 2 "Standard Grammatical Terminology," p. 14.) Some languages only make a two-way distinction in their morphology, between past and NONPAST or between future and NONFUTURE. For example, English verbs indicate tense by the presence or absence of *-(e)d*. The presence of *-(e)d* indicates past tense, its absence indicates nonpast, since this form is used both for present and future situations.

(2)   a. *I walk-ed.*
        b. *I (will) walk-Ø.*

Future time is distinguished from present by a separate auxiliary verb, *will,* not by tense morphology on the verb. (The null sign Ø in example (2) indicates the absence of any suffix in a particular position. Linguists sometimes talk about ZERO MORPHEMES in cases like this.) In addition to all these possibilities, languages sometimes subdivide past tense into RECENT PAST (e.g., earlier today) and REMOTE PAST (e.g., before today), or even three or four degrees of remoteness from the present moment.

ASPECT refers to the time of a situation in relation to its context. The two major distinctions that languages make are between PERFECTIVE and IMPERFECTIVE aspect. In imperfective aspect, the internal temporal structure of a situation (its beginning, middle, or end) is being presented as important, while in perfective, only the situation as a whole is important. Quite often, imperfective is

---

[1]In some languages, this 'present' moment can be shifted to another time, resulting in RELATIVE TENSE. See Comrie 1985b.

used for present events (which are not complete and whose internal structure is therefore of interest) while perfective is used for past events (which are usually presented as complete wholes). However, imperfective can also be used in past time, in contexts like this:

(3)   Imperfective   Perfective
      *While I **was wandering** through the maze, I **noticed**   a strange design on one wall.*

Since the time of noticing occurs entirely inside the time span of the wandering, the internal structure of the wandering is important. Thus *wander* would be presented in imperfective and *notice* in perfective. So, often, aspect presents the time of each verb with respect to the other verbs in context, not to a fixed present moment.

Sometimes a language also distinguishes between two types of imperfective aspect, called HABITUAL and PROGRESSIVE.[2] Habitual aspect refers to situations that occur repeatedly or typically, such as 'He empties the trash on Tuesdays'. Progressive refers to one-time or on-going events, such as 'He is emptying the trash right now'. English uses the *-ing* suffix for progressive aspect and a simple present tense verb form (like *empties*) to indicate present habitual aspect.[3]

You will often also encounter something called PERFECT ASPECT. It corresponds in meaning to the English auxiliary verb 'have' and is often translated 'have already'. It is not the same as perfective aspect; in fact, it is really more like a tense than an aspect, for it refers to a past situation that has present relevance. (For further examples of aspect, see chapter 2 "Standard Grammatical Terminology," p. 14.)

MOOD refers to the relationship between the situation reported by the verb and reality. I introduce only two types here: INDICATIVE (used for statements and questions, and concerned with how things actually are) and IMPERATIVE (used for commands, and concerned with how the speaker would like things to be). (I discuss mood in more detail in chapter 17 "Commands," pp. 235ff.)

The most common type of AGREEMENT is morphology on the verb that indicates something about the subject. For example, in English present tense verbs with third person singular subjects carry an *-s* suffix. If the subject is some other person or number, the suffix is absent.

(4)   a. *She/he/it ride-s fifteen miles a day.*
       b. *I/we/you/they ride-Ø fifteen miles a day.*

We say that English verbs 'agree with their subjects in person and number'. In many languages, the subject need not be present and the verbal-agreement marking communicates essentially the same information as a pronoun.

(5)   *Habla-n.*   (Spanish)
       speak-3Plural
       They are speaking.

(I return to agreement in detail in chapter 19 "Case and Agreement." Another type of agreement is illustrated below in (7).)

4.4. Stems and affixes

Morphology has to do with the various ways that morphemes are combined to form words. (Unfortunately, it's rather difficult to define WORD precisely, but for now you can assume it is a stretch of speech that is written surrounded by spaces or punctuation. We'll have to wait until

---

[2]For simplicity, I ignore the distinction that Comrie (1976) makes between continuous and progressive.
[3]To be precise, then, in (3) the *-ing* is used on *wander* because the situation is progressive, not because it is imperfective. It is imperfective, too, of course, but the morphology registers the distinction between progressive and nonprogressive, not between perfective and imperfective. The example is offered to illustrate the type of sentence that requires a contrast between perfective and imperfective in languages that mark this distinction morphologically.

chapter 20 "Word Division and Clitics" for a better explanation.) Usually, a word's structure is best described as consisting of a base, called either a STEM or a ROOT, and various additions or modifications to this base, called AFFIXES. You are doubtless already familiar with the two most common types of affixes, PREFIXES and SUFFIXES. (There are other types of affixes discussed in chapter 13 "Nonlinear Affixation" (p. 168ff.) which may occur inside or simultaneous with a stem. Also, there is a distinction between stems and roots in chapter 11 "Derivational Morphology" (p. 136ff.) but for now, we will talk about stems.)

Normally, making hypotheses about which morphemes are stems and which are affixes is fairly easy. Usually, if you are guided by what are stems and affixes in English and other languages, you will come up with the best hypothesis on the first try. Still, it is helpful to have some better 'rules of thumb' in making your analysis than just imitating the analysis of some other language. Languages differ too much to be able to copy an analysis from one to another without modification, or at least, without checking it out against the data.

There are three rules of thumb which can help form hypotheses about whether a morpheme is a stem or an affix:

(6)   a. the richness of its semantics
        b. whether it belongs to an open or closed class
        c. whether it is free or bound

Here's what they mean.

Stems usually have richer semantics than affixes. That is, stems usually have lexical meaning, while affixes often (not always) have grammatical meaning. Thus, stems can usually be glossed by a translation equivalent, while affixes often require technical linguistic terms.[4] For example, the Spanish word *cantas* 'you are singing' consists of two morphemes, the stem *canta,* which has the lexical meaning 'sing', and the suffix *-s,* which has the grammatical meaning 'second person singular present'.

Stems are usually members of OPEN CLASSES, while affixes are almost always members of CLOSED CLASSES. 'Open' and 'closed' refer partly to the number of members in a class, but more to the possibility of adding new members to the class. Take, for example, the word *harshness;* the stem *harsh* is a member of the open class of adjectives, while the suffix *-ness* is a member of the closed class of suffixes that attach to adjectives. There are hundreds of adjectives in English, but probably less than fifty suffixes that attach to adjectives. More important, new adjectives are being invented all the time, such as *spiffy* and *groovy* in this century; the class of adjectives is open to new members. New suffixes are much harder to invent; the class of adjectival suffixes is closed to new members.

Finally, affixes are always BOUND, while stems may be either bound or FREE. When we say that a morpheme is free, we mean that it can occur by itself as a word. A morpheme that is bound cannot be a word by itself, but must always be attached to some other morpheme. So, of course, affixes must be bound; if an affix were free, that would mean there would be a word that was all affix and no stem! Another way to look at this distinction is that (with very rare exceptions) a stem is always present in a word, while a word may or may not contain affixes.

Most stems in English are free. For example, the noun stem 'artichoke' can occur by itself, without any other morphemes attached, so it is free. (Of course, it can also occur together with the plural suffix, as in 'artichoke s', but this is irrelevant; it is still free because it can occur alone.) But, in Tzeltal (Mayan, Mexico), as in many other languages, this is not true for all nouns.[5] Some nouns must always be possessed. For example, you generally cannot talk about a hand in the abstract, you must say whose hand it is. The same is true for most other body parts, as well as many kinship terms. The possessor is expressed (in part) by prefixes on the noun. The word meaning 'hand' has three forms:

---

[4]This is not a hard and fast rule—one large class of affixes (derivational affixes) often has lexical meaning (see chapter 10 "Inflectional Morphology," pp. 114ff.).

[5]Tzeltal data in this book is from my own experience in the lowland dialect east of Ocosingo, Chiapas, Mexico; see Robles Uribe 1962, Slocum and Gerdel 1965, and Walter 1980 for published information on the language. Transcription is based on the practical orthography, but with IPA phonetic symbols substituted for some sounds.

(7)   *h-kap*   my hand
      a-kap   your hand
      s-kap   his hand

You will never hear the stem *kap* by itself, without one of these three prefixes. It is a bound stem. (This, incidentally, is the other type of agreement mentioned above: a noun agreeing with its possessor; see chapter 19 "Case and Agreement" (p. 264) for further analysis. For the syntactic side of possession, see chapter 7 "Embedding and Noun Phrase Structure," pp. 69ff.)

In summary, the distinction between stems and affixes is a distinction between the central and peripheral parts of a word. The normal characteristics of stems and affixes are summarized in the following chart:

Stems	Affixes
usually lexical meaning	usually grammatical meaning
usually from open classes	almost always from closed classes
either bound or free	always bound

4.5. Basic questions to ask about morphology

When we study the morphology of a language, that is, the structure of its words, there are two basic questions that we always need to be asking ourselves. Think of these questions especially when analyzing an affix.

(8)   a. What is its meaning?
      b. How is that meaning expressed?

Question (8a) has to do with semantics. It includes other questions, such as:

(9)   a. What meanings are being expressed?
      b. Are these meanings lexical or grammatical?

As you look at data from different languages, you will develop some sense of the most common meanings that are expressed morphologically, especially grammatical meanings.

Question (8b) has to do with phonology and grammar. It includes other questions, such as:

(10) a. What is the phonological material (e.g., the string of segments) that represents this meaning?
      b. Where is this material located with respect to the stem (prefixed, suffixed, etc.)?
      c. Is it always the same on every stem, or does it vary depending on context?
      d. What category of words is affected by this morphological process (nouns, verbs, etc.)?

The two basic questions in (8) guide discussions of morphology throughout the book. Some chapters will concentrate more on one, some on the other. But, you should always keep both clearly in mind and think through the answers to them whenever you are doing an analysis of word structure.

4.6. How different can morphological systems get?

The morphological systems of languages can be very different. This great variety of morphological systems contributed to a conclusion drawn by linguists in the 1940s and 1950s that languages can vary unpredictably and without limit. We know now that this is not true, but it did seem like it at the time.

There is a traditional way of classifying this variety, that is, a TYPOLOGY, which recognizes three main types of morphological systems, called ISOLATING, AGGLUTINATIVE, and FUSIONAL.

On one extreme are ISOLATING languages, which have the simplest possible morphology: practically every word consists of a single morpheme. Isolating languages are especially common in southeast Asia. Consider the following Vietnamese example:[6]

(11) *khi   tôi   đến   nhà   bạn   tôi,   chúng   tôi   bắt dầu   làm   bài.*
     when   I   come   house   friend   I   Plural   I   begin   do   lesson
     When I came to my friend's house, we began to do lessons.

There is no indication on the verb for person, number, or tense; *đến* could be translated either 'come', 'comes', or 'came', depending on context. There is similarly no distinction like that in English between 'I' and 'my'; the same word in Vietnamese is used in both contexts. The grammatical meaning 'Plural' is expressed by a separate word, *chúng,* not an affix.

In contrast, some languages have large numbers of morphemes per word, as in the following example from Chukchi (Paleosiberian, northeastern Siberia):

(12) *tə-meyŋə-levtə-pəyt-ərkən*
     1Sg-great-head-ache-Imperfective
     I have a fierce headache.

This one word in Chukchi corresponds to a whole sentence in many other languages. In languages like Chukchi, many sentences consist simply of a single long word. There are so many long words that it may be impractical to print literature in double-column format; too many words would be split across two lines, and some are even too long to fit in a single column!

In Chukchi, morphemes are easy to find; they are clearly separable from each other, and moreover, a given morpheme does not change very much when it appears in different contexts. Such languages are traditionally known as AGGLUTINATIVE (or AGGLUTINATING).

Other languages have several morphemes per word, but finding them is fraught with many and varied difficulties. There are not clear boundaries between morphemes, and such languages are called FUSIONAL. Most European languages are fusional. Consider, for example, the different forms of two Russian nouns. Try to make morpheme cuts before you proceed.

(13)

	table		lime-tree	
	Singular	Plural	Singular	Plural
Nominative	*stol*	*stoly*	*lipa*	*lipy*
Accusative	*stol*	*stoly*	*lipu*	*lipy*
Genitive	*stola*	*stolov*	*lipy*	*lip*
Dative	*stolu*	*stolam*	*lipe*	*lipam*
Instrumental	*stolom*	*stolami*	*lipoj*	*lipami*
Prepositional	*stole*	*stolax*	*lipe*	*lipax*

Notice that you cannot separate off one set of morphemes that indicates only number (singular and plural) and another set of morphemes that indicates only case (nominative, accusative, etc.), as you would probably be able to do in an agglutinative language. Instead, both number and case are combined into one large set of case/number suffixes, so that each suffix indicates both number and case. Further, there are different suffixes depending on the stem used; the genitive singular suffix is *-a* on *stol* but *-y* on *lip*. Again, this is unlike what normally happens in agglutinative languages, in which a single meaning tends to be represented the same way wherever it occurs.

---

[6]All examples in this section are from Comrie (1981:39–49).

4.7. Position classes

With this background, we're ready to take our analysis beyond identifying morphemes and their meanings, to look at the way they combine into words. We start with agglutinative languages; isolating languages don't have enough morphology to be interesting, and fusional languages involve complexities that we deal with later. Here's some data from a typical agglutinative language, Yagua (Peba-Yaguan, Peru).[7]

(14) a. *tsanta*   He plants.

      b. *tsantʃa*   He weaves.

      c. *tsantarṹũy*   He wants to plant.

      d. *tsantʃarṹũymáã*   He already wants to weave.

      e. *nã́ãntʃatsí*   She wove a week ago.

      f. *tsantaháy*   He planted yesterday.

      g. *nã́ãntarṹũyháymáã*   She was already wanting to plant yesterday.

      h. *tsantʃarṹũytsímáã*   He was already wanting to weave a week ago.

      i. *nã́ãntʃaháy*   She wove yesterday.

      j. *nã́ãnta*   She plants.

      k. *tsatúnurṹũy*   He wants to tie together.

      l. *nã́ãtunuháymáã*   She already tied together yesterday.

      m. *tsatúnurṹũytsímáã*   He was already wanting to tie together a week ago.

      n. *tsatúnu*   He ties together.

Make morpheme cuts and gloss morphemes now, before reading any further. (Remember to use pencil.)

As you can see, as many as one prefix and three suffixes occur together in the same word (e.g., sentences (14g, h, m)). And, they seem to occur in a fixed order; *-rṹũy* (whenever it occurs) immediately follows the stem and *-máã* (whenever it occurs) always comes last.

This ordering can be represented succinctly in a type of chart called a POSITION CLASS CHART.

−1 Person	0 STEM	+1 Desiderative	+2 Tense	+3 Aspect
nã́ã- she *tsa-* he		*-rṹũy* want	*-háy* recent past (yesterday) *-tsí* distal past (last week)	*-máã* perfect

Each column in the chart represents a POSITION CLASS, a class of morphemes that occur in the same position in a word. Any two morphemes that occur in the same position class will never occur in the same word; they are MUTUALLY EXCLUSIVE. (If they did occur together, one would have to

---

[7]Data from Elson and Pickett (1983:10–11), originally from Tom Payne. Transcription converted to IPA. Acute accent represents high tone; the slight variations in tone marking are not explained in the source, and I ignore them here.

precede the other, so they would be in different position classes.) When two affixes from different classes do appear together, they appear in the order given in the chart.

It is convenient to assign a number to each position class. One way of doing this starts with the stem as class 0 and numbers out from there, with prefix classes receiving negative numbers and suffix classes receiving positive numbers.[8] (Thus, if there are 3 prefix classes, the first (leftmost) one is numbered –3.)

The labels on the columns give some indication of the meanings of the affixes in that position class. The label 'Desiderative' refers to the meaning of *-rǘǘy*, 'want'. The label 'Tense' is based on the assumption that there are two past tenses, one for recent past (yesterday) and one for distant past (a week ago or more). The label 'Aspect' is used because 'Perfect' (the gloss of *-mǎâ*) is often classified as a type of aspect. Note there is also a column for the stem, but no stems are actually listed; being an open class, there may be hundreds of them, so we don't clutter the chart with them.

How do you make a chart like this? Start out with a small number of columns. (Hint: start with the same number of prefix columns as the *maximum* number of prefixes on any one word in the data, and do likewise for suffixes. For Yagua, you would start with one prefix class and three suffix classes. Often it turns out that this is an accurate estimate.) Then, ask yourself questions like these:

(15)   a. Which affixes (whenever they occur) are always first or last in the word, or always immediately precede or follow the stem?
        b. Which affixes are next in line in these positions, after the affixes found in question 1?
        c. More generally, for each pair of affixes that can occur together in a word, which one comes first?

Make hypotheses about which affix belongs in which column. Add or subtract columns, or move affixes to different columns, as needed, until all affixes have been included. Then check your chart once again against the data to make sure it covers all the facts correctly.

Position class charts are most useful when a language's morphology is of a certain specific type: it should be agglutinative (with several morphemes per word and clear divisions between them) and the morphemes must come in a fixed order. Chapter 10 "Inflectional Morphology" shows a way of representing morphological structure which works for all languages, including those that are not suitable for position class charts.

4.8. Review of key terms

MORPHEMES are unanalyzable (MINIMAL) clusters of SEMANTIC, PHONOLOGICAL, and GRAMMATICAL properties, often defined with the phrase 'minimal meaningful unit'. Their meanings may be either LEXICAL (easily glossed with TRANSLATION EQUIVALENTS) or GRAMMATICAL (defined primarily in reference to larger grammatical structure). Grammatical meanings commonly found in verbs include TENSE (PAST, PRESENT, FUTURE, NONPAST, NONFUTURE, RECENT/REMOTE), ASPECT (PERFECTIVE, IMPERFECTIVE, HABITUAL, PROGRESSIVE, as well as PERFECT 'ASPECT'), MOOD (INDICATIVE, IMPERATIVE), and AGREEMENT

Morphemes may be classified as STEMS or AFFIXES (e.g., PREFIXES or SUFFIXES), as BOUND or FREE, and as belonging to OPEN or CLOSED classes. The study of how morphemes combine to form words is called MORPHOLOGY.

The morphological systems of languages can be classified with the traditional TYPOLOGY that divides languages into three types: ISOLATING, AGGLUTINATIVE, and FUSIONAL.

Word structure in agglutinative languages can profitably be presented using POSITION CLASS CHARTS, which show how affixes are grouped into POSITION CLASSES, each of which contains a set of MUTUALLY EXCLUSIVE affixes.

---

[8]Following Joseph Grimes 1983.

4.9. Questions for analysis

In scientific research, it is often more important to know what questions to ask than to know what the answers are. To help you get a sense of important questions in linguistics, most chapters include a section called questions for analysis. The questions in these sections summarize the main things you should consider when applying that chapter to the analysis of real language data. Use them as a guide as you are learning how to do linguistic analysis.

1. What morphemes are found in the data?
2. What are their semantic properties (i.e., what do they mean)?
3. What are their phonological properties? (In the simplest cases, this question reduces to 'How are they pronounced?')
4. What are their grammatical properties? What types of words do they occur in? Do affixes group into position classes? How many classes are there, and what affixes are in each class?
5. Is the language isolating, fusional, agglutinative, or some combination of these?

4.10. Sample description

Beginning with this chapter, I include concise factual descriptions of the data covered in each chapter, which you can use as models in your own writing.[9] The first ones are quite short, like your first attempts probably will be. See chapter 24 "Hints for Linguistic Writing" for suggestions about how to write well for linguists; linguistic description differs from other writing you may have done.

Yagua verb structure

The verbal morphology of Yagua, an agglutinative language of the Amazon basin in Peru, can be represented in the following position class chart:

−1 Person	0 STEM	+1 Desiderative	+2 Tense		+3 Aspect
nãã- she		*-rũũy* want	*-háy*	recent past (yesterday)	*-mãã* perfect
tsa- he			*-tsí*	distal past (last week)	

4.11. For further reading

A more refined view of morphological typology can be found in chapter 2 of Comrie 1989. Comrie distinguishes two parameters along which morphological systems can vary; the index of synthesis (how many morphemes per word) and the index of fusion (how clear are the divisions between morphemes). The traditional isolating/agglutinative/fusional typology can be defined in terms of these two parameters.

Usually, position class charts are easy to construct, but when there are large numbers of morphemes and position classes, things can be complicated enough that a highly systematic method is needed. Such a method was developed by Joseph Grimes (1967) based on a suggestion by Frank Lister. (Lister, incidentally, was a student in one of Grimes' courses. One of the exciting aspects of linguistics is that there is relatively little distinction between students and teachers; it is not uncommon for people to make significant contributions to the field while they are still students.) This method is also described, somewhat more understandably, in Elson and Pickett (1983:12–16) and Daly, Lyman, and Rhodes (1981:171–77). It has been incorporated into a computer program called Paradigm (Joseph Grimes 1983), which also provides information about morpheme co-occurrence (which morphemes can occur with which others).

---

[9]I have found it helpful to ask students always to provide an informal description of any data they analyze for homework in my classes, using terminology that would be readily understood by linguists from all theoretical backgrounds.

Syntax Group 1

5
Introduction to Syntax:
Constituent Structure, Syntactic Categories, and Grammatical Relations

5.1. Goals and prerequisites

This chapter will help you do the following:

- ◉ use terminology for describing the structure of sentences (in English and other languages)
- ◉ state the two main criteria which are used to determine if a constituent belongs to a particular category, and use these criteria yourself when analyzing data
- ◉ diagram the structure of a sentence, using either labeled brackets or trees, and including information about syntactic categories and grammatical relations

It assumes that you are familiar with the following material:

- ✓ standard terminology used to describe syntax (chapter 2 "Standard Grammatical Terminology")
- ✓ techniques for identifying the meaning of morphemes (chapter 3 "Morphemes and Hypotheses")

If you have not already done so, you may want to read chapter 24 "Hints for Linguistic Writing" at the same time as this chapter.

5.2. Constituents and constituent structure

There are an infinite number of well-formed (or GRAMMATICAL) utterances in any language. Speakers cannot actually produce all of them (without living an infinite number of years), but they have internalized a system which has no limit on the number of sentences which can be produced or understood. In doing an analysis of a particular language, we as linguists try to discover what this system is. We want to discover the rules of the grammar which are available to speakers—rules which allow them to produce and understand grammatical utterances and to judge whether an utterance is grammatical or not.

However, before we can talk about the system of rules, we need to talk about the things that the rules describe: sentences and their structure. The fundamental concept in this chapter is that sentences are not just strings of words, but have a more complex structure, which linguists call CONSTITUENT STRUCTURE.

Consider the following sentence:

(1)   *John angered Mary.*

It consists of three words, two nouns separated by a verb. This may seem to fully describe its syntactic structure, but this is deceptive. Compare (1) with (2).

(2)   *The big dog angered the cat.*

Example (2) contains six words, yet it seems somehow parallel to (1). Three words, *the big dog,* seem to play the same role in (2) that one word, *John,* plays in (1). Similarly, *the cat* and *Mary* seem to play the same role. *The big dog* and *the cat* appear to be important chunks of material, which we can represent using BRACKETS.

(3)   *[The big dog] angered [the cat]*

Bracketed like this, we see that (3) has exactly the same overall structure as (1); it has three chunks, even though it has a different number of words.

Chunks of linguistic material like those enclosed in brackets in (3) are called CONSTITUENTS. The basic organization of (3) is not a string of six words, but rather a string of three constituents, two of which happen to consist of more than one word. Words are grouped together into constituents, and these are grouped together into still larger constituents. This pieces-within-pieces, or HIERARCHICAL, structure is found in many human activities, including all languages. The hierarchical structure of sentences and other utterances is called CONSTITUENT STRUCTURE.

5.3. Syntactic categories

We can also scramble things a bit and produce other sentences that are parallel to (2) and (3).

(4)   *The cat angered John.*
        Mary angered the big dog.

John, Mary, the big dog, and *the cat* are the same type of constituents, since they are MUTUALLY SUBSTITUTABLE for each other. By mutually substitutable, we mean that we can substitute one for another and still have grammatical sentences. Another way to say this is that they all have the same DISTRIBUTION, that is, they can all grammatically occur in the same places.

This type of constituent is traditionally called a NOUN PHRASE (NP), since it is a phrase built around a noun and optionally some 'lesser' elements MODIFYING the noun. The noun is the most important element in the phrase, so we call it the HEAD of the phrase; a noun phrase can be defined as a phrase whose head is a noun. To show the noun phrases in a sentence, we can label the brackets.

(5)   *[NP The big dog] angered [NP the cat]*

Here are some other noun phrases in English.

(6)   *many people*
        two big, bad bullies
        Arthur and his brother
        a shy antelope

All of these could be substituted for the noun phrases in (5). Since these phrases are mutually substitutable, we have evidence that they are all, in fact, in the same SYNTACTIC CATEGORY (or CLASS). A syntactic category is a set of constituents in a language which have several characteristics in common.[1] Sameness of distribution is one of the most important defining characteristics of a syntactic category.

The traditional PARTS OF SPEECH are also syntactic categories. The syntactic category of nouns (N) includes words such as *computer, volleyball,* and *lights;* all such words are mutually substitutable for each other. The syntactic category of verbs (V) includes words such as *marry, return,* and *walk.* The syntactic category of adjectives (A) includes words such as *big, ugly,* and *repulsive.*

ARTICLES such as *the, a,* and *an,* as well as DEMONSTRATIVES such as *this* and *that* together form another syntactic category, defined in part by the fact that they are mutually substitutable as the first word in a noun phrase.

(7)   ***the*** *old man*
       an *old man*
       this *old man*

In current linguistic studies, this category is usually called DETERMINER (D).

Finally, there are two larger constituents. The phrase 'angered the cat' in (5) is usually analyzed as a VERB PHRASE (VP), since its head is a verb. Also, every clause is a constituent, which belongs to the syntactic category commonly called S. (Originally S stood for SENTENCE, but it soon came to be used for all clauses, not just those clauses which were sentences. Thus, when you see S, think 'clause', not 'sentence'.)

With these additional syntactic categories, we can add more labeled brackets and identify all the constituents in (5). (Note that each word is a constituent, too, and so has its own pair of brackets.)

(8) $[_S$ $[_{NP}$ $[_D$ *The* $]$ $[_A$ *big* $]$ $[_N$ *dog* $]$ $]$ $[_{VP}$ $[_V$ *angered* $]$ $[_{NP}$ $[_D$ *the* $]$ $[_N$ *cat* $]$ $]$ $]$ $]$

As you can see, providing a full analysis of the constituent structure of a sentence using labeled brackets is cumbersome. A better way of representing constituent structure is introduced later in this chapter.

Bracketed this way, it is clear that certain strings in this sentence are not constituents. *Big dog* is not a constituent, because it is not complete. *The big dog angered* is not a constituent, because it has too many words to be a noun phrase and not enough to be a clause. For a string of words to be a constituent, there must be a matched pair of brackets that encloses the entire string and nothing but the string.

There is a special way to use the word CONSTITUENT which talks about the relationship of one constituent to the next larger one that encloses it. We can say that *the, big,* and *dog* are each CONSTITUENTS OF the first NP and *the* and *cat* are each constituents of the second NP. Also, the verb and the second NP are constituents of the VP. The individual words are not constituents of the clause, just of their respective phrases. The only two constituents of the clause are the first NP and the VP.

5.4. Comparing syntax and morphology

Some of the concepts introduced in chapter 4 "Introduction to Morphology" are also applicable to syntax.

Syntactic categories differ in size and expandability; some are OPEN CLASSES and some are CLOSED CLASSES. Most syntactic categories, like N and V, are open classes, since new nouns and

---

[1]In using the term 'set', I am making the standard generative assumption that languages, and thus syntactic categories, are recursively enumerable sets. For an alternate view, that languages are far larger than this, see Langendoen and Postal (1984).

verbs can be added freely to the vocabulary. A few syntactic categories, however, like D, are closed classes, since no new members are likely to be added. Some syntactic categories that are open in English, such as A (adjectives), are closed in other languages.

There is also a correlation between the openness of a class and the meaning of its members. Open classes like nouns almost always have LEXICAL MEANING, while closed classes like determiners usually have GRAMMATICAL MEANING. This is true both in syntax and morphology.

Finally, syntactic categories are like position classes in morphology. Recall that in every position class, the members are MUTUALLY SUBSTITUTABLE for each other. This is also an important criterion that we use to group words and phrases into syntactic categories.

5.5. Analyzing classes and categories

Certain categories are virtually universal. You can expect to find sentences, clauses, noun phrases, nouns, and verbs in any language. It is generally easy to identify these just on the basis of their meaning. Nouns in English, especially concrete nouns, tend to correspond to nouns in other languages, and vice versa. Other categories, such as adjectives, adverbs, and determiners, differ from language to language; even if they exist in a language, their membership may be very different from what you are familiar with. Further, in all categories, there may be words whose meaning may mislead you into an analysis which is not correct. For example, in Yuman languages (southwestern United States), kinship terms like 'mother' and 'brother' are verbs, and in Palauan (Austronesian, Republic of Belau), 'want' is a noun and 'not' is a verb. Position classes in morphology present even greater challenges, since they vary widely from one language to another.

When analyzing a language, it is necessary to examine the data carefully and set up categories based on characteristics of form that words and phrases have in common. Don't rely on meaning except to make a first hypothesis; after that look to characteristics of form to group elements into syntactic categories.

Recall that mutual substitutability (sameness of distribution) is one primary type of evidence we can use. Another is sameness of internal structure. When we group words into categories, we put together words that have the same morphological structure. For example, one characteristic that many adjectives in English share, in addition to their distribution, is that they have comparative (-er) and superlative (-est) forms.

When we group phrases into categories, we put together phrases that have the same constituent structure. For example, one thing that noun phrases in English have in common is that they contain head nouns, optionally preceded by a determiner and/or an adjective.[2] Thus, our analysis of English noun phrases is supported by facts about their shared internal structure as well as their sameness of distribution.

As you encounter data from diverse languages you will be exposed to a variety of categories, especially if you are using this book as part of a course that includes analysis of language data. Some of these may not correspond to anything that you are familiar with. In analyzing a particular language, if you have identified a category on the basis of mutual substitutability and/or sameness of internal structure, try to find an appropriate standard name for it if possible (ask someone if you need help); otherwise make up a name that reflects some general characteristic of the category, such as the meanings of its members. When writing about the language, be sure to explain any nonstandard terminology.

In short, then, don't use meaning to establish the categories in a language, but use it to name the categories once they are established by evidence about the morphological or syntactic form of utterances.

---

[2]As I often must do in the early chapters, I am oversimplifying here. Pronouns and conjoined noun phrases, both of which clearly belong to the category NP based on distributional evidence, do not have the structure described here. The larger point, however, still stands: there is a limited number of possibilities for the internal structure of an NP, and these possibilities are distinct from the structural possibilities for other phrasal categories.

5.6. Trees

As we have seen, sentences are not just strings of words. Words combine to make larger constituents called phrases, phrases combine to make still larger constituents called clauses, and so forth. A convenient device for displaying the constituent structure is called a TREE or TREE DIAGRAM (sometimes also called a phrase-marker or constituent structure tree).

(9)   a.   b.

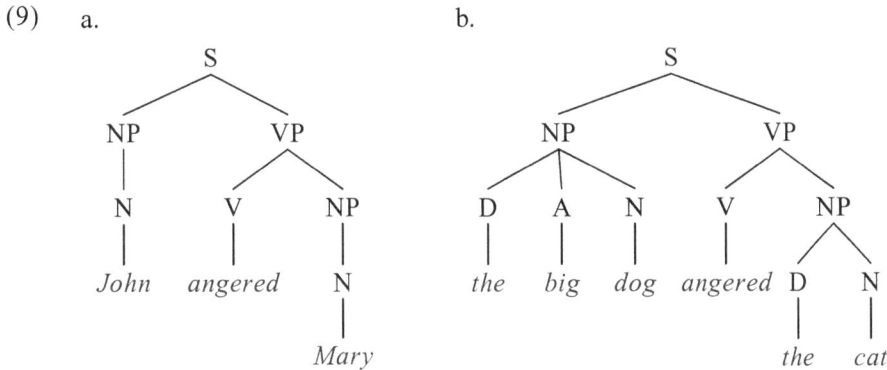

Compare the tree in (9b) to the labeled bracketing in (8), and see how much clearer (9b) is.

We need to define a number of terms in order to talk conveniently about the parts of a tree, the relationships between the parts, and the linguistic facts that they represent. As you read through this section, pay close attention to the examples of how the terms are used. Refer back to the diagrams frequently as you read the following definitions, so you can see immediately how each new term is used.

The lines in the trees are called BRANCHES, and the labeled places at the ends of the lines are called NODES. The topmost node on a tree is often called the ROOT node; the root nodes in the trees in (9) are labeled S. The bottommost nodes are called LEAVES or TERMINAL NODES; they are labeled with specific words like *the* and *angered*.

Every node which is not a terminal node is a NONTERMINAL node; nonterminal nodes always are labeled to indicate the syntactic category of the constituent underneath them. For example, in tree (9b), the leftmost NP node indicates that *the big dog* is an NP. The nodes immediately above the terminal nodes are a special type of nonterminal node called PRETERMINAL NODES; they show the syntactic category of an individual word. Every preterminal node has only one terminal node underneath it.

(Time out for a pep talk: Don't be discouraged if you don't understand all this terminology at first. It is normal to go through linguistic writing more than once before understanding it, especially technical material like this. Keep at it, and things will fall into place in a day or two.)

When we talk about trees, it is sometimes useful to use kinship terms. Thus, we can talk about one node as being the MOTHER of all the nodes immediately underneath it, which are its DAUGHTERS. Two nodes which have the same mother are SISTERS. Look back at (9b). The S node is mother to the first NP and the VP, and these two nodes are sisters to each other.

Any node is said to DOMINATE its 'descendants', and a lower node is said to BE DOMINATED BY any of its 'ancestors'. In (9b), the first NP and the VP are dominated by the S node. Conversely, the S node dominates the NP and VP nodes. The S node also dominates the second NP and all the D, A, and N nodes, although more remotely, and these nodes are dominated by S. The first D node is dominated by the first NP node, as are its sisters, an A and an N node.

If we want to zero in on the close relationship between a mother and its daughters, we say that the mother IMMEDIATELY DOMINATES its daughters and the daughters are IMMEDIATELY DOMINATED BY the mother. Thus in (9b), the leftmost NP node immediately dominates each of the three nodes D, A, and N, and that same NP is immediately dominated by S. The S node does not immediately dominate the D.

As mentioned earlier, the whole point in drawing trees is to have a convenient way to display a sentence's constituent structure. Note that if you start at any nonterminal node and trace from it down all the branches to the set of terminal nodes that it dominates (all its most remote descendants), you find a string of words that is a constituent; this constituent belongs to the syntactic category that is indicated by the node label. So, in (9b), the second NP node signifies that *the cat* is a constituent of type NP. The root node, S, signifies that the whole string *the big dog angered the cat* is a clause.

Another way to talk about the relationship of a node to a string of words which it dominates is to say that a node EXHAUSTIVELY DOMINATES a constituent. In (9b), the first NP node exhaustively dominates *the big dog* and thus we can see at a glance that *the big dog* is an NP. For a node to exhaustively dominate a string, the string must include all the terminal nodes dominated by the node and no others. Thus, the first NP in (9b) does not exhaustively dominate *big dog,* nor does it exhaustively dominate *the big dog angered.* To be exhaustively dominated by anything, a string must be a constituent.

Corresponding to the other use of the term CONSTITUENT (one constituent being a CONSTITUENT OF another), trees have one node immediately dominated by another. In (9b), the VP is immediately dominated by S, telling us that the verb phrase *angered the cat* is a constituent of the clause. For short, we say the VP is a constituent of the S.

To review, all this terminology gives us a way to represent our understanding of language as being hierarchically structured. Words in a sentence group together to form phrases, phrases group to form clauses, etc. A tree diagram is a convenient way to show this. A tree is like an "outline" of a sentence: it shows what the pieces are and which little pieces (e.g., words) go together to form bigger pieces (e.g., phrases and clauses).

Furthermore, we recognize that all pieces are not alike: some are verbs, some are noun phrases, some are clauses, etc. Thus, the tree also represents this information by means of the category labels at the nodes.

Finally, we want some way to talk about different parts of a tree and their relationships. For this reason we have terms such as NODE and DOMINATE, which give us precise ways of talking about constituents and their relationships.

5.7. Grammatical relations

But, there is more to basic clause structure than just constituency. The sentences *John angered Mary* and *Mary angered John* consist of identical categories and, except for the positions of two words, have identical constituent structures.

(10) a.   b.

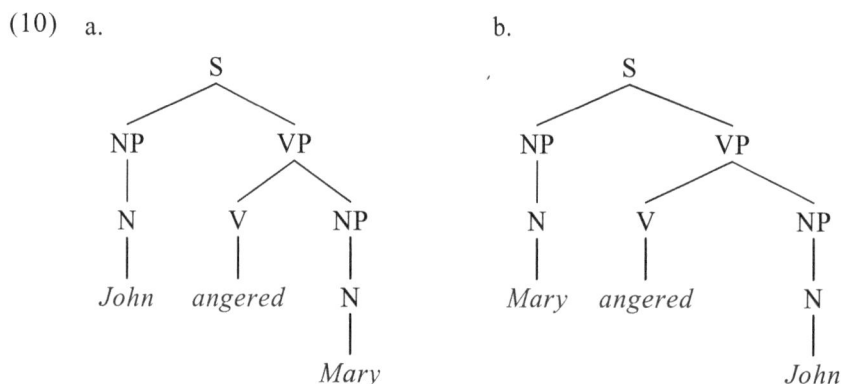

But, this change of word order makes a big difference in meaning. The two positions play a different role in the overall meaning of the sentence. Further, if we play around with the sentences a bit, we see several syntactic differences between the two positions too.[3]

---

[3]Thanks to Jim Meyer for suggesting this approach for introducing grammatical relations as an alternative to relying on meaning.

1. If we use pronouns, there are different forms of each pronoun depending on which position it is used in.

(11)   a. *He angered her.*
       b. *She angered him.*

2. In present tense, the verb changes form if we use 'they' as the first noun phrase, but it doesn't change if we use 'them' as the second noun phrase. That is, the verb agrees with the first noun phrase in number, but not with the second noun phrase (see the discussion of agreement in chapter 4 "Introduction to Morphology," p. 28).

(12)   a. *She angers him.*
       b. *They anger him.*
       c. *She angers them.*

3. If we question the second noun phrase, it is necessary to add *did* after the question word; this is not necessary for questioning the first noun phrase.

(13)   a. *Who did John anger?*
       b. *Who angered Mary?*

4. If we make what is called a 'tag' question, which ends with a pronoun, the pronoun always refers back to the first noun phrase, not the second.

(14)   a. *John angered Mary, didn't he?*
       b. *Mary angered John, didn't she?*
       c. **John angered Mary, didn't she?*

(Recall that the asterisk indicates that the example is unacceptable.)

There is something clearly different about these two noun phrase positions. The traditional way to distinguish them is by recognizing GRAMMATICAL RELATIONS (sometimes called GRAMMATICAL FUNCTIONS). In (15a), we say that *John* functions as the SUBJECT (Su) of the sentence and *Mary* functions as the DIRECT OBJECT (DO). In (15b), we say that *Mary* is the subject and *John* is the direct object. We can indicate grammatical relations in trees with the notation '[Su]' and '[DO]', as follows:

(15)   a.   b.

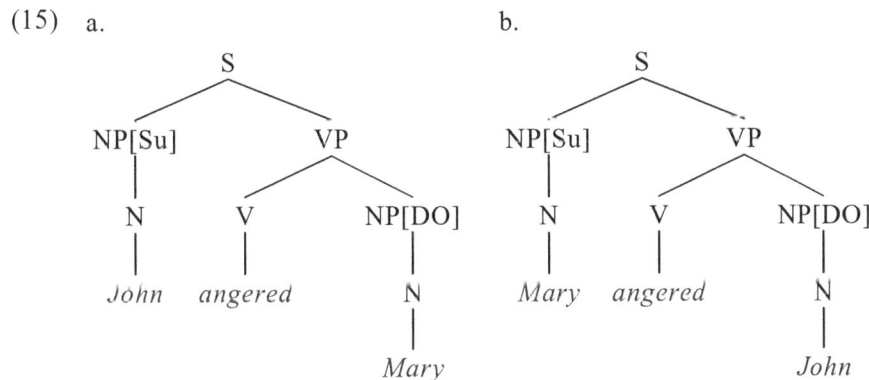

Chapter 6 ("The Base") explains more about this notation for grammatical relations.

As we have seen, there are quite a few syntactic differences between subjects and objects in English, and likewise in other languages there are often many differences between them. But, the details of those differences vary widely, and when you start working on a language, you don't know what those differences are. As a starting point for your analysis, you can assume the subject of a sentence to be the noun phrase that initiates the action and the direct object to be the noun phrase that is affected by the action. However, these are only preliminary hypotheses. As with setting up grammatical categories, you must find groups of NPs that behave alike in some respect; among these groups, one will typically be used for initiating an action and should be identified as subject, another will typically be affected by the action and should be identified as direct object. Thus, one of your first jobs as an analyst is to watch for syntactic differences that support a distinction between subject and object.

5.8. Analyzing other languages

Concepts such as constituent structure, syntactic categories, and grammatical relations are not confined to the analysis of English. These concepts are important to the study of all languages.

Consider the following pair of sentences from American Sign Language (North America).[4] ASL allows greater freedom of word order than English; the subject typically appears either first or last in the clause.

(16) a. *VISIT PARENTS I*
          I will visit (my) parents.
      b. *YESTERDAY I BUY TICKET*
          Yesterday, I bought a ticket.

(Since no practical orthography is in standard use for any signed language, examples are commonly transcribed using English glosses in capital letters to represent the individual words. This is only a crude representation of the richness of the language's structure, which is quite unlike English. Besides the differences in word order, note that, like many languages, spoken and signed, the verb is not marked for tense; time is indicated entirely by separate words like *YESTERDAY*.)

We can indicate the partial constituent structure and grammatical relations of these sentences with the following trees:

(17) a.   b.

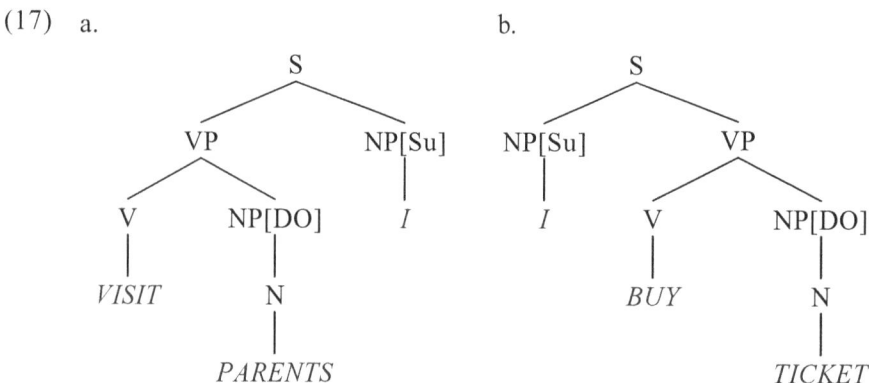

Note that each tree reflects the actual word order in each sentence, not the word order that you would find in English nor any standardized word order chosen arbitrarily.[5]

ASL also illustrates another pattern that is common in the world's languages: when a pronoun is understood in context, it may be omitted. In the following story, notice how few pronouns are overtly signed.[6]

---

[4]Data from Padden and Bendixen 1980:44.
[5]For simplicity, *YESTERDAY* is omitted from (17b); chapter 9 ("Obliques," pp. 101ff.) discusses how to handle it. Also, I haven't yet explained why pronouns are handled this way; that must wait for chapter 6 "The Base," pp. 54ff.
[6]Data from Karen Holte and Marilyn Plumlee (personal communication), with glosses simplified to hide details of ASL structure that are not relevant to the present discussion.

(18)   a. *LAST WEEK GUY PUT NEW L-I-N-O-L-E-U-M IN KITCHEN.*
          Last week, a man installed new linoleum in (my) kitchen.
       b. *NOW BUMP CORNER.*
          (But) then it was bulging out in the corner (lit., there was a bump in the corner).
       c. *CALL GUY; NOT.YET SHOW.UP.*
          (So) I called the guy, (but) he never showed up.
       d. *WAIT WAIT; CALL AGAIN.*
          I waited and waited, (and) called again.
       e. *HE FINALLY.SUCCEED COME YESTERDAY.*
          He finally came yesterday.
       f. *FIX FINISH.*
          He fixed it at last.

How do we draw trees when pronouns are present in the meaning but not overtly signed? Do we just omit the whole branch from the tree? Do we include the branch, but leave the terminal node empty? Or do we fill the terminal node with a silent pronoun? For reasons discussed later (in chapter 8 "Verbal Valence," p. 87), this book takes the silent-pronoun approach. A silent pronoun like this is often called *pro,* and it appears in trees like any other pronoun.[7]

(19)

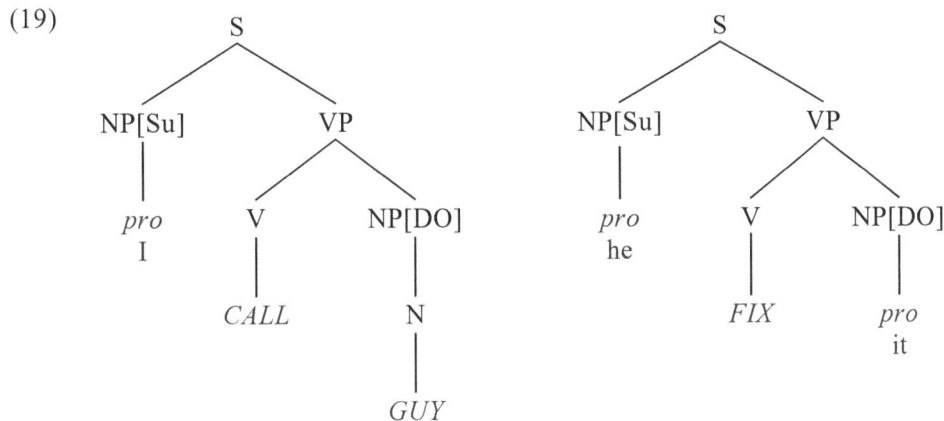

5.9. Review of key terms

One basic ability of a speaker of a language is the ability to judge whether utterances are GRAMMATICAL. Part of this ability consists in recognizing that sentence structure is HIERARCHICAL; it is not just strings of words. Words are grouped into phrases, phrases into clauses, and clauses into larger units like sentences and paragraphs. Each of these groups of material are called CONSTITUENTS, and all the constituents of a sentence taken together comprise its CONSTITUENT STRUCTURE.

Constituents belong to different SYNTACTIC CATEGORIES; some of the most common are CLAUSE (S), NOUN PHRASE (NP), VERB PHRASE (VP), DETERMINER (D), NOUN (N), VERB (V), and ADJECTIVE (A). We decide which constituents belong in the same syntactic categories not by paying attention to meaning, but rather finding constituents with shared characteristics of form, such as SAMENESS OF DISTRIBUTION (MUTUAL SUBSTITUTABILITY) and SAMENESS OF INTERNAL STRUCTURE. However, meaning is important for naming the categories that contain individual words, once their

---

[7]This approach does not share the assumption (cf. Radford 1997:522) that *pro* is limited to subject position, as there are many languages that allow direct object pronouns (or even other positions) to be omitted. Thus, as illustrated in chapter 8 "Verbal Valence" (p. 87), its distribution must be stipulated in its lexical entry.

membership has been determined. Then, we name the phrases after their central and most important member, or HEAD.

The constituent structure of a sentence can be represented in two ways, with LABELED BRACKETS and with TREES. Trees consist of a set of NODES connected by BRANCHES. Different types of nodes include ROOT NODES, TERMINAL NODES, PRETERMINAL NODES, and NONTERMINAL NODES. (These types overlap; some nodes belong to more than one type.) The relationships between nodes can be described with kinship terms such as MOTHER, DAUGHTER, and SISTER, or with terms like DOMINATES, IMMEDIATELY DOMINATES, and EXHAUSTIVELY DOMINATES. Finally, certain nodes, notably NP nodes, also carry labels for their GRAMMATICAL RELATION (or GRAMMATICAL FUNCTION), such as SUBJECT (Su) or DIRECT OBJECT (DO).

5.10. Questions for analysis

1. What syntactic categories are there for words and phrases?
2. What evidence supports your answer to question 1?

5.11. Sample description

The two largest classes of words in English are (not surprisingly) nouns and verbs. Verbs serve as the nucleus of a clause; nouns typically fill positions of subject, direct object, object of preposition, etc.

(1)   N   V   N   N
          The girl angered a cat under the porch

Adjectives modify nouns, usually occurring just before them as part of a noun phrase. The closed class of determiners (including *a/an* and *the*) precedes the adjectives.

(2)   D   A   N
          The sly dog

5.12. For further reading

Radford 1988, chapter 2, covers much the same material as this chapter. It is especially valuable for its numerous examples of the types of syntactic evidence that can be used to establish word-level and phrasal categories, spelling out what is referred to above as SAMENESS OF DISTRIBUTION.

Schacter 1985 provides a survey of the types of word-level categories that are commonly found in natural languages. It makes a very clear statement (pp. 3–4) about the role that meaning plays in the analysis of words into categories; this is the basis for the discussion above.

Most signed languages have been developed by deaf people to allow easy communication among themselves. Although over 100 are known to exist (Barbara Grimes 1996), relatively few have been studied extensively. Often, short vocabulary lists are available, but little else. American Sign Language has probably received more attention from linguists than any other signed language. For a linguistically-oriented introduction to this fascinating language, which is quite unlike English, see Klima and Bellugi 1979. For a more popular and much briefer treatment, see the segment 'Language' from the public TV series *The Mind*, available in the United States from PBS Videos (call 800-344-3337 for educational use, 800-531-4727 for home use).

6
The Base:
Phrase Structure Rules and the Lexicon

6.1. Goals and prerequisites

This chapter will help you do the following:

- ◎ explain the differences between formal and informal grammars
- ◎ draw a chart showing the base component of a generative grammar
- ◎ state three types of information contained in a lexical entry
- ◎ use phrase structure rules and lexical entries to construct simple sentences
- ◎ make reasonable hypotheses about phrase structure rules and lexical entries for data on simple clause structure
- ◎ describe such data informally, including stating the basic word order

It assumes that you are familiar with the following material:

- ✓ syntactic categories, grammatical relations, tree structures and other basic concepts for describing the structure of clauses (chapter 5 "Introduction to Syntax")

Some familiarity with phonetics and phonology is helpful at a couple of points. If you have not already done so, you may want to read chapter 24 "Hints for Linguistic Writing" at the same time as this chapter.

6.2. Formal versus informal grammars

Now we are ready to go a step beyond drawing trees for individual sentences; we will crystallize our hypotheses about syntactic structure into a FORMAL GRAMMAR. A formal grammar is a scientific model of a language which describes what is and what is not a grammatical (well-formed) sentence. It attempts to represent what a speaker of the language knows about its structure; this knowledge is also called a GRAMMAR. A formal grammar, then, is a model of a speaker's internal grammar.

Formal grammars are different from the books that you have usually seen called 'grammars', such as foreign language textbooks. These could be called INFORMAL GRAMMARS. They are usually easier to understand than formal grammars, but are usually less precise. Formal grammars attempt to represent a speaker's internal grammar much more accurately and in more detail than is usually

47

done in informal grammars. Many statements in informal grammars are not TESTABLE; they may be vague enough that it is difficult to tell whether they are right or wrong.

Since one goal of this book is to help you think clearly and precisely about languages, it makes use of formal grammars as tools for describing languages. The details of these grammars are based on a family of related linguistic theories which are collectively called GENERATIVE GRAMMAR. Generative grammar conceives of a language's grammar as a precise set of rules that specify which utterances are grammatical in a language and which are not.

Most generative grammars represent the structure of a sentence in the form of a tree, as we have been doing. The portion of a generative grammar which is responsible for building such trees is often called the BASE COMPONENT and consists of two parts, the PHRASE STRUCTURE RULES and the LEXICON.

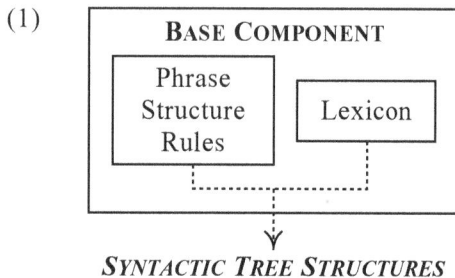

(1)

```
┌─────────────────────────────┐
│   BASE COMPONENT            │
│  ┌─────────┐  ┌──────────┐  │
│  │ Phrase  │  │          │  │
│  │Structure│  │ Lexicon  │  │
│  │ Rules   │  │          │  │
│  └─────────┘  └──────────┘  │
│            ↓                 │
└─────────────────────────────┘
```

SYNTACTIC TREE STRUCTURES

(This is only an approximate and incomplete diagram; there are several additions to it in later chapters.)

The phrase structure rules and lexicon divide their work this way: the phrase structure rules provide the syntactic structure of the sentence and the lexicon provides the vocabulary. Phrase structure rules provide precise statements about which trees are well-formed and which are ill-formed, with respect to such things as constituency and word order. The lexicon (a highly-refined dictionary) provides precise statements about whether the words in a tree are used in proper contexts, as well as providing information about their meaning and pronunciation. In short, the phrase structure rules build the nonterminal nodes of a tree and the lexicon adds the terminal nodes.

6.3. Phrase structure rules

To see how all this works, consider the following trees for sentences in Palantla Chinantec (Otomanguean, Mexico).[1] There are English glosses in the diagrams for readability, but the glosses are not part of the trees.[2]

---

[1]Based on Merrifield et. al. 1987, #137. Glosses and transcription are slightly modified. Ballistic stress is represented by *h* after a vowel; superscript numerals represent level tones (3=high, 1=low) and glides; other transcription is standard IPA.

[2]For now, we are ignoring inflectional morphology; chapter 10 "Inflectional Morphology" explains one way that it can be incorporated into a generative grammar.

(2)

```
                    S
        ┌───────────┼───────────┐
        V         NP[Su]       NP[DO]
        │         ┌──┴──┐         │
       se¹        N     A         N
    will.bathe    │     │         │
                 mih²  bã?²      tsi?²
                woman chubby    child
```

The chubby woman will bathe the child.

(3)

```
                    S
        ┌───────────┼───────────┐
        V         NP[Su]       NP[DO]
        │           │        ┌──┴──┐
      hɤh²          N        N     A
    will.see        │        │     │
                  kwɨ³      mih²  pã¹³
                  horse    woman  fat
```

The horse will see the fat woman.

(4)

```
                    S
        ┌───────────┼───────────┐
        V         NP[Su]       NP[DO]
        │           │            │
      zjã?¹²         N            N
    will.find        │            │
                  gju?¹³        tsi?²
                   man          child
```

The man will find the child.

(5)

```
                    S
        ┌───────────┼───────────┐
        V         NP[Su]       NP[DO]
        │         ┌──┴──┐      ┌──┴──┐
      zjã?¹²       N    A      N     A
    will.find      │    │      │     │
                 tsi?² pih?³  kwɨ³  bã?²
                 child little horse chubby
```

The little child will find the stocky horse.

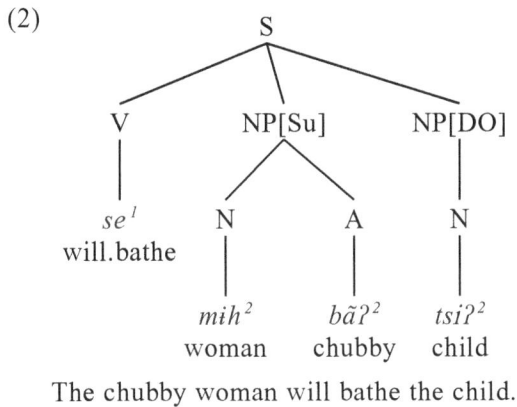

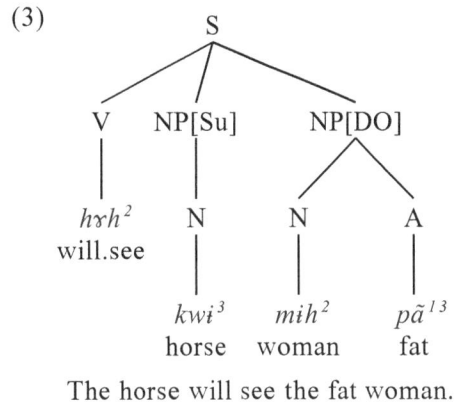

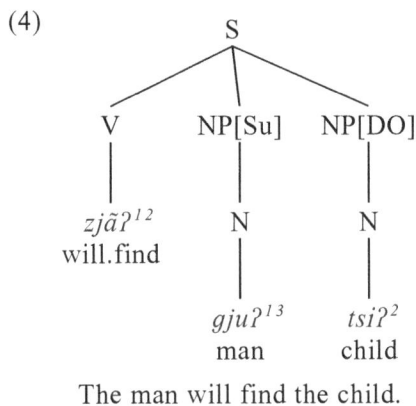

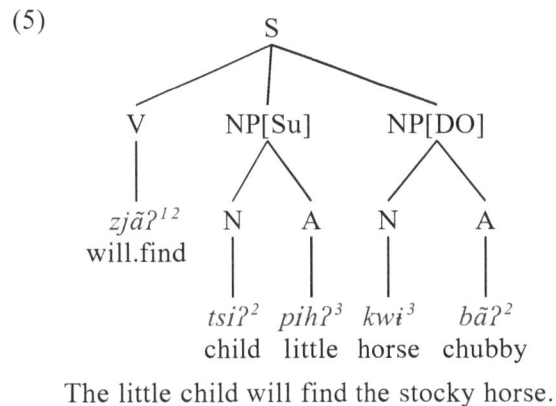

What observations and generalizations can we make about them?

First of all, we notice that in each case the order of elements directly below the S node is V NP NP. (Unlike English, we are not assuming that there is a VP node; more on this later.) Thus we can say, '(One kind of) Palantla Chinantec clause consists of a verb followed by two noun phrases'. We can formalize this statement in the form of a phrase structure rule as follows:

(6)   S → V NP NP

This is a first hypothesis about the clause structure; as we proceed, we will revise and refine it.

We also notice that the two noun phrases function as subject and direct object respectively. We incorporate this information into our rule.

(7)   S › V NP[Su] NP[DO]

The rule is now read, 'An S is composed of a verb followed by an NP functioning as subject followed by an NP functioning as direct object'.

Consider now the structure of the noun phrases. Some consist of a noun and a following adjective, while others consist of a single noun only. We write another phrase structure rule to express this observation, using parentheses to show the optionality of the adjective.

(8)   NP → N (A)

This rule says that a noun phrase consists of a noun, followed optionally by an adjective.

A complete grammar of Chinantec would need many parts and many more rules than are considered here. Our goal for the moment is simply to construct some small portion of a grammar.[3]

6.4. The lexicon

In order to account for the Palantla Chinantec data, we need more than phrase structure rules for S and NP. We also need a LEXICON, a precise listing of the basic units which occur in the language. The lexicon is very much like a dictionary, but there are some differences. Generally, a dictionary is a reference book written for a general audience. When linguists use the word LEXICON, however, they mean either a speaker's knowledge of the vocabulary of his language or a formal ANALYSIS of that knowledge (that is, a set of hypotheses about that knowledge). Such an analysis generally includes more information than is normally included in a dictionary (which is written for a general, nontechnical audience) and provides it in a form that is precise and testable.

The individual units in the lexicon are called LEXICAL ITEMS or LEXICAL ENTRIES. Roughly, each lexical entry corresponds to a single word, although we will refine this conception as we proceed through the book. For now, let us simply say that the lexicon contains lists of facts about words that are not predictable by general rule.

Each lexical entry contains three types of information: phonological information (about its pronunciation), grammatical information (e.g., its syntactic category and other properties that control how it combines with other elements), and semantic information (about its meaning). For example, the lexical entries for various words in Palantla Chinantec might be written something like this:[4]

(9)   *tsiʔ²*   N   child
       bã̃ʔ²   A   chubby, stocky
       kwi³   N   horse

Strictly speaking, the lexical entries of a language can be written in any order. If we were documenting a large portion of a lexicon (as in a dictionary), we might list the entries alphabetically according to their spelling. In this book, however, it is usually more convenient to group together all the entries that belong to the same syntactic category, as follows:

(10)   **A**
       bã̃ʔ²   chubby, stocky
       pã̃¹³   fat
       pihʔ³   little

       N
       tsiʔ²   child
       gjuʔ¹³   man
       kwi³   horse
       mih²   woman

---

[3]In fact, all formal grammars are incomplete, although of course some are more comprehensive than others. So-called 'complete' grammars are usually informal and even then leave some phenomena undescribed. The task of constructing a precise formal grammar for an entire language is extremely demanding, and few people have attempted it. Still, any progress one can make in understanding a language precisely is valuable, so linguists keep on producing incomplete formal grammars without apology.

[4]Verbs are omitted from this list because each of the verbs contains more than one morpheme, although this is not shown in the data here. They would need to be split up further before finding the pieces that would be listed as lexical entries.

6.5. How it all works

We can now run a check on our grammar to see what sentences it can GENERATE, or produce.[5] Our ultimate goal is to construct a grammar which generates all the grammatical sentences of a language and no ungrammatical (non)sentences. To achieve this goal, we want first to COVER THE DATA, i.e., make sure the grammar generates all the sentences in the data that we already know about and none of the sequences that we know native speakers find ungrammatical. Make a habit of checking your hypotheses thoroughly against the available data so that you can be confident they are correct.

However, when we write a formal grammar we are interested in more than covering the data; we want to have a model of what a speaker knows about the whole language, not just the data we have collected. A generative grammar makes predictions about further data, since it is capable of generating utterances not found in the data. Such predictions should be tested with a native speaker as a way of testing the grammar.[6] If some utterances are judged to be ungrammatical (that is, if they 'sound bad' to native speakers and this 'badness' cannot be attributed to other factors such as a nonsensical combination of words), the grammar is in need of revision. This happens often since our knowledge of a language is always incomplete.

Let's see how our grammar of Palantla Chinantec generates a sentence. Here are the rules again.

(11)   a.   S → V NP[Su] NP[DO]
       b.   NP → N (A)

We start by APPLYING THE S RULE (11a), which produces a structure like this:

(12)

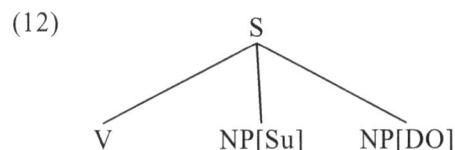

By APPLYING THE S RULE, we mean that we take the symbol on the left of the arrow and write it above the symbols on the right of the arrow; then we connect up the symbols with branches.

Next we apply the NP rule (11b). This rule gives us several choices and needs to be applied twice, once for the subject NP and once for the direct object NP. We can choose to rewrite both NPs as single nouns, or both as noun plus adjective, or one of each. All these possibilities are permitted by our grammar. For this sentence, let's generate an adjective only in the subject.

(13)

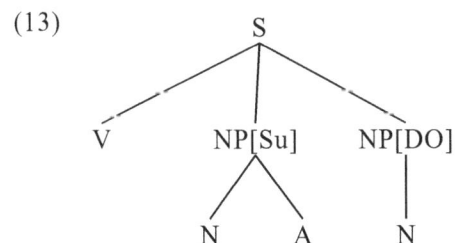

---

[5]Generative grammarians often draw a distinction between GENERATING sentences and PRODUCING them. Generating an utterance is what a grammar does: it specifies that it is grammatical. Producing an utterance is what people do when they speak (or write), including all sorts of details such as first deciding what they want to say and controlling their muscles. The practical matters of how they do this in their neurons is conceivably quite different from what happens in a generative grammar. What makes a grammar 'generative' is not that it has a set of procedures for constructing an utterance (although most generative grammars do), but that it precisely specifies which utterances are grammatical and which are not.

[6]There are many practical problems involved in getting reliable judgments from native speakers, such as convincing them not to just accept our mistakes politely and keeping boredom from introducing mistakes in their judgments. These concerns are covered in courses which are usually called 'Field Methods'.

This finishes the work of the phrase structure rules.

Next we choose items from the lexicon and insert them in the proper places. This process is called LEXICAL INSERTION.

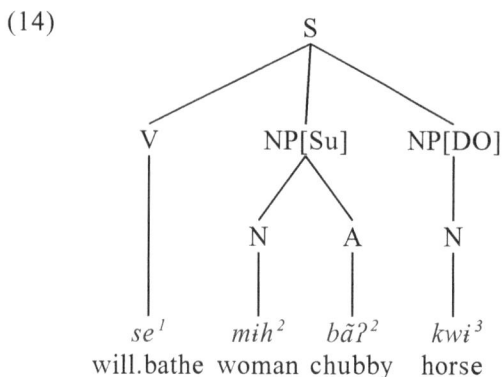

(14)

```
                          S
              ┌───────────┼───────────┐
              V        NP[Su]       NP[DO]
              │        ┌──┴──┐         │
              │        N     A         N
              │        │     │         │
             se¹     mih²   bã?²      kwɨ³
         will.bathe  woman  chubby    horse
```

The resulting sentence presumably means 'The chubby woman will bathe the horse'.

Notice that at virtually every step of the process, we had choices available to us. With only two rules and a small lexicon, we can generate quite a large number of different sentences. In fact, the total is 768.[7]

6.6. Basic word order

You certainly have noticed that the word order of Palantla Chinantec is different from that of English. English is considered an 'SVO' language, since the Subject normally comes first, then the Verb, then the Object (i.e., the direct object). Chinantec, on the other hand, is VSO. Given the subject, direct object, and verb, there are six logically possible orderings of these three elements, so there are six types of languages when classified according to word order in clauses.

SVO word order is one of the most common word orders, along with SOV and VSO. VOS is somewhat rare and only a handful of OSV and OVS languages are known. Notice that, in the three most common basic word orders, the subject precedes the objects.

All of this discussion refers to the BASIC WORD ORDER in a clause, i.e., the one that should be used when writing the phrase structure rules. In most cases, determining the basic order is not difficult. Quite often, it is also the most common word order, and in your initial analysis, it is safe to assume that the most common word order is the basic one.[8] However, all languages have one or more alternate word orders used for special purposes, and some languages allow more freedom of word order than others. It can sometimes be a challenge sorting all this out, so these issues are discussed again later in chapters 15 "Variable Orders of Constituents" (p. 214) and 17 "Commands" (p. 243).

6.7. Other types of noun phrases

Let us consider a slightly more complicated body of data in English.

---

[7]This total assumes three verbs, four nouns, three adjectives, and four distinct tree structures; it ignores morphology. Some of the resulting sentences would probably be unacceptable to native speakers, of course, but the point is how a very simple set of rules can produce a relatively large number of sentences.

[8]The most common word order in natural text may be a more reliable indicator than the order used in isolated examples, especially if the examples were developed by translation from another language.

(15) a. *John angered Mary.*
      b. *Mary angered John.*
      c. *John chased Mary.*
      d. *John chased the dog.*
      e. *The dog chased John.*
      f. *Mary chased John.*
      g. *Mary chased the cats.*
      h. *John walked.*
      i. *The big dog chased the cats.*
      j. *The dog runs.*
      k. *Cats hate dogs.*
      l. *The big dog chased the little cats.*
      m. *Little dogs chased the cats.*
      n. *I chased the cat.*
      o. *He loves her.*

What observations can we make about these sentences?

First, we notice that the order is uniformly SVO (subject-verb-direct object) and that the direct object is optional. Assuming (as we did in chapter 5 "Introduction to Syntax") that the verb and the direct object form a VP constituent in English, we incorporate our observations into two phrase structure rules.

(16)   S   → NP[Su] VP
       VP → V (NP[DO])

Second, we notice there are several types of noun phrases, including what are traditionally called COMMON NOUNS, PROPER NOUNS, and PRONOUNS. The formal analysis of these things is the topic for the next two sections.

Common nouns

One type of noun phrase consists of a COMMON NOUN (a generic name for a class of objects), optionally preceded by a determiner and/or an adjective, in that order.

(17)   NP → (D) (A) N

Other noun phrases consist entirely of a PROPER NOUN (a name of a particular individual). As you can see in the data above, proper nouns generally occur without modifiers and are usually singular. However, this is not necessarily the case.

(18) a. *There were two Alberts at camp.*
      b. *Practically every state in the union has a Madison.*
      c. *He is the largest Tim that I have ever seen.*

Of course, sentences like these are somewhat unusual. Even though they show that proper nouns seem to be able to combine with other words in the same ways as common nouns, most of the time proper nouns occur without any modifiers.

English common nouns, on the other hand, usually cannot appear unmodified when they are singular.[9]

(19)   **dog angered cat.*

---

[9]To be precise, it is common count nouns that are subject to this restriction.

This is ungrammatical, unless you understand 'dog' and 'cat' to refer to a specific individual, in which case they are being used as proper nouns (and would normally be capitalized in written English).

We need some way of representing these differences in our grammar. We do so by subdividing the category of nouns into two SUBCATEGORIES, one for common nouns and the other for proper nouns. This represents the fact that both types of nouns are still nouns and as such share many characteristics. It also represents the fact that they have minor differences.

To do this in our formal grammars, we use what is called a FEATURE along with the category label N. A feature is a formal way of representing some characteristic of a linguistic unit. (You may have encountered features already in phonetics and phonology, where they are used to express the various characteristics of sounds and how each sound is similar to and different from other sounds.) The feature we use in this case is [common], which has two values, [+common] (for common nouns) and [–common] (for proper nouns). Thus, our lexicon might look like this:

(20) **N[–common]**   **N[+common]**
      Mary   *dog*
      John   *cat*
      Mudville   *sentence*
      Manhattan   *linguist*
      ...   ...

This approach represents both the similarities of words (all are in the category N) and their differences (they differ in their value for [common]).[10]

Pronouns

How should pronouns, such as *I, he,* and *her,* be handled in a formal grammar? Traditional grammars often state that pronouns 'take the place of' nouns, implying that they are mutually substitutable for nouns and thus should be analyzed as a special type of N. But this not the case. Consider what happens if we try to use them as nouns, modified by adjectives, determiners, numbers, and the like.

(21) **A charming she loves the two us.*

Rather, pronouns are mutually substitutable for noun *phrases,* at least in most languages. A better analysis, then, is that they belong to the category NP, not the category N. We therefore list them in the lexicon as members of the category NP.[11] (These lexical entries are refined to account for the different forms of each pronoun in chapter 10 "Inflectional Morphology," pp. 128ff.)

---

[10]To be complete in our analysis, we would have to write rules to spell out exactly what the differences are between common and proper nouns; just creating the subcategories [+common] and [–common] does nothing unless we also formulate rules that spell out the characteristic behavior of each subcategory. As this particular area is complex and may well involve semantic and pragmatic considerations, I follow Chomsky (1965:82–83) and Radford (1988:338) and do not formulate the rules themselves. Doing so would only distract from the main purpose of the discussion, which is to introduce the concepts of subcategories and features in preparation for chapter 8 "Verbal Valence."

[11]In categorizing pronouns as NPs, I follow Radford (1988:78–82, cf. especially p. 232). It has not seemed necessary in this book to introduce a feature [+pro] distinguishing pronouns from NPs expanded by the phrase structure rules, although such a feature is necessary to handle binding conditions (Chomsky 1981:184–85). An alternative analysis of pronouns is that they are nouns with extremely strict subcategorization restrictions about what can occur with them inside their NP. However, such an analysis would require pronouns to exclude adjuncts to the NP as well as complements, obscuring the difference between complements and adjuncts.

(22) **NP**

I, me, my	first person singular
you, your	second person
she, her	third person singular feminine
he, him, his	third person singular masculine
we, us, our	first person plural

    ...

Don't be bothered by the fact that single words are being assigned to a 'phrasal' category; this is exactly what we want, since these single words replace whole noun phrases and refer to whole noun phrases. A phrase can consist of a single word, just like a word can consist of a single morpheme. Also, don't worry about the fact that phrasal categories are listed in the lexicon. Pronouns clearly belong in the lexicon (their meaning and form is not predictable by rule), and if putting them in a phrasal category gives the best account of the facts, then that's where we should put them.

When we are building a tree and encounter an NP node, we can either apply the phrase structure rule for NPs, as we did before, or we can insert a pronoun (an NP) from the lexicon. If we insert a pronoun, the result looks like this:

(23)

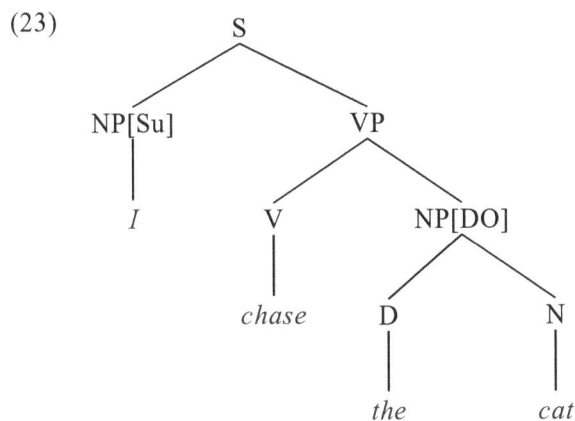

(For now, affixes like noun plurals and verb tense are not shown, since we have not yet discussed how to handle morphology in our formal grammars; this comes up in chapter 10 "Inflectional Morphology.")

6.8. Constituent structure in standard generative grammars

There are some differences between the generative grammars in this book and ones that you will find in most of the linguistic literature. I touch on a couple of the more obvious differences here, so that you have some idea about what you will find in further linguistic studies.

In some generative theories, grammatical relations are not written explicitly in phrase structure rules or trees. Instead, they are predictable from the shape of the trees. For example, look again at (23). In a tree like this, 'subject' can be defined as 'the NP immediately dominated by S' and 'direct object' as 'the NP immediately dominated by VP'. Grammatical relations are defined in terms of dominance and so do not need to be indicated explicitly in the tree.

This method of defining grammatical relations is adequate for a language with SVO order, such as English, in which we can have a VP node that includes the object but not the subject. But in languages with VSO or OSV orders, where the direct object and verb are separated by the subject, we can't follow this approach straightforwardly. Consider what would happen if we tried to adapt (23) to Palantla Chinantec (compare this to (4)).

(24)

```
                        S
              VP _____/|
          ____/\____     \
         V    NP[Su]    NP[DO]
         |      |          |
         |      N          N
         |      |          |
         |      |          |
       zjã?¹²  gju?¹³     tsi?²
      will.find  man      child
```

The man will find the child.

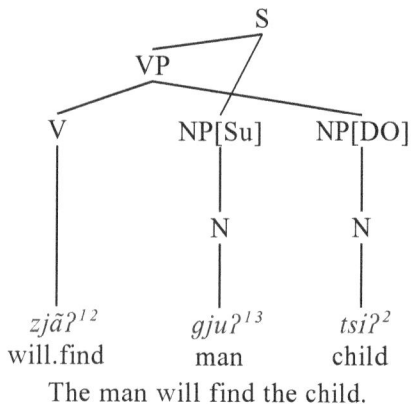

If we try to put the verb and the direct object together as a VP constituent which does not include the subject, we end up with crossed lines, which (most linguists assume) are forbidden in trees. But, without a VP constituent as in (4), we can't distinguish the subject and object by what dominates them, because both are dominated directly by S.

In the history of Generative Grammar, there have been many proposals for getting around this dilemma. One approach is to assume that in VSO (and OSV) languages, there is no VP constituent that includes the object. You can see this in the Chinantec trees earlier. That is, such languages have a FLAT CLAUSE STRUCTURE, in which the subject and direct object are sisters and both immediately dominated by S. The opposite type of structure, like that in (23), is sometimes called an ARTICULATED CLAUSE STRUCTURE. In an articulated structure, only the subject is immediately dominated by S; the direct object is under a VP node.

The difference is more than just a matter of convenience in writing rules; there are actual differences between languages that can be related to whether the verb and its object form a constituent.[12] However, they involve too many complexities to introduce here. Instead, this book takes the approach of adopting a reasonable hypothesis for each language, based on its word order type, and suggests that you do the same in your initial analysis. In SVO (and OVS) languages (e.g., English), we assume an articulated clause structure, and in VSO and OSV languages (e.g., Chinantec), we assume a flat one. These assumptions are reasonable because very often the data bears them out.

With SOV and VOS languages, the data varies more from one language to the next, so we may sometimes posit a flat clause structure, sometimes an articulated one, for them.

(25) SOV flat clause structure   SOV articulated clause structure

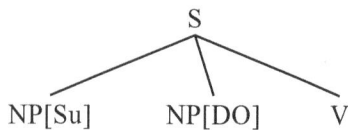

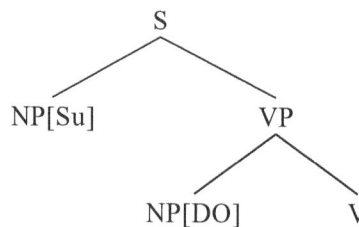

```
            S                                      S
        ____/|\____                            ___/ \___
       /     |     \                          /         \
   NP[Su]  NP[DO]   V                      NP[Su]        VP
                                                       __/ \__
                                                      /       \
                                                   NP[DO]      V
```

In summary, the following are good first hypotheses about the nature of the phrase structure in a language:

---

[12]See, for example, the papers in Marácz and Muysken 1989, especially the papers by Rebuschi, van Steenbergen, and Choe.

(26) Basic word order   First hypothesis

    SVO, OVS   articulated
    VSO, OSV   flat
    SOV, VOS   either

In actual fieldwork, these hypotheses would eventually need to be tested, just like the rest of the analysis, but it is generally hard to find relevant data that is appropriate for use with an introductory textbook. For now, we will content ourselves with a reasonable first hypothesis so we can move on to other aspects of the analysis.

Since we can't distinguish the subject from the direct object using dominance in a flat clause structure, we will follow the example of several generative theories and represent them explicitly in the tree, using the labels [Su] and [DO].[13] For consistency, we use them even in articulated clause structures, even though strictly speaking they are not necessary.

Incidentally, this way of representing subject and direct object in trees is not just an arbitrary system of labels. This book uses [Su] and [DO] as two instances of another type of feature, like [±common]. To be precise, it assumes a feature [GR] which represents grammatical relations and which has possible values that include [Su] and [DO], as well as others that we introduce later. (We could write these as [Su GR] and [DO GR], which makes their status as feature values more obvious, but usually we abbreviate them.)

6.9. What makes a good analysis

In constructing your formal grammars, how do you know which hypotheses are better than others? The first and foremost requirement is that the formal grammar should COVER THE DATA, as discussed above. The analysis should account for all the known facts—generating all known grammatical utterances and none that are known to be ungrammatical.

Second, the analysis must be CONSISTENT, both with itself and with the requirements of whatever theoretical framework you are using. Make sure the rules, lexical entries, etc., work together properly, given the theory's assumptions about how such rules work. For example, don't use 'N' as a symbol in the phrase structure rules and 'Noun' in the lexicon. Under standard assumptions in Generative Grammar, 'N' and 'Noun' are different symbols, and as a result, any words listed as 'Noun' in the lexicon cannot be inserted in the tree under the N nodes. Keep your abbreviations consistent, and when standard abbreviations are available, use them.

Once these two primary goals are achieved, there are two others: SIMPLICITY and NATURALNESS.

SIMPLICITY means you should avoid unnecessary symbols or rules. For example, for Palantla Chinantec, we did not posit a VP node to include the objects; further, there are no other words (in our data) which modify the verb and group together with it as a verb phrase. Thus, there is no need to include a VP rule in the analysis, and we would not want the following set of rules:

(27) S → VP NP[Su] (NP[DO])
    VP → V   *(wrong)*

To include a VP rule when it is not needed would depart from the goal of simplicity.

Simplicity also demands that when there is a generalization to be stated, it should be stated as such. For example, if the structure of a noun phrase is the same whether it is a subject or direct object, we should *not* write two almost identical rules like this:

---

[13]This is the norm, for example, in Lexical-functional Grammar (see especially Sells 1985:136) and Relational Grammar (Perlmutter 1983). Even in Government-binding Theory, abstract case is similar in many respects to grammatical relations. See, for example, Chomsky's (1981:128ff) demonstration that abstract case can substitute for constituent structure in a flat clause structure. Abstract case is necessary even in articulated clause structures, so there is not that great a step from standard transformational practice to the representations employed here. I use a feature for grammatical relations, however, rather than introducing the concept of abstract case, to avoid confusion with (superficial) morphological case.

(28) NP[Su]   → (D) (A) N   *(wrong)*
      NP[DO]   → (D) (A) N

Rather, we write just one rule that covers both subject and direct objects:

(29) NP → (D) (A) N   *(right)*

NATURALNESS means that the analysis should reflect what is known to be normally true about languages in general. It should highlight any similarities between this language and others, rather than obscure them.

For example, naturalness provides another reason for preferring (29) over (28). The internal structure of a subject NP is almost always the same as the structure of a direct object NP, so you should *not* write two different NP rules, even if, because of insufficient data, subjects and objects seem to differ.[14]

Also, all languages have modifiers of nouns, so that naturalness demands that you include an NP node dominating every N in every tree, even if, in some restricted set of examples, all the noun phrases consist of a single noun. To put it another way, every time you write an S rule, you should include NPs, not Ns, since you will certainly find them. As a temporary measure, make a partial rule like (30) to remind you to find out what the internal structure of noun phrases is.

(30) NP → ... N ...

One of the reasons that simplicity and naturalness are important is that we want our grammars to cover not just the data which we have already discovered, but also (as much as possible) to cover new data that we have not yet encountered. Of course, new data often requires revisions to our analysis, but if at each stage you work to keep your analysis simple and natural, it tends to keep the amount of revision you have to do later to a minimum. That is, grammars that are simple and natural tend to make more accurate predictions about further data.

Still, a caution is in order. Simplicity and naturalness should be sought only to the extent that the facts of the language allow. It does no good, for example, to have a simple and natural analysis which does not account for a complex set of facts. Covering the data and being consistent are more important than being simple and natural. However, given two analyses that both cover the data, the simpler and more natural one is generally the better one.[15]

6.10. Review of key terms

In describing a speaker's internalized GRAMMAR of a language, linguists may make INFORMAL descriptions in prose or construct FORMAL GRAMMARS, using the precise concepts and notation of a specific THEORETICAL FRAMEWORK. Although formal grammars are harder to understand, they have the advantage of being more explicit and thus more TESTABLE. A linguist makes a formal grammar by making hypotheses about the rules of the grammar, testing them against the data, and revising them as needed. The goal is to have an ANALYSIS which COVERS THE DATA and is CONSISTENT, SIMPLE, and NATURAL.

---

[14]The one major exception to this is case marking, but even then, the structure of subject and object noun phrases is similar enough that we would not want two separate but almost identical phrase structure rules. Instead, there is another approach which will account for these minor differences (see chapter 19 "Case and Agreement"), so that our phrase structure rules for NP can remain as simple and general as possible.

[15]In practice, all these factors must be weighed against each other and the choice is sometimes difficult. For example, if the theoretical framework you are using forces you into an analysis which is more complex than it needs to be to cover the facts, then it is probably time to revise the theory or look for a new one. On the other hand, sometimes people choose to ignore certain exceptional examples that don't fit their hypotheses to date, because they suspect the hypotheses are correct in their current simpler form and that some other explanation for the exceptions will arise later. So, people do legitimately disagree at times as to which of two analyses are better; that's one of the things that keeps linguistics (like all science) interesting.

The general theoretical framework adopted in this book is drawn from a family of linguistic theories known as GENERATIVE GRAMMAR. Most generative theories assume that the grammars of all languages include a BASE COMPONENT (or something similar) consisting of PHRASE STRUCTURE RULES and a LEXICON.

The phrase structure rules specify the possible trees that can be generated by the base, including the BASIC WORD ORDER of the language. The lexicon consists of LEXICAL ENTRIES (= LEXICAL ITEMS), each of which represents a unit, such as a word, which is not fully predictable by rule. These are grouped into CATEGORIES, like verbs, nouns, and PRONOUNS. These categories may be further divided into SUBCATEGORIES such as COMMON NOUNS and PROPER NOUNS. Membership in a subcategory is indicated by means of FEATURES. Lexical items are added to trees by a process of LEXICAL INSERTION.

Unlike some versions of generative grammar, we have assumed that some languages, especially those with VSO basic order, use a FLAT CLAUSE STRUCTURE, that is, that the subject, direct object, and the verb are sisters within the clause. Others, especially SVO languages, use an ARTICULATED CLAUSE STRUCTURE. Because it is not always possible to define grammatical relations in terms of the overall tree structure, we include an explicit feature for grammatical relation on each NP node.

6.11. Questions for analysis

1. What appears to be the basic word order in this language? Is it SVO, SOV, VSO, VOS, OSV, or OVS?
2. For each phrasal or larger syntactic category (e.g., for each S, VP, and NP):
    a. What constituents does it have? (That is, what category does each constituent belong to, and when relevant, what grammatical relation does each NP in it have?)
    b. What order do the constituents come in?
    c. Which are always present and which are optional?
3. Is there any evidence for subcategorizing nouns? Specifically, is there any difference in the syntactic behavior of proper and common nouns?
4. What category do pronouns belong in? (In most cases the answer is 'NP'.) What evidence is there for this analysis?

6.12. Sample descriptions

English
English has SVO basic word order, as seen in (1).[16]

(1)   a. *John chased the dog.*
        b. *The big dog chased the cats.*

Within a noun phrase, modifiers (determiners and adjectives) precede the noun. Adjectives are (of course) optional, as seen above. A determiner (an article or demonstrative) generally occurs with singular common nouns, but is optional with plurals, as in (2).

(2)   *Ferdinand was smelling (the) flowers.*

Determiners do not normally occur with proper nouns, such as 'John' in (1).

---

[16]This description of English is restricted to the facts that have been introduced in this chapter. The optionality of determiners is also conditioned by the mass/count distinction.

Palantla Chinantec

Palantla Chinantec is VSO, and in the noun phrase adjectives (when present) follow the head noun.

(1)   *se¹   mɨh²   bã́ʔ²   tsiʔ²*
      will.bathe woman   chubby   child
      The chubby woman will bathe the child.

6.13. For further reading

As mentioned earlier, Radford (1988, chapter 1) provides an excellent discussion of some of the most fundamental concepts in generative grammar. I have touched on some of them above, but Radford's treatment is more thorough than anything there is room for here. *If you read nothing else that we recommend for further reading, read this,* since it answers so many troublesome questions that usually arise at this stage. Sells (1985:1–17) covers roughly the same ground, although more briefly.

Object-initial languages (OSV and OVS) are quite rare. At one time, they were thought not to exist, but Derbyshire and Pullum (1981) present several that are clearly object-initial. As for the relative frequencies of the other word order types, see Dryer 1989.

Flat clause structures and a greater reliance on grammatical relations have been posited at various times and for various reasons. Among current theoretical frameworks, they are most prominently used in Relational Grammar (Perlmutter 1983, Perlmutter and Rosen 1984, Postal and Joseph 1990) and Lexical-Functional Grammar (Bresnan 1982). Blake (1990) provides an introduction to Relational Grammar and Sells (1985) does the same for Lexical-functional Grammar. For examples of the tests that can be used to determine whether a language has a flat or articulated clause structure, see Radford 1988, chapter 2, especially pp. 77–83. Radford uses these tests to demonstrate much of the phrase structure in English that we have largely assumed, including the claim that the clause uses an articulated clause structure, not a flat one.

For other syntactic theories within the school of Generative Grammar, Radford (1981, 1988, 1997) covers classic Transformational Grammar and more recent versions of it (Government-binding Theory and the Minimalist program) well. Haegeman (1991) and Sells (1985) also provide good introductions to Government-binding Theory. Sells also introduces Generalized Phrase Structure Grammar, a theory which later developed into Head-driven Phrase Structure Grammar (Pollard and Sag 1987, 1994). Newmeyer (1986) provides a historical survey of Generative Grammar as a whole.

7
Embedding and Noun Phrase Structure

7.1. Goals and prerequisites

This chapter will help you do the following:

- ◎ identify at least the following elements of noun phrase structure: D, Q, QP, Deg, A, AP, P, and PP, including possessors as instances of embedded NPs or PPs
- ◎ describe the structure of noun phrases, both informally (in prose) and formally (with trees and labeled brackets)
- ◎ state four constraints on phrase structure rules which are assumed by many linguists today, and determine if a set of phrase structure rules is consistent with them
- ◎ use the terminology that is needed to state the constraints
- ◎ construct a set of phrase structure rules for noun phrases (including demonstratives, possessors, and other embedded phrases) which is consistent with the constraints

It assumes that you are familiar with the following material:

- ✓ phrase structure rules and the concept of HEAD (chapter 6 "The Base")

7.2. Noun phrase structure in English

In this chapter, we turn from clause structure to noun phrase structure. We especially want to explore EMBEDDING, a principle underlying phrase structure in all languages. We start by looking at noun phrase structure in English, which illustrates embedding well.

We have assumed the following hypothesis about English noun phrases:

(1)   NP → (D) (A) N

This rule will generate noun phrases like the following:[1]

---

[1]Of course, the rules don't do this by themselves. We also need lexical entries and morphological rules to generate the plural forms. These latter rules are introduced in chapter 10 "Inflectional Morphology."

(2)   *artichokes*
       the artichoke
       the big artichoke
       big artichokes

However, there are many more noun phrase structures than this. Let's consider some of them and improve our hypothesis.
    A numeral can occur between the determiner and the adjective.

(3)   *two artichokes*
       two big artichokes
       the two artichokes
       the two big artichokes

Traditionally, numerals are classified as a type of adjective. However, they are not mutually substitutable for adjectives; for example, their ordering cannot be reversed.

(4)   **big two artichokes*

Therefore, we must recognize a separate category in the lexicon, called QUANTIFIER (Q), which includes numerals and other words which are mutually substitutable for them.[2]

(5) **Q**
       many
       few
       one
       two
       three
       ...

We also must add Q to the NP rule.

(6)   NP → (D) (Q) (A) N

    Also, words like *very, rather,* and *extremely,* which are called DEGREE WORDS (Deg), can occur just before an adjective.

(7)   *many **extremely** ripe artichokes*

What is the constituent structure of this example? There are two possibilities:

---

[2]Not all words that refer to quantity are Quantifiers. For example, 'some' in English is apparently a determiner ('some thirty boxcars'), and there is a category of words, including 'all', 'both', 'twice' (as well as words that don't refer to quantity, such as 'such' and 'what'), that precede the determiner ('all the students', 'both the fierce zebras', 'twice the fun'). I do not attempt an analysis of these elements in this book. John Roberts (personal communication) has observed a similar category in Amele (Papua New Guinea).

(8)   a.   b.

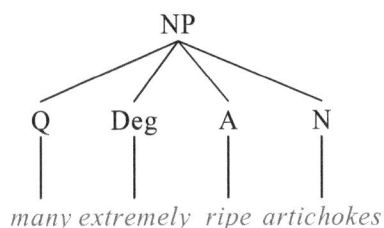
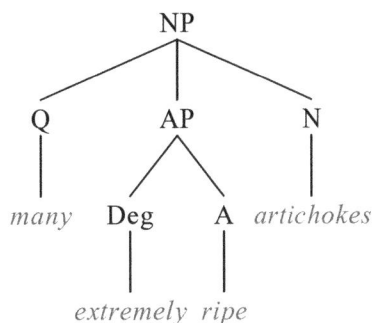

That is, do Deg and A together form an ADJECTIVE PHRASE (AP), as in (8b)? Or are they individually constituents of the NP, as in (8a)?

Extremely modifies *ripe,* rather than *many* or *artichokes.* That is, it is closer semantically to *ripe* than to the other words. This suggests that (8b) is the correct structure. But, is there any syntactic evidence supporting this conclusion?

For starters, *ripe* can occur without *extremely,* but *extremely* cannot occur without *ripe.*

(9)   *many ripe artichokes*
        ***many extremely artichokes.*

This can be explained easily if we assume (8b) is correct and that it is generated by the following set of rules:

(10)   Phrase structure rules for hypothesis in (8b)
        NP → (D) (Q) (AP) N
        AP → (Deg) A

These rules explicitly allow an A without a Deg, but not vice versa; the only way to get a Deg is to have an AP, and if you have an AP you also need an A. On the other hand, if we assume Deg is a daughter of NP, as in (8a), we would adopt an NP rule more like the following:

(11)   Phrase structure rule for hypothesis in (8a)
        NP → (D) (Q) (Deg) (A) N

This incorrectly allows a Deg to occur without an A. So, (10) and (8b) provide the better analysis.

Another fact: more than one adjective can occur in a noun phrase and each can have its own degree word.

(12)   *many ripe, juicy artichokes*
        many very ripe, very juicy artichokes
        many very ripe, very large, very juicy artichokes

We can account for this easily if we assume that there is an AP. All we need to do is add an asterisk to the AP in (10), which indicates that there can be any number of APs in the NP.[3]

(13)   Desirable phrase structure rules for (12):
        NP → (D) (Q) (AP)* N
        AP → (Deg) A

---

[3]Strictly speaking, the parentheses are unnecessary, since the asterisk normally means 'zero or more instances of the preceding item'; however, I include them as a reminder.

But, if we assume that Deg is a daughter of NP, as in (8a), we end up having to modify (11) into a horridly cumbersome rule.

(14)   Undesirable phrase structure rule for (12):
        NP → (D) (Q) (Deg) (A) (Deg) (A) (Deg) (A) N

And worse, this makes wrong predictions about further data; it allows a Deg word to follow an adjective.

(15)   *the moldy very artichoke*

As if all this isn't enough, adjectives can be modified by degree words in other contexts.

(16)   a. *The artichoke is **very mushy.***
        b. ***Very mushy** is a terrible condition for an artichoke to be in.*
        c. *He made it **very mushy.***

We haven't considered clauses like these before, but you can see that they contain adjective phrases that are not part of noun phrases. To handle such examples, we would simply have to include AP at appropriate places in other phrase structure rules that would generate these structures. But this assumes that we have an AP rule in our analysis; in an analysis like (14), there is no AP rule, and thus no easy way to generate sentences like those in (16).[4]

   All this evidence points to the conclusion that we need an AP and an AP rule. We've taken a crucial step in our analysis—we've recognized that one phrase can contain another.

   Let's look further. Quantifiers can be modified by degree words too.

(17)   ***too** many artichokes*
        ***approximately** 300 artichokes*

So, we also need to allow for the possibility of a QUANTIFIER PHRASE (QP) inside the NP, for the same reason that we recognized an AP.[5]

(18)   NP → (D) (QP) (AP)* N
        QP → (Deg) Q
        AP → (Deg) A

   What picture is beginning to emerge? All the major modifiers in an NP can be phrases; they are not limited to single words. And, if we push a little further, we find this true elsewhere. For example, the degree word (inside a QP or AP) can be replaced by a DEGREE PHRASE (DegP):

(19)   *[QP [DegP almost too] many] artichokes*
        many [AP [DegP very very] green] artichokes

So we need to change our rules again. (We will not try to figure out exactly what should be in the DegP rule, however; we have to stop this discussion somewhere!)

(20)   NP   → (D) (QP) (AP)* N
        QP   → (DegP) Q
        AP   → (DegP) A
        DegP → ... Deg

---

[4]In order to generate examples like (16) without having an AP rule, it would be necessary to repeat the details of the structure of adjective phrases in each rule that uses them, which is an unnecessary repetition and misses a generalization.

[5]There are other types of quantifier phrases, such as *more than two*, which unfortunately cannot be covered here.

This phrase-within-phrase structure is more visible if we draw a tree generated by these rules.[6]

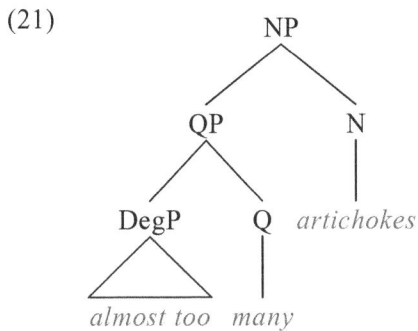

(21)

```
                    NP
                  /    \
                QP       N
               /  \      |
            DegP    Q   artichokes
             /\     |
            /  \   many
      almost too
```

(The triangle in the tree provides a way to draw the tree even though there are some details, like the internal structure of a DegP, that we don't know how to draw. The triangle is not part of the structure of the sentence, it's just in our diagram, leaving some part of the structure unstated. Triangles are also useful when part of the tree is irrelevant to the discussion, as a way of helping the reader focus on the main point, as in the next few trees below.)

Are there any other phrases that can occur inside a noun phrase? Yes, PREPOSITIONAL PHRASES (PPs) can.

(22)   *the artichoke [PP in the moon]*
        any artichoke [PP under the table]
        the man [PP with the artichoke]

A prepositional phrase consists of a PREPOSITION, like *in, under,* or *with,* together with a noun phrase. We need to do two things in our grammar: (a) add a rule defining what a PP is and (b) include an optional PP at the end of the NP rule.

(23)   PP   →   P NP
        NP   →   (D) (QP) (AP)* N (PP)
        QP   →   (DegP) Q
        AP   →   (DegP) A
        DegP   →   ... Deg

Since an NP can contain a PP, and a PP in turn contains another NP, this results in a tree structure with one NP node dominating another (with a PP node in between).

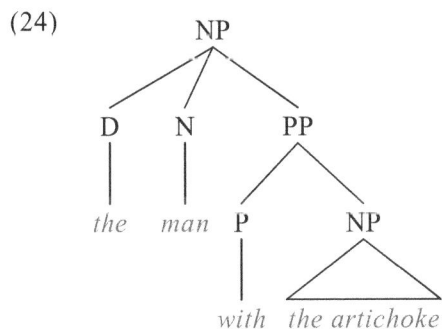

(24)

```
              NP
            / | \
           D  N  PP
           |  |   /\
          the man P  NP
                  |   /\
                with the artichoke
```

And since a PP can be added to the inner (lower) NP, you can see that English has the potential for producing some very large noun phrases.

---

[6]For simplicity's sake, I am ignoring details of the inflectional morphology. Technically, this is a surface tree, since an inflectional rule would have added *-s* to artichoke. See chapter 10 "Inflectional Morphology."

(25)

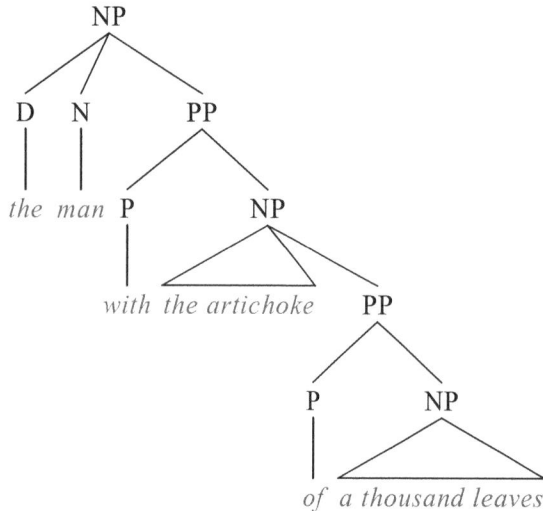

The grammar can continue adding more and more PPs to an NP forever; there is nothing in the grammar itself that imposes any limit on how many times this occurs. Thus, by allowing one phrase to occur inside another, we have created a small finite grammar that can produce an infinite number of sentences. In this way, we have provided a partial answer to a very basic question: 'How is it that speakers of English (or any other language) can recognize and produce such a large number of utterances?' They have internalized a grammar which provides enough options to do so. In particular, since phrases are allowed inside other phrases, their grammar can generate infinitely long utterances and an infinite number of them.

Of course, human limitations, like running out of memory or breath, do cause us to stop eventually; we never fully make use of the infinite potential in our grammar. At some point, we have to quit choosing the options which make an NP bigger and bigger. But, this is not a limit in the grammar itself; it is a limit imposed by other aspects of our humanness.

In the course of exploring English noun phrase structure, we have seen an example of how an analysis develops through a series of hypotheses, each one covering more data than the previous. Don't ever expect to get the 'right answer' on your first try at an analysis. Try instead to make a reasonable first hypothesis and work from there to improve it.

7.3. Embedding

The phrases-within-phrases structure that we have seen is called EMBEDDING. Embedding is the norm for phrase structure in all languages, although not all languages have as rich a set of possibilities for constructing large and complex phrases. Languages also differ in the extent to which they make use of these possibilities in practice; in many languages, noun phrases larger than a few words seldom occur, even when the grammar allows more complex phrases.

But still, all languages allow some possibilities for embedding. The point of looking at English noun phrases in such detail is to disprove the naive notion that phrases are just strings of words. Look back at the rules in (23) to see how false this is. Each phrase consists of its head (which is a word) plus any number of *phrases* (as well as miscellaneous words like D).

We can make the same point with Brôu (Mon-Khmer, Vietnam).[7] Look at the bracketed portions in the following noun phrases, which illustrate the embedding possibilities:

(26) [QP *klĭŋ   lĭʔ   ] *alik
           many   very   pig
       very many pigs

---

[7]Data from Miller 1964:68–75. Transcription adjusted to IPA symbols, based on the book's symbol guide (p. [i]).

(27)   *alik [*$_{AP}$ *tɔər lĭʔ   ]*
       pig   big   very
       very big pig(s)

(28)   *alik [*$_{PP}$ *paiŋ   [*$_{NP}$ *dŏŋ   ariaih]]*
       pig   above   house chief
       the pig(s) above the chief's house

The following set of phrase structure rules accounts for most of the facts in these examples:[8]

(29)   NP →   (QP) N (AP) (PP)
       QP →   Q (Deg)
       AP →   A (Deg)
       PP →   P NP

Again, each phrase is not a string of words, but a string of embedded phrases surrounding a head.

7.4. Constraints on phrase structure rules

Embedding is so important that in recent years a set of CONSTRAINTS ON PHRASE STRUCTURE RULES have developed which express the idea that phrases are not merely a string of words.[9] These constraints are rules for writing rules; they state requirements that all phrase structure rules must meet. Exactly which constraints are adopted by different linguists varies somewhat. This book adopts several constraints which should challenge you to dig into a language and find the full range of embedding possible. They do one thing that all good theories should do: help you ask the right questions about the languages that you will be investigating, so as to discover their structure.

Before presenting the constraints, we need some terminology. We have already used the word HEAD to refer to the central and most important daughter of a phrase. The head of NP is N, the head of VP is V, the head of AP is A, the head of PP is P, etc.[10] As you can see, the phrasal category is normally named after its head, but this is purely a matter of convenience. In fact, the head of S is often considered to be VP (or V, in a language without VPs). What matters is that each phrasal category has only one type of head, and each head is the head of only one type of phrase.

All phrasal categories have heads, but not all word-level categories can be the heads of phrases; this is another way of saying that not all word types can have modifiers. D is such a category in

---

[8]The ordering of the constituents in the NP is based on Miller's analysis; some variability in ordering is possible. Some of the embedding possibilities are inferred from her discussion and examples, since her terminology and formalism are quite different from that used here. For the possessor in (28), see footnote 18.

[9]These constraints constitute what is commonly known as X-bar theory, although as Pullum (1985) points out, it hardly merits being called a theory. I have found it easiest to explain them as constraints on phrase structure rules, while recognizing that others regard them as constraints on phrase markers (trees) themselves. Kornai and Pullum (1990) provide a valuable summary and critique of various types of constraints that have been proposed. They point out that naming the phrase after the head is far less important than is generally supposed; I therefore implicitly assume with them that an X-bar grammar should specify which categories are heads and what they are heads of. Further, they argue that the number of bar-levels allowed has little or nothing to do with the expressive power of the grammar. For this reason, and because more than two bar-levels are largely unnecessary for the type of data that students encounter in an introductory course, this book uses just two levels except for V/VP/S and skips the bar notation that is usually associated with X-bar theory. It concentrates, then, on elements of X-bar theory which reflect those fundamental properties of headedness and embedding that are recognized in most traditional approaches to grammar.

[10]It may not be obvious to everyone why the head of a PP is a P, since both the P and the NP are normally obligatory. In other categories, usually the head is obligatory and the other constituents are optional. However, Ps often show other characteristics of heads, for example, they can assign case marking to their object or even agree with it in a way that is analogous to verbs assigning case to or agreeing with their objects, and they often behave like heads with respect to word order (see chapter 9, "Obliques," p. 106ff.). There are exceptions, however. For example, there are some particles that have sometimes been analyzed as Ps (e.g., the case-marking 'postpositions' on subjects and objects in Korean) which might be better analyzed as a non-head constituent attached to a noun phrase; see Pollard and Sag 1994:44–46.

English; there are no modifiers for determiners and thus there are no determiner phrases for D to be the head of.[11] In some languages, there are no degree words or other categories that modify adjectives, and thus, there are no adjective phrases, just adjectives.

Any word-level category in a language which serves as the head of a phrase is called a MAJOR CATEGORY. Any word-level category which does not serve as the head of a phrase is called a MINOR CATEGORY. In English, D is a minor category, while N, P, V, A, Q, etc., are major categories.[12] Usually, minor categories are closed classes and major categories are open classes. For completeness, all phrasal categories are also considered to be major categories, like their heads.

Now, here are the constraints on phrase structure rules:

(30) a. Every phrasal category has a unique head.
      b. Every head is the head of only one type of phrase.
      c. Heads are never optional.
      d. All nonhead daughters are either phrasal categories or minor categories.

What do these mean? How do we apply them when we write phrase structure rules?[13]

The first two constraints (30a, b) require a one-to-one relationship between phrases and heads. On the right-hand side of every phrase structure rule, there must be one and only one head, and each head may appear on the right hand side of only one rule. You probably have already been doing this, without thinking about it. These two constraints forbid silly rules like the following:

(31) NP → AP   *(no head)*
      NP → N (QP) (AP) N   *(two heads)*
      AP → (DegP) N (NP)   *(N used as head of AP as well as NP)*

Always make sure that every phrase structure rule has a single head on the right-hand side and that no category serves as the head of more than one phrase.

The third constraint (30c) forbids us from using parentheses around the head. Thus, it forbids rules like the following:

(32) VP → (V) (NP[DO]) ...

If the head is optional, then the grammar will generate headless phrases, in violation of the spirit of (30a), if not the letter. Never put parentheses around the head in a phrase structure rule.[14]

The fourth constraint (30d) is perhaps the most important. It says that, except for the head, and except for word-level categories which have no corresponding phrasal categories, everything else on the right side of a rule must be a phrasal category. Because of it, we should never have considered the following rule for English noun phrases:

(33) NP → (D) (Q) (A) N

Since English has quantifier phrases and adjective phrases, the constraint (30d) requires us to use QP and AP, not Q and A.

(34) NP → (D) (QP) (AP) N

[11]That is, unless one considers D to be the head of a noun phrase, as is sometimes assumed in current work in Government-binding Theory.

[12]In most recent work in Government-binding Theory, D is analyzed as a major category, the head of a DP, as an alternative analysis for most of the constituents that this book analyzes as NPs. See Radford 1997:96, 152–7.

[13]These constraints do not apply in an obvious fashion to conjoined structures, which may be exceptions to them. Conjoining is discussed briefly in connection with embedded clauses in chapter 22 "Embedded Clauses" (p. 319).

[14]Of course, some account must be given of apparent headless NPs, such as in *Bill wants four sandwiches, but Harold only wants two ∅.* Similar facts, incidentally, are reported by Miller (1964:65) for Brôu. Since omission of the head noun is appropriate only when its reference is clearly understood in context, it seems best to posit a silent pronominal element as the head noun. Omitting the head entirely would lead to unconstrained overgeneration. Allowing silent (zero) elements is an important analytical device in generative grammar. See also footnote 19.

The reason this is important is that in some languages, categories like Q and A may be minor categories. That is, there may not be any words in the language that can modify them. In such a language, a rule like (33) might be perfectly appropriate. In other words, the constraint forces us to ask whether each type of word can be modified and thus serve as the head of a phrase. If it can, then (30d) forbids us from using it on the right-hand side of a rule except when it is the head. This makes a significant claim about all languages. It says that, for example, if a language has adjective phrases, then everywhere an adjective can appear, it should also be possible to get an adjective phrase.

So, if you are analyzing noun phrases and you find that there is a class of adjectives that modify nouns, you should immediately ask, 'Can adjectives themselves be modified?'. You can then find out if they can, while if you hadn't known about embedding and constraint (30d), you might have gone merrily on your way for years, perhaps even using the embedded structures correctly in your speech, without realizing that your analysis was inadequate.

You can write a set of rules to represent your hypothesis that you need an AP rule, even though you don't know yet what modifiers it contains.[15]

(35) NP → (D) (AP) N
      AP → ... A

The ellipsis ('...') represents your guess about where modifiers would occur and can serve as a reminder to look for modifiers on adjectives. If after several months, you find none, then you can simplify your hypothesis.

(36) NP → (D) (A) N

This is probably a better way to work than starting with a hypothesis like (36) and never bothering to find out if adjectives can be modified. That is, (35) is better as a first hypothesis, because it challenges you to look deeper into the structure of the language.

7.5. Possession

Now that we have recognized how embedding is essential to phrase structure in English (and every other language), we are ready to analyze possession. In English, there are two ways to express possession. One uses a PP (headed by the preposition *of*) embedded in an NP.

(37) *an artichoke [of mine]*
      the reign [of Herod the Great]

This type is already accounted for in our rules, which allow a PP to be embedded inside an NP.

The other way of expressing possession involves an NP embedded at the beginning of a larger NP.

(38) *[NP [NP the artichoke's] three shriveled leaves]*
      [NP [NP this book's] numerous artichoke examples]

Notice that the POSSESSOR NP (the inner one) takes the place of the determiner in the POSSESSED NP (the outer one). (We are, for now, ignoring the *'s* at the end of the possessor; in chapter 20 "Word Division and Clitics," pp. 282ff., we treat it as a type of suffix.)

Thus, to account for possession, we need to add an NP on the right side of the NP rule, as an option in place of the D. (In a phrase structure rule, we use braces {} to represent a choice between

---

[15]I recommend this approach for use in introductory courses, since in most exercises that are focused on other topics, phrase structure is kept extremely simple. This approach offers a constant reminder about the possible existence of embedding, even when it is not visible in the data.

items that can be used in the same horizontal position.) We label the new NP with the feature [Poss]; that is, we are adding POSSESSOR to the list of possible grammatical relations.[16]

(39)
$$NP \rightarrow \left(\left\{ \begin{matrix} D \\ NP[Poss] \end{matrix} \right\} \right) (QP) \, (AP)* \, N \, (PP)$$

This rule produces trees like the following:[17]

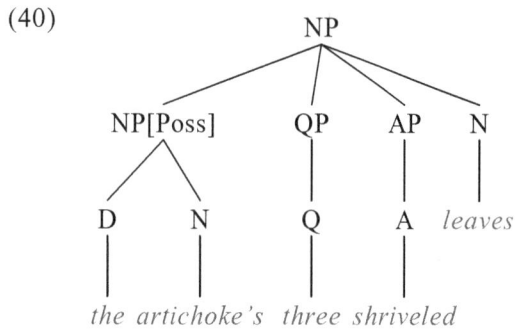

(40)

```
                         NP
            ┌─────────┬────────┬──────┐
        NP[Poss]      QP       AP     N
          ╱  ╲        │        │      │
        D     N       Q        A    leaves
        │     │       │        │
       the  artichoke's  three  shriveled
```

It may seem strange to have one NP inside another. (Remember that the arrow in the rule does not signify equality, but rather is an instruction for building a portion of a tree.) Yet, this is exactly what we want. For example, we can show that both the NPs in (40) are indeed NPs, because both can be used as subjects.

(41)   ***The artichoke*** *rolled down the street.*
       The artichoke's three shriveled leaves *blew down the street.*

Because (39) allows one NP to be inside another, it is capable of producing a long chain of NPs. Such multiply-embedded NPs can occur, for example, when talking about family relationships.

(42)   *[NP [NP [NP the butcher's] wife's] family]*

```
               NP
             ╱    ╲
        NP[Poss]   N
         ╱   ╲     │
    NP[Poss]  N  family
      ╱  ╲    │
     D    N  wife's
     │    │
    the butcher's
```

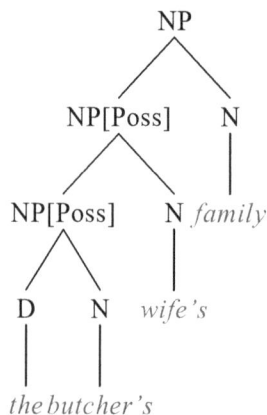

(43)   *Arthur's mother's father's sister's son's daughter*

---

[16]A more refined analysis might regard a possessor to be the subject of an NP. This would capture, for example, the parallel between *She discovered the letter* and *Her discovery of the letter,* in which the subject of the clause corresponds to the possessor of the NP. Thus, in place of [Poss], we could use [Su]. But, this book avoids such abstractions.

[17]The *'s* is added to the possessor NP by a later morphological rule, so this is actually a surface tree. See chapter 20 "Word Division and Clitics," p. 284.

As a challenge, see if you can add brackets to (43) and then draw a tree for it, following the same pattern as in (42).

Some languages, like Brôu (discussed earlier), use PPs as the primary means of indicating possession.[18]

(44)   *alik   phən   kĭʔ*
         pig   of   I
         my pigs

Languages vary as to whether they use NPs or PPs to indicate possession; some use only one or the other, some (like English) use both.

In closing, don't confuse POSSESSION (a syntactic concept) with OWNERSHIP (a semantic concept having to do with culturally-defined control of resources). Possession is often used to express ownership, but it can also express many other relationships.

(45)   *the artichoke's leaves*   part-whole relationship
        the artichoke's seedlings   kinship
        the artichoke's garden-mate   social relationship
        the artichoke's tremendous size   abstract quality
        the artichoke's startling achievement initiator of an action
        the artichoke's ultimate destruction the item affected by an action

7.6. Demonstratives

Most languages have a set of words with meanings like *this, that, these,* and *those*. These are called DEMONSTRATIVES because they 'point' at their referent. Demonstratives frequently occur as determiners within a noun phrase.

(46)   ***that*** artichoke
        these *silly, repetitious examples*

In English and many other languages, the same words can also be used in place of a whole noun phrase.

(47)   ***That*** *is an artichoke.*
        I'd like ***these.***

Apparently, demonstratives in such languages are both determiners and pronouns. Thus, in our formal grammar, they should be listed in the lexicon both in the category D and in the category NP. In other words, these two groups of words overlap.

---

[18]Data from Miller 1964:74. Since the phrase structure rule posited earlier already includes a PP after the noun, it already accounts for such phrases. It does not distinguish possessors from other types of PPs; however, this could be handled by introducing the feature [Poss] in the lexical entry for *phən* 'of'. This feature would be added to the tree when *phən* is inserted and would then be copied to the PP node by means of feature percolation (see chapter 19 "Case and Agreement," p. 256). So, it is unnecessary to include [Poss] in the NP phrase structure rule for the data shown here, although this might be necessary when other examples from Miller 1964 are considered. Further, the preposition is optionally omitted if the possessor immediately follows the head noun, as shown in (28). This could be accounted for by positing a silent variant of *phən* in the lexicon, with a restricted distribution requiring it to occur immediately following a head noun.

(48)

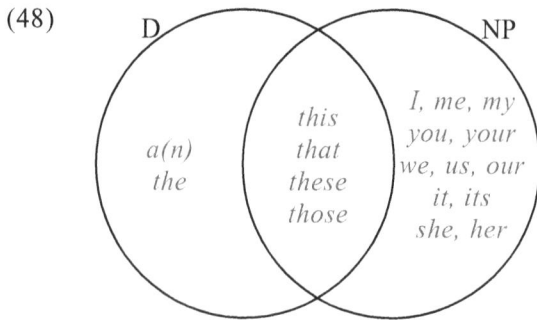

In our formal grammars, we can represent this as follows. List the demonstratives apart from the other Ds and NPs, like a separate category, and use braces in its title to show that these words can be inserted either at a D node or an NP node in a tree.[19]

(49)   **{D/NP}**

     this/these

     that/those

Warning: don't follow this advice without examining the data. In some languages, there are two different types of demonstratives. One type belongs to the category D, the other type belongs to the category NP. In these languages, the two categories D and NP do not overlap, and you should not analyze demonstratives as in (49). Just include the demonstrative determiners with the other Ds and the demonstrative pronouns with the other NPs.

7.7. Review of key terms

The essence of phrase structure is the EMBEDDING of one phrase inside another. Each PHRASAL CATEGORY contains one and only one HEAD. The set of all categories that are heads or have heads is called the set of MAJOR CATEGORIES; those word-level categories which do not serve as heads are called MINOR CATEGORIES. According to the CONSTRAINTS ON PHRASE STRUCTURE RULES presented in (30), there is a one-to-one relationship between phrases and heads, and within a phrase all constituents except the head must be either MINOR CATEGORIES or must themselves be PHRASAL CATEGORIES. In essence, these express our understanding that embedding is the norm for phrase structure in language.

Within noun phrases, languages typically have one or more of the following types of constituents: DETERMINERS (D), QUANTIFIER PHRASES (QP), ADJECTIVE PHRASES (AP), PREPOSITIONAL PHRASES (PP), or other noun phrases. Adjective phrases and quantifier phrases may in turn contain DEGREE PHRASES (DegP), which are headed by DEGREE WORDS (Deg). DEMONSTRATIVES generally are either determiners and/or pronouns. POSSESSION, not to be confused with OWNERSHIP, is typically indicated by the embedding of a POSSESSOR, which is either an NP or a PP, inside a larger POSSESSED NP.

7.8. Questions for analysis

1. Consider the following questions for each distinct type of phrase:
     a. What constituents can it have besides its head?
     b. Which of these constituents can themselves be phrases? That is, what are the possibilities for embedding?

---

[19]An alternative analysis of demonstrative pronouns is that they are simply determiners modifying silent noun heads.

2. Specifically with regard to noun phrase structure, how is possession expressed? Are possessors NPs or PPs? Do possessor NPs differ in any way from other NPs?

7.9. Sample description

In Brôu, a Mon-Khmer language of Vietnam, nouns may be modified by quantifier phrases, adjective phrases, and prepositional phrases (which indicate either location or possession).

(1) [_{QP} *klĭŋ   lĭʔ   ] *alik*
           many very   pig
     very many pigs

(2) *alik* [_{AP} *tɔər lĭʔ   ]
     pig   big   very
     very big pig(s)

(3) *alik* [_{PP} *paiŋ*   [_{NP} *dŏŋ   ariaih*]]
     pig   above   house chief
     the pig(s) above the chief's house

(4) *alik* [_{PP} *phən* [_{NP} *kĭʔ*]]
     pig   of   I
     my pigs

7.10. For further reading

The constraints on phrase structure rules presented here are a subset of proposals that have come to be known as X-bar theory. Radford (1988:167–225) presents other aspects of X-bar theory, including the reason for calling it that.

Ultan (1978b) provides a survey of different ways of marking possession in a representative sample of the world's languages. Although he concentrates primarily on morphological marking, he does make the following observation on the nature of embedding (as an explanation of why he doesn't say more about multiply-embedded possession, as in "George's friend's sister's dog's bone"): "…first, such constructions can be viewed as recursive [involving embedding] in probably all languages and will thus be accounted for by a basic typology; second, little descriptive matter is available on these constructions (although they certainly exist in all languages)" (p. 13). This represents the general assumption by most linguists that embedding provides the normal basis for building phrases in all languages.

8
Verbal Valence:
Subcategorization and Selectional Restrictions

8.1. Goals and prerequisites

This chapter will help you do the following:

- ◎ distinguish between ungrammaticality and other types of ill-formedness in specific examples from your native language
- ◎ explain why we need to subcategorize verbs based on their valence in a formal grammar
- ◎ state the semantic roles of specific noun phrases, and make hypotheses about their grammatical relations
- ◎ write phrase structure rules for clauses involving verbs, subjects, direct and indirect objects, and auxiliary verbs
- ◎ describe pro-drop phenomena informally, write an appropriate lexical entry for *pro*, and draw trees that contain *pro*
- ◎ express the valence of particular verbs, both informally (in prose) and formally (in lexical entries using SUBCAT features)

It assumes that you are familiar with the following material:

- ✓ phrase structure rules, lexical entries, and the use of features to represent subcategories of nouns (chapter 6 "The Base")
- ✓ embedding (chapter 7 "Embedding and Noun Phrase Structure")

8.2. Transitivity of clauses

In this chapter, we concentrate on verbs and how they are classified in the lexicon. The main thing to be learned here is that all verbs are not, strictly speaking, mutually substitutable. Although they share many characteristics, enough to group them together as one syntactic category, they also are fussy about the company they keep, that is, what other constituents can occur in the clause. Verbs that work with one combination of constituents may not work with another. In this chapter, first we look at some of the constituents that verbs are fussy about, then at the different types of verbs themselves, and finally at how we can account for all this in our formal grammars.

One of the main things that verbs are fussy about is the presence or absence of objects. We use terms like TRANSITIVE and INTRANSITIVE to describe these differences. Take a look at these sentences taken from Choapan Zapotec (Otomanguean, Mexico).[1]

Clauses that do not contain any objects are called INTRANSITIVE.

(1) *ujo   bẽʔ   naʔ*
     went   man   that
     The man went.

(2) *bdʒin   nigula*
     arrived   woman
     A woman arrived.

(3) *ureʔ   bekoʔ   ʒe   naʔ*
     sat   dog   big that
     The big dog sat.

(4) *ujasa   tu   ʒitu   daoʔ   naʔ*
     arose   one   cat   little that
     The one little cat arose.

Clauses which contain a direct object are called TRANSITIVE.

(5) *udao   bẽʔ   naʔ   [jeta naʔ]*
     ate   man that food that
     The man ate the food.

(6) *weʔe   tu   bekoʔ   daoʔ   naʔ   [nisa]*
     drank   one   dog   small   that water
     The one small dog drank water.

(7) *utʃaʔ   bẽʔ   naʔ   [tu   jaga   tona]*
     squared man that one   log   long
     The man squared a long log.

(8) *utʃugu   tʃopa   ʃkuidiʔ   naʔ   [tu   luba   ɾeo   naʔ]*
     cut   two   children that one   vine   thick that
     Those two children cut that one thick vine.

(9) *ulio   nigula   [nisa]*
     drew.out   woman   water
     A woman drew out water.

There is a special type of transitive clause which contains an INDIRECT OBJECT as well as a direct object. These are generally called DITRANSITIVE (or sometimes BITRANSITIVE).

(10) *beʔ   bẽʔ   naʔ   [nigula] tu   dumi   daoʔ*
     gave man that woman   one   money small
     The man gave a small coin to a woman.

---

[1]See footnote 2, p. 20.

(11)   *useʔlaʔ bẽʔ   naʔ [nigula] gitʃi*
       sent   man   that woman   paper
       The man sent a message to a woman.

(12)   *beʔlɛ   ʃkuidiʔ [tu nigula] diʔdzaʔ*
       gave.with child   one woman   word
       A child chatted with (lit. 'gave words with') a woman.

Indirect objects typically represent such ideas as the RECIPIENT of something (with verbs like *give* and *throw*) or the ADDRESSEE (with verbs like *mention, speak,* and *shout*).

In Choapan Zapotec, when there are two noun phrases following the subject, we can tell from the glosses that the first noun phrase after the subject is always the recipient or the addressee. We therefore make a hypothesis that this noun phrase is the indirect object of these clauses and that the last noun phrase in the clause is the direct object.

Similar reasoning has had a part in motivating many linguists to assume an analysis of English in which the highlighted phrases below are classified as indirect objects:

(13)   a. *He offered a mustache comb **to his girlfriend.***
       b. *She gave the ring back **to her former boyfriend.***
       c. *Lucy threw the ball **to Charlie Brown.***
       d. *Speak properly **to your mother.***

Their assumption is that indirect objects in English are PREPOSITIONAL PHRASES (PPs) consisting of the PREPOSITION *to* followed by an NP.

It would not be possible to justify this hypothesis fully here. Those of you familiar with traditional approaches to English grammar may note some differences at this point. But, because this analysis is reasonably standard in the linguistic literature, it is assumed in discussions of English throughout this book. One of the reasons this analysis is standard is that it is natural (see chapter 6 "The Base," pp. 57ff.); it shows how English is like other SVO languages in which the indirect object is a prepositional phrase (see (48) below for an example).[2]

We can see two differences between indirect objects in English and Choapan Zapotec. In Choapan Zapotec, indirect objects are noun phrases and precede the direct object. In English, they are PPs and follow the direct object (in normal word order). Taking these two differences into account, we write different phrase structure rules for Choapan Zapotec and English. For Choapan Zapotec, we have the following rule:

(14)   S   →   V NP[Su] (NP[IO]) (NP[DO])

This states that verbs come first, then subjects, then indirect objects (if any), and then direct objects (if any). For English, we have a slightly different set of rules, which show the indirect object as a prepositional phrase following the direct object.

(15)   S   →   NP[Su] VP
       VP →   V (NP[DO]) (PP[IO])
       PP →   P NP

---

[2]The traditional analysis considers **her** in *He offered **her** a mustache comb* to be the indirect object, based on its meaning. The analysis adopted here considers it a direct object, based on its syntactic characteristics (absence of any preposition and its position immediately following the verb, among other things). The phrase *A mustache comb* in this sentence is sometimes analyzed as a second direct object and sometimes as an example of some new grammatical relation, which some people call SECOND OBJECT and others call CHÔMEUR. Although there are differences in detail, many (perhaps most) linguists today agree that grammatical relations should be determined on the basis of form, not meaning, and a given meaning (such as recipient) may be expressed by more than one grammatical relation. If this concept is still hard to swallow, consider the fact that no one (even traditional grammarians) would analyze the recipient of *She was offered a mustache comb* as the indirect object. For grammatical relations to be useful syntactic terms, they must be defined in ways that do not tie them inextricably to semantics.

The rules introduced so far seem to do a good job in characterizing the differences between English and Choapan Zapotec.

8.3. Verbal valence

However, in another way, the rules are not working well enough yet. You can't take just any verb and put it in any clause. For example, the following sentences generally sound wrong to native speakers of English, but according to our rules so far, they should be grammatical.[3]

(16) a. *Mary rested the idea.*
      b. *The pilot put the airplane.*
      c. *Curious green ideas sleep furiously.*
      d. *The idea walked into the room.*

What is wrong with them? The exact answer varies, depending on the sentence. In general, the problem is that each verb requires certain phrases to be present or absent in its context. If the context is inappropriate for the verb, putting the verb in that context will sound wrong. This characteristic of verbs to be 'choosy' about their context is called VALENCE.

We consider two sides of verbal valence here. One has to do with syntactic properties of verbs and can be called SUBCATEGORIZATION.[4] The other concerns the semantic properties of verbs and is usually called SELECTIONAL RESTRICTIONS.

Syntactic valence: Subcategorization

Considering syntactic valence first, let's look again at Choapan Zapotec. If we attempt to use the rule (14) to form new clauses, some are rejected as incorrect by native speakers. Compare these to the ones earlier.[5]

(17) *utʃaʔa   bẽʔ   naʔ
       squared   man   that
       (The man squared.)

(18) *utʃugu tʃopa ʃkuidiʔ   naʔ
       cut   two   children that
       (Those two children cut.)

(19) *ulio   nigula
       drew.out   woman
       (A woman drew out.)

(20) *beʔɛ   bẽʔ   naʔ   nigula
       gave   man   that   woman
       (The man gave to a woman.)

---

[3]Here, the asterisks mean that the sentences are unacceptable, not necessarily ungrammatical; in some cases the problem is semantic. Often, the '*' is used only for ungrammaticality.

[4]It is common to refer to syntactic subcategorization as STRICT SUBCATEGORIZATION; however, this term tends to confuse students due to similarity in form (but not meaning!) with the term STRICTLY TRANSITIVE, so I avoid it in the text.

[5]Examples (20) and (21) are in fact grammatical, but not with the meaning given. The second noun phrase in each case is interpreted as the direct object, not the indirect object. Thus, the point still stands; these two verbs require direct objects, although indirect objects are optional.

(21)   *useʔlaʔ   bẽʔ   naʔ   nigula
         sent   man   that woman
       (The man sent to a woman.)

What is the difference between the grammatical and ungrammatical examples? The verbs in (17)–
(21) must be followed by a direct object. They can only be used in clauses that contain direct
objects; attempts to use them without a direct object result in ungrammaticality.

This phenomenon occurs in every language. Verbs differ in the number and type of phrases that
they can CO-OCCUR with ('coexist with' in the same clause). In terms of our formal grammars, we
say that verbs place requirements on the types of trees that they can be inserted into.

Verbs that occur only in intransitive clauses are called INTRANSITIVE VERBS. Looking at the data
in (1)–(4), we can assume that *ujo* 'went', *bdʒin* 'arrived', *ureʔ* 'sat', and *ujasa* 'arose' are
intransitive verbs. At least, they never take direct objects in our data, and in addition, it is difficult to
imagine situations in which verbs with these meanings could be used transitively. Still, to be sure,
we would want to try them out in some transitive clauses. If our hypothesis is correct, we would
expect native speakers to reject any attempt to use them transitively.

Verbs that occur in transitive clauses are called TRANSITIVE VERBS. *Utʃaʔ* 'squared', *utʃugu* 'cut',
and *ulio* 'drew out' are transitive verbs; they always occur with direct objects. Again, there are no
examples of them with indirect objects, so we will assume that they are STRICTLY TRANSITIVE, i.e.,
the only type of object they can take is a direct object, not an indirect object.

Verbs that can occur in ditransitive clauses are called DITRANSITIVE VERBS. Both *bɛʔ* 'gave' and
beʔlɛ 'chat' are ditransitive verbs; they take direct and indirect objects.

Some verbs are less picky; they can occur in either intransitive or transitive clauses. Compare the
intransitive clauses (22) and (23), below, with examples (5) and (6).

(22)   udao   bẽʔ   naʔ
         ate   man that
       The man ate.

(23)   weʔe   tu   bekoʔ   daoʔ   naʔ
       drank one dog   small that
       The one small dog drank.

These sentences involve two verbs of ingestion: *udao* 'ate' and *weʔe* 'drank'; verbs of ingestion in
many languages act this way. When they are used without direct objects, the actual food or drink
involved is left unspecified, usually because the speaker either doesn't know or does not consider it
important to specify.[6] Similarly, some ditransitive verbs can also omit the indirect object, leaving the
recipient or addressee unspecified. Compare (24) and (25) with (10) and (11).

(24)   bɛʔ   bẽʔ   naʔ   dumi   naʔ
       gave man   that money that
       The man gave that coin.

(25)   useʔlaʔ   nigula   naʔ   diʔdzaʔ
         sent   woman   that   word
       The woman sent a message.

We have seen that different verbs require different combinations of direct and indirect objects.
The category of verbs is thus subdivided into several smaller subcategories: intransitive verbs,
transitive verbs, etc. The usual way of saying this is that direct and indirect objects SUBCATEGORIZE

---

[6]This treatment of optional complements is oversimplified, since there are a variety of semantic effects that omission of a
complement may have (see Pollard and Sag 1987:132–34).

verbs. Or, we can say that verbs SUBCATEGORIZE FOR direct and indirect objects. This phenomenon is called (SYNTACTIC) SUBCATEGORIZATION, and it is one aspect of a verb's valence.

Verbs in different languages may have different valence, even if they have basically the same meaning. Take the word *chat,* for example. In English, this verb requires a subject (which is an Agent) and optionally takes an NP expressing who one is chatting with, which is expressed as the object of the preposition *with.* In Choapan Zapotec, however, the same idea is expressed by the verb *beʔle* 'give with', which takes two NPs. We have analyzed one as an indirect object; it corresponds to the object of *with* in English. The other is a direct object *diʔdzaʔ* 'word' that doesn't appear in English at all. Knowing the exact valence requirements of verbs is an important part of knowing a language. It can make the difference between success and failure, for example, in a translation into a language.

Semantic valence: Selectional restrictions

Syntactic subcategorization is distinguished from another type of verbal valence which involves semantics. Consider the following sentences:

(26)   a. *The lightning considered mopping the floor.*
       b. *The paramecium threaded its way through the maze.*
       c. *The lamppost was lecturing temperance.*
       d. *An idea flew into the room.*

All of them have an element of wrongness around them. Yet, this wrongness does not result from syntactic subcategorization, since there are parallel sentences, with the same combinations of direct and indirect objects, that are perfectly acceptable.

(27)   a. *The janitor considered mopping the floor.*
       b. *The rat threaded its way through the maze.*
       c. *The boss was lecturing Arthur.*
       d. *An idea flew into my mind.*

The problem with the sentences in (26) is that they describe situations which do not occur in the ordinary world. If we consider fairy-tale worlds, in which the nature of things like lampposts and ideas are different from the real world, then they can sound fine. For this reason, the sentences in (26) are generally considered grammatical; their wrongness, or UNACCEPTABILITY, is attributed not to grammatical rules but to other factors (like conflicts with our usual conception of the world).

That is, not all utterances which are judged unacceptable by native speakers are to be regarded as ungrammatical. Sentences like (26), or even ones that are perfectly well-formed but happen to be false, may be judged UNACCEPTABLE by a native speaker. A sentence is UNGRAMMATICAL only if it violates the grammatical rules of the language. Other forms of unacceptability need to be accounted for in other ways.

Getting back to the particular type of unacceptability illustrated in (26), the normal way to talk about it is to say that verbs place SELECTIONAL RESTRICTIONS on subjects and objects. For example, the verb *consider* requires that its subject refer to a being which is capable of thought. A verb's selectional restrictions are part of its meaning, and any complete description of its meaning must include some mention of these restrictions. Detailed study of this area belongs in a book on semantics, so we won't pursue the topic further here.

However, when we are doing syntactic analysis, we do sometimes need to keep track of the semantic structure of a verb in a rudimentary way. One common way to do this is through SEMANTIC ROLES, which are a kind of shorthand summary of common selectional restrictions.[7] Here are some of the semantic roles that are usually found with subjects, direct objects, and indirect objects:

---

[7]Semantic roles are often referred to as THEMATIC ROLES in recent literature.

(28) AGENT   a conscious, volitional causer of an event
      EXPERIENCER   a thinking being that experiences a mental event
      PATIENT   an entity that undergoes a change of state in an event
      THEME   an entity towards which an action is directed, without
                             being a patient (i.e., this is a miscellaneous category)
      RECIPIENT   a person who acquires control over a Theme as a
                             result of an event
      ADDRESSEE   the target of some communication

Look at the semantic roles associated with the noun phrases in the following Choapan Zapotec and English examples:

(29) a.   <u>Agent</u>   <u>Patient</u>
                weʔe   tu   bekoʔ daoʔ   naʔ   nisa
                drank   one   dog   small   that   water
                That one small dog drank water.

       b.   <u>Agent</u>   <u>Addressee</u>   <u>Theme</u>
                beʔlɛ   ʃkuidiʔ   tu   nigula   diʔdzaʔ
                gave.with   child   one   woman   word
                A child chatted with (lit., 'gave words with') a woman.

       c. <u>Experiencer</u>   <u>Theme</u>
           The old hunter   spotted   a three-point buck.

       d. <u>Agent</u>   <u>Theme</u>   <u>Recipient</u>
           My parents   give   too many presents   to our kids.

Semantic roles and grammatical relations

Up until now, when we have been making hypotheses about what are subjects, direct objects, and indirect objects, we have been relying to a large extent on semantic roles to do so. We have assumed Agents and Experiencers to be subjects, Patients and Themes to be direct objects, and Recipients and Addressees to be indirect objects. These associations of semantic roles and grammatical relations are frequent and typical, and they make good first hypotheses.

There are, however, plenty of exceptions. For example, in *receive,* the subject could be considered a Recipient rather than an Agent. In *break,* there are two possible associations of semantic roles, depending on its use as a transitive or intransitive verb. As a transitive verb ('He broke it'), the subject is an Agent and the direct object is a Patient. But, as an intransitive verb ('It broke'), the subject is a Patient and there is no Agent. So, we cannot completely predict semantic roles on the basis of grammatical relations, or vice versa. We can't write general rules of the form 'all subjects are Agents' or 'all Patients are direct objects'.

How, then, can we identify the grammatical relations in a language if we can't rely on semantic roles to do so? We take the same approach as in classifying words into syntactic categories (chapter 5 "Introduction to Syntax," pp. 40ff.). We look at the objective syntactic characteristics of the different elements in different clauses, such as their position relative to the verb and whether they are NPs or PPs. Then, we see which elements have the same characteristics; for those that do, we then assume they have the same grammatical relation. Finally, we label those grammatical relations as subject, direct object, and indirect object, based on the typical semantic roles that each expresses.

Every language has a set of syntactic and/or morphological characteristics which are typically used to express the semantic roles of Agent or Experiencer; these are the characteristics of subjects in that language. Typically, a different set of syntactic/morphological characteristics may be used to express the semantic roles of Patient or Theme; these are the characteristics of direct objects. And, if a third set of syntactic/morphological characteristics is used for Recipient and Addressee, those are the characteristics of indirect objects.[8]

However, most, if not all, languages have exceptional verbs like 'receive', which assign semantic roles to grammatical relations in unique ways, so these general correlations are only useful for naming grammatical relations, not for writing rules. Instead, semantic roles must be specified in the lexicon for each verb.[9] Chapter 21 ("Passive and Voice," p. 308ff.) introduces a notation that allows us to do so. For now, however, we formalize only syntactic subcategorization and leave semantic roles (as well as other selectional restrictions) unformalized.

8.4. Representing subcategorization in formal grammars

As mentioned above, in order to describe subcategorization, we must split the grammatical category V into smaller SUBCATEGORIES, one for intransitive verbs, one for transitive, etc. Recall (from chapter 6 "The Base," pp. 54ff.) how we split the category N into subcategories of common and proper nouns. We used a feature [±common]; some nouns are listed in the lexicon as [+common], others as [−common].

In recent years, features have become very important in several branches of generative grammar as a way of representing abstract characteristics of different constituents in a sentence. One theory that makes especially heavy use of features is known as Head-driven Phrase Structure Grammar. To subcategorize verbs, this theory proposes the use of a feature called [SUBCAT] . The purpose of this feature is to specify what type of tree a verb can be inserted into, specifically, what combinations of subject and objects it requires and/or permits. Unlike [±common], the [SUBCAT] feature needs to recognize several different types of verbs, rather than just two, so its value has to be something more than just a simple '+' or '−'. Instead, its value is a list of the constituents that a verb can co-occur with, which we write between ⟨angle brackets⟩. Look at the examples of different subcategories in this chart and how they would be expressed with the [SUBCAT] feature.

Informal name of subcategory	Corresponding formal notation with [SUBCAT] feature
intransitive verbs	V[SUBCAT ⟨ NP[Su] ⟩]
transitive verbs	V[SUBCAT ⟨ NP[Su], NP[DO] ⟩]
verbs that may be either transitive or intransitive	V[SUBCAT ⟨ NP[Su], (NP[DO]) ⟩]
ditransitive verbs	V[SUBCAT ⟨ NP[Su], NP[DO], NP[IO] ⟩] V[SUBCAT ⟨ NP[Su], NP[DO], (NP[IO]) ⟩] V[SUBCAT ⟨ NP[Su], (NP[DO]), NP[IO] ⟩] V[SUBCAT ⟨ NP[Su], (NP[DO]), (NP[IO]) ⟩]

Within the SUBCAT list, items are separated by commas to indicate that their order is unimportant.[10]

---

[8]In many languages, Recipients and Addressees have (virtually) the same syntactic characteristics as Patients and Themes. In such languages, it may be reasonable to assume that all four semantic roles are expressed as direct objects and that there is no need to posit indirect objects in the language at all.

[9]There is a more fundamental reason, too. Since the selectional restrictions for each verb are an integral part of its meaning, they must be specified in the lexicon. But, the selectional restrictions include the semantic roles. Not only would it be incorrect to specify semantic roles on the basis of general rules, it is entirely unnecessary to do so.

[10]This notation is borrowed from Head Driven Phrase Structure Grammar (HPSG) (Pollard and Sag 1987:67ff), although some of the details have been modified to mesh better with the other notational conventions in this book. By including explicit representation of grammatical relations, the order of constituents need not be fixed, as it must be in HPSG where the order is what represents the grammatical relations. In many cases in this book, the SUBCAT list could be streamlined by omitting mention of the grammatical relation or the category of each element; in some cases the facts might even require that we do so. I retain the full specification to simplify the exposition. Finally, I assume that associated with each element in the SUBCAT list is a specification of the appropriate selectional restrictions, including semantic roles. This idea is developed further in chapter 21 "Passive and Voice," pp. 308ff.)

Recall that some verbs may be either transitive or intransitive. This is represented by enclosing the NP[DO] in parentheses in their SUBCAT list. Similarly, there are a number of different types of verbs that could be considered ditransitive, depending on which object is optional, and each type thus has a different SUBCAT list. The formal notation is more precise (makes finer distinctions) than the informal terminology. This is one of the benefits of a good theory.

Each verb in the lexicon has its own value for SUBCAT. For Choapan Zapotec, the lexicon might be as follows:[11]

(30) **V[SUBCAT ⟨ NP[Su] ⟩]**

bdʒin	arrived
uɾeʔ	sat
ujasa	arose
ujo	went

V[SUBCAT ⟨ NP[Su], NP[DO] ⟩]

utʃaʔ	squared
utʃugu	cut
ulio	drew out

V[SUBCAT ⟨ NP[Su], (NP[DO]) ⟩]

| *weʔe* | drank |
| *udao* | ate |

V[SUBCAT ⟨ NP[Su], NP[DO], (NP[IO]) ⟩]

| *beʔ* | gave[12] |
| *useʔlaʔ* | sent |

Now let's generate a few sentences in our data in order to see in more detail how our verb subcategorization works. First, let's generate sentence (1).

(31)

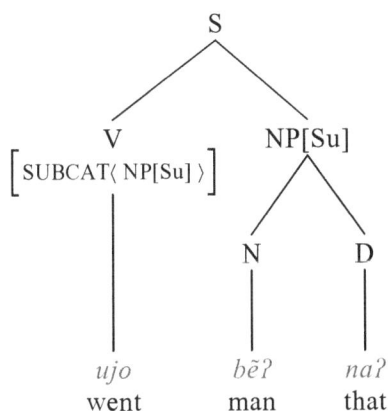

---

[11]One can, of course, arrange the verbs alphabetically, with the SUBCAT feature for each verb specified next to it rather than above a group of verbs. In this case, there would be just one list of verbs; the subcategorization would not be represented in the way the verbs are grouped on paper. The results mean the same thing, since the lexicon itself is regarded as an unordered list and any arrangement on paper is solely for the convenience of the readers.

[12]I do not know if the indirect object is optional with *beʔle* 'gave.with', so I omit it from the list. It would probably need to be listed as part of the idiomatic phrase *beʔle diʔdzaʔ* 'spoke words' anyway, which would require extra formalism that should not be introduced here. For a brief discussion of idiomatic phrases, see chapter 9 "Obliques," pp. 100ff.

Since no objects are present in the tree (31) above, we could not have chosen any verbs that require direct or indirect objects in their SUBCAT list. Since we are generating sentence (1), we choose *ujo* 'went', which requires only a subject.

Note that the SUBCAT feature is present in the tree, since a word that is inserted from the lexicon brings along all its features. We only show them in the trees when they are relevant, but we assume they are always there.

Now let's generate (5).

(32)

```
                                       S
              _____|_____
             |                        |                    |
             V                      NP[Su]                NP[DO]
  [SUBCAT⟨ NP[Su], NP[DO] ⟩]         / \                   / \
             |                      /   \                 /   \
             |                     N     D               N     D
             |                     |     |               |     |
           udao                   bẽʔ   naʔ            jeta    naʔ
            ate                   man   that           food    that
```

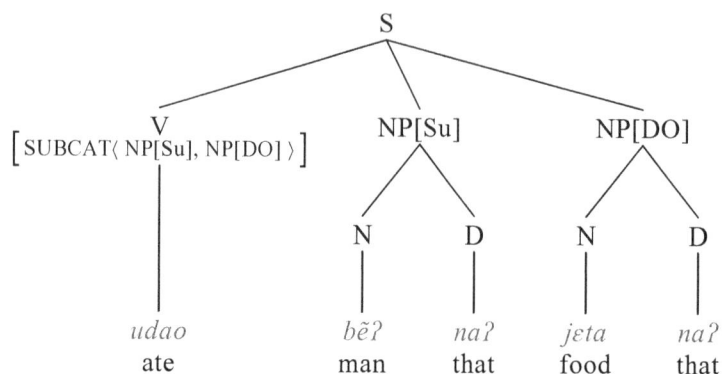

Since a direct object NP is present in tree (32) above, we could not use any verb that includes an obligatory indirect object in its SUBCAT list or any verb that does not allow a direct object.[13] Since *udao* 'ate' is [SUBCAT ⟨NP[Su], (NP[DO])⟩], we can use it and generate (5).[14]

Now let's generate (10).

(33)

```
                                       S
         _____|_____
        |                      |        |                         |
        V                    NP[Su]   NP[IO]                    NP[DO]
 [SUBCAT⟨ NP[Su], NP[DO], NP[IO] ⟩]    / \       |                /|\
        |                            /   \       |               / | \
        |                           N     D      N              Q  N  A
        |                           |     |      |              |  |  |
       bɛʔ                         bẽʔ   naʔ  nigula           tu dumi daoʔ
       gave                        man   that  woman           one money small
```

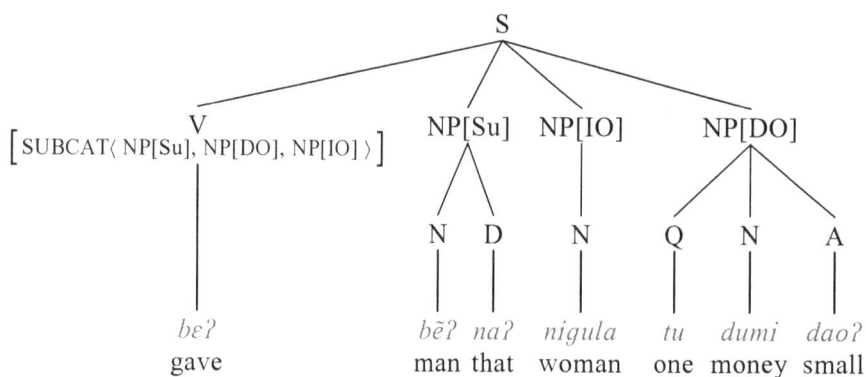

[13] Some explicit formal mechanism is needed to prevent verbs from being inserted in trees with extra complements, i.e., ones that do not occur in their SUBCAT list. Pollard and Sag (1987:71) do this by explicitly labeling certain constituents as complements and then requiring that every complement be sanctioned by an element in the SUBCAT list of its head. Since this book does not make a formal distinction between complements and adjuncts, another device is needed; let's assume (provisionally) that if an item occurs in a SUBCAT list for any verb in the lexicon, then such an item is automatically excluded for any verb that does not list it explicitly. Thus, because there are verbs that include NP[DO] in their SUBCAT list, any intransitive verb cannot be inserted in any clause that contains a direct object. We also need to restrict the scope of the SUBCAT mechanism to operate only locally; the usual assumption is that subcategorization operates within the maximal projection of the lexical head which carries the SUBCAT feature. In the case of verbal subcategorization, the maximal projection of V is S.

[14] The SUBCAT lists on the verbs in (32) and (33) do not have parentheses, reflecting the complements actually present in the tree. The assumption is that when a lexical entry specifies optional complements, the parentheses are a notational shortcut for a list of all the possible SUBCAT lists for that verb, each one containing a distinct list. (Often, the different subcategorization requirements correspond to different senses of the word.) Only the SUBCAT list that fits the tree exactly is actually inserted in any specific tree. Thus, when a transitive verb with an optional direct object (like *eat*) is inserted in an intransitive clause, the V node in the tree ends up with the feature [SUBCAT ⟨ NP[Su] ⟩].

Since both a direct object NP and an indirect object NP are present in tree (33), we could choose *only* from verbs having both NP[DO] and NP[IO] (at least optionally) in their SUBCAT list. We choose *bɛʔ* 'gave'.

Our grammar fragment is able to generate all the grammatical sentences and is unable to generate any of the 'sentences' which we know to be ungrammatical because they have the wrong combination of verbs and objects. It also makes predictions about other sentences that will be ungrammatical for the same reasons. This fulfills one goal of formal analysis: to construct a grammar for each language that not only generates all the grammatical utterances, but also does not generate anything else. A formal grammar is supposed to represent what a speaker of that language knows about its structure. Since native speakers know that some utterances are ungrammatical, a formal grammar must account for these judgments just as much as for utterances that actually do occur.

8.5. Auxiliary verbs

Many languages have a subclass of verbs called AUXILIARY VERBS or AUXILIARIES. Examples in English include words like *should, have,* and *be,* which are used in combination with other verbs and have special, usually grammatical, meanings. An auxiliary verb can be analyzed as the head of a VP that contains another VP embedded inside it.

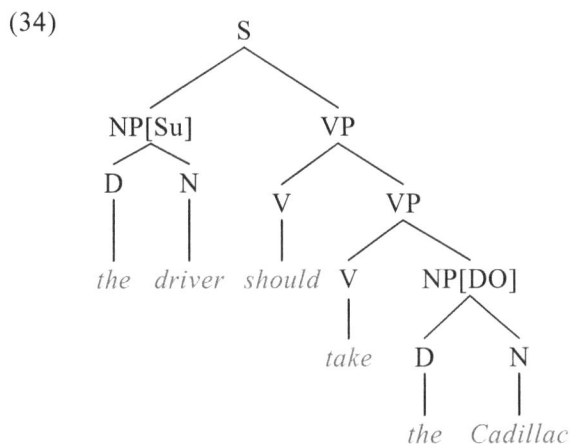

(34)
```
                         S
                       /   \
                  NP[Su]    VP
                   /  \    /  \
                  D    N  V    VP
                  |    |  |   /  \
                 the driver should V   NP[DO]
                              |     /  \
                             take  D    N
                                   |    |
                                  the  Cadillac
```

What is special about an auxiliary verb is that it requires a second VP to be present in the tree, just like a transitive verb requires a direct object to be present. In other words, auxiliaries subcategorize for VPs. In (34), the VP *take the Cadillac* occurs alongside the auxiliary *should,* thus satisfying its subcategorization requirement. It is this second VP that contains the 'main' verb (the one with lexical meaning).

Auxiliary verbs require just a few modifications to our formal grammar. First, the phrase structure rule for VP must allow for the possibility of one VP embedded inside another one.

(35)   VP → V (NP[DO]) (VP) (PP[IO])[15]

As in other cases of embedding, this rule correctly allows for chains of VPs involving two or more auxiliaries.

---

[15]The VP is placed after the direct object as a possible way of generating sentences like 'She sang the child to sleep'. If these sentences are generated in some other way, the order in the rule may be arbitrary. Although, for example, VP complements may not co-occur with indirect objects, the phrase structure rule does not need to state this by putting the choices within braces, since the subcategorization of no verb will allow them to co-occur.

(36)

```
                              S
                 ┌────────────┴────────────┐
              NP[Su]                       VP
              ┌──┴──┐              ┌────────┴────────┐
              D     N             V                 VP
              │     │             │          ┌──────┴──────┐
             the  driver        should       V             VP
                                            │        ┌──────┴──────┐
                                           have      V          NP[DO]
                                                     │          ┌──┴──┐
                                                   taken        D     N
                                                                │     │
                                                              the  Cadillac
```

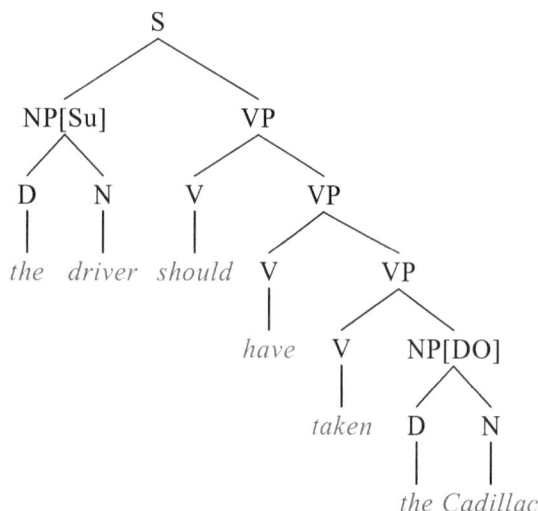

The second thing we need in our formal analysis is to identify the subcategory of auxiliary verbs. This can be done by giving auxiliary verbs the feature [SUBCAT ⟨ NP[Su], VP ⟩]. Note that there is no grammatical relation to specify on the VP in the SUBCAT list; not all subcategorization involves grammatical relations.[16] A similar analysis should work in many languages.[17]

8.6. Pro-drop

Many languages allow subject pronouns to be omitted, especially if there is agreement marking on the verb that expresses the same idea.

(37)   a. *Vemos   a   Jorge.*   (Spanish)
          see-1pl P Jorge
       b. *Nosotros   vemos   a   Jorge.*
          we   see   P Jorge

       We see Jorge.

(38)   a. *Geldi-m.*   (Turkish)[18]
          came-1sg
       b. *Ben geldi-m.*
          I   came-1sg

       I came.

This phenomenon is called PRO-DROP, and languages that allow it are called PRO-DROP LANGUAGES or NULL-SUBJECT LANGUAGES.

---

[16]In English, it is also necessary for auxiliaries to specify which inflected form the following verb assumes (base form, present participle, passive participle, etc.). See Pollard and Sag 1987:123–26, 1994:41–43. Also, some mechanism must be worked out so that the subject of the topmost auxiliary verb satisfies the subcategorization requirements of all the verbs in the auxiliary chain. Pollard and Sag 1987 only hint at the solution in one diagram, without commenting on it. Finally, there is the problem of how to enforce the proper ordering of auxiliaries in English, since sequences like '*is being had watched' are ungrammatical.

[17]In VSO and other languages with flat clause structures, I am at present not sure what to suggest, since I have not had the opportunity to think through the issue with data from such a language that has auxiliary verbs. It may be that, in such languages, auxiliary verbs take sentential complements rather than VP complements.

[18]Turkish data from Underhill 1976:47–49. Only relevant morphology is shown.

When a subject pronoun can be dropped, what do we do in the analysis? Do we omit the subject from the tree, make it optional in the phrase structure rules, and put parentheses around the subject in the SUBCAT list of all verbs? It's better not to, because this fails to express the generalization that omission of pronouns is a characteristic of subjects generally, not of particular verbs.[19] Also, it fails to explain why a missing subject still has the same meaning as a pronoun. What would a tree without a subject mean? It might have some vague meaning like 'someone' or 'something', or even that the event happened 'by itself' with no agent whatsoever.[20]

So, a better solution is the one introduced earlier (in chapter 5 "Introduction to Syntax," p. 45). We assume that Spanish and Turkish have a silent pronoun and write it as *pro*. It can be listed in the lexicon as follows:

(39) **NP**

    pro [Su]   (pronoun)

The gloss for *pro* is deliberately very general. It doesn't mention person and number since it can be used in place of any subject pronoun. (That is, any subject pronoun can be omitted, regardless of its person and number.) However, there is still meaning here; *pro* still refers to a specific person in the context, just like any other pronoun.[21]

Pro appears in trees just like other pronouns. Thus, the trees for examples (38a, b) are almost identical.

(40) a.   b.

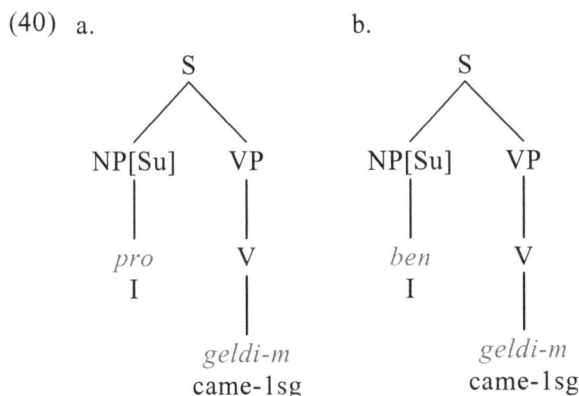

When we use *pro* in our analysis, we don't use parentheses around the subject in the phrase structure rule or in SUBCAT lists. In other words, this analysis makes the assumption that subjects are always present in trees.[22] The way we account for the absence of an overt subject in the data is by omitting

---

[19]Radford 1997:17–18 points out that languages do not allow individual verbs to control whether subject pronouns can be omitted; either subject pronouns can be omitted with all verbs or with none of them. Therefore, SUBCAT lists should not be used to account for the absence of pronominal subjects; if they were, this would suggest that verbs could differ from each other within one language in this respect.

[20]A third reason for using *pro* is discussed below: it allows us to easily characterize the difference between when a direct object is simply omitted because of properties particular to a verb and when it is omitted generally in the language but with a specific pronominal meaning. Finally, *pro* is required by the analysis of agreement features in chapter 19 "Case and Agreement" (p. 260). This analysis has the effect of introducing agreement features like person and number onto *pro*. Until then, these features are represented informally in trees by means of the glosses under *pro*.

[21]This is not to prevent *pro* from having person and number features in particular trees, however. For example, the use of the SUBCAT feature to account for agreement (in chapter 19 "Case and Agreement," p. 268) requires us to assign agreement features to *pro* in some cases, and it may well be that a full account would require that person/number features (or whatever is relevant to pronouns in a given language) be assigned in all cases. However, in most languages there is no reason for *pro* to be specified with these features *in the lexicon*. (Compare Pollard and Sag 1994:64.) However, in some languages only certain pronouns can be omitted. For example, in Modern Hebrew (Haegeman 1991:417), *pro* cannot be third person; it would be appropriate to specify this fact in the lexicon.

[22]This is a controversial assumption. There are, of course, some verbs that never have overt subjects, such as Spanish *llover* 'to rain'. Such verbs generally refer to ambient conditions (weather, etc.) and correspond to English verbs that must have the dummy pronoun *it* as their subject. In addition, many languages have impersonal verbs that likewise seem to be

only the phonological features from the subject, not the whole branch. For example, *pro* still has syntactic properties, such as the feature [Su] in its lexical entry; this feature prevents *pro* from being used for anything except subjects in Turkish and Spanish. (Compare (43) and (44) below.)

However, in some languages it is also possible to omit direct objects.[23] For example, recall the ASL example discussed in chapter 5 "Introduction to Syntax" (p. 45).

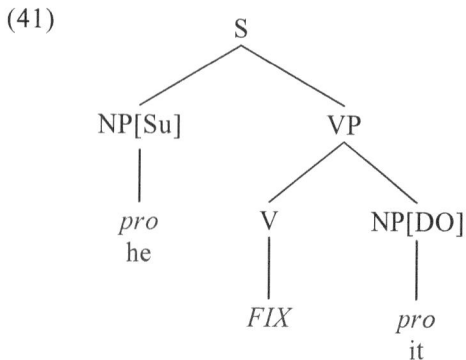

(41)

```
                           S
                  ┌────────┴────────┐
              NP[Su]              VP
                 │            ┌────┴─────┐
                 │            V        NP[DO]
                pro           │          │
                he           FIX        pro
                                         it
```

This raises a practical problem: If a particular transitive verb sometimes occurs without any overt direct object, how do we decide between the following two analyses for its absence?

(42)   a. The verb has an obligatory direct object in its SUBCAT list, but that direct object can be a silent pronoun *pro* (as illustrated in the tree).
       b. The verb has an optional direct object in its SUBCAT list, so that it can occur in an intransitive clause (not illustrated).

Compare this to the verbs of eating and drinking in Choapan Zapotec (22)–(23). For them, we chose the second analysis—we made the direct object optional in the SUBCAT list (see (30), p. 83). Why not use *pro* for these verbs and make the direct object obligatory? The reason is that when a direct object of these verbs is omitted, the meaning is completely unspecified. All we know about the thing that was eaten is that it was eaten, but this meaning comes completely from the verb. In contrast, the missing direct object in (41) has a very specific meaning, that of a pronoun referring to a particular item in the context.[24] Also, not all verbs in Choapan Zapotec allow the direct object to be omitted, so it is right to make the direct object optional in some SUBCAT lists but not in others. In contrast, all ASL verbs can occur without overt direct objects, so it is best not to specify this in each lexical entry.

More generally, there are two patterns that occur in languages, depending on whether the language has a pronoun *pro* that can occur as a direct object.

---

subjectless. One might be tempted to omit the subject from the SUBCAT list for these verbs. However, something needs to account for the fact that such verbs show agreement in some invariant form, usually third person singular. Therefore, a better approach would be to include the features [3 person, –plural] in the SUBCAT list, as in the treatment of agreement in chapter 19 "Case and Agreement" (p. 260), and include a silent dummy pronoun as subject. For a discussion of this issue, particularly as it relates to the analysis of impersonal passives, see Perlmutter and Postal 1984.

[23]In such cases, the lexical entry for *pro* would list other grammatical relations where *pro* can occur. Conceivably, if a pronoun could be omitted from absolutely any NP position, *pro* could be listed in the lexicon without any restrictions on its distribution. Although in some languages many different types of noun phrases can be omitted, it is an open question whether there is any language which would place no restrictions on the distribution of *pro*.

[24]More generally, we should be careful not to assume that silent elements exist unless we have some specific evidence for them. Besides the semantic consideration here (a missing subject or direct object functions as a pronoun with specific person/number features), other evidence might include presence of agreement markers on the verb, the ability of the 'missing' element to be the antecedent of another pronoun or an Equi-controller, to be passivized or raised, etc.

	Pattern A (no *pro* as DO)	Pattern B (DO can be *pro*)
intransitive verbs V[SUBCAT ⟨ NP[Su] ⟩]	never have overt DOs	never have overt DOs
transitive verbs V[SUBCAT ⟨ NP[Su], NP[DO] ⟩]	always have overt DOs	optionally have overt DOs; any 'missing' DO always has a pronominal meaning
verbs that can be either V[SUBCAT ⟨ NP[Su], (NP[DO]) ⟩]	may or may not have overt DOs	optionally have overt DOs; in some cases a 'missing' DO has a pronominal meaning while in other cases it has no meaning at all

If you find three classes of verbs as in pattern A, assume that the language does not allow *pro* to be a direct object (although it might still be possible as subject). If you find three classes as in pattern B and there are no verbs that always have a direct object, assume that *pro* can be a DO in this language. By allowing the possibility of having silent pronouns in our analysis, we can distinguish easily between the two types of languages.

One final variation on these patterns is that some languages do not have verbs in the third class. For example, in Turkish, even the verb 'eat' must always have a direct object. If necessary, a generic word is used as the direct object, one that adds little meaning other than that provided by the verb itself.[25]

(43)   *Adam   yemek   yedi.*
       man   food   he.ate
       The man ate.

(44)   *Orhan   yazi   yazdi.*
       Orhan   written.thing wrote
       Orhan wrote.

8.7. Typological notes: Marking of subjects and objects

There are several strategies that languages use to distinguish subjects, direct objects, and indirect objects from each other. We just saw one: sometimes languages can omit subject pronouns but not direct object pronouns. There are several other common ways that subjects and objects differ.

Some languages, like Choapan Zapotec and Kalkatungu (below), rely almost entirely on word order and meaning to indicate which NP in the clause is subject, which is direct object, etc.

(45)   *janiŋku   ntia   aña   wampa*   (Kalkatungu, Australia)[26]
       white.man   money   gave   girl
       The white man gave money to the girl.

Some languages use special morphological forms, called CASES, for nouns and pronouns, to indicate their grammatical relation. For example, in (46), the suffix glossed 'Dat(ive case)', shows that *ba* 'you' is the indirect object. In (47), the suffix glossed 'Acc(usative case)' shows that *filia* 'daughter' is the direct object.

---

[25]Data from Underhill 1976:52.
[26]Data from Blansitt 1986:33, citing Blake 1969:35. The transcription has been standardized.

(46) *cha kle bla   kete ba-ge*   (Bokotá, Panama)[27]
     I   be banana give you-Dat
     I am giving bananas to you.

(47) *mater filia-m   amat*   (Latin)
     mother daughter-Acc loves
     The mother loves the daughter.

English shows another type of case-marking, involving special forms of pronouns. For example, the first person singular pronoun has three forms: *I* is in nominative case (used for subjects), *me* is in objective case (used for direct and indirect objects), and *my* is in genitive case (used for possessors). (We come back to case marking again in chapter 10 "Inflectional Morphology" (p. 128) and especially chapter 19 "Case and Agreement" (p. 253), so don't bother to learn the names for the different cases now. The important point is knowing what case is and the role it plays in marking grammatical relations.)

Other languages (including English) mark the indirect object with a preposition, but leave the subject and direct object as bare noun phrases. (Another way to say this is that the indirect object in languages like English is a prepositional phrase.)

(48) *Lakilaki itu mengirim surat kepada wanita itu*   (Indonesian, Austronesian)[28]
     man   the sent   letter to   woman the
     The man sent a letter to the woman.

(49) *i³xi²   piy³bít² o'³ñĩm² je³'it² pe³*   (Munduruku, Brazil)[29]
     mother food   she.gave her.son to
     The mother gave her son food.

(When a 'preposition' follows its NP, as in (49), it is called a POSTPOSITION, and the PP is called a POSTPOSITIONAL PHRASE.)

Some languages even use PPs for direct objects, at least in some circumstances. (Here, I've used the gloss 'P' for prepositions that have no equivalent in English.)

(50) *Marta ve   [PP a Jorge].*   (Spanish)[30]
     Marta sees   P Jorge
     Marta sees Jorge.

(51) *Ng mədakt [PP ər a   dərumk].*   (Palauan, Austronesian, Belau)[31]
     He fears   P   thunder
     He is afraid of the thunder.

We return to this topic in chapter 21 "Passive and Voice," where it becomes crucially important to know what devices a language uses to mark different grammatical relations.

---

[27]Data from Blansitt 1986:32, citing Gunn 1975:95.

[28]Data from Chung 1983.

[29]Data from Blansitt 1986:32, citing Crofts 1973:50.

[30]Actually, the situation in Spanish is a bit complicated. PPs are used for direct objects in Spanish that are definite persons; otherwise NPs are used (i.e., the preposition *a* is omitted). I won't try to accommodate this type of fact in grammars in this book; the point here is to highlight some of the ways in which languages differ from each other.

[31]Palauan data from Josephs 1975:48. The rule governing the preposition *ər* is similar to Spanish; it is required (but only with imperfective verbs) when the object is specific. The word *a* in Palauan has no discernible meaning; it simply occurs at the beginning of most noun phrases.

8.8. Review of key terms

Clauses can be classified as INTRANSITIVE, TRANSITIVE, and DITRANSITIVE, depending on whether they contain DIRECT and/or INDIRECT OBJECTS. Verbs are also classified as INTRANSITIVE, TRANSITIVE, and DITRANSITIVE, based on the types of objects they can occur with. (Verbs that only take direct objects, and not indirect objects, are sometimes called STRICTLY TRANSITIVE.) This subdivision of verbs into SUBCATEGORIES according to the objects they can CO-OCCUR with is called (SYNTACTIC) SUBCATEGORIZATION; we say that objects SUBCATEGORIZE verbs. Many types of phrases can be involved in subcategorization; for example, AUXILIARY VERBS require a VP as a sister. Subcategorization is represented in this book with the [SUBCAT] feature, which takes as its value a list of grammatical categories identifying the phrases that the verb must or may co-occur with.

Subcategorization is the syntactic side to what is called VALENCE, the fact that a verb places requirements on the types of clauses it can be used in. There is also a semantic side to valence, called SELECTIONAL RESTRICTIONS; we have only concerned ourselves with those selectional restrictions which can be characterized as SEMANTIC ROLES of the different noun phrases in a clause, such as AGENT, EXPERIENCER, PATIENT, THEME, RECIPIENT, and ADDRESSEE.

When a verb's syntactic valence (subcategorization) is violated, the result is UNGRAMMATICAL. However, sentences can be UNACCEPTABLE for other reasons, such as when selectional restrictions are violated or when the sentence is false or obscene.

Subjects, direct objects, and indirect objects are marked in different ways in different languages: with word order, with PREPOSITIONS and POSTPOSITIONS, with noun morphology (CASES). They may also allow different possibilities for PRO-DROP; those that allow subject pronouns to be omitted are called NULL-SUBJECT or PRO-DROP LANGUAGES. When analyzing grammatical relations, we look for grammatical characteristics like these to identify types of constituents, then rely on semantic roles to make a hypothesis about which types are subjects, etc.

8.9. Questions for analysis

1. What grammatical category (NP or PP) is used for the subject, direct object, and indirect object? For the PPs, what preposition is used to indicate each grammatical relation?
2. What clausal constituents subcategorize verbs?
3. For each verb, which types of phrases must, may, or cannot be used with it?[32]
4. Is there a special subcategory of auxiliary verbs?
5. Is pro-drop possible? That is, can pronouns be omitted with pronominal meaning? For which grammatical relations is this possible? Under what conditions?

8.10. Sample description

The word order of Choapan Zapotec is VSO; the indirect object occurs between the subject and direct object. All three are bare noun phrases and are distinguished only by word order.

(1) *ujo bẽʔ naʔ*
     went man that
     That man went.

(2) *utʃugu tʃopa ʃkuidiʔ naʔ tu luba ɾeo naʔ*
     cut   two   children that one vine thick that
     Those two children cut that one thick vine.

[32]For a formal grammar to be complete, question 3 must in principle be asked for every verb. As a practical matter, people only publish a comprehensive list in a dictionary, and even then there are likely to be omissions.

(3)   *bɛʔ   bẽʔ   naʔ   nigula   tu   dumi   daoʔ*
       gave man   that woman   one   money small
       That man gave a small coin to a woman.

Verbs are subcategorized by their objects. Many are strictly transitive or intransitive, such as those in (1)–(2). There are a few verbs which can be either transitive or intransitive, such as verbs of ingestion.

(4)   *udao   bẽʔ   naʔ   (jɛta   naʔ)*
       ate   man   that (food   that)
       That man ate (that food).

Indirect objects are optional with many ditransitive verbs. Compare (5) with (3) above.

(5)   *bɛʔ   bẽʔ   naʔ   dumi   naʔ*
       gave man   that money   that
       That man gave that coin.

8.11. For further reading

Radford 1988, chapter 7, discusses subcategorization, selectional restrictions, and semantic roles in English in much greater detail, including some recent proposals about how to incorporate these ideas in a transformational grammar. Pollard and Sag (1987:115–46) provide an extensive, although somewhat technical, discussion of the types of elements that verbs (and other elements) can subcategorize for, including different grammatical categories, forms of the verbs that are complements of auxiliaries, cases on NPs, and prepositions in PPs. They develop the theoretical foundation of Head-driven Phrase Structure Grammar on which my treatment of subcategorization is based, including the SUBCAT feature itself.

The inventory of semantic roles presented here represents a selection from a number of different systems that have been used under labels such as 'semantic roles', 'thematic roles', 'theta roles', and 'case roles'. Cook (1998:4–5, 10–18) compares the most widely-known of these in the context of presenting his own system, as well as dealing with many other aspects of the semantic structure of verbs. Most textbooks on Government-binding Theory include a discussion of how thematic roles can be integrated into a transformational grammar; Radford (1988:372–92) gives one of the most readable introductions to this topic.

9
Obliques

9.1. Goals and prerequisites

This chapter will help you do the following:

- ◎ state the difference between the core constituents of a clause and the obliques, and between complements and adjuncts
- ◎ use semantic labels to identify the meanings of obliques in data
- ◎ list the structures commonly used for obliques, and identify the structure of obliques in data
- ◎ write a concise description of obliques found in a language
- ◎ construct a formal analysis of obliques that covers both their internal structure and their distribution

It assumes that you are familiar with the following material:

- ✓ noun phrase structure (chapter 7 "Embedding and Noun Phrase Structure")
- ✓ grammatical relations and syntactic subcategorization (chapter 8 "Verbal Valence")

9.2. Secondary information in a clause

Now that we've covered the primary constituents in the clause, it's time to move on to those that are in some sense 'less important'. Think of a clause as a movie. The verb represents the plot while the subject, direct object, and indirect object represent the main characters. The remainder of the clause supplies information about secondary characters, the setting, and the manner in which the main characters carry out the plot.

The topic of this chapter concerns this secondary information and the phrases which express it. These phrases are often called OBLIQUES. Let's define OBLIQUE as 'any of the phrases within a clause other than the subject, direct object, indirect object, or verb'.[1]

---

[1]The term 'oblique' is borrowed from Relational Grammar and Lexical-functional Grammar and is related to the term 'obliqueness' in Head-driven Phrase Structure Grammar. In all these frameworks, obliques are types of grammatical relations. For this book, the notion of oblique is in a sense a grammatical relation, or more precisely, the absence of a [GR] feature, and the different types of obliques are semantic entities only. Other common terms for OBLIQUES are ADVERBIALS and ADVERBIAL PHRASES, but these get easily confused with ADVERB PHRASE (below), which is only one type of oblique.

Obliques usually express a wider range of meanings than do subjects and objects. Some express secondary characters.

(1)   BENEFACTIVE
       He opened the door [for the small children.]
       Many nations provided funding [for the Persian Gulf War].

(2)   ACCOMPANIMENT
       He ate dinner [with his guests].
       Why don't you come [with me]?
       He mixed the dirt [with the manure].

(3)   INSTRUMENT
       Many people have learned to eat [with their fingers].
       The mill will not grind [with water that is past].
       We make a living [by what we get], but we make a life [by what we give].
       Let's go [on foot].

Others express setting.

(4)   TIME
       He awoke [late the next morning].
       It has been too hot [the whole week].
       Most successful sales come [after the fifth call].

(5)   LOCATION (of an object or an entire event)
       He saw the dog [over there].
       Little Miss Muffet sat [on a tuffet].

Others express locations of part of an event (with verbs of motion).

(6)   SOURCE (starting point)
       He came [from Alabama].
       Please take that silly hat [off your head].

(7)   PATH
       They passed [through many twisted corridors].
       One if [by land], two if [by sea]...

(8)   GOAL (endpoint)
       He ran [to the back of the room].
       I'll put the letter [on your desk].

Other obliques express abstract qualities characteristic of the event or of the speaker's attitude towards the event.

(9)   MANNER
       [Very slowly], she backed out of the cage.
       Sergeant Pepper dismantled the bomb [with great care].
       [Unfortunately], we cannot retain your services.

This is not in any way a complete list, but it covers the most common types. (A few more are introduced in chapter 22 "Embedded Clauses.")

9.3. Syntactic structures used for obliques

The meanings of obliques are comparable to semantic roles like agent, patient, experiencer, and recipient (see chapter 8 "Verbal Valence," pp. 80ff.). All languages have some way of expressing ideas such as the oblique meanings illustrated above, but as you can see just from these examples, there can be a variety of structures used to express any one idea. When you analyze a particular language, you need to examine its grammatical structures and then determine for each structure what range of meanings it can convey.

So, let's take a look at the variety of structures used for obliques, in English, Swahili (Bantu, East Africa),[2] and a few other languages. You will find that the internal structure of obliques is far more important than their distribution for establishing their syntactic category. This is because many obliques have the same distribution, but quite different internal structures.

Prepositional and postpositional phrases

The structure most used for obliques is a noun phrase combined with a PREPOSITION (such as *under*) to form a PREPOSITIONAL PHRASE (PP), such as *under the table*. Conversely, the most common use of PPs is as obliques, although we have also seen them used as possessors, indirect objects, and even direct objects. Languages tend to package noun phrases with attached prepositions (i.e., inside PPs) according to the following ranking:

(10)   Su DO IO Oblique
        NP ◄────────► PP

That is, PPs are used commonly for obliques, somewhat less often for indirect objects, quite rarely for direct objects, and almost never for subjects.[3]

The preposition plays a pivotal role in a PP, since it signals the relationship of the NP to the rest of the clause. For example, it is the preposition in the following examples that indicates the grammatical relation or meaning of the phrase.

(11) **to** *Arthur*   Indirect Object or Goal
      for *Arthur*   Benefactive
      with *Arthur*   Accompaniment
      on *Arthur*   Location
      through *Arthur*   Path

Of course, the meaning of the noun phrase itself also plays a factor, since many prepositions can be used to express more than one meaning:

(12) **in** *three minutes*   Time
      in *the candy dish*   Location
      in *a huff*   Manner

Swahili likewise uses prepositions for some obliques.

---

[2]Data from Vitale 1981 and Wilson 1985.

[3]This ranking, sometimes called an obliqueness hierarchy or relational hierarchy, has figured very importantly in certain theoretical frameworks, such as Relational Grammar, Lexical-functional Grammar, and Head-driven Phrase Structure Grammar. Pollard and Sag (1987:118–20) point out its empirical importance, which is far greater than the rather fuzzy correlation noted here. A variant of it comes back in chapter 23 "Relative Clauses," pp. 340 as the Noun Phrase Accessibility Hierarchy.

(13)   Time
    Fatuma alisimama kwa   muda   mrefu
    Fatuma she.stood for   period long
    Fatuma stood for a long time.

(14)   Goal
    aliingia   katika chumba kikubwa kile
    he.entered into   room   large   that
    He entered that large room.

(15)   Source
    kitabu kilianguka kutoka rafu-ni
    book   it.fell   from   shelf-Loc
    The book fell from the shelf.

(16)   Instrument
    chakula kililiwa   kwa kijiko
    food   it.was.eaten with spoon
    The food was eaten with a spoon.

(17)   Manner
    alikwenda kwa   haraka
    he.went   with haste
    He went quickly.

One Swahili preposition, *kwa,* is used to express several different meanings. Besides what are illustrated here ('for' and 'with'), it can mean 'to', 'towards', 'by', and 'by means of'. Structures used for obliques, such as particular prepositions, typically do not line up in a neat one-to-one fashion with the list of possible oblique meanings. That list is designed for use with all languages, but each language packages these meanings in its own way.

So, when you are analyzing prepositions, or more generally, when you are analyzing any obliques, you have to examine each structure's range of uses and compile a list of its different meanings. One consequence of this is that it is often impossible to translate obliques in a literal word-for-word fashion. You have to determine what the oblique means, then find a suitable structure in the target language that expresses the same idea.

In some languages (especially SOV languages), 'prepositions' follow the NP, in which case they are called POSTPOSITIONS (also P) and the phrases are called POSTPOSITIONAL PHRASES (also PP). For example, Turkish uses postpositions, not prepositions.[4]

(18) *Ahmet [ekmek için] dükkâna gitti.*
      Ahmet   bread   for   to.store   went
      Ahmet went to the store for bread.

(19) *Cevabı [yarına   kadar] bulurum.*
      answer   tomorrow   until   I.will.find
      I'll find the answer by (lit., until) tomorrow.

But, aside from word order, postpositions are identical in function to prepositions; they serve as a link between the NP and the rest of the clause.

In a PP, the preposition or postposition is the head and the noun phrase is called its OBJECT. The structure that is generally assumed for PPs is as follows:

---

[4]Data from Underhill 1976:157, 171.

(20) a.   PP   b.   PP

            P   NP   NP   P

            | /\   /\ |
           on   the computer   ekmek   için
                                                   bread   for

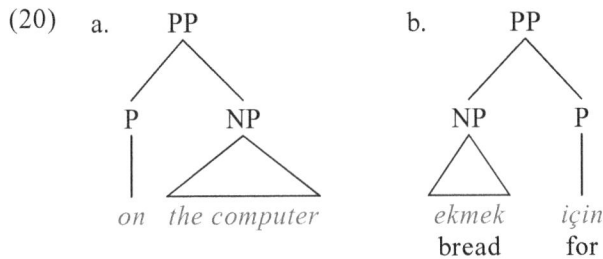

This means that a language will require a phrase structure rule similar to one of the following:

(21)   PP → P NP   OR   PP → NP P

In most languages, there is very little variation allowed from these two basic possibilities. The object is normally obligatory, it is usually just a noun phrase, and there are usually no other constituents possible in the phrase.[5]

Noun phrases

In Swahili, as in many languages, prepositions are not used to express certain oblique meanings, especially Benefactive, Time, and various types of spatial relationships (Location, Path, Goal). A bare noun phrase is used instead; even though there is no preposition it usually is obvious how the noun phrase relates semantically to the rest of the clause.[6]

(22)   Benefactive
      Juma   alimpikia   Ahmed   ugali.
      Juma   he.cooked.him   Ahmed   porridge
      Juma cooked some porridge for Ahmed.

(23)   Time
      jogoo   aliwika   mara   tatu
      rooster   he.crowed times three
      The rooster crowed three times.

(24)   Goal   Time
      Fatuma   huenda   msikiti-ni   ijumaa
      Fatuma   she.goes mosque-Loc   Friday
      Fatuma goes to the mosque on Fridays.

---

[5]English allows much more variation than this; see Radford 1988:246–53.

[6]The last /i/ in the verb of (22) is a separate suffix, commonly called an 'applicative', which is used in clauses that include a noun phrase interpreted as a Benefactive. Under some approaches, this example may be analyzed as an instance of advancement from Benefactive to direct or indirect object, hence not an 'oblique' at all as far as this book is concerned. See chapter 21 "Passive and Voice," p. 300ff. for more discussion of Benefactive 'voice' and other advancements. Especially consider the examples there from the related language Kinyarwanda, which allows clauses like (22) and also allows clauses with no applicative suffix and the Benefactive noun phrase following a preposition (hence apparently not involving advancement). I do not know if this second type of clause is possible in Swahili. At any rate, examples like this illustrate the importance of making a distinction between the different semantic concepts that can be expressed as part of a clause and the different ways that they can be expressed. In early field work, we depend rather heavily on semantics, while later understanding of syntactic structure may lead us to reanalyze some 'obliques' as having advanced to objects, based on their syntactic properties.

(25)   Location
 Juma   alimbusu   Halima dari-ni
 Juma   he.kissed.her Halima attic-Loc
 Juma kissed Halima in the attic.

(26)   Path
 Juma   haendi   njia-ni
 Juma   he.not.go path-Loc
 Juma did not go by the path.

(27)   Goal
 Siwezi   kufika   ng'ambo ya mto   ule
 I.not.able to.arrive far.side of river that
 I cannot go across (lit., arrive at the far side of) that river.

There are two other structures in Swahili that are similar to what you will find in other languages. First, notice the locative suffix *-ni* on several of the nouns above.[7] In some languages, special affixes are attached to certain oblique noun phrases to indicate their meaning within the clause; these are a type of case marking (see chapter 8 "Verbal Valence," p. 89, and chapter 19 "Case and Agreement," especially p. 257), but this time marking an oblique instead of a core grammatical relation. They function much like prepositions—they indicate the relationship of the noun phrase to the clause. But, their structure is different; they are affixes on nouns instead of separate words outside the noun phrase. Note too that this suffix again illustrates that one marker can have more than one function, since it is used for Location, Path, and Goal.

Second, notice the use of the possessed noun *ng'ambo* 'far side' in (27). This is an example of a RELATIONAL NOUN, a noun used to express a 'prepositional' idea. For example, in many Mesoamerican languages, body part nouns are used to express locative relations. To say 'behind him' you say literally 'at his back', to say 'in the cup' you say literally 'in the cup's belly', etc. Some languages have other relational nouns to express ideas like 'above (the area above something)', 'beyond (the area on the far side of something)', etc. In such languages, there may be few or no prepositions, since nouns express most of the meanings that we are used to thinking of as 'prepositional'. And finally, relational nouns in some languages are used in combination with a general-purpose (and virtually meaningless) preposition, such as *ər* in Palauan (Austronesian, Republic of Belau).[8]

(28) *a*[9] *bilis a maʔiuaiu* [PP *ər* [NP *a eungel   a tebəl*]]
       dog   is.sleeping   P   its.under.area table
      The dog is sleeping under the table (lit., in the table's under-area).

Indeed, *ər* is the *only* preposition in Palauan; virtually all of the meaning that is packed in prepositions in European languages is found in relational nouns in Palauan or is simply supplied from context.

Adverb phrases

You will sometimes hear obliques referred to as ADVERBIALS or ADVERBIAL PHRASES. These names come from the traditional conception of an adverb as a modifier of anything other than a

---

[7]There are a couple of quirks with this suffix. It can only be used on unmodified nouns; when a noun is modified by an adjective or demonstrative, as in (14), the synonymous preposition *katika* must be used instead of *-ni* (Wilson 1985:61). Also, it is sometimes used in combination with a preposition, as in (15). For simplicity, I will not attempt to handle these facts in the formal analysis.

[8]Data from Josephs 1975:280, transcription modified slightly to standard IPA symbols.

[9]This word is apparently meaningless; it serves only to mark the beginning of NPs and certain VPs.

noun. And, indeed, most obliques do function as a type of modifier within the clause, and some (like *quickly* and *far*) are indeed adverbs.

The term ADVERBIAL, however, leaves much to be desired. For one thing, the most common types of obliques are PPs and NPs, neither of which are adverbs. But worse, the traditional class of adverbs is an ill-defined conglomeration of very different types of words, many of which cannot be used as obliques. The core of this group, what we can call 'true ADVERBS', consists of words that can be modified (in English) by degree words; in this way they are like adjectives. The true adverbs thus include words like *possibly, quickly, well,* and *far,* and we reserve the word 'adverb' for a class of words that contains similar meanings.

Many other words traditionally called adverbs are clearly *not* in the same syntactic category as true adverbs. Degree words, for example, are traditionally considered adverbs, but they cannot be interchanged freely with true adverbs.

(29) a. *She ran very smoothly.*
      b. **She ran smoothly very.*
      c. **She ran quickly smoothly.*
      d. **She ran very so.*

(30) a. *Don't speak so fast.*
      b. **Don't speak fast so.*
      c. **Don't speak fast well.*
      b. **Don't speak very.*

This is why we have placed degree words in a separate category, Deg.

The word *not* is not an adverb, but (in English) is in a syntactic category by itself, since it can occur in several positions not open to true adverbs and vice versa. (We can represent the fact that one but not another word will work in a particular context by connecting them with a slash '/' and putting an asterisk in front of the one that doesn't work there.)[10]

(31) a. *He did not/? *quickly run the race yesterday.*
      b. *Not/*quickly even Harold knew about the impending catastrophe.*
      c. *She quickly/*not shut the door again.*
      d. *Run quickly/? *not downstairs and get me some ice cream; I'm desperate!*

In English, we can call this category Neg. In some languages the word meaning 'not' is a verb. The main point here is that a word meaning 'not' seldom behaves like adverbs.

Words like *here, there, now, then,* and *yesterday* are also not true adverbs, since they cannot be modified by degree words.

(32) a. **very yesterday*
      b. **rather here*

There is a very limited number of these words, i.e., they constitute a closed class, whereas the category of true adverbs in English is an open class. Later (p. 101) I suggest what category they might be placed in.

After distinguishing these different classes that traditional grammar lumps together, we find that the true adverbs that are left are very much like adjectives. Indeed, many English adverbs are derived from adjectives (see chapter 11 "Derivational Morphology," pp. 142ff.).

---

[10]The notation ?* means that an utterance is largely unacceptable, but this is not completely certain, either because of uncertainty on the part of individuals or disagreement between individuals. In (31a, d), the problem is that the construction is archaic, not used in modern speech, yet still familiar to some speakers.

(33)   Adjective   Adverb

        slow   slowly
        complete   completely
        happy   happily

Both adjectives and adverbs can be modified by degree phrases, to form adjective phrases and
ADVERB PHRASES (AdvP).

(34)   Adjective phrase   Adverb phrase

        very slow   very slowly
        quite complete   quite completely
        so happy   so happily
        almost too generous   almost too generously

This similarity is brought out in the phrase structure rules for AP and AdvP.

(35)   AP   →   (DegP) A
        AdvP   →   (DegP) Adv

And, adjective phrases function in noun phrases very much like adverb phrases do in clauses.

(36)   a. *their **excited** discussion of the candidates*
        b. *They **excitedly** discussed the candidates.*

Turning from form to function, adverb phrases are commonly used as obliques expressing
Manner (see examples above) and occasionally with other meanings, such as Time and Location.

(37)   *He left [(very) early].*
        Martha ran [(too) far] and collapsed.

Adverb phrases in Swahili can express the same meanings as in English.[11]

(38)   Time
        Halima aliamka   mapema
        Halima   she.awoke   early
        Halima woke up early.

(39)   Manner
        mwezi ulianza   vibaya   sana
        month   it.started badly   very
        The month started very badly.

Idiomatic phrases

    Some (perhaps all) languages have a limited set of idiomatic phrases that are used as obliques,
are learned as units, and are exceptional in some way. For example, *at college* appears to be a PP,
but lacks the determiner that is normally required for singular count nouns like *college*. Similarly,
last night appears to be an NP, but again is missing a determiner. Further, their meanings are not
completely predictable; *at college* does not mean 'located at some college campus', but rather

---

[11]However, we don't know if *mapema* 'early' can be modified by degree words like *sana* 'very'; if not, then it is most
likely not an adverb, but in the same class as words like 'here' and 'now'.

'studying at a college or university', and *last night* does not mean the same as *the last night* or *a last night*, but rather 'the night that preceded today'.

Because of these irregularities, they should not be generated by the phrase structure rules, which are meant to express regularities about phrase structure applicable to millions of NPs or PPs, not isolated idiosyncratic phrases. Instead, we list them with all their tree structure in the lexicon, which is where we keep track of information about expressions that have individual quirks and idiosyncrasies in form or meaning.[12] For example, the lexical entry for *last night* might be written as follows:

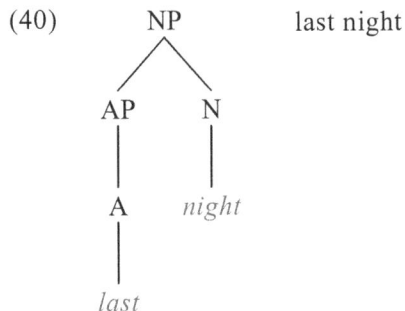

(40)   NP   last night

```
        NP
       /  \
      AP    N
      |     |
      A    night
      |
     last
```

Swahili appears to have idiomatic structures too, as in (41). This oblique seems to consist of either two nouns or possibly an adverb (*kesho* 'tomorrow') plus a noun. Whatever these words are, this pair is like no other constituent we've seen so far.

(41)

				Time	
wamasai	*watakuwa*	*wakicheza*	*dansi*	*kesho*	*usiku*
Masai	they.will.be	they.playing	dance	tomorrow	night

The Masai will be dancing (lit., playing a dance) tomorrow night.

So, this may be some sort of idiomatic NP. However, there is no way to be sure unless we first have a fairly complete analysis of the whole language; only when we know what the rules are can we spot the exceptions.

In summary, when doing an analysis of obliques, you may run across phrases that don't seem to fit your understanding of the way the grammar works. Set them aside for the moment, label them as apparent exceptions, and proceed with your analysis. You may discover some rule later that fully explains them, or you may ultimately have to assign them to the lexicon as idiomatic phrases.

Unmodifiable single words

In most languages, there are certain obliques consisting of single words which cannot take any modifiers. Most commonly, these indicate spatial relationships (Location, Goal, and Source) or Time. Typically they have meanings like 'here', 'there', 'to here', 'from there', 'now', and 'then', and possibly others like 'yesterday', 'noon', and 'home'.

In traditional grammars, such words are usually called 'adverbs'. But, since they are not mutually-substitutable for true adverbs (see discussion above, p. 99), they must be in some category other than Adv. In order to assign them to a category, recall what we did with pronouns. Pronouns are a small closed class of words which function as whole phrases, specifically noun phrases. Accordingly, we assigned them to the category NP.

Similarly, unmodifiable words used as obliques constitute a small closed class of words which function as whole phrases. But, unlike pronouns, they are not mutually-substitutable for just one type of phrase; as obliques, they have basically the same distribution as NPs, PPs, and AdvPs. So which are they? This may depend on the facts of the language, so in different languages the choice

---

[12]More generally, this is how I suggest you handle all idiomatic phrases. Jackendoff (1975:662–64) makes a similar proposal.

may be to assign them to any one of these three categories, treating them essentially as pronouns, pro-PPs, or pro-AdvPs.[13] As a first hypothesis, until you get further evidence, I suggest you classify them according to whatever category is used to express a similar meaning. Thus, if PPs are used to express location, put words like 'here' and 'there' in the category PP.

Thus, for Swahili, we might assume that certain words expressing Goal are listed either as NPs or PPs in the lexicon, since NPs and PPs are otherwise used to express location. Similarly, we might assume that *sasa* 'now' is a PP, NP, or AdvP.

(42)   <u>Goal</u>   <u>Goal</u>
uje   hapa upesi,   halafu   uende   pale   pia
you.come here quickly afterwards you.go there also
Would you (please) come here quickly, then go there also?

(43)   <u>Time</u>
lazima usiende   sasa
must   you.not.go   now
You must not go now.

However, this analysis must remain tentative, since we have not had the opportunity to test these words to see if they can be modified or to see what syntactic characteristics they might share with NPs, PPs, AdvPs, or other obliques. (Again, although meaning can be useful in forming hypotheses, it is generally not a good justification for a syntactic analysis.)

Analyzing obliques

Of the above structures used for obliques, the first three are the most important. Most obliques that you encounter will fit clearly in one of these three categories:

(44)   Primary syntactic categories used for obliques
       a. PP
       b. NP
       c. AdvP

Languages often have structures used for obliques which don't obviously fit in these three categories:

(45)   Other types of expressions used for obliques
       d. idiomatic versions of phrases that are still recognizable as one of the primary categories but don't quite fit all the rules that normally apply to them
       e. single words which are never modified and which have the same distribution as one or more of the primary categories above.

Ultimately, in a formal analysis, these two other types of structures generally should be assigned in the lexicon to one of the three syntactic categories in (44).

When you spot an oblique in a language that you don't know, how do you know what structure is being used? Here are some guidelines to help you in your first hypotheses:

---

[13]Radford 1988:79, for example, analyzes such words in English as pro-PPs.

(46)   a. If it looks like an NP, it's probably an NP.
       b. If it looks like an NP, with the addition of some extra word at the beginning or end, that extra word is likely a P and the whole phrase a PP. This is especially likely if the extra word expresses the relationship of the NP to the larger context.
       c. If it contains nothing that is likely to be a noun or pronoun, it's probably not an NP or PP.
       d. If it contains a modifier that could be a degree word, it's likely an AdvP and the word that is modified is likely an Adv.
       e. If it is a single word, it is probably not a preposition, since prepositions normally have objects. (It might, however, be an unmodifiable single word that could be classified as a PP.)
       f. If it is more than one word, it is not an unmodifiable single word. (Okay, that may seem obvious now, but sometimes it's hard to keep track of the obvious when you're doing analysis in a new language.)
       g. If it looks a great deal like what you've come to recognize as an NP or AdvP, but there are some minor differences from the norm, consider listing it in the lexicon as an idiom.

As we've seen, there is no neat one-to-one relationship between the different structures used for obliques in a language and their meanings. This means that you won't find neat correspondences between two languages either, so make sure you analyze the language, not the glosses! Just because one language uses a PP to express a certain idea, doesn't mean other languages will.

As you make hypotheses about the different obliques you find, you may find it useful to construct a chart something like the following to keep track of which structures are used for which oblique meanings. This one summarizes the facts we've seen in Swahili:

(47)

	PP	NP	AdvP	unmodifiable word
Ben		X		
Acc				
Instr	kwa			
Time	kwa	X	X?	X?
Loc		-ni		
Src	kutoka			
Path		-ni		
Goal	katika	X (-ni)		X?
Manner	kwa		X	

The X's mean that an example of a structure with a particular meaning has been found. If there is a specific morpheme (such as a preposition or suffix) that seems important to the meaning, you can put it in the chart too. If there is more than one such morpheme for a given meaning, list them all. Use a question mark for examples that you're less sure about. (Note that idiomatic phrases are left out of the chart; they need to be treated individually.)

This will help you to spot cases where the same structure (or the same morpheme) is used with more than one meaning. It will also help you find the different ways available for expressing the same idea (which could come in very handy when translating materials into the language). Note, however, that it is primarily for your own use in developing an analysis; it may not be very useful to your readers in a final write-up.

Be sure to compare the structures used for obliques with those used for subjects and objects too. For example, in some languages the notion benefactive may be expressed in the same way as the notion recipient. That is, there may be no difference in form between such phrases as *to the teacher* and *for the teacher;* the same preposition will be used for both or both will be bare noun phrases.

Something like this may be true in Swahili.[14] Compare the benefactive in (48) to the recipient in (49).

(48) *Juma alimpikia   Ahmed   ugali.*
      Juma he.cooked.him Ahmed porridge
      Juma cooked some porridge for Ahmed.

(49) *Badru alimwandikia Ahmed   barua*
      badru he.wrote.him   Ahmed letter
      Badru wrote a letter to Ahmed.

Note that both are noun phrases and the benefactive in (48) precedes the direct object. But, in all other examples obliques follow the direct object. Thus, the two meanings seem to be expressed by exactly the same structure, and one reasonable analysis would be as follows:

(50) a. This structure (the NP immediately following the verb) is an indirect object.
      b. Indirect objects express the semantic role benefactive as well as recipient and addressee.
      c. There is no separate oblique structure that we would call 'benefactive'.

9.4. The distribution of obliques

The discussion above has included a formal analysis of the internal structure of various types of obliques. What about their position within the clause? Quite often, obliques occur 'outside' of objects. That is, if they occur on the same side of the verb, the objects will be closer to the verb than the obliques. (See examples (48)–(49).) Wherever they occur, the relative order of the obliques to each other is usually free, while the order of subject, verb, and objects is often more fixed.

(51) a. *I went to sleep <u>in phonology class</u> <u>this morning</u>.*
      b. *I went to sleep <u>this morning</u> <u>in phonology class</u>.*
      c. **Went to sleep I in phonology class this morning.*

(52) a. *I was studying grammar <u>with some friends</u> <u>until two in the morning</u>.*
      b. *I was studying grammar <u>until two in the morning</u> <u>with some friends</u>.*
      c. **I grammar was studying with some friends until two in the morning.*
      d. **I was studying with some friends grammar until two in the morning.*

For English, we could write a VP rule like the following:

(53)
$$VP \rightarrow V\ (NP[DO])\ (VP)\ (PP[IO]) \left(\left\{ \begin{array}{l} NP \\ PP \\ AdvP \end{array} \right\} \right)*$$

In this rule, the obliques are enclosed with a starred pair of parentheses. Recall (from chapter 7 "Embedding and Noun Phrase Structure," p. 63) that this notation means that any number of such phrases (including zero) can occur, in any order with respect to each other. A similar rule could be given for the Swahili data above; try writing it.

---

[14]To be sure, more data than this would need to be considered. For this analysis to be maintained, the structures expressing the two semantic roles 'recipient' and 'benefactive' would have to have identical grammatical behavior in all respects. If there are significant grammatical differences between them, it would probably be best to distinguish them grammatically as indirect objects and benefactive obliques. Another possibility is that this may be an example of benefactive voice (see chapter 21 "Passive and Voice," p. 300).

There may also be more than one place where obliques can occur. In English, obliques can also occur in front of the subject. This fronting of obliques is very common at the beginning of discourse units, such as paragraphs, to introduce a new setting.

(54)   ***Last night,*** *I studied too long.*

Also, some obliques can occur just before the main verb.

(55)   *I was **gradually** waking up, when I realized how late it was.*

(Both alternate positions for obliques are probably best handled by a transformation, a type of rule that is introduced in chapter 15 "Variable Orders of Constituents," rather than inserting the obliques in every possible position with phrase structure rules.)[15]

9.5. Complements versus adjuncts

As noted above, most obliques serve as modifiers within the clause. One of the reasons for saying this is that most obliques can freely co-occur with all types of verbs, unlike direct and indirect objects. Recall that some verbs are intransitive (they can't have objects), some are ditransitive (they require two objects), etc. In contrast to this, the presence of most obliques is neither ruled out nor required by any verb.

Thus, a basic distinction is usually drawn between those phrases that are required by particular verbs, called COMPLEMENTS, and other phrases that freely occur with all verbs, called ADJUNCTS. The complements (such as direct and indirect objects) are those phrases that a verb subcategorizes for; all others are adjuncts.[16]

A traditional way of talking about the relationship between a verb and its complements is to say that a verb GOVERNS its complements. Linguists generally assume that a verb can only govern items within its own clause; it cannot subcategorize for anything outside its own clause.[17]

Most obliques are adjuncts, but not all are. Obliques expressing Source, Path, and Goal, in particular, are required by some verbs and cannot be used with others.

(56)   a.   *Polly put the kettle on the table.*
       b.   **Polly put the kettle.*

(57)   a.   *In a rage, Arthur killed the pesky fly.*
       b.   **In a rage, Arthur killed the pesky fly to the wall.*

Also, they cannot be used at the beginning of a clause; in this way they are unlike other obliques.

(58)   a.   **To her grandmother's house Little Red Riding Hood started out.*
       b.   **From Tucson she just arrived.*

---

[15]By using a transformation, we avoid mentioning the disjunction of structures {NP, PP, AdvP} in more than one place in the phrase structure rules. It should be noted too that there are some sharp restrictions on oblique fronting, for example, obliques may generally not be fronted in yes-no and content questions, nor in combination with topicalization. Such restrictions might be difficult to impose if obliques were base-generated clause-initially.

[16]The distinction is also sometimes applied within a noun phrase; the possessor is a complement, and the modifiers are adjuncts.

[17]More generally, a lexical head can only govern elements within its maximal projection (the largest phrase that it is the head of). Since V is the lexical head of S, verbs can only govern elements within their clause. Of course, as it stands, this claim is oversimplified, since it does not obviously account for cases of so-called subject-to-object raising, as well as cases where constituents are moved out of a clause by 'long-distance' movements. But it is a good starting place; compare, for example, similar claims in Chomsky 1965:96, 99, Gazdar, Klein, Pullum, and Sag 1985:34, and Pollard and Sag 1987:143–45.

Apparently, obliques of Source, Path, and Goal are complements, not adjuncts, at least in English. Further, the ability to move to the beginning of a clause in English is a property of adjuncts only, not all obliques. To distinguish oblique complements from oblique adjuncts, we need to include a PP (the structure used for Source, Path, and Goal) in the SUBCAT list for some verbs.[18]

(59)   *put*   [SUBCAT ⟨NP[Su], NP[DO], PP⟩]
       walk [SUBCAT ⟨NP[Su], (PP)⟩]

The following chart may help in summarizing many of the terms that have been introduced recently and their relationship to each other.

(60)   Normally complements   Normally adjuncts
       ⎧⎯⎯⎯⎯⎯⎯⎯⎯⎯⎯⎯⎯⎯⎯⎯⎯⎯⎯⎯⎯⎯⎯⎯⎯⎯⎯⎯⎯⎯⎯⎯⎯⎧   ⎧⎯⎯⎯⎯⎯⎯⎯⎯⎯⎯⎯⎯⎯⎯⎯⎯⎯⎯⎯⎯⎯⎯⎯⎯⎯⎧
              Agent   Source   Benefactive
              Experiencer   Goal   Accompaniment
              Patient   Path   Instrument
              Theme   Time
              Recipient   Location
              Addressee   Manner
       ⎩⎯⎯⎯⎯⎯⎯⎯⎯⎯⎯⎯⎯⎯⎯⎯⎯⎯⎯⎯⎯⎩   ⎩⎯⎯⎯⎯⎯⎯⎯⎯⎯⎯⎯⎯⎯⎯⎯⎯⎯⎯⎯⎯⎯⎯⎯⎯⎩
            Typically expressed   Typically expressed with obliques
            with grammatical
            relations: Su/DO/IO

9.6. Constituent-order universals:
How to write your PP rule before you see the data

Whether a language has prepositions or postpositions tends to correlate with facts about the order of constituents in other phrases. Broadly speaking, there are two types of languages with respect to constituent order in clauses and phrases, HEAD-INITIAL and HEAD-FINAL languages:[19]

(61)   Head-initial:

PREPOSITION	precedes	object	in PP
VERB	precedes	objects	in VP or S (SVO, VSO, VOS)
NOUN	precedes	possessor	in NP

       Head-final:

object	precedes	POSTPOSITION	in PP
objects	precede	VERB	in VP or S (SOV, OSV, OVS)
possessor	precedes	NOUN	in NP

Notice that it is the relative position of the objects to the verb that is important; the position of the subject is more variable.

Many languages fit very neatly into one of these two categories. Some, however, do not. For example, possessors in English precede the head noun, even though objects follow verbs and prepositions. In other words, these CONSTITUENT ORDER UNIVERSALS (as they are called) are not true for all languages but represent UNIVERSAL TENDENCIES that are true for most languages.

---

[18]These lexical entries are not complete, because they do not mention the selectional restrictions imposed on the oblique complements. For example, *put* requires its oblique complement to be a Goal, and *walk* requires its oblique complement(s) to be either Source, Goal, or Path.

[19]Thanks to Carl Harrison for inspiring this way of presenting Greenberg's generalizations graphically.

9.7. Summary of English grammar so far

We've gradually accumulated many pieces of a grammar for English. Let's bring our phrase structure rules together in one place and see how they work.

(62)   S   →   NP[Su] VP

VP   →   V (NP[DO]) (VP) (PP[IO]) $\left(\left\{ \begin{array}{c} \text{NP} \\ \text{PP} \\ \text{AdvP} \end{array} \right\} \right) *$

PP   →   P NP

NP   → $\left(\left\{ \begin{array}{c} \text{D} \\ \text{NP[Poss]} \end{array} \right\} \right)$ (QP) (AP)* N (PP)

AP   →   (DegP) A
AdvP   →   (DegP) Adv
QP   →   (DegP) Q
DegP   →   ... Deg

Given appropriate lexical entries, these rules will generate the following tree:

(63)   Gertrude cut the salami for my hungry children briskly there with a knife at the last minute.

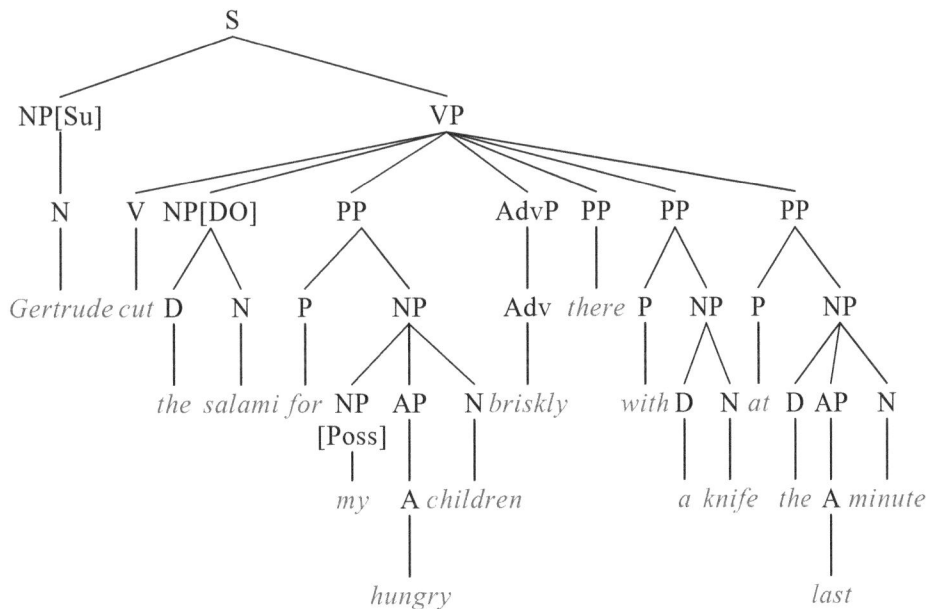

Bon appetit!

9.8. Review of key terms

OBLIQUES can represent a variety of meanings, including LOCATION, SOURCE, PATH, GOAL, TIME, MANNER, INSTRUMENT, BENEFACTIVE, and ACCOMPANIMENT. Most of these are ADJUNCTS, but a few may be COMPLEMENTS which are GOVERNED by particular verbs.

Obliques can have a variety of structures. One of the most common is a PREPOSITIONAL or POSTPOSITIONAL PHRASE (PP, consisting of a PREPOSITION or POSTPOSITION (P) as the head together with a noun phrase as its OBJECT). Noun phrases are also common, including cases where RELATIONAL NOUNS are used to express 'prepositional' meanings. Also, there may be ADVERB PHRASES (AdvP), consisting of an ADVERB (Adv) plus optional modifiers like degree words; these are analogous to adjective phrases. There may also be IDIOMATIC PHRASES (IDIOMS) and single words that cannot be modified.

There are some important CONSTITUENT ORDER UNIVERSALS, or more precisely, UNIVERSAL TENDENCIES in constituent order: the phrases within a language tend to be all HEAD-INITIAL or all HEAD-FINAL.

9.9. Questions for analysis

1. Where are obliques normally placed in the clause?
2. What structures are used for obliques?
   a. Are there PPs? Do they use prepositions or postpositions?
   b. Are noun phrases used as obliques? Are there any special morphemes (case markers) in oblique noun phrases? Are there relational nouns?
   c. Are there adverb phrases? What is their internal structure?
   d. Are there any idioms that fit only approximately into one of these three main categories?
   e. Are there unmodifiable single words?
3. For each of these structures, what meanings do they express?
4. How do the orders in different constituents (PP, NP, S, VP, etc.) correlate with each other? Are they all head-first, all head-last, or is there a mixture?

9.10. Sample description

Swahili normally places obliques at the end of the clause. Prepositional phrases are used for Instrument, Time, Source, Goal, and Manner.

(1) *Fatuma alisimama* **kwa muda mrefu**
    Fatuma she.stood   for   period long
    Fatuma stood for a long time.

(2) *kitabu kilianguka* **kutoka rafu-ni**
    book   it.fell   from   shelf-Loc
    The book fell from the shelf.

Noun phrases are used to express Benefactive, Time, Location, Path, and Goal. For the locative notions, a suffix -*ni* typically appears on the head noun.

(3) *Juma alimpikia* **Ahmed** *ugali.*
    Juma he.cooked.for.him Ahmed   porridge
    Juma cooked some porridge for Ahmed.

(4) *Fatuma huenda* **msikiti-ni** **ijumaa**
    Fatuma she.goes mosque-Loc   Friday
    Fatuma goes to the mosque on Fridays.

Adverb phrases (an adverb plus an optional degree word) are used to express Time and Manner.

(5) *Halima aliamka* **mapema**
    Halima she.awoke   early
    Halima woke up early.

(6)   *mwezi   ulianza   **vibaya   sana***
        month   it.started badly   very
        The month started very badly.

A few other words are used, without any modifiers, for Time and Goal.

(7)   *lazima   usiende   **sasa***
        must   you.not.go now
        You must not go now.

9.11. For further reading

Andrews 1985 provides an informal survey of obliques and other uses of NPs and PPs. Schachter 1985:20–23 touches on different types of adverbs and adverb phrases.

Within Transformational Grammar (one well-known type of Generative Grammar) the concepts of COMPLEMENTS and ADJUNCTS are more important than DIRECT OBJECT or OBLIQUE. Radford 1988, chapters 4 and 5, explores the internal structure of various types of phrases and the complement/adjunct distinction.

The complement/adjunct distinction and the related issue of subcategorization is also important in Head-driven Phrase Structure Grammar. Pollard and Sag (1987:134–37) point out a number of other distinctions between complements and adjuncts, which can be used as the basis of tests for analyzing this distinction in other languages.

The initial work on universal tendencies of constituent order was done by Greenberg (1966). Comrie (1989, chapter 4) provides an explanation and analysis of Greenberg's proposals, which have been extremely important in later typological and theoretical work. Dryer (1988) takes a second look at these correlations and proposes some modifications to them which are especially interesting in light of the distinction between major and minor categories. He claims that the tendencies noted above hold only for constituents which are phrasal. Thus, little can be said about adjectives and adverbs, for example, since in many languages they are not modifiable and thus do not have corresponding phrasal categories.

Morphology Group 2

10
Inflectional Morphology

10.1. Goals and prerequisites

This chapter will help you do the following:

- ◎ state at least two common differences between inflectional and derivational morphology
- ◎ make reasonable hypotheses about grammatical categories in data, organize data into paradigms, and express the grammatical categories using features
- ◎ draw a diagram showing how phrase structure rules, feature assignment rules, lexicon, and inflectional spellout rules are related to each other
- ◎ convert a position class chart into ordered sets of inflectional spellout rules and integrate them into a formal grammar which accounts for simple syntax and morphology
- ◎ account for irregular morphology in a formal grammar
- ◎ draw trees representing the different steps in generating a sentence with a formal grammar

This chapter ties syntax and morphology together, so it assumes that you are familiar with the basics of both, specifically:

- ✓ terminology for grammatical categories (chapter 2 "Standard Grammatical Terminology")
- ✓ morphological structure (chapter 4 "Introduction to Morphology")
- ✓ syntactic structure and the organization of a grammar (chapter 6 "The Base")
- ✓ possession (chapter 7 "Embedding and Noun Phrase Structure")
- ✓ case-marking (chapter 8 "Verbal Valence")

Some familiarity with phonological features is also helpful, but not essential, for learning about how features are used in morphology.

10.2. Inflection versus derivation

Recall the two basic questions in morphology introduced in chapter 4 "Introduction to Morphology," p. 30:

(1) a. What is its meaning?
     b. How is that meaning expressed?

In this chapter we look at one aspect of (1a), specifically the distinction between DERIVATIONAL and INFLECTIONAL morphology. Then we focus on how inflectional morphology can be integrated with syntax in a formal grammar, leaving the formal analysis of derivational morphology until later (chapter 11 "Derivational Morphology").

DERIVATIONAL MORPHOLOGY takes one word and changes it into another, creating new lexical entries. In the clearest cases, it creates a word of another syntactic category. For example, the suffix -ness changes adjectives into abstract nouns, as in *fat-ness, dry-ness,* and *red-ness.* The suffix -(e)r changes verbs into nouns, as in *teach-er, erase-r, farm-er,* and *tease-r.* The suffix -ify changes nouns or adjectives into verbs, as in *class-ify, pur-ify,* and *null-ify.*

INFLECTIONAL MORPHOLOGY, on the other hand, does not change one word into another and never changes syntactic category. Rather, it produces another form of the same word. For example, when the English inflectional suffix -(e)s is added to a noun, it produces the plural form of the same noun, not a new word. The same is true for other inflectional affixes:

(2)   *-(e)s*   third person singular present (on verbs)
       -(e)d   past (on verbs)

As it turns out, this is essentially all the inflectional morphology there is in English; most other affixes (dozens of them) are derivational.[1] Other languages have much more inflectional morphology than English does.

The essential difference between inflection and derivation is whether the addition of an affix creates a new word or just another form of the same word. There are three other important differences between inflection and derivation. One concerns PRODUCTIVITY: inflectional morphology is very productive, while derivational morphology usually is not. What this means is that if you take an inflectional affix that normally goes on verbs, you should be able to attach it easily to newly invented or borrowed words. English past tense marking is inflectional and so it is very productive—when new verbs are coined, their past tense is automatically available in the grammar. For example, English speakers added -(e)d to the new verb *digitize* to form *digitized* without blinking an eye.

Derivational affixes, on the other hand, often cannot be used with such generality. Indeed, they often cannot be used even on words that have been in the language for centuries. Consider the following examples of derivational affixes; some work and others fail. The ones that fail do so not because of any general rule, but simply because the resulting words don't happen to exist.[2]

(3)   Good   Bad
       same-ness   *different-ness*
       weak-ness   *strong-ness*
       mad-ness   *sane-ness*

One simply has to memorize which derived words contain -ness and which do not. This memory load is hardly ever necessary with inflection.

Of course, some derivational affixes are more productive than others. The suffix -er is relatively productive; word game players know that practically any verb can be turned into a noun by adding -(e)r. So, we aren't dealing with a hard and fast distinction, but in general inflection is more productive than derivation.

Another difference is that derivational affixes often have lexical meaning, while inflectional affixes usually have grammatical meaning. (The lexical/grammatical distinction is introduced in chapter 4 "Introduction to Morphology," p. 26.) For example, one meaning of the derivational suffix -er can be expressed as 'a person who...', but the meaning of the inflectional -(e)d is best expressed with the technical term 'past tense'.

---

[1]There are a few others that could be analyzed as inflectional. In chapter 20 "Word Division and Clitics" (p. 282), the possessive -'s is analyzed as a special type of inflectional affix. The participial suffixes (such as -(e)n and -ing) might, conceivably, also be treated as inflectional in some analyses. Some people regard the comparative *(-er)* and superlative *(-est)* forms of adjectives to be inflectional.

[2]Instead, there are other words with the expected meanings, such as *difference, strength,* and *sanity.* This phenomenon, called 'blocking', is similar to irregular inflection.

The third difference between inflection and derivation is that different inflected forms of a word can usually be usefully organized into a type of chart called a PARADIGM. For an example of this, we need to go to Spanish, a language that has more inflectional morphology than English. Most books about Spanish present the different forms of verbs in paradigms, like the following chart of the present tense of *andar* 'to walk'.

(4)   Singular   Plural
    first person   *ando*   *andamos*
    second person   *andas*   *andáis*
    third person   *anda*   *andan*

There are two GRAMMATICAL CATEGORIES shown in this paradigm: person and number. Each form is specified by some unique combination of some person and some number. For example, we identify *andas* as the second person singular present form of *andar* and *andan* as its third person plural present form. The two grammatical categories allow us to classify the six forms in a systematic way. This is the nature of paradigms: they consist of a set of forms which are cross-classified by means of a set of grammatical categories.

This cross-classifying of forms in paradigms is characteristic of inflectional morphology, but not of derivational morphology. Derivational morphology groups words together into pairs, like *march* and *marcher, farm* and *farmer,* but never into larger sets like the one in (4).[3]

Usually, the paradigms of different verbs in a language are similar or identical.[4] For example, person and number are relevant to all verbs in Spanish, not just *andar.* This means we can uniquely identify every form of every verb by specifying the verb involved and some combination of these grammatical categories.

Often the affixes used on different verbs are very similar to each other. Thus, we can generalize (4) to represent the inflection of all verbs like *andar* by only showing the affixes involved.[5]

(5)   Singular   Plural
    first person   *-o*   *-mos*
    second person   *-s*   *-´is*
    third person   *-Ø*   *-n*

A chart like this is an important step toward writing rules that account for the inflection of this class of verbs.

Actually, we need to distinguish two senses of the word PARADIGM. In one sense, a paradigm is a chart like (4) or (5), an informal means of presenting data, a way of using ink on paper. In the other sense, a paradigm is the set of inflected forms of some word, a set which is cross-classified by means of grammatical categories. A paradigm in this sense is part of the structure of the language itself. The two senses are related; a paradigm in the first sense is a way of representing a paradigm in the second sense.

The differences between inflection and derivation that we have discussed are summarized in the following chart:

---

[3]Of course, some inflectional paradigms may have only two forms, such as the singular and plural forms of nouns in English. So, just because forms come only in pairs does not mean that they are derivational. However, when you find any larger set of related forms, especially if more than one dimension (grammatical category) is involved, the type of morphology is almost certainly inflectional.

[4]The phonological material used to express the grammatical categories may differ for different verbs (see chapter 12 "Suppletion and Morphophonemics"), but generally the same grammatical categories will be relevant to all words in a class.

[5]I am assuming that the final /a/ of the stem deletes before the /o/ in the first singular and have adopted an informal notation for the stress shift to the final syllable of the stem in the second plural forms.

(6)   Inflection   Derivation

	Inflection	Derivation
Changes one lexical entry into another	no	yes
Changes syntactic category	no	often
Productivity	virtually total	partial at best
Organized in paradigms	yes	no
Type of meaning	grammatical	usually lexical

In broad terms, inflectional morphology tends to be systematic and regular; you can see this both in its productivity and its use of paradigms. Derivational morphology, on the other hand, is often irregular and full of exceptions. We return to this distinction in more detail in chapter 11 "Derivational Morphology." In the meantime, to help you distinguish inflectional morphology from derivational, you may find it helpful to refer to the list of grammatical categories in the appendix to this chapter (p. 133).

10.3. The importance of paradigms for inflectional morphology

Now that we know about paradigms, we can look at morphology from a new perspective. Agglutinative languages have morphemes arranged in a sequence like beads on a string, with clear morpheme cuts between them. Position class charts often provide a convenient way of summarizing their morphology, focusing on the relative ordering of the pieces of a word.

However, this analogy to beads on a string often breaks down. IRREGULAR (or SUPPLETIVE) verbs, which are found in most languages, cause it problems. In English, there is a large class of verbs which do not form their past tense using -(e)d.

(7)   Present   Past

        sing   *sang*
        think   *thought*
        have   *had*
        see   *saw*
        go   *went*
        is   *was*

Good consistent morpheme cuts are difficult at best, and there is little consistency from one verb to the next. Position class charts are useless for describing these verb forms. But, if we think in terms of paradigms and grammatical categories we can at least make some sense of the situation; all verbs have a paradigm which includes both present and past tense forms.

In a fusional language like Spanish, position class charts run into more problems. The endings (combinations of suffixes) on verbs in Spanish indicate not only person and number, but also tense, aspect (perfective versus imperfective), mood (indicative, subjunctive, and conditional), and the class the verb belongs to. Just giving a long list of the endings is not very instructive.

(8)   *-o*   first person singular present indicative
      -ieron   third person plural past perfective indicative, used with -*er* and -*ir* verbs
      -íamos   first person plural past imperfective indicative, used with -*er* and -*ir* verbs
      -rás   second person singular future indicative
      -e   third person singular present: indicative (with -*er* and -*ir* verbs) or subjunctive
                  (with -*ar* verbs)
      -ríamos   third person plural conditional

There are at least 50 more, one ending for practically every logical combination of grammatical categories. Some morpheme cuts are easy, but many are not, and if you know Spanish you know it would be difficult to organize the system into a neat position class chart. To make sense of such a system, we need an organized representation of the grammatical categories involved and their relationships. That is, the different endings should be arranged into paradigms, like the one in (5).

So, one advantage of using paradigms is that they help make sense of complex morphological systems with irregular verbs or in fusional languages, when position class charts aren't very helpful. But even in agglutinative languages, paradigms can be helpful; you have probably already discovered that it is easier to identify inflectional affixes and set up position class charts if the different forms of each word have first been arranged in some systematic way, in other words, organized in paradigms.

Thus, the first thing you should do when studying inflectional morphology is to arrange the data in paradigms and determine the grammatical categories involved. Only then make morpheme cuts. In some cases, you can carry the analysis further and construct position class charts; in other cases, this is impossible or unrevealing.

We have been contrasting two different perspectives on morphology.[6] One, called ITEM AND ARRANGEMENT, looks at morphology by focusing on individual morphemes, like beads on a string. Position class charts are examples of this perspective. The other perspective, called WORD AND PARADIGM, looks at morphology by focusing on grammatical categories and paradigms. It is useful for inflectional morphology in all types of languages and especially in fusional languages or where there is a lot of irregularity.

This book uses both perspectives. Item and arrangement can be very useful for presenting data informally, in position class charts, in some types of languages. But, since word and paradigm is useful for all languages, it is the basis for our formal grammars. Specifically, our grammars describe morphology using a theoretical framework that has been variously called Extended Word and Paradigm or A-morphous Morphology (Anderson 1982, 1992). The rest of this chapter explains how to handle inflectional morphology within such a system.[7]

10.4. Grammatical categories and inflectional features

The essence of the word and paradigm perspective is its focus on GRAMMATICAL CATEGORIES, like person, number, and tense. What exactly is a grammatical category? Grammatical categories are sets of abstract elements (like singular and plural) which are MUTUALLY EXCLUSIVE. Each grammatical category has only a small and fixed number of elements, that is, grammatical categories are closed classes. Thus, a grammatical category is a small, closed class of mutually exclusive grammatical properties.

How do we add this concept to our formal grammars? We do so with FEATURES. For example, to represent that a word is singular, we might assign it the feature [–plural]. To represent that a word is third person, we might assign it the feature [3 person].[8] In these examples, 'plural' and 'person' are the names of the features; '–' and '3' are their VALUES.

We've encountered features occasionally so far in this book. For example, in chapter 6 "The Basc" (p. 54), we used a feature [±common] to distinguish proper and common nouns. We have also used a feature [GR] to represent grammatical relations, with values [Su], [DO], etc. You may also have encountered features in phonology to represent the similarities and differences of sounds; for example, all sounds made with rounded lips have the feature [+round]. In the same way, features are used in morphology to represent the similarities and differences of words within a paradigm. Just

---

[6]The terminology comes from Hockett 1954, which is primarily concerned with contrasting item and arrangement with item and process (which in the discussion in this book has been subsumed under the heading item and arrangement), and which mentions word and paradigm only in passing.

[7]I have found that Anderson's approach to morphology is useful pedagogically because it provides formal expression for several important traditional concepts, such as paradigms, grammatical categories, inflection versus derivation, etc., and so reinforces them. As a bonus, it prepares people to understand transformational rules by showing how a sentence is built in several steps, even while students are still absorbing the basics of phrase structure. Although not without its critics (see for example Scalise 1984:191–97), it does reasonably well on descriptive adequacy, since it handles irregular verbs, morphology in fusional languages, and complex types of affixation more easily than item-and-arrangement approaches.

[8]I use the term 'feature' variously to refer either to the name of a feature ([plural]), to a specific feature value specification ([+plural]), or to the set of possible values for a feature ([±plural]). Context should always clarify which is meant.

as different combinations of phonological features represent different sounds, different combinations of morphological features represent different forms in a paradigm.

Many features are BINARY; they have only two values, usually '+' and '–'. Often this is because they represent grammatical categories that contain only two elements. For example, number (singular versus plural) is often represented with the binary feature [±plural]. At other times we deal with grammatical categories that have more than two elements, so a single binary feature will not do. The inflectional category of person is like this; it normally has three choices: first, second, and third person. One way to represent this formally is with a single feature that has three values: [1 person], [2 person], and [3 person].[9] Another is to use two binary features, such as [±me] and [±you].[10] These work as follows:

(9)   first person: [+me, –you]
        second person: [–me, +you]
        third person: [–me, –you]

One of the tasks in the morphological analysis of a language is making a precise hypothesis about the grammatical categories involved by choosing an appropriate set of features. For suggested features to use to represent different grammatical categories, see the appendix to this chapter (p. 133).

10.5. Inflectional morphology in a formal grammar

Now let's see how inflectional morphology can be fit together with syntax in a formal grammar. Recall (from chapter 6 "The Base," p. 48) that the base component builds trees with phrase structure rules, then fills in the terminal nodes from the lexicon.

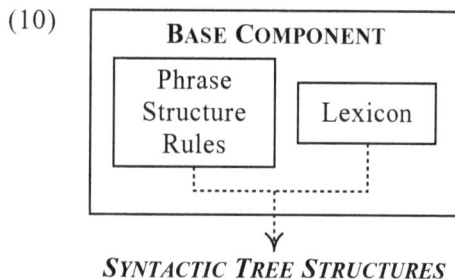

(10)
```
        ┌──────────────────────────────┐
        │  BASE COMPONENT              │
        │  ┌──────────┐                │
        │  │ Phrase   │  ┌───────────┐ │
        │  │ Structure│  │  Lexicon  │ │
        │  │ Rules    │  └───────────┘ │
        │  └──────────┘                │
        │         ┊        ┊           │
        │         └┄┄┄┄┄┄┄┄┘           │
        └─────────────┊────────────────┘
                      ▼
        SYNTACTIC TREE STRUCTURES
```

Morphology fits into this model by providing details about the terminal nodes.

We assume that the grammar builds a sentence in two phases: first syntax, then inflectional morphology. In the syntactic phase, the phonological material of inflectional affixes is not inserted from the lexicon. Instead, inflectional morphology is represented in trees produced by the base solely by inflectional features on preterminal nodes. For a sentence like *The boys cried,* the base would produce a tree that looks like this (using phonetic transcription to represent actual pronunciation more accurately):[11]

---

[9]I follow Generalized Phrase Structure Grammar (Gazdar, Klein, Pullum, and Sag 1985:22ff) in allowing non-binary features, although my notation for them is slightly different.

[10]For an example of the usefulness of binary features representing person, see Matthews 1972a:105–10, where these two features, with the addition of [±plural], are used to distinguish eight person/number combinations in Huave (Mexico), including such things as first plural inclusive/exclusive, and first dual inclusive.

[11]The broad phonetic (IPA) transcription of English in this book is based on upper Midwestern dialects in the United States, in a way that hopefully provides minimum distraction from the main point of the passage. Nothing depends on the exact choice of symbols used or the level of analysis represented.

(11)   Output of the base component for *The boys cried.*

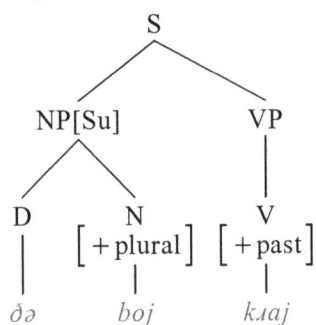

```
                    S
              /          \
          NP[Su]          VP
          /    \           |
         D      N          V
         |   [+plural]  [+past]
         |      |          |
         ðə    bɔj        kɹaj
```

The [+plural] on the N represents the plurality of *boys* and the [+past] on the verb represents the past tense of *cried*.[12] The only phonological material at the terminal nodes belongs to the stems, exactly as they are listed in the lexicon. A tree structure like (11), which is produced entirely by the base component, is called its DEEP STRUCTURE.

This, of course, is incomplete. Somehow, the inflectional features need to be 'spelled out' by adding phonological material to the stems, such as /z/ and /d/.

(12)   Structure of *The boys cried* after spelling out inflectional affixes

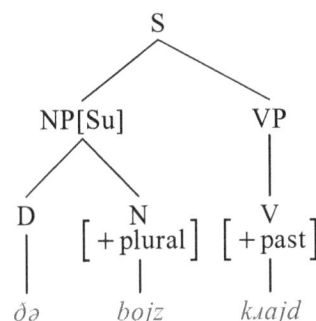

```
                    S
              /          \
          NP[Su]          VP
          /    \           |
         D      N          V
         |   [+plural]  [+past]
         |      |          |
         ðə    bɔjz       kɹajd
```

This completes the process of generating the sentence. A tree structure like (12), which matches the actual sentence we are trying to produce, is called its SURFACE STRUCTURE.[13]

The rules which convert the terminal nodes from one form to the other are described in the next section.

Inflectional spellout rules

To get from (11) to (12), we need one rule that adds *-z* to the end of any noun that is [+plural] and another that adds *-d* to the end of any verb that is [+past]. We call these rules INFLECTIONAL SPELLOUT RULES[14] and write them as follows:

---

[12]A binary feature for tense is adequate in English, because the morphology only distinguishes two forms: past and nonpast. Other so-called 'tenses' are handled by auxiliary verbs like *have* and *will,* so morphological features do not need to reflect them.

[13]Though the term SURFACE STRUCTURE is borrowed from Transformational Grammar and Anderson's (1982, 1992) work is couched in transformational terms, this approach to morphology could just as easily be combined with a nontransformational syntax.

[14]Inflectional spellout rules are half syntactic and half phonological. Like syntactic rules, they refer to syntactic information (like 'N' and '[+plural]' in (13). Phonological rules generally do not refer to syntactic information, only phonological information. However, inflectional spellout rules do not *change* syntactic information, only phonological information (like adding *-z*), and normally they act on only one word at a time. In this, they are like phonological rules and unlike syntactic rules. Inflectional spellout rules serve as a link between syntax and phonology, since they apply to the output of syntactic rules and their output becomes the input for phonological rules.

(13) Inflectional spellout rule for noun plurals

$$
\begin{array}{c}
\text{N} \\
[+\text{plural}] \\
[\text{X}]
\end{array} \quad \rightarrow \quad [\text{X}z]
$$

(14) Inflectional spellout rule for past tense on verbs

$$
\begin{array}{c}
\text{V} \\
[+\text{past}] \\
[\text{X}]
\end{array} \quad \rightarrow \quad [\text{X}d]
$$

In this notation,[15] the arrow represents the change made by the rule: the difference between its input (the left side) and its output (the right side). In (13), the rule takes as its input any N node in any tree which is [+plural]. The X in brackets on the bottom line stands for whatever phonological material happens to be under that node. In the surface structure tree, this is changed slightly by adding the suffix -z.[16] Look at the partial trees below.

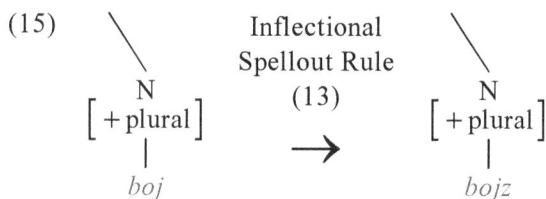

(15)   Inflectional
                       Spellout Rule
$$
\begin{array}{c}
\diagdown \\
\text{N} \\
\left[+\text{plural}\right] \\
| \\
\textit{boj}
\end{array}
\qquad
\begin{array}{c}
(13) \\
\longrightarrow
\end{array}
\qquad
\begin{array}{c}
\diagdown \\
\text{N} \\
\left[+\text{plural}\right] \\
| \\
\textit{bojz}
\end{array}
$$

Given this way of handling inflectional morphology, we can now refine our understanding of the lexicon. The lexicon does not need to contain the whole paradigm of a word (all its inflected forms), but only its stem, since this is what must be inserted in trees produced by the base.[17] Nor does it need to list any of the inflectional affixes, since these are spelled out later. The lexicon, then, is primarily a list of just *stems*, not of all morphemes in a language.

Feature assignment rules

We've seen how inflectional morphology is represented by inflectional features in trees, how those features are 'spelled out' with phonological material, and have noted what this means for the lexicon. But, we've skipped a step; we first need to make sure the right features get in the right places in the trees produced by the base. What puts them there?

There are some features, like [±past], which apply to all members of a particular word class. All English verbs have both Present and Past forms and every verb in every tree must be labeled either [+past] or [−past].[18] So we need a special type of phrase structure rule, a FEATURE ASSIGNMENT RULE, which puts the feature [past] on every verb.[19]

(16) V → [±past]

---

[15]This notation differs in a few details from that used by Anderson (1982), mostly in the use of brackets around feature bundles and for showing the constituent structure of phonological representations. Also, Anderson calls these rules 'Word Formation Rules', but I reserve this term for the derivational rules introduced in chapter 11 "Derivational Morphology."

[16]This suffix is variously pronounced [z], [s], and [iz], depending on the stem. See chapter 12 "Suppletion and Morphophonemics" (p. 153) for how to handle this variation and why only [z] is included in the inflectional spellout rule.

[17]This comment refers to regular inflection. For irregular inflection, see below.

[18]This is an oversimplification, since in some contexts, English verbs are not inflected for tense.

[19]The term 'feature assignment rule' is my own invention. Anderson attributes the idea for this type of rule to Chomsky's (1965:82–83) analysis of noun subcategorization. I depart from Anderson and Chomsky, though, in not positing feature assignment rules for features that are fully specified in the lexicon, as in (17). Feature assignment rules are similar to the feature co-occurrence restrictions of Generalized Phrase Structure Grammar (Gazdar, Klein, Pullum, and Sag 1985), with one difference: they build structure by adding features to trees, rather than just stating what combinations of features are possible.

Feature assignment rules are part of the base component and work together with the other phrase structure rules and the lexicon to build the trees. This rule says to add either [+past] or [–past] to a V node when building a tree.[20]

Other features are more limited in their distribution. For example, [+plural] can only be allowed to appear on certain nouns, called count nouns. Other nouns, like *software* do not have plural forms (i.e., *softwares* is not a grammatical English word).[21] This latter group is called mass nouns. This means, before we can talk about plural forms of nouns, we must first divide the class of nouns into two subcategories in the lexicon, using the features [+count] and [–count].

(17)   **N [+count]**   **N [–count]**
       sændwɪtʃ   sandwich   *sænd*   sand
       kəmpjutɹ   computer   *sɔftweɹ*   software

When a noun is inserted in a tree, we assume it carries with it all the features that it has associated with it in the lexicon (although we don't usually write all of them).[22] So, every N node in every tree ends up with a feature for [count].

(18)   Partial trees, just after lexical insertion

a.   b.

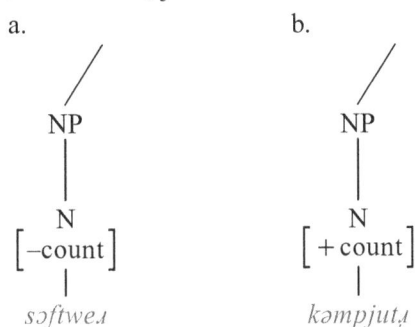

Then, we need feature assignment rules to add the feature [±plural]. But, this must be done selectively; mass ([–count]) nouns must always be [–plural], while count ([+count]) nouns can be either [+plural] or [–plural].[23]

(19)   **Feature assignment rules for English nouns**
       N[–count] → [–plural]
       N[+count] → [±plural]

---

[20]There is a possible ambiguity in the notation here; in this formulation, feature assignment rules, unlike other phrase structure rules, do not add new nodes underneath old ones, but only add new features to existing nodes. In practice, this is not a problem, since any time the right-hand side of the arrow consists of a single set of brackets (and what they enclose), the interpretation is to add features to an existing node; in all other cases the interpretation is to add new nodes to the tree. In Chomsky's (1965:82–83) original formulation, feature assignment rules actually added new nodes, but this resulted in a 'complex symbol' which in later generative work has been replaced by the notion of a bundle of features at a single node. The original notation is retained, rather than some novel notation, since in practice this is only a minor problem.

[21]Actually, this is oversimplified, since some mass nouns like *sand* do have corresponding count nouns with specialized senses. ('The soldiers trudged over the shifting *sands*.') The facts of the English count/mass distinction are complex, and I will not attempt to account for all of them.

[22]Anderson, in his presentation of A-morphous Morphology (1982:594, 1992:90–91), assumes that lexical insertion takes place at S-structure, not deep structure. However, the discussion here is not yet assuming a transformational framework, so the approach in the text is more typical of Chomsky (1977:10) in assuming that structures produced by the base contain phonological information.

[23]An alternate analysis would be not to assign any value for [plural] to nouns that are [–count]. This would correctly prevent inflectional spellout rules like (13) from applying to mass nouns. However, this would cause problems for the analysis of verb agreement, since mass nouns as subjects always require singular present tense forms of the verb. To leave mass nouns unspecified for number would allow them to co-occur with either singular or plural agreement, at least, given the approach to agreement adopted in chapter 19 "Case and Agreement." A third alternative would be to make [–plural] be the default value for [plural], but this may simply be a notational variant of the analysis given in the text.

When these rules are applied to the partial trees in (18), the choices in them allow any of the following results:

(20)   Completed deep structure trees, after all feature assignment rules have applied

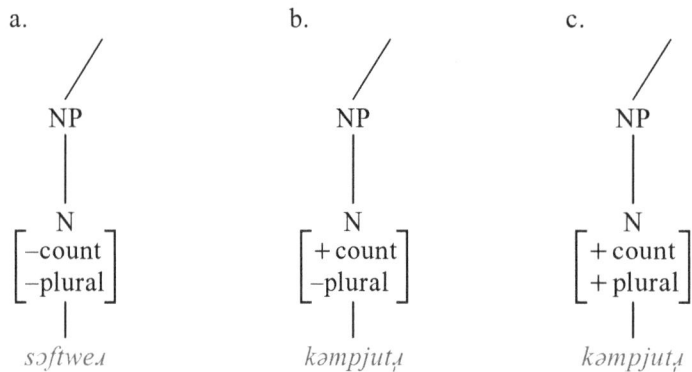

    a.   b.   c.

       NP   NP   NP

       N   N   N

$\begin{bmatrix} -\text{count} \\ -\text{plural} \end{bmatrix}$ $\begin{bmatrix} +\text{count} \\ -\text{plural} \end{bmatrix}$ $\begin{bmatrix} +\text{count} \\ +\text{plural} \end{bmatrix}$

     sɔftweɹ   *kəmpjutɹ*   *kəmpjutɹ*

Note that (18a) could never have been assigned the feature [+ plural]; it had to become (20a).

    After the inflectional spellout rule (13) applies, (20c) becomes (21); the other two, since they are marked [– plural], are left unchanged.

(21)   Surface structure for (20c)

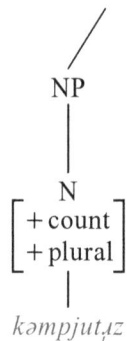

       NP

       N

$\begin{bmatrix} +\text{count} \\ +\text{plural} \end{bmatrix}$

    kəmpjutɹz

To summarize, we can add some detail to our diagram of a formal grammar.

(22)

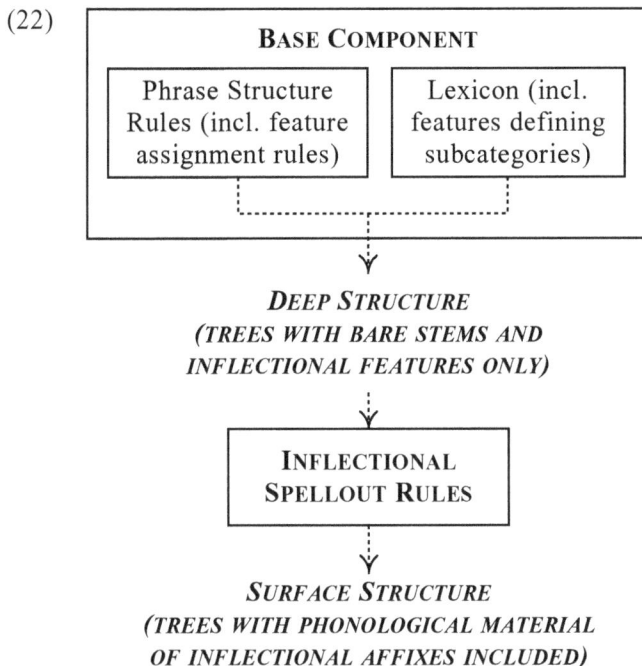

Some features relevant to inflectional morphology come from the lexicon along with the stems, while others are assigned by feature assignment rules. Wherever they come from, they end up as part of the initial trees built by the base. Thus, these trees contain all the information needed to specify the inflectional morphology, expressed as inflectional features. The actual phonological material of the affixes is not added until later by the inflectional spellout rules, which modify the terminal nodes produced by the base into surface structure based on the features that they find in the tree.

10.6. Building a formal analysis from a position class chart

Although position class charts are very useful in agglutinative languages, they do not tell us everything we need to know. For example, a language may have tense suffixes that are omitted in some contexts. Position class charts do not tell when to omit them, only where they occur when they are used. Position class charts also do not say anything about which affixes can co-occur with which others, only their relative order when they do co-occur. But, this type of information *should be* part of a formal grammar. So, to do a complete analysis, we should know how to take the information in a position class chart and construct a formal grammar, incorporating the extra information as we go.

Consider the following data from Fore (Trans-New Guinean, Papua New Guinea):[24]

1.	*natuwi*	I ate yesterday.	8.	*natuni*	We ate yesterday.
2.	*nagasuwi*	I ate today.	9.	*nagasuni*	We ate today.
3.	*nakuwi*	I will eat.	10.	*nakuni*	We will eat.
4.	*nata·ni*	You ate yesterday.	11.	*nagasusi*	We two ate today.
5.	*nata·naw*	You ate yesterday?	12.	*nakusi*	We two will eat.
6.	*nakiyi*	He will eat.	13.	*nata·wi*	They ate yesterday.
7.	*nakiyaw*	He will eat?	14.	*nata·si*	They two ate yesterday.

Notice some new variations on familiar grammatical categories. There appear to be two different past tenses, one used for events earlier today, the other for events yesterday (and possibly earlier).

---

[24]Data from Merrifield, et al., 1987, #26.

This is not uncommon: to divide past time into two tenses, often called recent and remote past. Also, the category of number has three values: singular, dual (two), and plural (three or more).

After making morpheme cuts, we can summarize the morphology in the following position class chart:[25]

(23) Stem	+1: Tense		+2: Subject Agreement		+3: Mood	
	-gas	recent past	*-uw*	first singular	*-i*	indicative
	-t	remote past	*-us*	first dual	*-aw*	interrogative
	-k	future	*-un*	first plural		
			-a'n	second singular		
			-iy	third singular		
			-a's	third dual		
			-a'w	third plural		

How do we construct a formal analysis of this data, building on what we know from the position class chart?

First, we decide on a set of features: both what features to use and how many values there are for each. For tense, we posit two features. One is [tense], with the three values [past tense], [pres tense], and [fut tense]. We assume that near and far past are distinguished by a feature of [±recent] and that this feature is used only on verbs that are [+past]. (Note that already we are clarifying something that is left unclear in (23), we are assuming that there is a present tense in Fore, even if we don't know how it is indicated.)[26] Similarly, for subject agreement we assume a feature of person, with three values: [1 person], [2 person], and [3 person]; and a feature of number, with three values: [sg number], [dl number], and [pl number].[27] Finally, for mood, we assume one feature with two values: [±interrogative].

Second, we incorporate these assumptions into feature assignment rules, as a formal hypothesis about Fore grammatical categories. To do so, we must consider which features can occur with which other features. Since the position class chart does not provide this information, we look back at the data. It appears that person, number, tense, and mood can freely occur with each other in any combination, except that [recent] is relevant only for [past tense]. (We don't have examples of all the combinations, but it is reasonable to assume that they can all occur, so we make that prediction in our analysis.)

(24)   **Feature assignment rules for Fore**

$$V \rightarrow \begin{bmatrix} \{1, 2, 3\} \text{ person} \\ \{\text{past, pres, fut}\} \text{ tense} \\ \{\text{sg, dl, pl}\} \text{ number} \\ \pm \text{ interrogative} \end{bmatrix}$$

$$V[\text{past tense}] \rightarrow [\pm \text{ recent}]$$

Notice the use of braces to list the possible values of features like person which have more than two values. The braces mean the same thing here as they do in regular phrase structure rules; they enclose a set of choices. The choices can either be arranged horizontally (as above, with commas separating them) or vertically.

---

[25]Although the agreement markers might conceivably split into separate morphemes for person and number, further division does not yield a simpler or more general analysis. The partial regularities are probably due to the history of the system, not to its current structure.

[26]Although we may have made the assumption that there is a present tense in Fore when we constructed (23), the chart itself does not make it explicit.

[27]This approach to features for agreement is adequate for the moment, but requires refinement if a verb agrees with two distinct nominals or if a noun shows agreement with a possessor. For now, if data like this must be analyzed in class, I suggest that you use makeshift features like [{1, 2, 3} personSu], [±pluralDO], or [{1, 2, 3} personPoss]. However, this is only slightly better; the best solution is in chapter 19 "Case and Agreement" (p. 259ff.).

(25)

$$V \rightarrow \begin{bmatrix} \begin{Bmatrix} 1 \\ 2 \\ 3 \end{Bmatrix} \text{person} \\ \begin{Bmatrix} \text{sg} \\ \text{dl} \\ \text{pl} \end{Bmatrix} \text{number} \\ \begin{Bmatrix} \text{past} \\ \text{pres} \\ \text{fut} \end{Bmatrix} \text{tense} \\ \pm \text{interrogative} \end{bmatrix}$$

The first notation is more compact; that's the only difference.

Third, we write inflectional spellout rules to add the phonological material for each affix. In simple cases like this, there is one rule for each affix. The rules for the first position class are as follows:

(26) a.   V
               [+ recent]   (for recent past tense)
                 [X]   →   [X*gas*]

      b.   V
               [− recent]   (for remote past tense)
                 [X]   →   [X*t*]

      c.   V
               [fut tense]   (for future tense)
                 [X]   →   [X*k*]

Notice that we did not need to refer to the feature [past tense] in (26a, b), because the feature [recent] only appears on verbs that are [past tense]. Thus (26a, b) can apply only to past tense forms.

The rules for the second suffix class are similar. Following is a partial list.

(27) a.   V
               $\begin{bmatrix} 1 \text{ person} \\ \text{sg number} \end{bmatrix}$ (for first person singular subject agreement)
                 [X]   →   [X*uw*]

      b.   V
               $\begin{bmatrix} 1 \text{ person} \\ \text{dl number} \end{bmatrix}$ (for first person dual subject agreement)
                 [X]   →   [X*us*]

      c.   V
               $\begin{bmatrix} 2 \text{ person} \\ \text{sg number} \end{bmatrix}$ (for second person singular subject agreement)
                 [X]   →   [X*a · n*]

      d.   ...   (similarly for other agreement markers)

And now, the rules for the third class of suffixes.

(28) a.   V
           $\begin{bmatrix} + \text{ interrogative} \end{bmatrix}$ (for interrogative mood)
                [X]   → [Xaw]

      b.   V
           $\begin{bmatrix} - \text{ interrogative} \end{bmatrix}$ (for indicative mood)
                [X]   → [Xi]

Fourth and finally, we state the order in which these rules apply, so we get the suffixes in the proper order.

(29) The rules in (26) apply first, then those in (27), and finally those in (28).

In other words, the ordering of the rules mirrors the ordering of the position classes.
    Let's see how this analysis works in a particular case, by generating the word *natuwi* 'I ate (yesterday)'. The initial tree produced by the base contains only the stem, *na*, plus a bundle of features provided by the feature assignment rules (24). These features indicate the specific form in the paradigm of *na* that will eventually be generated.

(30) Structure for *natuwi* produced by the base

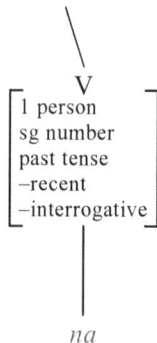

The three sets of inflectional spellout rules apply in order and add one affix at a time. The phonological form at the terminal node changes like this:

(31) a. Output of the base: *na*
      b. Output of rule (26b):   *nat*
      c. Output of rule (27a):   *natuw*
      d. Output of rule (28b):   *natuwi*

The resulting surface structure is thus:

(32)   Surface structure of *natuwi*

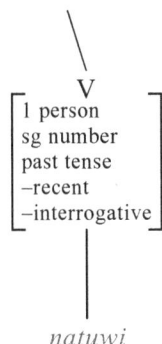

V
$$\begin{bmatrix} \text{1 person} \\ \text{sg number} \\ \text{past tense} \\ -\text{recent} \\ -\text{interrogative} \end{bmatrix}$$

natuwi

To recap, we need to do four things to build a formal analysis from a position class chart:

(33)   a. characterize the grammatical categories with a set of inflectional features
       b. write feature assignment rules to insert those features into trees
       c. write inflectional spellout rules to add the phonological material for each affix
       d. state the order in which the inflectional spellout rules apply

10.7. Irregular inflection in formal grammars

In every language, there are words that are INFLECTED IRREGULARLY, that is, which have some forms that do not follow the regular inflectional rules. These irregular, or SUPPLETIVE, forms must be listed in the lexicon, since they are not predictable by rule and must be learned individually. For example, the lexical entry of *go* might look like this:

(34)   **V**

go
went $\begin{bmatrix} + & \text{past} \end{bmatrix}$ go

The part of the lexical entry that provides phonological information is more complex than we have seen previously, since it includes both the stem *go*, which is the base for the regular forms *goes* and *going*, and also the irregular past tense form *went*. How do we make sure the right form gets in the tree? There are two parts to the answer.

First, if a tree contains a V[+past] node, the phonological form *went* must be inserted, since it is the one which carries the feature [+past]. If, on the other hand, the tree contains a V[−past] node, the form *go* must be inserted, since the [+past] feature of *went* is incompatible with the [−past] feature already in the tree. In other words, if there is more than one phonological form listed in a lexical entry, you insert the one that is most specific while still being compatible with the features already in the tree. This gets the right form of the verb into the tree in the first place.

Second, we also have to prevent the inflectional spellout rules from tacking on the regular past suffix to *went*, wrongly producing **wented*. To do so, we can rely on a general convention in Generative Grammar: whenever one rule is more specific than another and both could logically be applied in a given situation, the more specific one is applied and the less specific one is skipped. A lexical entry that specifies *went* as the past tense form of *go* is more specific than the inflectional spellout rule that adds *-(e)d* to any verb. Thus, inserting an irregular form in a tree automatically forces the regular inflectional spellout rule to be skipped. The more specific lexical entry wins and the inflectional spellout rule is prevented from interfering. On the other hand, if a tree has a V[−past] node, so that the form *go* is inserted, the inflectional spellout rule that adds *-(e)s* to form the third singular present is still allowed to apply, because the lexical entry for *go* says nothing about these other categories.

Nothing needs to be said in an individual grammar about the way suppletive stems are handled; the above 'rules' are assumptions about how all grammars work and thus only need to be stated once, in the general linguistic theory.[28]

10.8. Case marking on pronouns

In many languages, nouns and pronouns are marked for CASE, which means they have a different morphological form depending on where they occur in the clause. Case occurs minimally in English. It is most clearly seen in pronouns, each of which has three different forms.[29] Which form you use in a particular context depends on whether it is a subject (nominative case), an object (objective case), or a possessor (genitive case).

(35)   a. *I see a tiger.*
        b. *The tiger sees **me.***
        c. *It's time for **my** exit.*

In most languages whose pronouns are marked for case, it is impossible to identify distinct morphemes. Instead, there is one fused form that represents both the pronoun and its case, just as in irregular verbs. This is certainly true of English.

(36)

	Nominative	Objective	Genitive
first person singular	*I*	*me*	*my*
first person plural	*we*	*us*	*our*
second person	*you*	*you*	*your*
third person singular masculine	*he*	*him*	*his*
third person singular feminine	*she*	*her*	*her*
third person singular neuter	*it*	*it*	*its*
third person plural	*they*	*them*	*their*

No reasonable morpheme cutting is possible.

To account for case marking on pronouns, we can use the same mechanism as for irregularly inflected verbs. We list each form of a pronoun in the lexical entry and label it with a feature of [case].

---

[28]Anderson (1986) presents the two principles relied on here: the precedence of irregular lexical entries over regular inflectional spellout rules and the precedence of the more specific stem in lexical insertion over a less specific one. Both are instances of the disjunctive ordering principle first described by the ancient Sanskrit grammarian Pāṇini (Anderson 1982:593) and commonly referred to today as the 'Elsewhere Condition'.

[29]The possessive case suffix -'s used on nouns is discussed in chapter 20 "Word Division and Clitics."

(37) **NP**

$$
\left.\begin{array}{ll}
aj & [\text{Nom case}] \\
mi & [\text{Obj case}] \\
maj & [\text{Gen case}]
\end{array}\right\}
\begin{bmatrix}
1 \text{ person} \\
- \text{ plural}
\end{bmatrix}
$$

$$
\left.\begin{array}{ll}
ju & \\
juɹ & [\text{Gen case}]
\end{array}\right\}
\begin{bmatrix}
2 \text{ person}
\end{bmatrix}
$$

$$
\left.\begin{array}{ll}
hi & [\text{Nom case}] \\
hɪm & [\text{Obj case}] \\
hɪz & [\text{Gen case}]
\end{array}\right\}
\begin{bmatrix}
3 \text{ person} \\
- \text{ plural} \\
\text{m gender}
\end{bmatrix}
$$

$$
\left.\begin{array}{ll}
ʃi & [\text{Nom case}] \\
hɹ & [\text{Obj case}] \\
hɹ & [\text{Gen case}]
\end{array}\right\}
\begin{bmatrix}
3 \text{ person} \\
- \text{ plural} \\
\text{f gender}
\end{bmatrix}
$$

Notice that *ju* 'you' has been left unlabeled; this is because it is a regular form; just like nouns, it is unmarked for nominative and objective case.[30]

To complete the analysis, it is necessary to have some way of introducing the features for case on the proper nodes in trees. This matter is covered in chapter 19 "Case and Agreement" (p. 254), where there are rules that introduce [Nom case] on a subject NP, [Gen case] on a possessor NP, etc. For now, just assume that the features are there and don't worry about how they get there.

10.9. Summary of English grammar so far

Since we've added quite a few new elements to our grammar in this chapter, let's expand the summary of English grammar presented in chapter 9 "Obliques" (p. 107) to see how everything fits together. This grammar also handles some aspects of subject-verb agreement (in light of the similar analysis of Fore).[31]

I. Base

  A. Phrase structure rules

    S → NP[Su] VP

$$
\text{VP} \rightarrow \text{V} \ (\text{NP[DO]}) \ (\text{VP}) \ (\text{PP[IO]}) \left(\left\{\begin{array}{l} \text{NP} \\ \text{PP} \\ \text{AdvP} \end{array}\right\}\right)^{*}
$$

    PP → P NP

$$
\text{NP} \rightarrow \left(\left\{\begin{array}{l} \text{D} \\ \text{NP[Poss]} \end{array}\right\}\right) (\text{QP}) \ (\text{AP})^{*} \ \text{N} \ (\text{PP})
$$

    AP → (DegP) A

---

[30]Although the third singular feminine pronoun uses *her* for both objective and genitive case, it would unfortunately not work to list the form just once and leave it unlabelled for case. This would allow the regular genitive case suffix -'s to attach to it, producing an incorrect genitive form. See chapter20 "Word Division and Clitics" (p. 285).

[31]This is not ultimately a very satisfactory way of handling agreement. For a better approach, see chapter 19 "Case and Agreement."

AdvP → (DegP) Adv

QP → (DegP) Q

DegP → ... Deg

N[–count] → [–plural]

N[+count] → [±plural]

$$V \rightarrow \begin{bmatrix} \{1,2,3\} \text{ person} \\ \pm \text{ plural} \\ \pm \text{ past} \end{bmatrix}$$

B. Lexicon (sample lexical entries)

V[SUBCAT ⟨ NP[Su] ⟩]

wɔk	walk
go	
wɛnt [+ past]	go

V[SUBCAT ⟨ NP[Su], NP[DO] ⟩]

kloz	close
si	
sɔ [+ past]	see

N[+count]

bɔj	boy
tʃajld	
tʃɪldɹɛn [+ plural]	child

N[–count]

sɔftwɛɹ	software
wɔtɹ	water

NP

aj	[Nom case]	
mi	[Obj case]	[1 person, – plural]
maj	[Gen case]	
ju		
juɹ	[Gen case]	[2 person]

II. Inflectional Spellout Rules[32]

$$\begin{matrix} \text{N} \\ [+ \text{ plural}] \\ [\text{X}] \rightarrow [\text{X}z] \end{matrix}$$

$$\begin{matrix} \text{V} \\ [+ \text{ past}] \\ [\text{X}] \rightarrow [\text{X}d] \end{matrix}$$

$$\begin{matrix} \text{V} \\ \begin{bmatrix} 3 \text{ person} \\ - \text{ plural} \\ - \text{ past} \end{bmatrix} \\ [\text{X}] \rightarrow [\text{X}z] \end{matrix}$$

---

[32]As discussed in chapter 12 "Suppletion and Morphophonemics" (p. 154), the output of these rules becomes the input of phonological rules which modify the phonological material to produce the variant forms of the suffixes, such as [-s] and [-iz] for the noun plural.

10.10. Review of key terms

INFLECTIONAL MORPHOLOGY is distinguished from DERIVATIONAL MORPHOLOGY by producing different forms of the same word, by being more PRODUCTIVE, and by being organized according to GRAMMATICAL CATEGORIES into PARADIGMS. A WORD AND PARADIGM grammar takes this paradigmatic structure into account, while an ITEM AND ARRANGEMENT grammar looks primarily at morphemes like beads on a string.

Grammatical categories can be represented by FEATURES. Inflectional features may have just two VALUES (i.e., be BINARY) or more than two, but in all cases the different values for a feature are MUTUALLY EXCLUSIVE.

Features are placed in DEEP STRUCTURE trees by FEATURE ASSIGNMENT RULES, which are a type of phrase structure rule. For REGULAR inflection, the affixes corresponding to each combination of features are added by INFLECTIONAL SPELLOUT RULES, which result in a tree structure called SURFACE STRUCTURE. For IRREGULAR INFLECTION (i.e., SUPPLETIVE STEMS), the forms are provided in the lexicon. For example, the different CASE forms of English pronouns can be handled this way.

10.11. Questions for analysis

1.   What types of words are inflected?
2.   What is the paradigm for each type of word?
   a.   What grammatical categories are indicated on that class of word (person, number, tense, etc.)?
   b.   What are the choices within each grammatical category? (E.g., How many tenses are there and what are they? Does number include dual in addition to singular and plural?)
   c.   How are each of these choices indicated? In other words, what is the phonological material for each feature value (or for specific combinations of feature values) and where does it occur in the string of inflectional affixes?
3.   Are there any cases of irregular inflection? On what types of words? What grammatical categories are involved? In what way(s) are they irregular?

10.12. Sample description

(This description covers a broader range of facts than you would probably be writing about after reading only this far in the book. It is included to give you lots of examples of different ways of talking about morphology.)

English count nouns are inflected for number; singular is unmarked, plural is generally marked with a suffix that is spelled -s.

(1) | Singular | Plural |
      |----------|--------|
      | *boy* | *boy-s* |
      | *computer* | *computer-s* |
      | *hope* | *hope-s* |

There are, however, a few nouns with irregular plurals.

(2) | Singular | Plural |
      |----------|--------|
      | *child* | *children* |
      | *sheep* | *sheep* |
      | *man* | *men* |

English verbs are inflected for past versus nonpast tense and for the person and number of the subject. However, very few of the inflectional possibilities allowed by this system are actually realized. In nonpast forms (used in what is traditionally called the present tense), third person singular is indicated with a suffix -s. Other person/number combinations are all unmarked.

(3)   *I/we/you/they   see*
       he/she/it   see-s

The irregular verb *to be* shows slightly richer inflection.

(4)   *I   am*
       we/you/they   are
       he/she/it   is

Past tense (for all persons and numbers) is indicated by the suffix -*ed* for many verbs (the so-called 'weak' verbs).

(5)   Nonpast   Past

       walk   walk-ed
       exit   exit-ed
       shout   shout-ed

However, many verbs (the 'strong' verbs) have irregular past forms.

(6)   Nonpast   Past

       see   saw
       sing   sang
       think   thought

Only one verb, *to be,* shows agreement with the subject in the past tense. It has two past tense forms, *was* for first and third person singular, and *were* for other person/number combinations.

English pronouns are marked for person, number, and case. Third person singular forms are also inflected for gender. The marking is largely suppletive; little meaningful morpheme-cutting is possible.

(7) | | Nominative | Objective | Genitive |
|---|---|---|---|
| first person singular | *I* | *me* | *my* |
| first person plural | *we* | *us* | *our* |
| second person | *you* | *you* | *your* |
| third person singular masculine | *he* | *him* | *his* |
| third person singular feminine | *she* | *her* | *her* |
| third person singular neuter | *it* | *it* | *its* |
| third person plural | *they* | *them* | *their* |

10.13. For further reading

For more on the inflectional/derivational distinction, see Anderson (1985a) and Matthews 1974, chapter 3.

Matthews (chapter 12) also discusses the theoretical foundation on which this approach to inflectional morphology is based. In particular, it discusses the distinction between item and arrangement and word and paradigm approaches to morphology and how they relate to generative grammars. Anderson's work is an elaboration of the foundation that Matthews laid. Anderson (1982) provides a brief introduction to the Extended Word and Paradigm framework, while his later book entitled *A-Morphous Morphology* (1992) provides a thorough exposition of this approach and its rationale.

10.14. Appendix: Features for inflectional morphology

This appendix lists the most common distinctions which are used in languages as the basis for inflectional morphology, together with typical values and some suggestions for formalizing them in terms of features. It is not necessary (and probably not a good use of your time) to memorize these lists. Rather, use them to reinforce your understanding of the text and as a source of ideas when analyzing particular languages. Glance through them now, then refer back to them later as needed.

These are only suggestions, since the facts of the language will often dictate the type of feature system that must be used. Use them as a starting point for your analysis and adapt them as needed to fit the facts of the language.

Also, just because a distinction is listed here doesn't mean that it is always inflectional; in fact, some of these like gender, number, and aspect can be derivational (see chapter 11 "Derivational Morphology," especially p. 141ff.), though it is more common for them to be inflectional.

Inflectional categories commonly associated with nouns

2-way number	[±pl] OR [±sg]
3-way number	[Sg number] for singular, [Dl number] for dual, [Pl number] for plural; OR
	something like [–pl, –dl] for singular, [–pl, +dl] for dual, [+pl] for plural
2-way gender	[±masc] OR [±fem]
3-way gender	[{masc, fem, neut} gender]
Animacy	[±anim] OR [±human]
Honorifics	[±respect]
Person	[{1, 2, 3} person] OR [±me, ±you]
Inclusivity (in first person plural)	[±incl] (when using [{1, 2, 3} person]), OR
	[+me, +you] (for first person inclusive plural, when using [±me, ±you]
Definiteness	[±definite]
Distance	[±proximal] OR [1 distal], [2 distal], etc. (as many values as there are degrees of distance in the system)
Case	[Nom case], [Gen case], [Acc case], [Dat case], [Obj case], etc.

Inflectional categories commonly associated with verbs

Tense	[±past] OR [±future] OR (less likely) [{past, pres, fut} tense]
Remoteness	[±recent] (used in combination with tense features)
Aspect	[±perfective], [±habitual], [±progressive], OR some combination of these
Active versus Nonactive	[±dynamic] OR [±stative]
Mood	[±realis] AND/OR [±imperative]
Negation	[±positive]
Yes-No Question	[±YNQ] (OR just [±Q] if the same morphology is used in content questions too)
Transitivity	[SUBCAT ⟨ ... ⟩] (see chapters 8 "Verbal Valence" and 21 "Passive and Voice")
Voice	[±passive], [±reflexive], [±causative], [±impersonal], if these are relevant to syntactic or inflectional rules (often they aren't).
Agreement	For agreement in person, number, etc., with the subject or direct object, use noun features, positioned in either of two ways: see this chapter (p. 124) or chapter 19 "Case and Agreement" (p. 260ff.).

11
Derivational Morphology

11.1. Goals and prerequisites

This chapter will help you do the following:

- ◎ state at least five characteristics that typically distinguish derivational from inflectional morphology
- ◎ distinguish clear cases of derivation and inflection in data
- ◎ describe derivational morphology informally using the terminology introduced in this chapter
- ◎ write appropriate formal rules for derivational morphology
- ◎ analyze and describe compounding as well as derivational affixation
- ◎ explain the Lexicalist Hypothesis and state how it is represented in our formal grammars

It assumes that you are familiar with the following material:

- ✓ standard terminology used to describe morphology (chapter 2 "Standard Grammatical Terminology" and chapter 4 "Introduction to Morphology")
- ✓ syntactic structure and the organization of a grammar (chapter 6 "The Base")
- ✓ the distinction between inflection and derivation (chapter 10 "Inflectional Morphology")

It may also be helpful to refer to chapter 18 "Overall Structure of a Grammar" as each new part of the grammar is introduced in this and the next few chapters.

11.2. More on inflection versus derivation

Recall from chapter 10 "Inflectional Morphology" (p. 116) some of the typical differences between inflectional and derivational morphology.

(1)	Inflection	Derivation
Changes one lexical entry into another	no	yes
Changes syntactic category	no	often
Productivity	virtually total	partial at best
Organized in paradigms	yes	no
Type of meaning	grammatical	usually lexical

Derivational morphology changes one word into another, often changing it into a word of a different category. It tends to be irregular, both by being less productive than inflectional morphology and by lacking paradigms. Derivational morphology tends to have lexical meaning, while inflectional morphology has grammatical meaning (grammatical categories).

This chapter looks at this distinction in more detail and considers especially how to analyze derivational morphology formally.

Stems versus roots

You may recall (from chapter 4 "Introduction to Morphology," p. 29) that there are two words, STEM and ROOT, which are used to refer to the 'base' of a word, the part to which affixes attach. The distinction between them is based on the distinction between inflectional and derivational morphology.[1]

Consider a word like 'kickers'. It contains two suffixes, one derivational (-er), the other inflectional (-s). Strip both affixes off and you are left with *kick,* which we call a ROOT. Add back on the derivational suffix -er and you get *kicker,* which we call the STEM.

(2)

|←——Stem——→|

kick + *er* + *s*

Root   Derivational   Inflectional
        Suffix   Suffix

More generally, a root is any single morpheme which is not an affix. Normally, you can find a root by removing all the affixes (both derivational and inflectional) from a word.[2] The stem of a word, on the other hand, is found by removing all the *inflectional* affixes, but leaving any derivational affixes in place.

A root is always a single morpheme. A stem, on the other hand, may consist of more than one morpheme. Many stems, like *cat* consist of only a single root; the stem and the root are identical.

(3)

|←Stem→|

cat

Root

Others, like *kick-er,* consist of a root plus one (or more) derivational affixes.

Other stems consist of two or more roots, as in *view-point.* Neither *view* nor *point* is an affix and both are single morphemes, so they are both considered to be roots.

(4)

|←——Stem——→|

view + *point*

Root   Root

---

[1]This usage of STEM and ROOT follows Crystal (1991:303, 326). Not everyone uses these two words in this way, however. For example, STEM in this book corresponds to Matthews' (1974:40, 73) INFLECTIONAL ROOT, my ROOT corresponds to his SIMPLE ROOT, and his INFLECTIONAL STEM corresponds in this book only to an intermediate stage in the derivation of an inflected form by inflectional spellout rules.

[2]This procedure is useful but not foolproof. It runs into a problem when compounding is involved, since removing all the affixes will still leave more than one root, not a single root.

A stem containing more than one root is called a COMPOUND STEM or simply a COMPOUND; the process of forming such stems is called COMPOUNDING.

Compounding may, in some cases, involve derivational affixes too, as in *rabble-rouse-r;* this stem consists of two roots plus a derivational suffix.

(5)

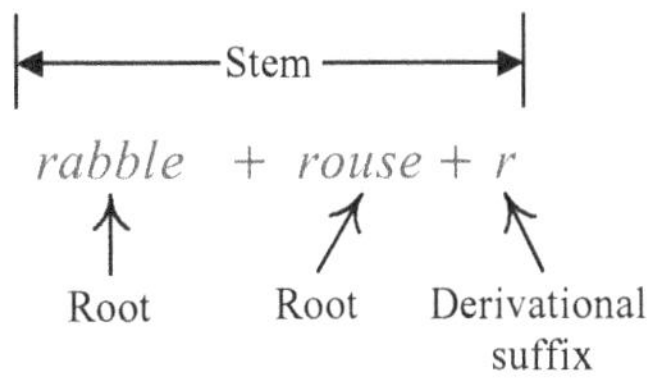

And, a stem may contain more than one derivational affix, as in *interlinearizer* (a type of computer program that is used by linguists for inserting interlinear word-by-word or morpheme-by-morpheme glosses in a text).[3]

(6)

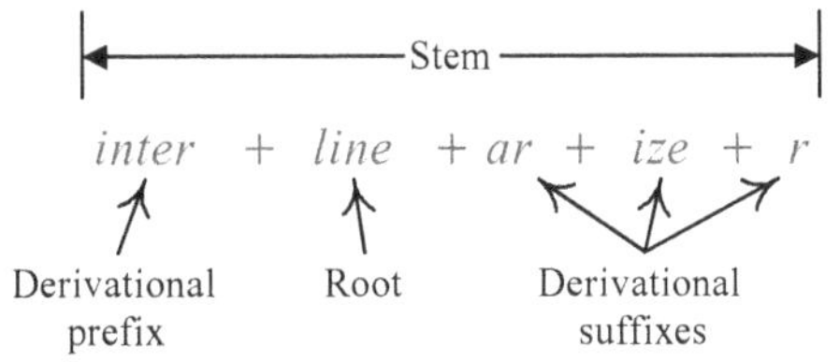

Thus, a stem consists of one or more roots, plus zero or more derivational affixes. A root, in contrast, is always a single morpheme.

All stems serve as the base to which inflectional affixes attach. So, for example, all the nouns mentioned above have plural forms.

(7) a. *cat-s*
     b. *kicker-s*
     c. *viewpoint-s*
     d. *rabble-rouser-s*
     e. *interlinearizer-s*

(8)

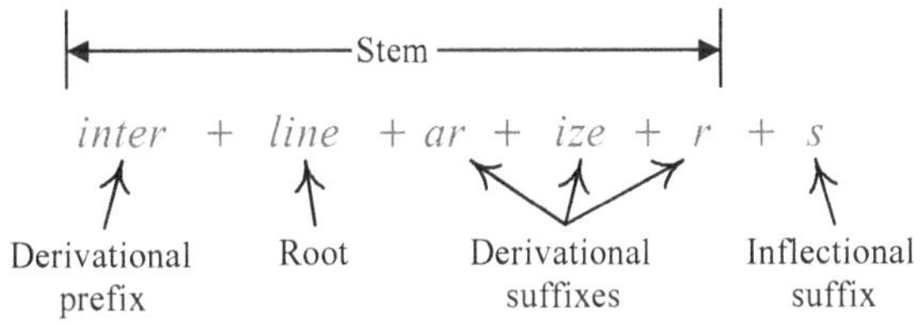

Virtually all roots are also stems and the simplest stems (those consisting of only one morpheme) are also roots.[4]

---

[3]The term 'interlinearizer' was not coined, to my knowledge, until software like the Interlinear Text Processor (Simons and Versaw 1988) and Shoebox (Wimbish 1990, Davis and Wimbish 1993) became available. It may not yet be in very widespread use even among linguists.

[4]Occasionally, there are roots that occur only in combination with other roots or derivational affixes, never by themselves as stems. English **aggress,* which occurs in *aggressive, aggressor,* and *aggression,* is such a root. See Jackendoff 1975:645–50 for their formal treatment.

(9)

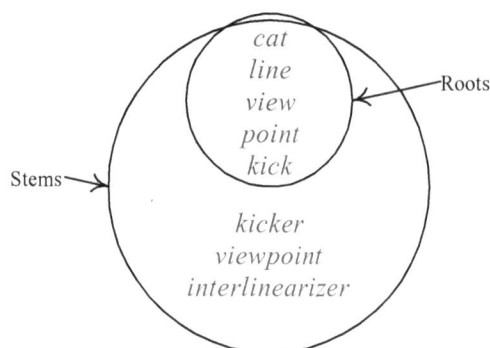

More differences between inflection and derivation

Let's consider some more differences between inflection and derivation, in addition to those discussed in chapter 10 "Inflectional Morphology."

One may be obvious from the examples so far. Derivational morphology normally occurs 'inside' inflectional morphology, that is, closer to the root. It is as if compounds are formed or derivational affixes are added before adding the inflectional affixes.

Recall that derivational morphology tends to have lexical meaning, while inflectional morphology has grammatical meaning. That is, the meaning of a derivational affix is often rich and complex, while the meaning of an inflectional affix is usually simple, often consisting of just a single abstract grammatical category. There is another side to the meaning of derivational morphology: the meaning of a derived word is often not fully predictable from the meaning of the morphemes involved. For example, a noun which is derived from a verb plus the *-(e)r* suffix generally refers to either the agent of the action or to the instrument.

(10)   Agent: *teach-er, lead-er, follow-er, greet-er*
         Instrument: *erase-r, compute-r, amplifi-er, elevat-or*

And, exactly which person or object is denoted by the derived form is unpredictable. For example, *computer* and *calculator* cannot be used interchangeably—they refer arbitrarily to distinct tools—even though both tools are used to compute and calculate. Finally, who could have guessed that a *twist-er* is a type of storm?

In semantics, when the meaning of the whole is not fully predictable from the meaning of its parts, we say that the meaning is CONVENTIONALIZED.[5] One characteristic of derivational morphology is that its meaning is often conventionalized, while the meaning of inflectional morphology is almost always fully predictable. This suggests that in a formal grammar, derivational morphology should be handled in the lexicon (where we place most idiosyncratic facts about elements of the language), while inflectional morphology can be handled by rules outside of the lexicon.

To summarize, let's expand the chart from (1). (The last item will be discussed in a moment.)

---

[5]Nunberg, Sag, and Wasow (1994), in their analysis of phrasal idioms, distinguish between CONVENTIONALIZED SEMANTICS and NONCOMPOSITIONAL SEMANTICS. They use COMPOSITIONALITY to refer to the degree to which the meaning of the whole can be analyzed in terms of the contributions of each of the parts. Thus, a linguistic unit like *computer* may be partially compositional, in that one can readily identify the contributions made by each of the parts *compute* and *-r;* at the same time it is conventionalized, in that the meaning of the whole is not totally predictable from the meaning of the parts. Many linguists do not distinguish the two concepts and label an expression as noncompositional whenever it is conventionalized in any obvious way.

(11)   Inflection   Derivation

     Changes one lexical entry into another   no   yes
     Changes syntactic category   no   often
     Productivity   virtually total[6]   partial at best
     Organized in paradigms   yes   no
     Distance from root   farther   closer
     Type of meaning   grammatical   usually lexical
     Conventionalized semantics   usually not   often yes
     Relevant to syntax   yes   no

While you are learning how to distinguish inflection from derivation, it may be helpful to review the list of grammatical categories at the end of chapter 10 "Inflectional Morphology" (p. 133). Become familiar with the types of meanings that are commonly expressed by inflectional morphology and use that list as a first hypothesis whether something is inflectional or derivational. If a particular meaning is listed there, it is probably inflectional; if not, it is probably derivational. After that, you can use the criteria in (11) to guide you as you gather evidence supporting or disconfirming your hypothesis.

Exceptions

The characteristics in (11) should not be applied rigidly; sometimes they will seem to conflict with each other. For example, although derivational morphology often results in a change of syntactic category, this is not always true. Consider *view-point* again. It is a compound noun consisting of two nouns. The process of compounding has produced a word that is in the same syntactic category as the words it is made up of. Or, consider the suffix *un-*, as in *un-kind*, which takes an adjective and turns it into another adjective. These are clearly derivational processes, because they involve lexical meaning which is conventionalized, they are not very productive, and they are not paradigmatic. Yet, they do not change syntactic category.

Sometimes, too, derivational morphology changes only the *sub*category of a word. For example, in many languages, there are CAUSATIVE affixes that change intransitive verbs to transitive. The suffix *-ish* in Swahili does this.[7]

(12)   Intransitive   Transitive (causative)
    kuhama   to move away   *kuhamisha*   to move (something)
    kufika   to arrive   *kufikisha*   to cause to reach/arrive
    kusimama   to stand   *kusimamisha*   to erect
    kula   to eat   *kulisha*   to feed

In chapter 21 "Passive and Voice" there are other examples of derivational morphology that changes the subcategory of a verb.

So, although the clearest cases of derivational morphology take words of one syntactic category and produce words of a different category, not all derivational morphology does so. Similarly, if you encounter a process that has limited productivity or whose meaning is not fully predictable, it is most likely derivational, yet there are exceptions. Sometimes derivational morphology is highly productive, and its meaning is very predictable from its parts. Sometimes inflectional morphology is highly irregular, even to the point of having gaps in paradigms. In deciding whether something is inflectional or derivational, think about the full range of characteristics listed in (11); don't rely on just one characteristic which may be misleading when considered by itself.

---

[6]Although some words may be inflected irregularly, they will almost always have some form for every position in the inflectional paradigm. On rare occasions, there may be words whose paradigms are DEFECTIVE, or missing certain forms, such as English *troops* 'soldiers', a noun which has only a plural form with no singular.

[7]Data from Wilson 1985:81–83. The *-a* is also a suffix, denoting mood.

Relevance to syntax

As we've seen, it is sometimes hard to tell the difference between inflection and derivation. Lists of typical characteristics like those in (11) may suggest contradictory conclusions when applied to specific cases. So, linguists have long sought for a single, more precise way of characterizing the difference between inflection and derivation.

One of the most helpful proposals in this regard is given by Anderson (1982:587).

(13)   Inflectional morphology is what is relevant to the syntax.

That is, inflectional morphology is sensitive to the larger syntactic context in which it occurs, while derivational morphology is not. To study it, you have to pay attention to other words in the sentence, while derivational morphology can be studied within a single word. Inflectional morphology is *syntactic* morphology. To see what this means, let's consider some examples.

Person and number in English are inflectional, because there is a rule in English which requires the verb to AGREE in person and number with the subject. That is, when you change the number (14) or person (15) of the subject, the morphological form of the verb must also change.

(14)   a. *A vulture **soars** more than it flies.*
       b. *Vultures **soar** more than they fly.*

(15)   a. *I **am** vivacious.*
       b. *You **are** vivacious.*
       c. *He **is** vivacious.*

This phenomenon is called AGREEMENT. Agreement morphology is relevant to the syntax because, in order to choose the right form of the verb, you have to look to another part of the sentence. According to (13), whenever you find agreement in a language, you know you are dealing with inflectional morphology.

The form of pronouns in English changes depending on whether they are used as subjects, objects, or possessors.

(16)   a. ***I** see an elephant.*
       b. *The elephant sees **me.***
       c. *It wants **my** apple.*

This sensitivity to grammatical relations is called CASE. In many languages, like Turkish, case is also marked on nouns.[8]

(17)   a. *Mehmet   kasaptır.*
          Mehmet   butcher
          Mehmet is a butcher

       b. *Mehmed-i   gördüm.*
          Mehmet-Obj   I.saw
          I saw Mehmet.

The suffix *-i* 'Obj' indicates that *Mehmet* is the direct object in (17b). The absence of this suffix in (17a) shows that *Mehmet* is the subject. Case, like agreement, is always inflectional, because it depends on the larger syntactic context of a word: the grammatical relation of the noun phrase of which it is the head. (We'll come back to case and agreement in chapter 19 "Case and Agreement.")

As a third example, tense marking on verbs is inflectional because the presence or absence of tense marking depends on the type of clause it occurs in. Look at these embedded clauses:

---

[8]Data from Underhill 1976, pp. 39, 51.

(18) a. *I believe [that she is   intelligent.]*
      b. **I believe [that she to be intelligent.]*
      c. *I believe [she is   intelligent.]*
      d. *I believe [her to be intelligent.]*

When an embedded clause (18a, b) begins with *that*, tense must be marked on the verb. The infinitive form *to be* (the form of the verb which does not have any tense marking) cannot be used. When the clause does not begin with *that*, either the form with tense marking (*is*) or the form without (*to be*) can be used. The presence of tense marking on the verb is conditioned by the presence of *that* earlier in the clause. Tense marking (in English, at least) is sensitive to the larger syntactic context and is therefore inflectional.[9]

A case study in Mexican Sign Language

Anderson's criterion (13) can be very useful to you as you do linguistic analysis. In Mexican Sign Language, there is a suffix consisting of a short, downward movement of the flat hand, palm down, at the side at waist level.[10] Here are some examples of the meanings of words without the suffix and the meaning that results when the suffix is added.

(19) Without suffix   With suffix

Without suffix	With suffix
'husband'	'wife'
'boyfriend'	'girlfriend'
'brother'	'sister'
'son'	'daughter'
'grandfather'	'grandmother'
'grandson'	'granddaughter'
'uncle'	'aunt'
'boy'	'girl'
'male friend'	'female friend'

In other words, it is added to a word which refers to a male, producing a word that refers to a female. Is this suffix inflectional or derivational?

Most of the criteria in (11) are not particularly helpful. This suffix does not change syntactic category and has predictable semantics, so it could be either inflectional or derivational by these criteria. It is the only suffix on these words, so we aren't helped by relative distance to the root. Its meaning could be considered either lexical, like the English suffix *-ess* (as in *princess, waitress*), or grammatical, as an instance of GENDER, one of the meanings that are often inflectional (see the end of chapter 10 "Inflectional Morphology," p. 133).

Productivity gives ambiguous results. This suffix is apparently only used with nouns referring to humans, unlike Spanish in which all nouns are either masculine or feminine, even those referring to objects with no innate gender. On the other hand, for at least some signers, it can be freely and spontaneously added to many words. In one interview when I was focusing on the use of this suffix, a woman spontaneously added the suffix to the word for 'devil' to produce 'she-devil'; the laughter this produced from her friends showed that it was a freshly-coined word.

So what about relevance to the syntax? To see how it helps, compare Mexican Sign Language to Spanish, in which the gender of a noun places requirements on the morphology of adjectives and determiners.

---

[9]These examples also illustrate again that case is inflectional, since the case on the subject of the embedded clause depends on whether the verb is inflected.

[10]Data on Mexican Sign Language is from my own fieldwork and from Karla (Faurot) Hurst, Steve Parkhurst, Dianne (Dellinger) Parkhurst, and Andy Eatough (personal communication).

(20) Masculine   Feminine

    el   palo largo   *la   rama   larga*
    the pole long   the   branch long

That is, Spanish adjectives and determiners agree in gender with the nouns they modify, and thus, Spanish gender is clearly inflectional. However, no such pattern of agreement occurs in Mexican Sign Language; the form of adjectives does not depend on the nouns they modify. The feminine suffix is relevant only to the noun of which it is a part, not the larger context. Thus, it is best considered derivational. (More generally, Mexican Sign Language and Spanish have very different grammatical structures; indeed, in most countries, the signed language is clearly distinct from the spoken language in the same country.[11])

This example illustrates the fact that a particular meaning (like gender) can be expressed with inflectional morphology in some languages and derivational morphology in others. Although the list of typically inflectional categories in chapter 10 "Inflectional Morphology" (p. 133) can give you a pretty good idea of whether something is likely to be inflectional or derivational, you can't rely on it 100%. The way you tell the difference is by checking for relevance to syntax.[12]

11.3. Derivational morphology in a formal grammar

In our formal grammars, we have incorporated the idea that inflectional morphology is relevant to the syntax by handling it with rules that are intermixed with syntactic rules. Recall from chapter 10 "Inflectional Morphology" (p. 118ff.) that feature assignment rules, which are a special type of phrase structure rules, assign inflectional features to nodes in trees. At first, inflectional affixes are represented in trees only by these inflectional features. The phonological form of these affixes are supplied later by inflectional spellout rules.

Derivational morphology, on the other hand, is idiosyncratic and irregular and thus appears to belong in the lexicon. The meaning of a compound word or a word containing a derivational affix is often not fully predictable from the meanings of the morphemes in the word. Since the meaning cannot be predicted by the rules alone, it must be supplied by a separate lexical entry. (Recall that similar facts led us in chapter 9 "Obliques," p. 101, to list idiomatic phrases in the lexicon.)

Lexical entries for derived words

So, this means many lexical entries contain more than one morpheme. The category Adv in English contains many words derived from adjectives with the derivational affix *-li,* as well as adverbs that consist of a single root.

(21) **Adv**
    [kwɪk]li   quickly
    [wik]li   weakly
    [ɛnθuziæstɪk]li   enthusiastically
    fæst   fast
    wɛl   well

Notice the use of brackets [ ] with the words that are derivationally complex.[13] This is done to keep track of the order in which derivational affixes are attached. For example, consider the word

---

[11]Mexican Sign Language is also different from the sign languages in Spain and other Latin American countries (Steve and Dianne Parkhurst and Ronald Henson, personal communication).

[12]For further examples, see Anderson 1982.

[13]Aronoff 1976:25 assumes that each bracket is labeled with a syntactic category.

inter-line-ar-ize-r mentioned above. The four derivational affixes are attached to the root in a definite sequence.[14]

(22) a.   *lajn*   line
      b.   [*lɪni*   ]   *əɹ*   linear
      c.   *ɪntɹ*   [[*lɪni*   ]   *əɹ*   ]   interlinear
      d.   [*ɪntɹ*   [[*lɪni*   ]   *əɹ*   ]]   *ajz*   interlinearize
      e.   [[*ɪntɹ*   [[*lɪni*   ]   *əɹ*   ]]   *ajz*   ]   ɹ   interlinearizer

Each affix adds a new element of meaning and produces a new word, which requires its own lexical entry. By using brackets, we show the full internal structure of each word—in essence, its derivational history.[15]

(23) **N**
      lajn   line
      [[ɪntɹ[[lɪni]əɹ]]ajz]ɹ   interlinearizer

      A
      [lɪni]əɹ   linear
      ɪntɹ[[lɪni]əɹ]   interlinear

      V
      [ɪntɹ[[lɪni]əɹ]]ajz   interlinearize

When a derived word is inserted in a tree, it is handled exactly like a simple word. Compare the following two noun phrases:

(24) a.   b.

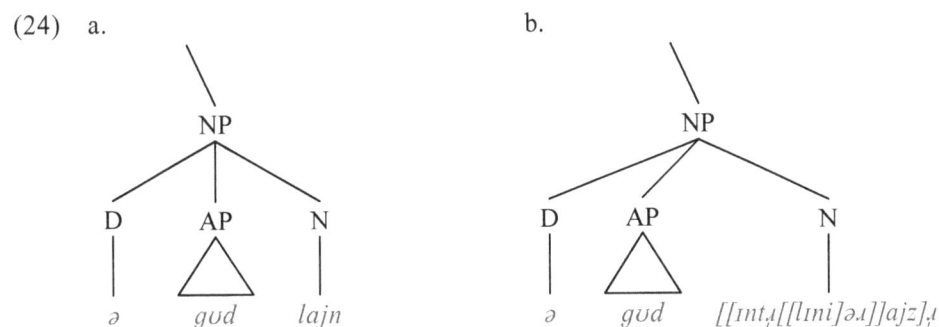

The entire phonological structure from the lexicon, including the brackets, is inserted underneath the N node.

Since all derivational morphology is listed in the lexicon, this means that the lexicon is primarily a list of *stems*. It is not a list of morphemes, because some lexical entries contain more than one morpheme, derivational affixes are not listed in separate lexical entries, and inflectional affixes are not included at all. (Although irregular inflection *is* included within some lexical entries, see chapter 10 "Inflectional Morphology," p. 127, these are still irregular *stems*.)

---

[14]Besides the bracketing, nothing about the phonological structure of these words is being claimed by the particular transcription here, which is impressionistic and unsystematic. This is especially obvious in vowel qualities in the root; the more abstract phonological analysis necessary to handle these is beyond what should be attempted here. The transcription practice is meant only as a reminder that lexical entries contain phonological segments, not practical orthography spellings.

[15]This is presumably important to the phonological analysis of these words, since phonological rules may need to refer to the brackets to produce the actual phonetic details of their pronunciation. For one thing, the brackets could be used to define cyclic application of phonological rules (see Aronoff 1976:23–27). However, Anderson (1992:256ff.) argues that they are not necessary, since the effect of cyclic application can also be achieved by limiting rules to applying in derived environments. I have retained them for this book, since they help focus students' attention on the derivational history of a word.

It is commonly assumed in much work in Generative Grammar today that derivational morphology is handled within the lexicon. Details of how this is handled vary; what this chapter presents is one of several possibilities. What is generally true of these approaches, however, is the assumption that derivational affixes are handled completely in the lexicon, are already present on a word before it is inserted in a tree, and that derivational morphology is thus independent from syntax.[16] This assumption is generally known as the LEXICALIST HYPOTHESIS.

Finding regularity amid irregularity: Word formation rules for derivational morphology

By including all derived words as lexical entries, we have fully accounted for the irregularity that is so common with derivational morphology. Each lexical entry provides all the information we need about the meaning and form of a derived word, no matter how irregular. This, without any special rules for derivational morphology, is enough to generate all grammatical utterances in the language.

But, this is only half the story for there is also a good deal of regularity with derivational morphology that, as linguists, we would like to express in the form of a rule and which native speakers can use to produce new words.

Consider the suffix -(e)r presented above in (10). This suffix consistently derives nouns from verbs. Although the meaning of the noun is not fully predictable from the meaning of the verb root, the meaning always has something to do with an agent or instrument commonly associated with the verb. Also, the pronunciation is consistently the same: [ɹ] (even though the spelling is inconsistent). Shouldn't there be some way to express these generalizations in the form of a rule? Further, we have to be able to account for people's ability to produce new nouns like *interlinearize-r*. Speakers do not just know the words which contain -(e)r, they also know a rule governing its use.

One way to write a rule for this suffix is like this:[17]

(25) $\uparrow [X]_V$ α

     $\downarrow [[X]_{\textit{ɹ}}]_N$ agent or instrument customarily associated with α

This rule expresses a speaker's ability to create new words; accordingly we call such rules WORD FORMATION RULES.[18] It also expresses the regularities between already existing words, like *play* and *player*.[19]

The brackets with subscripts in (25) show that one lexical entry is a verb, the other is a noun. The 'X' represents the phonological spelling of the verb; the '$[X]_{\textit{ɹ}}$' indicates that the corresponding noun is identical except for the addition of the suffix and the resultant bracketing. (Note that the 'X' does

---

[16]The assumption that inflectional morphology is handled by syntactic rules outside the lexicon is more controversial. The strict separation of inflection from derivation used in this book is based on the A-morphous Morphology of Anderson (1982, 1992). An alternative view (Scalise 1984:101–36, 191–96, and other references cited there) argues that inflectional morphology should also be handled in the lexicon, although still somewhat segregated from derivational morphology. Hammond and Noonan (1988) contain several papers on the issue. I have employed Anderson's proposal in this book because of its pedagogical value in reinforcing the inflectional/derivational distinction and in illustrating differing formal approaches (lexical and syntactic) to the problems of morphology.

[17]The notation for word formation rules is based largely on Jackendoff (1975), except that the rule is arranged vertically. This more clearly distinguishes word formation rules from inflectional spellout rules. The vertical arrangement also makes it somewhat easier to see the specific differences between the lexical items related by the rule, particularly in the formulation of passive in chapter 21 "Passive and Voice."

[18]This usage differs from Anderson (1992), who also uses the term 'word formation rule' to refer to rules for inflectional morphology, what I call 'inflectional spellout rules'.

[19]In this matter I follow Jackendoff 1975, Aronoff 1976:22–34, Bybee 1985, and others, in rejecting the assumption that any fact which can be predicted by rule should not be listed separately in the lexicon. For a broader perspective on this issue, Langacker (1987:29, 42; 1990:264–65; and especially 1988) has argued that this approach should be extended to all areas of grammar. The formulation here most closely resembles Aronoff's, so it adopts his name for the rules, although it uses notation based on Jackendoff. Word Formation Rules play a dual role in our grammars: (1) synchronically, to express regularities between lexical entries and (2) diachronically, to produce new lexical entries from old. (The two roles are related: pairs of entries which are synchronically related by a rule are, in most cases, the result of its diachronic operation.) For simplicity, I depart from Aronoff in not allowing Word Formation Rules to play any direct role in generating individual sentences; all words to be inserted in trees must exist previously in the lexicon.

not require the verb to be a single morpheme; the rule can apply easily to a complex verb like *interlinearize* to produce *interlinearizer*.) The 'α' (alpha) represents the meaning of the verb; whatever this meaning is, the noun refers to an agent or instrument customarily associated with the verb's meaning.[20] Thus, just like a lexical entry, a word formation rule includes grammatical, phonological, and semantic information.

The place of word formation rules in the grammar

Word formation rules are not used directly to generate sentences.[21] Lexical insertion simply takes an established lexical entry, which may or may not contain derivational affixes, and inserts it in a tree. Rather, word formation rules operate independently of specific sentences; they simply take a word like *interlinearize* and produce a new lexical entry *interlinearizer*. A particular lexical entry only needs to be created once by a word formation rule; from that time onward, it is available to be inserted into many different sentences without further involvement by the word formation rule.[22]

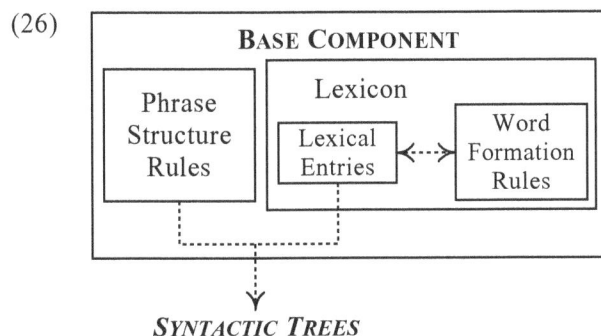

(26)

```
          BASE COMPONENT
 ┌─────────────────────────────────────┐
 │             Lexicon                  │
 │ Phrase   ┌──────────────────────┐    │
 │Structure │ Lexical  <--> Word    │    │
 │ Rules    │ Entries       Formation│   │
 │          │               Rules    │   │
 │          └──────────────────────┘    │
 └─────────────────────────────────────┘
              │
              ▼
       SYNTACTIC TREES
```

Though word formation rules are not needed to generate individual sentences, they are important for two reasons:[23]

- expressing the generalizations that native speakers know about the relationships between words in the lexicon
- accounting for native speakers' ability to create new words following the same pattern

Once the new lexical entry is created (in the process of historical change), it takes on a life of its own independent of the rule and may change further in ways that are inconsistent with the rule. For example, consider the *-th* suffix in English, used on many nouns derived from verbs, adjectives, and other nouns.[24]

---

[20]In this book, the characterization of the meaning change effected by word formation rules is informal and approximate.

[21]Given two grammars, identical except that one contains Word Formation Rules and the other does not, both can produce exactly the same sentences. Of course, the grammar which has Word Formation Rules can make new lexical entries and thus generate new sentences that cannot be generated by the grammar without such rules. But by making new lexical entries it is, technically speaking, no longer the same grammar. It is a third grammar, which can create new sentences because it contains additional lexical entries that the first two grammars lack. Thus, in comparing the synchronic ability of two grammars to generate a set of sentences, we must specifically ignore the diachronic functioning of Word Formation Rules.

[22]Of course, derivational processes differ in productivity. It is not clear how to characterize varying degrees of productivity in formal grammars like these. For derivational processes that are completely nonproductive (such as English *-th* in *warmth*, *breadth*, *birth*) it would be most correct not to include a word formation rule in the formal grammar. However, it may still be useful to write one as a descriptive device capturing whatever regularity may still exist in the lexicon.

[23]The exact role and function of word formation rules, as explained here, is accepted by many but not all linguists. Aronoff (1976:43ff), for example, suggests that only those derived forms which are irregular in some respect should be listed in the lexicon; those which are fully predictable should not be listed and thus must be generated by rule each time they are needed.

[24]Thanks to Ben Unseth (personal communication) for providing most of these examples.

(27)   Verbs   Nouns

        smite   smith
        heal   health
        steal   stealth
        bear   birth
        weigh   weight
        brew   broth

(28)   Adjectives   Nouns

        warm   warmth
        true   truth, troth
        long   length
        high   height
        wide   width
        deep   depth
        well   wealth
        sly   sleuth

(29)   Nouns   Nouns

        heart   hearth
        ire   wrath

This suffix is not currently productive, although presumably it was at one time. Although the same suffix apparently occurs in all examples, there is quite a bit of irregularity in form: there are vowel changes in the stem and occasionally the suffix appears as -t. The meaning of the derived noun is largely unpredictable, often referring to an abstraction (*warmth*), sometimes to an event (*birth*), sometimes a product (*broth*), sometimes an occupation (*smith,* 'a metalworker, one who smites metal'), sometimes just an object that has some vague association (*hearth*). It is often the case, especially with old and nonproductive derivational affixes like -*th*, that the meaning or form of individual lexical items has changed from what the word formation rule originally created. Our task in this case is to try to uncover as many regularities as possible, while at the same time to be sensitive to the unique characteristics of individual words. The following rule represents the regularities that exist, using the phonetic symbol θ to represent the most common form of the suffix.

(30) $\uparrow$ $[X]_{\{V,N,A\}}$ α
        $\downarrow$ $[[X]\theta]_N$ something associated with α

This rule doesn't explain everything and has many exceptions, but this is no problem, because the details about each word are given in its lexical entry. Indeed, the best analysis may be that the rule itself is not a part of modern English grammar; all that are left are the lexical entries that the rule once produced and which have subsequently changed.

Word formation rule for Mexican Sign Language feminine suffix

Recall the feminine suffix in Mexican Sign Language discussed above (p. 141). A word formation rule for it could be written as follows (using '⟨PALM.DOWN⟩' as a makeshift representation for the gesture used):

(31) $\uparrow$ $[X]_N$ male (human) α
        $\downarrow$ $[[X]\langle\text{PALM.DOWN}\rangle]_N$ female (human) α

As always, this rule assumes that each word containing the suffix must be listed individually in the lexicon. This means that there may easily be exceptions to the rule and, indeed, there are. The signs for 'woman' and 'mother' are single roots not related to the signs for 'man' and 'father'. This sort of irregularity is normal with derivational morphology and it is easily handled by simply listing in the lexicon all the words that are actually used.[25]

Word formation rules for compounding

Now what about compounding? A word formation rule for compounding must show the relationship between two or more roots and a compound stem. Consider Alamblak (Papuan, Papua New Guinea),[26] in which verbs are often compounded. This often means that the two events occur simultaneously or in sequence.

(32) ***muh-hambrë***-*më-r-m*
      climb-search.for-RemotePast-3sMascSu-3pDO
      He climbed (it) searching for them. OR He climbed (it) and (then) searched for them.

Sometimes the semantic relationship between the two roots is one of causation or an indication of degree.

(33) ***tat-noh***-*më-an-r*
      hit-die-RemotePast-1sgSu-3sMascDO
      I hit him (and he) died.

(34) ***dbëhna-noh***-*më-r*
      sick-die-RemotePast-3sMascSu
      He was sick and died. OR He was deathly sick.

Although the semantic relationships between the roots (and thus the meaning of the compound) vary, the phonological and syntactic properties of the compound are regular and can be expressed by the following word formation rule. Note that three lexical entries are involved; one for the compound and two for the words that comprise it.

(35)
$$
\begin{cases}
[X]_V & \alpha \\
[Y]_V & \beta
\end{cases}
$$
$$
[[X][Y]]_V \quad
\begin{cases}
\alpha \text{ and } \beta \text{ simultaneously or sequentially} \\
\alpha \text{ causes } \beta \\
\alpha \text{ done to the degree that } \beta \text{ might happen}
\end{cases}
$$

The semantic portion of the rule approximates the range of meanings expressed by verbal compounding.[27]

Word formation rules and inflectional spellout rules contrasted

Inflectional spellout rules and word formation rules are similar, since they both add affixes to stems. However, there are many differences, summarized here.

---

[25]The model predicts such irregularity to be greater for derivation than for inflection. Irregular inflection always requires a more complicated lexical entry (see chapter 10 "Inflectional Morphology," p. 127) than for regular inflection. Irregular derivation, on the other hand, simply requires a different, but no more complex, lexical entry. Irregular derivational morphology is less costly and thus is expected more often.

[26]Data from Les Bruce (personal communication).

[27]A more refined semantic analysis could certainly be given.

(36)

Inflectional spellout rules	Word formation rules
account for inflectional morphology	account for derivational morphology
operate on the output of the phrase structure rules and lexicon and before phonological rules	operate in the lexicon
generate inflected forms of a word that are not listed in the lexicon (unless irregular)	express correspondences between stems that are each listed independently in the lexicon
apply to stems after they are inserted in the tree, as part of the derivation of individual sentences	are not directly involved in producing individual sentences, but rather produce new lexical entries (modifying the grammar itself)
do not change grammatical and semantic information	can change grammatical and semantic information
our notation: →	our notation: ↕

11.4. Review of key terms

DERIVATIONAL MORPHOLOGY is distinguished from inflectional morphology by the characteristics in (11). Besides the characteristics discussed in chapter 10 "Inflectional Morphology," derivational morphology is usually closer to the root and often has CONVENTIONALIZED SEMANTICS. We noted, too, that although it often produces words that are in a different syntactic category, this is not always true; sometimes the change is only in subcategory, as with CAUSATIVES. One clear criterion separating inflection from derivation is RELEVANCE TO THE SYNTAX; on these grounds, CASE and AGREEMENT are always inflectional, although other specific meanings like GENDER may be expressed by inflection in some languages and derivation in others.

We have expanded our understanding of the lexicon considerably. In chapter 6 "The Base" (p. 50), we saw that the lexicon consists of lexical entries, each of which contains grammatical, semantic, and phonological information. Some types of lexical entries are complex, such as those for idiom phrases (chapter 9 "Obliques," p. 101) and suppletive stems (chapter 10 "Inflectional Morphology," p. 127). We have seen in this chapter, following one variety of the LEXICALIST HYPOTHESIS, that each lexical entry typically represents a STEM, that is, it may contain DERIVATIONAL AFFIXES or be a COMPOUND STEM. Stems are thus distinguished from ROOTS, which are always single morphemes.

Besides the lexical entries, there are also WORD FORMATION RULES, which express the regular and predictable characteristics (grammatical, semantic, and phonological) of a derivational affix or a pattern of compounding and which help account for its PRODUCTIVITY, or the ability to produce new words with it.

11.5. Questions for analysis

Is there any derivational morphology? For each derivational process, consider the following:

1. What is the phonological effect of the process? (For example: adding an affix, compounding two roots.)
2. What class of words does the process apply to? What class of words results from the process?
3. What difference of meaning results?
4. How productive is the process? Is it still possible to make new words with the rule or is it only a historical process that is no longer active? Are there many examples already in the lexicon or only a few?

11.6. Sample descriptions

English agentive/instrumental nominalization

Many English nouns are derived from verbs by the addition of a suffix *-r* (which is also spelled *-er* and *-or* in the standard orthography). The resulting noun refers to the agent of the verb or to some instrument typically associated with the action. For example, a *teach-er* is a person that *teaches* and a *strain-er* is used to *strain* things. But even at that, the resulting word usually refers to something more specific than the generalization would suggest. An *act-or* is a person who *acts* (but only in the narrow sense of a dramatic performance) and a *twist-er* is not someone who does the twist, but a tornado. The process is productive; it is frequently used as a tactic to gain a few extra points in word games and can be used freely on newly-coined verbs such as *digitize* to produce *digitizer*.

The feminine suffix in Mexican Sign Language

The so-called 'feminine' suffix consists of a short, downward movement of the flat hand, palm down, at the side at waist level. It is used to derive nouns referring to females from nouns referring to males, as in words with the following meanings:

Without suffix	With suffix
'husband'	'wife'
'boyfriend'	'girlfriend'
'brother'	'sister'
'son'	'daughter'
'grandfather'	'grandmother'
'grandson'	'granddaughter'
'uncle'	'aunt'
'boy'	'girl'
'male friend'	'female friend'

Its use seems to be largely limited to human nouns, although signers who know Spanish tend to use it more productively than those who do not, apparently in partial imitation of the Spanish gender distinction. (Unlike Spanish, Mexican Sign Language has no agreement in gender.)

11.7. For further reading

Characterizing the distinction between inflection and derivation is a classic problem; besides the readings suggested at the end of chapter 10 "Inflectional Morphology," you may especially want to look at Anderson's (1982:585–91) discussion of this topic, including the issue of categories that may be inflectional in one language and derivational in another. Bybee (1985, chapter 4) presents a rather different view from the one adopted here, arguing that the distinction between derivation and inflection is a continuum with no abrupt distinction between them.

For different types of derivational morphology, Anderson (1985b) surveys a variety of derivational processes, Comrie and Thompson (1985) look especially at the semantics of NOMINALIZATION (deriving nouns from other words), and Matthews (1974:188–95) discusses how to distinguish compounds from multiword lexical items.

The lexicalist hypothesis was proposed by Chomsky (1970) in his article "Remarks on Nominalization" and has been preserved in some form or another in most generative work on morphology since that time. Although this article is worth reading, it is somewhat involved and technical; a more readable summary, together with an explanation of its importance in the development of Generative Grammar, is provided by Newmeyer (1980:114–21 and 1986:106–10, 139–69) in his history of Generative Grammar.

12
Suppletion and Morphophonemics

12.1. Goals and prerequisites

This chapter will help you do the following:

- ◉ identify any of the following different types of allomorphy:
  - • morphophonemics versus suppletion
  - • suppletion of stems versus affixes
  - • lexical versus phonological conditioning
- ◉ write informal descriptions of the facts for data illustrating these different types
- ◉ incorporate these facts in appropriate places in a formal analysis

It assumes that you are familiar with the following material:

- ✓ inflectional morphology (chapter 10)
- ✓ derivational morphology (chapter 11)
- ✓ certain phonological concepts, such as COMPLEMENTARY DISTRIBUTION, MORPHOPHONEMICS, and UNDERLYING FORM

12.2. English noun plurals: Morphophonemics and stem suppletion

So far in our work in morphology, almost all morphemes have had only one phonological shape. But, all morphemes are not like this; the same meaning may be expressed by different forms in different contexts. This subject is called ALLOMORPHIC VARIATION or ALLOMORPHY.

We'll take a look at some specific examples in three different languages. Let's start with examples from English of two main types: MORPHOPHONEMICS and STEM SUPPLETION. MORPHOPHONEMICS refers to allomorphy which results from regular phonological rules; STEM SUPPLETION refers to irregular inflection, which has already been discussed in chapter 10 "Inflectional Morphology" (p. 127).

The data

Consider number on English count nouns. Most nouns form their plurals by adding a suffix -(e)s, which has three different forms: /-z/, /-s/, and /-iz/. (These differences are only partially represented in ordinary spelling.)

(1) a. /bɔj-z/   *boy-s*
         /tɹi-z/   *tree-s*
         /kaw-z/   *cow-s*

     b. /tap-s/   *top-s*
         /bʊk-s/   *book-s*
         /hɪp-s/   *hip-s*

     c. /baks-ɨz/   *box-es*
         /ɹoz-ɨz/   *ros-es*
         /pitʃ-ɨz/   *peach-es*

However, other nouns have irregular plurals. A few have identical singular and plural forms.

(2)   Singular   Plural
       sheep   *sheep*
       fish   *fish*

With others, the singular and plural forms differ in the stem vowel.

(3)   Singular   Plural
       foot   *feet*
       mouse   *mice*
       woman   *women*
       man   *men*

With a few, the plural has a suffix that no other stem in the language has. Some nouns have both an irregular suffix and a vowel change.

(4)   Singular   Plural
       /aks/   /aks-ən/   *ox(en)*
       /tʃajld/   /tʃɪld-ɹən/ *child(ren)*

Others retain the singular/plural inflection from Latin, although this pattern is being regularized, i.e., some irregular forms have been replaced by regular ones.

(5)   Singular   Plural
       alumnus   *alumni*
       octopus   *octopi*   (traditional, irregular form)
                   octopuses   (colloquial, regularized form)

In English, then, there are at least seven different ways to mark plurality on nouns.

Morphemes and allomorphs

Unlike what people often think, the irregularity that exists in English is normal. Many (perhaps most) languages exhibit considerable variation in the way they express a single grammatical category; this is ALLOMORPHY. Analyzing the allomorphy in a language is an important part of understanding its morphological system. As a practical matter when we are learning a language, we want to speak and recognize the different forms of a morpheme correctly, and any translated materials we produce should be morphologically correct.

Sometimes, it is useful to talk about one morpheme having several different variants, called its ALLOMORPHS. The different allomorphs of a morpheme all have the same meaning. However, they are in complementary distribution, just like the allophones of a phoneme; in any given context, only one allomorph of the morpheme is possible.[1]

So, then, we must refine our understanding of what a morpheme is. Recall that in chapter 4 "Introduction to Morphology" (p. 27) MORPHEME was defined as: A morpheme is 'a consistent and unanalyzable association of phonological, grammatical, and semantic information'. Up until now, the phonological information has been a single sequence of segments, such as in the English suffix *-tion*. Now we need to recognize that the association of phonological material may be more complex. A single morpheme, like the English plural, may have more than one phonological form (its different allomorphs).

Morphophonemics

There are several kinds of allomorphy in English noun plurals. The most widespread is the variation in pronunciation of the regular suffix *-(e)s,* as illustrated in (1). We can attribute it to two phonological processes:

(6)   a.   assimilation in voicing (/z/ → /s/ after a voiceless segment)

  b.   insertion of /i/ to break up clusters of alveolar and alveopalatal consonants

This type of allomorphy is called MORPHOPHONEMICS and is considered to be a part of phonology, since it has to do purely with the interactions of sounds. We should not account for morphophonemics with morphological rules, since it is best handled by phonological rules.[2]

However, the grammar does need to supply the phonological rules with the proper input, since the phonological rules operate on the output of the grammar. The input to the phonological rules is called an UNDERLYING FORM. An underlying form is meant to represent only those aspects of a morpheme's pronunciation which are not predictable by phonological rules. In the case of the *-(e)s* suffix, we can assume that the underlying form is /-z/. The two phonological rules in (6) modify /-z/ to produce the other two variants /-s/ and /-iz/. Together, the three forms /-z/, /-s/ and /-iz/ are the SURFACE FORMS for the plural morpheme.

With phonological rules available to handle morphophonemic variation, all morphemes mentioned anywhere in the grammar can (and should) be underlying forms. This includes both stems in the lexicon and the phonological material introduced by word formation rules and inflectional spellout rules. This is why chapter 10 "Inflectional Morphology" (p. 120) gives the following as the inflectional spellout rule for noun plurals:

(7)   N
    [+ plural]
      [X]   →   [X*z*]

The other two allomorphs did not need to be mentioned, because they are derived by phonological rules.

For example, suppose we want to generate *cats, dogs,* and *roses.* The deep structures are as follows:

---

[1]This represents the typical case; allomorphs may sometimes be in free variation, such as the two pronunciations of the word 'to' ([tu] and [tʊ]).

[2]This is a bit of oversimplification. Some minor differences in the form of a morpheme can be attributed to surface phonetic variation, what has sometimes been called POST-LEXICAL RULES or ALLOPHONICS. Allophonic rules, unlike morphophonemic rules, are insensitive to morphemic structure. On the other hand, such variations are so trivial that they are often not even considered in discussions of allomorphy. Regardless of how they are classified, the overall point remains the same. Some allomorphic variation can and should be accounted for by phonological rules operating on the output of the grammar, and the grammar should only refer to the morpheme by means of its phonological underlying form.

(8)
```
        NP            NP            NP
        |             |             |
        N             N             N
   [+plural]      [+plural]      [+plural]
        |             |             |
       kæt           dɔg           ɹoɹ
```

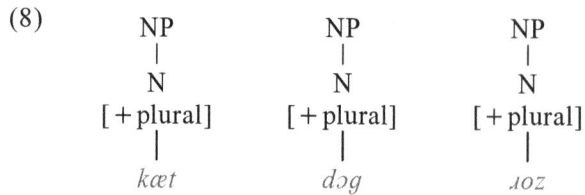

The rule in (7) applies to produce (syntactic) surface structure:

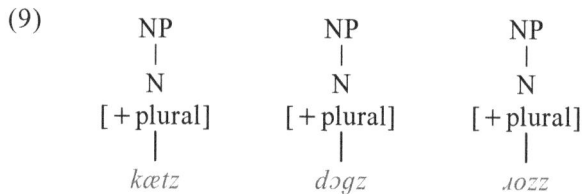

(9)
```
        NP            NP            NP
        |             |             |
        N             N             N
   [+plural]      [+plural]      [+plural]
        |             |             |
       kætz          dɔgz          ɹozz
```

These are the input to the phonological rules, which modify the terminal nodes to produce the correct (phonological) surface forms.[3]

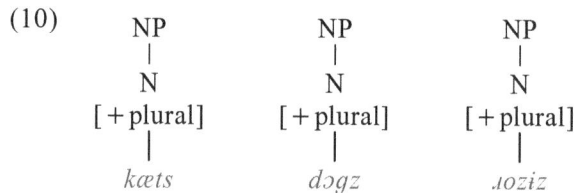

(10)
```
        NP            NP            NP
        |             |             |
        N             N             N
   [+plural]      [+plural]      [+plural]
        |             |             |
       kæts          dɔgz         ɹoziz
```

Morphophonemics in derivational morphology

Morphophonemics occurs with both inflectional and derivational morphology. Let's look at an example involving derivation. Consider the pairs of adjectives listed in (11).[4]

(11) a. *elegant*   *inelegant*
        eligible   *ineligible*
        tolerant   *intolerant*
        direct   *indirect*
     b. *possible*   *impossible*
        perfect   *imperfect*
        practical   *impractical*
        movable   *immovable*
     c. *correct*   *incorrect*
        capable   *incapable*
     d. *legal*   *illegal*
        legible   *illegible*
        legitimate   *illegitimate*
     e. *reverent*   *irreverent*
        regular   *irregular*
        reversible   *irreversible*

---

[3]In Lexical Phonology, these would presumably be what are called 'lexical rules', although the name does not fit well with our assumptions about the location of inflectional morphology in the grammar. Lexical Phonology assumes that all affixes, inflectional as well as derivational, are added in the lexicon. For our purposes, the important point about them is not where in the grammar they are located, but *when* they apply (immediately after each affix is added, in cyclic fashion) and their *range of application* (within words only).

[4]This prefix is considered derivational because it has lexical meaning, the process is not productive and applies to only a subset of all adjectives, and it is irrelevant to the syntax (see chapter 11 "Derivational Morphology," p. 139).

There are five allomorphs of the same prefix here: /ɪn-/, /ɪm-/, /ɪŋ-/, /ɪl-/, and /ɪɹ-/. The variation is phonologically predictable. If we assume that /ɪn-/ is the underlying form, then it is easy to explain the other four allomorphs as a case of assimilation to bilabial /m/ before a bilabial, to velar /ŋ/ before a velar, to /l/ before /l/, and to /ɹ/ before /ɹ/.

When we describe this process with a word formation rule, we mention the underlying form of the prefix in the rule.

(12) $\updownarrow$ $\begin{array}{ll} \uparrow [X]_A & \alpha \\ \downarrow [ɪn[X]]_A & \text{not } \alpha \end{array}$

Phonological rules then immediately change /ɪn-/ to /ɪm-/ before a bilabial stop, etc., so that in the lexical entries, we show the different allomorphs of the prefix.[5]

(13)   **A**

ɪn[ɛlɪgŋt]	not elegant
ɪm[pɹæktɪkl̩]	not practical
ɪŋ[koɹɛkt]	not correct
ɪl[ligl̩]	not legal
ɪɹ[ɹɛgulɹ̩]	not regular

In the study of grammar, when we encounter morphophonemics, we are only concerned with the underlying form of a morpheme. We talk about what the phonological rules should do to it to produce the correct surface forms, but leave it up to a specific phonological theory to work out the details.

Stem suppletion (review)

Not all allomorphic variation is morphophonemic; any that cannot be handled by regular phonological rules is called SUPPLETION or SUPPLETIVE ALLOMORPHY. Chapter 10 "Inflectional Morphology" (p. 127) discusses one type of suppletion: words that have irregular forms in their paradigms. This is called STEM SUPPLETION. Most of the allomorphy of the English noun plurals discussed above is of this type, involving irregular patterns of suffixation and vowel changes. Recall how we list these irregularities in the lexicon.

(14)   **N**

fʊt	[− plural]	
fit	[+ plural]	foot
tʃajld	[− plural]	
tʃɪldɹen	[+ plural]	child
maʊs	[− plural]	
majs	[+ plural]	mouse

The correct surface form is inserted directly from the lexicon in deep structure.

---

[5]Phonological theories differ in their assumptions about when phonological rules apply to morphology that is generated in the lexicon. Classical Generative Phonology assumed that all phonological rules applied to the output of the transformational component, i.e., to the terminal nodes of surface structure trees. Lexical Phonology assumes that phonological rules apply immediately after each affix is applied, hence lexical entries for derived forms show the results of phonological rules, as shown in the text. Either is compatible with the general approach presented here. However, details of specific phonological theories and analyses may require revision of some of the assumptions presented in the text, particularly the underlying forms of specific morphemes and the way that words are spelled in the lexicon.

We also adopted an understanding about how these complex lexical entries interact with the regular inflectional spellout rules. We don't want the grammar to add the regular suffix *-(e)s* to the irregular stems; this would produce incorrect forms like *childrens* and *mices*. To avoid this, we have assumed that whenever the feature [+plural] is spelled out in the lexicon, we skip the regular inflectional spellout rule for that feature.

12.3. Suppletive affixation with lexical conditioning

We've considered two types of allomorphic variation so far: morphophonemics and stem suppletion. Now we turn to a different type of suppletion called SUPPLETIVE AFFIXATION. This describes cases where an affix has several allomorphs, each used with different stems. First, we look at a case where the choice of allomorph used with each stem is arbitrary.

Kiowa subject agreement

The following verb paradigms are from Kiowa (Tanoan, Oklahoma).[6]

(15) a. *à-bá·nmà*   I go   f. *yá-táy*   I wake up
        èm-bá·nmà   you go   *gyát-táy*   you wake up
        bá·nmà   he goes   *án-táy*   he wakes up
     b. *gyàt-kʰɔ́·mɔ̀*   I read   g. *gyàt-hí·nmɔ̀*   I dig
        bát-kʰɔ́·mɔ̀   you read   *bát-hí·nmɔ̀*   you dig
        gyá-kʰɔ́·mɔ̀   he reads   *gyá-hí·nmɔ̀*   he digs
     c. *gyàt-píɔ́·mɔ̀*   I cook   h. *yá-yáy*   I am busy
        bát-píɔ́·mɔ̀   you cook   *gyát-yáy*   you are busy
        gyá-píɔ́·mɔ̀   he cooks   *án-yáy*   he is busy
     d. *yá-tɔ́·zá·nmà*   I talk   i. *à-pɔ́ttɔ*   I eat
        gyát-tɔ́·zá·nmà you talk   *èm-pɔ́ttɔ*   you eat
        án-tɔ́·zá·nmà   he talks   *pɔ́ttɔ*   he eats
     e. *à-pʰɔ́*   I stand up   j. *gyàt-gúttɔ*   I write
        èm-pʰɔ́   you stand up   *bát-gúttɔ*   you write
        pʰɔ́   he stands up   *gyá-gúttɔ*   he writes

We see that each subject agreement prefix has several different forms and that the variation is too irregular to be accounted for by simple phonological rules. Therefore, it is suppletive. This time, however, the suppletion involves affixes, not stems. That is, these are not irregular verbs. There are several classes of verbs, each with a different paradigm, but within each class the inflection is perfectly regular.

How do we analyze a system like this? The first step is to list the different sets of allomorphs as in (16). Each set is used by a different class of verbs.

(16)
	Set 1	Set 2	Set 3
first person	*à-*	*gyàt-*	*yá-*
second person	*èm-*	*bát-*	*gyát-*
third person	*Ø-*	*gyá-*	*án-*

Each row in this chart contains the different allomorphs of one morpheme. Each column contains the set of allomorphs (one from each morpheme) which occurs with a particular class of stems.

---

[6]Data from Merrifield et. al. 1987, #46. Though Merrifield gives only masculine glosses for third person, I have assumed in the analysis that the forms are genuine third person (undifferentiated for gender). Merrifield's transcription is based on the Americanist phonetic tradition: *y* represents IPA *j*, and the polish hook under certain vowels presumably represents nasalization.

Now that we have identified the different sets of allomorphs, we can determine which class each verb belongs in, based on which set of allomorphs it uses.

(17)   Class 1, used with *à-, èm-, Ø-:*
       bá·nmà   go
       pʰ̀ɔ́   stand up
       pɔ́ttɔ̀   eat

(18)   Class 2, used with *gyàt-, bát-, gyá-:*
       kʰɔ́·mɔ̀   read
       píɔ́·mɔ̀   cook
       hí·nmɔ̀   dig
       gúttɔ̀   write

(19)   Class 3, used with *yá̱-, gyát-, a̱n-:*
       tó̱·zá·nmà   talk
       táy   wake up
       yáy   be busy

The next step in the analysis is to look at these classes and find out the conditioning factor for the allomorphy, if any. Is there any special reason why a given set of prefixes is used with a given verb or is the choice just arbitrary? So, we check if there is anything that all the verb stems in each class have in common.

(20)   Phonologically: Do they begin with the same or similar segments?
       Semantically: Do they have similar meanings?
       Grammatically: Are they in the same subcategory (e.g., all transitive or intransitive)?

In each case, the answer seems to be 'no'. There is no property common to all the stems in a class; the groupings of stems into classes is arbitrary.

This means that, for every verb, you have to memorize which set of prefixes it takes; there is no general way to know what set it takes based on its meaning or form. Arbitrary classes of words like these are called INFLECTIONAL CLASSES and this type of allomorphy is said to be LEXICALLY-CONDITIONED.

Formal analysis of suppletive affixation

The formal analysis of suppletive affixation is straightforward. The three inflectional classes are three subcategories of verbs.[7] In the lexicon we use a feature [class] to represent them, with numbers as its values.

(21)   **V[1 class]**
       bá·nmà   go
       pʰ̀ɔ́   stand up
       pɔ́ttɔ̀   eat

---

[7]These subcategories are not the same as the subcategories for transitivity which are discussed in chapter 8 "Verbal Valence." Within each inflectional class, some verbs are intransitive, some transitive, etc., so if we were to consider all the details, each inflectional class would be subdivided further according to transitivity. In other words, subcategorization by valence and subcategorization by inflectional class represent two independent ways to subdivide the class of verbs. In practice, there are enough different ways of subcategorizing verbs that it may be simplest to list all verbs in alphabetical order, each with its own set of features to indicate which subcategories it belongs to.

(22) **V[2 class]**

$k^h\acute{\varsigma}\cdot m\grave{\varsigma}$	read
$p\acute{\iota}\acute{\varsigma}\cdot m\grave{\varsigma}$	cook
$h\acute{\iota}\cdot nm\grave{\varsigma}$	dig
$g\acute{u}tt\grave{\vartriangle}$	write

(23) **V[3 class]**

$t\acute{\varsigma}\cdot z\acute{a}\cdot nm\grave{a}$	talk
$t\acute{a}y$	wake up
$y\acute{a}y$	be busy

When the verb gets inserted in a deep structure tree, it brings along with it a value for the feature [class], and the feature assignment rules add a value for the feature [person]. The following is the deep structure for *án-tǫ́·zá·nmà* 'he talks':

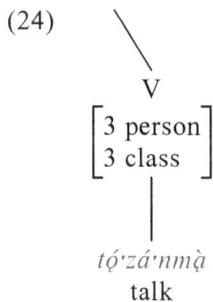

(24)

$$
\begin{array}{c}
\backslash \\
\text{V} \\
\begin{bmatrix} 3 \text{ person} \\ 3 \text{ class} \end{bmatrix} \\
| \\
t\acute{\varsigma}\cdot z\acute{a}\cdot nm\grave{a} \\
\text{talk}
\end{array}
$$

It is not necessary to write a feature assignment rule stating that verbs carry a feature for [class]; this information is already available in the lexicon and is inserted into the tree along with the other features for the stem. Feature assignment rules are only necessary when all stems of a syntactic category can have any value for a particular feature.

Now, we need to guarantee that the right allomorphs get placed on each stem by the inflectional spellout rules. We do so by including the feature [class] in each spellout rule. Since there is no suffix in third person for class 1, there is no need to write a rule for this combination of features.

Rules for class 1

(25)
$$
\begin{array}{c}
\text{V} \\
\begin{bmatrix} 1 \text{ person} \\ 1 \text{ class} \end{bmatrix} \\
[\text{X}] \quad \rightarrow \quad [\grave{a}\text{X}]
\end{array}
$$

(26)
$$
\begin{array}{c}
\text{V} \\
\begin{bmatrix} 2 \text{ person} \\ 1 \text{ class} \end{bmatrix} \\
[\text{X}] \quad \rightarrow \quad [\acute{e}m\text{X}]
\end{array}
$$

Rules for class 2

(27)
$$
\begin{array}{c}
\text{V} \\
\begin{bmatrix} 1 \text{ person} \\ 2 \text{ class} \end{bmatrix} \\
[\text{X}] \quad \rightarrow \quad [gy\grave{a}t\text{X}]
\end{array}
$$

(28)
$$
\begin{array}{c}
\text{V} \\
\begin{bmatrix} 2 \text{ person} \\ 2 \text{ class} \end{bmatrix} \\
[\text{X}] \quad \rightarrow \quad [b\acute{a}t\text{X}]
\end{array}
$$

(29)
$$
\begin{array}{c}
\text{V} \\
\begin{bmatrix} 3 \text{ person} \\ 2 \text{ class} \end{bmatrix} \\
[\text{X}] \quad \rightarrow \quad [gy\acute{a}\text{X}]
\end{array}
$$

Rules for class 3

(30)
$$V$$
$$\begin{bmatrix} 1\ person \\ 3\ class \end{bmatrix}$$
$$[X] \rightarrow [y\acute{a}X]$$

(31)
$$V$$
$$\begin{bmatrix} 2\ person \\ 3\ class \end{bmatrix}$$
$$[X] \rightarrow [gy\acute{a}tX]$$

(32)
$$V$$
$$\begin{bmatrix} 3\ person \\ 3\ class \end{bmatrix}$$
$$[X] \rightarrow [\acute{a}nX]$$

After applying rule (32) to (24), we get the following surface structure:

(33)

$$V$$
$$\begin{bmatrix} 3\ person \\ 3\ class \end{bmatrix}$$

ą̀ntǫ́·zá'nmà
he talks

12.4. Tzeltal possessor agreement: Suppletive affixation with phonological conditioning

In Kiowa, the conditioning factor for the suppletion was arbitrary. This is the most common situation with suppletive affixation, but it is not always true. For example, consider possessor prefixes in Tzeltal (Mayan; Chiapas, Mexico).[8] There are two sets of these prefixes, one used by the nouns in (34a), one by the nouns in (34b).

(34)

		first person	second person	third person
a.	father	h-tat	a-tat	s-tat
	mother	h-nan	a-nan	s-nan
	machete	h-matʃit	a-matʃit	s-matʃit
	self	h-ba	a-ba	s-ba
b.	older brother	k-itsin	aw-itsin	j-itsin
	leg	k-ok	aw-ok	j-ok
	inside(s)	k-util	aw-util	j-util
	tooth, edge	k-eh	aw-eh	j-eh

Here, unlike what we saw in Kiowa, there is an independent reason why the stems group into the two classes. The nouns in (34a) all begin with consonants, while the ones in (34b) all begin with vowels.

(35)

	first person	second person	third person
C-initial stems	h-	a-	s-
V-initial stems	k-	aw-	j-

[8]See footnote 5, p. 29.

In other words, this allomorphy is PHONOLOGICALLY-CONDITIONED.

Note that this is *not* a case of morphophonemics, even though the conditioning environment is a phonological one. Despite the phonological similarities of some of the allomorphs, no other morphemes in Tzeltal show this pattern of allomorphy, so this is not a result of a general phonological process.[9] It is suppletive.

Therefore, we write an inflectional spellout rule for each affix, as we did in Kiowa, and do not write phonological rules. But, unlike Kiowa, the inflectional spellout rules make reference to the phonological structure of the stem, rather than an arbitrary feature [class]. Thus, we include a 'C' or 'V' in the rule at the beginning of each stem.[10]

(36) a.   N $\begin{bmatrix} 1\ \text{person} \\ [\text{CX}] \end{bmatrix} \rightarrow [h\text{CX}]$ d.   N $\begin{bmatrix} 1\ \text{person} \\ [\text{VX}] \end{bmatrix} \rightarrow [k\text{VX}]$

    b.   N $\begin{bmatrix} 2\ \text{person} \\ [\text{CX}] \end{bmatrix} \rightarrow [a\text{CX}]$ e.   N $\begin{bmatrix} 2\ \text{person} \\ [\text{VX}] \end{bmatrix} \rightarrow [aw\text{VX}]$

    c.   N $\begin{bmatrix} 3\ \text{person} \\ [\text{CX}] \end{bmatrix} \rightarrow [s\text{CX}]$ f.   N $\begin{bmatrix} 3\ \text{person} \\ [\text{VX}] \end{bmatrix} \rightarrow [j\text{VX}]$

The form *htat* 'my father' is derived as follows. Rule (36a) is used to derive the surface structure, rather than (36d), because the stem begins with a consonant.

(37)   Deep: Surface:

          N   N
     [1 person]   [1 person]

         tat   *htat*
     my father   my father

12.5. Analyzing allomorphic variation in general

These three languages have provided examples of the most common types of allomorphy that you are likely to encounter. Let's take a more systematic look at how to go about analyzing allomorphy. (See also questions for analysis, p. 162.)

The first question to consider concerns the differences between the variants: is the allomorphy morphophonemic, suppletive, or a mixture of the two? If possible, we want to account for the differences by positing general phonological rules. If this can be done, we just indicate one

---

[9]Contrast this with the situation with English noun plurals. The variation in this suffix also occurs in at least four other morphemes: the third person singular present suffix on verbs, the possessive *'s* on noun phrases, and the homophonous contracted forms *'s* of *is* and *has*. The variation of the past tense suffix *-(e)d* can also be seen as an instance of the same pattern. Since the rules apply in many morphemes, they express legitimate generalizations about the language. No such generalization exists in Tzeltal. The changes are drastic enough that it would take at least three separate (and rather unnatural) phonological rules to derive one set of prefixes from the other, hardly a gain in simplicity over introducing the allomorphs directly by morphological rules.

[10]In these rules, I am assuming that there is a feature assignment rule which marks a possessed noun for a feature of [person]. This is a makeshift approach; a better treatment is presented in chapter 19 "Case and Agreement (p. 264) ."

underlying form in the grammar which (together with the phonological rules) accounts for several variants. This can simplify the grammar.[11]

However, many times no general phonological rule can be written, because the variation is too drastic (as in Kiowa) or it is confined to a single morpheme (as in Tzeltal). In these cases, we posit one phonological underlying form for *each* suppletive allomorph or irregular stem.

The next question to consider is whether the suppletion occurs in stems or in affixes. If a word has an irregular paradigm, then we say the suppletion is in the stem. We list the irregular forms in the lexicon, together with bundles of inflectional features indicating when to use each form (example: English irregular noun plurals).

If the suppletion is in an affix, then we write the inflectional spellout rules[12] in such a way that the correct allomorph is attached to each stem. This means we must find out what environment conditions the allomorphy, or to put it another way, what it is about a stem that requires one allomorph rather than another. If the stems that take one set of affixes have some phonological or other characteristic in common, we include this information in the inflectional spellout rule (example: Tzeltal). If they have nothing else in common except what allomorphs they take, then we say the allomorphy is lexically-conditioned. We group verbs in arbitrary inflectional classes in the lexicon and make reference to them in the inflectional spellout rules (e.g., Kiowa).

In some cases, a combination of approaches is necessary. For example, the allomorphy of English plurals can be accounted for partly by listing suppletive stems in the lexicon (for irregular plurals), partly by phonological rules (for the morphophonemic variants of the *-(e)s* suffix), and partly by inflectional classes of nouns (the small classes of nouns that take affixes derived from Latin).[13]

So, there are three main factors that distinguish different types of allomorphy:

(38) a. type of variation: morphophonemics versus suppletion
      b. what varies: stems versus affixes
      c. conditioning environment: lexical (arbitrary) or something else (e.g., phonological)

In principle, all three can vary independently, but usually they combine to produce the following four types:

Type	Examples
Morphophonemics affecting stems and/or affixes with phonological conditioning	Regular English noun plurals English derivational prefix /ɪn-/
Suppletion of stems	Irregular English noun plurals
Suppletion of affixes, phonological conditioning	Tzeltal possessor agreement
Suppletion of affixes, lexical conditioning	Kiowa subject agreement

---

[11]Of course, this simplification comes at the cost of some additional phonological rules. Usually, however, the savings are worth the cost, and the overall analysis (morphology plus phonology) is simplified. When the savings do not outweigh the costs, then it is simpler to treat the variation as a case of suppletion, as in the case of Tzeltal possessor agreement.

[12]Derivational morphology is usually not described as being suppletive, and thus this possibility is not discussed in the main text. Usually, each separate phonological form is treated as a separate derivational affix, rather than an allomorph. The reason is that derivational morphology is usually not systematic enough to be able to establish that two distinct forms are allomorphs of the same morpheme. It usually lacks an overall structure analogous to inflectional paradigms which can provide the basis for making this identification. There are exceptions, however. Aronoff (1976:98–110) discusses a clear case of suppletive derivational affixation, involving the different forms of the English suffix *-ion*. Still, this possibility only applies to suppletive affixation; the possibility of derivational suppletion of stems is never considered because it is always simpler to analyze such cases as two unrelated lexical items.

[13]Rather than using the feature [class], this class of nouns could be labeled [+Latinate] in the lexicon, whereas most nouns would be [–Latinate]. We would also need separate inflectional spellout rules to add the correct singular and plural suffixes to [+Latinate] stems.

12.6. Review of key terms

ALLOMORPHY (ALLOMORPHIC VARIATION) refers to variations in the form of a particular morpheme depending on its context; each of these variants is called one of its ALLOMORPHS. There are two types of allomorphy: MORPHOPHONEMICS and SUPPLETION. Suppletion can occur either in the form of IRREGULAR STEMS (STEM SUPPLETION) or in SUPPLETIVE AFFIXATION, which is the use of different SETS of affixes with different INFLECTIONAL CLASSES of stems. Suppletive affixation can be LEXICALLY CONDITIONED or PHONOLOGICALLY CONDITIONED.

If the allomorphy is morphophonemic, then only the UNDERLYING FORM is included in the lexicon or morphological rule; the allomorphy itself is handled by phonological rules which produce the correct SURFACE FORM. If it is suppletive, then the underlying form of each suppletive allomorph is included in the lexicon and/or morphological rules.

It may be helpful to refer to chapter 18 "Overall Structure of a Grammar" to help visualize how morphophonemic rules relate to the morphological rules in the grammar.

12.7. Questions for analysis

The considerations in §12.5 (p. 160) can be incorporated into a step-by-step procedure that you can use when analyzing allomorphy. This procedure also incorporates the questions for analysis (in italics) for this chapter, which identify the information to include in a description of the data for others.

1. If the morphology is inflectional, first organize your data into paradigms and make hypotheses about the grammatical categories involved. If it is derivational, list pairs of related words in parallel columns. Make tentative morpheme cuts and glosses. Make clear cuts first. Rely on contrast more than recurring partials.
2. If you find allomorphic variation, list the allomorphs of each morpheme. *Which grammatical categories or derivational affixes are involved in the variation? What classes of words do they occur on? What aspects of the variation are morphophonemic, and what aspects are suppletive?*
3. If you find morphophonemics: *What phonological processes are responsible for the variation? What is the underlying form of each morpheme?* Include only the underlying form in the grammar rules or lexicon. Do as much with phonology as you reasonably can.
4. If, after doing this, there is still some allomorphy unaccounted for, treat it as suppletive.[14] *Does this suppletion primarily affect stems or affixes?*
5. If the allomorphy is in stems:
    a. *What parts of the paradigm are irregular?*
    b. List the irregular forms in the lexicon, with the appropriate inflectional features.
6. If the allomorphy is in affixes:
    a. Group the allomorphs of several related affixes into sets, one set for each class of stems. *How many inflectional classes are there?* Make a list of the stems in each class.
    b. *What is the conditioning factor for the variation?* Check each class of stems for phonological or other similarities that might define them as a class. If you find them, refer to these similarities in the inflectional spellout rules. If you find no similarities, you will have to treat the class as an arbitrary lexical subcategory. This means using a feature like [class] to identify each subcategory in the lexicon, then referring to this feature in the inflectional spellout rules.

This procedure is summarized in the following chart:

---

[14]Since most suppletion is inflectional, the following questions presuppose this. But to handle derivational suppletion of affixes (see footnote 12), the grammar would require a separate word formation rule for each variant. If there is a clear conditioning factor, this can be mentioned in the word formation rule. If the choice of variant is arbitrary, then nothing more needs to be done by rule since the lexical entries of the derived forms will show which variant is used in each case.

(39)

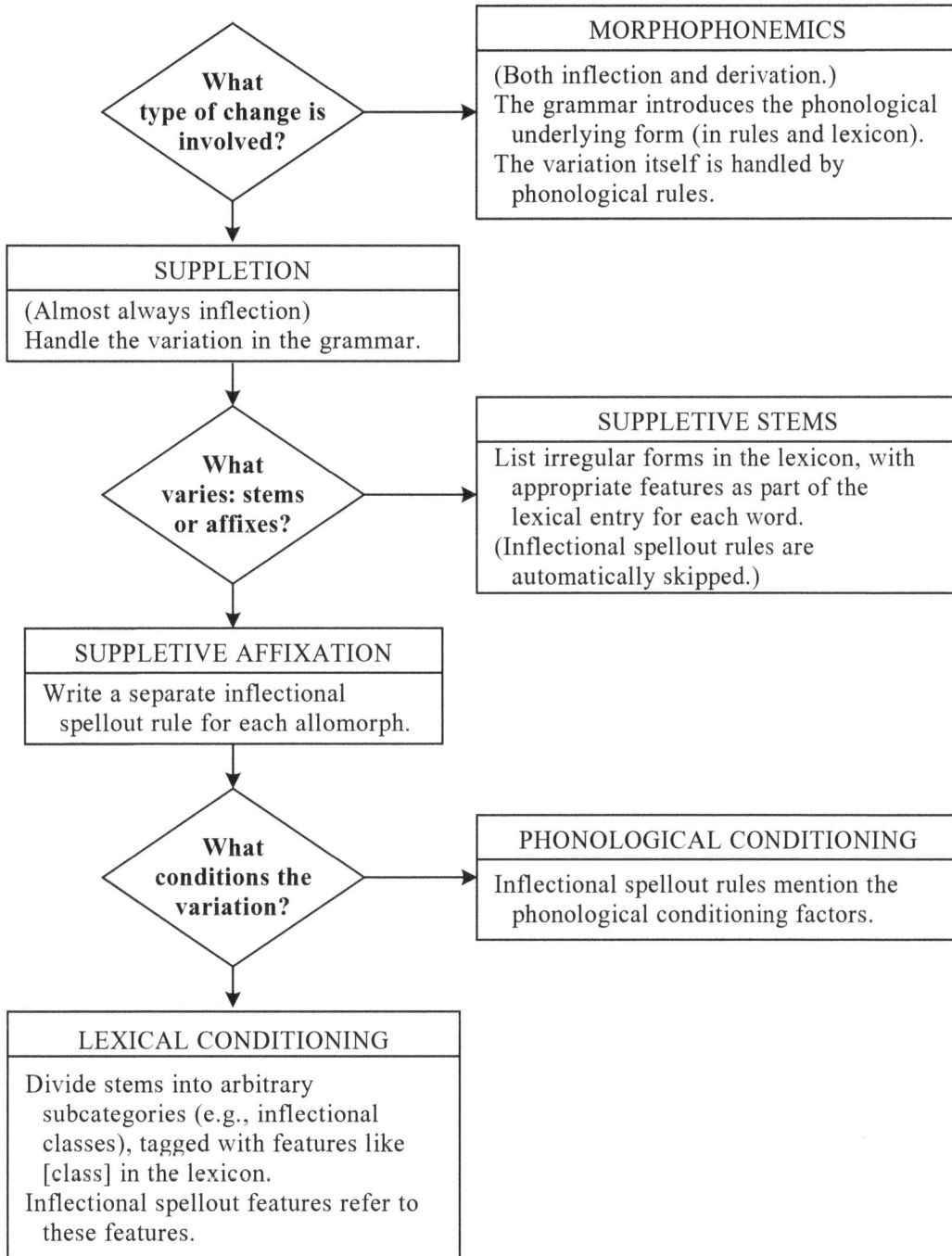

12.8. Sample descriptions

English noun plurals

Most English count nouns form plurals by adding a suffix /-z/, which has two morphophonemic variants, /-s/ and /-ɪz/.

(1)   *dɔg-z, bɔj-z, gˌɪl-z, kaɹ-z*   dogs, boys, girls, cars
       kæt-s, kəp-s, ɹejk-s   cats, cups, rakes
       hoɹs-ɪz, wɔtʃ-ɪz, wɪʃ-ɪz   horses, watches, wishes

One small subcategory of nouns marks number following a Latin pattern, with /-əs/ for singular and /-aj/ for plural.

(2)   *ələmn-əs*   *ələmn-aj*   alumnus, alumni
       hɪpopatom-əs *hɪpopatom-aj*   hippopotamus, hippopotami

Several others have various irregular patterns involving suffixal material and changes of stem vowels.

(3)   *mæn*   *mɛn*   man, men
       wʊmən   *wɪmən*   woman, women
       tʃajld   *tʃɪld-ɹən*   child, children
       aks   *aks-ən̩*   ox, oxen
       maus   *majs*   mouse, mice

Still others are irregular in not marking number at all, such as *sheep* and *fish*; their singular and plural forms are identical.

Kiowa subject agreement

In Kiowa, agreement with person of the subject is indicated with verbal prefixes. There are three sets of prefixes, one for each inflectional class of verbs.

	Set 1	Set 2	Set 3
first person	à-	gyàt-	yá̗-
second person	èm-	bát-	gyát-
third person	Ø-	gyá-	á̗n-

Classification of verbs into inflectional classes is entirely arbitrary.

Tzeltal possessor prefixes

In Tzeltal, the person of the possessor is indicated on possessed nouns with two sets of prefixes. One set is used for consonant-initial noun stems, the other for vowel-initial stems.

	first person	second person	third person
C-initial stems	*h-*	*a-*	*s-*
V-initial stems	*k-*	*aw-*	*j-*

12.9. For further reading

A discussion of morphophonemics can be found in practically any textbook on Generative Phonology (or more recent approaches). Kenstowicz and Kisseberth (1979:45–75), for example, devote a full chapter to showing why morphophonemics should be handled by phonological rules and not in the same way as suppletion. Along the way, they provide several examples of phonological rules and underlying forms.

For more examples of allomorphy of different types, see Matthews (1974:77–115). Jensen (1990) presents an alternative theoretical approach to the one explained here, which places inflectional rules in the lexicon alongside word formation rules. His discussion includes suppletion and inflectional classes (pp. 120–23) and morphophonemics (pp. 157–90).

13
Nonlinear Affixation

13.1. Goals and prerequisites

This chapter will help you do the following:

- ◉ identify and describe the following types of nonlinear affixation: infixation, mutation, subtraction, suprafixation, reduplication, discontinuity, and total fusion
- ◉ construct a formal analysis to account for them

It assumes that you are familiar with the following material:

- ✓ inflectional morphology, feature assignment rules, and inflectional spellout rules (chapter 10 "Inflectional Morphology")
- ✓ derivational morphology and word formation rules (chapter 11 "Derivational Morphology")
- ✓ suppletion and morphophonemic variation (chapter 12 "Suppletion and Morphophonemics")

13.2. Other types of affixation

Up to this point, we have conceived of morphemes as discrete chunks of material that can be strung together like beads on a string, one after another. This way of combining one morpheme with another can be called LINEAR; it includes prefixation, suffixation, and compounding. Although much morphology is linear, some is not.

In this chapter, we look more closely at NONLINEAR MORPHOLOGY.[1] Nonlinear morphology is, unusual (that is, most morphology is linear), but at the same time it is not uncommon for a language to have at least one or two instances of it, and in some languages it is quite widespread.

As we get into the topic, we encounter a small problem with the presentation. Rules for nonlinear morphology often need to make reference to the internal phonological structure of words. How this would be done depends on the phonological theory that is being used. I've tried to use a fairly generic notation for the phonological details, one that should not be too difficult to adapt to any phonological framework. Modify it as needed, to fit your theoretical assumptions and the details of the language you're working on.

---

[1]In this chapter, the term NONLINEAR is used somewhat loosely. It includes some things that might, under some sets of phonological assumptions, actually be considered linear, but which have not always been regarded as such. As a practical matter, the chapter attempts to include all morphological marking strategies other than straightforward prefixing, suffixing, and compounding, and to provide an overall typology of such strategies (see the questions for analysis).

Infixation

An INFIX is an affix which occurs inside the stem to which it is attached. One of the most famous examples of an infix is in Chontal of Oaxaca (Hokan, Mexico).[2]

(1)		Singular	Plural
	squirrel	*cece*	*cełce*
	foreigner	*tuwa*	*tułwa*
	woman	*akanʔoʔ*	*akałnʔoʔ*
	possum	*łipo*	*łiłpo*
	flower bud	*łekutuʔ*	*łekułtuʔ*
	small gourd jar	*lalipu*	*laliłpu*
	mole	*afuʔwa*	*afułʔwa*
	lizard	*kwepoʔ*	*kwełpoʔ*

The infix is *-ł-*, which is added inside the stem to form the plural. Note the use of hyphens on both sides of the form to identify it as an infix.

When analyzing infixes, it is important to determine exactly where in the stem the infix is placed. Here, it appears that the infix is placed before the final syllable. This can be expressed in the following inflectional spellout rule (assuming that number in Chontal is inflectional).

(2)
$$\begin{array}{c} N \\ [+\text{plural}] \end{array}$$
$$[\;\; \underset{1}{X} \;\; \underset{2}{\sigma} \;\;] \rightarrow [\;\; \underset{1}{X} \;\; ł \;\; \underset{2}{\sigma} \;\;]$$

Note that it has to refer to the internal structure of the stem in order to pick out the final syllable (represented here by σ). To keep track of the different pieces of the stem, we sometimes include numbers underneath; these are called INDICES.

The following chart shows how the rule applies to two different stems above:

(3)
X	σ	→	X	ł	σ
1	2		1		2
ce	ce		ce	ł	ce
aka	nʔoʔ		aka	ł	nʔoʔ

Note how the X in the rule can refer to one or more syllables.

Palauan (Austronesian, Republic of Belau) has a derivational infix, used to derive abstract nouns from verbs.[3]

(4)
	V		**N**	
،	*bəkeu*	be brave	*bləkeu*	bravery
	bulak	be deceitful	*blulak*	lie
	kasoes	see each other	*klasoes*	relationship (seeing each other)

This can be expressed in the following word formation rule:

---

[2]Data from Viola Waterhouse (personal communication); some examples were published previously in Merrifield, et al. 1987, #17. Transcription modified along the lines of Jensen (1990:64) in his retranscription of the data from Merrifield; /c/ is IPA /ts/; /nʔ/ is phonetically [nʔ]. The infix *-ł-* illustrated here is one of several strategies for marking plurality in Chontal; other nouns use suffix-infix combinations (a type of discontinuity, as discussed later). See Waterhouse (1962:95) for further data and discussion.

[3]Data from Josephs (1975:191ff). For simplicity, the discussion ignores many irregularities of the data. The class here characterized as V might be better characterized as [+V], i.e., including both verbs and adjectives; see the analysis of Palauan in chapter 14 "Nonactive Complements" (p. 193).

(5)
$$\begin{array}{c} \uparrow \\ \downarrow \end{array} \quad \begin{array}{ccc} [& C & X &]_V \quad \alpha \\ & 1 & 2 \\ [& C & l & X &]_N \quad \text{abstraction related to } \alpha \\ & 1 & & 2 \end{array}$$

Do not confuse infixes with prefixes or suffixes that occur in inner positions in a word. An affix is an infix only if it occurs inside *the stem;*[4] it is not enough just to be surrounded on both sides by other parts of the word. For example, recall the Fore word *natuwi* 'I ate (yesterday)' (from chapter 10 "Inflectional Morphology," p. 123).

(6)   *na   -t   -uw   -i*
       eat   -far.past   -1sg   -Indic
       I ate (yesterday).

The morphemes *-t* and *-uw* are suffixes, not infixes, because they occur *after* the stem *na,* not inside it. Thus we write them with only one hyphen each, not with hyphens on both sides.

Mutation

Sometimes affixation results in a change, or MUTATION, of material already present, rather than the addition of new material. Consider plurals in one class of German nouns.[5]

(7)
	Singular	Plural
father	*fatəʀ*	*fetəʀ*
mother	*mutəʀ*	*mytəʀ*
cloister	*klostəʀ*	*kløstəʀ*

Plurals are formed by fronting the stressed vowel of the stem.[6]

(8)
$$\begin{array}{c} N \\ [+\text{plural}] \end{array}$$

$$[\quad X \quad \acute{V} \quad Y \quad] \rightarrow [\quad X \quad \acute{V} \quad Y \quad]$$
$$ 1 \quad 2 \quad 3 1 \quad 2 \quad 3$$
$$[-\text{back}]$$

Typically these are called MORPHEME PROCESSES or are even classified as a type of morpheme called a PROCESS MORPHEME.

Subtraction

In rare cases, instead of adding segments, affixation removes them. The perfective forms of verbs in Tohono O'odham (Uto-Aztecan, Arizona)[7] have one less consonant than the stems.

---

[4]Or, more precisely, inside whatever it attaches to, whether that be a root, stem, or even some partially-derived inflected form.

[5]Data from Jensen 1990:72, retranscribed broadly with IPA phonetic symbols.

[6]Adjustments to this rule would be necessary for longer stems. The change in height from /ɑ/ to /e/ can be handled by a regular phonological rule operating on the output of the inflectional spellout rule.

[7]Data and analysis from Dean Saxton (personal communication). Other allomorphs of this affix involve both the subtraction of the final consonant and the addition of a suffix *-i.*

(9)   Stem   Perfective
        happen   *tʃuʔidʒ*   *tʃuʔi*
        drip   *ʔoʔot*   *ʔoʔo*
        taste   *dʒɯɯk*   *dʒɯɯ*

One might be tempted to say that things are the other way around, that the 'stem' form has an added suffix which is not in the Perfective. However, this 'suffix' could be any consonant in the language! It is a much simpler analysis to say that the perfective form removes the final consonant from the stem, i.e., that this is a process of SUBTRACTION and that the 'morpheme' involved is a SUBTRACTIVE MORPHEME.

(10)   V
        [+perfective]
        [X   C   ]   →   [X   ]
            1   2   1

Suprafixation

Affixes can also occur 'on top of' the stem, or more precisely, simultaneous with it. Such affixes are called SUPRAFIXES; they consist of SUPRASEGMENTAL elements like tone, stress, and nasalization.

English appears to have a derivational suprafix consisting of a stress shift, which derives nouns from verbs.

(11)   **V**   **N**
        addréss   *áddress*
        convért   *cónvert*
        knock óut   *knóckout*
        permít   *pérmit*
        pervért   *pérvert*
        rejéct   *réject*
        repéat   *répeat*
        subjéct   *súbject*

One possible analysis of this is in terms of a word formation rule that shifts the stress.[8] In the following rule, each σ represents a distinct syllable.

(12)   ↑[X   σ   σ́   ]$_V$ 'α'
        ↓[X   σ́   σ   ]$_N$ 'outcome or product of α'

Many languages rely on tone for inflection. Consider these verbs from Atatlahuca Mixtec (Otomanguean, Mexico).[9] High tone is indicated by an acute accent; mid tone is unmarked.

(13)   Realis   Irrealis
        weave   *kųnų*   *kų́nų*
        swallow   *koko*   *kóko*
        call   *kąną*   *ką́ną*
        hit   *kąnį*   *ką́nį*

---

[8]Other analyses are possible. Chomsky and Halle (1991:96ff), for example, offer one in which the category of the word is basic and it controls which syllable stress is assigned to.

[9]Data from Ruth Mary Alexander (personal communication). Polish hook represents nasalization.

The realis forms have all mid tones; the irrealis forms have a high tone on the first syllable. At first glance, this appears to be a mutation—a change of tone—and that is one possible analysis. But, it can also be analyzed as a type of prefixation, given the right analytical approach.

Tone behaves rather independently of other characteristics of a segment and usually is represented today on a separate level called the tonal tier. Tones on the tonal tier are linked to individual segments with what are called 'association lines'.[10] For example, the realis form of 'weave' might be represented as follows (where M stands for mid tone):

(14)   M
         ⌃
     k ų n ų

Note that one tone can be linked to more than one segment.

To account for the data in (13), we assume that the underlying form of this class of verbs has the tone pattern found in realis forms: all mid tones. We also assume the underlying form of this class of verbs does not include the association lines, so it appears in the lexicon as follows:

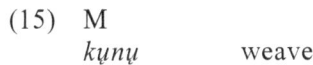

(15) M
      kųnų   weave

For the realis form, little more is necessary. The association lines would be supplied later by automatic principles (part of the phonology) in such a way that each vowel is associated with a tone. Since two vowels can share the one mid tone, this produces the surface form kųnų, as in (14).

How does the grammar generate the irrealis form? The deep structure for the irrealis of 'weave' would look like this (using brackets around the terminal node):

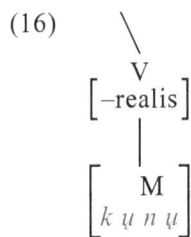

(16)   \
           V
       $\begin{bmatrix} -realis \end{bmatrix}$
           |
       $\begin{bmatrix} M \\ k\ ų\ n\ ų \end{bmatrix}$

Now we need an inflectional spellout rule, which adds an H (high) tone to the tonal tier:

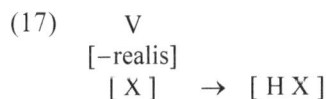

(17)   V
       [−realis]
         [X]   →   [H X]

This would modify (16) to produce the following (syntactic) surface structure:

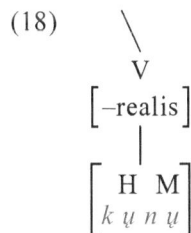

(18)   \
           V
       $\begin{bmatrix} -realis \end{bmatrix}$
           |
       $\begin{bmatrix} H\ M \\ k\ ų\ n\ ų \end{bmatrix}$

The association principles in the phonology would then link up tones with vowels, producing the correct surface form, with high tone on the first syllable and mid tone on the second.

---

[10]For ease of presentation, I adopt the simplest autosegmental assumptions about what levels exist and how they are linked.

(19)

$$
\diagdown
$$
$$
V
$$
$$
\begin{bmatrix} -\text{realis} \end{bmatrix}
$$
$$
\mid
$$
$$
\begin{bmatrix} \text{H} & \text{M} \\ k\ u\ n\ u \end{bmatrix}
$$

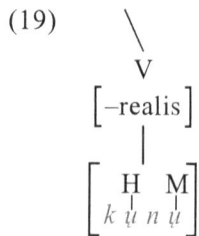

Notice that in an analysis like this, the rule (17) is essentially a prefixing rule which only has the *appearance* of changing the tone on the first syllable. The difference from prefixes we have seen before is that this is a prefix on a suprasegmental tier; the traditional label SUPRAFIXATION is based more on appearances than on a specific analysis.[11]

Reduplication

REDUPLICATION is a type of morphological marking which involves a partial or complete repetition of a stem. In Sierra Popoluca (Mixe-Zoquean, Mexico),[12] a verb stem is reduplicated to indicate repetitive aspect.

(20) *hoks-pa*   he hoes
      hoks-oʔj-pa   he hoes here and there
      *hoks-**hoks**-oʔj-pa*   he keeps on hoeing here and there

      pet-pa   he sweeps
      ped-oʔj-pa   he sweeps here and there
      *pet-**ped**-oʔj-pa*   he keeps on sweeping here and there

      wiʔk-pa   he eats
      *wiʔk-**wik**-neʔ-pa*   he keeps on eating over and over

Although the reduplication is very productive and does not change word class, it is best analyzed as derivational because it is irrelevant to syntactic rules and it occurs inside two other suffixes with similar meanings (*-oʔj* and *-neʔ*) which are more clearly derivational. The following word formation rule expresses the process:

(21) $\uparrow$ [X]$_V$ α
      $\downarrow$ [XX]$_V$ α continuously

When only part of a stem is reduplicated, the reduplicated portion is usually one phonological unit, such as a segment or a syllable. In Ilocano (Austronesian, Philippines), a reduplicated syllable indicates plural.[13]

---

[11]One of the benefits of recent work in phonology has been that types of affixation formerly thought to be nonlinear turn out to be prefixes or suffixes, given the proper assumptions about phonological structure. In general, a morpheme's classification as a prefix, suffix, infix, etc., depends to some extent on the particular theoretical framework used to describe it.

[12]Data from Ben Elson (personal communication, cf. Elson 1960:86–87, 101–2), who notes two details apparent in the data. One, a stem-final consonant voices before certain suffixes, changing /pet/ to [ped] (cf. Elson 1960:12). Two, a glottal stop deletes in the unstressed syllable of a reduplicated form. Morphological or phonological rules handling these details would need to be ordered after the word formation rule. Transcription based on the practical orthography, but using standard IPA symbols.

[13]Data from Jensen 1990:70, citing Gleason 1955:28.

(22)   Singular   Plural

    dish   *píŋgan*   *piŋpíŋgan*
    field   *tálon*   *taltálon*
    road   *dálan*   *daldálan*
    life   *bíag*   *bibíag*
    carabao   *nuá*   *nunuá*
    head   *úlo*   *ulúlo*

Partial reduplication can be thought of as addition of an affix which is only partially specified for phonological features. Here, we have a reduplicative prefix consisting of a CVC syllable. This can be represented in the following inflectional spellout rule, which prefixes an empty CVC syllable to the stem:

(23)   N σ
       [+plural] $\bigwedge$
        [X]   →   [CVC X]

(Syllable structure is represented by a syllable node σ which is connected with association lines to individual segments.)

This rule assumes that there is some mechanism available for filling in the specific segments in the prefix. One way to do this is to assume that a reduplication rule is automatically followed by a rule which copies in adjacent segments from the stem.[14] Sometimes a C or V position cannot be filled because the stem is missing a consonant or vowel in the right position and thus is dropped from the surface form.

(24)   fields   lives   heads
    Underlying form of stem   *talon*   *biag*   *ulo*
    Add CVC prefix   CVC-*talon*   CVC-*biag*   CVC-*ulo*
    Copy segments into empty CVC slots *tal-talon*   *biC-biag*   *Cul-ulo*
    Drop remaining empty slots   *taltalon*   *bibiag*   *ululo*

Chickasaw (Muskogean, USA) provides examples of two variations on reduplication, a reduplicative infix and a more complete specification of the reduplicated portion.[15]

(25) *yopi*   he's swimming   *toksali*   he's working
    yo-hõ-pi he goes swimming all the time   *toksa-hã-li* he works all the time

This infix consists of /h/ plus a nasalized copy of the second to last vowel; only the vowel quality is left unspecified. It is inserted just before the final syllable.[16]

(26)   V
       [+repetitive]
        [X σ] → [X σ σ]

            1   2   1   h   V   2
                                  [+nasal]

A single segment can also be reduplicated. Some adjectives in American Sign Language have intensive forms which consist of a pause at the initial position of the movement, followed by a faster

---

[14]Presumably part of universal grammar, so it doesn't need to be specified in each language.

[15]Data from Anderson (1985a:169). The letter *y* presumably represents IPA [j].

[16]For completeness, some stipulation or general principle would have to specify that the reduplicated vowel gets its features from the vowel to the left.

than normal movement. For example, 'slow' consists of drawing the right fingertips along the back of the left hand from fingertips to wrist, with both hands palm down and fingers spread. The intensive form, meaning 'very slow', involves a pause of the right hand over the fingertips of the left, followed by a faster movement back to the wrist. (Ironically, this results in a fast movement expressing the idea 'very slow'.)

In signed languages, movements are analogous to vowels and their endpoints (called 'locations' or 'holds') to consonants. Thus, this process can be seen as lengthening of the initial 'consonant' (a pause at the initial position), followed by a shorter 'vowel' (faster movement). The lengthening of the initial location can be represented as reduplication of a single consonant segment.[17]

(27)   ↑[CX]$_A$ α
       ↓[CCX]$_A$ very α

Unlike other types of affixation, reduplication tends to express a fairly narrow set of meanings, such as plurality, intensity ('very'), or some type of aspect, especially repetitive or habitual. There seems to be a natural tendency to use repetition of form to symbolize quantity of an object, degree of an abstract quality, or repetition of an event. Reduplication shows that the association between meaning and form is not entirely arbitrary.

13.3. Discontinuous affixation

Sometimes, a morpheme involves two or more of the operations we've discussed so far. For example, in Kaiwá (Tupí-Guaraní, Brazil),[18] negation is expressed by prefixing ^{n}d- and suffixing -i simultaneously. (Sometimes this is referred to as a CIRCUMFIX.)

(28)   a. *o-gʷapi-se*   he/she wants to sit
           3-sit-want

       b. ^{n}*d-o-gʷapi-se-i*   he/she doesn't want to sit
           Neg-3-sit-want-Neg

       c. *o-gʷata*   he/she is walking
           3-walk

       d. ^{n}*d-o-gʷata-i*   he/she is not walking
           Neg-3-walk-Neg

Since there is a prefix (*o-* 'third person') inside the negative prefix (closer to the stem) and '3 person' is almost certainly inflectional, a good initial hypothesis is to treat the negative affix as inflectional too. We need a feature assignment rule and two inflectional spellout rules for these examples.[19]

---

[17]Signed language researchers usually use M and H to represent 'movement' and 'hold'. Though the analogy of M and H to vowels and consonants is widely-recognized, some researchers are not yet ready to say that they are exactly the same thing. Following an analysis by David Perlmutter (personal communication) I have used C in the rule to represent 'hold' so that students will have sample rules to look at that are more like what they might encounter in spoken languages; this also reinforces the point that signed languages are very similar to spoken languages. The shortening of the following movement can be handled by a phonetic rule of 'compensatory shortening', analogous to what happens in some spoken languages, which shortens vowels after doubled consonants and keeps the overall length of the syllable approximately the same. An alternative analysis can be given for the initial hold, which lengthens it (a mutation) instead of reduplicating it. In some current phonological theories, there is no formal difference between the two approaches.

[18]Data from John Taylor (personal communication); based on a lab problem attributed to Lorraine Bridgeman.

[19]The form *gʷapi-se* 'wants to sit' is presumably a derived form listed separately in the lexicon; the word formation rule and lexical entry for it are omitted.

(29)

$$V \rightarrow \begin{bmatrix} \pm \text{ negative} \\ \begin{Bmatrix} 1 \\ 2 \\ 3 \end{Bmatrix} \text{person} \end{bmatrix}$$

(30)

$$\underset{[\,\text{X}\,]}{\overset{\text{V}}{[3\text{ person}]}} \rightarrow [\,o\text{X}]$$

(31)

$$\underset{[\,\text{X}\,]}{\overset{\text{V}}{[+\text{negative}]}} \rightarrow [\,{}^{n}d\text{X}i\,]$$

Rule (31), which attaches the negative prefix/suffix, must be applied after (30), since the negative prefix appears outside the prefix for person.

In Choctaw (Muskogean, USA),[20] negation is indicated by a combination of a prefix *ak*-, an infix -*ʔ*-, and a mutation of the final vowel to /o/. For the sake of illustration, let's assume negation is inflectional in Choctaw.

(32)		
	malili	he/she is running
	akmaliʔlo	he/she is not running

(33)

V
[+negative]

[	X	C	V	]	→	[	*ak*	X	*ʔ*	C	*o*	]
	1	2	3					1		2	3	

In German, in addition to the class of nouns mentioned above, there is another similar class which lacks /əʀ/ in the singular; the class shown above in (7) has it in both singular and plural. Both classes have a vowel change in the plural.

(34)		Singular	Plural
	forest	*valt*	*veldəʀ*
	book	*bux*	*byçəʀ*

These examples can be accommodated by modifying the earlier rule to add /əʀ/ if it is not there already. The parentheses allow it to work with both sets of examples; if the stem already ends in /əʀ/, as in (7), the ending is left unchanged.[21]

(35)

N
[+plural]

[	X	V́	Y	(*əʀ*)	]	→	[	X	V́	Y	*əʀ*	]
	1	2	3	4				1	2	3	4	
									[−back]			

[20]Data from Doris Payne (personal communication).

[21]A phonological rule devoicing word-final obstruents must apply after (35). Also, /ç/ in the plural of *buch* 'book' in (34) is palatalized from /x/, due to a phonological rule that also applies after (35).

The most elaborate use of discontinuous affixation occurs in Semitic languages like Classical Arabic.[22] Roots in Semitic languages typically consist of three consonants, with no vowels; the vowels in the stems are supplied by discontinuous derivational affixes. Compare the different stems derived from the root *k_t_b* 'write'. Notice how vowels and other consonants are filled in around the root consonants *k*, *t*, and *b* in each of the following:

(36) a. ***katab***   write
      b. ***kātab***   write to (someone)
      c. ***ʔaktab***   dictate, cause to write
      d. ***takātab***   correspond, write to each other
      e. ***ktatab***   be registered
      f. ***staktab***   ask someone to write

Each derivational affix is discontinuous; it consists of a combination of prefixed, suffixed, and infixed material. Many other roots can receive the same affixes; they represent regular derivational processes. Like most derivational morphology, the patterns are not completely productive and not all the meanings are easily predictable, but they do form a vital part of the structure of the language.[23]

13.4. Total fusion

Recall that one type of suppletion is irregular inflection of stems. This can be viewed as a case of TOTAL FUSION between a stem and one or more affixes, so that their individual identities have been obscured or lost.

Total fusion can also take place between two stems or two affixes. The classic example of this is from French. Whenever the preposition *à* [a] 'to' occurs with the masculine definite article *le* [lə] 'the', they fuse to form what is sometimes called a PORTMANTEAU form.[24] One never says [a lə]; instead one says [o].

(37) Syntactic structure
      Standard spelling   *a   le   chien*
      Phonetic transcription   *a   lə   ʃjɛ̃*
                                      to   the   dog
      Actual pronunciation
      Standard spelling   *au   chien*
      Phonetic transcription   *o   ʃjɛ̃*
                                      to.the   dog

One way to account for this is to posit a rule that readjusts the strings in the terminal nodes.[25]

(38)   P   D
       [a] [lə]   ⇒ [o]

Do not confuse total fusion of two morphemes, which is quite rare, with the very common case of a single affix representing more than one inflectional feature. For example, the suffixes on verbs in

---

[22]Data from Anderson (1985b:34–39).

[23]For an analysis of such patterns, see McCarthy 1981.

[24]The term 'total fusion' is better than 'portmanteau' for this class of phenomena because 'portmanteau' as it is customarily used is rather ill-defined. Also, it calls attention to the similarities between portmanteau and other phenomena like irregular inflection and fusion of two affixes. The specific morphological phenomenon of 'total fusion' has no particular relation to the general category of 'fusional' languages discussed in chapter 4 "Introduction to Morphology" (p. 31).

[25]Such a rule probably must be ordered after certain phonological rules, since the rule that deletes the vowel in the article before a vowel-initial noun blocks (38): *a l'oncle* 'to the uncle', not **au oncle*.

Spanish and other European languages *regularly* indicate a combination of person, number, and tense.

(39)   *anda-s*
       walk-2SgPresent

There are not separate suffixes for 'second person', 'singular', and 'present'; these features are always represented together by one suffix, so this is not a case of total fusion. What is meant by 'total fusion' is an *irregular* interaction between two distinct morphemes, each of which can occur independently of the other.

Also, do not confuse total fusion with the obscuring of morpheme boundaries that sometimes results from the operation of regular phonological rules. What we are talking about here happens to specific morphemes, not to any pair of morphemes that happen to have certain phonological characteristics.

13.5. On the definition of 'morpheme'

The material in this chapter illustrates again why it is important not to think naively about a morpheme as a 'minimal meaningful unit'. For example, a discontinuous affix is not obviously a single unit; rather it appears to be two or more units. It is not at all obvious how processes like mutation or subtraction are 'units' at all. Of course, one could stretch the definition to accommodate these cases (as people do when they use the term PROCESS MORPHEME). However, whenever we start stretching the definition of a technical term so that it no longer has the obvious meaning that people would first suspect, it may be time to look for a new definition.

Recall that in chapter 4 "Introduction to Morphology" (p. 27) we provided one.

(40)   A morpheme is 'a consistent and unanalyzable association of phonological, grammatical, and semantic information'.

This is carefully worded so that the 'phonological...information' in the morpheme need not be a single string of segments, but may be several such strings (discontinuity), a phonological string that is not fully specified (reduplication), or a morphological process (mutation, subtraction).

All the types of morphological marking presented in this chapter clearly fall under the revised definition. They all represent consistent associations which we can describe precisely by writing rules. All involve a three-way association of phonology, grammar, and semantics; the rules all refer to grammatical categories like N and V, details of pronunciation, and meaning (either directly or indirectly via inflectional features). All the associations are unanalyzable; we can't break up the morpheme further into any parts that have this three-way association.

13.6. Review of key terms

In contrast to LINEAR affixation, such as prefixation, suffixation, and compounding, we have considered several different types of NONLINEAR affixation in this chapter: INFIXATION, MUTATION (= PROCESS MORPHEME or MORPHEME PROCESS), SUBTRACTION, SUPRAFIXATION, and REDUPLICATION. Any of these can be the only expression of a particular meaning, or they may be combined with each other in DISCONTINUOUS AFFIXATION (CIRCUMFIXES). As a postscript, we also expanded our understanding of TOTAL FUSION to include such things as PORTMANTEAU.

To handle this type of morphology, inflectional spellout rules and word formation rules need to mention the internal phonological structure of the stem. Often, numerical INDICES are necessary to keep track of the different elements involved in the rule. In the case of suprafixes, the rule must refer to SUPRASEGMENTAL elements.

13.7. Questions for analysis

Is there any morphology that is not a straightforward matter of adding a prefix or suffix to a stem/root? Specifically, are there any instances of the following:

1. infixation: What material is inserted? Where, exactly, is it inserted?
2. mutation: What material changes? To what?
3. subtraction: What material is removed?
4. suprafixation: What suprasegmental tier is affected: tone, stress, nasalization, or something else? What changes take place? Are they best analyzed as a matter of adding a new element to the tier or as a change of material that is already present on the stem?
5. reduplication: Is this total reduplication or partial? If partial, how much of the affix is invariant and how much does it depend on the phonological shape of the stem?
6. discontinuity: Are there any affixes that consist of two or more 'pieces'? What are they? What are the properties of each piece (as indicated by the other questions about morphological marking in the previous question and in other chapters)?
7. total fusion: Are there any cases where what appears to be one morpheme is better analyzed as a fusion of two other morphemes, each of which can occur separately?

In all these cases, of course, also ask the usual questions about what the affix means, under what conditions it occurs, and whether there is any suppletive or morphophonemic variation.

13.8. Sample descriptions

Palauan abstract nominalizer

Palauan has a derivational infix *-l-* 'nominalizer' which is inserted after the first consonant of a verb. The resulting noun generally refers to some abstract quality or an event, although the meaning is not fully predictable.

V		N	
bəkeu	be brave	*bləkeu*	bravery
bulak	be deceitful	*blulak*	lie
kasoes	see each other	*klasoes*	relationship (seeing each other)

German noun plurals

Formation of plural nouns in German often involves fronting a back vowel in the stem in addition to the plural suffix *-əʀ*.

	Singular	Plural
forest	*valt*	*veldəʀ*
book	*bux*	*byçəʀ*

Some nouns, curiously, also have what appears to be the plural suffix in the singular form; in these, vowel fronting is the only indication of number.

	Singular	Plural
father	*fatəʀ*	*fetəʀ*
mother	*mutəʀ*	*mytəʀ*
cloister	*klostəʀ*	*kløstəʀ*

13.9. For further reading

Matthews (1974:116–35) and Jensen (1990:63–85) cover roughly the same ground as in this chapter. Spencer (1991:133–72) reviews various proposals that have been made for analyzing such things as discontinuous affixation, reduplication, and suprafixation.

As illustrated above, Semitic languages like Hebrew and Arabic have some of the most elaborate examples of discontinuous morphology in the world. Anderson (1985b:34–35) provides an introduction to them. Indeed, that whole chapter taken together with another chapter in the same book (Anderson 1985a) provide a good overview of morphological marking. These two chapters tie together the whole subject while illustrating important concepts in detail in several specific languages. (Be aware, though, that 'word formation' in those chapters includes inflection as well as derivation, while in this book 'word formation rules' are only for derivational morphology.)

Anderson (1992:48–72) discusses the range of problems that plague traditional conceptions of MORPHEME (and with them most item and arrangement approaches to morphology). It presents a word and paradigm conception of morphology which is built around words and morphological processes (rules) rather than morphemes. (This is the theoretical basis on which the discussions of morphology in this textbook are based.) This position is not universally accepted, however; Spencer (1991:12–21) summarizes the two perspectives about morphemes in terms of 'Morphemes: Things or rules?'.

For more on the segmental analysis of signed languages, see the first three papers in Fischer and Siple 1990. These are somewhat technical, but may be of interest because they provide a review of literature on the subject, draw out the similarities between signed and spoken languages, and include discussion about some of the nonlinear morphological processes presented above, especially reduplication.

Syntax Group 2

14
Nonactive Complements

14.1. Goals and prerequisites

This chapter will help you do the following:

- ◉ identify different types of nonactive complements, distinguishing them from other complements, from adjuncts, and from each other
- ◉ identify special clause structures used to assert location, existence, and possession
- ◉ use appropriate terminology to describe both their meaning and structure informally
- ◉ see past misleading glosses to make good hypotheses about structure
- ◉ provide a formal analysis for clauses with nominal, adjectival, and locative complements
- ◉ list at least four ways that languages can differ in the way they express states

It assumes that you are familiar with the following material:

- ✓ basic NP structure (chapter 7 "Embedding and Noun Phrase Structure")
- ✓ strict subcategorization (chapter 8 "Verbal Valence")
- ✓ structures used for obliques and the complement/adjunct distinction (chapter 9 "Obliques")

It's also helpful, but not essential, to have covered the following, since there are passing references to them:

- ✓ inflectional features and irregular inflection (chapter 10 "Inflectional Morphology")
- ✓ derivational morphology (chapter 11 "Derivational Morphology")
- ✓ infixes (chapter 13 "Nonlinear Affixation")

14.2. Nonactive complements

Up to this point, we have considered clauses that consist of a subject, a verb, and various types of complements. Depending on the verb, there may be a direct object, an indirect object, or an oblique complement. In addition, there may be adjuncts, phrases that are fully optional with any verb. This description covers sentences like the following, in which the complements are bracketed:

(1)   a. *Mary saw [Harry].*
       b. *John offered [a peanut] [to the monkey] yesterday.*
       c. *The big boy ran [to town] very slowly.*
       d. *Julie will come on time.*
       e. *He wept.*

This chapter introduces a wider variety of complements, which we call NONACTIVE COMPLEMENTS. In the following examples, the nonactive complements are bracketed:

(2)   a. *My green pencil is [long].*
       b. *The boy seemed [unusually large].*
       c. *Heidi became [sick] at the circus yesterday.*

(3)   a. *Maria is [a happy woman].*
       b. *Reagan was [the president of the USA] from 1981 to 1989.*
       c. *She became [one of the most influential people in the world].*

(4)   a. *A trapeze artist will be [at the circus].*
       b. *Joan is [here] now.*
       c. *John was [on time] yesterday.*
       d. *The party is [tomorrow].*
       e. *That artichoke is [mine]!*
       f. *This spud's [for you].*

Each clause contains a verb such as *be, become,* or *seem,* followed by some phrase such as an AP, NP, PP, or AdvP. Clearly, these extra phrases are not objects, which are always NPs.[1] Yet they *are* complements, since these verbs cannot occur without them.

(5)   a. **My green pencil is.*[2]
       b. **She became.*
       c. **The boy seemed.*

Many examples have more than one phrase after the verb, but all except the first are optional and therefore are adjuncts.

(6)   a. *Heidi became sick (at the circus) (yesterday).*
       b. *Reagan was the president of the USA (from 1981 to 1989).*
       c. *Joan is here (now).*
       d. *John was on time (yesterday).*

Nonactive complements are classified based partly on their syntactic category and partly on their meaning. In (2), the complements are adjective phrases. Accordingly, they are called ADJECTIVAL COMPLEMENTS. In (3), the complements are noun phrases. They are called NOMINAL COMPLEMENTS. In (4), the complements have a variety of structures and meanings, but most correspond to oblique adjuncts such as location and time. There is no standard term for them as a class, but (depending on their function) they might be called LOCATIVE COMPLEMENTS, TEMPORAL COMPLEMENTS, POSSESSIVE COMPLEMENTS, etc.[3]

---

[1]Even those that are NPs are not direct objects. For example, in English, they are not eligible for passivization or Object-to-object raising. In Latin, NP complements are in nominative case, not accusative like direct objects. Grimshaw (1982:146, note 24) cites other evidence that nominal complements are not objects.

[2]Examples like this occasionally occur in philosophical discussions, as an alternative to *My green pencil exists.* However, this usage is ungrammatical in ordinary speech, which is what we are describing.

[3]There is a definitional problem that surfaces here. According to the definition of 'oblique' in chapter 9, nonactive complements are also obliques, since they are not subjects, direct objects, or indirect objects. However, standard usage does not use the term 'oblique' to refer to nominal and adjectival complements, and it may even be uncommon to refer to a locative complement as an 'oblique'.

Nonactive verbs

In most languages, only a small number of verbs can take nonactive complements. Let's call them NONACTIVE VERBS. Such verbs may take a different set of affixes from the 'ordinary' ACTIVE VERBS, or they may take only some of the affixes that are used with active verbs. Their syntactic properties may be unusual too. One purpose of this chapter is to help you become aware of their syntactic and morphological peculiarities and account for them in your analysis.

Nonactive verbs often have little meaning. The least meaningful is *be*, which can be described simply as a 'grammatical equals sign', since it expresses a close identification of the subject with the complement. Many languages have a verb meaning 'be', and when they do, it has a special name: a COPULA. When a language has a copula, it is usually the most common nonactive verb. However, there is so little meaning to a copula that many languages dispense with using it at all, at least part of the time.

(7) *Biz Türküz*   (Turkish, Altaic)[4]
     we Turk
     We (are) Turks.

(8) *ihintumo kabholosino   kamokulando*   (Muna, Austronesian, Indonesia)[5]
     you   their.replacement their.parents
     You (are) the substitute of their parents.

Some languages have more than one copula, used for different purposes. Plus, most languages have other nonactive verbs with meanings such as 'seem', 'become', and 'have'.

Actions versus states

NONACTIVE CLAUSES (clauses with nonactive complements) generally have meanings that are different from the clauses we've seen so far. Most of the clauses we have considered referred to ACTIONS, while most of the ones in (2)–(4) refer to STATES. The difference between an action and a state is that an action refers to a situation that changes over a relevant period of time, whereas a state refers to a situation that does not change over the relevant period.[6]

(9) Action: *The truck crashed through the store window.*
     State: *The driver was drunk.*

During the relevant time period (a few moments), both the truck and the window underwent significant changes, but the driver's state of inebriation did not change.

Normally languages use different clause structures and different verbs to express actions and states. That is, languages generally make a distinction in form between active and nonactive (sometimes called STATIVE) clauses and verbs,[7] which roughly mirrors the semantic distinction between actions and states. We say 'roughly' because the subcategories of verbs in a language do not generally line up precisely with the action/state distinction. For example, consider *become;* although it expresses an action (i.e., a *change* of state), it takes many of the same complements as clear cases of nonactive verbs like *be* and *seem*. Hence, we classify it as a nonactive verb.

---

[4]Data from Underhill 1976:37. Although the noun *Türküz* 'Turks' carries a morpheme that is sometimes glossed as if it is a clitic copula, Underhill regards it as an agreement marker that is attached to nouns in nominal complements, since it does change form completely depending on the person and number of the subject.

[5]Data from van den Berg 1989:171.

[6]This is an approximate characterization; for a more precise one, see Comrie 1976:48–51.

[7]I prefer the term 'nonactive' to 'stative', because 'stative' is used in so many ways. It can be used narrowly to refer only to verbs that take adjectival complements or to adjectives (and verbs with 'adjectival' meanings). It can be used more broadly to include verbs that express semantic states (even those like 'know' that take direct objects) or as a synonym for 'nonactive' as used here. 'Nonactive' is so infrequently used that I can give it one consistent definition and let students put off coping with the ambiguity of 'stative' for their later studies, when they have a better foundation and will be less likely to be confused by it.

As always, we use facts about syntactic form to make our categories, then use the typical meaning of each category to name it. This principle is very important when analyzing clauses that express states because there are quite a few different structures that languages can use to express them. Let's consider such clauses in more detail, starting with the different types of nonactive complements.

Adjectival complements

ADJECTIVAL COMPLEMENTS (complements that are adjective phrases) typically express an abstract quality of the subject.

(10)   *Martha seems [pensive].*
       That outhouse is [almost too repulsive].

The function of adjective phrases as complements is almost the same as their function as modifiers within a noun phrase. The difference is that, within a noun phrase, adjectives are used only to identify what the noun phrase refers to; in an adjectival complement they provide new information about the subject.

Not all languages have a category of adjectives, and even languages that have them may have very few. Ideas that we may think of as 'adjectival' (adjective-like) are often expressed with intransitive verbs (11) or even nouns (12).[8]

(11)   *neige   nühaizi   piaoliang*   (Mandarin Chinese)
       that   girl   be.beautiful
       That girl is beautiful (lit., 'that girl beautifuls').

(12)   *yana   da   alheri*   (Hausa, Afro-Asiatic, Nigeria)
       he.is   with kindness
       He is kind (lit., 'he is with kindness').

When you encounter clauses like (11) which consist only of a noun phrase and a word that would be translated in English with an adjective, but no copula, you have to consider two possible analyses. One is that the 'adjectival' words are really a special type of intransitive verb.[9] Although they may have special morphological patterns that distinguish them from active verbs, they may still have enough in common with them to be considered verbs. The other possible analysis is that the 'adjectival' words really are adjectives, and that there really is a copula but it is silent.

If there is no overt copula, it can even be hard sometimes to tell a noun phrase from a clause with an adjectival complement. Usually, though, word order provides a good clue. In Swahili (Bantu, East Africa),[10] for example, nouns are first and determiners are last in a noun phrase. Use this fact to identify the constituent structure of the following examples and their meanings. One means 'this nice tree'; the other means 'This tree is nice.' See the footnote for a hint.[11]

(13)   *mti   huu   mzuri*
       tree this nice

(14)   *mti   mzuri   huu*
       tree nice   this

---

[8]Discussion based on and data from Schachter 1985:15–20.
[9]Such verbs are sometimes called stative verbs, even though they don't have nonactive complements, because they express states. Even in English there are several similarities between the syntactic behavior of verbs and adjectives, so it is reasonable to consider them as two subcategories of a larger category which is usually called just [+ V]. For a historical review of this line of analysis, with references to key literature, see Cook 1998:8–9.
[10]Data from Wilson 1985:52.
[11]Hint: Use the determiner to find the right edge of the noun phrase. In one example, all three words form a noun phrase ('this nice tree'); in the other (which means 'this tree is nice'), only the first two words do.

We'll come back to clauses without overt copulas later in this chapter, where there are some suggestions about how to decide if a word is an adjective or a verb.

Nominal complements

NOMINAL COMPLEMENTS express either that the subject is a member of a group or identifies the subject as a specific individual.

(15)   a. *I am [a pacifist].*
       b. *Kangaroos are [some of the most fascinating creatures on earth].*
       c. *That woman is [the culprit]!*
       d. *Arthur is [my favorite uncle].*

In many languages, nominal complements occur in clauses without any overt copula, as illustrated above in examples (7) and (8). This results in clauses consisting of two noun phrases.

Don't confuse nominal complements which contain adjectives with adjectival complements. They have distinct structures.

(16)   Nominal complement containing an adjective: *My mother is [a tall woman].*
       Adjectival complement: *My mother is [tall].*

The meanings are so similar, you might be tempted to think that both are adjectival complements. Not so! If there is a head noun in the complement, it's a nominal complement. If the head is an adjective, it's an adjectival complement.

This similarity of meaning can fool you in your analysis if you rely naively on glosses, because adjectival complements in other languages are sometimes glossed with nominal complements and vice versa. Even though the gloss may have an adjectival complement, the structure in the language you're investigating might be different. For example, in Hua (Papua New Guinea),[12] adjectival complements do not exist. Instead, Hua uses a nominal complement containing an adjective.

(17)   **bura fu nupa baie*
       that pig black is
       (That pig is black.)

(18)   *bura fu nupa fu baie*
       that pig black pig is
       That pig is black (lit., that pig is a black pig).

In Malayalam (Dravidian, south India),[13] what seems to be an adjectival complement is in fact a noun that is derived from an adjective. (This involves derivational morphology, see chapter 11.)

(19)   **kuTTi nalla aaNə*
       child good is
       (The child is good.)

(20)   *kuTTi nallawan aaNə*
       child good.one is
       The child is good (lit., the child is a good-one).

Thus, *nallawan* is a nominal complement, not an adjectival complement, despite the translation. Make sure you analyze the structures, not the glosses!

---

[12]Data from Schachter 1985:16.
[13]Data from Mohanan 1982:520. Capital letters here represent retroflex consonants (written with underdot in the original).

Other nonactive complements

Recall from chapter 9 "Obliques" (p. 105) that some obliques may be complements, especially those that occur with verbs of motion and placement (e.g., 'go' and 'put') to express meanings such as Source, Path, and Goal. With other verbs, obliques that express Location are usually adjuncts. However, many languages have one or more nonactive verbs like 'be' that are used to express where some object is located. These verbs require obliques of Location, which are thus their complements. Specifically, they can be called LOCATIVE COMPLEMENTS. Compare the following examples to see the difference between Location as an adjunct or a nonactive complement.

	Locative adjunct	Locative complement
PP	I saw her **at the concert.**	Three hundred people were **at the concert.**
Unmodifiable single-word.	He was reading a book **here.**	He is not **here.**
Idiomatic NP	She bought a dress **downtown.**	My wife is **downtown.**

Typically, any phrase that can express location as an adjunct in an active clause can also express it as a complement in a nonactive clause. Thus, locative complements are typically PPs, NPs, AdvPs, single-word obliques, or idioms, depending on the specific possibilities in the language.

Languages may have a general purpose copula, like English 'be', that works both with locative complements and other types. Or, there may be a special verb meaning 'be located', which is used only with locative complements. (For an example of the latter, see the discussion of Palauan on p. 193.)

However, here's another place where you have to be careful not to be fooled by the meanings. Some languages don't have special nonactive verbs for expressing location; instead they use ordinary (active) intransitive verbs like 'sit', 'stand', 'lie', or 'live'.[14]

(21) *šuul **winit** tugumbalaap*   (Tubatulabal, Uto-Aztecan, California)[15]
      star   stand   in.sky
      The stars are (lit., stand) in the sky.

(22) *xuan **tsi:nap** tuhugum*   (Sayula Popoluca, Mixe-Zoquean, Mexico)[16]
      John   he.sits   in.house
      John is (lit., is sitting) in the house.

Besides locative complements, you may run into nonactive complements with other oblique meanings, such as Time or Benefactive.[17]

(23) *La   fiesta es   miercoles.*   (Spanish)
      The party   is   Wednesday.
      The party is (on) Wednesday.

(24) *[soomo kamarano] watu*   (Muna, Austronesian, Indonesia)[18]
        for   his.room   that
      That room is for him (lit., That is for his room).

Also see the English examples (4c–f).

---

[14]I don't know whether the locative obliques that occur with these verbs are adjuncts or complements. Conceivably, this might vary, depending on the language.

[15]Data from Langacker 1977:41.

[16]Data from Daly, Lyman, and Rhodes 1981:48.

[17]Such sentences are not often mentioned in descriptive grammars, so I don't know how common they are. It may be that they are very common but usually overlooked by linguists as they write up their findings. Temporal complements may be considered a special type of locative complement, cf. Lyons 1968:388–89.

[18]Data from van den Berg 1989:172.

Existence and possession

There are two other meanings, EXISTENCE and POSSESSION, that are often expressed with structures that resemble nonactive clauses containing locative complements.

Languages have different ways to express EXISTENCE. In the simplest cases, a language may have a special EXISTENTIAL VERB meaning 'exist'.

(25)   ***Hay***   *tortillas*   *en*   *la*   *canasta.*   (Spanish)
              exist   tortillas   in   the   basket
              There are tortillas in the basket.

However, many languages have special clause structures to express existence, which may be called EXISTENTIAL CLAUSES. Often, existential clauses are very similar in form to clauses with locative complements. Consider the following English examples:

(26)   Existential clause   Ordinary clause with locative complement

      There's flies in my soup.   *The fly is in my soup.*
      There is a Santa Claus.   *Santa Claus is in the chimney.*

There are some differences between the two clause types, however. The existential clauses have a dummy (meaningless) subject *there,* and the 'logical' subject occurs after the copula. Also, existential clauses seem to tolerate the omission of the locative oblique more easily than ordinary clauses with locative complements.[19]

In terms of meaning, an existential verb or clause asserts that the subject exists, often (but not always) specifying a location in which the existence is asserted. Establishing that something exists is normally prerequisite to talking further about it, so such assertions usually occur at the first mention of an item in a discourse.

(27)   *Once upon a time, there were three bears.*

A clause with a locative complement, however, presupposes that the subject's *existence* has already been established and asserts its *location*.

(28)   *They were in the forest picking berries.*

Such clauses normally do not occur when an item is first mentioned in a discourse.[20]

POSSESSION is similar to existence and location in many ways. Like existence, languages may have a special verb to assert possession, such as the word *have* in English.

(29)   *The baby bear had a wee, tiny chair.*

Or, they may have special structures to express the same idea. For example, there may be an existential verb with a possessed noun as subject.

(30)   *aj*   *s-bankil.*   (Tzeltal, Mayan, Mexico)[21]
          there.is   your-older.brother
          You have an older brother (lit., your older brother exists).

---

[19]Lyons 1968:390 regards existential sentences as 'implicitly locative', and classifies the locative oblique as a complement, even though under some circumstances it can be omitted.

[20]Compare Clark's (1978) discussion of definiteness in existential and locative clauses.

[21]See footnote 5, p. 29.

Some languages may use more than one structure. For example, classical Latin[22] and Spanish each use at least three.[23]

(31) a. *Johannes habet librum.*   (possessive verb; possessor as subject)
      John   has   book
      John has a book.

   b. *Est   Johanni   liber.*   (copula; possessor in dative case)
      is(3s) John(Dative) book
      John has a book (lit., it is to John a book).

   c. *Liber est   Johannis.*   (copula; possessor in genitive case)
      book is(3s) John(Genitive)
      John has a book (lit., the book is of John).

(32) a. *Mi hermana tiene una falda negra.*   (possessive verb; possessor as subject)
      my sister   has a   skirt black
      My sister has a black skirt.

   b. *La falda pertenece a mi hermana.*   (possessive verb; possessor as indirect
      the skirt belongs   to my sister   object)
      The skirt belongs to my sister.

   c. *Este falda es de mi hermana.*   (copula; possessor as object of *de*)
      this skirt is of my sister
      This skirt is my sister's.

Like existential clauses, special possessive clause structures are often similar to nonactive clauses with locative complements. For this reason, linguists often express this similarity somehow in their formal grammars. This formal analysis often requires some fancy theoretical footwork, so this book does not attempt it. However, you should be able to recognize when a language has one of these special nonactive clause types, name it appropriately, describe its structure informally, and identify what other clause types it resembles and how it resembles them.

14.3. Formal analysis of nonactive complements

How do we account for the differences between active and nonactive clauses in our formal grammars? We need to do two things. One, we must expand the phrase structure rule for S to include nonactive complements which are NPs, APs, or various other phrases. Two, we must have some way of identifying nonactive verbs in the lexicon, to indicate that they (and only they) take nonactive complements.

So far in this book, we have developed the following phrase structure rules for English clauses:

(33) S → NP[Su] VP

$$VP → V \ (NP[DO]) \ (VP) \ (PP[IO]) \left(\left\{ \begin{array}{l} NP \\ PP \\ AdvP \end{array} \right\} \right)*$$

---

[22]Latin data from Lyons 1967:391–92 and Lyons 1968:392.
[23]Clark 1978 points out that it is very common to have two possessive constructions in a language. One is like (31a) and (32a), having the possessor as subject; it asserts the existence of some (usually indefinite) item belonging to the possessor, and thus, often has similarities to existential clauses. The other is like (31c) and (32c), having the possessed item as a definite subject; it identifies who owns an item, and often has similarities to clauses with locative complements. In both cases the possessor seems to be treated as an abstract animate location.

To handle nonactive complements, we add a choice of NP, AP, PP, or AdvP to the VP rule, flagged with feature [NC] to represent the grammatical relation 'nonactive complement'.[24]

(34)
$$VP \rightarrow V \left(NP[DO]\right) \left(VP\right) \left(PP[IO]\right) \left(\begin{Bmatrix} NP \\ AP \\ PP \\ AdvP \end{Bmatrix} [NC] \right) \left(\begin{Bmatrix} NP \\ PP \\ AdvP \end{Bmatrix} \right) *$$

As for the lexicon, nonactive verbs subcategorize for different types of nonactive complements. As we've seen in examples (2)–(4), the copula *be* can occur with any nonactive complement. *Become* is different; it occurs only with adjectival and nominal complements. *Seem* occurs only with adjectival complements.[25]

(35) a. *He became worried.*
      b. *He became a man.*
      c. **He became in(to) the park.*
      d. **He became there.*

(36) a. *She seems worried.*
      b. **She seems a professional.*
      c. **She seems in the park.*
      d. **She seems there.*

These subcategorization requirements can be indicated in the lexicon as follows:

(37) *be*[26]   V[SUBCAT ⟨ NP[Su], [NC] ⟩]

      become $V \left[SUBCAT \left\langle NP[Su], \begin{Bmatrix} AP \\ NP \end{Bmatrix} [NC] \right\rangle \right]$

      seem   V[SUBCAT ⟨ NP[Su], AP[NC] ⟩]

Note that the SUBCAT feature for *be* states only that it requires a nonactive complement, but does not specify its category, thus all types of nonactive complements allowed by the phrase structure rules can be used with *be*. The SUBCAT lists for the other two verbs need to be more specific, since they are more restrictive about what type of complements they can take.[27]

Let's draw some trees that illustrate these rules. In sentence (2b), we have an adjectival complement.

---

[24]The feature [NC] corresponds roughly to the grammatical functions ACOMP and NCOMP of Grimshaw (1982:95), who posits a similar phrase structure rule. The order specified with respect to the objects is largely arbitrary. It is not necessary to list nonactive complements in braces with the objects; impossible combinations can be excluded by the subcategorization requirements of verbs as easily as in the phrase structure rules.

[25]Sentences like 'She seems a kind woman' are apparently grammatical in some dialects.

[26]Of course, irregularly inflected forms of these verbs would also need to be spelled out in the lexicon. This detail is omitted in order to concentrate on the subcategorization.

[27]As assumed in chapter 8 "Verbal Valence" (p. 84, fn. 13), if a complement type is mentioned in some verb's SUBCAT list, then it cannot occur with any other verb that does not specifically mention it.

(38)   Deep structure tree for (2b)[28]

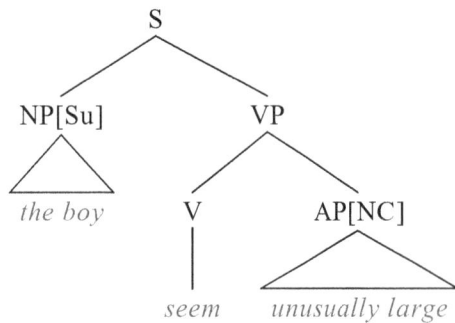

```
                    S
            ┌───────┴───────┐
        NP[Su]             VP
          △          ┌──────┴──────┐
       the boy       V           AP[NC]
                     │              △
                   seem      unusually large
```

Besides *seem,* we could also have inserted *be* or *become,* since all three include adjectival complements in their SUBCAT list.

In sentence (3c), we have a nominal complement.

(39)   Deep structure tree for (3c)

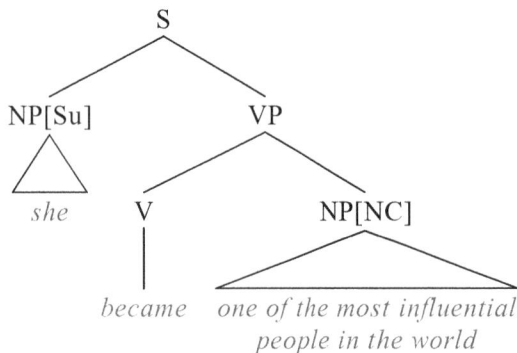

```
                    S
            ┌───────┴───────┐
        NP[Su]             VP
          △          ┌──────┴──────┐
         she         V           NP[NC]
                     │              △
                  became   one of the most influential
                            people in the world
```

Besides *become,* we could have inserted *be,* but the subcategorization feature for *seem* prevents it from being inserted.

In sentence (4b), we have a locative AdvP complement, as well as an adjunct expressing time.

(40)   Deep structure tree for (4b)

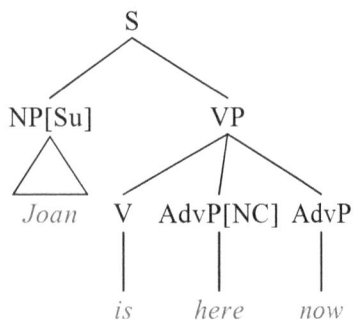

```
                   S
            ┌──────┴──────┐
        NP[Su]           VP
          △         ┌─────┼─────┐
        Joan        V  AdvP[NC] AdvP
                    │     │      │
                   is    here   now
```

Neither *become* nor *seem* allow AdvP complements, so *be* is the only verb we can insert.

---

[28]Since these are deep trees, there is no regular inflectional morphology in them, although the fully-inflected form of suppletive stems such as *became* is included (see chapter 10 "Inflectional Morphology"). I omit the inflectional features from the diagrams for simplicity and to make it easier to study this chapter before chapter 10, if so desired.

14.4. Nonactive complements in Palauan

Nonactive clauses in English are quite uniform. For data with some more variety, let's consider nonactive complements in Palauan (Austronesian, Republic of Belau).[29] First we'll look at active clauses, so we can compare them to nonactive clauses later.

(41) *ak məŋa ər a ŋikəl*
      I   eat   P fish
      I am eating fish.

(42) *ak mləŋa ər a ŋikəl*
      I   Past/eat P   fish
      I ate fish.

(43) *a sensey a məʔiwayu*
         teacher   sleep
      The teacher is sleeping.

(44) *a sensey a mləʔiwayu*
         teacher   Past/sleep
      The teacher slept.

There are a few basic facts to explain. The basic word order appears to be SVO. The direct object is a PP; the preposition *ər* which is used with the direct object is the only preposition in Palauan, so the gloss can just be 'P'. Within a noun phrase, there is always an initial determiner *a*, which is apparently meaningless, so it is unglossed. This word also occurs between a subject noun and a verb. The past tense of verbs is formed by inserting the infix *-l-* after the first consonant of the stem. (See chapter 13 "Nonlinear Affixation," p. 168, for a formal analysis of infixes; we don't need the formalities now.)

Now let's consider different types of nonactive complements in Palauan.

Adjectival complements

One type of clause has the meaning that we might expect with an adjectival complement, but there is no overt copula.

(45) *a kall a bədərəʔuis*
         food   spoiled
      The food is spoiled.

(46) *ak smeʔər*
      I   sick
      I am sick.

That is, each clause consists of a subject noun phrase and a word with an adjectival meaning. Are these words verbs or adjectives? If they are adjectives, how do we account for the absence of the verb in our rules? Answers begin to emerge if we look at past tense forms.

(47) *a kall a mle bədərəʔuis*
         food   spoiled
      The food was spoiled.

---

[29]Data from Josephs 1975.

(48) *ak   mle   sme?ər*
       I   sick
       I was sick.

Unlike clear cases of verbs, these words do not form their past tense with *-l-*. Instead, there is an extra word, *mle*, preceding them. This suggests that these 'adjectival' words are indeed in a separate category from verbs, since they have a different pattern of morphology (they are not inflected directly for tense) and a different distribution (clear cases of verbs don't occur after *mle*). Given their meaning, it's reasonable to call this category adjectives.

These new examples also suggest a way of accounting for the missing copula. It is reasonable to assume that Palauan really does have a copula; *mle* is its past tense form, and *Ø* (phonologically empty) is its present tense form.[30] It is an irregular verb (see chapter 10 "Inflectional Morphology," p. 127) and can thus be represented in the lexicon as follows:

(49) $\emptyset$ $\begin{bmatrix} -\text{past} \end{bmatrix}$
        mle $\begin{bmatrix} +\text{past} \end{bmatrix}$ $V\begin{bmatrix} \text{SUBCAT} \langle \text{NP[Su], [NC]} \rangle \end{bmatrix}$ to be

Like all lexical entries, this entry contains phonological, morphosyntactic, and semantic information. The only thing unusual is that, in the present tense, the phonological information is *silence*; there are no phonological features.

You may ask, "Why not just make the verb optional in the phrase structure rule?" One reason is that this would violate the constraints on phrase structure rules introduced in chapter 7 "Embedding and Noun Phrase Structure" (p. 68). However, this isn't a very strong reason; one could also legitimately ask if those constraints might simply be wrong. But, there would be two undesirable consequences of just leaving the verb out of the rule. One, it would allow the verb to be omitted from any type of clause, not just those with nonactive complements, and would thus surely generate ungrammatical sentences. Two, it would be difficult to state what a clause without a verb would mean. On the other hand, by assuming that there is a silent verb in (49), we have a way of stating what the absence of an overt verb means (through the semantic information in the lexical entry) and when it can occur (through the SUBCAT list). So, the better analysis is the one that has an obligatory verb in the phrase structure rules. The constraints we adopted earlier have been vindicated.

The phrase structure rules must allow for adjectives and adjectival complements.[31]

(50) S   → NP[Su] VP
      VP → V (PP[DO]) (AP[NC])
      NP → D N
      AP → ... A

This hypothesis will generate the following tree for (46):

---

[30]A similar situation is reported by Rapaport (1985) for Hebrew, but with an interesting twist: the silent copula in present tense still bears inflectional features, so it surfaces in a form that is identical to the third person nominative pronoun.

[31]This analysis assumes for now that adjectives can be modified, even though we don't know what an AP would look like.

(51)

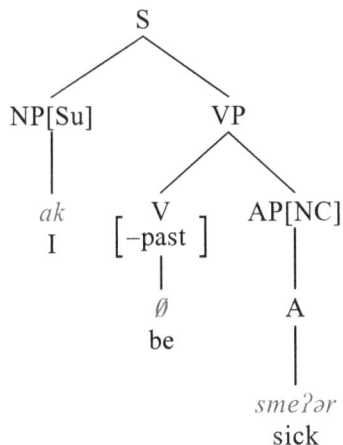

Reinforcing this analysis, there is a verb *mo* 'become', which can also take what we have assumed is an adjectival complement. Its behavior seems completely parallel to *mle,* except that it forms its past tense regularly.

(52) *ak   mo   sme?ər*
      I   become sick
      I am getting sick.

(53) *ak   mlo   sme?ər*
      I   became sick
      I got sick.

Its lexical entry is as follows:

(54) *mo*   V[SUBCAT ⟨ NP[Su], AP[NC] ⟩]   to become

Nominal complements

If we look at nominal complements, a similar pattern emerges, suggesting that we are on the right track.

(55) *ak   sensey*
      I   teacher
      I am a teacher.

(56) *ak   mle   sensey*
      I   was   teacher
      I was a teacher.

(57) *ŋ   mlik*
      it my-car
      It's my car.

(58) *ŋ   mle   mlik*
      it was   my-car
      It was my car.

Again, there is no (overt) copula in present tense, but *mle* occurs in past tense.
    All we need to do to handle these new examples is to add a nominal complement to the VP rule.

(59)

$$\text{VP} \rightarrow \text{V} \left(\text{PP[DO]}\right) \left(\begin{Bmatrix} \text{NP} \\ \text{AP} \end{Bmatrix} \text{[NC]}\right)$$

The lexical entry (49) for Ø/*mle* still works, since we planned ahead and allowed this verb to occur with any nonactive complement.

Locative complements

Locative complements provide a bit of a surprise—there is a new verb, *ŋar*/*mla* 'be located'.

(60) *a Droteo a ŋar   ər a sers*
     Droteo   is.located P   garden
     Droteo is in the garden.

(61) *a Droteo a mla   ər a sers*
     Droteo   was.located P   garden
     Droteo was in the garden.

(62) *a ŋikəl a ŋar   ər a daob*
     fish   is.located P   ocean
     The fish is/are in the ocean.

(63) *a ŋikəl a mla   ər a daob*
     fish   was.located P   ocean
     The fish was/were in the ocean.

It is not uncommon for a language to use a copula for adjectival and nominal complements but have a different verb meaning 'be located' for locative complements.

These sentences require us to add a PP complement to the VP rule and to create a lexical entry for *ŋar*/*mla* 'be located'. We also have to revise the entry for Ø/*mle* to limit it to adjectival and nominal complements.

(64)

$$\text{VP} \rightarrow \text{V} \left(\text{PP[DO]}\right) \left(\begin{Bmatrix} \text{NP} \\ \text{AP} \\ \text{PP} \end{Bmatrix} \text{[NC]}\right)$$

(65) $\left.\begin{array}{l} \text{ŋar} \\ \text{mla} \;\; \text{[+past]} \end{array}\right\}$ V$\left[\text{SUBCAT} \langle \text{NP[Su]}, \text{PP[NC]} \rangle \right]$ to be located

(66) $\left.\begin{array}{l} \text{Ø} \\ \text{mle} \;\; \text{[+past]} \end{array}\right\}$ V$\left[\text{SUBCAT} \left\langle \text{NP[Su]}, \begin{Bmatrix} \text{NP} \\ \text{AP} \end{Bmatrix}\text{[NC]} \right\rangle \right]$ to be

Existential clauses

Finally, there is a separate clause structure that is used to assert existence. It uses the same verb as the clauses with locative complements, but with the addition of two dummy pronouns: *ŋ* before the verb and *ŋii* in a PP after the verb.

(67) *ŋ ŋar ər ŋii a ŋikəl ər a daob*
     3   P   3   fish P   ocean
     There are fish in the ocean.

(68) ŋ mla ər ŋii a ŋikəl ər a daob
      3 P   3   fish P   ocean
      There were fish in the ocean.

(69) ŋ ŋar ər ŋii a blai   ər tiaŋ
      3 P   3   house P here
      There is a house here.

(70) ŋ mla ər ŋii a blai   ər tiaŋ
      3 P   3   house P here
      There was a house here.

Existential clauses are also used to assert possession by expressing the existence of a possessed noun.

(71) ŋ ŋar ər ŋii a uldəsaek
      3 P   3   my-idea
      I have an idea (lit., my idea exists).

Even though we are not attempting a formal analysis of existential clauses, you can see how we still were able to give a relatively precise informal description of them and distinguish them from other similar structures.

14.5. Intransitive verbs rather than nonactive complements

Recall that sometimes what we would expect to be adjectives turn out to be verbs. There is an extra twist on this possibility to consider. In some languages, adjectival and nominal complements do not exist or are not often used, even though the language has adjectives and, of course, nouns. Instead, nouns and adjectives are changed into verbs, using derivational affixes, and the derived verbs are used to express the ideas in intransitive clauses. For example, in Russian the verb *belet'* 'to be white' is derived from the adjective *bel* 'white' and the verb *carstvovat'* 'to be tsar, to reign' is derived from the noun *car'* 'tsar, emperor'.[32]

Here's how you spot this situation. If you know there are adjectives and nouns, but they cannot be modified when they seem to be used as nonactive complements, if there is no overt copula, and especially if they have an extra affix in this use, then they are probably better analyzed as derived intransitive verbs, not nonactive complements. They would thus be listed in the lexicon with other intransitive verbs. (See chapter 11 "Derivational Morphology" for more details about the formal analysis of the derivational process itself.)

Here are some more hints for telling adjectives from verbs. As we saw above with Palauan, it is especially important to consider these factors when there is no overt copula to make the analysis obvious.

1. If words with 'adjectival' meanings always or often occur with a word that could be analyzed as a copula and words with 'verbal' meanings do not, then there probably are two separate categories: adjectives and verbs.

2. If adjectival meanings can be expressed simply in nonactive clauses, but when expressed as modifiers in a noun phrase, extra morphemes are needed that could be analyzed as parts of a relative clause (see chapter 23 "Relative Clauses"), then words with adjectival meanings are probably just verbs. If a relative clause is needed for only some words with adjectival meanings, then the ones that require extra morphemes are probably verbs, and the rest adjectives.

---

[32]Data from Comrie 1985a:345–46.

3. If words with adjectival and verbal meanings have the same pattern of inflection (the same grammatical categories and affixes), then there is probably just one category of verbs. If they have completely different morphology, then there are probably two categories: adjectives and verbs. If the morphology is similar, but the 'adjectival' words have simpler inflection, there is probably just one category of verbs that includes a subcategory of 'stative verbs'.

Even if there are two separate categories of adjectives and verbs, the exact membership of them may not correspond to languages you are familiar with. Some things you would expect to be adjectives may be verbs, and vice versa.

14.6. Summary of typological variation

As we have seen, there is quite a bit of variation from one language to the next in the structures that are used to express states. Here's a summary of them.

a. There may be significant differences in word order in clauses with nonactive complements, compared to ordinary clauses.
b. There may be different types of phrases which can serve as nonactive complements in different languages.
c. A nonactive verb in one language may subcategorize for a different set of complements than a synonymous verb in another language.
d. Verbs with nonactive complements may have different morphology from active verbs.
e. There may not be an overt verb meaning *to be,* at least not in some environments. If not, one option for analysis is to posit a silent copula, particularly if a copula appears in some environments or tenses, but not in others. Even if there is no overt copula, there may be other nonactive verbs, with meanings like 'become' and 'seem', which are overt and take nonactive complements; these will help you identify the nonactive complements.
f. Some or all of the meanings that we think of as 'adjectival' may be expressed as intransitive verbs.
g. Nominal complements containing an adjective may be used rather than adjectival complements. Or, adjectives may be changed into nouns (by derivational morphology), so that they end up as nominal complements. Similarly, intransitive verbs may be derived morphologically from nouns or adjectives.
h. There may or may not be distinct clause structures to assert existence and possession. If there are, they may resemble each other or clauses that contain locative complements.

Because there are so many different possibilities, wait a bit before doing much analysis on nonactive complements and other ways of expressing states. You need to have a clear idea of basic active clause structure before you can decide which of the above possibilities are actually used to express states in a language. It's easy to jump to conclusions, so don't get permanently attached to a hypothesis. Stay prepared to try out several different possibilities to see which one works best.

14.7. Review of key terms

Most languages have a few special verbs, called NONACTIVE (or STATIVE) verbs, which typically take NONACTIVE COMPLEMENTS (NC) and express STATES. They are distinct from active verbs, which generally express ACTIONS. Clauses are also called ACTIVE or NONACTIVE, depending on the type of verb they contain. Many languages have a special nonactive verb meaning 'be', which is called a COPULA, although others do not, leaving a gap where the verb should be.

We have considered three main types of nonactive complements: ADJECTIVAL COMPLEMENTS (APs), NOMINAL COMPLEMENTS (NPs), and LOCATIVE COMPLEMENTS (using the same structures as obliques of location). Sometimes languages have special verbs or clauses with special structures for asserting EXISTENCE (called EXISTENTIAL VERBS and CLAUSES) and POSSESSION.

14.8. Questions for analysis

1. What structures are available for expressing states? Look for clauses without complements and for clauses with adjectival, nominal, and locative complements. What are the details on each structure and what range of meanings does it express? How do they differ from active clauses?
2. How does the language assert existence and possession?
    a. Is there an existential verb that means 'exist'? Are there special clause structures used to assert existence?
    b. Is there a possessive verb, like English *have?* Are there special clause structures used to assert possession?
    c. Are any of these structures used to express any other meanings?
    d. How are these structures similar to each other and to clauses with locative complements?
3. Is there an overt copula? Are there any other verbs that take nonactive complements? Which verbs are used with which types of complements?
4. Is there any special inflectional morphology on nonactive verbs?
5. Is there any derivational morphology that is used to express states (to derive nouns or verbs from adjectives, or verbs from nouns)?
6. Is there a category of adjectives distinct from verbs? What properties distinguish them?

14.9. Sample description

(The following description assumes that the reader is familiar with the basic facts of Palauan clause structure, so that it can focus on nonactive clauses. It is typical of what you might find in one section of a whole grammar sketch.)

Palauan allows adjectival, nominal, and locative complements after the verb. The copula is *Ø* (phonologically null) in present tense, but *mle* in past tense, and is used with adjectival and nominal complements. Other verbs like *mo* 'become' also take these complements.

(1) *ak Ø/mle sensey*
     I   be   teacher
     I am/was a teacher.

(2) *ak Ø/mle smeʔər*
     I   be   sick
     I am/was sick.

(3) *ak mlo   smeʔər*
     I   became sick
     I got sick.

Locative complements use a separate verb, *ŋar/mla* 'be located'.

(4) *a Droteo a mla   ər a sers*
       Droteo   was.located P   garden
     Droteo was in the garden.

Existential clauses are similar, but involve dummy third person pronouns before and after the verb.

(5) *ŋ ŋar   ər ŋii a blai   ər tiaŋ*
     3 is.located P   3   house P   here
     There is a house here.

14.10. For further reading

There is relatively little written on nonactive clauses and what exists tends to be in bits and
snatches tucked in around the edges of some other topic. Comrie (1985a:345–46) discusses
derivational morphology that derives nouns from adjectives, verbs from nouns, etc. Schachter
(1985:7, 11, 13–20) has an especially helpful discussion of adjectives and the ways of expressing
adjectival meanings in languages that have few or no adjectives. Clark (1978) surveys locative,
existential, and possessive clauses in a number of languages, and points out several systematic
similarities and differences between them; Ultan (1978b:33–35) also has some useful observations.

One exception to this lack of information is the literature that has grown up around what are
called 'small clauses': nonactive clauses without overt copulas in languages that normally use
copulas. Radford (1988:324–31) provides an introduction to them and an analysis that differs in
significant ways from the one given here.

15
Variable Orders of Constituents

15.1. Goals and prerequisites

This chapter will help you do the following:

- ◎ make a reasonable hypothesis about basic order when the data contains variable orders of constituents
- ◎ describe such data informally
- ◎ construct a formal analysis that accounts for variable order (especially phrase structure rules and movement transformations)
- ◎ draw deep and surface structure trees consistent with your analysis
- ◎ state where movement transformations fit in the overall outline of a transformational grammar and how the different levels of structure are related to each other
- ◎ distinguish FOCUS and TOPICALIZATION and state some common devices that languages use to express them

It assumes that you are familiar with the following material:

- ✓ basic syntactic structure (earlier chapters on syntax through chapter 9 "Obliques")
- ✓ how to handle regular and irregular inflection in a formal grammar (chapter 10 "Inflectional Morphology")
- ✓ nonactive complements (chapter 14)

15.2. English particle movement

In this chapter, we examine a basic fact about all languages: words do not come in a single, fixed order. Some languages allow more freedom of word order than others, but all allow some. We start by considering 'particle movement' in English.

Many verbs in English can combine with prepositions to form what are called verb-particle constructions. In these constructions, the preposition can be separated from the verb.

(1)   a. *He gave **away** the ball.*
       b. *He gave the ball **away.***

(2)   a. *He put **out** the fire.*
       b. *He put the fire **out.***

These verb-particle constructions do not involve prepositional phrases, even though they look like this at first glance. There are major semantic differences between verb-particle constructions and ordinary PPs. For example, "He threw in his two cent's worth" does not mean that he was located (even figuratively) in his two cent's worth when he threw something or that he threw (something) into his two cent's worth, but that his two cent's worth was thrown into something else, i.e., the conversation. The verb *throw* is not the same as the verb-particle construction *throw in.*

Another difference: the preposition can be moved away from the verb only when it is part of a verb-particle construction.

(3)   Verb-particle   Verb with PP
        Next to verb: a. *He ran up a big bill.*   c. *He ran up a big hill.*
        Moved later: b. *He ran a big bill up.*   d. **He ran a big hill up.*

So you see, virtually identical sequences of words can have different syntactic and semantic properties. In our study of a language, we want to become aware of these differences, understand them, and develop an analysis that accounts for them.

A typical analysis of verb-particle constructions is that they are syntactic compounds of a verb stem and a preposition, which together form a complex verb. At the same time, these compounds are not indivisible single words, since the preposition can be moved away from the verb.[1] The compound *run up* would thus be listed in the lexicon as a V which consisted of two parts, a V and a P. (Compare the discussion of idiomatic oblique phrases in chapter 9 "Obliques," p. 101.)[2]

(4)

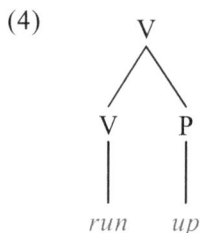

This means that the tree structures of (3a) and (3c) are different.

---

[1]The assumption here is that syntactic rules can't refer to the internal structure of a word; this can only be done by morphological rules. For example, it is impossible for a syntactic rule to take part of a word and move it elsewhere. This claim is generally true; with most lexical entries, you can't move just part of it around. There are, however, a few odd ones like verb-particle constructions that are different and do allow movement of their pieces; by allowing fragments of trees as lexical entries, we make it possible to represent how they are different from ordinary lexical entries.

[2]Syntactic compounds and idiomatic phrases are unlike morphological compounds (chapter 11 "Derivational Morphology," p. 147), because the internal structure of a morphological compound is invisible to syntactic rules. Morphological compounds occupy a simple terminal node in a tree, while syntactic compounds and idioms are analyzed as fragments of trees that are listed as wholes in the lexicon.

(5)

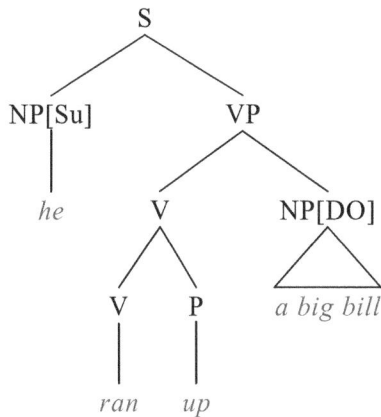

(6)

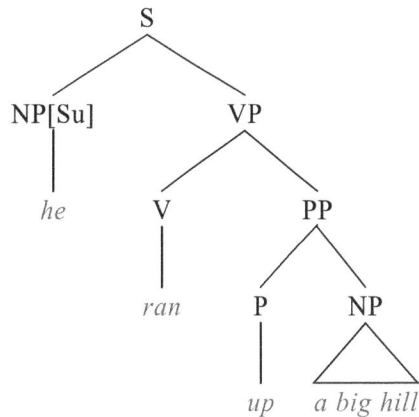

We see again that sentences are not merely strings of words. In (5) the preposition forms a complex verb with the preceding V; in (6) it forms a PP with the following NP. Two apparently similar strings can have quite different constituent structures, and these different structures are the key to understanding their different properties.

But, before we can account for the movement of the preposition, we need to add a new type of rule to our formal grammars.

15.3. Transformational rules and transformational grammars

Generative Grammar grew out of an attempt to account for constructions like verb-particle movement in as simple and general a fashion as possible. The basic problem is that there are lots of pairs of sentences like those in (3a, b) in which the only difference is the position of the preposition. How can we have a grammar that generates the preposition in either of two positions with general rules that relate them to each other?

One of the earliest approaches was to build a sentence like (3b) in two steps. In the first step, the preposition is placed right after the verb, as in (3a).

(7)

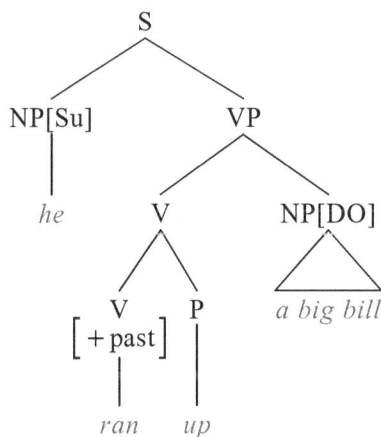

In the second step, the preposition is moved after the direct object.

(8)

```
                              S
                            /   \
                      NP[Su]      VP
                        |        / | \
                       he      V  NP[DO]  P
                              |    /\     |
                              V   /  \    up
                          ┌──────┐ a big bill
                          │+ past│
                          └──────┘
                              |
                             ran
```

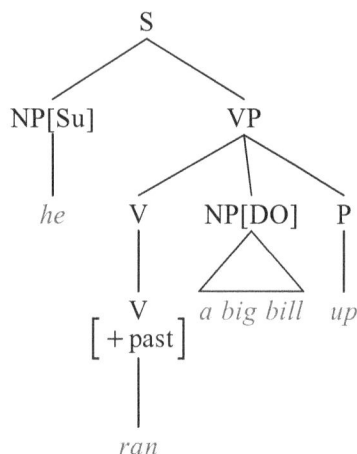

The type of rule that moves an element from one place in the tree to another is called a TRANSFORMATION. Those generative grammars which include transformations are called TRANSFORMATIONAL GRAMMARS.

Where exactly do transformations fit in the outline of grammar introduced earlier? Transformations apply to the output of the base component; this output is usually called DEEP STRUCTURE. We will also assume that they apply before the inflectional spellout rules, so that the syntax is complete before the inflectional morphology is spelled out. Together, the transformations and inflectional spellout rules produce the SURFACE STRUCTURE of a sentence.

(9)

```
┌─────────────────────────────────────┐
│        BASE COMPONENT                │
│  ┌──────────┐                        │
│  │ Phrase   │  ┌──────────┐          │
│  │ Structure│  │ Lexicon  │          │
│  │ Rules    │  └──────────┘          │
│  └──────────┘                        │
└─────────────────────────────────────┘
                 ↓
          DEEP STRUCTURE
                 ↓
      ┌──────────────────────┐
      │   TRANSFORMATIONS     │
      └──────────────────────┘
                 ↓
      ┌──────────────────────┐
      │   INFLECTIONAL        │
      │   SPELLOUT RULES      │
      └──────────────────────┘
                 ↓
          SURFACE STRUCTURE
```

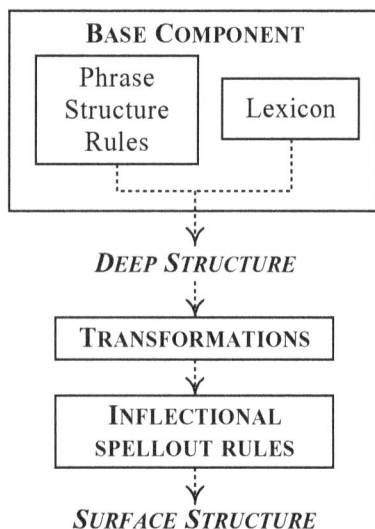

Each sentence in a language has associated with it a deep structure and a surface structure, although in some cases (when the transformation and inflectional spellout rules make no changes) the deep and surface structures may be identical.

To get back to English particle movement—we need a transformational rule that converts (7) into (8). Let's call it PARTICLE MOVEMENT. All that Particle Movement does is to remove the particle from the V and reattach it directly under the VP at the end of the clause.[3]

Except for the compound verb, (7) looks like the deep structure for an ordinary transitive clause. Indeed, if we don't apply Particle Movement to this tree, then the result is the grammatical sentence *He ran up a big bill*. If we do apply Particle Movement, the result is (8), for *He ran a big bill up*. Notice that the same tree (7) serves as the deep structure for both sentences (3a, b). This is the

---

[3]There is nothing in the data here to determine the exact target of the movement: to the end of the clause or to the right of the direct object. The discussion assumes (without evidence) that the target is the end of the clause. However, see footnote 5.

transformational explanation for the fact that they are identical except for the position of the preposition. They are, in fact, derived from the same deep structure and differ only in whether Particle Movement has applied.

The structure in (8) then becomes the input to the inflectional spellout rules. In this particular case, the spellout rules have nothing to do, since the irregular form *ran* is listed in the lexicon as the past tense form of *run*. (Recall the treatment of irregular inflection in chapter 10 "Inflectional Morphology," p. 127.) Thus, (8) is also the surface structure of *He ran a big bill up*. However, a sentence with a regular verb would be derived in three steps:

(10)   *Deep:*   *He look[+past] up her name in the telephone directory.*

                                          Particle Movement

          He look[+past] her name up in the telephone directory.

                      Inflectional spellout for past tense

       Surface: *He looked[+past] her name up in the telephone directory.*

How do we write movement transformations? Although a formal notation for transformations exists,[4] most writers just give a clear prose statement of what the transformation does. So, for Particle Movement, we could write the following:

(11)   **Particle Movement** (optional)
       Take a P dominated by V and move it to the end of VP.[5]

This concisely states three important facts:

(12)   a. What moves?
       b. Where?
       c. Under what conditions?

The statement in (11) that the rule is optional requires further comment. Transformations are of two types: obligatory and optional. This rule is optional because in the data the particle occurs in either position: just after the verb or at the end of the VP. (More on this shortly.)

Note that Particle Movement moves Ps only when they are part of a compound V. It will not take the head of a PP and produce ungrammatical strings like '*He ran a big hill up'. This completes the explanation of why a preposition can move after a direct object only when it is part of a verb-particle construction, not when it is the head of a PP.

To sum up, we have considered a new type of syntactic rule, a transformation. Unlike the phrase structure rules, transformations don't build structure, but instead modify existing structures. To make an analogy: the phrase structure rules and the lexicon are responsible for growing trees, and the transformational rules prune and graft the branches.

15.4. Fronting in Choapan Zapotec

Sometimes, two different word orders are apparently synonymous. Such seems to be the case with English Particle Movement. Whether the particle occurs next to the verb or at the end of the clause, the meaning is essentially the same. Meaning includes such subtleties as the relative emphasis or prominence of different elements in the clause, but even in this respect there is little or no discernible difference in meaning.

---

[4]See, for example, Baker 1978:66ff or Akmajian and Heny 1975:140ff.
[5]This statement reflects the hypothesis that the particle moves to the end of the clause. In fact, this is not the correct generalization, as can be seen in (10), but I leave it to a classroom exercise to correct the rule. See, for example, Daly, Lyman, and Rhodes 1981:229, which was originally adapted from Akmajian and Heny 1975:176.

Such is not always the case. Languages often place constituents in special positions to highlight them. We look at one such example in some detail, involving fronting in Choapan Zapotec (Otomanguean, Mexico).[6]

Fronting obliques

The basic word order in Zapotec is verb-initial, as in (13).

(13) *ujo   bẽʔ   naʔ taɾia   tʃoapan   nioge*
      went man   that quickly   Choapan   yesterday
      The man went to Choapan quickly yesterday.

However, an oblique may optionally be moved to the beginning of the clause (i.e., FRONTED) as in (14)–(16).

(14) *taɾia   ujo   bẽʔ   naʔ tʃoapan   nioge*
      quickly   went man   that Choapan   yesterday
      The man went to Choapan *quickly* yesterday.

(15) *tʃoapan   ujo   bẽʔ   naʔ taɾia   nioge*
      Choapan   went man   that quickly   yesterday
      The man went *to Choapan* quickly yesterday.

(16) *nioge   ujo   bẽʔ   naʔ taɾia   tʃoapan*
      yesterday   went man   that quickly   Choapan
      The man went to Choapan quickly *yesterday*.

In Choapan Zapotec, fronting highlights a constituent; that is, the speaker is calling special attention to it and is placing special emphasis on it.[7] Fronting gives a subtle shift in meaning. It does not affect the basic 'plot' of the clause; the same person is going to the same place at the same time in all four examples. Rather, the difference is in the relative prominence of the different elements of the clause.

In Choapan Zapotec, as in many other languages, this special prominence is indicated by means of MOVEMENT, i.e., a departure from the basic word order. In transformational grammar, departures from the basic word order are accounted for by writing transformations that move elements from one part of a sentence to another.

Before we can write a transformation, however, we must decide what the base component does. Why? Recall that transformations only modify trees, they do not build them. Thus, in order to write a transformation, we must know about the trees it will be modifying; this generally means that we must know what the base is, since it builds the trees in the first place. In other words, our decisions about how to write phrase structure rules, lexical entries, and transformations depend on each other and must be made to work together.

We can write a simple set of phrase structure rules which is adequate for the data so far.

(17)
$$S \rightarrow V\ NP[Su] \left(\left\{ \begin{array}{c} AdvP \\ NP \end{array} \right\} \right)^{*}$$

NP $\rightarrow$ N (D)
AdvP $\rightarrow$ Adv ...

---

[6]Data from Larry Lyman. See footnote 2, p. 20 for information about transcription.

[7]Fronting in Zapotec languages is sometimes used to indicate focus, sometimes new topic, and sometimes just temporal or locative discontinuity (Chuck Speck, personal communication). I follow Lyman's suggestion in glossing the Choapan fronted constituents with English heavy stress, as if they were contrastive focus, but this is probably not the only discourse function they have.

As for the lexicon, we can assume that *taria* 'quickly' is an Adv, that *tʃoapan* 'Choapan' is an N, and that *nioge* 'yesterday' is an AdvP (compare chapter 9 "Obliques," p. 101).

This minimal base component generates the tree in (18), which is the deep structure for all four sentences (13)–(16).[8]

(18)   Deep structure for (13)–(16)

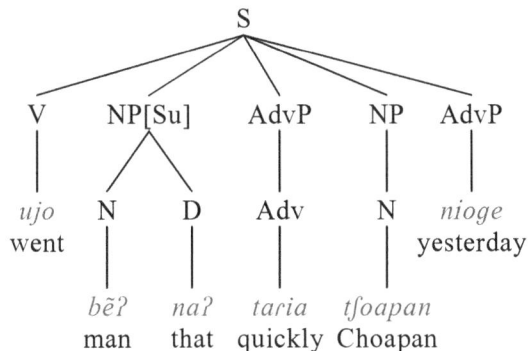

```
                           S
        ┌──────┬───────┬───────┬───────┐
        V    NP[Su]   AdvP    NP     AdvP
        │     ╱ ╲      │       │       │
       ujo   N   D    Adv      N     nioge
       went  │   │     │       │    yesterday
             bẽʔ naʔ  taria  tʃoapan
             man that quickly Choapan
```

This, of course, is also the surface structure tree for sentence (13). (When no transformations apply, the surface structure tree is identical to the deep structure tree.)

In order to produce the surface structures for the three with fronted constituents, we need a transformation which takes any single oblique in (18) and moves it to the left of the verb. For example, to produce (14), we want it to move the *taria* 'quickly' in front of the verb, as in (19).

(19)   Surface structure for (14)

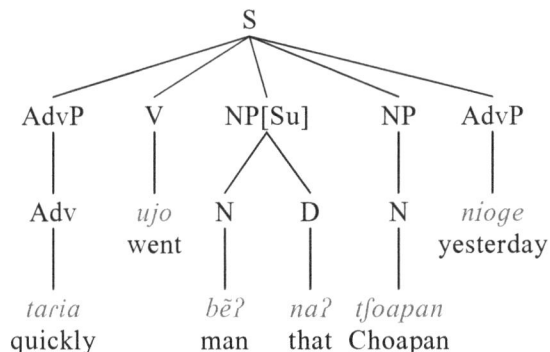

```
                            S
        ┌──────┬───────┬───────┬───────┐
       AdvP    V    NP[Su]    NP      AdvP
        │      │     ╱ ╲       │       │
       Adv    ujo   N   D      N     nioge
        │    went   │   │      │   yesterday
      taria         bẽʔ naʔ  tʃoapan
     quickly        man that Choapan
```

How do we write the transformation that derives (19) from (18)? Again, we'll just state what the rule does in prose:

(20)   **Fronting** (optional)
       Move AdvP or NP to the left of V.

Let's look at each part of this rule.

Fronting is the name of the transformation. We give informal labels to transformations as memory aids, using names that give some indication of what the rule accomplishes. In this case, the title refers to the change in structure.

The rule is labeled OPTIONAL, which means that if we don't apply it to a tree that is eligible, we still get a grammatical sentence. For instance, the tree in (18) is eligible for the Fronting rule, but if we choose not to apply the rule, we still get the grammatical sentence (13). If a transformation is OBLIGATORY, that means we have no choice about applying it; if we tried not to apply it, the result would be ungrammatical. We present examples of obligatory rules in later chapters.

---

[8]I am, for this chapter, ignoring Choapan Zapotec inflectional morphology.

It is essential to remember, when deciding whether a rule is obligatory or optional, to consider only grammaticality. Don't start thinking this way: 'Well, if I want to produce sentence (14), I have to apply the Fronting rule, so I guess that makes it obligatory, at least in this case.' That's not what the term means! A rule is not obligatory or optional with respect to individual trees; it is simply obligatory or optional in general. If we don't apply the Fronting rule to get (14), we still get a grammatical sentence (even though it may not be the one we want). Grammaticality is all that counts in determining optionality.

The rest of the rule in (20) means 'find an AdvP or NP, pull it off the tree, and stick it back on just to the left of the V'. This is the part of the rule that actually specifies what it does. There is some technical wording here: 'to the left of V' means that we reattach the moved item to the node that dominates V, that is, to the S. This is how reattachment works whenever we move something to the 'left' or 'right' of something else. In this case, an alternate wording is also possible: 'Move an AdvP or NP to the beginning of S'. This means to reattach it to the S node, in front of whatever daughters may already be there.[9]

There are three different ways to apply the rule in (20) to the tree in (18), one for each oblique that can be fronted. We have already seen how it applies to *taria* 'quickly' to produce (19). Suppose we want to produce sentence (15), in which *tʃoapan* 'Choapan' has been fronted. The rule can also do this, producing the tree in (21).

(21)   Surface structure for (15)

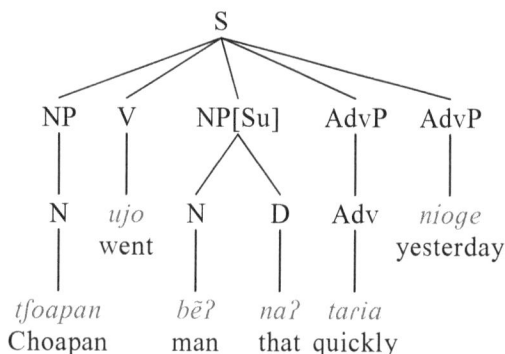

Similarly, the rule can be used to front *nioge* 'yesterday', as in (16). As an exercise, try drawing the resulting tree; see the footnote for an answer.[10] Thus, one rule can generate three different orders, represented in (14)–(16), all from the same deep structure tree (18).

---

[9]Both wordings have the same effect in this case, but in other cases they won't. Specifically, if the target of the movement is in the middle of a constituent, it is only possible to use the 'left/right' wording. Note, too, that moving something 'to the left of X' does not have the same effect as moving it 'to the beginning of X'; in the first case, the moved constituent ends up outside X, as its sister; in the second case the moved constituent ends up inside X, as its daughter. Formally, 'left/right' reattachment is known as 'sister adjunction' and 'beginning/end' reattachment as 'daughter adjunction'.

[10]The surface structure of (16) is as follows:

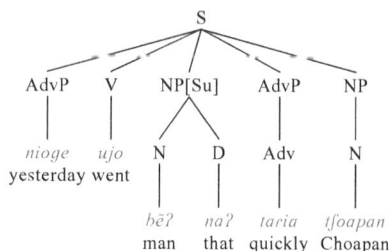

Restrictions on Fronting

Actually, the analysis so far is not quite right, because this rule (as written) could also move more than one constituent to the left of the verb, one at a time. In fact, however, such sentences are ungrammatical, as we see in (22) and (23).

(22) *nioge   taria   ujo   bẽʔ   naʔ   tʃoapan
      yesterday quickly   went   man   that Choapan
      (The man went to Choapan *quickly yesterday.*)

(23) *taria   nioge   ujo   bẽʔ   naʔ   tʃoapan
      quickly   yesterday went   man   that Choapan
      (The man went to Choapan *quickly yesterday.*)

Choapan Zapotec does not allow more than one oblique to be in front of the verb.

We don't want our grammar to produce these ungrammatical 'sentences', yet in its current form it does. There are various ways to stop the rule from applying twice. One way is simply to state that it must not reapply to its own output. Another is to require that it only operate on clauses that are (still) verb-initial, which has the effect of preventing it from applying twice.[11] How we do it, however, is less important than that it be done somehow.

One important point, though, is that the rule can only move one constituent at a time. We don't have to worry about blocking a derivation in which the Fronting rule moves two obliques at the same time, because this is ruled out by theoretical assumptions that we say more about a little later.

Fronting other constituents

Now consider the following additional data:

(24) bɛʔ   bẽʔ   naʔ nigula naʔ dumi
      gave person that woman   that money
      The man gave money to the woman.

(25) bẽʔ   naʔ bɛʔnɛʔ nigula   dumi
      person that gave   woman   money
      The man gave money to the woman.

(26) nigula   naʔ bɛʔ   bẽʔ   naʔ dumi
      woman   that gave person   that money
      To the woman the man gave money.

(27) dumi   bɛʔ   bẽʔ   naʔ nigula naʔ
      money   gave person that woman   that
      (It was) *money* (that) the man gave to the woman.

These sentences show us that we can also front subjects and objects in the same way as obliques.[12] Further investigation would show us that we could front practically any constituent in the following sentence:

---

[11]A third way would be to posit a filter (a quality control check on the output of the rules) which would check surface structure clauses to see if they have more than one constituent in front of the verb. If they did, the filter would mark them as ill-formed.

[12]I ignore one detail in (25): the extra *-nɛʔ* on the verb when the subject is fronted. This is a pronominal clitic copy, which is required whenever the subject is fronted. For simplicity of presentation, the rules in the text do not account for this detail.

(28) *bɛʔ   bẽʔ   naʔ   nigula   dumi   luegozi   ʒan   juʔ   ᴋɪɛ...*
      gave   man   that   woman   money   right.away   in   house   of.him   yesterday
      The man gave money to the woman right away yesterday in his house.

We can account for fronted NPs with only a slight modification to our grammar. We need to revise our phrase structure rule for S to include direct and indirect objects. We assume that obliques normally follow the objects, as in (28).

(29)
$$S \rightarrow V\ NP[Su]\ \big(NP[IO]\big)\ \big(NP[DO]\big) \left(\left\{ \begin{matrix} NP \\ AdvP \end{matrix} \right\} \right) *$$

Rule (20) will work exactly as we had it before, since it already fronts NPs and will front subjects and objects just as well as it did oblique NPs.

Actually, the 'or' in rule (20) suggests that perhaps any constituents could be fronted.[13] We could represent this hypothesis as follows (where 'XP' stands for any phrasal node):

(30) **Fronting** (optional)
      Move XP to the left of V.

Then, of course, we would look for data either confirming or disconfirming this new hypothesis.

15.5. Some (more) nitty gritties of transformations

There are four main things to include in an informal description of a transformation:

(31) a. What's the title?
      b. Is it optional or obligatory? (If you don't apply it, is the result grammatical?)
      c. What does the transformation do? (For movement rules: 'What moves where?')
      d. Does the tree have to meet any special conditions before the rule can apply?

Remember to consider all these things when you write a transformational rule.

Movement rules

Most of the transformations in this book involve some constituent being moved someplace in the tree.[14] There is one very important restriction on movement rules: a rule can move only one constituent at a time. Movement rules in languages around the world do not move more than one constituent at a time. If two or more constituents move together, that is usually regarded as evidence that those constituents group together to form a larger constituent.

For example, in sentence (26), two words are fronted by the same rule; this is evidence that they together form some sort of phrase. Up until now, if we found an N followed by a D which translated as an NP in English, we (probably unconsciously) made a hypothesis that this was an NP in the foreign language as well. Now we have evidence to back up our hypothesis: the N and D move together to the left of the V, which would be expected if they grouped together as an NP.

---

[13]Normally, linguists get suspicious when they see 'or' in a rule, especially if there is a whole list of alternative items that the rule may apply to. Often these ways of writing the rule mask a broader generalization that should be sought out and captured in one simple statement, as we do in (30).

[14]In fact, so many transformations are movements that the most recent versions of transformational grammar concentrate almost exclusively on movement transformations.

Revised outline of a transformational grammar

Current versions of transformational grammar distinguish between transformations that can change meaning and those which cannot. They do this by positing two new tree structures as part of the derivation of a sentence, in addition to Deep Structure and Surface Structure.

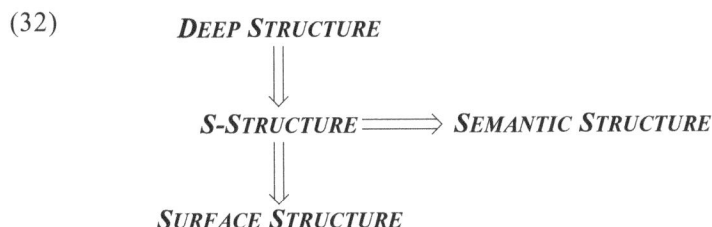

(32)   **DEEP STRUCTURE**
                    ⇓

        S-STRUCTURE ⟹ **SEMANTIC STRUCTURE**
                    ⇓

        SURFACE STRUCTURE

One, which we'll call SEMANTIC STRUCTURE, provides a basis for representing the meaning of the sentence, in the same way that Surface Structure provides a basis for representing its pronunciation.[15] The other, called S-STRUCTURE (Shallow Structure), is the intermediate step that connects Deep Structure with Surface Structure and Semantic Structure.[16] Deep Structure is first transformed to produce S-Structure, then S-Structure is transformed in one way to produce Semantic Structure and in another way to produce Surface Structure.

To get from one structure to the next, we need transformations. If you compare this chart to the one given earlier in (9), you will see that the various rule types are omitted from (32). This is because diagrams like (32) are usually drawn to represent the way transformations are organized and all three arrows represent transformations of various types. As an exercise, see if you can determine where the other types of rules in (9) belong in (32); see the footnote for an answer.[17]

We won't concern ourselves here with Semantic Structure or the transformations that derive it from S-Structure, except for this: Any transformations which apply before S-Structure can have an impact on meaning, since S-Structure is the basis for constructing Semantic Structure. Any changes that are made between S-Structure and Surface Structure cannot affect the meaning in any way, only the pronunciation, because these changes will not be reflected in Semantic Structure. Thus, we can distinguish in our grammar between grammatical rules which change meaning, like Fronting, and rules that don't, like English Particle Movement. Fronting would have to apply between Deep Structure and S-Structure; Particle Movement probably applies between S-Structure and Surface Structure.

There are two important consequences of this distinction. One is that any transformation that affects meaning must precede any other transformation that does not affect meaning. The other is related to a further claim made by current transformational grammars: all transformations that apply before S-Structure must be movements. Consequently, the only transformations that can change meaning are movement rules. Between S-Structure and Surface Structure other changes can be made, like deleting a constituent, but these can never change the meaning of a sentence.[18]

---

[15]Semantic structure is usually called 'logical form'. In place of 'surface structure' in this diagram, one often sees the label 'phonetic form', but this tends to confuse syntactic surface structure, which is the input to phonological rules, with the output of those rules, which is what would properly be called 'phonetic form'.

[16]According to Chomsky (1977:6), the term 'shallow structure' was originally suggested by Paul Postal. It was apparently soon abbreviated to 'S-structure', which is the name most commonly found in the literature.

[17]The phrase structure rules and lexicon together produce Deep Structure, and thus should be inserted at the top of the diagram. Transformations occur wherever there is a double-shafted arrow. Inflectional spellout rules apply after all syntactic transformations and thus apply just before Surface Structure. For more details, see chapter 18 "Overall Structure of a Grammar."

[18]Theoretical claims like these must be treated with caution. They can't be rejected simply by presenting an analysis of a set of facts that has, for example, a deletion transformation that changes meaning. The reason is that there may well be another analysis of the facts that is consistent with the claims. Claims like these are like the rules of a game; you have to make a conscientious effort to play the game according to the rules, to find an analysis of the facts that is consistent with the claims. Only if that leads to unsatisfactory results should you raise questions about revising the rules.

This conception of grammar also cannot be rejected on the basis that it is not reasonable to assume that people construct sentences in this manner. This is a model of competence (what people know about language), not performance (how they

15.6. Focus and topic

Recall that Fronting in Choapan Zapotec gives special prominence to an item. There are two main types of special prominence that may be placed on a noun phrase, called FOCUS and TOPIC. Both have to do with subtle shifts in meaning[19] that are important in making a sentence fit well within its larger discourse context.

An item is put in FOCUS to contrast it with some other item within an assumed context. For example, (33) would be appropriate in a conversation where it was obvious I had said something, but the hearer didn't hear it correctly the first time.

(33)   *I said* 'bees', *not* 'peas'.

Everybody agrees that something was said; the focus on *'bees'* provides information about *what* was said, in contrast to other possibilities. For this reason, focus is sometimes called CONTRASTIVE FOCUS.

The most common way in English to express contrastive focus is through heavy stress, which is usually realized by higher than normal pitch. For example, imagine how you would say (34).

(34)   *I like* volleyball *but not* tennis.

Heavy stress is often written with italics, underlining, or boldface; this is one of the few cases where we indicate pitch in written English.

There are at least four common strategies that languages use to express contrastive focus.[20] Heavy stress is one, as in (34). Another common device is moving an item to some special position in the sentence (usually the beginning); this is one of the reasons for fronting in Choapan Zapotec, as reflected in the glosses of the examples above.

A third common strategy for expressing focus is by inserting a 'focus' morpheme next to the focused constituent. English reflexive pronouns can serve this purpose, as shown in (35).

(35)   *The director* **himself** *made the meals, since he didn't think the fledgling school could afford a cook.*

Himself in (35) is not used with the usual reflexive sense; the director is not doing anything to himself. Rather it places focus on *the director,* indicating that he, in contrast to any of his subordinates, personally cracked the eggs and flipped the pancakes.

A fourth common strategy is to use what is called a CLEFT construction. Clefts contain both a nominal complement and a relative clause referring to the same person or thing. (See chapter 14 "Nonactive Complements," p. 187, for nominal complements; see chapter 23 "Relative Clauses" for more on relative clauses.) Four different types of cleft structures are shown in (36); the relative clauses are bracketed and the nominal complement is in boldface.

(36)   a. *It was* **Dave** *[who saved the day].*
       b. *[What I want] is* **a long weekend.**
       c. *The one [who means the most to me] is* **Mildred.**
       d. **Penelope** *is the one [who took us to the airport].*

---

make use of that knowledge to produce or interpret sentences). Again, the only reasonable refutation is to show that the theoretical assumptions make it difficult or impossible to state all relevant generalizations in a satisfactory manner.

[19]Here I use 'meaning' broadly, to include what is usually called pragmatics, or the study of meaning as it relates to a specific communicative situation with a particular speaker and hearer. It is distinguished from 'semantics proper', which has to do with meaning in the abstract. Focus and topic are generally considered to be pragmatic notions. Also, I use 'focus' and 'contrastive focus' interchangeably, although some scholars distinguish them.

[20]There may be other common strategies, too. I am not aware of any cross-linguistic survey of ways of expressing focus and so can offer nothing more at this point than an impressionistic list of things I have observed.

The sentences in (36) are similar in meaning to those in (37), but without special focus on any constituent.

(37) a. *Dave saved the day.*
      b. *I want a long weekend.*
      c. *Mildred means the most to me.*
      d. *Penelope took us to the airport.*

Languages may employ more than one of these strategies, even in the same sentence.

(38) *It was* John himself *who I saw peeking in the window.*

And, if a language has more than one such strategy, there may be subtle differences in meaning between them.

It is helpful to understand focus in terms of new and old information in a discourse. The focused element introduces new information; the rest of the sentence recapitulates old information. This is especially obvious by comparing certain types of questions to some possible answers.

(39) *Who did you meet?*
      a. *I met the stage director.*
      b. *I met the president himself.*
      c. *It was the stage director that I met.*

Each of the three responses repeats the old information that I met someone, information which is assumed by the question. The focused element provides the new information that answers the question.

On the other hand, we often need to say things in which one element in the sentence is old information and most or all of the rest is new. In the following example, the only piece of information that carries from one sentence to the next is 'I'.

(40) *Yesterday, I wandered down into the canyon to look for wildflowers. I had just reached the little stream at the bottom when I heard a gunshot bounce off the far wall. Of course, I hit the ground fast, getting mud all over my new T-shirt.*

The old information that carries through from one sentence to the next within a paragraph is commonly called the TOPIC.[21] The topic indicates what the sentence is talking about; the rest of the sentence provides information about it.

In most cases, the subject is also topic. Indeed, in some languages this is a requirement; it is part of the function of subjects in those languages to express the topic.

When the topic changes, languages may have special devices to call attention to the NEW TOPIC. English does this with the words *as for*.

(41) *Arthur was delighted to have been chosen as the class president.* **As for** *his rival, her opinion was somewhat different.*

Sometimes topicalized elements are moved to special positions, just like focused elements. For example, although English normally puts the topic in the subject, it can also put it in the direct object. When it does, the direct object may be fronted.

(42) a. *When did you last see "Gone with the Wind"?*
      b. **That movie** *I last saw in April.*

---

[21]Of course, there may be more than one piece of old information that carries from one sentence to the next. One of these is generally more important to the context than the others; it is selected by the speaker as topic and is placed in each sentence in positions of greater prominence.

Fronting of the object is especially appropriate when a series of topics are being compared.

(43)   a. *What types of vegetables do you like?*
       b. ***Beans*** *I like.* ***Broccoli*** *is horrible.* ***Corn*** *I can eat any day of the week.*

Each sentence in (43b) introduces a new vegetable as topic. The vegetable is either topicalized by being fronted or it appears as the subject (the default topic). This use is very similar to contrastive focus, since each new topic introduces new information. However, there is something lacking for this to be focus; there is no assumed context of old information. Hence, the transformation that fronts objects in English is normally called TOPICALIZATION.

We've thus seen that the same device can be used for two different purposes. Fronting may either indicate focus or it may identify a new topic in contrast to other topics.

The discussion above points out the difference between movement rules, on the one hand, and semantic notions like focus and topic on the other. It is true that movement is often used to express focus or topic, but they are not the same as movement. As we have seen, not all instances of them involve movement transformations, and movement can happen for reasons other than contrastive focus or topicalization (as in Particle Movement).

This can create a bit of a problem when you analyze syntax. If you only look at isolated sentences, it may not be possible to determine whether a movement rule affects meaning, and if so, what affect it has. Usually, you need examples of sentences in some larger context to figure out what subtle shifts of meaning (if any) are expressed by variations in constituent order. Yet (especially in exercises that may be used with this textbook), you may not have this context. Sometimes the free glosses may contain underlining; this often indicates contrastive focus, but you can't be sure. In other cases, you may have no information as to meaning. In such a case, you just have to name the rule after the change in structure that it makes, with a name like **Fronting,** and leave open the question of whether it precedes or follows S-Structure. In the field, the best thing to do is to collect lots of texts and study them to see how special positions of constituents within sentences express relationships of the sentences to each other.

15.7. Picking a basic word order

When analyzing variable orders of constituents, you need to pick an order which is generated by the phrase structure rules and appears in deep structure. We call this the BASIC ORDER, that is, the order produced by the base.

How do you decide which order is basic? We can't consider a complete answer yet, since we need to cover the material in the next few chapters first. (We come back to the problem in chapter 17 "Commands," p. 243.) But, there are some rules of thumb that will help in the meantime. One of these has already been mentioned in chapter 6 "The Base" (p. 52). As a first hypothesis, pick the order that occurs most frequently in your data.[22] However, this guideline can be misleading, because sometimes data can be biased toward an order that is not the basic order. Here are three other rules of thumb to consider, which will help you zero in on the best data for choosing basic order.

First, base your first hypothesis on clauses which have neutral semantics. For example, we've seen above that placing special prominence on one constituent is often expressed by a deviation from the basic word order. Also watch out for clauses whose order may be determined by some other semantic or discourse factors. Clauses that occur at the beginnings of paragraphs or sections in English narrative tend to have fronted time or location obliques (see chapter 9 "Obliques," p. 105), as a way of calling attention to a change in time or location. Noun phrases that have special prominence (such as topic or focus) are often fronted or moved to some other special position. In

---

[22]The concept of 'basic word order' presented in this book comes from a generative perspective. It differs from the concept used in functional-typological approaches, which typically choose the most frequently occurring word order in running text as the 'basic word order'. Also, these approaches often pay more attention to main clauses than subordinate ones. This sometimes leads generative and functional-typological approaches to propose different 'basic word orders' for the same language, but of course they are really talking about different things.

Biblical Hebrew, clauses on the narrative plot-line are verb-initial, while other clauses are SVO.[23] Questions often involve special constituent orders (see chapter 16 "Questions"). Watch out for all these factors and pick a basic order that reflects as little special semantic conditioning as possible.

Second, avoid pronouns. Pronouns often move around more freely than do nouns[24] and may easily be confused with agreement markers. Base your hypothesis about basic word order on the positions that nouns occupy.[25]

Third, look at the order of elements in embedded clauses, not main clauses. The reason is that there is often more freedom in word order in main clauses than in embedded clauses, thus more complications in their analysis. Because main clauses are sometimes called 'upstairs clauses', this consideration has been summarized 'more goes on upstairs than downstairs' and thus is sometimes called the PENTHOUSE PRINCIPLE.[26]

To illustrate, consider its application to German.[27] At first glance, German appears to be SVO.

(44) *Hans **ass** die Kartoffeln.*
       Hans ate the potatoes
       Hans ate the potatoes.

However, when there is an auxiliary verb, it is in second position and the main verb appears at the end of the clause.

(45) *Hans **hat** die Kartoffeln **gegessen.***
       Hans has the potatoes   eaten
       Hans has eaten the potatoes.

(46) *Hans **sollte** die Kartoffeln **essen.***
       Hans should the potatoes   eat
       Hans should eat the potatoes.

Inside embedded clauses, all verbs come at the end, but the verb in the main clause is still in second position.

(47) *Ich weiss...*
       I   know
       a. ... [*dass Hans die Kartoffeln **ass**].*
              that Hans the potatoes   ate
       b. ... [*dass Hans die Kartoffeln **gegessen hat**].*
              that Hans the potatoes   eaten   has
       c. ... [*dass Hans die Kartoffeln **essen sollte**].*
              that Hans the potatoes   eat   should

This is strange; where do verbs really belong in our rules?

The Penthouse Principle suggests that we should take the order in embedded clauses as our guide and assume that the basic order is SOV. That is, our phrase structure rules should assume SOV order and all deep structure trees will be SOV, even in main clauses. Then, all we need is a transformation that moves the highest verb (the auxiliary if there is one, otherwise the main verb) to just after the

---

[23]Shin Ja J. Hwang, personal communication.

[24]This is especially true if they are clitics (see chapter 20 "Word Division and Clitics").

[25]In some languages, clauses with more than one overt noun are rare or extremely awkward. For example, with transitive verbs, either the subject or object will always be a pronoun or completely absent. Further, when a noun is present, it may often be topicalized or focused, so by the first rule of thumb, such clauses should not be used as evidence for basic order. The concept of basic order may not be very important in such languages or may need to be determined based on subtle evidence. In such a case, pick the one that is most reasonable as a first hypothesis and turn your attention to other matters. Keep your eyes and ears open for evidence that may help decide the matter.

[26]Ross 1973.

[27]For a more extensive discussion of the German facts within Government-binding Theory and for further references, see Haegeman 1991:520–37.

subject, generating the surface word order. (We are assuming an articulated clause structure, since the main clauses are SVO. See chapter 8 "Verbal Valence," p. 85, for the analysis of auxiliary verbs with articulated clause structures.)

(48)   *Deep:*   *Hans [_{VP} [_{VP} die Kartoffeln essen] ___ sollte.]*

   Surface: *Hans [_{VP} sollte [_{VP} die Kartoffeln essen.]]*

As a challenge, try writing that transformation. See the footnote for one way of doing so.[28]

Here, again, are the four rules of thumb for making a good first hypothesis about basic order:

(49)   a. choose the order which is most common
       b. examine semantically neutral clauses (no topicalization, focus, questions, etc.)
       c. examine the position of nouns, not pronouns
       d. if there is a difference, use the order in embedded clauses, not main clauses

However, these are just for making a *first* hypothesis. Ultimately, you have to choose a basic order that works best for your overall analysis. So, you may have to try more than one possibility, see what adjustments you have to make in your overall grammar for each one, and then choose the hypothesis that gives the best grammar overall. (For more explanation, see chapter 17 "Commands," p. 243.)

15.8. Review of key terms

All languages allow some MOVEMENT of the constituents of the clause, or departure from the BASIC ORDER. Often a constituent is moved to some prominent position to give it (CONTRASTIVE) FOCUS; especially common is the use of FRONTING for this purpose. Movement may also be used for TOPICALIZATION, especially to identify NEW TOPICS. Other times, there is no apparent meaning to the movement, as in PARTICLE MOVEMENT. As noted by the PENTHOUSE PRINCIPLE, movements are more common in main clauses than in embedded clauses, so that the order in embedded clauses is a better guide for choosing a BASIC ORDER.

In a TRANSFORMATIONAL GRAMMAR, alternative orders are accounted for using MOVEMENT TRANSFORMATIONS. Transformations are operations that change DEEP STRUCTURE trees into SURFACE STRUCTURE. Halfway between Deep and Surface is a level called S-STRUCTURE, which forms the basis for semantic interpretation. Thus, transformations that apply before S-Structure can have an effect on meaning; those that apply between S-Structure and Surface Structure cannot. Transformations may be OBLIGATORY or OPTIONAL, depending on whether the result is grammatical if they are not applied to a particular tree.

Besides using movement, focus can be expressed by heavy stress, insertion of a 'focus' morpheme, and CLEFTING.

---

[28]The simplest way to get the verb in second position is to move it to the beginning of its VP. (This is one of the advantages of using an articulated clause structure, as opposed to a flat one.) This rule must be worded carefully, though, so only the topmost VP in a tree is affected. Here is one way of stating this requirement:

Verb-second in main clauses (obligatory)

Within VP immediately dominated by a root S, move V to beginning of that VP.

The mention of the 'root S' limits the transformation to apply only in main clauses. The requirement that the VP be immediately dominated by S means that only the topmost VP within that clause will be affected. The transformation is obligatory, because once the necessary conditions are met, the transformation must apply in all trees in order for the result to be grammatical.

15.9. Questions for analysis

1. What word order is basic? Is this an articulated or flat clause structure?
2. What other word orders are there? Specifically, what constituents can occur in what non-basic positions?
3. What effect do the non-basic orders have on the meaning of the sentence, if any?
4. How does this language express contrastive focus?
   a. By a change in word order?
   b. By a special morpheme associated with the focused element?
   c. By intonation?
   d. By clefting?
   e. By some other device?
   f. By various combinations of these?
5. Is there any special marking for topics (either new or established)? What is it?
   a. By putting the topic in a special position in the clause?
   b. By always or usually encoding the topic as the subject?
   c. By a special morpheme associated with the topic?
   d. By some other device?

15.10. Sample description

Choapan Zapotec has VSO basic word order; this is observed in sentences with a neutral reading.

(1) *bɛʔ   bẽʔ   naʔ nigula naʔ dumi*
    gave person that woman that money
    The man gave money to the woman.

One variation on this order is to place a constituent at the beginning of the sentence, immediately preceding the verb. Any NP or oblique can be fronted in this way.

(2) *taɾia   ujo   bẽʔ naʔ tʃoapan nioge*
    quickly went man that Choapan yesterday
    The man went to Choapan *quickly* yesterday.

(3) *nigula naʔ bɛʔ   bẽʔ   naʔ dumi*
    woman   that gave person that money
    To the woman the man gave money.

However, only one constituent may precede the verb.

(4) **taɾia   nioge   ujo   bẽʔ naʔ tʃoapan*
    quickly yesterday went man that Choapan
    (The man went to Choapan *quickly yesterday*.)

15.11. For further reading

The most famous early work in Transformational Grammar is Chomsky's 1965 monograph *Aspects of the Theory of Syntax*. It's heavy going in some places, but by now you've covered enough material that you might want to tackle it. Chapter 1 covers a number of foundational issues, such as competence versus performance, the overall organization of a transformational grammar, the type of data that we need to determine the best grammar for a language, and what constitutes 'best' in a grammar and a theory. Chapter 2 discusses the base, including the use of features to represent syntactic and morphological properties of words. Chapter 3 discusses transformations, in a form that is similar to the way they are presented here (although the formulation in this book has been modified somewhat by subsequent work). For an easier introduction to the basic elements of Transformational Grammar at this stage of its development, see Perlmutter and Soames 1979.

Most transformations discussed in current versions of Transformational Grammar are movements. Indeed, there are quite a number of things that can move around in most languages. Radford (1988, chapters 8–10) covers several of them in English and uses them to build up to a rather startling proposal assumed in most recent transformational work. It may be that there is only one movement rule in all languages: move anything anywhere. The apparent large number of different movement rules may simply be the result of independent conditions that strictly determine what can move where, with different conditions applicable in different languages. If this intrigues you, check out Radford's discussion, which makes the rationale behind it quite clear. (However, demonstrating that such a sweeping claim is actually correct is quite a bit more than can be done in one book, but that's just one of the things that makes linguistics interesting these days.)

Most languages allow some variation in word order, either for some specific purpose (such as focus or topicalization) or just for stylistic variety, and some languages allow more freedom than others. Steele (1978:585–623) surveys a number of languages and draws several conclusions about factors that can influence how free or rigid word order can be and what optional word orders tend to be allowed in sentences with various basic word orders.

For more further discussion about notions like FOCUS and TOPIC, see Andrews 1985:77–80 and Comrie 1981:56–59. Harries-Delisle (1978:419–86) surveys the variety of structures that are used to express contrastive focus in a variety of languages and notes some consistent correlations with basic word order.

16
Questions

16.1. Goals and prerequisites

This chapter will help you do the following:

- ◉ distinguish between the form and function of statements, questions, and commands; classify them according to their structural characteristics (form), not necessarily according to the way speakers actually use them (function)
- ◉ state the primary functions of yes-no and content questions and the strategies that are most commonly used to express each type
- ◉ describe the structures used in a particular language to express each type of question
- ◉ construct a formal analysis which generates these structures (including appropriate lexical categories, phrase structure rules, and/or transformations)

It assumes that you are familiar with the following material:

- ✓ basic clause structure from earlier chapters on syntax
- ✓ handling of inflectional morphology (chapter 10)
- ✓ movement transformations (chapter 15 "Variable Orders of Constituents")

16.2. Questionable beliefs

Up to now, we have been considering the structure of STATEMENTS, sentences which are normally used to convey information. In this chapter and the next we consider two variations on sentence structure: QUESTIONS (normally used to request information) and COMMANDS (normally used to influence the behavior of others). Although you are certainly familiar with the distinction, you may have been taught to think too simplistically about them. In the next two sections, we look at two important distinctions that are often overlooked in basic grammar education.

Form and function

Your prior education probably implied a very simple relationship between the form of a sentence (its grammatical structure) and its function (what people use it for). It is not true that questions always request information or that any sentence which requests information is a question. Questions can also be used to influence others' behavior, a function normally associated with commands.

(1)   a. *Why don't we start now?*
      b. *How many times do I have to tell you to stop whistling in the house?*

Sometimes people ask a question when they really aren't asking for information; such questions are called RHETORICAL QUESTIONS. Often these are used to introduce a topic, prepare an audience for stating an important claim, or otherwise make explicit the structure of the discourse. This function is more like that of statements.

(2)   a. *How should we understand this problem? I will suggest a way...*
      b. *Could we find a better solution than the one Maria has proposed? Certainly not!*
      c. *What do we need in a formal analysis to handle this data? First we should...*

Similarly, statements and commands are sometimes used with the function of questions: to request information.

(3)   a. *I'd like to find out more about your dried artichoke collection.*
      b. *Tell me everything you remember about the robber's appearance.*

So, then, it is important to distinguish the form of an utterance from its function. The form is its grammatical structure, whether it is a statement, question, or command. Each form has a primary function, but in English each can also be used for functions typical of the others.

(4)

	Primary function	Secondary functions
Statement	Convey information	Request information Influence others' behavior
Question	Request information	Influence others' behavior Convey information Introduce topics and otherwise make explicit the structure of the discourse
Command	Influence others' behavior	Request information

The distinction between primary and secondary functions is important for three reasons. One, the primary function is what we use as the basis for naming a form. That is, if in our analysis, we find a particular sentence structure that is primarily used for requesting information, then we can call that structure a 'question'. (As always, we do the analysis on the basis of form and choose labels for structures on the basis of meaning.) On the other hand, just because a structure can be used to request information doesn't mean that it is a type of question; to be appropriately called a question, requesting information has to be its primary function.

Two, primary functions are what allow us to identify a structure in one language as being in some sense 'the same as' a structure in another. That is, there are certain cross-linguistic generalizations about questions (discussed in the rest of the chapter) that can help you in your analysis of a new language, but they are valid only for structures which have the primary function of requesting information.

Three, although the primary functions of questions will be the same in all languages, the secondary functions vary quite a bit from one language to the next. Although English (like many European languages) uses rhetorical questions quite freely, other languages may use questions only to request information or for purposes unlike any that English uses.

What all this means is that the primary functions are the 'core' of a grammatical description. Of course, the secondary functions of questions are important objects of study too. An entire subdiscipline, called PRAGMATICS, is devoted to the study of how people use language to communicate. This includes the different uses that statements, questions, and commands can be put to. To speak a language effectively, we need to do more than assemble grammatical sentence structures, we must use the different structures to communicate the way native speakers do. A full description of a language includes pragmatic information about the secondary uses of statements, questions, and commands.

Still, since this is a book about grammar, not pragmatics, the rest of this chapter (and the next) concentrates on the form of questions and commands and their primary functions.

Intonation: Distinguishing two types of questions

Children are also often taught that 'your voice goes up' at the end of a question. However, this statement, like so many taught about language in schools, is only partly true. Say the following questions to yourself:

(5) a. *Who killed Cock Robin?*
     b. *Where did you park the car?*
     c. *How old were you when you were born?*

(6) a. *Is that your great Uncle Harold?*
     b. *Does this course count toward your degree?*
     c. *Did you bake that blueberry pie?*

Only the questions in (6) are normally said with rising intonation.[1] The idea that all questions have rising intonation is a myth.

These two intonation patterns point out that there are really two types of questions with two different meanings. The questions in (5) are used to ask a question such as 'who?', 'what?', 'where?', 'when?', 'why?', and 'how?', we call them CONTENT QUESTIONS or INFORMATION QUESTIONS. (Because so many of these words in English begin with *wh*, content questions are often called WH QUESTIONS.) The questions in (6) have an expected 'yes' or 'no' answer and we call them YES-NO QUESTIONS or TRUTH-VALUE QUESTIONS. Yes-no questions are like true-false questions on an exam (only two answers are normally expected), while content questions are like fill-in-the-blank questions (any of a number of answers are possible).

16.3. Content questions

Consider the following pairs of content questions and statements in Choapan Zapotec:

(7) a. *gaʒi   ɾao   ʒua   ʒubaʔ*
         where? eats John corn
         Where does John eat corn?

     b. *ɾao   ʒua   ʒubaʔ   uga*
         eats John corn   there
         John eats corn there.

(8) a. *bataʒi   ɾao   ʒua   ʒubaʔ*
         when?   eats John corn
         When does John eat corn?

     b. *ɾao   ʒua   ʒubaʔ   zila*
         eats John corn   early
         John eats corn early.

---

[1]The questions in (5) are sometimes said with rising intonation when a person repeats a question that he has just been asked. Normally, however, when sincerely asking for information, these questions are said with falling intonation or a quick rise on the initial interrogative phrase followed by a gradual fall. The resulting pattern is more like that used for statements than it is like the questions in (6).

(9)   a. *cabiʒi ɾao ʒua ʒubaʔ*
          how? eats John corn
          How does John eat corn?

      b. *ɾao ʒua ʒubaʔ tsolaʔdjiʔ*
          eats John corn   slowly
          John eats corn slowly.

There are two differences to note between the questions and statements. One is that the questions include what is traditionally called an INTERROGATIVE ADVERB, a word like 'where?', 'when?', or 'how?', each of which is used to question a particular type of constituent. We will call them and other similar words (see below) INTERROGATIVE WORDS. In content questions, we sometimes say that the interrogative word allows us to QUESTION a particular category, function, or meaning. For example, (7a) questions an AdvP of location and (8a) questions time.

The second difference between the questions and statements is that interrogative words questioning obliques occur at the beginning of the clause, but ordinary obliques occur at the end. As we saw in chapter 15 "Variable Orders of Constituents," the basic word order in Zapotec places obliques at the end of the clause; constituents are moved in front of the verb only for special purposes. Thus, we see that content questions, like sentences with focus, involve fronting.[2]

Formal analysis of content questions

Our overall approach to the analysis of content questions in Choapan Zapotec will be to generate interrogative obliques at the end of the clause, like other obliques, and later move them with a transformation to the beginning of the clause. As in all cases of movement, we need to consider three different parts of the grammar: the phrase structure rules, the lexicon, and a transformation.

The phrase structure rule we developed in chapter 15 "Variable Orders of Constituents" (p. 210) is still adequate. It introduces an AdvP into the deep structure tree, making a place for the interrogative adverbs to be inserted.

(10)
$$S \rightarrow V\ NP[Su]\ (NP[IO])\ (NP[DO]) \left(\left\{ \begin{matrix} NP \\ AdvP \end{matrix} \right\} \right) *$$

In the lexicon, we categorize interrogative adverbs as AdvPs, since they appear to be mutually-substitutable for other AdvPs (compare chapter 9 "Obliques," p. 101).[3] That is, they are mutually-substitutable, except for the fact that they occur at the beginning of the clause, but we can take care of that later with a transformation. However, we do need to keep track of the fact that interrogative words are not ordinary AdvPs, so when we get around to moving them later we won't inadvertently move just any AdvP. We do this by putting interrogative adverbs in a special subcategory within the category AdvP. As we have done before, we use a feature to identify the members of the subcategory. (Compare what we did to distinguish common and proper nouns in chapter 6 "The Base," p. 54.) The feature we use is [±WH]. All interrogative words are [+WH]; all others are [−WH].[4]

(11) **AdvP[+WH]**   **AdvP[−WH]**
      gaʒi   where?   *uga*   there
      bataʒi   when?   *nioge*   yesterday
      cabiʒi   how?

---

[2]Indeed, focus and content questions frequently share structural traits, most likely because an interrogative word is generally in contrastive focus. The common structure here suggests that Focus and WH Movement in Choapan Zapotec could be given a unified treatment.

[3]Equivalently, we could have classified these unmodifiable words (both the interrogative and non-interrogative ones) as PPs rather than AdvPs.

[4]To avoid clutter, I normally omit the feature value [−WH] from lexical entries in this book and only mention the feature [WH] when its value is '+'. The value [−WH] should be assumed whenever a value for [WH] is not mentioned.

Thus, when we are ready to insert items from the lexicon, we have a choice whenever we find an AdvP node. Either we can (1) use the regular AdvP rule to build an ordinary adverb phrase, (2) insert an ordinary single-word AdvP (such as *uga* 'there') from the lexicon, or (3) insert an interrogative word from the special subcategory AdvP[+WH]. If we take the last option, this makes the sentence into a content question.

For example, here is the deep structure of (7a):

(12)

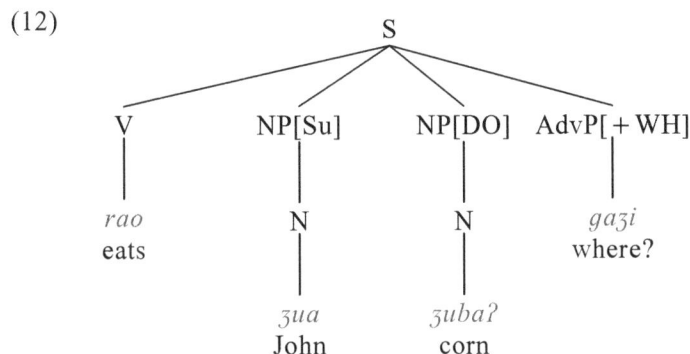

This tree has the same words as the surface sentence (7a), but in a different order. The order in the deep structure tree (12) is the basic word order, with the oblique at the end. In order to produce the surface tree for (7a), we need a transformation which moves the interrogative word to the beginning of the sentence. This transformation is generally called WH MOVEMENT.[5]

As far as we know, interrogative words in Choapan Zapotec must occur at the beginning of the sentence. (This is a reasonable assumption, since many, perhaps most, languages that front interrogative words do so all the time.) This means that if we allowed the tree (12) to surface without modification, we would predict the result to be ungrammatical. Thus, we are assuming that the WH Movement transformation is obligatory.

We are now ready to write the transformation.

(13) **WH Movement** (obligatory)
      Move AdvP[+WH] to beginning of S.

When an interrogative oblique is inserted from the lexicon, (13) will move it to the front of the sentence. Applying the transformation to (12) produces the following:

(14)   Surface structure of (7a)

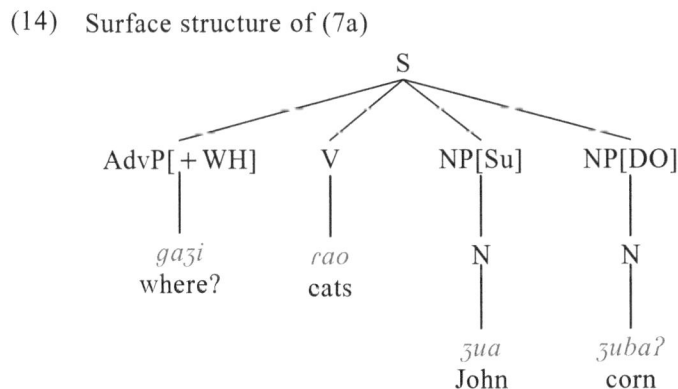

---

[5]The name WH Movement and the feature [WH] are used even in other languages, whose interrogative words, of course, don't contain 'wh'. These labels are admittedly based on the structure of English and one could object to them on that basis. We should, of course, be very cautious about assuming that other languages are like English in their structure (the actual formulation of the rules and lexicon), but names of rules or features are relatively harmless. 'WH' has one advantage in being commonly-recognized as referring to content questions.

Questioned NPs

What about questioning elements of a sentence besides obliques? This too is possible.

(15) a. *nuʒi   ɾao   ʒubaʔ*
          who? eats corn
          Who eats corn?

      b. *ɾao   ʒua   ʒubaʔ*
          eats John corn
          John eats corn.

(16) a. *biʒi   ɾao   ʒua*
          what? eats John
          What does John eat?

      b. *ɾao   ʒua   ʒubaʔ*
          eats John corn
          John eats corn.

(17) a. *nuʒi   bɛʔ ʒua   dumi*
          to.whom? gave John money
          To whom did John give money?

      b. *bɛʔ ʒua   nigula   dumi*
          gave John woman money
          John gave the money to the woman.

These sentences show how NPs are questioned with what are traditionally called INTERROGATIVE PRONOUNS.

Their formal analysis is similar to interrogative adverbs. They can be listed in the lexicon as a subcategory of pronouns.

(18) **NP[+ WH]**
      nuʒi   who?
      biʒi   what?

Note that we use the same feature [+ WH] as we did with interrogative obliques. Using [+ WH] for both subcategories allows us to use the same transformation to front interrogative pronouns as well as interrogative obliques, just by referring only to [+ WH], not AdvP or NP.

(19) **WH Movement** (obligatory)
      Move [+ WH] to beginning of S.

Using this rule, (15a) and (16a) are derived like this:

(20)   Deep structure of (15a)   Deep structure of (16a)

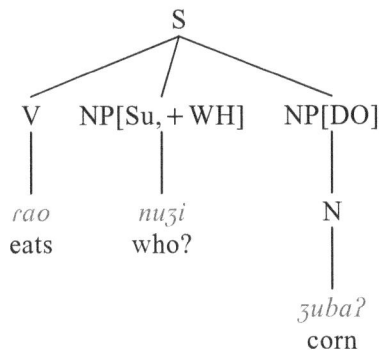

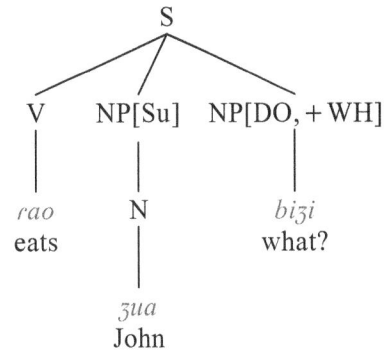

```
               S                                          S
        ┌──────┼──────┐                          ┌────────┼────────┐
        V   NP[Su,+WH]  NP[DO]                    V     NP[Su]   NP[DO,+WH]
        │      │        │                         │       │          │
      ɾao     nuʒi      N                        ɾao       N         biʒi
      eats    who?      │                        eats      │        what?
                        │                                  │
                      ʒubaʔ                               ʒua
                       corn                               John
```

(21)   Surface structure of (15a)   Surface structure of (16a)

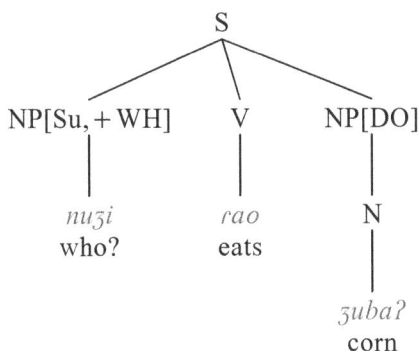

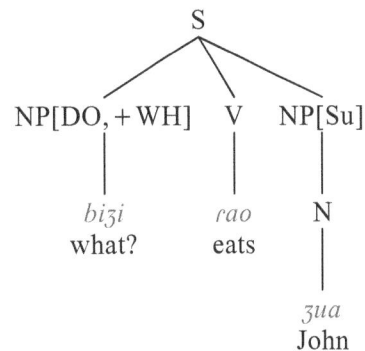

```
               S                                          S
        ┌──────┼──────┐                          ┌────────┼────────┐
   NP[Su,+WH]  V    NP[DO]                    NP[DO,+WH]   V     NP[Su]
        │      │     │                            │        │        │
       nuʒi   ɾao    N                           biʒi     ɾao       N
       who?   eats   │                           what?    eats      │
                     │                                               │
                   ʒubaʔ                                            ʒua
                    corn                                            John
```

(The two features on the subject come from two different sources; [Su] is inserted by phrase structure rules, while [+WH] comes with *nuʒi* 'who?' from the lexicon.)

Movement transformations and gaps

Let's briefly consider an alternative analysis, which will point out one important fact about content questions, as well as illustrate why we need transformations in our grammar. Suppose we try to generate content questions without a transformation, by modifying the S rule to generate an interrogative word in clause-first position.

(22)   S → ([+WH]) V NP[Su] (NP[IO]) (NP[DO]) (AdvP)*

This rule would allow us to generate surface trees with an initial interrogative word directly from the base, skipping the transformation (19).

The problem with this analysis is that it fails to explain the absence of the questioned constituent after the verb. That is, the rule (22) can also generate an ungrammatical sentence like (23).

(23)   *nuʒi   ɾao   ʒua   ʒubaʔ
       who?   eats   John   corn
       (Who does John eat corn?)

The key fact is that every clause-initial interrogative word is paired with a later GAP, which (22) does not account for. On the other hand, an analysis which moves the interrogative word with a transformation does account for the gap, as the place from which the interrogative word was moved. Therefore, an analysis using a transformation accounts for the facts better than one which just uses phrase structure rules.[6]

---

[6]This is a simplified account of the issues. See the comments in "For Further Reading" for a fuller picture.

Overlapping categories in the lexicon

The feature [±WH] in essence sets up a category of interrogative words that cuts across the other categories in the lexicon. As we can see from English interrogative words, many different categories and functions can be questioned:

(24) a. ***Who*** *came? (NP subject)*
      b. ***Who(m)*** *did the director appoint? (NP direct object)*
      c. ***Who*** *did you give the report to? (NP object of preposition)*
      d. ***Which*** *do you want? (demonstrative NP)*
      e. ***Which*** *book do you want? (D)*
      f. ***Where*** *are we going? (AdvP or PP of location)*
      g. ***When*** *will we ever get there? (AdvP or PP of time)*
      h. ***How*** *are you feeling? (AdvP of manner)*
      i. ***How*** *long is it? (DegP)*

Each of the categories like NP or AdvP contains one or more interrogative words, as well as other words. That is, each category is split into two subcategories by the feature [±WH]. This can be represented as follows:

(25)

	NP	{NP, D}	DegP	AdvP
[+WH]	*who?/whom?/whose?* *what?*	*which?*	*how?*[7]	*where?* *when?* *why?* *how?*
[–WH]	*I/me/my* *you/your* *she/her* *it/its* *...*	*this/these* *that/those*	*very* *somewhat* *rather* *...*	*here* *there* *now* *then* *...*

This shows that categorization is not just a matter of finding mutually-exclusive categories, because categories can actually overlap. The category of interrogative words [+WH] overlaps with other categories like NP and AdvP, just as (in categorizing people) the category of females overlaps with other categories like painters and Chinese citizens. This overlapping categorization is exactly what we need in order to write our rules efficiently; in some cases we need to refer to groups of words such as NP or AdvP (as in phrase structure rules); in other cases we need to refer to groups such as [+WH] (as in a movement transformation).

Note that not all major categories in English contain interrogative words. There are no interrogative verbs in English; when we want to question a verb, we must use a paraphrase structure with the dummy verb *do,* and then we question its direct object. Likewise there are no interrogative quantifiers or quantifier phrases; instead, we use the interrogative DegP *how?* to modify *many* or *much.*

(26) *What did you do?*
      How many/much did you buy?

Languages differ in what categories can be questioned directly with interrogative words. For example, Spanish has an interrogative quantifier, *cuantos* 'how many?'; English has nothing like this. Southern Paiute has interrogative verbs with meanings like 'to do what?' and 'to say what?'.[8]

---

[7]The word *how?* occurs in two categories, DegP and AdvP. For simplicity of presentation, I have placed it in two places in the chart, but in the lexicon it would be better to list its category membership as {DegP, AdvP}.
[8]Sadock and Zwicky 1985:184.

Part of the analysis of content questions in a language is determining which main category each interrogative word belongs in and how to question categories that don't contain interrogative words.

Typological variation in content questions

Fronting is a very common strategy for forming content questions. In many languages, you can use the exact same analysis, except for the phonological details in the lexical entries; the [WH] feature and the transformational rule will be the same. Other languages will use basically the same analysis, with only slight variations. There is a remarkable consistency in the way that content questions are formed.[9]

The most common variation on the above is that many languages do not front their interrogative words. Instead, interrogative words occur just exactly where we would expect them to occur in the basic word order; no movement is involved. For example, consider Turkish.[10]

(27) *Bugün kim   geldi?*
      today who?   came
      Who came today?

(28) *Fatma   kimdir?*
      Fatma   who?
      Who is Fatma?

(29) *Kitabı kimden   aldınız?*
      book   from.whom? you.got
      Who did you get the book from?

The analysis in such a case is simple: do as above, except don't write a transformation. The interrogative word is generated in the proper place by the phrase structure rules, so no further positioning is necessary.

16.4. Yes-no questions

There are three main strategies used to form yes-no questions: by a special intonation pattern, by a special particle or affix, and by a change in word order. Different languages use different strategies. Some languages use more than one, either in combination in a hybrid strategy or as two alternative ways of asking a yes-no question.

Special intonation

The simplest and most common strategy is just a special INTONATION PATTERN. Recall that, although content questions in English use an intonation pattern similar to statements, with overall falling intonation,[11] yes-no questions generally use RISING INTONATION. In many languages, intonation can be the only difference between statements and the corresponding yes-no questions. For example, consider French.

---

[9]More generally, because of the close semantic connection between focus and content questions, I expect that whatever structure is used for focus in a language will also be available for content questions. My informal observations support this expectation.

[10]Underhill 1976:107.

[11]Intonation in content questions in English is not exactly like intonation in statements. Content questions typically start at a fairly high level on the interrogative word, before starting to fall. Statements do not start as high, unless there is contrastive focus (see chapter 15 "Variable Orders of Constituents," p. 212). However, after this initial peak, the falling intonation to the end of the sentence is similar.

(30)   a. *Pierre est là?*
           Is Pierre there?

       b. *Pierre est là.*
           Pierre is there.

In such a case, a formal analysis is usually not presented; all that is done in a published description is to state the facts, as done here.[12]

Use of a special intonation contour is probably the most common way to construct yes-no questions. Even if a language uses some other device (like the two discussed below), it will often also use special intonation in addition. Almost always, the special intonation contour for yes-no questions involves a higher pitch somewhere in the pitch contour, compared to the intonation used in statements. Usually this occurs at or near the end of the sentence, resulting in rising intonation.[13]

Question particles and affixes

The second strategy for forming yes-no questions is to include a special (YES-NO) QUESTION (YNQ) particle or affix in the sentence. Consider the following examples from Turkish, in which the question particle occurs after the verb:[14]

(31)   *gittí   mi?*
       he.went   YNQ
       Did he go?

(32)   *gazete   geldi   mi?*
       newspaper it.came YNQ
       Did the newspaper come?

(33)   *meyva aldık   mı?*
       fruit   we.bought YNQ
       Did we buy fruit?

In other languages, the same function may be assumed by an affix, as in Hua (Papuan, Papua New Guinea), although this is less common.[15]

(34)   *bai-sa-pe*
       be-Subj-YNQ
       Will you be (here)?

(35)   *kgaimo rivzamo   za   rivzamo   riroka   a-pe*
       you   firewood tree firewood you.took you.came-YNQ
       Did you bring firewood?

The question particle or affix functions like a question mark does in written English. In fact, if a language uses such devices for yes-no questions, it may not be necessary to use a question mark '?'

---

[12]Ideally, of course, a complete formal grammar should account for intonation as well as all other aspects of structure, but I am not aware of any attempts to do this within a generative framework.

[13]For discussion, see Ultan 1978a:219–20, who also distinguishes several subtypes of 'rising intonation'.

[14]Data from Underhill 1976:58. The question particle in this case is actually an enclitic (see chapter 20 "Word Division and Clitics," p. 281) and is subject to vowel harmony rules. For the sake of discussion, I arbitrarily assume *mi* as the underlying form. Like question particles in many languages, it can also be inserted after a noun phrase or other constituent, resulting in a focused yes-no question.

[15]Data from Haiman 1980:165. Haiman gives the form of the YNQ suffix as *ve;* regular rules account for the surface form *pe*. For simplicity in the discussion, the surface form is used in the rules.

or any other special punctuation on questions in a practical orthography; the question particle or affix itself makes it clear that an item is a question without any special punctuation.

When a yes-no question particle occurs as a separate word in a language, we can insert it with a phrase structure rule and an appropriate lexical entry. For Turkish, this would be:

(36)   S → (NP[Su]) (NP[DO]) V (YNQ)

(37)   **YNQ**
       mi   yes-no question

In some languages a transformation may be needed to position the question particle correctly;[16] normally, however, the above is all that is necessary.

In the case of a YNQ affix, as in Hua, this can be added by rules of inflectional morphology.

(38)   V → [±YNQ]

(39)   V
       [+ YNQ]
          [X]   →   [X*pe*]

Do not confuse question particles used in yes-no questions with interrogative words used in content questions. The two categories of words are generally not mutually substitutable.

Change in word order

Another strategy for forming yes-no questions is a change in word order, typically placing the main verb at or near the beginning of the sentence.[17] This is not very common worldwide, but it is worth mentioning if only because it is common in European languages which you may be familiar with. As an example, take Swedish.

(40)   a. *kan jag gå?*
          can I   go
       b. *jag kan gå.*
          I   can go

(41)   a. *kan jag gå nu?*
          can I   go now
       b. *jag kan gå nu.*
          I   can go now

(42)   a. *kan jag inte gå nu?*
          can I   not go now
       b. *jag kan inte gå nu.*
          I   can not go now

---

[16]Here, I am thinking of cases where the question particle is a clitic whose position cannot be easily fixed by phrase structure rules, such as second position clitics. (See chapter 20 "Word Division and Clitics," p. 287.) Sadock and Zwicky (1985:182) cite Latin *-ne* as also having considerable mobility. There are also more elaborate cases like Hidatsa (Sadock and Zwicky 1985:181), in which the last vowel of the last word of a yes-no question is interrupted by a glottal stop. This could be analyzed as a phrasal affix which is an infix or a morpheme process.

[17]Sadock and Zwicky (1985:181) claim "Invariably, the change is such as to place the verb at or near the beginning of the sentence and is thus impossible in a language whose basic word order has the verb first." Ultan (1978a:222) likewise notes that, in his sample, languages showing verb inversion in yes-no questions are primarily SVO, with only one SOV example and no other word-order types represented.

In the statements (b sentences), the basic order is SV, and there is an auxiliary verb preceding the main verb. In yes-no questions (a sentences), the order of the subject and the auxiliary is reversed.

To account for these facts, we first account for the word order in statements, using phrase structure rules. (For the analysis of auxiliary verbs, see chapter 8 "Verbal Valence," p. 85.)

(43) S   → NP[Su] VP
      VP → V (Neg) (VP) (AdvP)*

This analysis assumes that auxiliary verbs are distinguished from other verbs in the lexicon by carrying the feature [+Aux], which gets incorporated into deep structure trees such as the following for both (42a) and (42b).[18]

(44)

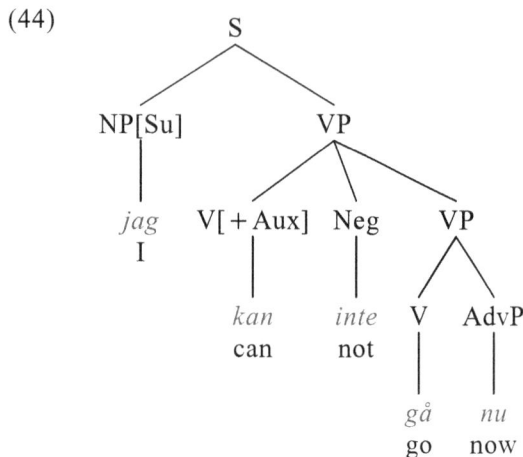

To form the statement (42b), this tree is left unchanged. To form the yes-no question (42a), we need an optional transformation which moves the auxiliary verb to the front of the sentence.

(45) **Aux Fronting in Questions** (optional)
      Move [+Aux] to left of [Su]

(46)

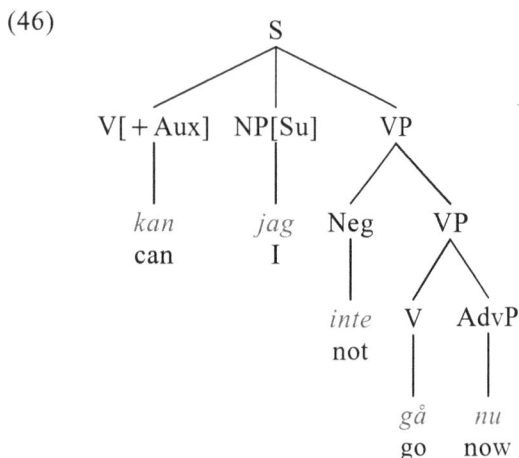

This rule is optional because, if it does not apply and the deep structure tree in (44) is allowed to surface unchanged as (42b), the result is still grammatical. Both the statement and the yes-no

---

[18]The feature [+Aux] is probably best regarded as a shorthand for the SUBCAT feature used in chapter 8 "Verbal Valence" (p. 86) to identify auxiliary verbs. The SUBCAT feature would probably also need to specify that the negative particle *inte* can only be used after an auxiliary.

question are built out of the same deep structure. The optionality of the transformation determines which is produced.

16.5. Shared strategies between question types

Languages often use very different strategies for content and yes-no questions, but sometimes there are similarities between the two. For example, in Germanic languages like English and Swedish, the auxiliary appears before the subject not only in yes-no questions but also in content questions.

(47) a. *You will give a big party next week.*
      b. *Will you give a big party next week?*
      c. **When you will give a big party?*
      d. *When will you give a big party?*

This means that an auxiliary fronting rule like (45) should really be generalized to apply in content questions too. When an interrogative word is present, the fronting is obligatory, as shown in (47c).[19]
   So, for English at least, the rule should really be revised more like this:[20]

(48) **Aux Fronting in Questions**
      (Obligatory if the first constituent of S contains [+ WH], optional otherwise)
      Move [+ Aux] to left of [Su]

This rule obligatorily fronts the auxiliary if an interrogative [+ WH] word has already been fronted by WH Movement (13). If there is no interrogative word, rule (48) is optional. If it applies, the result is a yes-no question; if it doesn't, the result is a statement.
   Such strategy sharing between question types is relatively common. For example, in some languages, a special question particle may occur by itself in yes-no questions, but in addition to an interrogative word in content questions. When there is strategy sharing between question types like this, it is easy to get confused, think all questions are exactly alike, and miss seeing the differences. To guard against this, you should sort your questions into types initially based on their meaning (yes-no versus content question). Study the types separately until both similarities and differences become apparent.

16.6. Review of key terms

QUESTIONS are special clause structures that languages use primarily to request information, in contrast to STATEMENTS that convey information. Some languages allow questions to be used for other purposes, such as RHETORICAL QUESTIONS; this is one of the things studied in the discipline of PRAGMATICS.
   The two most important types of questions are YES-NO QUESTIONS (also called TRUTH-VALUE QUESTIONS) and CONTENT QUESTIONS (also known as INFORMATION QUESTIONS or WH QUESTIONS). Yes-no questions typically are expressed with some special INTONATION PATTERN (usually RISING INTONATION), an overt QUESTION PARTICLE OR AFFIX, and/or a change in word order. Content questions typically are formed by including an INTERROGATIVE WORD (such as an INTERROGATIVE PRONOUN or INTERROGATIVE ADVERB) as the questioned constituent; they may also have some

---

[19]When the interrogative word is the subject, it is not obvious that the auxiliary has been fronted, as in *Who will give the big party next week?* However, such sentences can easily be produced if we assume that both Aux Fronting and WH Movement apply, in that order, just as they must do when questioning nonsubjects. The result of these two rules, when applied to a clause that contains a questioned subject, is to cancel each other out; the resulting word order is the same as in deep structure (although the tree structure is different). The rules still work properly as given, although in a seemingly round-about fashion.
[20]Some provision is also needed so that this rule applies in main clauses only.

characteristics of yes-no questions. The category of interrogative words cuts across other categories in the lexicon; that is, categories overlap. In many languages the questioned constituent is moved to a prominent position by a transformation of WH MOVEMENT, but some languages simply leave it in the place you'd expect to find a nonquestioned constituent in a statement.

16.7. Questions for analysis

1. How do yes-no questions differ from statements? Is it in intonation, the use of a question particle or affix, change in word order, or what? What combinations of these strategies can or must be used?
2. How are content questions expressed? How are they different from statements and from yes-no questions?
    a. What categories (NPs, PPs, AdvPs, etc.) and meanings can be questioned? What interrogative words are available in each category?
    b. Are these words fronted, or do they remain in the same position as ordinary (noninterrogative) words? If they can be fronted, must they always be fronted?
    c. What special intonation (if any) is used for content questions?
    d. Do content questions share any characteristics with yes-no questions?
3. What other communicative functions (besides their primary function of requesting information) do questions have?

16.8. Sample descriptions

Choapan Zapotec content questions

Choapan Zapotec, which has VSO basic word order, can question both NPs and obliques. In both cases, the interrogative word appears at the beginning of the clause, immediately before the verb.

(1) *bataʒi ɾao ʒua ʒuba?*
     when? eats John corn
     When does John eat corn?

(2) *nuʒi ɾao ʒuba?*
     who? eats corn
     Who eats corn?

Yes-no questions in Turkish

Turkish (an SOV language) forms yes-no questions by including the particle *mi* (or its variant *mı*) immediately following the verb.

(1) *gazete geldi mi?*
     newspaper it.came YNQ
     Did the newspaper come?

(2) *meyva aldık mı?*
     fruit we.bought YNQ
     Did we buy fruit?

16.9. For further reading

There are many different types of questions besides those covered here. For some broader surveys of them and structures typically used for them, see Sadock and Zwicky 1985:178–86 and

Ultan 1978a. Ultan concludes with a "Field Worker's Guide" summarizing the different devices that languages use to mark questions, intended for use as a checklist when analyzing a language.

For a more extensive list of question types that occur in various languages, see Comrie and Smith 1977:11–13. Actually, this work is a large outline of questions for analysis which covers a wide range of grammatical phenomena besides questions. It can provide a rich resource of ideas of what to investigate in a language. However, be cautious about using this outline as the basis for organizing your own writing on the language; it is usually better to let the organization of a grammatical description arise out of the actual facts of the language, rather than a general-purpose outline designed for all languages.

For simplicity of presentation, this textbook sticks with the classical transformational analysis of WH movement. However, more recent versions of Transformational Grammar take other factors into consideration, and the result is a bit more involved than what is presented here. Radford (1988:462–79) is a good preparation for reading about WH movement in the general linguistic literature. One major difference between the classical and current approaches to analysis is that, currently, the gaps left behind when a constituent is moved are represented explicitly by TRACES. What traces are and some of the reasons for using them are presented in Radford 1988:553–62; that passage presupposes some familiarity with earlier parts of that book.

It should also be noted that phrase structure rules can, in fact, be made to account for gaps without transformations, at the expense of a bit more complexity in the way they are written. One easily-available example of this approach is Gazdar, Klein, Pullum, and Sag 1985:137–68.

17
Commands

17.1. Goals and prerequisites

This chapter will help you do the following:

- ◎ list and define four grammatical categories that are examples of MOOD
- ◎ state the elements of meaning that are normally present in commands
- ◎ state at least three strategies that languages commonly use to express commands
- ◎ describe the facts about commands in a language, including the omissibility of the subject and any special verbal morphology
- ◎ construct a formal analysis that accounts for those facts
- ◎ construct a hypothesis about basic constituent order based on clause types with a variety of constituent orders

It assumes that you are familiar with the following material:

- ✓ the formal analysis of inflectional morphology (chapter 10 "Inflectional Morphology")
- ✓ transformations (chapter 15 "Variable Orders of Constituents")
- ✓ the pragmatic uses of commands (chapter 16 "Questions")

17.2. Mood

This chapter looks at the special structures that languages use to express commands. We are entering the domain of what is traditionally called MOOD, which is a grammatical category used in many languages to indicate something about the relationship of a sentence's meaning to the facts of the real world (or some imaginary world). Usually it is marked on verbs, occasionally elsewhere. A mood that is used primarily in statements (to communicate information about the world) is called INDICATIVE MOOD. A mood that is used primarily in commands (to exert some influence over the world) is called IMPERATIVE MOOD.

Other languages don't make the division so much between statements and commands, but have two moods that distinguish between what is real (REALIS MOOD) and what is less than real (IRREALIS MOOD). Depending on the language, IRREALIS may include commands, wishes, hypothetical and/or contrafactual statements, future time (which is not yet real), and statements over which the speaker indicates doubt or uncertainty. That is, if a language has a special irrealis mood, it would typically be used in the translations of some or all of the following clauses:

(1)   **Command**
      Go to bed!
      God, please make it rain!
      Live like a king!

(2)   **Wish**
      May my baby go to bed early!
      (I hope) it rains tomorrow...
      Long live the king!

(3)   **Purpose**
      (Get dressed) so you can go to bed.
      (The shaman offered a sacrifice) to make it rain.
      (He worked very hard) to become king.

(4)   **Hypothetical**
      If you go to bed...
      If it rains tomorrow...
      If he becomes the next king...

(5)   **Contrafactual**[1]
      If you had gone to bed...
      If it had rained yesterday...
      If I was king...

(6)   **Future**
      You will go to bed at 8:00.
      It will rain later this week.
      He will become king on the death of his mother, the current queen.

(7)   **Uncertain**
      (I think) that he may have gone to bed.
      (It is reported that) it rains every day in June (but I will not vouch for this fact personally).
      His reign will (probably) be long and illustrious.

If a language has a morphological form that is used for several of these purposes, it may be appropriate to call it 'irrealis'.

The term 'mood' is most properly used as a way of describing verbal morphology. By extension, however, terms such as INDICATIVE, IMPERATIVE, REALIS, and IRREALIS are sometimes used to refer to whole clauses and sentences, either describing their meanings or the syntactic structures that are used to express them. Indeed, a complete analysis of how this set of meanings is expressed in a language typically requires attention to both morphology and syntax. This is especially true for commands, as you will see later through examples in two very different languages, English and Hebrew.

17.3. Prototypical semantics of commands

There is a surprising similarity in the way languages form commands. This seems to stem from two basic semantic facts about commands:[2]

---

[1] Formal English has special irrealis ('subjunctive') forms, used for certain hypothetical/contrafactual conditions *(If he were in bed..., if it were to rain tomorrow..., if I were king...)*. The data here represents the facts in more informal usage.

[2] Many languages also have special structures for 'hortatives', that is third person (e.g., *Let them eat cake)* or first person plural commands (e.g., *Let's play volleyball)*. They may also have special structures for negative commands (what Sadock and Zwicky 1985:175ff call 'prohibitives') or special ways for expressing differences between commands, warnings,

- the subject of a command is second person
- a command refers to future time

These can be seen in English not just in the meanings of commands, but also in their grammatical structure.

Why do we say that the subject of a command is second person, when the subject is normally omitted? Of course, that is the understood meaning of a command. For instance, in the English commands below, the agent who is intended to perform the action is clearly *you*.

(8) a. *Shut up!*
     b. *Stop it!*
     c. *Please brush your teeth—your breath stinks!*
     d. *Come here at once or you'll get a spanking!*
     e. *Don't talk to my best friend that way!*

But, what evidence do we have that a second person pronoun is actually present as a *syntactic* subject, not just an element in meaning (e.g., an agent)? Consider REFLEXIVE PRONOUNS, a special type of pronoun used in many languages if and only if the pronoun's antecedent (the NP it refers to) is in the same clause. In English, these are used in place of the regular object pronouns when a direct object pronoun is COREFERENTIAL WITH (refers to the same person as) the subject.

(9) a. *You can dress yourself.*
     b. **You can dress you.*

(10) c. *He can dress you.*
     d. **He can dress yourself.*

When we look at reflexive pronouns in commands, we see the same distribution of reflexive pronouns as in (9).

(11) a. *Dress yourself*
     b. **Dress you!*

This is evidence that the subject of (11) is a second person pronoun, even though it does not appear overtly.

More evidence for second person as a syntactic subject is provided by the possibility of (emphatically) expressing the subject of a command. When the subject is overt, it is always second person.

(12) a. **I be quiet!*
     b. *You be quiet!*
     c. **He be quiet!*

Commands act like statements with second person subjects in these two respects. This provides evidence that the subjects of commands are second person, that second person is part of the syntactic as well as the semantic structure of commands.

Why do we say that commands refer to the future? It is, of course, pointless to command anything about the past or even about the exact moment of speech. There is nothing that we can say which will change anything except the future.[3] Given that time flows in only one direction, there is no other choice.

---

suggestions, etc. For brevity, this chapter covers only positive second person commands. These are, after all, the most commonly-studied, so more is known about them cross-linguistically, and the most significant and robust cross-linguistic generalizations concern them alone. Presumably, the others can be handled adequately with no new theoretical apparatus.

[3]This statement requires some clarification. Actually, it *is* possible to change the present situation through speech, beyond the trivial fact that the speaking itself is part of the present moment. There are some sentences which become true as a result

But, in addition to these philosophic concerns, there is some linguistic evidence in English that commands are grammatically future. Future time is indicated in English with the auxiliary verb *will*. It is omitted from an imperative clause, but it reappears when a tag is added to a command, such as *will you* in (13).

(13) *Come here, will you!*

So, there is syntactic evidence in English that the subjects of commands are second person and they relate to future time. In fact, all commands in all languages have these elements. They may not always have a direct impact on form, but often they do. Indeed, there are several things that one can reasonably expect about the structure of commands; let's consider them now.

17.4. English commands

Commands in English differ from statements in three ways, all related fairly directly to the universal factors noted above. The first is syntactic, the other two morphological.

(14) a. The subject NP is usually omitted.
      b. All overt indication that the subject is second person is removed from the verb.
      c. The verb is not marked for tense.

We have already discussed the omission of the subject NP. What about the morphology?

The lack of agreement and tense morphology can be seen most clearly with the copula *to be*. This verb has more forms than most verbs; it varies depending on tense and the person and number of the subject.

(15) *I*   ***am***
      he/she/it   ***is***
      we/you/they   ***are***
      I/he/she/it   ***was***
      we/you/they   ***were***

However, in commands we find none of these forms. Instead, we get only the stem form *be*, sometimes called the INFINITIVE.[4]

(16) ***Be*** *quiet!*

Whenever this form *be* is used, it expresses nothing about person, number, or tense. In other words, imperative verbs use a special morphological form, the infinitive, which does not mark as many grammatical categories as ordinary verb forms.

Of course, this special morphology is only visible on the verb *be,* since for all other English verbs, the second person form of the verb is identical to the infinitive. Thus, the morphological differences between indicative and imperative in English are really quite minor. Mostly we rely on the syntactic difference (the absence of the subject) to signal the difference between a statement and a command. As we see below, other languages rely much more on morphological differences.

Given these morphological and syntactic differences, let's consider how to incorporate commands into our formal analysis of English. First, how do we account for the use of the infinitive in English? We assume that the reason infinitives are not inflected is because they do not carry any

---

of being spoken by someone with the proper authority, such as a parent naming a child with a sentence like *His name is John*. By speaking such sentences, the world at the moment of speech is changed. However, such sentences are usually not expressed as commands. In a second person command, the hearer must necessarily hear the command before he can obey it, so the event referred to by the command is future with respect to the command itself. Therefore, all commands imply future time for the situation that is commanded.

[4]Sometimes called the 'bare infinitive', to distinguish it from the phrase 'to be'.

features for tense or agreement. As a result, the inflectional spellout rules ignore them and the stem remains unchanged.

We can capture this insight by introducing a new feature for verbal morphology, [±imperative]. Then we need to revise our earlier feature assignment rules (from the summary of English grammar at the end of chapter 9 "Obliques," p. 107). They need first to assign this new feature; then they assign tense and agreement features only if a verb is not imperative.[5]

(17)   V → [±imperative]

(18)
$$\underset{[-\text{imperative}]}{V} \rightarrow \begin{bmatrix} \{1,2,3\}\text{person} \\ \pm\text{plural} \\ \pm\text{past} \end{bmatrix}$$

As a result of (18), any verb that is [+imperative] does not have any features for person, number, or tense. The inflectional spellout rules that add the tense and agreement suffixes ignore them, resulting in the verb form which has traditionally been called the infinitive. That takes care of the morphology.

Second, what about syntax? As noted earlier, in English commands the subject NP (*you*) is usually omitted. How do we account for this? We don't want to make the subject optional in the phrase structure rules, because this would allow all subjects to be optional, not just the subjects of commands. We need some way of stating that it is just in commands that the subject can be omitted.

What we need is a transformation, one which deletes the subject *you* only in commands. That is, we assume that the deep structure of a command always has *you* as its subject and that the transformation, called IMPERATIVE SUBJECT DELETION, optionally deletes the subject if the verb has been marked [+imperative]. We write this rule semi-formally as follows:

(19) **Imperative Subject Deletion** (optional)
       In [s NP[2 person] V[+imperative] ...]: Delete NP[2 person].

Note the introductory clause ('In...:'), which restricts the deletion to clauses in which the verb is [+imperative]. (Why is the transformation optional?)[6]

As an example of how this rule works, consider how we might generate the command *'Go home!'* Our phrase structure rules and lexicon would produce the following deep structure:

---

[5]The way of handling agreement features is provisional; a better approach using the SUBCAT feature is presented in chapter 19 "Case and Agreement" (p. 260). However, nothing in the analysis of commands depends crucially on this; the important point at present is to introduce agreement features only on nonimperative verbs. To be complete, something in the analysis would have to limit the distribution of [+imperative] to main clauses and certain embedded clauses (so-called 'embedded commands').

[6]The transformation is optional because *you* can be retained with an imperative verb form *(You be quiet!)* and the sentence is still grammatical.

(20) Deep structure

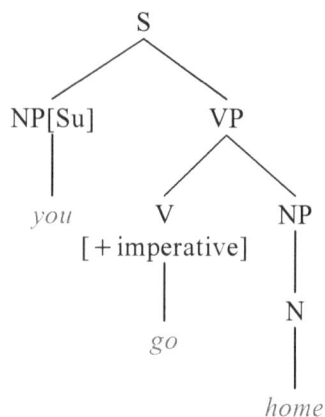

```
              S
           /     \
       NP[Su]     VP
         |       /   \
        you     V     NP
             [+imperative]  |
                |           N
                go          |
                           home
```

Note that the inflectional features on the verb are the only difference between (20) and the deep structure of the corresponding statement *'You go home'*.

If this tree is allowed to surface without being affected by Imperative Subject Deletion, the eventual result is the grammatical command *'You go home!'* More commonly, however, the transformation does apply and the result is a sentence with the following structure:

(21) Surface structure

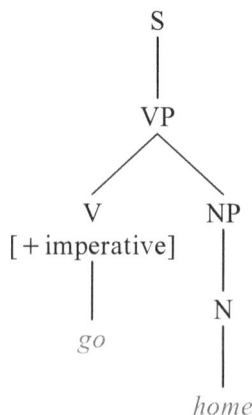

```
        S
        |
        VP
       /   \
      V     NP
 [+imperative]  |
      |         N
      go        |
               home
```

The inflectional spellout rules have nothing to change on this tree and it surfaces as *'Go home!'* This is exactly what we want.

17.5. Commands in languages with richer morphology

To illustrate another variation on the same theme, consider Biblical Hebrew (Semitic).[7] Hebrew is quite different from English in both morphology and syntax. It optionally omits subject pronouns in statements; when they occur, they typically follow the verb and indicate special emphasis (probably contrastive focus). The morphology is richer and more complicated than English. Number and gender (masculine vs. feminine) are marked on both pronouns and verbs. On verbs they are marked with a complex combination of prefixes, suffixes, and stem vowel changes. (Ignore the

---

[7]Information on Hebrew provided by Elizabeth Willett. The discussion here applies only to positive commands. See Simon, Resnikoff, and Motzkin 1992:195–97 and Kautzsch and Cowley 1910:124–25 for further details on the morphology. Hebrew verb forms are only approximately called 'tenses'; they seem rather to express a combination of aspect and mood; cf. Kautzsch and Cowley 1910:309–19.

details of the morphemes; just notice that the verb form changes depending on the gender and number of the subject.)

(22)   *tiʃmor*   *(atta)*
        2ms/guard/Imperf   2ms
        You (masc. sg.) will guard.

(23)   *tiʃməriy*   *(att)*
        2fs/guard/Imperf   2fs
        You (fem. sg.) will guard.

(24)   *tiʃməru*   *(attem)*
        2mp/guard/Imperf   2mp
        You (masc. pl.) will guard.

(25)   *tiʃmornah*   *(atten)*
        2fp/guard/Imperf   2fp
        You (fem. pl.) will guard.

Yet, in commands, we see devices that are familiar from English. The subject pronoun is normally omitted and the morphology is simplified. Specifically, a prefix *ti-* is omitted, although the verb forms are otherwise very similar to the imperfect tense, inflecting for the gender and number of the subject.

(26)   *ʃmor*
        ms/guard/Imper
        Guard (masc. sg.)!

(27)   *ʃimriy*
        fs/guard/Imper
        Guard (fem. sg.)!

(28)   *ʃimru*
        mp/guard/Imper
        Guard (masc. pl.)!

(29)   *ʃəmornah*
        fp/guard/Imper
        Guard (fem. pl.)!

We can incorporate these generalizations in our feature assignment rules as follows:

(30)   a.
        $$V \rightarrow \begin{bmatrix} \pm \text{ imperative} \\ \{m, f\} \text{ gender} \\ \pm \text{ plural} \end{bmatrix}$$

        b.
        $$\begin{matrix} V \\ [-\text{ imperative}] \end{matrix} \rightarrow \begin{bmatrix} \{1,2,3\} \text{ person} \\ \pm \text{ perfective} \end{bmatrix}$$

Just as in English, person is only marked on [–imperative] verbs.

Then, we need an inflectional spellout rule to add *ti-* '2nd person imperfect' to all verbs that are marked [2 person] and [–perfective]. Because of (30b), only [–imperative] verbs have a feature for person, so *ti-* won't be added to an imperative verb.

(31)   V
$$\begin{bmatrix} 2 \text{ person} \\ - \text{ perfective} \end{bmatrix}$$
$$[\text{X}] \quad \rightarrow \quad [ti\text{X}]$$

Other inflectional spellout rules take care of the other person/gender marking in the imperfect and the imperative, but these are complex enough that we omit them here. (See chapter 13 "Nonlinear Affixation" for discussion of how these rules might be written.)

This is all that is needed to account for the facts. There is no need to write a transformation to delete the subject in commands. Because subjects are optional in statements, we would assume that *pro* can occur as the subject in Hebrew. (See chapter 8 "Verbal Valence," p. 87.) If so, then presumably *pro* can also occur as the subject of a command. This accounts for the apparent absence of the subject without having to delete it with a transformation.[8]

17.6. How languages construct commands

Let's summarize what we've covered so far about how languages construct commands and add a few more details about other variations in certain languages.

There is just one main syntactic strategy for expressing commands, which is used either by itself or in combination with one or more morphological devices. The overwhelming pattern is for languages to omit the subject NP in commands, regardless of whether subject pronouns can be omitted in statements.[9] English and Hebrew represent the two variations on this theme; the difference is in the optionality of the subject in statements, since this affects the analysis of commands. In English, the subject is always overtly present in statements, while in Hebrew subject pronouns can be omitted. As a result of this difference, the formal analysis of English requires a transformational rule to delete the subject in commands, while the formal analysis of Hebrew does not.

In addition, languages generally have a different pattern of verbal morphology in commands. Usually this involves omitting the affixation that normally indicates agreement in person with the subject, omitting the normal tense/aspect marking, and possibly other reductions. In such a case, we can posit a mood feature like [±imperative] on the verb and assign person, tense, etc., features to a verb only if it is [–imperative]. This automatically prevents the unwanted affixes from showing up on imperative verbs.

The widespread use of these syntactic and morphological devices is not at all surprising, since they basically involve omitting explicit reference to those elements of meaning which are typical for commands. Once a sentence is determined to be a command, there is normally no need to mention that the subject is second person or that the time is future.[10]

---

[8]This analysis assumes that it is, in fact, possible to have a subject NP present in a command. If, in fact, this was impossible, then probably the simplest way to account for the facts would be to write a filter (a type of quality control check) which requires the subject to be *pro* if the verb is imperative. I do not know if this is required in any language, let alone Hebrew.

[9]This is not universally true, however. Zapotec languages retain the subject pronoun if it is plural (Chuck Speck, personal communication). Sadock and Zwicky 1985:174 note "In our sample, only one language, Onandaga, was not described as lacking either some subjects or some concord markers in the imperative." Rick Thiele (personal communication) reports that in Yanomám (Yanomami, northwestern Brazil and southeastern Venezuela), subject pronouns are obligatory in imperatives.

[10]Of course, there are certainly times when languages require explicit and 'unnecessary' mention of the obvious, so this does not provide a full explanation of why subject and tense marking is normally omitted in commands. It does explain, however, why (as far as I know) no language can omit the subject noun phrase in statements but not in (second person) commands.

In some languages, the absence of the subject pronoun and/or the absence of person and tense/aspect morphology is all that explicitly identifies a command as a command. However, many languages employ a third morphological device: some explicit indication of mood, such as a special imperative affix. We account for it formally by writing an inflectional spellout rule which attaches it to a [+imperative] verb.[11]

Finally, there is one strategy that is very simple grammatically, which shifts the handling of commands to semantics and pragmatics. Some languages use future tense statements (or imperfective aspect) to communicate the same idea as a command. For example, in Ozumacín Chinantec (Otomanguean, Mexico),[12] such statements are used as a mild way of telling someone to do something. The translation can function the same way in English.

(32)   *hme·^{H}*   *=?*   *ta^M*   *?ø·^{BH}*
       Fut/do   2   work   tomorrow
       You will work tomorrow.

Both English and Chinantec have other structures used only for commands. However, in other languages this may not be true; there may be no way to express a command other than using a future tense statement. If that's the case, no grammatical analysis of commands is necessary, because they do not exist as a separate structure. Rather, we can simply say that future tense has two related but distinct uses:

- to convey information about the future
- to influence others' behavior

This, of course, is another instance of the importance of pragmatics, as discussed in chapter 16 "Questions" (p. 220). A given grammatical structure can often be used for a variety of purposes besides its primary one. Part of understanding a structure is understanding the different ways it is used.

17.7. Determining basic constituent order

Now, we have accumulated experience with enough different variations on clause structure to return to one final suggestion on how to determine the basic constituent order (which is the order we put in the phrase structure rules), in addition to those presented in chapter 15 "Variable Orders of Constituents" (p. 214). Among the variety of clause structures that we have seen for English, there are quite a few different orders, which are shown in the following chart. Looking ahead to chapter 22, some embedded clauses are included in the list.

---

[11]Some languages use one affix for hypothetical and/or conditional statements as well as commands; in this case, it is better to call it 'irrealis mood' and use a feature [±realis]. Even in this case, there may be need for a special feature of [±imperative], assigned only to [−realis] verbs, in order to control subject deletion or the assignment of person and tense features.

[12]Data from Nadine Rupp and James Rupp (personal communication). Transcription is IPA, except that superscript letters refer to tones (High, Mid, Ballistic High) and the equals sign represents a clitic pronoun.

(33)   Constituent order   Examples

Statement		S VO Obl	*She stuck the needle in his leg yesterday.*
Topicalization	O	S V Obl	*The needle she stuck in his leg.*
Change of setting (see p. 105)	Obl	S VO Obl	*Yesterday, she stuck it in his leg.*
Yes-no question		Aux S VO Obl	*Did she stick it in his leg?*
Content questions	S	VO Obl	*Who stuck the needle in his leg?*
	O	Aux S V Obl	*What did she stick in his leg yesterday?*
	Obl	Aux S VO	*Where did she stick the needle?*
	Obl	Aux S VO	*When did she stick the needle in his leg?*
Command		VO Obl	*Stick it in his leg.*
Relative clauses	S	VO Obl	*...(the nurse) who stuck the needle in his leg...*
	O	S V Obl	*...(the needle) which she stuck in his leg...*
Complement clause	C	S VO Obl	*...that she stuck the needle in his leg.*
Oblique clause	C	S VO Obl	*...when she stuck the needle in his leg.*

Is English SVO, as we have supposed, or is it rather OSV as in the case of topicalization? Since the auxiliary, a type of verb, can occur before the subject in some clauses, does this mean that English is VSO? Where do obliques belong—at the beginning or the end of the clause?

Surveying this variety, there is still quite a bit of regularity, which is obvious when we line up the constituents in columns as in the chart above. In most clauses, the subject precedes the verb, the verb precedes the objects, and the obliques occur at the end. Putting this all together, we get SVO Obl; this then is the best hypothesis for basic order. This does not mean that most clause types have exactly SVO Obl order, but this order does recur as a theme throughout all clause types. Most clauses in fact have some minor variation on the SVO theme, but it is clearly a variation on SVO order rather than some completely different order.

Recall that one goal in constructing an analysis is to be as simple and general as possible. The simplest analysis overall is that English is SVO: all sentences have SVO Obl order in deep structure and movement transformations generate the other orderings. The derivation of each alternative ordering is fairly simple, since only one or two constituents need to be moved and only for clearly defined reasons. If we had chosen OSV as the basic order, for instance, then most clauses would require a transformation to move the object after the verb, in addition to any other transformations that apply to it, and there would be no apparent reason for the movement. Choosing SVO order as basic rather than OSV allows us to move the object only under very specific circumstances: when it is topicalized.

In summary, then, the earlier advice still stands: look for the orderings of constituents which occur most often. However, there is a subtle twist: 'most often' does not refer to statistical frequency in texts, but to the order that occurs in the greatest *variety* of constructions.[13] Once you find it, search for what special circumstances (focus, questioning, being the main clause, etc.) are causing some clauses to deviate from this order.

17.8. Review of key terms

The area of MOOD reflects the relationship of the meaning of a clause to the real world and includes such meanings as INDICATIVE versus IMPERATIVE and IRREALIS versus REALIS. Specifically, we have looked at the differences between COMMANDS and STATEMENTS. Syntactically, commands almost always lack overt subjects, yet the presence of a second person subject can be demonstrated by evidence from REFLEXIVE PRONOUNS. (Since they must be COREFERENTIAL WITH the subject, a second person reflexive pronoun in a command shows that the subject is second person.)

---

[13]See footnote 22 (p. 214) for discussion of different ways the term BASIC WORD ORDER is used in different theoretical frameworks.

In some languages commands can be derived by a transformation that DELETES the subject of an imperative clause. Morphologically, verbs in commands tend to have simpler morphology, as in English's use of the bare stem or INFINITIVE. Typically, imperative verbs omit overt reference to person (which is understood to be second person) or time (which is understood to be future); they may also have a special IMPERATIVE affix.

17.9. Questions for analysis

1. Is the subject in a command always omitted or may it be optionally expressed? Is this different from what happens in statements? Is there any difference of meaning in a command when the subject is expressed or not?
2. What grammatical categories are marked on indicative verbs which are not marked on imperatives, and vice versa?
    a.   Is there a special imperative affix or a specialized sense of some other grammatical category (such as future or irrealis)?
    b.   If indicative verbs are marked for tense, aspect, or the person of the subject, are these features omitted on imperative verbs?
3. How are these categories marked?
    a.   What are the specific affixes?
    b.   Are they the same set as in indicative verbs, or is there a suppletive set used only in imperatives? If a special set, what is it?

17.10. Sample description

The verb form in Hebrew commands is very similar to the form in second person imperfect statements, but with omission of the *ti-* prefix and some vowel changes. Like the imperfect, it inflects for the person and gender of the subject.

(1)		Imperfect	Imperative
	2 Sg. Masc.	*tiʃmor*	*ʃmor*
	2 Sg. Fem.	*tiʃməriy*	*ʃimriy*
	2 Pl. Masc.	*tiʃməru*	*ʃimru*
	2 Pl. Fem.	*tiʃmornah*	*ʃəmornah*

Subject pronouns are normally omitted.

17.11. For further reading

Perlmutter and Soames (1979:8–23) discuss reflexive pronouns and imperatives in English from an early transformational perspective. They include several exercises that focus on the evidence for including *you* as the underlying subject of imperatives in English. The emphasis is on helping the reader develop the ability to construct arguments to decide between competing hypotheses. This theme is carried through the whole book, which covers many of the major syntactic structures of English and issues that were important in generative grammar during the 1960s and 1970s.

Although positive second person commands are in some sense the most important, there are many other ways in which we may use language to influence the world around us. Languages often have a variety of other 'imperative' structures for these other purposes. Sadock and Zwicky (1985) provide a brief survey of a number of them, as well as providing examples from a number of different languages. Their article would be a good next step if you want a broader survey of this subject.

18
Overall Structure of a Grammar

18.1. Goals and prerequisites

This chapter will help you do the following:

◉ visualize the overall structure of the transformational grammars presented in this book and how the different parts relate to each other

It may be especially useful to refer to this summary diagram starting with chapter 11 "Derivational Morphology" and continuing through chapter 17 "Commands," referring to it as each new element in the grammar is introduced.

18.2. A chart of the grammar

The following diagram covers all the different rule types that are mentioned in the book, even if only in passing.[1] It might usefully be used along with chapter 11, although some rule types (especially transformations) have not yet been introduced at that point.

---

[1]The positioning of phonological rules follows the standard assumption in lexical phonology that phonological rules apply immediately after the addition of each affix. Lexical phonology usually assumes that all morphology (inflectional as well as derivational) happens in the lexicon and hence calls all such rules 'lexical rules'. In a model of morphology that adds the phonological material of inflectional affixes after transformational rules, some of these so-called 'lexical rules' actually apply outside the lexicon. However, they are still to be distinguished from the 'post-lexical' rules which apply across word boundaries, after all morphology has been added, and which introduce noncontrastive (allophonic) phonetic details.

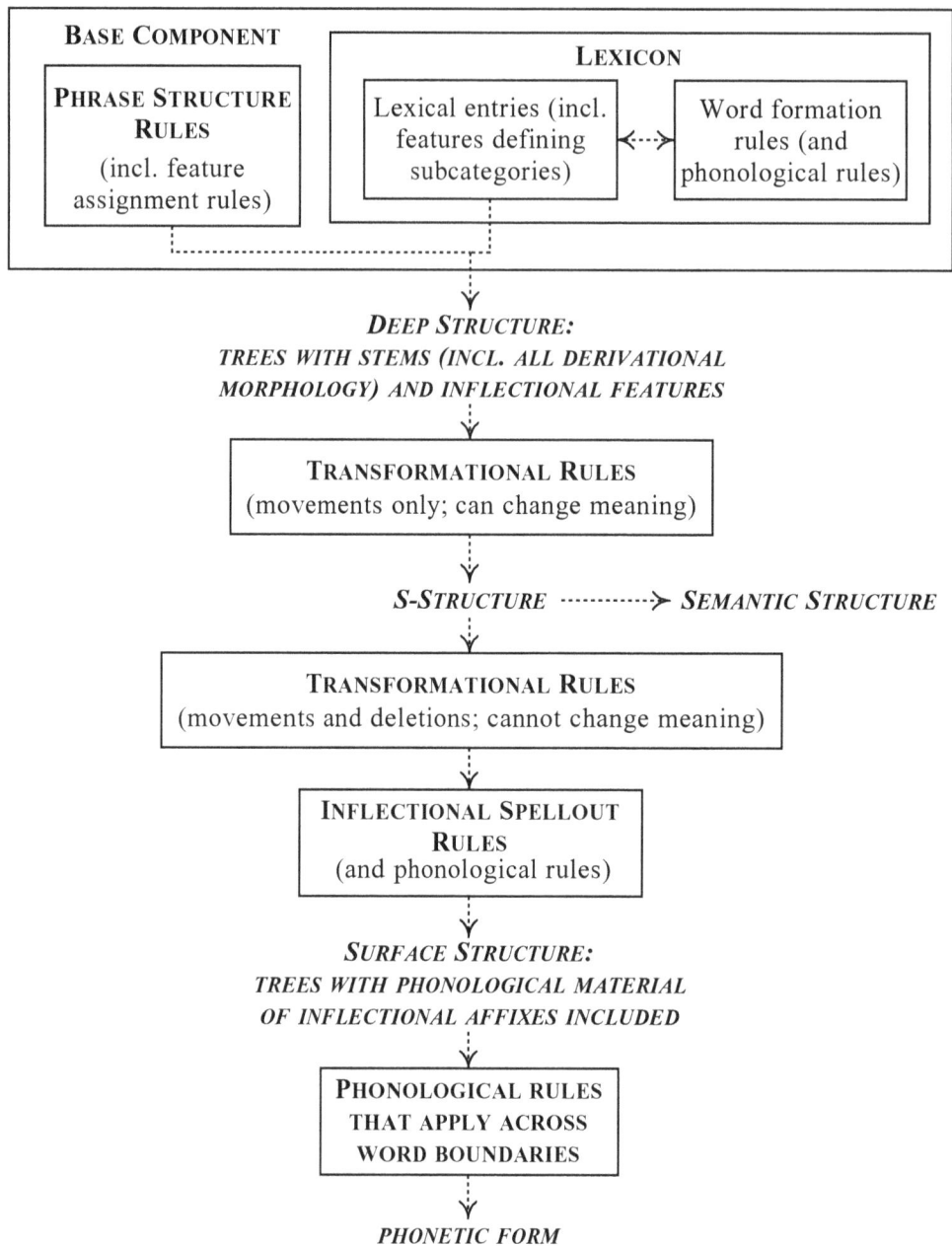

Morphology Group 3

19
Case and Agreement

19.1. Goals and prerequisites

This chapter will help you do the following:

- ◎ identify case and agreement phenomena in data and distinguish them from each other
- ◎ describe data involving case marking on nouns and pronouns
- ◎ describe data involving agreement of verbs with subjects and objects, nouns with possessors, and modifiers with head nouns
- ◎ construct formal analyses that account for case marking of noun phrases in nominative-accusative systems
- ◎ construct formal analyses that account for agreement with complements in nominative-accusative systems
- ◎ explain the function of feature percolation in the formal analysis of case and agreement
- ◎ describe data involving ergative-absolutive patterns of case and agreement

It assumes that you are familiar with the following material:

- ✓ bound and free morphemes, agreement marking on verbs and nouns (chapter 4 "Introduction to Morphology")
- ✓ phrases and their heads, possession (chapter 7 "Embedding and Noun Phrase Structure")
- ✓ semantic roles, grammatical relations, the SUBCAT feature, and case marking (chapter 8 "Verbal Valence")
- ✓ complements vs. adjuncts (chapter 9 "Obliques")
- ✓ the formal analysis of inflectional morphology (feature assignment rules, inflectional spellout rules, etc.), especially the partial analysis of agreement on verbs and case on English pronouns (chapter 10 "Inflectional Morphology")
- ✓ why agreement and case are inflectional, not derivational (chapter 11 "Derivational Morphology")
- ✓ allomorphy, especially suppletion with lexical conditioning (chapter 12 "Suppletion and Morphophonemics")
- ✓ nominal and adjectival complements (chapter 14 "Nonactive Complements")

19.2. The morphology of grammatical relations

In this chapter, we discuss two types of inflectional morphology that are sensitive to grammatical relations: case and agreement. We have touched on them several times in previous chapters, but there is more to them than what we have seen so far. Especially, we need to examine their formal analysis in more detail.

They are important, because together with word order, they can provide important evidence about grammatical relations as you do your analysis of a language. This is particularly important when analyzing clauses in which semantic roles do not line up with grammatical relations in the 'normal' way (see chapter 21 "Passive and Voice"). In such clauses, the only things we can rely on for making hypotheses about grammatical relations are facts about the form of the utterance, such as word order, case, and agreement.

19.3. Case

Recall what we assumed early in the book (chapter 6 "The Base," p. 57)—that all noun phrases are alike. That's why we do not write separate phrase structure rules for subject and object NPs. This assumption is correct as far as syntactic structure is concerned. But, in many languages there are morphological differences in noun phrases, depending on what role they play in the larger structure; this type of morphology is called CASE. In such languages, we say that the noun phrases are MARKED FOR CASE.

Case helps identify the grammatical relations in a clause. For example, case marking on pronouns in English helps speakers determine the grammatical relations, and thus the meaning, of poetic sentences like the following:

(1)   a. *She me loved.* (SOV)
       b. *Her I did not love.* (OSV)

We have already seen an analysis of case marking on English pronouns in chapter 10 "Inflectional Morphology" (p. 129), which lists the different case forms of pronouns in the lexicon. Each form is tagged with a feature for case, and this feature forces the form to be inserted in a tree at an NP that has an identical case feature. We did not, however, write the rules that determine how the case features got on the NPs in the tree in the first place. That is one of the topics for this chapter.

Case on nouns in Latin

Typically case is indicated in one of two ways. One, there may be suppletive forms of pronouns, as in English. Two, there may be affixes (called CASE MARKERS) on the head noun of a noun phrase. Case markers are like little flags on a noun which help identify its grammatical relation.

To show examples, we must look at a language that marks case on its nouns. Latin serves this purpose well, since it has a well-developed case system. In the following examples, notice how the same noun has different suffixes, depending on its function in the clause.

(2)   *puella columba-m ama-t*
       girl   dove   love-3sg
       The girl loves the dove.

(3)   *columba puella-m ama-t*
       dove   girl   love-3sg
       The dove loves the girl.

(4)   *puella columba-m libera-t*
      girl   dove   free-3sg
      The girl is letting the dove go.

(5)   *filia   femina-e aqua-m columba-e da-t*
      daughter woman   water   dove   give-3sg
      The woman's daughter is giving water to the dove.

(6)   *femina grammatica-m puella-e doce-t*
      woman   grammar   girl   teach-3sg
      The woman teaches grammar to the girl.

The suffixes indicate something about the grammatical relation of the noun. What appears to be the direct object (the patient) is marked with *-m,* what appear to be indirect objects (recipients and addressees) or possessors are marked with *-e,* and what appears to be the subject (the agent) has no suffix.[1] We can thus make two interdependent hypotheses:

(7)   a.   The grammatical relations are what we would expect them to be, based on semantic roles. (Thus we assume agents and experiencers are subjects, patients and themes are direct objects, etc.)
      b.   There is case marking on the nouns:
           -∅   for subjects
           -m   for direct objects
           -e   for indirect objects and possessors

Traditionally, a case which is used for subjects is called NOMINATIVE, a case for direct objects ACCUSATIVE, a case for indirect objects DATIVE, and a case for possessors GENITIVE. All these different cases are required for the analysis of Latin. (Although the nouns above have the same form for indirect objects and possessors, other nouns do have distinct forms for these two functions, so we must recognize a distinction between dative and genitive case.)[2]

The reason that we need terminology for case in addition to terms for grammatical relations is that usually one case is used for more than one purpose. For example, in Latin, nominative case is used for nominal and adjectival complements as well as for subjects, and accusative case is used for the objects of many prepositions.[3]

(8)   *Lydia-∅   **puella-∅** est*
      Lydia-Nom girl-Nom   is
      Lydia is a girl.

(9)   *Lydia-∅   **pulcra-∅** est*
      Lydia-Nom pretty-Nom is
      Lydia is pretty.

---

[1]The *a* at the end of all the nouns is traditionally analyzed as part of the case suffix. I present it here as part of the stem, because this is what it appears to be on the basis of this limited data. More generally, I attempt to sidestep the issues that must be raised in a full analysis of Latin case morphology. Thus, the analysis is very incomplete; the aim is to provide only enough detail to illustrate the main points about case systems generally. For a much more complete analysis of Latin morphology in a word-and-paradigm model, see Matthews 1972b.

[2]If Latin really did use the same forms for indirect objects and possessors for all nouns, we would assume that there was only one case that was used for both. We might call it either GENITIVE or DATIVE (but not both), since either label would work equally well in characterizing how the case is used.

[3]Other prepositions require a fifth case, called ablative. So, even if we know a noun phrase's general role in the whole clause (e.g., as the object of a preposition), we can't predict its case, since it sometimes depends on properties of individual lexical items. This is another argument for the point made in the main text.

(10) *puella-Ø* ***ad villa-m***   *ambulat*
     girl-Nom to   country.house-Acc walks
     The girl is walking to the country house.

Another reason is that different classes of nouns take different suffixes for the same cases. Just to give you some flavor of the system, here are some of the suffixes used for various classes of nouns.

(11)

Noun class:	I	II	III	IV
Nominative	*-Ø*	*-us*	*-Ø*	*-us*
Genitive	*-e*	*-ī*	*-is*	*-ūs*
Dative	*-e*	*-ō*	*-ī*	*-uī*
Accusative	*-m*	*-um*	*em*	*-um*

In short, there is not a simple, direct mapping from function (grammatical relation or other position in the clause) to the individual suffixes. Grammarians have long recognized that in order to compute the morphology for a noun correctly we must use a two-step process with case-marking as the intermediate step. First we state what functions should be represented by each case, and then we state how to spell out each case for each class of nouns.[4]

Formal analysis of case marking

Let's consider how to formalize this analysis in a grammar of Latin. The phrase structure rules are straightforward. (These rules ignore verbal morphology and assume a flat clause structure.)

(12)   S → NP[Su] (NP[DO]) (NP[IO]) V
        NP → N (NP[Poss])

Next, we need to get case features on the NPs. When case is determined directly by grammatical relation,[5] this can be done in the feature assignment rules, part of the phrase structure rules. (This chapter shows the features for grammatical relations [GR] in full to emphasize that they are features; elsewhere, for example, [Su GR] is abbreviated as [Su].)

(13) $\begin{bmatrix} \begin{Bmatrix} Su \\ NC \end{Bmatrix} GR \end{bmatrix}$ →   [Nom case]

       [DO GR]   →   [Acc case]

       [IO GR]   →   [Dat case]

       [Poss GR]   →   [Gen case]

These add the case features to the NP nodes, alongside the [GR] features.
      Finally, we need inflectional spellout rules, to get the proper case markers on the nouns.[6]

---

[4]Compare Pollard and Sag's (1987:128–29) concern to maintain the traditional distinction between form (case) and function (grammatical relations).

[5]When case is assigned by specific prepositions, a formal grammar can represent the case assignment with a SUBCAT feature on the preposition. For example, *ad* 'to' can take the feature [SUBCAT ⟨ NP[Acc case] ⟩]; this states that the object of *ad* must be in accusative case.

[6]These rules account only for the nouns discussed here. A separate set of rules is needed for each inflectional class of nouns. That is why each rule here has a feature to limit its application to nouns from the first inflectional class (traditionally called FIRST DECLENSION). See chapter 12 "Suppletion and Morphophonemics" for more discussion about suppletive allomorphy of affixes.

(14)   N

$$\begin{bmatrix} \text{Acc case} \\ \text{I class} \\ \quad [\text{X}] \end{bmatrix} \rightarrow [\text{X}m]$$

(15)   N

$$\begin{bmatrix} \left\{\begin{matrix} \text{Dat} \\ \text{Gen} \end{matrix}\right\} \text{case} \\ \text{I class} \\ \quad [\text{X}] \end{bmatrix} \rightarrow [\text{X}e]$$

But, wait a minute—there's a glitch. To see what it is, look at the tree that the base rules build for sentence (5).

(16)   Output of base component for (5)

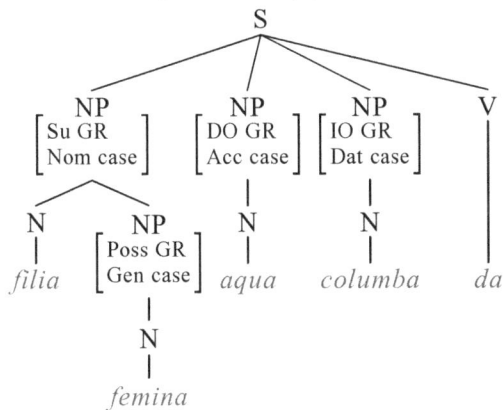

The feature assignment rules (13) put case features on NP nodes, but the inflectional spellout rules (14)–(15) need them on N nodes.[7] How do we get the case features from the NP nodes to the N nodes?

The answer goes back to what was discussed in chapter 7 "Embedding and Noun Phrase Structure." Recall that an N is the head of its NP. One characteristic that most linguists assume about phrases and their heads is that they share many important features, including features for case. One way of thinking about this is that anytime an inflectional feature is assigned to a phrasal node, it is automatically copied down to the head. So, the structure of (5) should really be shown as follows:

---

[7]Note that the case marking is definitely on the head noun, not on the final word in the noun phrase. So, we do not have the option of treating case marking as a phrasal affix, as with English possessive -'s, and rewriting the inflectional spellout rules to refer to NPs instead of Ns.

(17)   Output of base component for (5), with copied features displayed

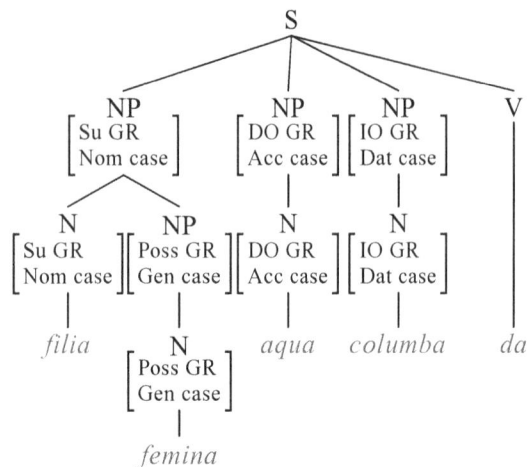

With this understanding, the inflectional spellout rules apply properly to the nouns, producing the following surface structure:

(18)   Surface structure for (5) after application of inflectional spellout rules

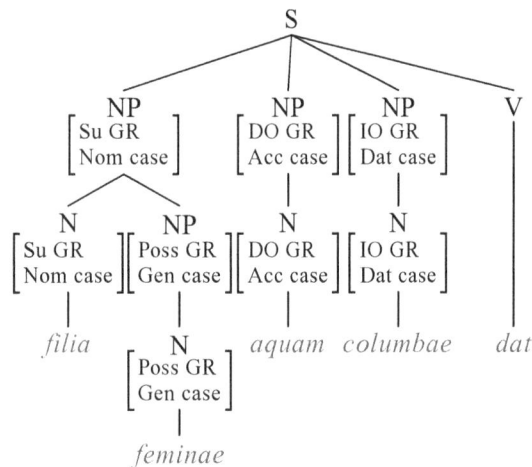

The automatic copying of features from a phrase to its head is sometimes called FEATURE PERCOLATION. Our theory assumes it happens automatically, whenever it is needed. There is no need to write rules for it; we simply take advantage of it in our analysis.[8] Feature percolation is also important in our analysis of agreement, later in this chapter (p. 260).

Case marking versus prepositions and postpositions

In many languages, prepositions or postpositions function in many ways like case markers. In Japanese (for example) the subject, objects, etc., are all postpositional phrases; the particular postposition used is dependent on the grammatical relation of the PP. In such a language, the gloss of the P is simply the appropriate feature for the grammatical relation of the PP ([Su], [DO], etc.). Likewise, in English, indirect objects are PPs, with the preposition *to* being identified in the lexicon as [IO].[9]

---

[8]Strictly speaking, we would need to specify which features are HEAD FEATURES, i.e., the ones that are automatically copied between a phrasal node and its head. For our purposes, let's assume that any features needed for case and agreement are head features. In the trees that follow, feature percolation is represented only when it is relevant to the discussion.

[9]Any time a tree contains a PP[IO], the feature [IO] is copied down to the P, forcing us to choose *to* from the lexicon, since it is the P with the most specific set of features which are consistent with the features already in the tree.

Conversely, in some languages there are special case markers that occur on obliques and which serve the same function as a preposition or postposition. Consider the following examples from Dəmʌna (Chibchan, Colombia).[10]

(19) *íngwi kən   kaŋgəmám-**ba*** gágə   kə́ma uyá*
      one   wood   earth-**Obl**   placed InfW did
      He laid a stick on the ground.

(20) *pwebrú-**ba*** naká awín*
      village-**Obl** came did
      He came to the village.

(21) *šerá-**ba***   nəkəkó awín*
      machete-**Obl**   cut.me did
      He cut me with a machete.

In this case, an affix /-ba/ 'Obl' is functioning in a role that is usually assumed by prepositions and postpositions.

Despite the similar functions of prepositions, postpositions, and case markers, it is important to distinguish them because their structure is different. This book uses 'case marker' for affixes and 'preposition/postposition' for syntactically separate words. One reason for maintaining this distinction is that prepositions or postpositions may occur in the same language with case marking. For example, Latin has both case markers as suffixes on nouns and prepositions as separate words in front of the noun phrase. (See example (10).)

19.4. Agreement

We have encountered AGREEMENT several times already in this book, especially in the morphology of verbs. Any affix on a verb which indicates the person, number, or some other characteristic of the subject is an AGREEMENT AFFIX (or AGREEMENT MARKER). In agreement, the morphology of some word 'points' to some noun phrase in the clause and redundantly indicates one or more of its features. The number suffix on English present tense verbs is an example. If the subject noun phrase is third person singular, the verb ends in -*s*. Otherwise, the verb has no ending.

(22) a. *The boy   runs/*run.*
      b. *I/we/you/they *runs/run.*

We say that in English the verb AGREES WITH the subject in person and number. By this, we mean that there are different forms of every verb; to determine the correct form in a particular clause, we must consider the person and number of the subject. The morphology of the verb is sensitive to features that are not logically part of the verb itself, but which are logically part of the subject. This is what we mean when we say that the morphology of the verb points to the subject and redundantly indicates its person and number.

This is important, because it can help us identify the subject in unclear cases. Consider, for instance, the following two (highly poetic) sentences:

(23) a. *God the years controls.*
      b. *God the years control.*

---

[10]Examples are from Cindy Williams 1993:34–35, whose transcription follows Americanist practice. Only the relevant morphological structure is shown. The oblique case marker -*ba* is an enclitic, probably a phrasal affix (see chapter 20 "Word Division and Clitics," p. 282, footnote 22). It is used on addressees and recipients as well as obliques.

Sentences (23a) and (23b) make very different theological claims. What is there about their almost identical structures that gives them such different meanings? It is the agreement marking on the verb. In the first sentence, the verb has an -*s* suffix, indicating that the subject is third person singular. The only third person singular noun phrase is *God,* so that we know that it is the subject, despite the unusual word order. In the second sentence, the verb tells us that the subject is not third singular. Again, there is only one noun phrase, *the years,* that could be subject. The agreement has allowed us to identify the grammatical relations of the noun phrases, despite the use of a non-basic word order.

In informal descriptions of languages, agreement may be described using one of several formulas. The first is the easiest to use.

(24)   The subject and verb agree in person and number

The others are a little trickier, because they require that you identify the *source* of the features, i.e., the constituent to which they logically belong. For example:

(25)   The verb agrees with the subject in person and number.

One would *not* say that 'The subject agrees with the verb in person and number' because the features of person and number are inherent characteristics of things (nouns), not actions and states of affairs (verbs). The thing that 'does the agreeing' is always the category which has the agreement marking (e.g., the verb), and the thing it 'agrees with' is always the logical source of the features, i.e., the noun phrase that the agreement morphology points to (e.g., the subject).

Finally, a third way to describe agreement is like this:

(26)   The person and number of the subject are marked (or registered) on the verb.

Formal analysis of verb agreement

To provide a formal analysis of agreement, we need to improve a bit on what we've done so far. Until now, we've written feature assignment rules to make verbs carry certain features of the subject, such as person and number in English. (Compare chapter 10 "Inflectional Morphology," p. 124.)

(27)   Feature assignment rule for English verb agreement (until this chapter)

$$V \rightarrow \begin{bmatrix} \{1,2,3\} \text{ person} \\ \pm \text{ plural} \\ \pm \text{ past} \end{bmatrix}$$

This results in a tree like the following:[11]

(28)   Output of base component (until this chapter)

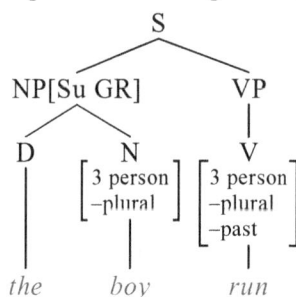

---

[11]For this chapter only, I make explicit the assumption that all nouns carry the feature [3 person].

Then we've written inflectional spellout rules to add the agreement affixes themselves.

(29)   Inflectional spellout rule for English verb agreement (until this chapter)

$$
\begin{array}{c}
\text{V} \\
\begin{bmatrix} 3\ \text{person} \\ -\ \text{plural} \\ -\ \text{past} \end{bmatrix} \\
[\text{X}]
\end{array}
\quad \rightarrow \quad [\text{X}z]
$$

These operate on the tree to produce the correct surface structure.

(30)   Surface structure (until this chapter)

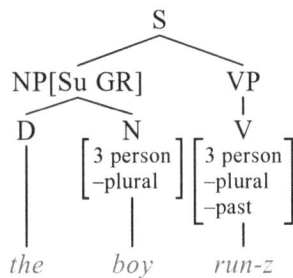

This is all very good, as far as it goes. However, what part of our grammar guarantees that the right combination of features appears on the V? What forces the features for person and number on the V to match those on the subject? What prevents the grammar from generating a tree like the following, in which the verb has the wrong features and, thus, fails to get the right agreement suffix?

(31)   Incorrect surface structure (wrongly permitted by the analysis in previous chapters)

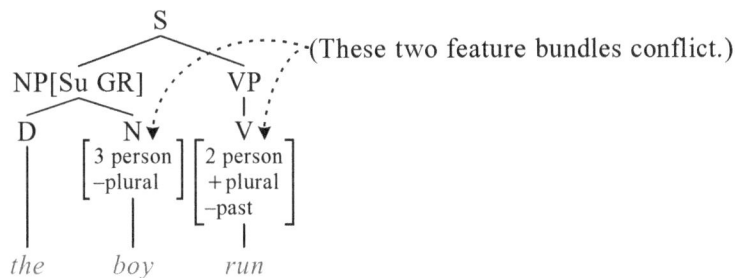

Somehow, we have to prevent this from happening.

There's a second problem too. The approach we've used so far doesn't work very well in languages whose verbs agree with both subjects and direct objects. For example, in Chichewa (Bantu, Malawi),[12] verbs carry agreement prefixes that indicate (among other things) the person and number of both the subject and direct object. The following two examples are identical, except for the object agreement prefix.

(32)   a.   *ndi-ku-**mu**-ona*
           1sgSu-Pres-**3sgDO**-see
           I see him/her.

       b.   *ndi-ku-**wa**-ona*
           1sgSu-Pres-**3plDO**-see
           I see them.

---

[12]Chichewa data is from Corbett and Mtenje 1987.

In a formal analysis of Chichewa, the verb must be marked with two sets of features for person and number, one set for the subject and one for the direct object. How is a grammar supposed to keep the two sets of features from getting confused with each other?

Fortunately, there is an easy solution to both problems. We can take advantage of the SUBCAT feature introduced in chapter 8 "Verbal Valence" (p. 82) and put it to a new use. For subject agreement, we can position the agreement features in that part of the SUBCAT list that requires a subject. In other words, we want to have the phrase structure rules and lexicon produce a tree like the following:

(33)   Output of base component (using agreement features in SUBCAT list)

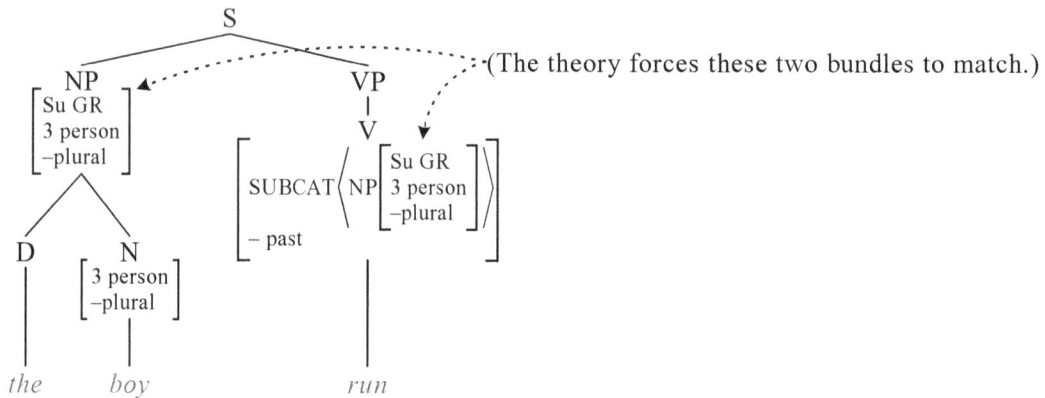

This solves both problems at once. For the first problem, it automatically guarantees that the subject agreement features on the verb will match the features on the subject, since our theory requires the SUBCAT list on a verb to match the actual nodes in the tree.[13] Note that, to make this work properly, we have again relied on feature percolation, but this time going upward. In building (33), the person and number features from the subject noun were copied up to the NP node, where they could be checked against the SUBCAT list. For the second problem, in languages that have verbal agreement with both subjects and direct objects, the SUBCAT list provides a way of keeping subject and object inflectional features separate from each other on the verb, because it refers separately to the subject and object of a transitive verb.

(34)   Partial deep structure for (32b): Chichewa *ndikuwaona* 'I see them'

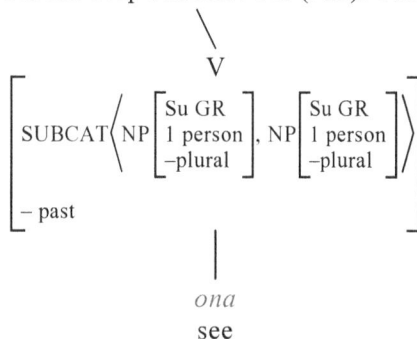

Now we just need to revise our rules to accommodate the new location for the agreement features. We rewrite the English feature assignment rule (27) so that it can help build (33). In order

---

[13]To be precise, any feature that is specified for the subject in the SUBCAT list must match a feature that is on the subject NP of the clause. If necessary, a feature that is assigned by rule to the SUBCAT list is copied to the appropriate node in the tree. On the other hand, there are many features that are part of the subject NP in the tree that are not mirrored in the SUBCAT list. Thus, the feature assignment rules have the effect of specifying exactly what features are the basis for agreement, by assigning only those features to the SUBCAT list.

to simplify the notation, we split it into two rules, writing the one that adds the agreement features to the SUBCAT list in an abbreviated form.[14]

(35) a. V → [±past]

     b. in V[SUBCAT]: [Su GR] → $\begin{bmatrix} \{1,2,3\} \text{ person} \\ \pm \text{ plural} \end{bmatrix}$

To see how this works, recall that the SUBCAT feature comes originally from the lexicon with the verb. Once it is in the tree, (35b) adds features for person and number alongside the feature for grammatical relation ([Su GR]) that is already there in the list. To illustrate, the diagrams in (36) show these steps in building the tree (33).

(36) Steps in assigning features to the verb in (33): *runs (3sg.)*

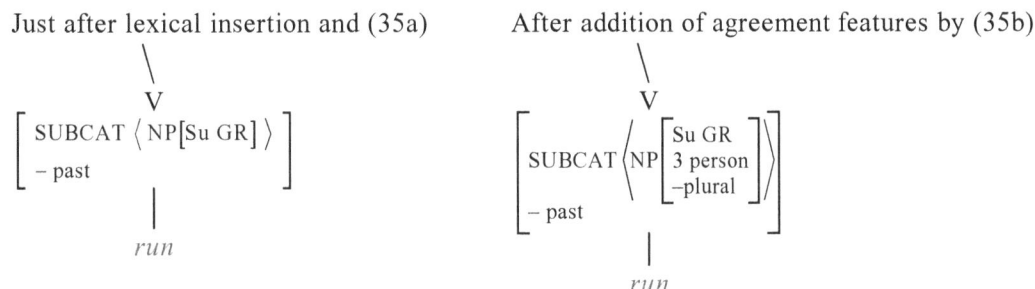

   Just after lexical insertion and (35a)   After addition of agreement features by (35b)

$$\begin{bmatrix} \text{SUBCAT} \langle \text{NP[Su GR]} \rangle \\ -\text{past} \end{bmatrix}$$

run

$$\begin{bmatrix} \text{SUBCAT} \langle \text{NP} \begin{bmatrix} \text{Su GR} \\ 3 \text{ person} \\ -\text{plural} \end{bmatrix} \rangle \\ -\text{past} \end{bmatrix}$$

run

We also revise the inflectional spellout rule (29) which adds the /-z/ suffix so it can refer to the new, improved SUBCAT feature.

(37)
$$\begin{bmatrix} \text{SUBCAT} \langle \text{NP} \begin{bmatrix} \text{Su GR} \\ 3 \text{ person} \\ -\text{ plural} \end{bmatrix} ... \rangle \\ -\text{past} \end{bmatrix}$$
$[\text{X}]$ → $[\text{X}z]$

This will attach /-z/ to the verb in (33), producing the proper surface sentence 'The boy runs'. The ellipsis (3 dots) inside the SUBCAT list in the rule allow it to apply equally well to transitive verbs.

For languages like Chichewa that have object agreement, we need to do something similar. The rules we wrote for English in (35) also work for Chichewa, but we need an additional feature assignment rule to position the object agreement features in the correct place in (34). As an exercise, write it. Also, write an inflectional spellout rule for the third person plural object prefix that would

---

[14]Without the abbreviation, the rule would have to be written like this:

$$\text{V}\left[\text{SUBCAT}\langle \text{NP[Su GR]} ... \rangle\right] \rightarrow \begin{bmatrix} \text{SUBCAT} \langle \text{NP} \begin{bmatrix} \text{Su GR} \\ \{1,2,3\} \text{ person} \\ \pm \text{ plural} \end{bmatrix} ... \rangle \end{bmatrix}$$

need to be added to this tree to help produce the surface structure of (32b). How would this rule be ordered with respect to the rules for the other affixes in (32b)? For the answers, see the footnote.[15]

In summary, by refining the way we represent agreement features on the verb, we've been able to account for agreement fully without any new rules, just refinements of old ones. In the rest of this chapter, we look at other types of agreement and the way the SUBCAT feature can be used to account for them.

Gender agreement in Imyan Tehit

In English and most European languages you may be familiar with, the verb agrees in PERSON and NUMBER with the subject. These features are often used in agreement systems. Some languages, however, base their agreement systems on other features of noun phrases, such as GENDER.

GENDER is an arbitrary or semi-arbitrary system for classifying nouns and pronouns, which is often based on sex, animacy, or shape. In English a distinction is made in personal pronouns on the basis of sex, i.e., *he* (masculine), *she* (feminine), and *it* (neuter). In Spanish there are only two classes, 'masculine' and 'feminine', and all nouns are either one or the other, so that both classes include nouns which English speakers would probably regard as neuter. Other languages have gender classifications based upon other distinctions, such as animate versus inanimate or the size and shape of an object.

Gender plays a relatively minor role in English, since it is relevant only to the choice of pronouns. In many languages, however, gender is also an integral part of the agreement system. For example, the verb may agree in gender with the subject as well as person and/or number. One such language is Imyan Tehit (West Papuan, Irian Jaya).[16] The following examples illustrate the possibilities for a single verb:

(38) a. *tet*   *toso*   *wale*   *qyet*
         1SgPro   hear   already   news
         I heard the news already.

      b. *nen*   *noso*   *wale*   *qyet*
         2SgPro   hear
         You (sg.) heard the news already.

      c. *Maria*   *moso*   *wale*   *qyet*
         Mary   hear   already   news

      d. *Yoel*   *woso*   *wale*   *qyet*
         Joel   hear   already   news

      e. *faf*   *foso*   *wale*   *qyet*
         1PlInclPro   hear   already   news

      f. *mam*   *moso*   *wale*   *qyet*
         1PlExclPro   hear   already   news

---

[15]The following feature assignment rule for Chichewa states that verbs agree with their direct objects in person and number:

$$\text{in } V[\text{SUBCAT}] \quad [\text{DO GR}] \rightarrow \begin{bmatrix} \{1,2,3\} \text{ person} \\ \pm \text{ plural} \end{bmatrix}$$

The inflectional spellout rule for the third plural object prefix is below. Two sets of ellipses are included, the first one so it will ignore the subject and the last one to allow ditransitive verbs to show agreement.

$$\begin{matrix} & V & \\ \begin{bmatrix} \text{SUBCAT} \left\langle \begin{matrix} / \\ \\ \backslash \end{matrix} \dots \text{NP} \begin{bmatrix} \text{DO GR} \\ 3 \text{ person} \\ + \text{ plural} \end{bmatrix} \begin{matrix} \backslash \\ \dots \\ / \end{matrix} \right\rangle \end{bmatrix} & \\ [X] & \rightarrow & [waX] \end{matrix}$$

This rule must apply before the inflectional spellout rules for the other prefixes, since *wa-* is in the innermost position class.

[16]Data from Ron Hesse (personal communication). Transcription follows the practical orthography, in which /y/ is an approximant (IPA /j/); /f/ is a bilabial fricative (IPA /ɸ/); /q/ is a uvular stop (IPA /q/), which is pronounced voiced and/or velar in most positions in these examples.

	nan	*noso*	*wale*	*qyet*
g.	2PlPro	hear	already	news

	na-i	*yoso*	*wale*	*qyet*
h.	person-Pl	hear	already	news

Note the different forms of the verb 'hear' (identify the agreement affixes if you wish). In order to pick the right form, we need to know several things about the subject. Its person and number are always important. First person plural is subdivided into INCLUSIVE ('we including you') and EXCLUSIVE ('we but not you'). Third person singular is subdivided by gender: masculine and feminine. To summarize in a paradigm:

(39)

	Singular		Plural	
	Masculine	Feminine	Inclusive	Exclusive
1	*toso*		*foso*	*moso*
2	*noso*			
3	*woso*	*moso*	*yoso*	

Note that number is irrelevant for agreement in second person, even though there are distinct pronouns for second person singular and plural. Also, the third singular feminine and first plural exclusive forms are both *moso;* this however appears to be a coincidence. This ambiguity normally causes no problems, because the full meaning is available from the context, normally from the subject noun phrase itself.[17]

We can express these facts about agreement in the following feature assignment rules:[18]

(40)   in V[SUBCAT]:

$$\left[\text{Su GR}\right] \rightarrow \begin{bmatrix} \{1,2,3\} \text{ person} \\ \pm \text{ plural} \end{bmatrix}$$

$$\begin{bmatrix} 1 \text{ person} \\ + \text{ plural} \end{bmatrix} \rightarrow \left[\pm \text{ inclusive}\right]$$

$$\begin{bmatrix} 3 \text{ person} \\ - \text{ plural} \end{bmatrix} \rightarrow \begin{bmatrix} \begin{Bmatrix} m \\ f \end{Bmatrix} \text{ gender} \end{bmatrix}$$

These three rules, all of which apply within the verb's SUBCAT list, require the verb first to agree with the subject in [person] and [plural], then if the subject is first plural, also to agree in [inclusive], and if the subject is third person singular, also to agree in [gender].

This takes care of the agreement features on the verb. But, this is just half of the story; we also need to be sure the proper features get on the subject NP in the first place. We need a feature assignment rule (41) to give every noun a feature for singular or plural.

(41)   N → [±plural]

Then, all nouns must be marked in the lexicon as third person and each noun as either masculine or feminine, as in (42).[19]

---

[17]Subject pronouns may be omitted from the clause when the meaning is clear from context.

[18]For gender, I use a feature with two values (m or f), rather than ones like [±feminine] and [±masculine]. Partly this is to avoid irrelevant discussions about gender bias in the analysis (discussions which are irrelevant because the choice of feature names is, from the point of view of the formal grammar, completely arbitrary). More significantly, this approach provides an easy way to add more genders for languages that require them.

[19]Normally, nouns are always third person. However, in Spanish, nouns can apparently be used as the subjects of first person plural verbs: *Los Hijos del Sol no aguantamos eso.* 'We, the children of the sun, don't tolerate that.' (Example from Eugene Loos, personal communication.) This suggests that they may be unmarked for number. However, there is a possible alternative analysis, pointed out to me by Colleen Ahland, in which the noun phrase *Los Hijos del Sol* is an appositive to *pro.*

(42) **N[3 person]**

Maria	[f gender]	Mary
Yoel	[m gender]	Joel
qyet	[f gender]	news[20]

Finally, every pronoun must carry an appropriate combination of features, as in (43).

(43) **NP**

faf	$\begin{bmatrix} \text{1 person} \\ +\text{ plural} \\ +\text{ inclusive} \end{bmatrix}$	we (inclusive)
nen	$\begin{bmatrix} \text{2 person} \\ -\text{ plural} \end{bmatrix}$	you (sing.)
nan	$\begin{bmatrix} \text{2 person} \\ +\text{ plural} \end{bmatrix}$	you (pl.)
...		

When words are inserted into a tree, they carry with them any features that they have in the lexicon. Any features on nouns are then automatically copied to the NP nodes. Thus, the structure of (38d) looks something like this:

(44)

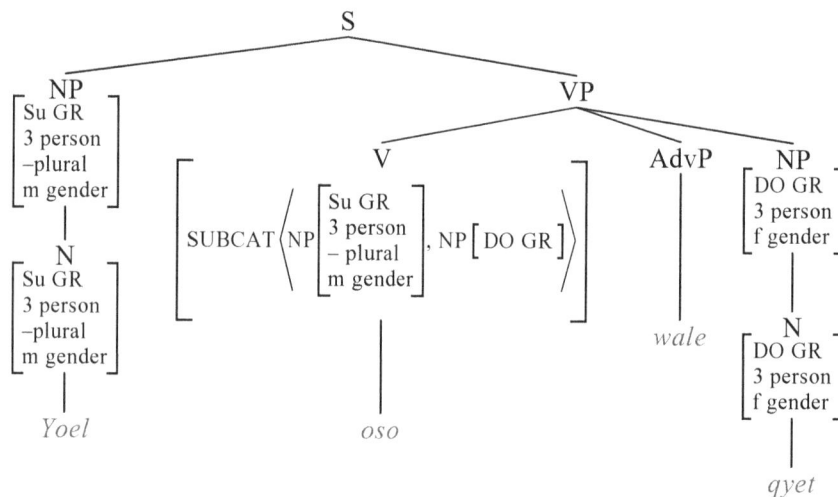

Finally, we need inflectional spellout rules to produce the correct verb forms. But, this is largely routine, and I leave it to you as an exercise, if you wish.

Possessor agreement in Tzeltal

Agreement between the verb and its subject is probably the most common type of agreement, but there are several others. In many languages, the head noun of a noun phrase often has affixes indicating the person and/or number of its possessor; this is another type of agreement. For example, consider the following paradigms from Tzeltal (Mayan, Mexico).[21]

(45)

	'hand/arm'	'house'
first person ('my')	*h-kap*	*h-na*
second person ('your')	*a-kap*	*a-na*
third person ('his/her/its')	*s-kap*	*s-na*

---

[20]Nothing in the data shows that *qyet* is feminine; this information is directly from Ron Hesse.
[21]See footnote 5, p. 29.

Viewed in isolation, it may not be obvious that the prefixes are agreement markers. But look at how the third person forms are used in context.

(46)   *s-kap   markos*
       3-hand   Mark
       Mark's hand

We see the same thing as in a verb agreeing with its subject; the head noun *kap* has a prefix *s-* that redundantly indicates the person of its possessor *markos*. (In fact, exactly the same prefixes are used in Tzeltal to show verb agreement with subjects of transitive clauses.) So, we can say informally that nouns agree with the person of their possessor (if any).

The formal analysis here is like the one for verb agreement. We use the SUBCAT feature on the head noun to keep track of the agreement features of the possessor; in this case it states that the possessor is third person.

(47)

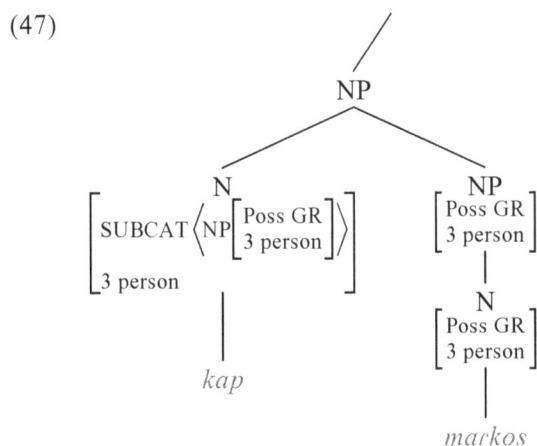

Notice that *kap* has its own feature for third person, too; the SUBCAT feature enables the head noun to have a record both of its own person and the person of its possessor, without confusing the two.

This works especially well, because we need the SUBCAT feature on nouns for another purpose anyway. Some nouns in Tzeltal, like *kap* 'hand', require possessors, just as many verbs require direct objects. Other nouns, like *na* 'house', permit possessors but do not require them. In other words, the possessor in a noun phrase is a complement of the head noun. So, we need to subcategorize nouns with the SUBCAT feature just like we subcategorize verbs.

(48)   **N[SUBCAT ⟨ NP[Poss GR] ⟩]**   **N[SUBCAT ⟨ (NP[Poss GR]) ⟩]**
       kap   arm/hand   *na*   house

Any NP that contains a possessor can have a head noun from either class; any NP that doesn't have a possessor can only have a head noun from the second (optionally possessed) class.[22]

What do we need to generate (46)? First, we need a feature assignment rule (49) to add the agreement feature of person to the possessor in the SUBCAT list of a possessed noun.

(49)   in N[SUBCAT]: [Poss GR] → [{1,2,3} person]

This, together with other parts of the base component, will produce the tree (47). The theory will make sure that (49) assigns [3 person] to the SUBCAT list, since the possessor is [3 person].

---

[22]As with verbs that take optional complements, this approach assumes that when an optionally possessed noun is inserted in a tree, its SUBCAT feature is adjusted so that it exactly matches the tree. The parentheses around the possessor in the SUBCAT list are removed if the noun has a possessor, while the possessor is removed from the SUBCAT list if the noun does not have a possessor.

Then, to produce the proper surface structure, we need an inflectional spellout rule like the one in (50).

(50)
$$\begin{bmatrix} N \\ \text{SUBCAT} \left\langle \text{NP} \begin{bmatrix} \text{Poss GR} \\ \text{3 person} \end{bmatrix} \right\rangle \\ [\text{X}] \end{bmatrix} \rightarrow [s\text{X}]$$

For practice, try writing the inflectional spellout rules for first and second person.[23]

Modifier agreement within a noun phrase

The types of agreement we have seen so far all involve a head (a verb or noun) agreeing with its complements. There is another type of agreement, however, in which the head noun of a noun phrase controls the form of other words in the phrase, such as adjectives and determiners.[24] For example, in Spanish, articles and adjectives change form depending on the gender of the head noun.

(51)   a. *un hombre alto*
           a   man   tall
           a tall man

       b. *una mujer alta*
           a   woman tall
           a tall woman

Some of the most striking examples of modifier agreement come from Bantu languages (Africa), in which the same prefixes occur both on the noun and on its modifiers, indicating the gender class of the noun.

(52)   a. *ki-su   ki-refu*   (Swahili)[25]
           knife   long
           a long knife

       b. *wa-tu   wa-refu*
           people tall
           tall (lit., long) people

Indeed, these same prefixes are also used on verbs to indicate agreement with the subject.

(53)   a. *ki-su   ki-meanguka*
           knife   has.fallen
           The knife has fallen.

       b. *wa-tu   wa-meanguka*
           people have.fallen
           The people have fallen.

---

[23]As shown in chapter 12 "Suppletion and Morphophonemics" (p. 159), the actual rules in Tzeltal must also be sensitive to the phonological shape of the noun. This particular set of affixes is used only on consonant-initial stems. The rule should probably be generalized to apply to subjects of transitive verbs also, but it is not immediately obvious how to do this.

[24]The SUBCAT feature cannot be used to account for modifier agreement. For a formal analysis within Head-driven Phrase Structure Grammar, see Pollard and Sag 1994:83–84, 88–91.

[25]Data from Gregersen 1967:1.

The term CONCORD is often used to refer to this type of agreement system, in which the same prefixes are used repeatedly on different types of words.

Pronouns versus agreement markers

This book carefully distinguishes two types of morphemes, agreement markers and pronouns, which are sometimes confused. It reserves the term PRONOUN for free morphemes which are mutually-substitutable for noun phrases. Affixes on the verb which indicate the person and number of some noun phrase are not pronouns but AGREEMENT MARKERS. Confusion can arise because they communicate the same information; pronouns in one language often correspond to agreement markers in another. For example, compare the following pairs of Spanish and English sentences:

(54) a. *Juana corr-e.*   *Jane is running.*
      b. *Corr-e.*   *She is running.*
      c. *Corr-es.*   *You are running.*
      d. *Corr-o.*   *I am running.*

In the Spanish sentences (54b)–(54d), there are no overt subjects, while the corresponding English sentences have pronouns as subjects. The agreement suffixes on the Spanish verbs communicate the same information about the subject that the English pronouns communicate.

Despite this similarity in meaning and use, there are two clear syntactic differences between pronouns and agreement markers. First, pronouns are separate words, while agreement markers are affixes. Second, agreement markers can co-occur with a full noun phrase, while pronouns cannot.

(55) *Juana corr-e.*   **Jane she is running.*

This contrast is most striking when the subject is a pronoun, co-occurring with the agreement markers on the verb.[26]

(56) *Ella corr-e.*   **She she is running.*

So, just as case markers are distinguished from postpositions (see p. 256), agreement markers are distinguished from pronouns. Though the functions and meanings of two morphemes may be quite similar, grammatical analysis is concerned with identifying their form.

The following chart may help you sort all this out:

Function	Separate word	Affix
Indicates the relation of a constituent to its larger context (grammatical relation or semantic role)	preposition or postposition	case
Indicate features (like person, number, and gender) of other constituents	pronoun	agreement

For further suggestions about how to tell these things apart in unclear cases, see the discussion in chapter 20 "Word Division and Clitics" (especially p. 279ff., p. 282, and footnote 22).

While we're clarifying terminology, let's tackle SUBJECT MARKER. Sometimes it is used to mean 'verbal affix indicating agreement with the subject' and sometimes to mean 'case marker used for subjects'. For this reason, it's probably best to avoid terms like SUBJECT MARKER and OBJECT MARKER. When necessary, say 'subject agreement marker', 'nominative case marker', etc.

---

[26]In Spanish, this usage generally corresponds to an English pronoun with heavy stress: ***She*** *is running.*

Agreement and pro-drop

Recall (from chapter 8 "Verbal Valence," p. 86) that many languages permit subject (or other) pronouns to be omitted, and that they are often called pro-drop languages. There are two further issues to explore about pro-drop in light of the information in this chapter.

Roughly speaking, pro-drop languages tend to have richer sets of agreement markers than do non-pro-drop languages like English. For example, Spanish has separate verb forms for all six combinations of person and number of the subject. Almost all English verbs, on the other hand, have only two forms: one for third singular and the other for all other person/number combinations. English agreement morphology does not tell much about the subject, so pronominal subjects cannot be dropped without significant loss of information about the subject. Thus, it is understandable why English does not allow pro-drop. Spanish, with its much richer agreement system, can safely allow pro-drop without losing the ability to communicate the person and number of the subject. So, the richer the system of agreement in a language, the more likely it is to allow pro-drop. However, this is not a hard-and-fast rule; some pro-drop languages do not have any verb agreement, and some languages with fairly rich verbal agreement cannot freely omit the subject.[27]

In the formal analysis of pro-drop phenomena, we accounted for the absence of the subject by assuming that the language had a silent pronoun *pro* which could appear as subject. So, for example, the base for Spanish might generate a tree like the following:

(57)   Deep structure for *Corre* 'he/she/it runs'

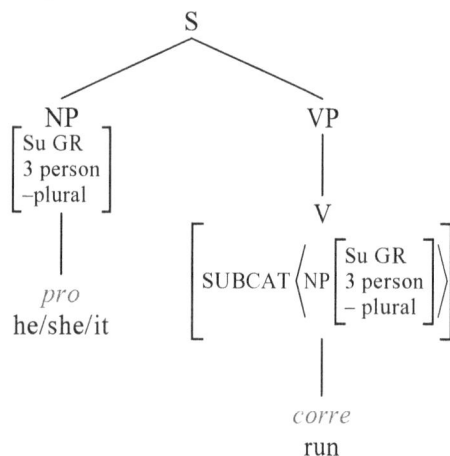

Notice that there are person and agreement features on *pro*. These get copied there automatically when the features for agreement are placed in the SUBCAT list. This is an aspect of the analysis using *pro* that hasn't been explicit yet, but we have assumed it (and represented it informally in trees with glosses). That is, even though *pro* does not have features for person, number, etc., in the lexicon, it can eventually get them in a specific tree as a result of agreement features in the SUBCAT feature.[28]

19.5. Ergativity

In the examples considered so far, both case and agreement treat subjects of intransitive clauses the same as subjects of transitive clauses. Both types of subject had the same case markers and triggered the same pattern of agreement, regardless of transitivity. However, many languages treat subjects of intransitives in the same way as the direct objects of transitives for the purposes of case

---

[27]Haegeman 1991:418 provides useful discussion and references on this point.

[28]Indeed, it may be necessary to see that pronominal features get assigned to *pro* even when it is not involved with agreement, in order for semantic interpretation rules to work properly, but we don't need to resolve that issue here.

or agreement. For example, in Dəməna (Chibchan, Colombia),[29] the subject of a transitive clause has a case suffix -*ga,* but the subject of an intransitive clause is unmarked, like a direct object.

(58) *ranžáde-∅   nayá*
      my.father   went
      My father left.

(59) *ranžadé-ga   dumágə-∅   gwagá   awín*
      my.father   lion   killed did
      My father killed a lion.

The same thing can happen with agreement. In Tzotzil (Mayan, Mexico),[30] one set (Set A) of verbal affixes indicates agreement with the subject of a transitive clause, while another set (Set B) indicates agreement with either the direct object of a transitive or the subject of an intransitive.

(60) *Ch-*   *a-*   *mil*   *-on.*
      Incompletive **2A** kill   **1sgB**
      You're going to kill me.

(61) *Tal*   *-em*   *-on.*
      come   Perfect   **1sgB**
      I have come.

This phenomenon is called ERGATIVITY. In ergative case and agreement systems, it is convenient to have a special term ABSOLUTIVE that means 'subject of an intransitive clause or direct object of a transitive clause'. Similarly, the term ERGATIVE means 'subject of a transitive clause'. These terms make it easier to describe the facts of the language.

(62) Dəməna case marking
      a. ergative noun phrases are case-marked with -*ga* (ERGATIVE case)
      b. absolutive noun phrases are unmarked (ABSOLUTIVE case)

(63) Tzotzil verb agreement
      a. Set A affixes indicate agreement with the ergative of the clause (ERGATIVE agreement)
      b. Set B affixes indicate agreement with the absolutive of the clause (ABSOLUTIVE agreement)

Although it may seem strange for a language to treat intransitive subjects as if they were direct objects, it really isn't if you look at it in terms of the needs of communication. Languages often treat subjects and direct objects differently with respect to case or agreement; this helps distinguish them for the listener. In intransitive clauses, however, the subject doesn't need to be distinguished from a direct object, so it doesn't matter how it is treated. Sometimes languages treat it the same as the subject of a transitive clause, according to what is called a NOMINATIVE-ACCUSATIVE PATTERN, as in (64a). Sometimes they treat it the same as a direct object, according to an ERGATIVE-ABSOLUTIVE PATTERN, as in (64b).

---

[29]Data from Cindy Williams 1993:29, whose transcription is based on Americanist practice. Only the relevant morphological structure is shown. The ergative marker -*ga* is an enclitic, probably a phrasal affix (see chapter 20 "Word Division and Clitics," p. 282, footnote 22.). It is also used on certain nominals that trigger indirect or direct object agreement (Cindy Williams 1993:30–31) but which could conceivably be analyzed as subjects at some level.
[30]Data from Aissen 1987:44–45.

(64)   Intransitive: a.   b.
        Transitive:

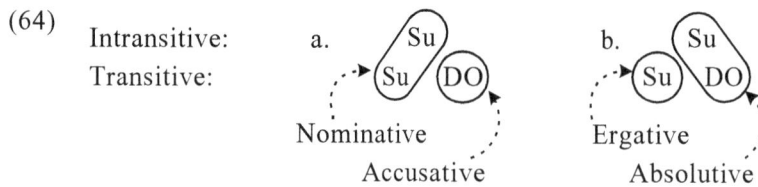

In most theoretical frameworks, the formal analysis of ergative case and agreement systems is more complicated than the analysis of nominative-accusative systems. For this reason, I will not attempt to provide a formal analysis for ergativity here.[31] However, you should be able to recognize ergative case and agreement systems when you find them and to describe them informally.

19.6. Review of key terms

CASE and AGREEMENT are two types of inflectional morphology that are sensitive to grammatical relations. Thus they help us take our analysis beyond just guessing at the grammatical relations based on the semantic roles involved. In both, FEATURE PERCOLATION is important in making our formal grammars work correctly.

Case represents the grammatical relation of a noun phrase. Both nouns and pronouns may be MARKED FOR CASE. Affixes on nouns that indicate case are called CASE MARKERS. Possible cases include NOMINATIVE, ACCUSATIVE, DATIVE, GENITIVE, ERGATIVE, and ABSOLUTIVE.

Agreement, which is typically marked on verbs but can also be marked on other types of words, indicates something about the features of some other constituent in the clause; grammatical relations are used to state which other constituent is important. Quite frequently, for example, the verb AGREES WITH the subject and/or direct object, a noun agrees with a possessor, or a modifier agrees with its head. Features of GENDER, NUMBER, and PERSON (including INCLUSIVE versus EXCLUSIVE in first person plural) typically are involved in agreement.

Both verb agreement and case marking can manifest ERGATIVITY. That is, they can follow an ERGATIVE-ABSOLUTIVE pattern instead of the more familiar NOMINATIVE-ACCUSATIVE pattern.

AGREEMENT MARKERS (= AGREEMENT AFFIXES) should not be confused with PRONOUNS, despite their similarity of meaning. Pronouns, for example, may be optional (in pro-drop languages), but agreement markers usually are not. Similarly, CASE MARKERS should not be confused with prepositions and postpositions. Finally, I suggest avoiding terms like SUBJECT MARKER and OBJECT MARKER, even though they occur in the literature, since they may refer to either case or agreement.

19.7. Questions for analysis

For case:

1. On what words in a noun phrase is case marked? (head noun only? modifiers, too? only pronouns?)
2. How is case marked? That is, what are the forms of the case markers?
3. Does case-marking follow a nominative-accusative or ergative pattern?

For agreement:

1. On what word is the agreement marked? (the verb? the head noun of a noun phrase? an adjective or other noun phrase modifier?)
2. In what features does it agree? (person? number? gender? case?)
3. What is the source of these features? (subject? direct object? possessor? head of the NP?)

---

[31] Pollard and Sag 1994 do not offer any suggestion on how to handle ergativity within a Head-driven Phrase Structure Grammar. One possibility might be to add ergative and absolutive case features in appropriate places in the SUBCAT feature on the verb, which would then get automatically copied to the subject and direct object NPs. Inflectional spellout rules for case and agreement could refer to these features rather than to grammatical relations.

4. How is the agreement marked? (What are the morphological forms of the agreement markers?)
5. Does verb agreement follow a nominative-accusative or ergative pattern?

19.8. Sample descriptions

Subject-verb agreement in Imyan Tehit

In Imyan Tehit, the verb agrees with the subject in person, number, and (in third person singular) gender.

(1) *tet   t-oso   wale   qyet*
     1SgPro 1Sg-hear already news
     I heard the news already.

(2) *faf   f-oso   wale   qyet*
     1PlInclPro 1PlIncl-hear already news
     We (incl.) heard the news already.

(3) *Maria m-oso   wale   qyet*
     Mary   3SgFem-hear already news

(4) *Yoel   w-oso   wale   qyet*
     Joel   3SgMasc-hear already news

The complete paradigm of the agreement prefixes is as follows:

(5)

	Singular		Plural	
	Masculine	Feminine	Inclusive	Exclusive
1	*t-*		*f-*	*m-*
2	*n-*			
3	*w-*	*m-*	*y-*	

Latin case

Latin (an SOV language with relatively free word order) exhibits case on nouns, by means of case/number suffixes. There are at least four cases: nominative (for subjects and nominal complements), accusative (for direct objects and the objects of certain prepositions), dative (for indirect objects), and genitive (for possessors).

(1) *filia-Ø   femina-e   aqua-m   columba-e   dat*
     daughter-NomSg woman-GenSg water-AccSg dove-DatSg gives
     The woman's daughter is giving water to the dove.

19.9. For further reading

This chapter relies heavily on features to do the work necessary to describe case and agreement. This approach is largely based on work in Generalized Phrase Structure Grammar (Gazdar, Klein, Pullum, and Sag 1985) and Head-driven Phrase Structure Grammar (Pollard and Sag 1987). For a basic introduction to GPSG, including a discussion of feature percolation, see Sells (1985:77–134).

For more extensive discussion of such matters as case, agreement, gender, and other inflectional categories, see Anderson 1985a.

20
Word Division and Clitics

20.1. Goals and prerequisites

This chapter will help you do the following:

- ◎ state syntactic guidelines and a few basic phonological guidelines for developing hypotheses about word boundaries
- ◎ use these guidelines to identify clitics in written data, regardless of whether they are written attached to adjacent words or separately
- ◎ classify clitics, using standard terminology
- ◎ describe clitics informally, including stating the reasons for considering a morpheme to be a clitic and for classifying it as a bound word or phrasal affix
- ◎ construct a formal analysis that accounts for a clitic's distribution (except clitic doubling)

This chapter assumes that you are familiar with the following material:

- ✓ bound versus free morphemes (chapter 4 "Introduction to Morphology")
- ✓ embedding in noun phrases (chapter 7 "Embedding and Noun Phrase Structure")
- ✓ different structures used for obliques (chapter 9 "Obliques")
- ✓ the formal analysis of inflectional morphology, especially the analysis of case-marking on English pronouns (chapter 10 "Inflectional Morphology")
- ✓ the distinction between inflection and derivation (chapter 11 "Derivational Morphology")
- ✓ morphophonemics, especially for English -(e)s, and suppletion (chapter 12 "Suppletion and Morphophonemics")
- ✓ portmanteau forms (chapter 13 "Nonlinear Affixation")
- ✓ movement transformations (chapter 15 "Variable Orders of Constituents")
- ✓ the formal analysis of agreement and case, the distinction between case-marking and prepositions, and the distinction between agreement-marking and pronouns (chapter 19 "Case and Agreement")

(Is it beginning to be clear that the different parts of a grammar can be extremely interrelated?)

20.2. Word boundaries

So far, we have maintained a clear distinction between morphology (the structure of words) and syntax (the structure of sentences). We have assumed we knew what a WORD was and where the WORD BOUNDARIES (or WORD BREAKS) were in a sentence. Now it's time to question those assumptions. It is one thing to divide a sentence into words when there is an established written tradition for a language; people simply learn to write spaces where everyone else writes them. It is quite another thing to identify word boundaries in an unwritten language and to help speakers develop their own conventions for writing them.

So, what exactly is a word, and how do we make reasonable hypotheses about word boundaries? First off, we need to recognize at least three different senses of the word 'word'.

(1) a. 'word in a dictionary' OR   a stem, together with all its inflected forms (i.e.,
         'lexical entry'   its entire paradigm)
     b. 'word form' OR   a particular inflected form from the paradigm of
         'fully inflected word'   some word (in sense a)
     c. 'word in a sentence'   a string of material in a sentence that forms one
                                               of the basic building blocks of the sentence

Earlier chapters (especially chapter 10 "Inflectional Morphology") have focused on senses a and b, which are concerned with words as objects within a grammar. This chapter is concerned with clarifying sense c, that is, with finding word boundaries in specific sentences. We will be asking the following types of questions:

(2) a. How do we make an analysis of boundaries between words in a sentence?
     b. How do we decide if a morpheme is a word or an affix, if it is bound or free?
     c. How many terminal nodes do we need in a tree? How do we distribute the phonological material of a sentence among them?
     d. What do we treat as syntax and what as morphology?
     e. Where do we write spaces in a practical orthography?

There are quite a few guidelines, both syntactic and phonological, to use in answering these questions. In most cases analyzing word boundaries is straightforward, but sometimes the syntactic guidelines suggest different word breaks than the phonological ones. Thus, we must distinguish PHONOLOGICAL WORD BOUNDARIES and SYNTACTIC WORD BOUNDARIES; these are discussed in the next two sections.

Phonological word boundaries

The traditional conception of word boundaries is phonological—a word in sense (1c) is a minimal utterance.[1]

(3) **Phonological guideline #1**
     No utterance can be shorter than a single phonological word.

If native speakers do not recognize a morpheme out of context or would never pronounce it by itself, then it is not a word. If they can, it probably is.[2] For example, the minimal reply to a question is a single word, not part of a word.

---

[1]Notice the similarity to the definition of MORPHEME in chapter 3 "Morphemes and Hypotheses" (p. 19) as a minimal meaningful unit. The same considerations about 'minimal' apply here as are discussed in chapter 4 "Introduction to Morphology" (p. 25).

[2]This guideline has to be used with caution when speakers have an established written or grammatical tradition. In the course of learning to read or analyze their own language, they may also have learned how to pronounce bound forms in isolation. In these cases, looking at normal responses to questions is a much more reliable test than just discussing words as words to see if they can be spoken in isolation.

(4)   *How many children do you have?*

Possible answers: Impossible answers:

Nineteen   **-teen*
Lots   **-s*

When you learn a word in isolation (which is normally what happens), this guideline alone can give you a pretty good idea about word boundaries. When you hear the same word in a sentence, a reasonable hypothesis is that there are word boundaries on either side of it (allowing for any affixes, of course).

A second phonological guideline is that pauses are generally impossible inside words.

(5)   **Phonological guideline #2**
       Pauses are only possible at word boundaries.

If there is a pause at a certain point in a sentence or if a pause is possible there, then that point is probably a phonological word boundary. For example, consider how an irritated elementary school teacher might speak to the class, pausing for effect between each word, but not within words.[3]

(6)   a.   [bojz... ʔænd... gɹlz]   'boys and girls'
       b. *[boj... z... ʔænd... gɹl... z]

The problem with (6b) is that the plural suffixes, which are bound morphemes, have been pronounced as separate words.

Once you begin to apply these guidelines in a language, you may find phonological rules whose behavior is affected by word boundaries. You can use them as additional diagnostic tests.

(7)   **Phonological guideline #3**
       Look for phonological rules that provide information about word boundaries, then use them to help define word boundaries in unclear cases.

For example, the rules in English which account for the variation in voicing of the plural suffix -*s* do not operate across word boundaries. There is good reason to believe that the underlying form of this suffix is /-z/. There is a phonological rule that causes /z/ to devoice after a voiceless segment (as in *bats*), but a /z/ which begins a separate word (as in *the bat zoomed*) does not devoice in that environment.

(8)   'bats'   'the bat zoomed'
       Input to phonological rules: bæt-z   ðə bæt zumd
       Output of phonological rules: bæt-s   ðə bæt zumd

So, if you find a /z/ at the beginning of some morpheme which sometimes becomes [s] because of this rule, then the rule is treating the morpheme as a suffix, not a separate word. That is, the rule provides evidence that the morpheme is a suffix. As another example, the rules of English require full words to have at least one vowel, but this requirement does not apply to morphemes like the plural -*s,* which often occur without vowels. This is evidence that it is a suffix, not a separate word.

Specific rules like this can be very useful in identifying phonological word breaks. To find them, work from clear cases to unclear ones. First develop a hypothesis about a phonological rule which is sensitive to obvious word breaks, and refine it until it works well in clear cases. Then, use this hypothesis to help you make further hypotheses about word breaks in other cases that are less obvious. Use what you know to discover what you don't know.

---

[3]The phonetic transcription of English here is an approximate broad phonetic transcription of one upper Midwestern U.S. dialect, not based on any particular phonological analysis. It is used at several points to focus on the phonological system of the language rather than irrelevant details of the practical orthography.

Exercise: Phonological word boundaries

Consider the following facts about Tohono O'odham (Uto-Aztecan, Arizona):[4]

(9) a. All stressed syllables are word-initial, but not all words are stressed.
    b. All words begin with one or more consonants.
    c. Within a word, many vowel sequences are forbidden, such as /ao/, /ou/, and /ai/.
       They are forbidden even when the vowels are separated by a glottal stop /ʔ/ or /h/.

We can use the guidelines to identify the phonological word boundaries in the following clause, even without identifying morphemes.

(10) *číhiaʔohúhuʔidhígaimíistol*
     The girl is chasing the cat.

Before reading on, try using the guidelines in (9) to insert phonological word boundaries in (10). If you need help, consult the footnote.[5]

Syntactic word boundaries

When we turn to syntactic word boundaries, we are essentially trying to determine what to put on separate terminal nodes in a tree. Our first hypotheses about syntactic word boundaries are based on what we know about the phonology.

(11) **Syntactic guideline #1**
    Any phonological word break is generally also a syntactic word break.

So, once we have decided that there is a phonological word boundary before *zoomed* in *the bat zoomed,* we are largely committed to recognizing a syntactic word boundary there, too, and putting *zoomed* on a separate terminal node. (Warning: the opposite is not true, as discussed below; some syntactic word breaks are not phonological ones!)

But, there are purely syntactic reasons for making syntactic word breaks too. One of the strongest is based on the overall structure of the tree.

(12) **Syntactic guideline #2**
    Any major constituent break (e.g., the beginning or end of a phrase) is also a syntactic word break.

This, together with our understanding of noun phrase structure (chapter 7 "Embedding and Noun Phrase Structure," p. 65), explains why there are word boundaries between the different morphemes in NPs like the following. Between almost every pair of morphemes is a phrase boundary, hence also a syntactic word boundary.

(13) *[NP the [QP two] [AP [DegP very] little] dogs]*

Other guidelines may also be helpful in deciding whether a morpheme is an affix or a separate syntactic word.

---

[4]Information about Tohono O'odham (formerly known as Papago) from Dean Saxton; based on an illustration by Langacker (1972). Transcription based on Americanist practice.
[5]By (9a), we need a word break somewhere before each stressed vowel. By (9b), we must locate each word break just before a consonant. This gives us *číhiaʔo húhuʔid hígai míistol.* (Placing the second word break between /d/ and /h/ is a guess, although a reasonable one.) By (9c), our first 'word' needs to be divided further, since /aʔo/ is not permitted within words. By (9b), the glottal stop belongs with the /o/: *číhia ʔo húhuʔid hígai míistol.*

(14) **Syntactic guideline #3**
      Affixes tend to occur next to only a single type of word (their stems) and in a fixed order;
      words occur more freely in various combination with each other.

This means words can often be moved with respect to each other; this is usually not possible for
morphemes within a word.

(15) a. *I see the tiny, little people down there on the ground.*
      b. *I see the little, tiny people down there on the ground.*

(16) a. *teach-er-s*
      b. **teach-s-er*

It also means a syntactic word or phrase can usually be inserted between two other morphemes only
at syntactic word breaks; trying to insert a word between a stem and an affix usually results in the
affix being attached to the wrong type of word.[6] So, for example, to find out if the English plural
marker *-(e)s* is a word or affix, we could try inserting adjectives (which we already know to be
separate syntactic words) and PPs between the noun and the plural marker.

(17) a. *the dog-s*
      b. **the dog-big-s*
      c. **the dog [in the manger]-s*[7]

This doesn't work, so according to both phonological and syntactic guidelines, *-(e)s* is bound.
     Finally, one can often tell the difference between words and affixes by sniffing out the irregular
forms in the language.

(18) **Syntactic guideline #4**
      Morphology often shows great irregularities, while combinations of separate syntactic words
      do not.

We have seen this morphological irregularity often (especially in chapter 12 "Suppletion and
Morphophonemics"). In contrast, irregular combinations of separate syntactic words (which I have
called TOTAL FUSION, see chapter 13 "Nonlinear Affixation," p. 176) hardly ever occur. For
example, there are irregular noun plurals like *oxen* in place of **oxes*, but there are not any irregular
combinations of the definite article *the* with particular nouns. So, by this guideline, the plural *-(e)s* is
an affix and *the* is probably not (although we can't tell for sure, because it might be a perfectly
regular affix).

Exercise: Syntactic word boundaries

     Justify as many of the spaces in the following examples as you can, by citing specific syntactic
evidence that each represents a syntactic word boundary. Where there are morpheme breaks inside
words, cite the evidence that they are not syntactic word boundaries. See the footnote for a partial
answer.[8]

---

[6]This criterion needs to be used with caution, because of compounding (see chapter 11 "Derivational Morphology," p. 137)
and noun incorporation (chapter 21 "Passive and Voice," p. 302). So, before concluding that a particular boundary is a word
boundary just because a word can be inserted at that point, one must eliminate these two possibilities.
     [7]That is, this is ungrammatical when the *-s* is interpreted as the plural marking on *dog,* not the possessive *'s* or the plural of
manger.
     [8]First, construct a tree for each sentence. Every phrase boundary is also a word boundary; this takes care of many of the
spaces. However, this is somewhat circular (until we become sure of our hypothesis about phrase structure), since we may
have used our hypotheses about word boundaries to help justify our phrase structure rules. So, we should consider other
criteria. Several substrings of the sentences can be used as answers to questions, such as 'Arthur', '(a) cactus', 'all', 'over',
'his', 'please', and 'choose', and are phonological words by other guidelines; this provides evidence for syntactic word

(19)   a. *Arthur grabbed a cactus, and he has prickers all over his hand!*
       b. *Hand me the calculator, please.*
       c. *Which 'un did ya' choose?*

20.3. Clitics: When the guidelines disagree...

Word breaks are not always obvious. Sometimes the different guidelines don't even agree; some guidelines may suggest that a certain morpheme is bound, while others may suggest that it is free. If it is unclear whether a morpheme is a word or an affix, it is generally called a CLITIC. In some ways (especially by phonological guidelines), clitics are like affixes; in other ways (especially by syntactic guidelines), they are like words.

As examples, consider two homophonous morphemes in English, both of which are spelled *'s:*

(20)   Contracted *'s* (from *is*)
       a. *hu-z gɔn*   Who's gone?
       b. *hwət-s ðæt*   What's that?
       c. *hwɪtʃ-ɪz jɔrz*   Which's yours?

       Possessive *'s*
       d. *ðə mæn-z opɪnjən*   the man's opinion
       e. *ði kæt ɪn ðə hæt-s opɪnjən*   the cat in the hat's opinion
       f. *ðə pitʃ-ɪz pɪt*   the peach's pit

Should we analyze them as affixes or words? Phonological guidelines suggest that both are affixes.

(21)   a. They are never pronounced in isolation.
       b. They cannot be preceded by pause.
       c. They do not contain vowels (at least in some environments), unlike clear cases of words.
       d. They undergo devoicing, like the plural suffix in (8).

Syntactic guidelines suggest that they are separate words.

(22)   a. Contracted *'s* functions as the verb in a clause (as a contraction of *is* or *has*).
       b. Possessive *'s* always attaches to the end of a noun phrase, not always to the head noun (look again at (20e)).
       c. Both can attach to a variety of word types (see (24) below).
       d. Contracted *'s* is completely regular; there is no stem suppletion.

On the other hand, at least one syntactic guideline suggests that possessive *'s* is an affix.

(23)   There are irregular possessive forms of pronouns, like *my*, which are found in place of regular combinations like **I's*.

---

breaks at their edges. Most of the spaces mark places where large chunks of material can be inserted which are clearly word-sized or larger, as seen in (i).
   (i)   ***Hand*** *over to **me,** won't you, **the** electronic **calculator** in the corner, **please?***
Many pieces between spaces can be rearranged freely.
   (ii) *Ya' did choose 'un, didn't ya'?*
Finally, for every item between spaces which has lexical meaning, we can substitute other items, without running across any irregular changes or combinations with neighboring items with grammatical meaning (the ones that could conceivably be affixes). Compare (iii) to (19a).
   (iii) *My daughter bumped a bucket of paint, and she has dark brown splotches all over her new clothes!*

These morphemes are not clearly words or affixes, but have some characteristics of each. They are PHONOLOGICALLY BOUND like affixes and (at least partially) SYNTACTICALLY FREE like words. So, in order to have some label for them until we figure out exactly what they are, we call them clitics.

20.4. Finding clitics

Cross-linguistically, clitics generally have grammatical meaning, rather than lexical meaning. Most belong to closed classes like pronouns, prepositions, auxiliary verbs, and conjunctions. They usually attach to the edges of words, outside of derivational and inflectional affixes. They almost always are clearly-defined strings of segments, like prefixes and suffixes (rather than infixes, morpheme processes, or other nonlinear affixes discussed in chapter 13 "Nonlinear Affixation").[9]

Still, clitics are not always obvious, because analysts tend to jump to conclusions about whether something is a word or an affix. When you get data in written form, decisions about where to put spaces have already been made. Clitics may be written either as words or affixes, perhaps inconsistently. Sometimes even clear cases of words or affixes are written the 'wrong' way. You can't assume that written words always correspond to phonological or syntactic words, although most of the time they will.

When you collect your own data, be equally suspicious. Be on the lookout especially for apparent affixes that have some word-like properties and, thus, might need special analysis as clitics. Just because something is phonologically bound does not mean that it should always be analyzed as an affix. On the other hand, clitics are relatively uncommon. Don't assume something is anything other than a straightforward affix or word unless you have good evidence to the contrary. If it looks like an affix and sounds like an affix, then assume it *is* an affix, unless you know that it also has some characteristics of a word. Do the same for apparent words. So, what is good evidence that something is a clitic rather than an affix?

One type of clitic that is easy to spot is one that attaches to a variety of different types of words. An example is the possessive = 's, as it is used in colloquial spoken English.[10] (Linguists sometimes use an equals sign rather than a hyphen on clitics, to distinguish them from affixes.[11])

(24) a. *[the woman]'s tennis racket*
      b. *[anyone who likes children]'s ideas about child-rearing*
      c. *[the one with red on]'s atrocious behavior*
      d. *[people who hurry]'s ideas about politeness*
      e. *[someone who types quickly]'s job prospects*

Here, = 's attaches to a head noun, a nonhead noun, a preposition, a verb, and an adverb. This property of many clitics is sometimes called PROMISCUOUS ATTACHMENT. Affixes, on the other hand, usually attach to only one type of word. But, there is a generalization about possessive = 's; it always attaches to the last word in the noun phrase (whatever it may be). A better way to say this is that it attaches to the whole phrase.

Promiscuous attachment can also be illustrated by a morpheme which occurs in Huichol (Uto-Aztecan, Mexico).[12]

---

[9]One exception is noted by Zwicky 1987:138, in Tongan, for a phrasal affix. Barbara Hollenbach (personal communication) and I have even encountered bound words which are realized as morpheme processes in a few Otomanguean languages. These are clearly subject pronouns in terms of their syntax, with the same distribution as the subject pronouns in other Otomanguean languages (of which the Peñoles Mixtec data in (26) is typical). However, they are apparently realized on verbs as processes, such as the laryngealization of all vowels from the stem vowel to the end of the word. (It is possible that an autosegmental representation of the bound word, with appropriate spreading rules, might avoid the need to posit that a bound word can be a process.)

[10]Because this construction is not sanctioned in standard English, many of these seem odd, if not ungrammatical, when encountered in writing. However, such constructions commonly occur in natural speech and for that reason should be considered grammatical, in at least some dialects.

[11]See, for example, Klavens 1985 and Spencer 1991:379ff.

[12]Data based on Merrifield et. al. 1987, #186, with clarifications (chiefly tone and vowel length) supplied by Joseph Grimes (personal communication). Transcription follows Americanist conventions. According to Grimes, =cíe, like certain other

(25) a. *ʔákí*   canyon
      b. *ʔákí ʔamïpáa*   big canyon
      c. *ʔákícíe*   in the canyon
      d. *ʔákí ʔamïpáacíe*   in the big canyon

The morpheme *=cíe* 'in' seems to be an affix, since it is phonologically bound. But, it attaches to either a noun or an adjective, again whichever is last in the noun phrase. Its location is defined with respect to the whole phrase, rather than with respect to a single word. This is word-like behavior, like a postposition. Thus, *=cíe* can be called a clitic.

Another type of clitic that is easy to spot appears at first glance to be an agreement marker, but disappears whenever a full noun phrase appears, as seen in the following examples from Peñoles Mixtec.[13] In this case a morpheme that looks like an agreement affix, *=ší* '3f', is mutually-substitutable for a full noun phrase.

(26) *ní-šinu=ší*
      Cmp-run-3f
      She ran.

(27) *ní-šinu   šeči-áⁿ*
      Cmp-run   girl-that
      That girl ran.

However, clear cases of agreement markers do not disappear when there is a full noun phrase as subject. (See the various examples in chapter 19 "Case and Agreement," pp. 257ff., and the discussion on p. 267.) In other words, *=ší* '3f' has the syntactic properties of a pronoun (a separate word), even though it is phonologically bound. Thus, it is better to analyze *=ší* not as an agreement marker but as a pronoun, because it is mutually-exclusive with some category of free forms (for example, noun phrases).[14]

Often, clitics are variant forms of morphemes that are clearly separate words, but the clitics are phonologically reduced (missing one or more segments, vowels changed to schwa, stressless, etc.). For example, English ['ʔænd] 'and' has a shortened clitic form [n̩=] (usually spelled *'n*). The full and reduced forms are sometimes simply variants of the same lexical entry; the two forms are identical in meaning and grammar; they differ only in their phonological properties. The reduced form acts phonologically like an affix, but in all other respects is a separate word.[15]

Again, if it looks like an affix and sounds like an affix, analyze it as an affix, unless you have good reason to suspect otherwise. Some good reasons to analyze a morpheme as a clitic are as follows:

(28)   Evidence   Probable type of clitic

Promiscuous attachment	bound word or phrasal affix
Mutually-substitutable with a category of free forms	bound word
Phonologically-reduced variant of some free form	bound word

(This chart also suggests which of two types a clitic might be; these are discussed below.)

---

enclitic postpositions in Huichol, forms a separate phonological foot, while other enclitic postpositions become part of the final foot of the item to which they attach.

[13]Data from Peñoles Mixtec provided by John Daly. Transcription follows Americanist conventions. Superscript *n* represents nasalization.

[14]For more on distinguishing agreement markers from pronouns, see chapter 19 "Case and Agreement" (p. 267).

[15]Be cautious though. The reduced form may be a completely separate lexical entry, with only a historical relationship to the full form. As a result, there may some differences in semantics or syntax. Also, some clear cases of affixes may bear similarities to free words that are their historical ancestors, so not all phonologically-reduced forms are clitics. See, for example, Zwicky's (1987) analysis of English *n't* as a suffix.

20.5. Types of clitics

Clitics are often classified based on two dimensions:

- where they attach
- how word-like versus affix-like they are

Let's consider each of these classifications.

Where does it attach? Proclitics and enclitics

Clitics may be classified based on whether they attach at the beginning or end of another word. A PROCLITIC is a clitic that is phonologically attached to the beginning of some other item, like a prefix. Many phonologically reduced forms in English are proclitics.

(29)   *... ði= pɛnsl̩ ...*
        (Where did) the pencil (go?)

(30)   *... n̩= æpl̩, n̩= ə= tʰɹək, n̩= ə= bɔl*
        (Santa brought me) 'n apple, 'n a truck, 'n a ball...

(31)   *gɪt n̩= ði= kaɹ*
        Git 'n th' car.

An ENCLITIC is a clitic that is phonologically attached to the end of some other item, like a suffix. The two clitics *'s* in (20) are enclitics, as is *=cie* 'in' in (25) and *=ši* '3f' in (26).

How word-like or affix-like is it? Unstressed words, bound words, and phrasal affixes

However, it is far more significant to classify clitics based on how word-like or affix-like they are. Some clitics are essentially words with the phonological properties of affixes, others are essentially affixes with a few syntactic properties of words.[16]

Of those clitics that are essentially words, we can distinguish two subtypes. Some are simply words that are never stressed or can occur without stress, such as the reduced forms of *the* and *in* mentioned in (29)–(31). These have all the properties of words, except that they (the reduced forms) are never pronounced in isolation, since they are stressless. Although these are sometimes considered to be clitics, most recent discussions assume that a morpheme should not be considered phonologically bound simply because it is stressless.[17] We call such morphemes UNSTRESSED WORDS, and consider them to be clitics only marginally.

Rather, we should concentrate on syntactic words that are phonologically bound in more interesting ways than unstressed words. For example, English has two homophonous contractions *'s* (from *is* and *has*); both are clearly verbs and thus are syntactically free. But, both undergo the same morphophonemic alternation [s/z/ɨz] as the noun plural *-(e)s* and the verb third person singular *-(e)s*. Since these rules only apply within phonological words, these contractions are phonologically

---

[16]Following a proposal by Nevis (1986) with later refinements by Zwicky (1987), I assume that ultimately all clitics can either be analyzed as words with some affix-like properties (bound words) or affixes with some word-like properties (phrasal affixes). That is, the term CLITIC does not refer to a principled class of linguistic objects, but rather a pretheoretic amalgamation of two very different types of morphemes. Nevertheless, it can be a useful concept, if defined as 'a morpheme which is not clearly either a word or an affix'. This is particularly true in early stages of analysis.

[17]For example, Zwicky (1987:133) states, "I propose here to reserve the term [clitic] for elements whose description requires more than the stipulation that they may or must be prosodically dependent," and again (1985:287), "[the accentual test of clitichood] is most unreliable; it should never, I think, be used as the sole (or even major) criterion for a classification." Nevis (1986:68–70) echoes, "It is true that a large number of grammatical function words do not bear stress or accent as a matter of principle. But these can be distinguished from true clitics, which have additional properties." Besides the existence of unstressed words that are not clitic, both point out the existence of stressed clitics.

bound. Thus they are clitics, for more reasons than just being unstressed. They are called BOUND WORDS, since they are essentially words which happen to be phonologically bound.

As another example, Telugu (Dravidian, south India) has two types of postpositions. Some are free; they are clearly separate words.[18]

(32)   *kaaru   rooḍḍu   miida   unnadi*
        car   road   on   it.is
        The car is on the road.

(33)   *kaayitaalu   peṭṭe   kinda   unnaay*
        papers   box   under   they.are
        The papers are under the box.

Others are bound, but otherwise have essentially the same syntactic traits as the free postpositions.[19]

(34)   *atanu   madraasu=nunci   waccæcæḍu*
        he   Madras=from   he.came
        He came from Madras.

(35)   *waaḍu   kukkanu   karra=too   koṭṭæcæḍu*
        he   dog   stick=with   he.beat
        He beat the dog with the stick.

For this reason, the simplest analysis seems to be to consider both the bound and free forms to be postpositions. Those that are phonologically bound are examples of bound words.

In contrast to bound words, some clitics are essentially affixes, but they have the odd characteristic that they attach to a whole phrase, rather than a specific word. The English possessive =*'s* discussed above in (24) is the standard example of this type of clitic.[20] Such clitics are called PHRASAL AFFIXES.

Another example of phrasal affixes is provided by case markers in Dəmənə[21] mentioned in chapter 19 "Case and Agreement" (pp. 257 and 269). These are enclitics, not suffixes, since they display promiscuous attachment. They always occur at the end of a noun phrase, attaching either to a pronoun, the head noun, or a following adjective.[22]

---

[18]Data from Krishnamurti and Gwynn 1985:93–95. Underdot on alveolars represents retroflexion.

[19]The analysis here is tentative. Krishnamurti and Gwynn 1985:95 do not specify in what sense the free postpositions are free, except that they can "occur as independent words." In other words, the bound postpositions appear to be clitics, but their exact phonological properties are not specified. When I had the opportunity to consult a native speaker from Hyderabad, it appeared that free postpositions began with a rise in pitch (stress?), while bound ones did not. At least one bound postposition, =*too* 'with', has a corresponding free form *tooṭi*. My consultant also noted that bound postpositions are written attached in the practical orthography and that these examples represent very informal usage. Krishnamurti and Gwynn also mention that there are some syntactic and morphological differences between the free and bound postpositions, but their exact nature is unclear.

[20]Compare also Radford's (1988:65) description of *'s* as a "phrasal inflection."

[21]Data from Cindy Williams 1993:29, 33–35, whose transcription follows Americanist conventions. Only the relevant morphological structure is shown.

[22]I assume that these case markers are best analyzed as phrasal affixes rather than clitic postpositions for the following reasons: (1) If the ergative marker is a suffix, then the phrase structure rules can be stated more simply, since subjects will always be NPs regardless of transitivity. (2) The ergative marker can be omitted from transitive subjects in some circumstances (Cindy Williams 1993:33–34), which is not typical behavior for a postposition. (3) If the genitive enclitic was a postposition, it would be more difficult to formalize agreement of the head noun with the possessor (which occurs with inalienable possession, Cindy Williams 1993:36–38), since the SUBCAT feature for agreement on the head noun would then have to refer to the object of a PP rather than to a bare NP. To put this another way: from a typological perspective, the object of a PP usually does not control agreement outside the PP. Hence, possessors are probably better analyzed as NPs, and the genitive enclitic as a phrasal suffix. (4) There is a distinct set of locative postpositions (Cindy Williams 1993:80) which have a different distribution from the oblique case marker. Two of these are free forms; the other, =*ka* 'in, on, at', is apparently a clitic. As evidence that they are distinct from the case markers, (a) the oblique case marker can co-occur with one of the free postpositions (Larry Williams 1995:109); (b) the ergative and oblique case markers precede the Topic clitic =*ru* (see examples in Cindy Williams 1993:152 and Larry Williams 1995:7, 44, and elsewhere), which can attach to a variety

(36) a. *íngwi kən   [kaŋgəmám]=ba gágə   kə́ma uyá*
          one   wood   earth=Obl   placed InfW did
          He laid a stick on the ground.

      b. *[iŋgúna zukwegá]=ba nə́ngwi*
          trail   good=Obl   he.stands
          He is standing on the good road.

(37) a. *[ranžadé]=ga   dumágə gwagá awín*
          my.father=Erg   lion   killed did
          My father killed a lion.[23]

      b. *[súži bənší]=ga zeŋ   məkənakúki   kə́ma kekwá*
          bird white=Erg fear don't.let.come.for.you InfW said
          The white bird said to her, "Don't let fear come for you."

(38) a. *[nawin]=že urága*
          we=Gen   house
          our house

      b. *[ména   tšukkwegán]=že məŋkəsára*
          woman   big=Gen   clothes
          a big woman's clothes

We have seen that the term CLITIC refers to two quite different types of morphemes: bound words and phrasal affixes. In fact, these two types probably shouldn't both be called by the same label. When we use the term CLITIC for both, it implies that they have significant characteristics in common. In fact, about all they have in common is that they tend to get confused with each other. So, the term CLITIC is useful only as a temporary way of talking about a morpheme which is not obviously either a word or an affix; it does not ultimately shed much light on what it actually is. It is better to use terms like BOUND WORD and PHRASAL AFFIX whenever possible.

20.6. How to handle clitics in a formal grammar

The formal analysis of different types of clitics is straightforward, with only a couple of slight twists on what we've seen before. Unstressed words and bound words are handled like other words, while phrasal affixes are handled like inflectional affixes.

Clitics that are essentially words (bound words)

Since bound words (and unstressed words) are just a special type of syntactic word, they are listed in the lexicon with all the other words. You may want to include an equals sign on bound words as a way of showing that they are phonologically bound.

(39) **P**   (Huichol)
      =cíe   to

(The equals sign is just an informal notation, not an official part of a formal grammar. To be complete, we would need to explain how bound words 'change' from being free to bound as they move from the syntactic to phonological parts of the grammar.[24] The equals sign is only a reminder that our grammar is incomplete in this respect.)

---

of different phrases and thus is probably a bound word; (c) the clitic locative postposition generally follows the Topic clitic (see examples in Larry Williams 1995:20, 28, and elsewhere) and, thus, is probably also a bound word.

[23]Presumably a large wildcat such as a mountain lion or jaguar.

[24]Nevis (1986), for example, discusses a process of 'liaison', which attaches a clitic phonologically to a neighboring word between the syntactic and phonological components, and discusses similar proposals by others.

It's probably best not to include the equals sign for unstressed words, since these are not phonologically bound in any significant sense. Thus, for the English preposition *in*, we list the reduced form /n̩/ next to the full form in the lexicon. When it comes time to insert some form of this word in a tree, we are free to choose either the full or reduced form.

(40) **P**   (English)

  ɪn, n̩ location in a place

Similarly, if bound words are alternate forms of ordinary (free) words, we list both forms, as in the verb *be*.[25]

(41) **V [SUBCAT ⟨ NP[Su], [NC] ⟩]**

  bi

  æm, =m [1 person, –plural, –past]

  ɪz, =z [3 person, –plural, –past] ⎫ (copula)

  aɹ, =ɹ [–past]

As always, we list *'s*, the contracted form of *is*, in its phonological underlying form /=z/, since phonological rules will account for its allomorphs [=s] and [=ɪz]. (Compare the way we handled the plural suffix *-(e)s* in chapter 12 "Suppletion and Morphophonemics," p. 153.)

Clitics that are essentially affixes (phrasal affixes)

Phrasal affixes are handled in the grammar like any other inflectional affix; they are added with an inflectional spellout rule. The only unusual thing about the rule is that it refers to a *phrasal* category—in this case, NP.[26]

(42) NP

  [Gen case]

   [X] → [Xz]

This rule applies in the following way to add the possessive suffix to the possessor NP *the king of England*:

(43) Deep structure   Surface structure

---

[25]There are some restrictions on when the bound forms can occur, which are not accounted for here.

[26]I assume that all possessors carry the feature [Gen case]. The rules that introduce case features are discussed in chapter 19 "Case and Agreement" (p. 254).

Like all inflectional spellout rules, (42) does not apply to possessive pronouns, whose forms are listed explicitly in the lexicon like all irregular stems. (See chapter 10 "Inflectional Morphology," p. 129.)

(44) **NP**

aj	[Nom case]	
maj	[Gen case]	$\left.\begin{array}{c}\end{array}\right\}$ $\begin{bmatrix}1\text{ person}\\-\text{ plural}\end{bmatrix}$
mi	[Obj case]	

hi	[Nom case]	
his	[Gen case]	$\left.\begin{array}{c}\end{array}\right\}$ $\begin{bmatrix}3\text{ person}\\-\text{ plural}\\ \text{m gender}\end{bmatrix}$
him	[Obj case]	

...

When the irregular forms are inserted in the tree, this automatically blocks the regular inflectional spellout rule (42) from applying and thus prevents ungrammatical forms like the following:

(45) **my's*
      *his's
      *her's
      *their's

On the other hand, one English pronoun is completely regular: *it*. Only one form must be listed in the lexicon. When *it* is inserted as a possessor, the inflectional spellout rule (42) adds /-z/ to it, just as it does to all ordinary NPs. After the application of regular phonological rules, the surface form *its* results. The only thing 'irregular' about this form is that its spelling does not include an apostrophe, but this is a fact about the writing system, not about the spoken language, which is the primary focus of our analysis.

Distinguishing bound words from phrasal affixes

Phrasal affixes may appear at first glance to be syntactically free, like bound words, because they attach to a variety of different types of words. However, on closer examination, it may become apparent that the simplest analysis is to treat them as inflectional affixes, not as bound words on a separate terminal node. Compare, for example, the English possessive suffix in (24) to the Huichol postposition in (25). Both exhibit promiscuous attachment. But, we have analyzed them differently: English *'s* as a phrasal affix (42), while Huichol *=cíe* as a bound word (39). Why?

The only way to be sure in cases like this is to try both possible analyses (bound word versus phrasal affix) and see which one works best. Suppose we analyzed English *'s* as a bound word. Then we would have to put it in some category in the lexicon; the best choice might be to consider it a postposition. (See chapter 19 "Case and Agreement," p. 256, for the parallel between case markers and pre/postpositions.) But, this would force us to complicate our PP rule to allow the NP to occur either before or after the head P.

(46) PP → (NP) P (NP)

Further, we would need to mark each P in the lexicon as to whether it was a preposition (most of them) or postposition (*'s*), rather than letting the PP rule take care of this detail for everything at once. Finally, possessive pronouns (*my, your,* etc.) would have to be assigned to the category PP, rather than NP, since under this analysis possessors are PPs; this is weird, since usually pronouns are NPs, not PPs.[27] Clearly, it is simpler and more natural to treat *'s* as a phrasal affix.

---

[27]Many of these difficulties are not insurmountable, given other theoretic assumptions. It might be the case, under other assumptions, that the analysis would work out better by treating possessive *'s* as a bound word. So, like most analytical decisions, this one is dependent on the theoretical assumptions being used. We can't say absolutely that *'s* is a phrasal affix, only that under certain assumptions, this is the best analysis.

On the other hand, in Huichol, it works just fine to analyze *=cíe* as a postposition (a bound word), as far as we know. Further, bound words are more common than phrasal affixes, so our first hypothesis about a clitic should always be that it is a bound word; we analyze it as a phrasal affix only if doing so simplifies the analysis.

There's another reason, too, to treat *'s* as a phrasal affix. Recall (from chapter 9 "Obliques," p. 95) that there is a tendency for PPs to be used mostly for obliques and rather rarely for subjects and objects.

(47)   Su   DO   IO   Oblique
       NP ←———————→ PP

Case markers, on the other hand, are more commonly used for subjects and objects and quite rarely used for obliques. Possessors tend to be like subjects and objects in this regard. So, naturalness suggests that it is better to treat English *'s* as a case marker (a phrasal affix) and Huichol *=cíe* as a postposition (a bound word).[28]

These, then, are some of the considerations that can be relevant when you try to classify a clitic as a bound word or a phrasal affix, specifically, as a pre/postposition or a case marker. Of course, the arguments based on simplicity of the analysis are stronger than the ones based on naturalness. But, since all these arguments point in the same direction, we can be reasonably sure of the conclusion.

20.7. Special properties of some clitics

Some clitics, specifically bound words, have special grammatical properties that need to be accounted for in addition to their status as clitics.

Some bound words don't appear in the position that you'd expect, but rather move someplace else. For example, the direct object pronouns in Spanish are bound words. They are attached to the left of a verb (as proclitics), instead of following the verb like objects that are full noun phrases.

(48)   a. *Manuela   tiró   el   voleibol.*
          Manuela   threw   the   volleyball
          Manuela threw the volleyball.

       b. *Manuela   lo=   tiró.*
          Manuela   3sgDO=   threw
          Manuela threw it.

Even though they appear in a different part of the clause, they do not co-occur with full direct object noun phrases; as in Mixtec (26), this is evidence that they are pronouns, not agreement markers.

(49)   **Manuela   lo=   tiró   el   voleibol.*
        Manuela   3sgDO=   threw   the   volleyball
        (Manuela threw the volleyball.)

These facts can be handled easily by generating the object pronouns in deep structure in the normal place after the verb, then obligatorily moving them with a transformation to precede the verb.[29]

---

[28]Naturalness is relevant in another way, too. Huichol is a Uto-Aztecan language, a family which is predominantly head-final. Although Huichol may not be head-final (noun phrases are head-initial), postpositions are not out of place in the family as a whole. In European languages like English, however, postpositions are quite rare.

[29]Such a transformation would need some way to distinguish pronouns, inserted from the lexicon, from full NPs developed by the phrase structure rules. The most natural way to do this is to mark all pronouns in the lexicon as NP[+pro], while NPs with noun heads are [–pro]. This feature is needed anyway for the binding conditions (Chomsky 1981:184–85). The facts of

(50)   a. Deep structure   b. Surface structure

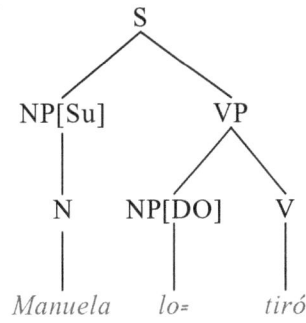

```
              S                                          S
           /     \                                    /     \
      NP[Su]      VP                             NP[Su]       VP
        |        /  \                              |         / | \
        N       V   NP[DO]     ⇒                   N    NP[DO]   V
        |       |     |                            |      |      |
     Manuela  tiró    lo=                       Manuela   lo=   tiró
```

In many languages, clitics tend to cluster just after the first word in a constituent. These are commonly called SECOND POSITION CLITICS. In Latin, for example, the conjunction =que 'and' is an enclitic. Unlike most conjunctions, it does not appear between the two conjoined constituents (in this case, two nouns), but one word later.

(51)   *senātus populus =que rōmānus*
       senate   people   and   of.Rome
       the senate and people of Rome

If the second conjoined constituent contains more than one word, =que is still placed after the first word and thus ends up inside the constituent.[30]

(52)   [*Meīs cōpiīs*   ] [*meō =que exercitū*] *rēgna*   *vōbīs*   *conciliābō*
           my   resources   my   and   army   kingdoms for.you   I.will.obtain
       (With) my resources and my army, I will obtain kingdoms for you.

Such examples can be handled by generating the clitic between the two conjoined constituents and then moving it one word to the right with an obligatory transformation.[31]

(53)   Deep structure

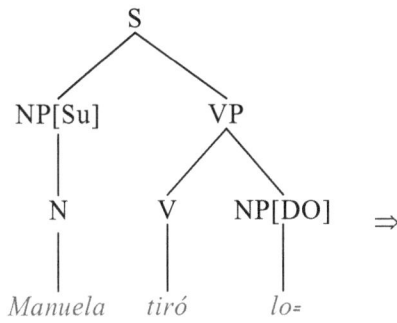

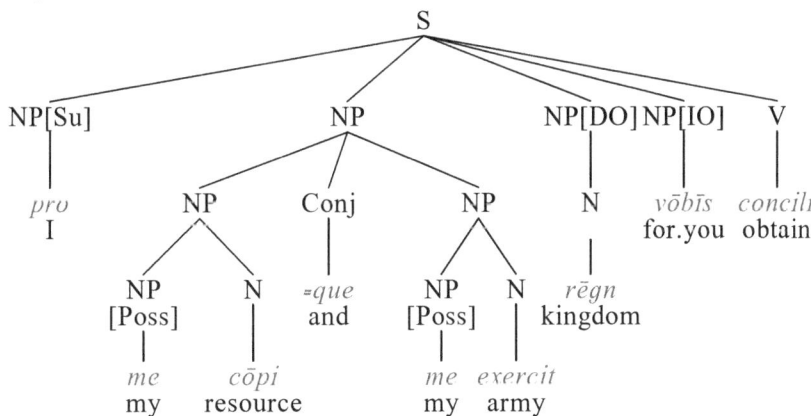

```
                                       S
                    /            |          |       |     \
               NP[Su]            NP      NP[DO] NP[IO]    V
                 |             /  |  \       |      |      |
                pro         NP  Conj  NP     N    vōbīs  concili
                 I         / \   |   / \     |    for.you obtain
                         NP   N =que NP  N  rēgn
                       [Poss] |  and [Poss]| kingdom
                         |   cōpi      |  exercit
                         me  resource  me  army
                         my            my
```

Spanish are a bit more complex than discussed here, however, since object pronouns are proclitics only when the verb is finite; on nonfinite verbs they are enclitics.

[30]From Hines, Welch, and Hopkinson (1966:207), which is an adaptation from Caesar's Gallic War, Book 1, chapter 3. The meaning 'with, by means of' comes from the ablative case marking on the nouns; this structure is normal for instrument obliques in Latin.

[31]The discussion here makes the standard assumption that conjunctions join two constituents of the same type to form a larger constituent of that same type. In addition to the transformation that moves the clitic, there are inflectional spellout rules; for simplicity of presentation, I omit the inflectional features from the trees. The stem forms in the deep structure are based on the traditional analysis of the morphology. The tree assumes a flat clause structure for Latin, but this is not crucial.

(54)   Surface structure

$\Rightarrow$

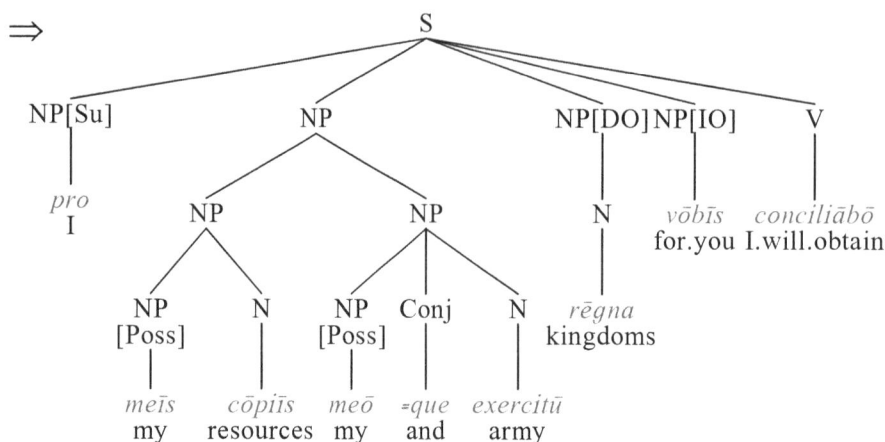

Another type of complication sometimes occurs with pronoun clitics, which may sometimes act just a bit like agreement markers. For example, indirect object clitics in Spanish, unlike the direct objects, sometimes do co-occur with an overt indirect object PP.

(55)   a.   Full indirect object PP only
             Martín dió   la   rana   a   su   madre.
             Martin give(3sgPast) the frog   to his mother
             Martin gave the frog to his mother.

       b.   Clitic indirect object pronoun only
             Martín le=   dió   la   rana.
             Martin 3sgIO=   give(3sgPast) the frog
             Martin gave the frog to her.

       c.   Clitic pronoun together with a full PP
             Martín le=   dió   la   rana   a   su   madre.
             Martin 3sgIO=   give(3sgPast) the frog   to his mother
             Martin gave the frog to his mother.

This makes them look more like agreement markers (affixes) and not pronouns (separate syntactic words). Yet, they are not fully like agreement affixes, either, since they are optionally absent when a full PP is present; agreement markers are present at all times.[32] When a language allows a pronoun clitic to co-occur with a full NP or PP, we say the language allows CLITIC DOUBLING.

Formal treatment of clitic doubling is too complicated for this book. Don't try to write formal rules to account for it; just describe informally what word-like and affix-like traits each clitic has, and list it in some appropriate category in the lexicon. The same is true for the many other special behaviors that clitics exhibit, which are too numerous to discuss here. Describe the full range of facts informally, take the formal analysis as far as you can, and start reading in the literature for ideas on how to proceed further.

20.8. Writing clitics in practical orthographies

One important practical consideration that comes up when analyzing clitics is how to write them in a practical orthography: as separate words or affixes. (There's more to designing a practical orthography than inventing an alphabet; you must also consider how to use spaces, hyphens, and other punctuation marks.) When you are making a first attempt at designing a practical orthography,

---

[32]Full noun phrases can occur without a doubling clitic only when they have the semantic roles of recipient or addressee. For a presentation and analysis of the facts, see J. Albert Bickford 1985.

a good rule of thumb is to use spaces to reflect syntactic word boundaries. That is, phrasal affixes should probably be written attached and bound words written as separate words.

However, the reaction of native speakers is usually a very important factor in orthography design, not just the linguistic facts. In many languages speakers prefer to write bound words attached, since that is the way they sound. (You may want to try using a hyphen or an equals sign with bound words in this case.)

As with all orthography design, this is more than just asking people about their preferences. You should also consider ease of learning (for new readers) and ease of use (for experienced readers and writers). Evaluating these factors may require careful testing, helping people learn to read and monitoring their progress, to see which of several options gives the best results overall. The final decisions on practical orthographies should normally be made not by linguists but by the people who are going to have to live with them: those who depend on the language as their primary means of communication.[33]

20.9. Review of key terms

When dividing a sentence into WORDS by finding WORD BOUNDARIES (or WORD BREAKS), we can identify either PHONOLOGICAL WORD BOUNDARIES or SYNTACTIC WORD BOUNDARIES, depending on whether we are concerned with phonological or syntactic characteristics. When a morpheme has some characteristics of words and some of affixes, it is commonly called a CLITIC; clitics are typically PHONOLOGICALLY BOUND but SYNTACTICALLY FREE. Clitics often display other traits such as being members of closed classes with grammatical meaning, occurring at the edges of words, PROMISCUOUS ATTACHMENT, and (for pronoun clitics) mutual-substitutability for full noun phrases.

Clitics may be classified as PROCLITICS or ENCLITICS and as BOUND WORDS or PHRASAL AFFIXES. (UNSTRESSED WORDS are sometimes also considered clitics, but we have not done so.) Sometimes clitics have special grammatical properties, such as appearing in an unexpected position (especially SECOND POSITION CLITICS) or CLITIC DOUBLING.

20.10. Questions for analysis

For each morpheme that is phonologically bound:
1. Is there any evidence that it is syntactically free? (Is it a bound word?)
2. If not a bound word, is it positioned with respect to a phrase instead of a word? (Is it a phrasal affix?)
3. What syntactic and phonological properties does this morpheme share with clear cases of words? What ones does it share with clear cases of affixes?
4. Does it have any special grammatical properties, such as occurrence in an unexpected position or clitic doubling?

20.11. Sample descriptions

Latin -que

Latin has a conjunction, *=que,* which is an enclitic. Rather than occurring between the two conjoined phrases, it attaches to the end of the first word in the second phrase.

---

[33]Exactly how to go about making such a decision in a particular society (or encouraging and enabling others to make it) is not something that I pretend to give advice on, nor do I mention here all the relevant factors to be considered in designing a useful practical orthography.

(1)   *senātus populus =que rōmānus*
       senate   people   and   of.Rome
       the senate and people of Rome

(2)   *Meīs cōpiīs   meō =que exercitū rēgna   vōbīs   conciliābō*
       my   resources my and army   kingdoms   for.you   I.will.obtain
       With my resources and my army, I will obtain kingdoms for you.

Spanish object pronouns

   Spanish direct and indirect object pronouns are proclitics attached to the verb, rather than occurring in the normal object position after the verb. Indirect object clitics precede direct object ones.

(1)   a. *Manuela lo=   tiró.*
           Manuela   3sgDO=   threw
           Manuela threw it.

       b. *Le=   dió   la   rana.*
           3sgIO=   gave the frog
           He gave the frog to her.

       c. *Me=   lo=   dió.*
           1sgIO= 3sgDO=   gave
           He gave it to me.

Indirect object clitics sometimes exhibit clitic doubling, but this does not occur (in most dialects) with direct objects.

(2)   a. *Le=   dió   la   rana a   su   madre.*
           3sgIO=   gave the frog to his mother
           He gave the frog to his mother.

       b. **Manuela lo=   tiró   el   voleibol.*
           Manuela   3sgDO=   threw the volleyball
           (Manuela threw the volleyball.)

20.12. For further reading

   Matthews 1974:20–36 has an extensive discussion of the three different senses of WORD and the importance of distinguishing among them.
   For more discussion of cliticization and several recent theoretical approaches to understanding it, see Spencer 1991:350–94. This chapter includes detailed descriptions of clitic systems in three Slavic languages, which illustrate many of the characteristics commonly associated with clitics around the world (some of which have not been introduced here).
   The way of classifying clitics introduced in this chapter is based largely on work by Arnold Zwicky in collaboration with various others. Three of his articles might be especially interesting at this point. Zwicky and Pullum 1983 provides half a dozen criteria that can be used for deciding whether a word is a clitic or an affix. It illustrates how these criteria can be applied to data by arguing that the English contraction *n't* is not a clitic (and thus not like the contracted form *'s* of *is*), but rather an ordinary suffix that occurs only on auxiliary verbs. Zwicky 1985 provides a number of other such guidelines; perhaps more importantly it discusses the proper role of guidelines like these in linguistic analysis. It also discusses (and dismisses) the related notion of 'particle' as a useful linguistic concept. Zwicky 1987 provides an analysis of the fact that the English possessive *'s* is

absent after the plural suffix -*s*. These articles are somewhat more technical than works recommended in other chapters, and two use classifications of clitics that differ from what is used here (this chapter follows Zwicky 1987). But you do have the background now to understand much of what they contain, and they are well worth reading as examples of how to apply linguistic theories to analytic problems in individual languages, as well as providing helpful perspectives on larger issues within the field.

Although most of the factors that affect the design of practical orthographies come from other disciplines like phonology, sociolinguistics, and education, some aspects of morphology and syntax may also be relevant, as discussed above. There are several books available that provide a reasonably comprehensive treatment of the subject, including a number of case studies in specific languages showing the practical application of the basic principles of orthography design. Venezky 1970 provides a compact summary of principles of orthographic design, especially letter choice and spelling conventions. For more details, there are some book-length treatments. Smalley 1963 is a collection of previously-published articles which includes a couple of articles specifically on word division. Though it discusses many linguistic issues in terms of older theoretical frameworks, the issues themselves are still relevant. Fishman 1977 builds on the earlier book, including perspectives from work in Generative Phonology in the 1960s and 1970s. It examines especially the role of social, political, and other nonlinguistic factors in design, revision, and acceptance of writing systems. Finally, Weber (1993, to appear), especially chapter 2, provides an extensive case study of how one might apply such principles to specific languages and illustrates some of the sharp differences of opinion that can arise over practical writing systems, which are often very controversial and politically-sensitive issues.

21
Passive and Voice

21.1. Goals and prerequisites

This chapter will help you do the following:

- ◎ find syntactic and morphological characteristics that can be used as tests to help make hypotheses about grammatical relations
- ◎ construct reasonable hypotheses about passive clauses in data, and support the analysis with arguments based on tests for grammatical relations
- ◎ represent an analysis of passive with a word formation rule, and write lexical entries consistent with it
- ◎ recognize several other types of morphology that can affect the subcategorization requirements of verbs: dative shift, benefactives and applicatives, reflexives and reciprocals, causatives, and noun incorporation

It assumes that you are familiar with the following material:

- ✓ verbal valence: strict subcategorization, selectional restrictions, semantic roles, the SUBCAT feature, and *pro*-drop (chapter 8 "Verbal Valence")
- ✓ obliques, complements versus adjuncts (chapter 9 "Obliques")
- ✓ derivational morphology and word formation rules (chapter 11 "Derivational Morphology")
- ✓ contrastive focus and topicalization (chapter 15 "Variable Orders of Constituents")
- ✓ case marking and agreement as tests for grammatical relations (chapter 19 "Case and Agreement")
- ✓ the facts of Spanish pronoun clitics (chapter 20 "Word Division and Clitics")

More than any other chapter, this chapter shows the way that different parts of a grammar interact and how your knowledge of one part can be useful in analyzing another part.

21.2. Nonprototypical associations of semantic roles and grammatical relations

Recall (from chapter 8 "Verbal Valence," p. 81) that we can get an approximate idea of what the grammatical relations in a language are by describing their PROTOTYPICAL (normal or usual) semantic roles. Subjects are prototypically agents or experiencers, direct objects are prototypically patients or themes, and indirect objects are prototypically recipients or addressees. However, these

293

prototypical meanings are not adequate as definitions, since many verbs provide exceptions. For example, the subject may sometimes express other semantic roles.

(1)   Patient
      The branch   broke.

(2)   Recipient
      Maurice   received a care package from his mother.

Sometimes there are regular rules for creating verbs with exceptional semantic roles. One that we look at in this chapter is called PASSIVE. Here's a passive clause in English:

(3)   *Arthur was startled by Lancelot.*

Clearly, the subject of this clause is *Arthur*. Why? What is our evidence for this claim? *Arthur* has the syntactic and morphological characteristics of a subject. That is, it acts like other clear examples of subjects with respect to word order, agreement, and case. First, it occurs in the normal position for subjects in English: preceding the verb. Second, the verb *be* agrees with it, as can be seen by comparing (3) with (4).

(4)   *The knights were startled by Lancelot.*

Third, if we replace *Arthur* with a pronoun, we get the subject case, not the object case of the pronoun. (Notice the abbreviated way of showing the correct form in a particular position, using a slash to separate two possibilities and a star in front of the incorrect one.)

(5)   *He/*him was startled by Lancelot.*

But, even though *Arthur* is the subject, it does *not* refer to the agent, but rather to the patient. Again we see that the traditional definition of the subject as the 'doer of the action' (the agent) has so many exceptions that it must be rejected as incorrect.

On the other hand, the NP referring to the agent, *Lancelot,* is clearly *not* the subject, since it is part of an oblique PP, it occurs after the verb, it does not determine agreement on the verb, and any pronoun in that position is in the object case.

(6)   a.   *Arthur was/*were startled by the knights.*
      b.   *Arthur was startled by him/*he.*

So, the subject is not the agent and the agent is not the subject.

This illustrates one of the most interesting facets of grammar: there is not a simple one-to-one mapping from meaning to form. In this case, there is not a simple one-to-one mapping from semantic roles to grammatical relations. Indeed, one of the most general and important questions to answer about a language is how native speakers can figure out what a sentence means, given the complexity of the mapping from meaning to form.

Thus, it is important to make a careful distinction between form and meaning, between grammar and semantics, when we discuss language. Meaning provides misleading information about grammatical relations in some types of clauses. Grammatical relations are a part of grammar, so we must look to grammatical patterns rather than meaning to help us form hypotheses about the syntactic structure of clauses.

This book has introduced several basic phenomena that are closely tied to grammatical relations: word order, syntactic category membership (NP versus PP), omissibility of pronouns (pro-drop), case, and agreement. This chapter shows how to make use of what we have learned about these phenomena to discover more about grammatical relations. The basic strategy is to find out how grammatical relations are involved in specific grammatical rules, based on the clearest examples in the data. When we find such rules, we then have GRAMMATICAL TESTS that we can use to help determine grammatical relations in less clear examples, such as when semantic roles are associated with grammatical relations in nontypical ways.

21.3. Passive

Let's look at passive clauses in a bit more detail. Each of the following clauses is passive.

(7) a. *The Titanic was sunk by an iceberg.*
     b. *The town clock was struck by lightning at midnight last Saturday.*
     c. *Many new books were published this year.*
     d. *This course has been taught differently every semester.*

Passives in English have several things in common. The subject typically has the semantic role of patient or theme, roles that we would normally expect of a direct object.[1] The agent or experiencer is not necessarily expressed at all, but if it is, it occurs after the verb as the object of the preposition *by*. There is no syntactic direct object in a passive; passives are intransitive.[2]

As for morphology, the verb always appears in a form which has traditionally been called the past participle, i.e., the form which in regular verbs is formed by adding the suffix *-(e)d*. The participle is preceded by some form of the auxiliary verb *be*. (Notice that the marking for subject agreement and tense in English is always carried on the first verb in a clause; if there is an auxiliary verb, the first such auxiliary shows tense and agreement. Thus, in a passive, *be* shows tense and agreement, and the participle does not.)

Which aspects of English passives are universal, and which are peculiar to English? As linguists have analyzed many languages, they frequently find a type of verbal morphology which is like the English passive in certain ways. This type DETRANSITIVIZES a verb (i.e., turns a transitive verb into an intransitive) by doing two things:

(8) a. the direct object of the transitive verb becomes the subject of the intransitive
     b. the subject of the transitive either becomes an oblique with the intransitive verb
        or is omitted entirely

When this morphology has been found, it has generally been called PASSIVE. The transitive verb is called the ACTIVE VERB, and the intransitive one is called the PASSIVE VERB or sometimes the PASSIVE FORM of the verb. The clauses are also named ACTIVE and PASSIVE, depending on the type of verb they contain. (Caution: ACTIVE as the opposite of passive has nothing to do with its meaning in chapter 14 "Nonactive Complements," where ACTIVE is the opposite of NONACTIVE. The term ACTIVE is, unfortunately, used in both ways, but usually context will reveal which meaning is intended.)

Passive is often considered to be a derivational process, rather than an inflectional one, for several reasons:

- it changes the subcategory of the verb (it changes a transitive verb into an intransitive one) or even the category (from verb to adjective, see next section)
- it involves a relatively major change in the meaning of the verb (in terms of the semantic role of the subject)

---

[1]In addition to the types of passive discussed here, there are also English examples like *He was given the book by the teacher*, in which the subject is a Recipient, a semantic role prototypically associated with indirect objects. Such passives are usually considered to be derived by a combination of Dative Shift (see p. 299) and passive.

[2]J. Albert Bickford 1987 argues that this is universally true, despite claims that transitive passives do in fact exist (for example, see Postal 1986:81). The evidence supporting claims for transitive passives is weak, since alternative analyses are possible.

- there is no syntactic rule that needs to refer to the distinction between active and passive verbs (it is irrelevant to the syntax)[3]

This is the approach taken in this book. Linguists are not entirely in agreement on this matter, however.[4]

Not all languages have passives; even when they do, the form and function of passives may be very different from what it is in English. The next three sections discuss some of the different types of passives you may find in other languages.

Adjectival and verbal passives

In English, the verb form used in the passive is called the 'past participle' of the verb. Usually the past participle is identical to the past tense form of the verb, but not always.

(9)   Stem   Past tense   Past participle

        create   *created*   *created*
        destroy   *destroyed*   *destroyed*
        pinch   *pinched*   *pinched*
        bring   *brought*   *brought*
        say   *said*   *said*

        give   *gave*   *given*
        write   *wrote*   *written*
        sing   *sang*   *sung*

The past participle has a variety of uses; when used in a passive, it is actually an adjective. It cannot occur by itself as a verb, but instead must follow nonactive verbs like *be* and *seem*. Also, it can modify nouns in noun phrases.

(10)   a. *The police officer was **startled** by the condition of the room.*
        b. *The occupant seemed **puzzled** by the search warrant.*
        c. *They arrested the **confused** man.*

Passive in English apparently derives an adjective from a verb. However, this is an adjective that can have indirect objects and obliques associated with it as part of an adjective phrase, parallel to what happens in a verb phrase.[5]

(11)   *The reward was [AP presented to the informant at the ceremony yesterday].*

In many other languages, passives are clearly verbs, not adjectives. For example, in SiSwati[6] (Bantu) passives are formed by the addition of the suffix *-w* to the verb, forming another verb.

---

[3]Anderson 1982 specifically excludes subcategorization information as being 'relevant to the syntax'.

[4]For example, early transformational accounts (e.g., Chomsky 1965:103ff.) derived passive clauses with syntactic rules. Starting from deep structures that were essentially active clauses, they moved the direct object to subject position, the subject to an oblique, etc. Relational Grammar likewise treats Passive as a phenomenon that is reflected directly in the syntactic structures of sentences. Government-binding Theory adopts a compromise position, positing a word formation rule which derives passive verbs from active ones in the lexicon (as is done here). However, these verbs still have the Patient/Theme in object position in deep structure, with no deep structure subject; a transformation moves the object to subject position in S-structure. The result is that passive is handled by a combination of morphological and syntactic rules. (See Haegeman 1991:169–77, 282–85.)

[5]This suggests that we should have one 'generic' phrase structure rule that covers both VPs and APs, but this book does not go into the details of how to do that.

[6]Data from De Guzman 1986.

(12) a. *John u-nik-e   sinini banana*
        John SuAgr-give-Past friend banana
        John gave a banana to a friend.

     b. *banana u-nik-w-e   sinini ngu John*
        banana SuAgr-give-Pass-Past friend by John
        The banana was given to a friend by John.

Thus, passives in some languages are ADJECTIVAL; in other languages VERBAL.

Long and short passives

In many languages the agent (or other 'former' subject) may be expressed in a passive clause by some sort of oblique. This is true in English and SiSwati, for example. This type of oblique is generally called an AGENT PHRASE. (This term is somewhat misleading, because the semantic role is not always that of agent; it may be an experiencer or any other semantic role normally associated with a subject.) The agent phrase is generally optional, which is appropriate for its status as an oblique.

(13) a. *The banana was given to a friend (by John).*
     b. *He was seen (by the police).*

(Note that an agent phrase is a new type of oblique, one that was not mentioned in chapter 9 "Obliques."[7])

However, in some languages, there is no way to express the agent in a passive. This is true, for example, in Latvian.[8]

(14) *Es tieku macits (*no mates)*
     I   am   taught (by   mother)

When a language has a way of expressing an agent phrase in a passive clause, it is said to have a LONG PASSIVE (even in sentences which omit the agent phrase). A language like Latvian that has no way to express the agent in a passive is said to have a SHORT PASSIVE. Here, the terms LONG and SHORT PASSIVE refer not to individual sentences, but to the type of passive construction that is used in a language. Thus, an English passive clause without an agent phrase, such as 'Superman was seen in Bombay' is still considered to be an example of a long passive, because English allows the possibility of expressing an agent.

The meaning and function of passives in discourse

Typically, passive is used to deemphasize the agent or experiencer when it is unimportant to the discussion or when the speaker wants to hide the information. For example, consider the following three sentences:

(15) a. *Caviar is considered to be a delicacy.*
     b. *Harold considers caviar to be a delicacy.*
     c. *Caviar is considered by Harold to be a delicacy.*

---

[7]As Keenan 1985a:261ff. points out, agent phrases may occur with nonpassive verbs, as in *Cheating* **by students** *is punishable with expulsion.* As such, he does not consider them to be integral parts of the passive construction itself. Thus, terms like 'long passive' and 'short passive' are somewhat misleading, as they seem to imply that the possibility of an agent phrase is a property of the passive construction, whereas it seems rather to be an independent fact about whether this type of oblique exists in the language.

[8]Data from Keenan 1985a:249, citing Lazdina 1966.

The passive in (15a), by omitting the agent phrase, is able to talk about caviar and its status as a delicacy without mentioning who considers it such. It could be anyone; indeed, it may be irrelevant who considers it a delicacy. In contrast, when the agent is mentioned in the active clause (15b), there is attention focused on Harold; (15b) is really a sentence about Harold, while (15a) is about caviar. Even if the passive includes an agent phrase, as in (15c), the sentence is still more about caviar than about Harold. It would be appropriate in a discussion about caviar, while the active clause (15b) would fit less naturally in such a context.

There is a general discourse rule in English (and many other languages) that the topic of a discourse unit tends to be indicated by the subjects of the sentences in that unit. The rule is not a hard-and-fast one, but in a well-formed discourse, it is often followed. (For further discussion, see chapter 15 "Variable Orders of Constituents," p. 213.)

Passive, then, provides a way of taking a topic which would normally be the direct object of some verb and presenting it, instead, as the subject. In this way, the topic of the discourse is clarified for the hearer by keeping it in subject position. This is especially helpful when what would normally be the subject of a verb is completely irrelevant to the context. For further examples of how this technique is used, look at the passive constructions in this paragraph and how they help keep your attention focused on the topic (passive) rather than on the agents (the speakers who use it).

However common this function of passive may be, passive has other functions in some languages. For example, in Thai (Mon-Khmer, Thailand),[9] the passive is only used to refer to undesirable or unpleasant experiences. Thus, in Thai, a passive clause like 'We were invited to the party by the mayor' implies that we expect it to be at best a boring affair. In Southern Tiwa (Tanoan, New Mexico),[10] passive has an entirely different function. A grammatical constraint forbids any clause to have a third person subject and a first or second person object. Thus, one cannot say the literal equivalent of 'The man saw me'; instead, one must use a passive 'I was seen by the man'. Such a use of passives has nothing whatsoever to do with topicality or any other meaning; it is determined entirely by syntactic concerns. Even when passive seems to be used in a 'normal' fashion to keep the topic in subject position, there may be subtle differences in meaning in different languages. For example, in Nomatsiguenga (Arawakan, Peru)[11] the use of a passive means that the speaker is an uninvolved observer who is just reporting a story as he heard it.

All this means that we must be very careful when translating passive clauses. A passive clause in the source language may not have the same meaning as a passive in the target language. A 'literal' translation of one passive to another may actually have the effect of distorting the meaning, rather than translating it faithfully.

This also means that it is often quite useless to request native speakers to produce passive clauses, unless they are well-educated and know what you mean by 'passive'. Asking them to translate a passive clause from some language to their own may or may not result in a passive clause (if, indeed, passive even exists in their language). The best way to find passives in a language you are studying is to look for them in natural texts. Then, once you've collected several examples of a construction that you think might be a passive, begin exploring its syntactic and morphological characteristics by making systematic changes to existing examples.

21.4. Voice: Valence changing morphology

Passive belongs to a class of phenomena which are referred to generally as VOICE, that is, derivational morphology which changes the valence of a verb, the semantic roles of its complements, or both.[12]

---

[9]Filbeck 1972:331ff. reports this for Thai and T'in (Mon-Khmer, Thailand and Laos) and cites a claim by Householder that this is common for languages from East Africa to Southeast Asia.

[10]Information from Allen and Frantz 1983:305.

[11]Information from Wise 1971:5.

[12]Usually the word VOICE is used in a more narrow sense, including only passive, reflexive/middle, causative, and possibly one or two others. However, formal definitions of the term are usually worded in such a way as to include other valence changing operations, such as dative shift, applicatives, and noun incorporation, even if these are not listed as typical

Languages vary in terms of how much variety they allow in the mapping from semantic roles to grammatical relations. In some languages, the mapping is very straightforward—agents are always subjects, patients are always direct objects, and so forth. Such languages do not have passives or other types of voice. So, don't expect to find passives or other examples of voice in every language. But, the following are some of the more common types that occur.

Dative shift

In many languages, there is a way of upgrading an indirect object to a direct object, which is sometimes called DATIVE SHIFT. For example, in Chamorro (Austronesian, Guam),[13] a VSO language, verbs that take indirect objects may appear in one of two types of clauses:

(16) a. *Hu tugi' i   kätta pära i   che'lu-hu*
     1s write the letter to   the sibling-my
     I wrote the letter to my brother.

    b. *Hu tugi'-i   i   che'lu-hu ni kätta*
      1s write-DativeShift the sibling-my Obl letter
      I wrote my brother the letter.

In (16a), *kätta* 'letter' is the direct object and *pära i che'lu-hu* 'to my sibling' is the indirect object, as we might expect. Notice that the direct object is an NP and the indirect object is a PP using the preposition *pära* 'to'. In (16b), things are different. The recipient, 'sibling', is an NP, while the theme, 'letter', is the object of the preposition *ni* which is used for a variety of obliques. The most reasonable hypothesis is that the direct object of (16b) is the recipient, 'sibling'. Notice that there is an extra suffix -*i* on the verb. This suffix apparently derives a simple transitive verb from a ditransitive one by changing the indirect object into a direct object. This is what is called DATIVE SHIFT.

As further evidence for this, there are passive clauses that correspond to both clauses in (16); the passive (17a) corresponding to (16a) has *i kätta* 'the letter' as subject, while the passive (17b) corresponding to (16b) has *i che'lu-hu* 'my sibling' as subject.

(17) a. *Ma-tugi' i   kätta pära i   che'lu-hu*
     Pass-write the letter to   the sibling-my
     The letter was written to my brother.

    b. *Ma-tugi'-i   i   che'lu-hu ni kätta*
     Pass-write-DativeShift the sibling-my Obl letter
     My brother was written the letter.

In other words, passive treats *i che'lu-hu* 'my sibling' in (16b) as if it is the direct object, even though it is the recipient.

Because of the prevalence of dative shift in the world's languages, many linguists analyze the following pair of English sentences to be an example of dative shift, even though there is no overt morphology on the verb. (Compare these to the glosses of the Chamorro sentences.)

(18) a. *Mary gave a kiss to John.*
    b. *Mary gave John a kiss.*

examples of the category (Crystal 1991:135, Trask 1993:299). Thus, this book uses the term in a wider sense, since the whole class of valence changing operations share many properties.
[13]Data from Gibson 1980:31–37, 158.

Specifically, this analysis regards *John* in (18b) as a syntactic direct object, even though it is the recipient. This is somewhat different from the traditional analysis, which considers *John* in (18b) to be an indirect object, following what one might expect on the basis of semantics.

We won't try to settle the issue for English here. But, there are two points to be made: (1) It's not uncommon to find the same data analyzed in more than one way. (2) It is legitimate to propose an analysis in which a direct object is a recipient. That is, when we analyze voice, we should pay attention to the grammatical characteristics of the various constituents in the clause. When we do, we may arrive at an analysis that we would not expect based solely on meaning.

Benefactives and applicatives

Some languages provide ways of changing obliques to direct or indirect objects. For example, in Spanish, it is possible to add an indirect object to a verb which has the meaning of a BENEFACTIVE.[14]

(19) a. *Mi   esposa   hace   comida   para   muchas   familias   pobres.*
          my   wife   makes   food   for   many   families   poor
      b. *Mi   esposa   les=   hace   comida   a   muchas   familias   pobres.*
          my   wife   to.them makes   food   to   many   families   poor

     My wife prepares food for many poor families.

In (19a), 'many poor families' is syntactically a benefactive, with the preposition *para* 'for'. In (19b), however, it has at least two characteristics typical of indirect objects: it is marked with the preposition *a* 'to' and the verb is preceded by an indirect object pronoun *les=*. A derivational process has changed the subcategorization requirements of 'make' to allow an indirect object that has the meaning of a benefactive. (The process itself is often called BENEFACTIVE.) Like dative shift in English, there is no overt morphology on the verb that indicates the change in valence; although languages often signal changes in valence with overt morphology, they don't always do this.

Some languages have ways of promoting other obliques to direct object. In Kinyarwanda (Bantu, Rwanda),[15] a locative oblique can be promoted to direct object by adding a suffix to the verb. In (20a), 'cook' is direct object and 'market' is a locative oblique. Sentence (20b) has the same meaning, but 'market' is the direct object (it is immediately after the verb and has other characteristics of direct objects).

(20) a. *umugóre   y-oohere-je   umubooyi   kw'=   iisóko*
          woman   she-send-Asp   cook   to   market
      b. *umugóre   y-oohere-jé-ho   isóko   umubooyi*
          woman   she-send-Asp-to   market   cook

     The woman sent the cook to market.

Such verb forms involving an oblique promoted to objecthood are sometimes called APPLICATIVES.

Reflexives and reciprocals

Most languages use some special device when the subject and object of a verb refer to the same person(s) or thing(s). That is, a special device is used to express situations that are REFLEXIVE (acting on oneself) or RECIPROCAL (acting on each other).

---

[14]For further discussion of this construction and its analysis, see J. Albert Bickford 1985.

[15]Data from Kimenyi 1980:89–96. There are three possible suffixes with different meanings, with some resemblances to locative prepositions with the same meanings. The evidence that 'market' in (20b) is the direct object comes from the possibilities for object pronoun incorporation, passivization, reflexivization, relativization, and clefting; all these processes treat the locative nominal as direct object and do not treat 'cook' as direct object.

(21) a. *I see **myself** in the mirror every morning.*
      b. *You will find **yourself** in a dimly-lighted room.*
      c. *They were beating **themselves** with freshly-cut branches.*

(22) a. *Now that it was getting light, we began to see **each other**.*
      b. *I think you will find **each other** to be very attractive.*
      c. *They were beating **each other** with freshly-cut branches.*

Many languages have a special verb form, called a REFLEXIVE VOICE, which indicates that the subject and direct object refer to the same person or thing. For example, in Coatlán Mixe (Mixe-Zoquean, Mexico),[16] the prefix *naj-* indicates that the verb is reflexive.

(23) Reflexive
      Ø-naj-pupeht-ip
      3Intr-Refl-help-NCCont
      He/she is helping himself/herself.

(24) Nonreflexive
      j-pupeht-p-j
      3Trans-help-NCCont-Trans
      He/she is helping him/her (i.e., someone else).

An important thing to note here is that the reflexive verb is *intransitive* in form, even though the meaning (at least from one perspective) is still transitive. This can be seen easily in Mixe, which has distinct forms of the agreement prefixes for transitives and intransitives; it also has an extra *-j* suffix only in transitive forms. This is, in fact, the normal pattern in languages that express reflexives and reciprocals by derivational morphology on the verb; the reflexive/reciprocal affixes convert the verb from a transitive to an intransitive form.

All languages have ways of expressing a reflexive/reciprocal situation, but not all languages use special derivational morphology. The other device that languages often use is a special object pronoun that refers back to the subject. English, for example, has REFLEXIVE PRONOUNS like *himself* and *themselves,* as seen in (21) and uses *each other* as a RECIPROCAL PRONOUN, as in (22). Unlike morphological reflexives and reciprocals, clauses that use separate reflexive and reciprocal pronouns are generally transitive. That is, in these languages an ordinary transitive verb is used with a special pronoun, rather than using morphology to derive an intransitive reflexive verb.

Causatives

In some languages there is a verbal suffix meaning roughly 'to cause' which derives CAUSATIVE verbs; these have more complements than the verbs they are derived from. In the following Turkish examples,[17] the causative suffix *-dür* is used to derive a transitive verb from an intransitive one. Notice that the object of the transitive verb corresponds to the subject of the intransitive. This same suffix may also be used to derive ditransitive verbs from transitive ones.

(25) a. *Hasan öl-dü*
         Hasan die-Past
         Hasan died.

---

[16]Data from Coatlán Mixe is from Hoogshagen and Bartholomew 1993:373 and from Searle Hoogshagen (personal communication); compare also Van Haitsma and Van Haitsma 1976. However, the analysis is my own, based on fieldwork in the nearby Guichicovi dialect. Data has been rewritten morphophonemically using standard IPA symbols. Single voiced stops are voiced between sonorants and a /j/ immediately preceding or following a consonant is realized as palatalization on that consonant. Reflexive forms use a special form *-ip* of the Nonconjunct Continuous suffix; this form also occurs in other constructions.

[17]Data from Comrie 1985a:323, with transcription conventions modified to match Turkish data cited from Underhill 1976 elsewhere in this book.

b. *Ali   Hasan-ı   öl-dür-dü*
   Ali   Hasan-DO   die-Cause-Past
   Ali killed Hasan (caused Hasan to die).

Just as with reflexives, all languages have a way of expressing causation, but not all do it with special morphology. Many simply have one or more verbs meaning 'cause' which take embedded clauses as their direct objects. This is true in English, for example.[18]

(26)   a. *John ate supper.*
       b. *His mother made/had [John eat supper].*
       c. *His mother caused/forced [John to eat supper].*

Only the morphological causatives, like those in Turkish, are examples of CAUSATIVE VOICE.

Noun incorporation

Some languages have a way of combining nouns with verbs called NOUN INCORPORATION or OBJECT INCORPORATION. Typically, a verb is combined with a noun that represents its direct object, as in (27b), from Chuckchi (Siberia).[19]

(27)   a. *tumg-e   na-ntəwat-ən   kupre-n*
          friends-Erg   3sg-set-Trans   net-Abs
          The friends set the net.

       b. ***kupra**-ntəwat-g'at*
          tumg-ət
          friends-Nom   net-set-Intrans
          The friends set nets (lit., were net-setting).

As a by-product of incorporating the noun *kupra* 'net' into the verb, the new verb is intransitive. The evidence for this comes from two facts: (1) The verbal suffixes indicate transitivity directly. (2) Since the case-marking on the subject in Chukchee follows an ergative pattern, it changes when the transitivity of the clause changes (see chapter 19 "Case and Agreement," p. 268).

It is common for object incorporation to have this effect of detransitivizing the verb. However, sometimes the resulting compound is transitive and can have a syntactic direct object in addition to the incorporated noun, as in this example from Mohawk (Iroquoian, USA):[20]

(28)   *kwískwis   y-aʔ-t-ho-ʔnyukwal-íhshta-ʔ*
       pig   Trs-Aor-Dpl-3M.3M-snout-grab-Punc
       He grabbed the pig's nose (lit., he snout-grabbed the pig).

For this to work, the meanings of the two nouns must be compatible; in other words, the incorporated noun adds a selectional restriction to the verb which must be satisfied by the syntactic direct object. The verb *ʔnyukwal-íhshta* 'snout-grab' in (28) presumably requires that its direct object refer to an animal with a snout. (See chapter 8 "Verbal Valence," p. 80, for more about selectional restrictions.)

---

[18]Such syntactic causatives sometimes behave like compound verbs in a single clause. For discussion, see Comrie 1985a:331–32 and especially the relational grammar literature on causative clause union (e.g., Gerdts 1990, Gibson and Raposo 1986).

[19]Data from Payne 1997:221–22.

[20]Data and analysis from Rosen (1989:297, 301), whose transcription follows Americanist conventions. Rosen provides additional arguments that this type of incorporation results in transitive verbs, even though the direct object is often not overt. She also reviews attempts to account for incorporation with movement transformations (or other syntactic devices) and argues, instead, that noun incorporation is a lexical process.

Although many languages have ways of combining nouns and verbs in various types of compounds (see chapter 11 "Derivational Morphology," p. 137), the terms 'noun incorporation' and 'object incorporation' are usually only used for a process that is very productive, produces new verbs, and changes valence (syntactic subcategorization or selectional restrictions).

21.5. Making and supporting an analysis of passive

Analyzing voice can be challenging, because you cannot rely on semantics to give you information about grammatical relations. Instead, you must rely on word order, case marking, agreement, and other properties that you already know are linked to grammatical relations, based on clear-cut examples. When you get to less clear examples (such as passives), you use your knowledge about these things to determine what the grammatical relations are. To illustrate this process, consider Spanish, which has a passive construction that is similar in many respects to English, but which provides richer evidence about grammatical relations than English does.

Passive in Spanish

Spanish exhibits the same prototypical associations of semantic roles and grammatical relations as most languages:[21]

(29)   <u>Agent</u>   <u>Patient</u>
       Juana hizo las tortillas.
       Jane made the tortillas
       Jane made the tortillas.

(30)   <u>Experiencer</u>   <u>Theme</u>
       Marcos vió a Chabela en la cocina.
       Mark   saw   Chabela in the kitchen
       Mark saw Chabela in the kitchen.

(31)   <u>Agent</u>   <u>Patient</u>   <u>Recipient</u>
       Mario dió unos regalitos a su novia ayer.
       Mario gave some gifties   to his girlfriend yesterday
       Mario gave some 'affectionate little gifts' (tokens of affection) to his girlfriend yesterday.

However, some verbs can appear in their past participle form preceded by the auxiliary verb *ser* 'to be'. Their semantic roles are different; the patient or theme is not a direct object, but rather appears to be the subject.

(32)   *El conductor fue asesinado (por Jorge).*
       the driver   was murdered (by George)
       The driver was murdered (by George).

This construction is parallel to the English passive and has been traditionally called a passive in Spanish. However, just because someone calls a construction 'passive' doesn't mean that it *is* a passive. We need to ask 'What is the evidence that this construction is a passive?'

When we encounter clauses that we suspect may be examples of passive (or some other voice), it is often helpful to give them a temporary neutral name that allows us to talk about them without

---

[21]Special thanks to José Álvarez and Irma Ritter for helping polish the Spanish examples. Passive is rather nonproductive in Spanish, and it can be hard to find verbs that tolerate it. Further, it is not used as often as passive in English, so some of the examples still come out somewhat stilted. However, to the extent that passive is possible and allowing for occasional oversimplifications for the sake of clarity, the generalizations and rules stated here are well known in school grammars and are generally regarded as correct.

prejudicing us about their analysis. For the moment, let's call this type of clause a SER + participle clause.

Is the patient or theme really the subject of a SER + participle clause? How would we find out? The first step is to make a precise hypothesis about such clauses:

(33) a. the patient/theme of a SER + participle clause is its subject
      b. the agent/experiencer is neither the subject nor the direct object
      c. a SER + participle clause has no direct object; it is intransitive

In short, this hypothesis states that (32) and other SER + participle clauses are passives.

The next step is to consider the evidence. The process of systematically presenting evidence for an analysis is called ARGUMENTATION. The following sections illustrate several arguments, both to show how to support an analysis of passive and to give you an extended example of linguistic argumentation.

The form of all the arguments is essentially the same. First we establish some generalization that makes reference to grammatical relations, such as word order, case, or agreement, based on simple clear-cut examples. We state this as a hypothesis of some grammatical rule, which can be used as a GRAMMATICAL TEST for grammatical relations. Then we look at how that rule applies in SER + participle clauses and use this as evidence in support of our analysis of SER + participle clauses as passives.

Evidence from word order

The normal word order in Spanish is: Su V DO IO Obl. That is, in the clearest examples the subject precedes the verb, so we would like to say that any noun phrase which precedes the verb is the subject. However, this test must be used carefully, since other orders are also possible. We must control for certain conditioning factors: no contrastive focus, no special discourse context, etc. Still, once we do so, we find that the patient/theme in a SER + participle clause precedes the verb, as seen in the examples above; this is evidence that it is the subject. Similarly, the agent/experiencer does not precede the verb; this is evidence that it is not the subject.

Evidence from subject-verb agreement

Verbal suffixes in Spanish indicate agreement with the subject in person and number.

(34) *Manuel dió   un regalito a su   novia.*
      Manuel gave(3sg) a giftie   to his girlfriend
      Manuel gave an affectionate gift to his girlfriend.

(35) *Manuel y Abel dieron   un regalito a su   madre.*
      Manuel and Abel gave(3pl) a giftie   to their mother
      Manuel and Abel gave an affectionate gift to their mother.

The verbal suffixes do not mark agreement with the objects. Compare (34) with (36); the verb form is the same even though the objects are plural.

(36) *Manuel dió   unos regalitos a sus novias.*
      Manuel gave(3sg) some gifties   to his girlfriends
      Manuel gave some affectionate gifts to his girlfriends.

Since (in clear examples) the verb agrees only with the subject, not with the objects, we can, thus, use this test to help identify the subject in SER + participle clauses.

(37) *La campana fue/*fueron   oída por los niños.*
      The bell(3s) was(3sg)/*were(3pl) heard by the boys
      The bell was heard by the boys.

(38) *Las campanas *fue/fueron   oídas   por el   niño.*
      The bells(3pl) *was(3sg)/were(3pl) heard   by   the boy
      The bells were heard by the boy.

The verb agrees with the patient/theme rather than with the agent/experiencer. This is evidence that the patient/theme is the subject.

Evidence from pronouns: Case marking, positioning, and omissibility

Spanish has different forms of pronouns, depending on their grammatical relation. That is, pronouns are marked for case.

(39) Case marking on third person pronouns

	Subject	Direct Object
Singular masculine	*él*	*lo=*
Singular feminine	*ella*	*la=*
Plural masculine	*ellos*	*los=*
Plural feminine	*ellas*	*las=*

There are also two other important ways in which the subject and object pronouns differ.

(40) Subject pronouns

occur in the same positions as a subject which is a full noun phrase

are usually omitted; their presence indicates contrastive focus

Direct object pronouns

are always attached as clitics to the verb; in statements, they appear preceding the verb, while full noun phrases normally occur after the verb

cannot be omitted; their presence does not indicate contrastive focus

These facts are illustrated in the following examples.

(41) a. **Él**   *dió   unos regalitos a   su   novia.*
          He(Su) gave(3Sg) some gifties   to his girlfriend
          He (contrastive focus) gave some affectionate gifts to his girlfriend.

      b. **0** *Dió   unos regalitos a   su   novia.*
               gave(3Sg) some gifties   to his girlfriend
          He gave some affectionate gifts to his girlfriend.

(42) a. *Mario **los=**   dió a   su   novia.*
          Mario   them(DO) gave to his girlfriend
          Mario gave them to his girlfriend.

      b. **Mario **0** dió a   su   novia.*
           Mario   gave to his girlfriend
          (Mario gave (them) to his girlfriend.)

In the clear examples above, pronouns distinguish subjects from direct objects by the form of pronoun, its position in the clause, and the possibilities for omitting it. When we apply the same tests to SER + participle clauses, we find more evidence the patient/theme is the subject, since it uses subject pronouns which have an emphatic sense when present and which can be freely omitted.

(43) a. *Él/*Lo=* *fue* *asesinado.*
   he(Su/*DO) was murdered
   He (emph.) was murdered.

  b. *Ø* *Fue* *asesinado.*
    was murdered
   He was murdered.

Evidence from grammatical category: noun phrases versus prepositional phrases

Sometimes there are special idiosyncrasies in a language's rules which can also be used as tests for grammatical relations. For example, Spanish is a bit more complicated than other languages we have seen in how it determines whether the direct object is a noun phrase or a prepositional phrase.

(44) a. Subjects are always noun phrases.
  b. Direct objects vary:
   • A direct object which refers to a specific person is a prepositional phrase whose head is the preposition *a* (which is also used for indirect objects).
   • Any other direct object is a noun phrase.

These rules are illustrated in the following examples:

(45) a. DO is a specific person
   Mario busca ***a*** *su novia.*
   Mario look.for his girlfriend
   Mario is looking for his girlfriend.

  b. DO is not a specific person
   Mario busca *una novia.*
   Mario look.for a girlfriend
   Mario is looking for a girlfriend.

Don't worry how this would be represented in formal rules, just notice how this fact can serve as evidence in the analysis of SER + participle clauses.
  This grammatical test can tell us the following things about grammatical relations:

(46) a. A noun phrase (i.e., one not accompanied by *a*) referring to a specific person must be the subject, not the direct object.
  b. Other noun phrases (i.e., nonspecific or nonhuman) could be either the subject or the direct object.
  c. A prepositional phrase which uses *a* is clearly not the subject; if it refers to a specific person then it might be the direct object (although there are other possibilities).

Applying this test to the SER + participle clauses above, such as (32), note that the patient/theme is a bare noun phrase, even when it refers to a specific person; it thus appears to be the subject. The agent/experiencer is a prepositional phrase, using the preposition *por;* this is clearly not the subject.

Summary and final cautions

All the tests that we have tried above point to the same conclusion: SER + participle clauses are indeed passives. By assuming an analysis of passive, we can retain the rules about case marking, agreement, etc., in a simple and straightforward form while still explaining the facts about SER + participle clauses. All the pieces of the grammar work together neatly and account for the observed facts about the language.

Careful argumentation, in which the logical steps are clearly laid out, is especially important when analyzing passive and other types of voice. In particular, there are two pitfalls to avoid. One, be careful to distinguish between observable facts about form and your assumptions (based on semantics) about the grammatical relations of various noun phrases. Your first guess may easily be wrong. Rely on what you know independently about the grammar and morphology of the language, then use these grammatical tests to help identify grammatical relations. Be ready to adjust your hypotheses about grammatical relations in individual sentences if you find the grammatical tests suggesting a hypothesis that is different from what you'd expect based on meaning.

Two, just because you (or someone else) have labeled a construction 'passive' or glossed a particular affix as 'passive' doesn't constitute evidence that it really is passive. It could easily be the case that the analysis and gloss are incorrect. Determining the gloss is the goal of the analysis, not an argument for it. As a way of avoiding getting 'locked in' to an analysis based on an early incorrect gloss, it is good to develop the habit of using temporary, neutral names for constructions and affixes that may reflect valence changes until you have a good idea what they are. This is what we did above with the name 'SER + participle' in Spanish.

However, such careful and explicit argumentation may not always be necessary, especially in basic descriptive work. For a concise example of how to summarize the same facts, see the sample description on p. 313.

21.6. The formal analysis of passive

Now it is time to integrate the analysis of passive into our formal grammars. To do so, the grammar must first have some way to specify what semantic role is associated with what grammatical relation. Until now, our formal grammars have dealt with strict subcategorization only, using the SUBCAT feature (chapter 8 "Verbal Valence," p. 82). Now, by expanding our use of the SUBCAT feature, we can also use it to represent semantic roles, thus accounting for both types of valence. After that, we look at how to use the expanded SUBCAT feature in an analysis of passive.

Including semantic roles in lexical entries

Recall why we want to include semantic roles in the lexical entries for verbs. Two verbs may have the same complements (the same strict subcategorization), but different semantic roles, such as in the pairs of verbs below.[22]

(47)

	Subject	Direct Object	Indirect Object
walk	Agent		
break	Patient		
make	Agent	Patient	
see	Experiencer	Theme	
give	Agent	Theme	Recipient
tell	Agent	Theme	Addressee

Or, a verb such as *break* may be either intransitive or transitive, but the semantic role of the subject will be different.

---

[22]Because exact definitions of semantic roles are hard to agree on, not all linguists will agree on the specific semantic roles presented here. That is not the point; the point is that each verb must specify something about the semantic relationship of its complements to the overall meaning of the clause of which the verb is the head. Characterizing that relationship precisely is the job of semantics; the purpose for using semantic roles here is to provide some approximate characterization of the semantics so that we can talk about the relationship of semantics to syntax. Nothing crucial to the analysis of passive depends on the specific semantic roles assigned to a particular verb. Also, the verbs illustrated here have other uses which, in some cases, involve different semantic roles.

(48)
		Direct
	Subject	Object
break	Patient	
break	Agent	Patient

Thus, if we want a complete account of a verb's meaning and usage, it is not enough to say that a verb is transitive or intransitive. We must also say something about the meanings of the subjects and objects that are used with that verb.

   One way to do this is to modify the SUBCAT list for each verb to also show the semantic roles of its complements.[23] For example, the following SUBCAT feature says that the verb assigns the semantic role of agent to its subject and the role of patient to its direct object. That is, the subject of this verb is understood as its agent and the direct object as its patient.

(49)
$$\begin{array}{cc} Agent & Patient \\ | & | \end{array}$$
[SUBCAT ⟨ NP[Su], NP[DO] ⟩]

To illustrate further, the following lexical entries show how this would be done for a variety of Spanish verbs, some of which involve nonprototypical associations of semantic roles to grammatical relations.

(50)

anda
$$\begin{array}{c} Patient \\ | \end{array}$$
[SUBCAT ⟨ NP[Su] ⟩]   walk

quebra[24]
$$\begin{array}{c} Patient \\ | \end{array}$$
[SUBCAT ⟨ NP[Su] ⟩]   break

hace
$$\begin{array}{cc} Agent & Patient \\ | & | \end{array}$$
[SUBCAT ⟨ NP[Su], NP[DO] ⟩]   make

ve
$$\begin{array}{cc} Experiencer & Theme \\ | & | \end{array}$$
[SUBCAT ⟨ NP[Su], NP[DO] ⟩]   see

da
$$\begin{array}{ccc} Agent & Theme & Recipient \\ | & | & | \end{array}$$
[SUBCAT ⟨ NP[Su], NP[DO], PP[IO] ⟩]   give

---

[23]The notation and formalization here is based loosely on Pollard and Sag (1987:115–45).

[24]To be precise, this usage of *quebrar* is always reflexive in form, though not in meaning; this fact is not accounted for in the text.

$$\text{recibi}^{25} \quad \left[\text{SUBCAT} \langle \quad \underset{\mid}{\overset{\textit{Recipient}}{\text{NP[Su]}}}, \quad \underset{\mid}{\overset{\textit{Theme}}{\text{NP[DO]}}}, \quad \underset{\mid}{\overset{\textit{Source}}{\text{(PP)}}} \quad \rangle \right] \quad \text{receive}$$

This makes it very clear, for example, what is the difference in meaning of the subjects of verbs like 'give' and 'receive'.

Notice that we have rearranged the lexical information so that all verbs are listed together in one large category and each verb has its own SUBCAT list. What's done in earlier chapters (grouping verbs together in subcategories and giving only one SUBCAT feature for the whole subcategory) has been a useful abbreviation. But, since verbs vary quite a bit in how they assign semantic roles to grammatical relations, we really need to give each verb its own SUBCAT feature, with its own specification of semantic roles. So, now that we're taking semantics into account, it's more convenient to just arrange all verbs together in one large group; the SUBCAT feature for each tells what subcategory they belong in.

Lexical entries for passives

Now we can come back to passives and their analysis. Since we are treating passive as a type of derivational morphology (see chapter 11), we need to do two things. One, we need to decide what the lexical entries for passive verbs look like and how they differ from the lexical entries for the corresponding active verbs. Two, we need to summarize those differences in a word formation rule.[26]

Here are some lexical entries for active and passive verbs in Spanish, showing how their SUBCAT lists express their different semantic roles and complements:

(51) a.

$$\text{[asesina]}_V \quad \left[\text{SUBCAT} \langle \quad \underset{\mid}{\overset{\textit{Agent}}{\text{NP[Su]}}}, \quad \underset{\mid}{\overset{\textit{Patient}}{\text{NP[DO]}}} \quad \rangle \right] \quad \text{murder}$$

b.

$$\text{[[asesina]d]}_A \quad \left[\text{SUBCAT} \langle \quad \underset{\mid}{\overset{\textit{Patient}}{\text{NP[Su]}}}, \quad (\underset{\mid}{\overset{\textit{Agent}}{[_{PP} \textit{ por } \text{NP}]}}) \quad \rangle \right] \quad \text{be murdered}$$

(52) a.

$$\text{[oí]}_V \quad \left[\text{SUBCAT} \langle \quad \underset{\mid}{\overset{\textit{Experiencer}}{\text{NP[Su]}}}, \quad \underset{\mid}{\overset{\textit{Theme}}{\text{NP[DO]}}} \quad \rangle \right] \quad \text{hear}$$

b.

$$\text{[[oí]d]}_A \quad \left[\text{SUBCAT} \langle \quad \underset{\mid}{\overset{\textit{Theme}}{\text{NP[Su]}}}, \quad (\underset{\mid}{\overset{\textit{Experiencer}}{[_{PP} \textit{ por } \text{NP}]}}) \quad \rangle \right] \quad \text{be heard}$$

Within each pair, the differences in the SUBCAT list show that the active verb is transitive, taking a subject and a direct object, while the passive form is intransitive, taking a subject and an optional PP

---

[25]It is not necessary to specify in the SUBCAT list for *recibi* 'receive' the specific preposition used in the PP. There is only one preposition in Spanish that can express Source, the preposition *de* 'of, from'. Thus, it must be used as the head of the PP required by this verb. This choice of preposition can be determined automatically, as long as we assume a robust enough semantic component. In the lexicon, *de* is the only preposition whose meaning is compatible with the semantic role of Source and, thus, the only preposition that can be inserted as the head of a PP which is the Source complement of a verb like *recibir*.

[26]This treatment of passive thus is very similar to what is done in Lexical-functional Grammar, although it manipulates SUBCAT lists instead of predicate argument structures.

complement (which is always headed by the preposition *por*). As for the semantic roles, the subject of the active verb always has the same role as the PP headed by *por,* and the direct object of the active verb always has the same role as the subject of the passive form.

Since Spanish, like English, uses an adjectival form for passives, we have assigned the passive forms to the category of adjectives. (In a language with verbal passives, the passive forms would be in the category V.) The SUBCAT list of an adjective works just like that of a verb and controls what type of tree it can be inserted into. In the case of passive forms, they can be inserted in any clause which contains a subject. (We are assuming that there is an AP rule which generates the adjective phrases below. The full form of the adjective *asesinado* would be handled by inflectional spellout rules later.)

(53)

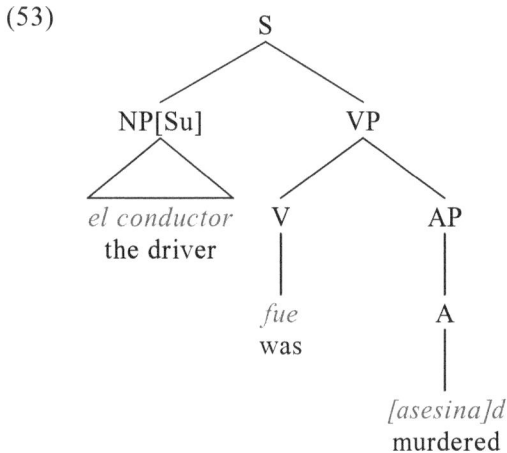

The AP may or may not contain a PP headed by *por;* if it does, then the SUBCAT list in (51) specifies that the PP is interpreted as the Agent of the verb.

(54)

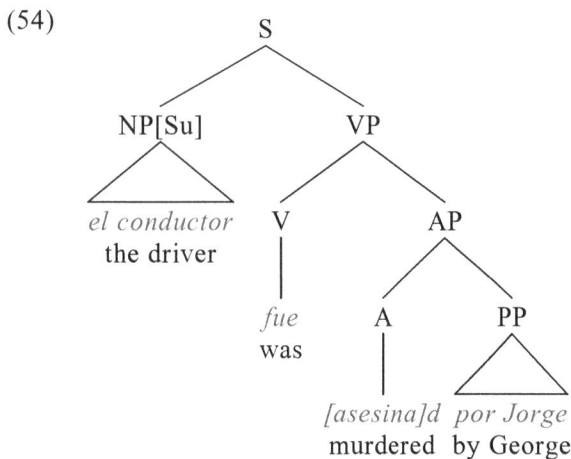

Word formation rule for passive

Since passive is derivational morphology, recall (from chapter 11 "Derivational Morphology," p. 145) that what we have done above is all we need to actually generate passive clauses. The lexical entries for the passive forms are all we need to construct trees without needing any *rule* for Passive. However, it is useful to write a word formation rule for Passive in order to express the regularities between the active and passive forms that exist in the lexicon and so that the grammar can create new passive forms that might not already exist.

(55)

$$\uparrow \quad [X]_V \quad \left[SUBCAT \left\langle \overset{\overset{\alpha}{|}}{NP[Su]}, \ \overset{\overset{\beta}{|}}{NP[DO]} \dots \right\rangle \right]$$

$$\downarrow \quad [[X]d]_A \quad \left[SUBCAT \left\langle \overset{\overset{\beta}{|}}{NP[Su]}, \ \left(\left[_{PP} \overset{\overset{\alpha}{|}}{por} NP \right] \right) \dots \right\rangle \right]$$

To understand the rule, notice the difference in the way semantic roles (represented by α and β[27]) are assigned to specific elements in the SUBCAT list. The subject of the transitive verb has the same semantic role as the PP in the passive; the direct object of the transitive has the same semantic role as the subject of the passive. So, for example, to apply the rule to (51a), you essentially change the NP[Su] in its SUBCAT list into an optional PP headed by *por,* change the NP[DO] into NP[Su], and adjust the phonological form by adding *-d*. The result is (51b).

The rule refers to semantic roles with variables, rather than specific roles like Agent and Patient, since it has to be able to refer to all transitive verbs, regardless of what semantic roles are assigned to each complement. The rule applies equally well to (52a) to produce (52b), even though the semantic roles are different from those in (51). The semantic roles stay the same when you apply the rule; the thing that changes is the type of complement that expresses each semantic role.

Further, this rule also works for other types of verbs. For example, ditransitive verbs can also have passive forms, as shown in the following lexical entries for the Spanish verb *dar* 'give'.

(56) a.

$$[da]_V \quad \left[SUBCAT \left\langle \ \overset{\overset{Agent}{|}}{NP[Su]}, \ \overset{\overset{Theme}{|}}{NP[DO]}, \ \overset{\overset{Recipient}{|}}{PP[IO]} \ \right\rangle \right] \qquad \text{give}$$

  b.

$$[[da]d]_A \quad \left[SUBCAT \left\langle \ \overset{\overset{Theme}{|}}{NP[Su]}, \ \overset{\overset{Recipient}{|}}{PP[IO]}, \ \left(\left[_{PP} \overset{\overset{Agent}{|}}{por} NP \right] \right) \ \right\rangle \right] \qquad \text{be given}$$

The Word Formation Rule for passive (55) applies equally well to this pair of verbs as it does to the ones above. Notice that the rule includes ellipses ('...') to indicate that it can apply to verbs that may have other complements besides just a subject and direct object.

Formal analysis of other types of voice

The above examples show how the analysis works for adjectival passives. The analysis of verbal passives is very similar, as illustrated here using the SiSwati data from (12). The main difference in the lexical entry for the passive form *nikw* 'be given' is that it is a verb, not an adjective. A few other adjustments need to be made to accommodate other differences between the two languages, but essentially the SUBCAT lists are the same as for the corresponding Spanish verbs in (56).

---

[27]To be precise, the greek letters represent not just semantic roles, but all the selectional restrictions associated with a complement.

(57) a.

$$\qquad\qquad\qquad\qquad\quad \textit{Agent} \quad\ \textit{Theme}\quad\ \textit{Recipient}$$

$$[nik]_V \qquad [\text{ SUBCAT}\ \langle\ \text{NP[Su]},\quad \text{NP[DO]},\quad \text{NP[IO]}\ \rangle\ ]\qquad\qquad \text{give}$$

b.

$$\qquad\qquad\qquad\qquad\quad \textit{Theme}\quad\ \textit{Recipient}\qquad \textit{Agent}$$

$$[[nik]w]_V \quad [\text{ SUBCAT}\ \langle\ \text{NP[Su]},\quad \text{NP[IO]},\quad (\ [_{PP}\ ngu\ \text{NP}\ ])\ \rangle\ ]\qquad \text{be given}$$

Notice that the lexical entries only include the derivational affixes; the inflectional agreement and tense marking affixes visible in (12) are added by inflectional spellout rules after these verbs are inserted in specific trees.

The word formation rule for passive in SiSwati is likewise very similar to the one for passive in Spanish (55).

(58)

$$\qquad\qquad\qquad\qquad\qquad \overset{\alpha}{|}\qquad\ \overset{\beta}{|}$$

$$[X]_V \qquad [\text{SUBCAT}\ \langle\ \text{NP[Su]},\ \text{NP[DO]} \ldots \rangle]$$

$$\qquad\qquad\qquad\qquad\qquad \overset{\beta}{|}\qquad\qquad\ \overset{\alpha}{|}$$

$$[[X]w]_V \quad [\text{SUBCAT}\ \langle\ \text{NP[Su]},\ (\ [_{PP}\ ngu\ \text{NP}\ ])\ \ldots \rangle]$$

The same notation can be easily adapted to handle other types of voice. For example, the analysis of dative shift in English discussed above (p. 299) can be summarized in the following word formation rule:

(59)

$$\qquad\qquad\qquad\qquad\qquad \overset{\alpha}{|}\qquad\ \overset{\beta}{|}$$

$$[X]_V \qquad [\text{SUBCAT}\ \langle\ \ldots\ \text{NP[DO]},\ \text{PP[IO]} \ldots \rangle\ ]$$

$$\qquad\qquad\qquad\qquad\qquad \overset{\beta}{|}\qquad\qquad\ \overset{\alpha}{|}$$

$$[X]_V \qquad [\text{SUBCAT}\ \langle\ \ldots\ \text{NP[DO]},\ \text{NP[Obj2]} \ldots \rangle]$$

(Here, 'Obj2' represents the grammatical relation that the former direct object assumes in the dative shifted clause, since the former indirect object has 'taken over' the grammatical relation of direct object; different grammatical theories use different names for this grammatical relation.)

21.7. Review of key terms

In this chapter, we have resumed the discussion of verbal VALENCE that began in chapter 8 "Verbal Valence." Languages often have DERIVATIONAL MORPHOLOGY that manipulates the STRICT SUBCATEGORIZATION or SELECTIONAL RESTRICTIONS of verbs; this type of morphology is called VOICE. For example, PASSIVE VOICE is a DETRANSITIVIZING process, i.e., one that derives an INTRANSITIVE verb from a TRANSITIVE one in such a way that the SEMANTIC ROLE of the subject of the PASSIVE VERB is the same as the semantic role of the direct object of the corresponding ACTIVE VERB. (The relationship between active and passive verbs is so close in many languages that sometimes people speak of ACTIVE and PASSIVE FORMS of the same verb.)

Not all languages have passives. Those that do may have either LONG or SHORT passives (depending on whether it is possible to include an AGENT PHRASE in a PASSIVE CLAUSE), and the passive form may be either VERBAL or ADJECTIVAL.

Passive represents a systematic departure from PROTOTYPICAL associations of semantic roles with grammatical relations (such as agent with subject), but there are also individual verbs that do not follow them. Because of the existence of these exceptions, it is important to rely on GRAMMATICAL TESTS such as WORD ORDER, CASE, and AGREEMENT, rather than meaning, to construct analyses of grammatical relations. The systematic presentation of such arguments in support of a particular analysis is called ARGUMENTATION.

Because of nonprototypical associations of semantic roles with grammatical relations, the lexical entries of verbs must specify the semantic roles of their complements. One way to do this is by including semantic roles as part of the SUBCAT FEATURE of a verb. For passive, which is a systematic derivational process, we can also write a WORD FORMATION RULE that expresses the regular relationships between actives and passives.

Other examples of voice include DATIVE SHIFT, BENEFACTIVES, APPLICATIVES, CAUSATIVES, REFLEXIVES, RECIPROCALS, and NOUN INCORPORATION. (However, languages don't always use voice morphology to express the same ideas; for example, some languages have special sets of REFLEXIVE and/or RECIPROCAL PRONOUNS, and some have separate verbs meaning 'cause, make'.)

21.8. Questions for analysis

1. What characteristics do subjects and direct objects have in clear examples? Especially consider basic word order, categorial status (NP versus PP), optionality, case marking, and agreement.
2. Is there any evidence for passive in this language?
   a. What observable differences are there between passive and active clauses? Especially note verbal morphology and the semantic roles of the different noun phrases and prepositional phrases.
   b. Which of these facts support your hypothesis that these are indeed passives? For example, are there any ways in which the patient or theme in a passive clause behaves like clear examples of subjects and fails to behave like clear examples of direct objects?
   c. Why are passives used instead of actives in some contexts? What role, if any, do they play in discourse?
3. Is there any evidence for any other types of morphology that changes the subcategorization or semantic roles of verbs? (If so, ask questions like those listed above for passives.)

21.9. Sample description

Spanish has passives, as seen by comparing the active clause in (1a) with the corresponding passive in (1b). The passive agent may optionally be expressed as the object of the preposition *por* 'by'.[28]

(1) a. *Todos oyeron el gerente.*
        all   heard the manager
        Everyone heard the manager.

     b. *El gerente fue oído por todos.*
        the manager was heard by all
        The manager was heard by everyone.

There are two verbs in a passive clause: the auxiliary verb *ser* 'to be', followed by the main verb. The main verb is in a special adjectival form (traditionally called the passive participle) which uses the suffix *-d* and a gender/number suffix in place of the person/number/tense suffix that it carries in the active clause. The auxiliary verb *ser* is inflected for person, number, and tense (unless preceded by some other auxiliary).

---

[28]Data based on Gonzalez 1985:101.

There are several arguments that *el gerente* is the subject in (1b), not the direct object. One, *el gerente* is a bare NP, like clear examples of subjects. It cannot be the object of the preposition *a,* as it would be if it were the direct object. Two, it often precedes the verb, like clear examples of subjects, rather than following it, the typical position of direct objects. Three, if a pronoun is used in place of *el gerente,* the subject form of the pronoun is used, not the clitic form used for direct objects.

(2)   *Él/*lo fue oído por todos.*
      he   was heard by   all
      He was heard by everyone.

Four, like all clear examples of subjects, *el gerente* determines agreement on the auxiliary verb *ser* and on the participial main verb. The verbs do not agree with the object of *por*. Compare (3) with (1).

(3)   *Los gerentes fueron oídos por todo el mundo.*
      the   managers were   heard by   all   the world
      The managers were heard by everyone (lit. the whole world).

21.10. For further reading

Three articles in the Shopen (1985) series, which surveys basic linguistic structures around the world, may be of interest if you want to study further about passive and voice in general. Keenan (1985a) writes specifically about the ways that languages differ in passive constructions (including a few things under the heading 'passive' that not all linguists would use that term for). Comrie (1985a) presents other types of voice, with particular emphasis on causatives. Foley and van Valin (1985) consider the role that passive and other phenomena play in expressing the relative prominence of different noun phrases in a sentence.

As just noted, people sometimes legitimately disagree on what is appropriately called 'passive'. However, there is some value in trying to come up with a standard definition for 'passive' that brings together under one name phenomena that really are alike in some significant and important sense. In one of the most well-known attempts to do so, Perlmutter and Postal (1983) propose a characterization similar to what is given above. They argue first that this definition in terms of grammatical relations is superior to definitions that are based on word order, case marking, or agreement, then go on to lay out the basic elements of the theory of Relational Grammar which focuses on voice phenomena and was especially influential during the 1970s and 1980s. Other linguists, however, prefer to characterize passive very differently—in terms of its meaning and its affect on information packaging. This is the approach of Foley and van Valin (1985). The larger question here is a basic one for linguistic theory: if there are two constructions in two different languages, are they (despite their superficial differences) essentially the same? How do we know? This is all part of the search for what all languages have in common and how they differ from one another.

If you're interested in learning more about the different meanings that passive constructions can have in other languages and the resulting problems in translating them, Filbeck (1972) provides some suggestions for translators in light of the 'unpleasant passives' of Thai mentioned above (p. 298), both to avoid connotations of unpleasantness when this is not warranted and to exploit this meaning of passive when it is appropriate.

Syntax Group 3

22
Embedded Clauses

22.1. Goals and prerequisites

This chapter will help you do the following:

◎ identify different types of embedded clauses and state each type's function within its matrix clause
◎ describe the differences between matrix and embedded clauses in language data
◎ indicate the constituent structure of sentences involving embedded clauses, using either trees or labeled brackets
◎ modify phrase structure rules in a formal grammar so as to introduce embedded clauses in deep structure
◎ identify instances of conjoining and conjunctions in data

It assumes that you are familiar with the following material:

✓ embedding (chapter 7 "Embedding and Noun Phrase Structure")
✓ obliques (chapter 9 "Obliques")
✓ movement transformations (chapter 15 "Variable Orders of Constituents")

This chapter also makes brief reference to chapter 17 "Commands."

22.2. Embedding (review)

This chapter gives a brief introduction to embedded clauses and to sentences that contain more than one clause.

Throughout the book, we have been working with embedded structures. Consider a typical PP rule.

(1)   PP → P NP

This rule states that an NP is embedded inside a PP. Or, consider the NP rule we assumed for English in chapter 7 "Embedding and Noun Phrase Structure" (p. 70).

(2)   NP → $\left(\left\{ \begin{matrix} D \\ NP[Poss] \end{matrix} \right\} \right)$ (QP) (AP)* N (PP)

This states that several different types of phrases are embedded inside an NP. In particular, both a PP and an NP (the possessor) can be embedded inside another NP.

(3)

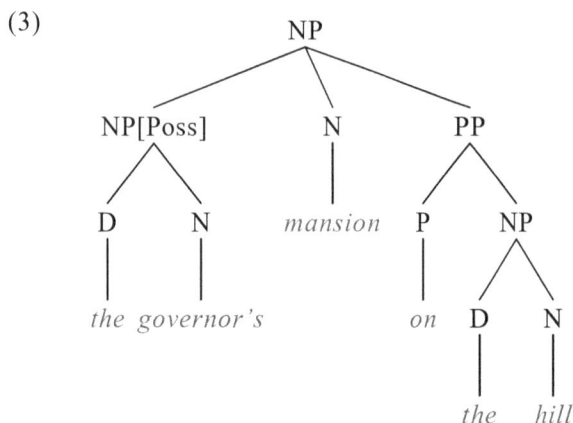

So, embedding is nothing new. Indeed, we have assumed that it is the norm for phrase structure. All constituents in a phrase (except for the head and minor categories like D) are other phrases (see chapter 7 "Embedding and Noun Phrase Structure," p. 68). This insures, for example, that the object of a preposition is always an NP, not just an N. One phrase is embedded inside another.

Embedding becomes more striking when *clauses* are embedded. There are many interesting things that could be discussed about embedded clauses, and some of the most important advances in linguistics in the latter part of this century have been in the area of embedded clauses. This book can only scratch the surface of this subject. This chapter does just two things: it introduces some of the traditional terminology for embedded clauses and gives examples of how to draw trees for them.

22.3. Embedded clauses

The following sentences exemplify three different kinds of embedded clauses. Brackets have been used to indicate the embedded clauses.

(4)   a. *John suspects [that Philomena likes him].*
       b. *Murgatroyd will work [when he has eaten lunch].*
       c. *I love the music [which is broadcast by the public radio station].*

In (4a), the embedded clause is acting as the complement (specifically the direct object) of the verb *suspects* and so is often called a COMPLEMENT CLAUSE. In (4b), the embedded clause is an oblique of time and so can be called an OBLIQUE CLAUSE (also known as an ADVERBIAL CLAUSE). In (4c), the embedded clause occurs inside a noun phrase modifying the head and is called a RELATIVE CLAUSE.

The above terminology describes the different subtypes of embedded clauses. There are also traditional terms which refer to the larger distinction between embedded clauses and other clauses.

Embedded clauses are traditionally called SUBORDINATE CLAUSES, because they are included in some other clause. In a tree diagram, the main clause is the topmost S and the other clauses are 'subordinate' to it (i.e., dominated by it).

(5)

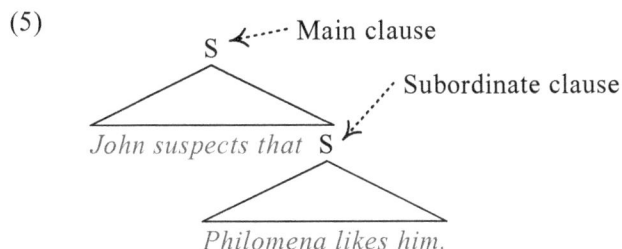

(Note the liberal use of TRIANGLES to represent part or all of a constituent. They are especially useful when drawing trees with embedded clauses to avoid the distraction of too much detail.)

Embedded clauses are also often called DEPENDENT CLAUSES, since they typically have minor differences inside of them which prevent them from standing on their own as main clauses. For example, the relative clause in (4c) is grammatical when it is embedded, but ungrammatical by itself as a full sentence.

(6)   *Which is broadcast by the public radio station.

Clauses which can stand alone as main clauses are called INDEPENDENT CLAUSES.

However, just because a clause *can* stand alone does not mean that it *does* stand alone in all cases. Besides embedding, there is another way of combining constituents, called CONJOINING. Roughly speaking, conjoining links together two constituents of the same type, to make another constituent of the same type.[1] It connects them with words like *and* and *or*, which are traditionally called CONJUNCTIONS. For example, the following sentence consists of two conjoined independent clauses. The two clauses, when conjoined with *and,* form a larger clause.[2]

(7)   [s [s John sings] and [s Mary plays the tuba]].

Even though they are combined as part of a larger clause, they are both considered to be independent clauses, because they have the right structure to stand alone as main clauses.

Two dependent clauses can also be conjoined. In the following, two complement clauses have been joined into a larger complement clause which is the direct object of the main clause.

(8)   I believe [[that he is guilty] and [that they will convict him]].

Finally, it is sometimes useful to refer to the relationship between an embedded clause and the next bigger clause that contains it, that is, the next higher S in the tree. The higher S is called the UPSTAIRS or MATRIX clause; the lower S is called the DOWNSTAIRS or embedded clause. So, in (9), the second S from the top is embedded (downstairs) with respect to the topmost S (the main clause), but matrix (upstairs) with respect to the third S from the top.

---

[1] In most languages, a wide range of constituents can be conjoined, not just clauses.

VP:	*John [[sings] and [plays the tuba]].*
NP:	*[[the director] and [her husband]]*
N:	*the older [[boys] and [girls]]*
AP:	*Its coat was [[red] and [sky blue]].*
PP:	*You should look for it [[in the attic] or [outside the garage]].*

[2] I leave open the question of how the conjunction fits into the overall structure; whether it is an immediate constituent of the conjoined clause or forms an intermediate constituent together with the second conjunct.

(9)

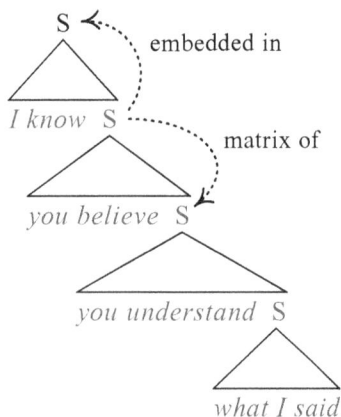

In summary, there are a number of terms traditionally used to describe different types of clauses. SUBORDINATE, EMBEDDED, and DEPENDENT mean roughly the same thing: that a clause is either a complement, oblique, or relative clause. A MAIN CLAUSE, on the other hand, is not embedded in (or subordinate to) any other constituent; since it is the whole sentence. INDEPENDENT clauses have the internal structure of a main clause, whether or not they actually are the main clause in a particular tree; the opposite of DEPENDENT is INDEPENDENT, not MAIN. Finally, when a clause is embedded in another clause, the second is the MATRIX CLAUSE of the first; this matrix clause may be a main clause or embedded in a third, higher clause.

Let's consider each type of embedded clause in more detail.

Complement clauses

A complement clause occurs embedded as the subject or direct object of another clause.[3] Consider the following sentences, in which the complement clauses are bracketed:

(10)   a.   *[That John kept practicing so long] surprised me.*
       b.   *She thought [that Bill brushed his teeth with garlic sauce].*

The words which introduce complement clauses are called COMPLEMENTIZERS. There are several different complementizers in English; *that* is the clearest example. Linguists generally assign complementizers to a minor category called C, which joins together with an S to form a constituent called S′ (read 'S-PRIME'). Sometimes you will see $\bar{\text{S}}$ ('S-BAR') in place of S′.[4]

(11)   *She was surprised [$_{S'}$ that [$_S$ Bill's breath smelled so fresh.]]*

S′ is used not just for complement clauses, but for all embedded clauses. An S′ constituent is generally used in an analysis whenever a particular type of embedded clause in a language is customarily introduced by some special word, e.g., the complementizer for a complement clause; the introducing word is labeled C.

---

[3]The term COMPLEMENT CLAUSE is used in a variety of different ways, as Crystal's (1991:67) discussion of COMPLEMENT points out. The usage of this term in this book, though relatively standard, is not entirely satisfactory, since there are some types of oblique clauses (see note 6, p. 323) which are also complements of the verb, but which often do not have the same internal structure as what here are called complement clauses (clauses embedded as subject or object of a verb). Further, the term 'complement clause' should probably include clauses which are the objects of nouns (*the notion [that the earth is flat]*), adjectives (*afraid [that she would fall]*), and prepositions (*in [that he never received the letter]*), since these have many of the same properties as clauses which are objects of verbs.

[4]There is disagreement in the current literature about the nature of S′ and C constituents. Work in Government-binding theory generally assumes that C is the head of S′, i.e., that S′ is a synonym for CP. (See, for example, the discussion in Haegeman 1991:106–12.) Pollard and Sag (1994), however, assume that S is the head of S′, as implied by the notation. In this book, the question is left open. Also, it should be noted that previous chapters have not made a distinction between S and S′, at times using S when, in light of the discussion here, it would be more precise to use S′.

Trees help you visualize the concept of embedding. Notice in the following trees how one clause is included in another; the embedded clause is functioning as subject or direct object within the matrix clause. Grammatical relations can be represented with the same features [Su] and [DO], but they are attached to the S′ node, rather than an NP.

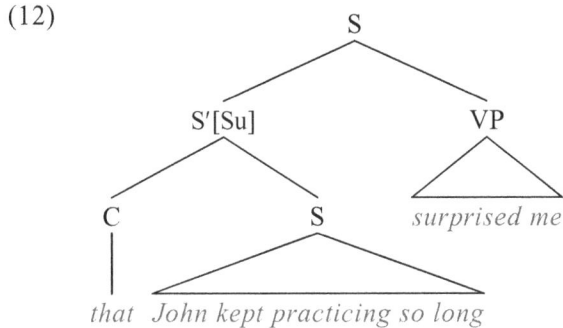

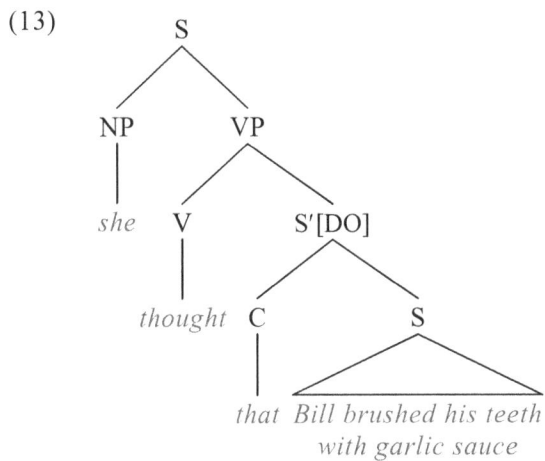

(12)

```
                    S
            _____|_____
         S′[Su]              VP
        ___|___             /___\
       C       S        surprised me
       |      /___\
     that  John kept practicing so long
```

(13)

```
              S
          ____|____
        NP         VP
        |        ___|___
       she      V       S′[DO]
        |      |       ___|___
    thought   C       S
                |     /___\
              that  Bill brushed his teeth
                    with garlic sauce
```

In some languages, there is no introducer in some clause types, as is the case in some complement clauses in English. In one sense there is no need to assume an S′ constituent; you could conceivably just use the S, as in the following tree.

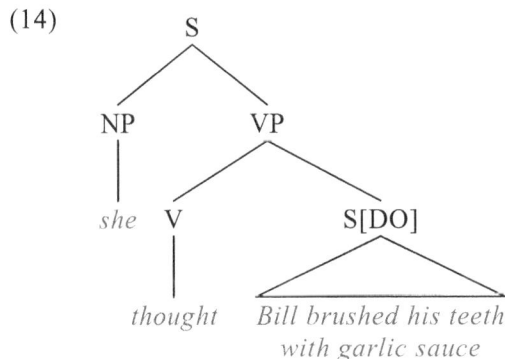

(14)

```
              S
          ____|____
        NP         VP
        |        ___|___
       she      V       S[DO]
        |      |       /___\
    thought        Bill brushed his teeth
                    with garlic sauce
```

Still, many linguists assume an S′ constituent for all embedded clauses in all languages, as part of their theory of universal grammar. When there is no explicit complementizer, they assume an empty C, represented as ∅.

(15)

```
              S
           /     \
         NP       VP
          |      /   \
        she    V     S'[DO]
                |     /    \
            thought  C      S
                     |      /\
                     Ø   Bill brushed his teeth
                          with garlic sauce
```

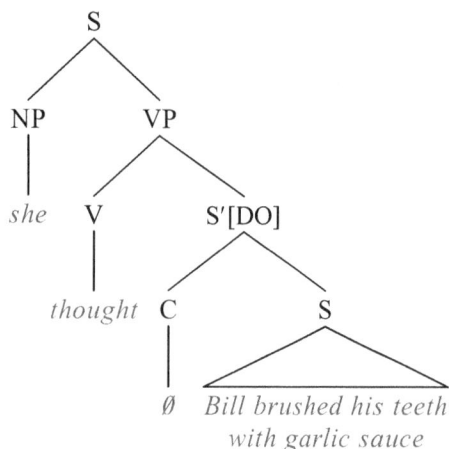

On the other hand, in some languages there may not be any evidence favoring either approach. In your analysis of other languages, then, it may depend on which theoretical approach you are following whether to include it or not, if you don't actually see a complementizer in the data. On the other hand, if there *is* a clause introducer (a C), be sure to include the S' node.

In other languages, complement clauses often correspond fairly closely to complement clauses in English. The following sentences illustrate complement clauses in Peñoles Mixtec (Otomanguean, Mexico):[5]

(16) *ní-šiní   =dé [sá   ñúʔú   ndìkutu =dé itú   ]*
      Cmp-see he   that Cnt/be.in ox(en) his field
      He saw that his oxen were in the cornfield.

(17) *sàní iní =dé [sá   bá-kádá   čiuⁿ =í]*
      Cnt/think he   that not-Pot/do work I
      He thinks that I won't work.

In each sentence, the object is a complement clause introduced by a complementizer *sá*. The structure of sentence (16) can be represented this way:

(18)

```
                  S
           /     |      \
         V    NP[Su]    S'[DO]
         |      |       /    \
      ní-šiní  =dé     C      S
       saw     he      |      /\
                       sá   ñúʔú ndìkutu =dé itú
                      that  his oxen were in the cornfield
```

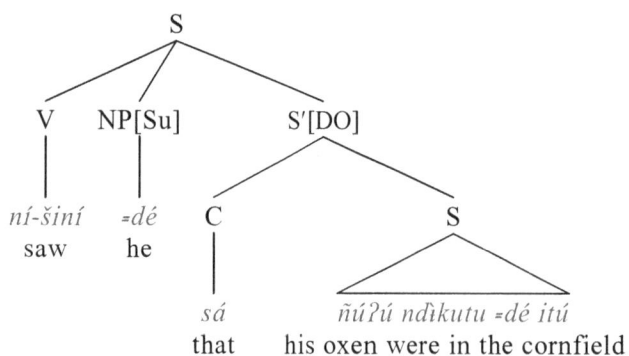

[5]Data from Peñoles Mixtec is from John Daly (personal communication) and is partly based on Daly 1973. Transcription follows Americanist practice; diacritics are tone marks, based on the analysis in Daly 1977; superscript ⁿ indicates nasalization. The three aspects glossed on the verbs are Cmp (completive), Cnt (continuative), and Pot (potential).

Oblique clauses

Oblique clauses are embedded clauses which are obliques within their matrix clauses.[6] Along with PPs, AdvPs, NPs, etc., they are used to express typical oblique notions such as time, location, and manner. Consider the following sentences, in which the oblique clauses are bracketed:

(19) a. *My heart goes [where the wild goose goes].*
     b. *John will leave [when he finishes breakfast].*
     c. *[Having won the battle], Caesar marched into Rome triumphantly.*
     d. *[If John keeps practicing], he'll be famous.*
     e. *[Because Mary kept practicing so faithfully], she did become famous.*
     f. *[Although John kept on practicing faithfully], he didn't become famous.*
     g. *Be quiet [so that you can get an ice cream cone].*

For example, we might draw the following tree to show a clause embedded in the VP as an oblique.

(20)

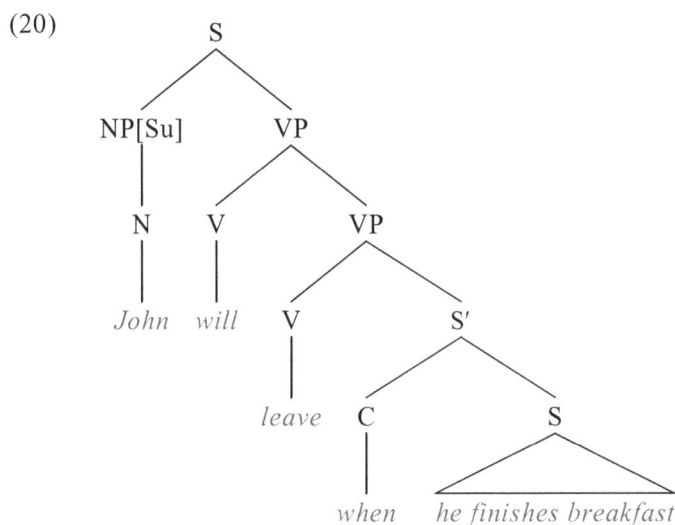

Note that the category C includes words such as *when, where, if,* and *because,* even though these would traditionally be called 'subordinating conjunctions' rather than complementizers. C is used for any particle that introduces a clause, because all such particles (regardless of their traditional labels) share the property of introducing a embedded clause.[7]

Some of the examples in (19) above involve semantic notions that we did not discuss earlier in connection with obliques, such as condition *(if)*, purpose *(so that)*, reason *(because)*, etc. All of these ideas can also be expressed by PP obliques.

(21) a. Condition: ***In case of fire,*** *you should run and holler, scream and shout.*
     b. Purpose: *He pulled the fire alarm just **for fun.***
     c. Reason: *He paid a heavy fine **for his stupidity.***

Even with these additions, this is probably not a complete list of semantic functions of obliques. For now, it's enough to say that obliques can express a variety of meanings and these meanings can be expressed by a variety of structures, including PPs, AdvPs, NPs, and embedded clauses.

---

[6]Oblique clauses are sometimes called 'adjunct clauses', but this term is not completely appropriate, because such clauses can be complements of certain verbs, as in (19a). See also footnote 3 (p. 320).

[7]In some traditional approaches to grammar, oblique clauses are not considered to be subordinate to a matrix clause, but rather somehow equal to it. This traditional conception, however, ignores the fact that oblique clauses function as obliques, expressing many of the familiar oblique notions, especially time, location, and manner, as well as other oblique functions (noted in the text above) which may be expressed with PPs as well as embedded clauses.

Oblique clauses are also affected by many of the same rules that affect PPs and AdvP obliques. Oblique clauses in English occur either at the beginning or the end of their matrix clause, just like 'ordinary' obliques. Recall that when obliques occur at the beginning of a clause, this normally indicates the beginning of a new episode or paragraph in discourse. The same is true of oblique clauses.

(22)   a. *[When he finished rolling the oats], he made oatmeal.*
       b. *He made oatmeal [when he finished rolling the oats].*

Sentence (22a), in which the oblique clause is fronted, would fit very naturally at the beginning of a new episode in the continuing saga of a family obsessed with a desire for self-sufficiency, while (22b) would fit more naturally in the middle of an episode. Thus, in this way, oblique clauses act just like other obliques.

As examples of oblique clauses in another language, consider the following Peñoles Mixtec oblique clauses:

(23)   *ndèku =dé [núú ndékú tătá =dě]*
       Cnt/be he   where Cnt/be father his
       He is where his father is.

(24)   *kada čìu^n =dé [òré kuu žačí =dé]*
       Pot/do work he   when Pot/be time he
       He will work when he has time.

(25)   *[dàtá^n kìde čìu^n tátá =dě] kìde čìu^n =dé*
         like Cnt/do work father his   Cnt/do work he
       He works like his father works.

In sentence (23), the oblique clause expresses location, in sentence (24), time, and in sentence (25), manner.

Relative clauses

Relative clauses are modifiers within noun phrases. Consider the following sentences with the relative clauses bracketed:

(26)   a. *The man [who came to dinner] stayed too long.*
       b. *The tree [that grew in Brooklyn] finally withered and died.*
       c. *What did you bring the book [I don't want to be read to out of] up for?*

They perform the same function as adjectives, either describing or helping to identify a participant in a discourse, and thus they are sometimes called ADJECTIVAL CLAUSES.

Relative clauses have the same basic structure as other embedded clauses: they consist of an (optional) introducer followed by an S. Thus, we analyze them as being one more instance of the category S′ and the introducer as C. Relative clauses are discussed in more detail in chapter 23.

22.4. Finite versus nonfinite in embedded clauses

There are frequently minor differences between main clauses and embedded clauses. Languages often place complementizers at the beginning of embedded clauses, but generally not in main clauses. Verbs in embedded clauses may have special morphology. Relative clauses typically have other differences, described in chapter 23.

Still, all clauses have essentially the same structure. All have constituents like subjects, verbs, objects, and obliques; they generally involve the same or similar patterns of case and agreement; all have similar options for ordering of constituents. Generative Grammar has expressed this overwhelming similarity by using the symbol S to represent all types of clauses. The differences between independent clauses and embedded clauses are then accounted for in other ways. For example, the presence of a special particle introducing an embedded clause is accounted for by positing a category S′ consisting of a C plus an S.

Another difference between independent and embedded clauses concerns the morphology on the verb. Some languages, like English, omit many morphological distinctions in certain embedded clauses. For example, the verb in a complement or oblique clause may use a noninflected form— what is often called an INFINITIVE (the bare stem, preceded by *to*). Recall from chapter 17 "Commands" (p. 238) that the infinitive form of the verb lacks any indication of person, number, or tense.[8]

(27) a. *John sincerely expects [Mary **to kiss** him].*
      b. *John wants [Ø **to kiss** Mary, too].*
      c. *She turns her back [Ø **to get** [him **to stop** acting so obnoxious]].*

Often the infinitive is used because the subject is omitted, something that happens in some embedded clauses, especially when the subject of the clause is coreferential with the subject of the main clause.[9]

Languages often make a similar distinction between two types of verb forms. One type is fully inflected, that is, it is marked for all the inflectional features that the language normally marks, such as tense, aspect, person, and number of the subject, etc. There may be a large number of these forms; they are called FINITE verb forms. Other verb forms, like the English infinitive, may not make any indication of some or all of these features; these are called NONFINITE verb forms. Clauses are also called FINITE or NONFINITE, based on whether their verbs are finite or nonfinite. As we have seen, embedded clauses are often nonfinite; indeed, nonfinite clauses are almost always embedded clauses.

22.5. Extraposition

Clauses are striking examples of embedding because they are relatively large constituents. Often, they are so large that they don't fit comfortably where one might expect them. For example, in English, subject complement clauses usually don't show up as subjects in surface sentences.

(28) a. *[That he would do such a thing] shocked me.*
      b. ***It** shocked me [that he would do such a thing].*

Although (28a) is a possible sentence, (28b) is more natural. In (28b), the subject complement clause has been moved to the end of the clause. In its place is a dummy subject *it*. Such clauses are said to be EXTRAPOSED. Native speakers feel that clauses are usually too big to fit comfortably just before the verb and prefer them at the end of the clause.

Sometimes clauses are extraposed for no obvious reason.

(29) a. *I believe [that he could be president next year].*
      b. *I hate **it** [that he could be president next year].*

---

[8]The bracketing in these examples follows assumptions in Government-binding Theory, which generally assumes that words like *Mary* in (27a) and *him* in (27c) are surface constituents of the embedded clause. Other approaches, however, assume that *Mary* is moved outside the embedded clause by a transformation called 'Raising'.

[9]This is sometimes referred to as Equi-NP deletion or just Equi, after the early transformational approaches that assumed there was a transformation that deleted the subject of an embedded clause if it was identical with the subject of the matrix clause. More recent transformational approaches have analyzed this phenomenon in terms of 'control structure'; they have assumed that such clauses contain a special silent pronominal element called 'PRO' (sometimes called "big" PRO to distinguish it from the silent pronoun "little" *pro*). See Radford 1988:313–17, 320–24; Radford 1997:131–35; Haegeman 1991:242–64; or Borsley 1991:146–58.

In (29b), the object complement is extraposed to the end of the clause, leaving the dummy *it* behind, even though it was already at the end of the clause in deep structure.

Relative clauses can also be extraposed out of the NPs that they logically belong to. Compare the following two sentences, in which the first has a small relative clause, the second a heavy one.

(30)   a. *I haven't seen [$_{NP}$ the movie [$_{S'}$ that you recommended]] yet.*
       b. *I haven't seen [$_{NP}$ the movie] yet [$_{S'}$ that you recommended to me last week*
          while we were sitting across the river next to the music building].

The relative clause in (30b) still is interpreted as modifying the direct object *movie,* but it is not a surface constituent of that NP. This can clearly be seen because the time oblique *yet* is stuck between the head and the clause. Note that when the relative clause is extraposed, there is no dummy pronoun inserted in its place, unlike what we saw for the extraposition of subject and object clauses.

22.6. Phrase structure rules for embedded clauses

One aspect of the analysis of embedded clauses is quite straightforward. We need to add a phrase structure rule for S′ to our grammar of English (chapter 9 "Obliques," p. 107), and then we insert S′ in subject and object position (for complement clauses), as an additional type of oblique (for oblique clauses), and as a modifier in the noun phrase (for relative clauses).

(31)   S′ → C S

$$(32) \quad S \rightarrow \begin{Bmatrix} NP \\ S' \end{Bmatrix} [Su] \; VP$$

$$(33) \quad VP \rightarrow V \left(\begin{Bmatrix} NP \\ S' \end{Bmatrix} [DO] \right) (VP) \left(PP[IO] \right) \left(\begin{Bmatrix} NP \\ PP \\ AdvP \\ S' \end{Bmatrix} \right) *$$

$$(34) \quad NP \rightarrow \left(\begin{Bmatrix} D \\ NP[Poss] \end{Bmatrix} \right) (QP) \, (AP) * N \, (PP) \, (S')$$

These rules are assumed by the trees drawn for English sentences in this chapter.

This accounts for the most obvious facts about their distribution. This book does not attempt to cover other facts in the formal grammars, such as finite versus nonfinite clauses, extraposition, and the internal structure of relative clauses. In your work at this stage, beyond writing phrase structure rules, I suggest you concentrate on providing a clear and accurate description of the facts for the data you may encounter, rather than writing formal rules.

22.7. Embedding and the infinite use of finite means

Embedding goes a long way towards explaining why people can produce an infinite number of sentences with only a finite grammar in a finite mind. Now that we have looked at embedding of clauses, you can appreciate this point more fully.

First, recall that possessors can be recursively embedded within NPs and that NPs and PPs can be recursively embedded inside of each other.

(35)

```
                    NP
              ┌──────┴──────┐
          NP[Poss]          N
         ┌────┴────┐        │
     NP[Poss]      N      muzzle
    ┌────┴────┐    │
NP[Poss]      N   dog's
    │         │
   my      mother's
```

(36)

```
          NP
     ┌────┼────┐
     D    N    PP
     │    │   ┌─┴──┐
 the smile   P    NP
             │  ┌──┴──┐
            on  D  N   PP
                │  │  ┌─┴──┐
            the face P    NP
                     │  ┌──┼────┐
                    of  D  N    PP
                        │  │   ┌─┴──┐
                       the man P    NP
                               │   △
                              in the moon
```

Complement clauses and relative clauses can be embedded down to many levels. No matter how much embedding there is in a sentence, it's always possible to stick in one new embedded clause.

(37) a. *Sally thought [that he wanted [her to see [whether the movie was showing]]].*
      b. *This is [ₙₚ the cat [ₛ' that chased [ₙₚ the rat [ₛ' that ate [ₙₚ the malt [ₛ' that lay in [ₙₚ the house [ₛ' that Jack built]]]]]]]].*

Conjoining also makes it possible to produce arbitrarily long sentences, as children usually discover sometime during their preschool years.

(38) *We saw zebras and ducks and elephants and ostriches and giraffes and monkeys and rhinos and...*

Sentences that provide several examples of different types of embedding and conjoining are really quite common. Consider, for example, the first sentence from the preface to Radford 1981.

(39)   *The aim of this book is to provide a clear, simple introduction to recent work in syntax*
       by Chomsky and his followers, for all those who find Chomsky unintelligible.

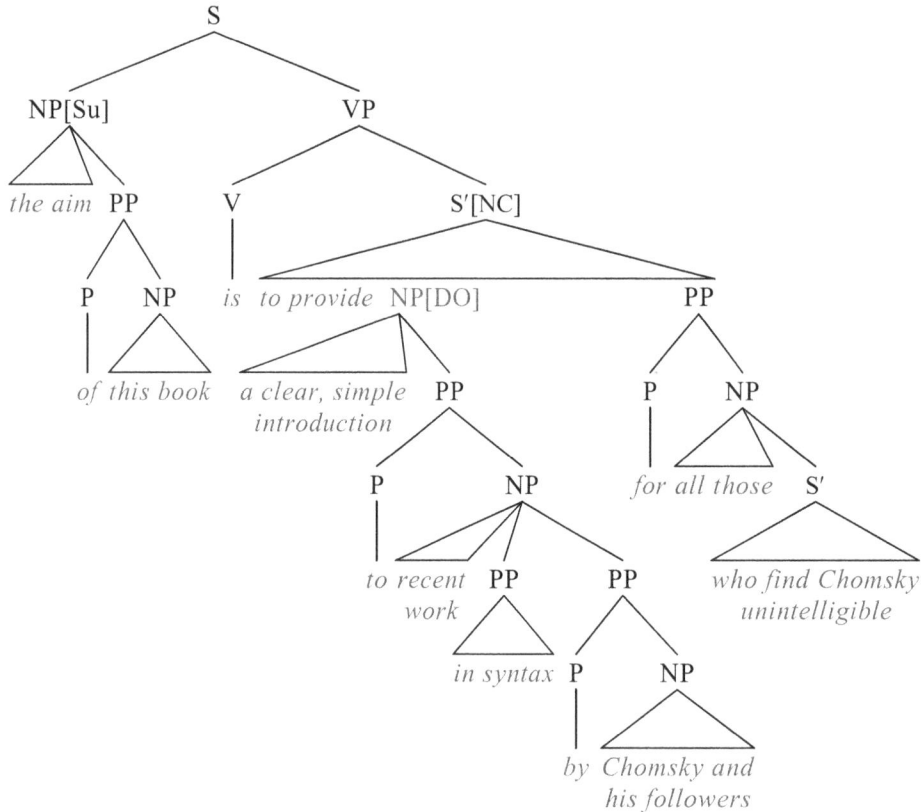

```
                              S
                      ┌───────┴───────┐
                   NP[Su]            VP
                    /△\         ┌─────┴─────┐
              the aim  PP       V          S'[NC]
                      /△\       |      ┌────┴────────────┐
                     P   NP    is  to provide  NP[DO]          PP
                     |   /△\                   /───△\         /\
              of this book  a clear, simple  PP           P      NP
                            introduction    /△\      for all those  /△\
                                           P    NP                     S'
                                           |   /△\              /────△────\
                                      to recent  PP      PP    who find Chomsky
                                        work    /△\     /\      unintelligible
                                           in syntax  P    NP
                                                      |   /△\
                                                 by Chomsky and
                                                  his followers
```

The grammar places no limit on the amount of embedding and conjoining possible in a sentence and, thus, no limits on the length or complexity of a sentence or the number of sentences that the grammar can generate. Other human limitations (memory, lung capacity, etc.) do place restrictions on how long a sentence we can produce and understand, but even with these limitations, we can easily handle sentences that are considerably more complex than the ones illustrated here. The linguistic capacity of the human mind is truly amazing.

22.8. Review of key terms

We have considered EMBEDDING, especially embedding involving SUBORDINATE or DEPENDENT clauses. The clause in which they are embedded is called the MATRIX or UPSTAIRS clause, to distinguish it from the EMBEDDED or DOWNSTAIRS clause. Clauses which have a structure that can stand alone are called INDEPENDENT clauses; the clearest example of an independent clause is the topmost S in a tree diagram of a sentence, that is, the whole sentence itself. Besides embedding, clauses (and other constituents) can be linked together by CONJOINING, in which two constituents of the same type are linked together with a CONJUNCTION to form a larger constituent of the same type.

Embedded clauses can be classified by their function in the matrix clause, as COMPLEMENT, OBLIQUE (or ADVERBIAL), or RELATIVE (or ADJECTIVAL) clauses. In languages with significant morphology, it is often useful to distinguish between FINITE and NONFINITE (or minimally inflected) clauses, since embedded clauses often have different morphology on the verb from main clauses. Embedded clauses are often different from independent clauses, too, in that they contain a COMPLEMENTIZER (a word that identifies them as embedded and expresses something of their relation to the matrix). Finally, some embedded clauses may be EXTRAPOSED, or moved out of their deep structure position, particularly if they are large (= HEAVY).

In our trees, we have introduced S′ as the constituent that includes the embedded S and its introducer, called C.

22.9. Questions for analysis

1. Examine each type of embedded clause (complement, oblique, and relative) to identify the differences between it and main clauses.
    a. Does this type of clause have complementizers? What are they and (especially for oblique clauses) what are their meanings? Where do they occur in the clause? Are they obligatory or optional?
    b. Is there any special verbal morphology in such clauses? Is there a special nonfinite form used or different affixes than would be used in a main clause?
2. With respect to conjoining: What types of constituents can be conjoined? What conjunctions are available for each?

22.10. Sample description

Peñoles Mixtec complement and oblique clauses are essentially identical in structure to main clauses. A variety of complementizers are used to introduce embedded clauses, depending on the clause type.

(1) *sàní ini =dé [sá   bá-kádá   čìu^n =í]*
     Cnt/think he   that not-Pot/do work I
     He thinks that I won't work.

(2) *ndèku =dé [núú   ndèkú tătá =dĕ]*
     Cnt/be he   where Cnt/be father his
     He is where his father is.

(3) *[dàtá^n kìde čiu^n tátá =dĕ] kìde   čiu^n =dé*
        like   Cnt/do work father his   Cnt/do work he
     He works like his father works.

There is no special morphology in embedded clauses. The interpretation of the tense/aspect morphology in an embedded clause depends on the tense/aspect in the main clause. For example, in (4) a continuative form (normally used for present time) is used in the embedded clause to indicate that the oxen were in the cornfield at some time in the past, specifically, at the same time as they were seen (as indicated by the completive form in the main clause).

(4) *ní-šiní =dé [sá   ñúʔú   ndìkutu =dé itú]*
     Cmp-see he   that Cnt/be.in ox(en) his field
     He saw that his oxen were in the cornfield.

22.11. For further reading

Much, perhaps most, of the work done in the early days of generative linguistics dealt with embedded clauses. Although other areas of structure have also come under scrutiny more recently, the structure of sentences with more than one clause still remains very important in the literature. Perlmutter and Soames (1979) cover many of the issues that were important through the 1970s and which remain relevant today (although dressed in different theoretical clothing): 'missing' subjects in embedded clauses, sharing of complements between two clauses (known as 'raising' and 'Equi'), principles that control the order in which rules are applied, barriers that limit how far things can be moved, the interpretation of pronouns, and so forth. Their book is especially helpful because it adopts a 'learning-by-doing' approach to learning syntax, guiding the reader through a series of exercises (with sample answers) that develop both an understanding of syntactic structure and skill in developing arguments in favor of a particular analysis. For a more recent transformational perspective, both Radford 1988 and Haegeman 1991 include substantial material on embedded clauses.

Shopen (1985), volume 2 is devoted to 'complex constructions', with separate chapters on conjoining, complement clauses, relative clauses, adverbial (= oblique) clauses, and overall sentence structure as a complex of clauses. Like all of the chapters in the three volumes of this collection of helps for field workers, the emphasis is on providing a survey of structures used in a wide variety of languages, organized and discussed in a way that introduces a minimum of formal theoretical apparatus, but does include semi-theoretical distinctions that are important for the area under study.

23
Relative Clauses

23.1. Goals and prerequisites

This chapter will help you do the following:

- ◎ use terms like HEAD and RELATIVIZED POSITION to talk about the parts of relative clauses
- ◎ describe the devices that languages typically use to form relative clauses (how relative clauses in one language might differ from those in other languages)
- ◎ state how the Noun Phrase Accessibility Hierarchy is relevant to relative clauses
- ◎ identify the relative clause strategy or strategies in a language and describe each
- ◎ provide a partial formal analysis by writing phrase structure rules and drawing deep and surface structure trees for relative clauses

It assumes that you are familiar with the following material:

- ✓ basic noun phrase structure (chapter 7 "Embedding and Noun Phrase Structure")
- ✓ case marking (chapters 8 "Verbal Valence" and 10 "Inflectional Morphology"; chapter 19 "Case and Agreement" is optional but recommended)
- ✓ embedded clauses (chapter 22 "Embedded Clauses")

There are also passing references to the following:

- ✓ content questions (chapter 16 "Questions")
- ✓ passive (chapter 21 "Passive and Voice")

23.2. Semantics of relative clauses: Restrictive and nonrestrictive

A relative clause is a clause which is embedded in a noun phrase and which modifies the head noun. It functions like an adjective, in that it helps to specify what the head noun refers to or provides further information about it.

(1)

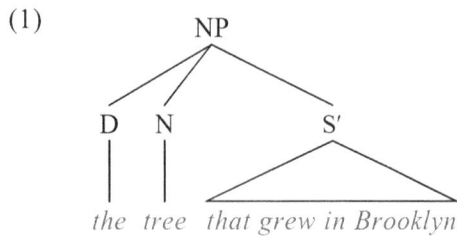

When we consider the exact contribution that a relative clause makes to the meaning of a noun phrase, we can distinguish two types of relative clauses, called RESTRICTIVE and NONRESTRICTIVE (or APPOSITIVE). A restrictive relative clause specifies or narrows down the class of entities referred to by the head noun.

(2)   a. *The man [who ran over our Frisbee in his pickup truck yesterday] came by to apologize.*
      b. *I wish I could see a movie about whales [that doesn't romanticize them].*

Each relative clause identifies which individual in some large class is the one that is being referred to in this particular case. For example, in (2a), if we just said 'the man', we could be talking about millions of different people; the relative clause identifies which one of those millions we're talking about.

In contrast, a nonrestrictive relative clause provides additional information about the head noun, but does not help identify who or what we are talking about, usually because the identification is complete without the relative clause. In English, nonrestrictive relative clauses are surrounded by pauses, which we write with commas.

(3)   a. *My oldest brother, [who is a famous piccolo player], will perform in Kalamazoo next week.*
      b. *I really enjoyed that movie about whales, [which I've seen five times].*

In (3), if we left out the relative clauses, it would still be clear who or what we were talking about. In (2), by contrast, if we left out the relative clause it would not be clear who or what we were talking about. If we just said 'The man came by to apologize,' as an opener to a conversation, people would probably ask 'What man?' On the other hand, starting a conversation with 'My oldest brother will perform in Kalamazoo next week' would not cause this problem.

This semantic difference has an impact on what type of noun phrase each type of relative clause can be used in. For instance, a restrictive relative clause, which is supposed to help identify who we are talking about, is usually not acceptable with proper names and other noun phrases that fully specify an entity by themselves.

(4)   a. **Clarence who is a real swinger likes jazz.*
      b. *Clarence, who is a real swinger, likes jazz.*

On the other hand, a noun phrase of the form [NP any ... N], which doesn't fully specify anything by itself, cannot be used with a nonrestrictive relative clause.

(5)   a. *Any linguist who can't make morpheme cuts is going to have problems.*
      b. **Any linguist, who can't make morpheme cuts, is going to have problems.*

Differences like this between restrictive and nonrestrictive relatives are probably universal, but there are also differences peculiar to English. For instance, only restrictive relative clauses can be introduced with *that;* nonrestrictive relative clauses cannot (at least in standard dialects).

(6)   a. *The car that ran over our Frisbee....*
      b. **My car, that is bright orange,....*

Nonrestrictive relative clauses must always be introduced with a WH word: *who, whose, which,* etc.

In this chapter, we concentrate on restrictive relative clauses, since much less is known about nonrestrictive relative clauses (although some of what follows is also relevant to them). When analyzing a language, it is generally important to distinguish the two, since their structures may differ. The reason for knowing the difference between them is so you can recognize and distinguish them in language data that you may be analyzing.

23.3. Terminology for describing relative clauses

First, let's introduce some terminology that is commonly used to describe relative clauses.

Head

The noun that the relative clause modifies is called its HEAD. This usage of 'head' is different from the use of HEAD that was introduced earlier when talking about embedding (chapter 7 "Embedding and Noun Phrase Structure," p. 67). The 'head' of a relative clause (in this new sense) is not the central constituent inside the relative clause; rather it is the noun that the relative clause modifies.[1]

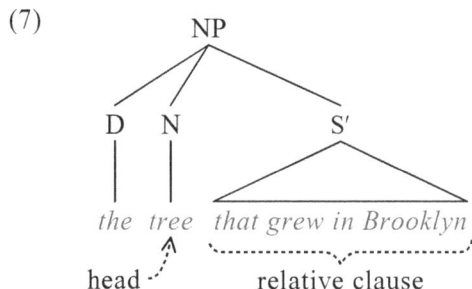

(7)

The head of a relative clause has a unique role in its meaning, because even though it is outside the clause, it figures semantically inside the clause.[2] For example, in (7) *tree* is interpreted as the subject of the relative clause, even though it is outside the clause.

One (almost) never sees a relative clause in which a copy of the head shows up inside the relative clause.[3]

(8)   ***The Frisbee [that he ran over the Frisbee]** ...

Instead, we find that there is a gap in the relative clause (represented in (9) by Ø) where we would expect to find a copy of the head. This gap acts like a pronoun that refers back to the head noun.

(9)

The Frisbee [that he ran over Ø] ...

---

[1]Actually, the two senses are related. The head of a relative clause (in the new sense) is the head (in the old sense) of the noun phrase which the relative clause is part of.

[2]There are occasional exceptions, such as *I like a handout [that you can tell what the paper was]* or this elaborate example from a Garrison Keillor radio monologue: *I can tell that, of all the surprising haircuts I've received, this is going to be one [that I'll have to wear a hat for a week].* In these cases, there is not even a resumptive pronoun (see p. 339) inside the relative clause to link it to the head. Instead, the connection is purely semantic, as the embedded clause restricts the domain of reference of the head without making direct reference to it. This suggests that it is the semantic function of restrictiveness that is the defining characteristic of relative clauses; most relative clauses also contain some sort of syntactic link between the head noun and some constituent of the relevant clause, but not all do. Although Keenan (1985b) does not seem to discuss such clauses, his description (p. 142) would classify them as relative clauses, since it is semantically-based.

[3]Keenan (1985b:152) gives a few examples in which a copy of the head noun (or something very much like it) does occur inside the relative clause.

This is one general characteristic of relative clauses in most or all languages: the head noun is not repeated in the relative clause, even though it is understood as part of that clause semantically. Instead, there is some pronominal element (often simply a gap) in the clause that refers to the head.

Relativized position

Relative clauses are often classified with respect to the function this pronominal element has inside the relative clause. An easy way to think of this is to substitute the head into the relative clause, replacing the gap or other pronominal element. That is, ask, "What grammatical relation would the head have inside the relative clause, if it appeared there?" For example, in (7) the head would have to be inserted in subject position ('the tree grew in Brooklyn'), and so we say that the subject position is RELATIVIZED. Alternatively, we can say that the RELATIVIZED POSITION is subject. Here are some more examples in which the relativized position is subject.

(10) a. *the woman [that Ø talked to us last night]*
      b. *the clock [that Ø stands in the corner]*
      c. *the first person [that Ø made me an offer]*

Note that it is the grammatical relation *inside the relative clause* that is important. The grammatical relation of the head in the matrix clause is not what you should consider. In (11), the subject is relativized, because the head, *woman,* is understood as the subject of the relative clause; it is irrelevant that *woman* is the direct object of the matrix clause.

(11) *I like the woman [that Ø talked to us last night].*

It's what's inside the clause that counts for determining what position is relativized.
    If the head would be the direct object of the relative clause, as in (12), we say that the direct object is relativized or that the relativized position is the direct object.

(12) a. *the laser printer [that he bought Ø yesterday]*
      b. *attractive documents [that he has already produced Ø with it]*
      c. *the one [that my brother recommended Ø]*

This terminology works the same for any position in the relative clause. For example, we can talk about relativizing the indirect object, as in (13a), or the possessor of the direct object, as in (13b).

(13) a. *The man [that I gave a scolding to Ø]*
      b. *The little boy [whose Frisbee he had destroyed Ø]*

There is a subtle distinction to make here. In (13b), note that it is *whose* that refers back to the head *(boy); whose* is the possessor of the direct object, so the relativized position is a possessor. There is also a gap, but this gap is different—it corresponds to the whole direct object, not just the relativized position. This gap arises because the whole direct object (relativized possessor included) has been fronted within the relative clause. So, don't assume that a gap always shows you what position is relativized; often it will, but you have to ask yourself, "What element inside the relative clause refers back to the head? What is its grammatical relation within the relative clause?"

Relative pronouns and relativizers

Recall that there are sometimes minor differences between independent and embedded clauses. In English relative clauses, there are two differences. Besides the presence of a gap, relative clauses also are usually introduced by what are traditionally called RELATIVE PRONOUNS, such as *who(m), which, whose,* and *that.*

Modern linguistics generally draws a finer distinction, though, reserving the term RELATIVE PRONOUN for those words which vary depending on context. For example, if the head is human, most English speakers use *who(m)*, but if the head is nonhuman, they use *which*.

(14)   *the man* $\left\{ \begin{array}{l} who \\ *which \end{array} \right\}$ *ran over the frisbee*

(15)   *the car* $\left\{ \begin{array}{l} *who \\ which \end{array} \right\}$ *ran over the frisbee*

This is analogous to the personal pronouns *he* and *she*, which are used for humans, and *it*, which is used for nonhumans. Furthermore, relative pronouns, like other pronouns in English, are marked for case. If the subject is relativized, we use *who*, if a possessor is relativized, we use *whose*, and if an object is relativized, we use *whom* (at least, in formal dialects).

(16)   a.   *the man **who** ran over the Frisbee*
        b.   *the man **whose** car got sprayed with shaving cream*
        c.   *the man **whom** I scolded*

In contrast, *that* may be used in many different contexts without varying for gender or case.

(17)   a.   *the man **that** ran over the Frisbee*
        b.   *the car **that** ran over the Frisbee*
        c.   *the man **that** I scolded*

As such, *that* is usually not called a relative pronoun, but rather is called a RELATIVIZER or RELATIVE PARTICLE, a special type of complementizer for relative clauses. This is just like its use as a complementizer in complement clauses—it introduces the clause, period.

There are many reasons for classifying *that* as a relativizer and distinguishing it from relative pronouns. If *that* is not a pronoun, it is not surprising that it does not vary in form like a relative pronoun. If it isn't a pronoun, it doesn't refer to the head (as a pronoun would); therefore, there is no reason that it would vary in form depending on the humanness of the head or be marked for case. The relative pronouns *who, whose, which* can all be used as interrogative pronouns as well as relative pronouns; that is, there is one class of WH pronouns in English that are used both in content questions and relative clauses. *That* cannot be used as an interrogative word and, thus, is clearly not part of this class. The relative pronouns can be used with prepositions; *that* cannot, which is what we'd expect if it isn't a pronoun.

(18)   a.   *the car under which the Frisbee perished*
        b.   **the car under that the Frisbee perished*

There is, of course, a pronoun *that*, but it is pronounced differently. The demonstrative pronoun *that* has secondary stress; the *that* which introduces a complement clause or relative clause is unstressed.

(19)   a.   *I saw **thát** man.*
        b.   *the man **that** I saw*

These and many more reasons justify classifying *that* as something other than a relative pronoun.[4]

---

[4]In some dialects, *that* cannot be used with human antecedents; in all dialects, it cannot be used to relativize the possessor. These facts make it seem a bit more like the relative pronoun *which*. However, there are still numerous differences that fully justify not classifying it as a relative pronoun. See Radford 1988:482ff.

Some native speakers of English may claim to have intuitions that *that* indeed *does* refer to the head, as a pronoun. Remember, however, that these 'intuitions' have been strongly biased by education under the traditional analysis, so that they are not valid evidence in favor of that analysis. In fact, native speakers' 'intuitions' about grammatical rules are notoriously unreliable; they must be tested against objective evidence. On the other hand, we should not question native speaker judgments about the grammaticality of individual sentences or their meaning, since these are the object of our study. The point here is that most native speakers do not consciously know the rules that control their unconscious linguistic behavior; any 'knowledge' that they claim about how the rules work must be tested against the evidence just like any other hypothesis. (At the same time, if native speakers volunteer explanations for the rules of the language, it is important for politeness sake to listen to them graciously and not 'correct' them with our 'better' analysis. Indeed, they might actually be right—or their explanation might provide clues to a more satisfactory analysis.)

23.4. Typological variation

When you encounter relative clauses in a language, there are several basic questions that you should ask about their structure. The next few sections discuss them and indicate the most common answers you will find to them. This is not a complete survey of the different ways that languages form relative clauses, but these sections do mention the most common types and a few related generalizations.[5]

The first question to ask is about word order. In most languages, the relative clause follows the head, as in English. Such relative clauses are called POSTNOMINAL. When the basic word order is verb-initial (VSO or VOS), relative clauses are virtually always postnominal (only two partial exceptions are known). In SVO languages, the overwhelming tendency is for the relative clause to follow the head.

Only in SOV languages will you find PRENOMINAL relative clauses (preceding the head), as in Basque (isolate, Spain).[6]

(20) [*gizon-a-k   liburu-a eman dio-n   ] emakume-a*
         man-the-Su   book-the   give   has-Rel   woman-the
      the woman that the man has given the book to

Still, many SOV languages use postnominal relative clauses.[7]

Some languages, such as German, appear to have both prenominal and postnominal relative clauses.[8]

(21) *der [in seinem Büro arbeitende] Mann*
      the   in his   study working   man
      the man who is working in his study

(22) *der Mann, [der   in seinem Büro   arbeitet]*
      the   man   who(MascSgNom) in his   study   works
      the man who is working in his study

---

[5]For further information on these typological generalizations, see Keenan 1985b, which is the basis for the discussion in this section and (unless otherwise stated) is the source of the non-English examples.

[6]There aren't enough OSV and OVS languages known to make any generalizations about them.

[7]SOV languages also sometimes have a third type, in which it seems that the noun that would be the head in most languages appears inside the relative clause, and there is no external head. This can, perhaps, be regarded as the use of a prenominal relative clause together with a variation on the resumptive pronoun strategy discussed later in this chapter. Because the relativized position comes first, it appears explicitly, while there is a zero resumptive pronoun as head. See Keenan 1985b:143.

[8]The bracketed clause in (21) might also be analyzed as a VP embedded inside the NP, rather than a full clause.

A second question concerns morphology. Some languages use special morphology on verbs in relative clauses. For example, note above that in prenominal relative clauses in German (21), a nonfinite form of the verb is used, but in postnominal relative clauses (22), a finite form is used. In some languages there may be a different affix when relativizing the subject, another when relativizing the direct object, etc.

The third question concerns how the relative clause differs syntactically from an independent clause. It is so important that the whole next section is devoted to it.

23.5. Gaps, relativizers, and relative pronouns

There are two interrelated matters to consider about any relative clause—what type of clause-introducer there is (if any) and how the relativized position is represented. There are three main options used in the world's languages:

(23) a. Use a gap in the relativized position, with or without a relativizer
      b. Use a relative pronoun in the relativized position (usually the relative pronoun appears at the beginning of the relative clause)
      c. Use a resumptive pronoun in the relativized position with or without a relativizer

Let's discuss each of these in turn.

Gaps

Many times, there is simply nothing inside the relative clause in the relativized position. That is, the relativized position is represented by a GAP. This pattern has been illustrated extensively above; every relative clause which begins with the relativizer *that* has a gap in the relativized position.

Although relative clauses formed with gaps are often introduced with a relativizer, this is not always the case.

(24) *the Frisbee [he ran over Ø]*

In some languages a relativizer is always used with a gap, in others never, and in others (like English) both possibilities are used.

Representing the relativized position with a gap is common in other languages. For example, consider the following relative clauses in Choapan Zapotec (Otomanguean, Mexico). Despite the lack of a relativizer, it is easy to see where the relative clause begins just by finding the verb, since Zapotec is VSO.[9]

(25) *ɾao tu nigula [bɛ Ø mala]*
      eats one woman   did   bad
      One woman [who did bad] is eating.

(26) *bginu juʔ [bɛ benɛʔ Ø]*
      fell house   made people
      The house [that the people made] fell down.

(27) *ɾao nigula [bɛ benɛʔ juʔ kjɛ Ø]*
      eats woman   made people house of
      The woman [whose house the people made] is eating.

There is no relativizer or relative pronoun in these relative clauses, just a gap where we would expect to find a noun phrase in an independent clause.

---

[9]Data from Larry Lyman (personal communication). See footnote 2, p. 20 for transcription conventions.

Relative pronouns

Relative clauses with relative pronouns look very much like those that simply use a gap, except that in place of a relativizer, there is a relative pronoun. The English relative clauses above which use the relative pronouns *who(m)*, *which*, and *whose* are examples.

Recall that the way to tell a relativizer from a relative pronoun is that a relative pronoun agrees with the head in some features and may also be marked for case (depending on its position inside the relative clause). Often, relative pronouns have the same form as interrogative (WH) or demonstrative pronouns. For example, in German, the relative pronouns are similar in form to the demonstrative pronouns and, like them, vary in form depending on number, gender, and case. (Compare also (22) above.)

(28) *der Mann, **den**   Marie liebt*
      the man   **whom**(MascSgAcc) Mary loves
      the man whom Mary loves

(29) *die Frau, **die**   er liebt*
      the woman **whom**(FemSgAcc) he loves
      the woman whom he loves

On the other hand, a relativizer is invariant, does not behave in any significant way like a pronoun, and is often also used as a complementizer in other types of embedded clauses.

Relative pronouns are generally fronted and, thus, provide an explicit marker of the beginning of the relative clause. When a relative pronoun is fronted, of course it leaves a gap behind, but this is not the same as a gap that represents the relativized position. As mentioned earlier, sometimes not just the relative pronoun is fronted, but some larger constituent that contains it. The gap then corresponds to the whole fronted constituent, not just to the relative pronoun. In this case, you can't just find the gap to identify the relativized position; you have to look at the relative pronoun and ask about its function. For example, in (30a), only the object of the preposition *in* is relativized, even though the gap corresponds to the whole PP; you can see this by looking at where *the suitcase* occurs in (30b). Similarly, in (30c), a possessor is what is relativized, not the subject of *fall*, as can be seen in (30d).

(30) a. *the suitcase [in which he hid the loot Ø]*
      b. *He hid the loot in **the suitcase**.*
      c. *the traveler [whose suitcase I saw Ø fall from the luggage rack]*
      d. *I saw **the traveler**'s suitcase fall from the luggage rack.*

This is different from what happens when there is no relative pronoun; when there is only a gap, the gap is always in the relativized position.

Resumptive pronouns

A third option for dealing with the relativized position is similar in some respects to the use of a gap, except that the relativized position is filled by an overt pronoun, called a RESUMPTIVE PRONOUN, rather than leaving it empty. This option is not usually recognized in traditional grammars of English, but is quite common in informal speech and, occasionally, even in well-edited writing. Listen to people around you, and you will hear many examples such as the following real-life examples, provided for your enjoyment.[10] (The resumptive pronoun is in boldface.)

---

[10]The examples of resumptive pronouns were all collected from native speakers who used them naturally in conversation. Examples like these are too common and consistent to be speech errors, even though they seem strange when presented out of context. Sometimes they even occur in professional journals and other well-edited writing. Garrison Keillor (of *A Prairie Home Companion* on public radio in the USA) deserves credit for the last two; the rest are from colleagues, friends, or relatives who shall remain nameless.

(31) a. *She is one [that her friends come to **her** for counseling].*
       b. *Sharon is the only person [that Micah cries*[11] *when **she** leaves].*
       c. *A tradition [that nobody knows what **it**'s based on] will, sooner or later, fall apart.*
       d. *I saw a car coming down the hill [that I wondered if **that** might be him].*
       e. *Voice is troublesome, because it's one of those things [that you can't tell ahead of time whether **it**'s derivational or inflectional].*
       f. *...it sounds like a possible English sentence, one [that even if you don't say **it** that way, you would not be particularly surprised to hear someone else say **it** that way or to see **it** written].*[12]
       g. *What words do you have in your language that we don't have...words [that English would be a better language if we stole **them** from you]?*
       h. *He jumped over the fence (of the cattle yard) and into something [that, if he had known what **it** was, he would have jumped farther left].*

Note that it would be ungrammatical to use a gap in place of the resumptive pronoun in many of these examples. (Some of them can be rearranged and paraphrased so the same idea can be communicated with a relative clause that does use a gap, but that's not the point. When the above complex structures are used, a resumptive pronoun is the only option.) Resumptive pronouns tend to be used when the relativized position is buried deep in the relative clause; relative pronouns and gaps cannot be used in these cases.

A resumptive pronoun is normal in relative clauses in some languages.

(32) *ha-sarim*   *[she-ha-nasi*   *shalax* **otam** *la-mitsraim]*   (Hebrew)
       the-ministers   Rel-the-President sent   **them** to-Egypt
       the ministers [that the President sent (them) to Egypt]

(33) *Man zan-i*   *râ* *[ke   John be* **u** *sibe zamini dâd] mishenasam* (Persian)
       I   woman-the DO   that John to **her** potato   gave   know
       I know the woman [that John gave the potato to (her)].

Correlations with word order

There are some interesting correlations between word order and how the relativized position is represented. Relative pronouns are found mostly in SVO languages, whereas gaps are found in all word-order types. Relativizers and relative pronouns, when they occur, generally appear on that edge of the relative clause which is toward the head. Since relative pronouns are found almost entirely in SVO languages and in such languages the clause typically follows the head, relative pronouns usually (perhaps always) occur at the beginning of the relative clause.

23.6. Relative clause strategies and noun phrase accessibility

We have seen that languages may use a variety of devices to form relative clauses, usually drawn from some combination of the following options:

(34) a. relative clauses may precede or follow the head
       b. relative clauses may be separated from the head by a relativizer or not
       c. the relativized position may be represented by a relative pronoun, a resumptive pronoun, or nothing (a gap)
       d. there may be special morphology on the main verb of a relative clause

---

[11]Note that the relative clause is not *that Micah cries for θ when she leaves*, which uses a gap in the relativized position (the object of the preposition *for*). Without the preposition, the meaning is slightly different, and the pronoun *she* is the only element in the relative clause that refers back to the head noun.

[12]This example appeared as part of the text (not data!) in a linguistic article in a reputable, well-edited journal, as a striking example of a sentence inadvertently describing itself.

In any one language, there may be more than one type of relative clause. Each way of forming a relative clause is called a RELATIVE CLAUSE STRATEGY. To describe a strategy, we specify which of the options in (34) it uses, as well as any special language-particular characteristics it may have. For example, we saw above in (21)–(22) and (28)–(29) that German has two strategies:

(35)   Strategy A, as in (21)   Strategy B, as in (22) and (28)–(29)

   prenominal (specifically, between the   postnominal
       determiner and the head noun)
   gap in relativized position and no   relativized position is a relative pronoun,
       relativizer   which introduces the clause
   verb is nonfinite (specifically, it is a   verb is finite (same as in an independent
       present participle)   clause)

Once each strategy is defined and distinguished from the others, there is one further fact to determine about it. Each strategy generally has limits as to which positions it can relativize. For example, the English relative pronoun strategy can relativize subjects, direct objects, indirect objects, obliques, and possessors.

(36)   a. subject   *the man [who Ø ran over the Frisbee]*
       b. direct object   *the man [who I saw Ø]*
       c. indirect object   *the man [who the police gave a ticket to Ø]*
       d. oblique   *the man [who we pinned the blame on Ø]*
       e. possessor   *the man [whose truck Ø ran over the Frisbee]*

The gap strategy can relativize all these positions except possessors.

(37)   a. subject   *the man [that Ø ran over the Frisbee]*
       b. direct object   *the man [that I saw Ø]*
       c. indirect object   *the man [that the police gave a ticket to Ø]*
       d. oblique   *the man [that we pinned the blame on Ø]*
       e. possessor   **the man [that Ø's truck ran over the Frisbee]*

The relativizer is optional with the gap strategy, but if it is omitted, the subject cannot be relativized either.[13]

(38)   a. subject   **the man [Ø ran over the Frisbee]*
       b. direct object   *the man [I saw Ø]*
       c. indirect object   *the man [the police gave a ticket to Ø]*
       d. oblique   *the man [we pinned the blame on Ø]*
       e. possessor   **the man [Ø's truck ran over the Frisbee]*

So, part of describing a relative clause strategy is stating which positions it can and cannot relativize.

There seem to be some fairly strong universal generalizations about what positions a given strategy can relativize, which are based on what has been called the NOUN PHRASE ACCESSIBILITY HIERARCHY:[14]

---

[13]The asterisks in (38a, e) indicate that this structure is ungrammatical *as a noun phrase*. These strings of words are grammatical as whole clauses (*the man ran over the Frisbee, the man's truck ran over the Frisbee*), but they cannot be used as a noun phrase in a larger structure (**the man ran over the Frisbee came by to apologize*). Thus, *ran over the Frisbee*, without a relativizer, cannot be a relative clause.

[14]Keenan and Comrie (1977) include Object of Comparison as the last item in the noun-phrase accessibility hierarchy. See their paper for details of their claims about the hierarchy and supporting data.

(39)   Su > DO > IO > Oblique > Possessor

First, every language appears to have a strategy that can relativize subjects, most can relativize direct objects, and some can relativize farther down the hierarchy. That is, subjects are the most 'accessible' to relativization, direct objects are next most accessible, etc. Some languages push this to an extreme and relativize only subjects. This is true, for example, in Malagasy (Austronesian, Madagascar). If one wants to relativize the direct object, one must instead paraphrase by using a passive in the relative clause, as in (42).[15] (Malagasy is VOS.)

(40)   *ny mpianatra [izay nahita ny vehivavy]*
       the student   that saw   the woman
       the student that saw the woman

(41)   **ny* vehivavy [izay nahita ny mpianatra]*
       the woman   that saw the student
       (the woman that the student saw)

(42)   *ny vehivavy [izay nohitan'ny   mpianatra]*
       the woman   that seen(Passive).the student
       the woman that was seen by the student

Second, it appears that in most languages, any given strategy can only relativize a continuous segment of this hierarchy. Thus, if a particular language has a relative pronoun strategy and you know that it can relativize subjects and indirect objects, you can be reasonably confident that you'll find relative pronouns with direct objects too, even if you don't have the data yet. However, you have no information about relativizing obliques and possessors.

23.7. Formal analysis of relative clauses

We have seen three strategies used to form relative clauses in English. How are they analyzed? We will not go into full details, but let's at least look at the outline of a formal analysis of them by looking at deep and surface trees.

For all three strategies, we'll assume the phrase structure rules that were introduced in chapter 22 "Embedded Clauses" (p. 326):

(43) $NP \rightarrow \left(\left\{ \begin{matrix} D \\ NP[Poss] \end{matrix} \right\} \right) (QP) (AP)* N (PP) (S')$

(44) $S' \rightarrow C\ S$

Rule (43) accounts for the postnominal position of relative clauses in English, and rule (44) accounts for the location of the relativizer or relative pronoun at the beginning of the clause, in the C position. But, we still have to account for the relativized position inside the clause. There is a slightly different explanation for each strategy.

First, consider the strategy that uses only a gap in the relativized position. This strategy often introduces the clause with the relativizer *that,* which we analyze the same way as we do for complement clauses, as a C. The gap in the relativized position is often represented with a null sign 'Ø', but this is only an informal, temporary notation until we figure out what causes the gap.

[15]Data from Keenan and Comrie (1977:70). Presumably (41) is grammatical in the reading 'the woman that saw the student', in which the subject is relativized, although Keenan and Comrie do not state this. Glosses in (42) modified slightly to clarify the exposition.

(45)   Gap strategy with relativizer (partial analysis, deep and surface)

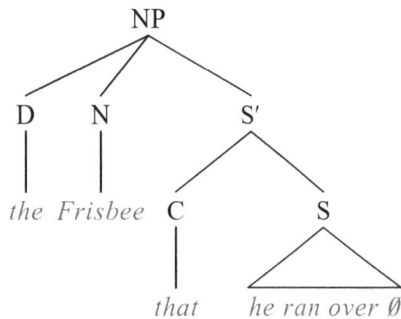

Throughout this book, we've seen that gaps can arise from a variety of causes. In other words, saying that there is a gap in a sentence is just a way of saying that something is missing in a certain position that we might otherwise expect to be there. (We expect something to be there because of our general knowledge of the structure of the language. In the case of (45), we know that *run over* normally takes a direct object and that *the Frisbee* is understood as its direct object even though it is not part of the relative clause.) So, saying that there is a gap in a sentence doesn't explain anything; it just describes some exception to the general rules of a language that we need to explain.

Whenever we find a gap in a sentence, there are a number of different approaches available to us for making a formal grammar. In the course of this book, we've introduced four:

(46)   a.   The gap really is nothing—the grammar simply does not put anything into the tree (e.g., a 'zero' affix).

b.   The gap arises because something was there in deep structure, but it got deleted (e.g., the missing subject noun phrase in a command).

c.   The gap arises because something was there in deep structure, but it got moved someplace else (e.g., the gaps that arise from WH-movement).

d.   The gap is a 'silent something'—a morpheme that has syntactic and semantic properties, but its phonological properties are *silence* (e.g., silent copulas and *pro*).

In the case of relative clauses, which of these four approaches is the best explanation for a gap in the relativized position? We can't just leave the direct object out of the tree completely (option a), because the lexical entry for *run over* requires a direct object. That means we have to have a direct object in deep structure. We could say that the direct object got deleted (option b), but this approach has fallen out of favor.[16] There is nothing that could have been moved (option c). So, we're left with an analysis that this gap is a special 'silent something'; it has syntactic and semantic properties but is silent. Specifically, it is a special type of pronoun which is sometimes represented as *'O'*.[17] *'O'* is listed in the lexicon as a pronoun and is inserted into the tree in deep structure in the relativized position. The following shows the same tree, with an explicit *'O'* to account for the gap. This tree would be both deep and surface structure.[18]

---

[16]In earlier transformational work, deletion transformations were used more than they are now. One problem with them is that there could conceivably be many deep structures for the same surface sentence if the only difference between them was in the constituent that gets deleted. Another problem is representing the semantic relationship of the head to the relative clause. If the relative clause contains a silent pronominal element, then it can represent this relationship directly.

[17]The *'O'* stands for 'operator'. 'Operators' are words which act in some respects like mathematical operators in terms of their meaning; they include the WH words.

[18]There are reasons, however, for preferring a more elaborate analysis involving fronting of the silent pronoun *'O'*, just like fronting with overt relative pronouns; see Radford 1988:487ff.

(47)   Gap strategy with relativizer (with analysis of gap as a silent pronoun)

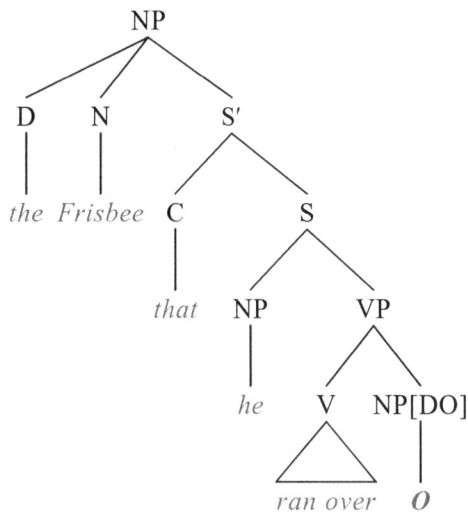

In cases where the relativizer is absent, linguists generally assume that the C node is still present in the tree (just as they do for complement clauses, see chapter 22 "Embedded Clauses," p. 321), but that there is nothing under it in deep structure.[19]

(48)   Gap strategy without relativizer (deep and surface)

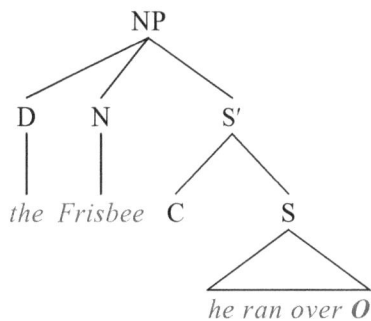

In contrast to the gap strategy, the relative pronoun strategy has an overt relative pronoun in the relativized position, which presumably occurs in the normal place in deep structure. Note that it, too, has an empty C position in deep structure.

---

[19]For the most part, this book has not left terminal nodes empty in deep structure. However, this approach is commonly used in current versions of transformational grammar. In other words, lexical insertion is now considered optional. This provides a fifth possible analysis of a gap—the preterminal node is present, but its terminal node is unfilled. This is different from the 'silent something' approach because an empty terminal node does not have any semantic or morphosyntactic features, while a 'silent something' does.

(49)   Relative pronoun strategy (deep structure)

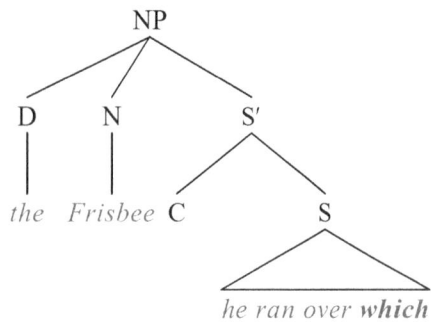

This must then be moved to the empty C position at the beginning of the clause, with the following result as its surface structure:[20]

(50)   Relative pronoun strategy (surface structure)

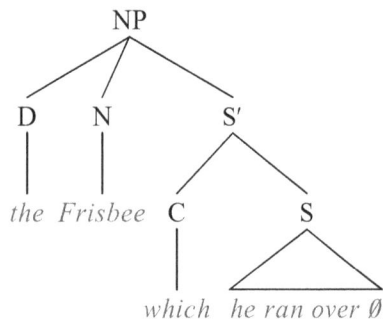

Of course, the movement leaves a gap behind, just like all movements do. This is written informally as ∅ in (50). However, this gap is quite different from the one we find in the gap strategy. In the gap strategy, we analyzed the gap as a silent pronoun *'O'* in deep structure; in the relative pronoun strategy, the gap results only as a side-effect of fronting the relative pronoun.[21] This difference in analysis explains something we noted earlier: when there is a relative pronoun, the gap does not always correspond to the relativized position, while in the gap strategy, it always does.

   Turning now to the resumptive pronoun strategy, it is the simplest of all to analyze. Like the other two strategies, it has a pronoun in the relativized position in deep structure, but this is an ordinary pronoun rather than *'O'* or a relative pronoun.[22]

---

   [20]Though the relative pronoun is often assumed to move under the C node in surface structure, it is not classified as a C in the lexicon and would not be considered a relativizer. This is one area where informal terminology and formal analysis seem to be at odds with each other.

   [21]Since the 1970s, it has been assumed in Transformational Grammar that when an element is moved, it leaves behind an empty node, called a 'trace', which does not have the same syntactic properties as *'O'*. Analyzing 'empty' categories like these has become very important in recent years, as people have asked the question "When there is a gap in a sentence, why is it there?"

   [22]Note that the resumptive pronoun is buried two clauses down from the head, inside of an embedded question. This is one type of complexity that makes it impossible to use the other two strategies, for reasons that are discussed in Radford (1988:487–88).

(51)   Resumptive pronoun strategy (deep and surface)

```
                      NP
          ┌───────────┼───────────┐
          D           N           S'
          │           │        ┌───┴────┐
          │           │        C        S
       a tradition             │      ╱───╲
                                │    nobody knows  S'
                            that              ╱───╲
                                          what it's based on
```

The ordinary pronoun *it* is inserted in deep structure in the relativized position. That's all that is needed to account for the surface structure; no movements or other transformations are necessary.

23.8. Review of key terms

A RELATIVE CLAUSE is a clause which is embedded inside a noun phrase, modifying the head noun. It may help identify the head noun, as a RESTRICTIVE relative clause, or simply provide additional information about it, as a NONRESTRICTIVE (or APPOSITIVE) relative clause.

The noun which the clause modifies is called its HEAD. In some languages, relative clauses are PRENOMINAL (before the head), but more commonly they are POSTNOMINAL.

Inside the clause, the position which corresponds to the head (subject, direct object, etc.) is called the RELATIVIZED POSITION. Alternatively, we can say that such-and-such position inside the clause is RELATIVIZED. There are three main ways that languages use to fill the relativized position. It is often simply a GAP; it may also be a RESUMPTIVE PRONOUN or a RELATIVE PRONOUN. In the first two cases, there may be a RELATIVIZER (or RELATIVE PARTICLE) introducing the clause. When there is a relative pronoun, the relative pronoun itself usually occupies that clause-initial position.

Languages may have more than one way to form relative clauses; each different type is called a RELATIVE CLAUSE STRATEGY. Any one strategy usually can only be used to relativize certain positions within a relative clause. These are not random, but appear always to be a continuous segment along the NOUN PHRASE ACCESSIBILITY HIERARCHY.

23.9. Questions for analysis

1.   What different relative clause strategies are there?
2.   For each strategy, how does the relative clause differ from an independent clause?
     a.   Do relative clauses precede or follow the head?
     b.   How is the relativized position represented? By a relative pronoun, a resumptive pronoun, or a gap?
     c.   If there are relative pronouns, what are they? In what features do they agree with the head? Do they vary for case or any other grammatical category?
     d.   Does this strategy involve a relativizer? What is it? Where does it come with respect to the relative clause? What other uses does it have in the language?
     e.   Does this strategy involve any special morphology on the verb?
     f.   Along what segment of the noun phrase accessibility hierarchy does this strategy operate? That is, what positions in the relative clause can be relativized using this strategy?

23.10. Sample description

In English, relative clauses follow the head.

(1)   *anyone [who eats purple cabbage]*

There are two commonly-used relative clause strategies in standard dialects. In one, the clause is introduced by the relativizer *that,* and there is a gap in the relativized position.

(2)   a. *the game [that Ø entertains me most] is chess*
        b. *the bear [that I saw Ø over there]*
        c. *a house [that I can live with Ø]*

The relativizer *that* may be omitted unless the subject is relativized.

(3)   a. **the game [Ø entertains me most] is chess*
        b.   *the bear [I saw Ø over there]*
        c.   *a house [I can live with Ø]*

Some speakers restrict the use of *that* to nonhuman heads.
    In the other strategy, a relative pronoun (and sometimes a whole phrase which contains it) is fronted within the clause, leaving a gap.

(4)   a. *the man [**who** Ø beats me at chess]*
        b. *the person [**who(m)** I abhor Ø most]*
        c. *a house [**which** I can live in Ø]*
        d. *anyone [**whose** room Ø looks like this]*

Who and *whom* are used for humans, *which* for nonhumans. In the standard prescriptive dialect, *who* is used only for subjects, *whom* for objects, *whose* for possessors, although informal usage allows *who* for both subjects and objects.
    The two strategies can relativize any noun phrase position within a single clause, with the exception of the gap strategy, which cannot relativize possessors.

(5)   **anyone [(that) Ø's room looks like this]*

There is no special verbal morphology in any relative clauses in English.

23.11. For further reading

The study of relative clauses cross-linguistically illustrates the concern of much of modern linguistics—to identify how all languages are alike and how they may differ from each other. The first step in such a study is to identify an area in which languages do seem to be alike yet different; in this case, they all have something that is recognizably a relative clause, but there is an interesting amount of variety from one language to the next. The next step is to examine a broad variety of languages and make a fairly precise, but still informal, statement of what exactly they have in common and how they differ. This is what Keenan (1985b) does for relative clauses, providing a definition that works well cross linguistically and a characterization of the different devices used to form them. Finally, theorists attempt to construct precise formal analyses and theories that account for the observed facts about language variation and the different devices used. They ask questions like "Why are these devices used and not others?" and "Why are these devices used in the way that they are and not in other logically-possible ways?"
    In a formal analysis of relative clauses, it usually makes sense to handle them with the same rules as are needed for content questions (chapter 16 "Questions," p. 222ff.), since in many languages the

structure of questions and relative clauses is very similar. In one common approach, WH movement is used to move relative pronouns to the beginning of a relative clause, leaving a gap. Radford (1988:480–92) develops this approach in some detail for English. He includes several arguments that *that* is a complementizer (=relativizer) in relative clauses, not a relative pronoun. His discussion also introduces constraints that limit how far a constituent can be moved; these have been an extremely important issue in research on embedded clauses since the late 1960s. Once you've finished this section, you may be interested in glancing through Radford's (1988:601–4) summary of the transformational literature on relative clauses; not that it will all be perfectly clear, but it will give you an idea of the range of options that people have considered in developing analyses to account for them.

Practical Helps

24
Hints for Linguistic Writing

24.1. Goals and prerequisites

This chapter will help you do the following:[1]

◎ state how an informal description differs from a formal analysis and why both are important
◎ write short (2–3 sentence) factual descriptions of linguistic data without relying on theory-specific terminology or formal rules

24.2. The importance of informal analysis

One important skill of a linguist is the ability to write clearly and concisely about a language's structure. Accordingly, an analysis of data can be done in two ways. On the one hand, you could make a FORMAL ANALYSIS, involving rules, lexical entries, trees, and other concepts that are used in some theoretical framework. On the other hand, you could give an INFORMAL DESCRIPTION of the facts, similar to what you might find in many pedagogical grammars, written so that most linguists should be able to understand it, regardless of their theoretical orientation.

Most people find it easier to write the informal descriptions after they've worked out the formal analysis. There's something about a careful analysis in a formal theoretical framework that really helps us zero in on what's going on in the language. That's why this book uses formal analysis.

However, formal grammars are hard to understand without informal explanations about the data they are supposed to cover and how the rules work. This is especially true if your readers are not familiar with the particular framework you're using. Even if they are, it often helps them to be able to read a summary description or introduction in ordinary language before looking at a formal rule. (That is, let the readers read the informal statement first, even though you might write it last.) So, we need both ways of presenting an analysis: an informal approach for ease of initial understanding and communication to a wide audience and a formal one for precision.

The rest of this chapter gives some suggestions to help you with informal descriptive writing, especially constructing good paragraphs. Chapter 25 ("Guide to Writing a Grammar Sketch") deals with the larger-scale organization of a whole grammar sketch.

---

[1]Some courses may want to use this chapter as early as chapter 4 "Introduction to Morphology," which is where the sample descriptions start and where students can begin writing their own brief descriptions. However, I suggest waiting to read it until chapter 6 "The Base," partly to give students some experience with linguistic writing before they read about it and partly because the present chapter talks about elements of formal analysis that aren't introduced until chapter 6.

351

24.3. Communicate with your audience

In any writing that you do, it's important to keep clearly in mind who your audience is and how best to communicate to them. For example, if you are using this book as part of a course, assume that you are writing for fellow students who have covered all the material you have, but who are not familiar with the particular language that you are writing about.

Write so that most of these readers will understand without making them reread several times. Use common words that your readers will readily understand whenever possible. Obscure words may seem impressive, but readers are usually much more impressed by clear communication. Make it easy to understand; write to communicate, not to impress people with your education. On the other hand, don't make it so easy to understand that your average reader is bored or insulted. The important thing is to strike a balance that is appropriate for the people you want to communicate to.

Test your writing; step back and read it as if you were someone else. It's also useful to have others read and comment on your work while you still have a chance to revise it. Ask one or two of your fellow students to read a draft and give you comments about what they find clear or unclear, helpful or not.

24.4. Linguistic style

There are a few aspects of style which are relatively standard in linguistic writing, which are mentioned briefly here. I've also tried to model them in the sample descriptions throughout this book.

Avoid using terminology that is specific to a theoretical framework, such as Transformational Grammar or any other generative approach. Theory-specific terms like 'phrase structure rule', 'base', etc., are best reserved for a discussion of your analysis, not of the data the analysis is supposed to cover. Strive for objectivity; this is supposed to be a statement of the facts that anyone could agree with, regardless of whether they accept your formal analysis or the theory in which it is expressed.

Unlike creative writing, which may have been the focus of much of your prior instruction about how to write, technical writing strives for clear, objective, and conventional ways of saying things. So, avoid statements like "Perengano is a very expressive language," because there's no way to know what "expressive" means in terms of the details of language structure. Rather, say something like "The inventory of words expressing abstract qualities, especially adjectives and adverbs, is unusually large" or "Good narrative style employs frequent reference to the emotional state or attitude of the speaker by means of a set of sentence initial particles which have meanings like 'happily', 'unfortunately', and 'luckily'."

To take another example, consider the following, which appeared in a newspaper editorial defending the slang use of *like* in American English:

(1)   *Much more than the random misfire of a stunted mind, "like" is actually a rhetorical device that demonstrates the speaker's heightened sensibility and offers the listener added levels of color, nuance, and meaning.*

As entertaining as this wording is, it's not very useful to us as linguists—how could we ever know if it is true?

Unlike creative writing, technical writing uses parallel wording for parallel situations and the same word consistently if the same meaning is intended.

Strive for a balance between conciseness and clarity. Long, elaborate, or complicated sentences should be avoided, no matter how impressive they sound. On the other hand, if you make your writing too choppy, you will sacrifice readability. Similarly, don't be afraid to say something twice if you think your readers will need it, but also avoid going on for several sentences without introducing any significant new information.

A frequent mistake in an attempt to be concise is to introduce too many abbreviations: "The BCs require PNPs to be bound in their DPC." Write it out and take the drain off the reader's memory, except possibly for abbreviations that are widely understood (such as 'NP') or for a few select concepts which are so important in the discussion that the reader will have no trouble remembering what they stand for. Of course, any abbreviations that are not well known should be explained the first time they are used. The main exception to this would be abbreviations used as interlinear morpheme glosses; for these, it is best to provide a table of abbreviations, use standard abbreviations whenever possible, and be sure to include commentary in the text whenever understanding a particular abbreviation in a particular example is crucial to the argument.

Finally, a common mistake as people start writing about linguistics is to let their uncertainty about their analytic and writing skills bleed through into their writing. Don't be wishy-washy in your statements or apologize for what you don't know (or even call attention to it). Avoid statements like the following:

(2)   *Although I've only worked with this language a few months...*
      There are a lot of things that I don't understand yet...
      This is a topic for further research.

Self-conscious statements like these irritate readers; they want to learn what you know, not what you don't know. It may be appropriate to point out problem examples that don't fit your analysis, but don't dwell on the problem. Concentrate on what you *do* know and what your analysis *does* accomplish, and state it plainly, simply, and confidently.

24.5. Example data

All significant claims about the language should be backed up with data. People want to know why you say the things that you do about the language, and often readers need an illustration of your point before they can understand it.

In most linguistic papers, examples larger than a single phrase are set off from the rest of the text, are numbered sequentially, and are referred to by number.[2]

(3)   *Sino ang titser   para sa ikalawang grado*
      who is   teacher for   second   grade
      Who is the teacher for the second grade?

Always supply adequate glosses with the data, unless you are certain that all your readers are so familiar with the language that they won't need them. There are two types of glosses that are normally included for numbered examples like (3): a morpheme-by-morpheme (or word-by-word) gloss and a free (or semi-free) translation.

Short forms (such as individual phrases, words, or morphemes) are usually cited within the text, rather than being set off from it as in (3). They are highlighted in some way, either with underlining, boldface, or italics. (Whichever you choose, be consistent.) Their glosses are normally in single quotes immediately after the word: *ikalawang* 'second'.

24.6. What to include: Using the questions for analysis

A question frequently arises about what information should or should not be included in an informal description. In general, be guided by the questions for analysis in each chapter; include answers to those that are relevant, plus any background information (such as basic word order) which may be necessary to prepare the reader to understand the rest of what you have written.

Do not adhere mechanically to the questions, however. Some of the questions for analysis will be irrelevant for some languages, and there may be special features of some languages which are

---

[2]Data from Tagalog (Schachter and Otanes 1972:124).

relevant to the topic, but which are not mentioned in the questions. Organize the paragraph(s) in some logical fashion, but not necessarily the same order in which the questions are asked. Write in such a way that anyone reading your work would be able to answer the questions, based just on what you have written.

24.7. Learning how to write

Although linguistic writing may feel unfamiliar and awkward at first, you'll soon get the hang of it. Learning to write is very much like learning to speak a new language, so the very same things that help in learning a language will help you as you learn to write:

- Relax and have fun.
- Pay attention to how others express themselves and imitate them. (This is the purpose for the sample descriptions in this book.) Don't concern yourself with being creative; that comes later. Slavish imitation is just fine!
- Have your teachers and fellow students comment on your work, and try out their suggestions.
- As you get more comfortable, experiment with different ways of saying things, and pay attention to the reactions you get from others (and even from yourself the next day).

Do these things and writing about language for linguists will quickly become second nature.

24.8. For further reading

Strunk and White (1979) provides a readable and very concise set of suggestions for general writing. If you would like more specific guidance on details, there are several good style manuals for technical writing and publication; *The Chicago Manual of Style* (University of Chicago 1993) is one of the most complete. If you will be writing a thesis or dissertation, Turabian (1996) provides a customization of *The Chicago Manual of Style* as it applies to writing by graduate students; be sure also to check the requirements of your graduate school and department.

For matters specific to linguistics, see the style sheet of any major linguistic journal. The style sheet for *Language* is the most widely used; it is published each December in the *LSA* (Linguistic Society of America) *Bulletin*, which should be available at most university libraries and can also be downloaded from the LSA's web site at http://www.lsadc.org. The stylesheet by itself is also available from the following two URLs:

- http://semlab2.sbs.sunysb.edu/Language/langstyl.html
- http://www.tamu-commerce.edu/swjl/stylesheet.html

25
Guide to Writing a Grammar Sketch

25.1. Goals and prerequisites

This chapter will help you do the following:

- ◉ write a description of some aspect of the grammar of a language, incorporating both informal description and formal analysis
- ◉ organize several such descriptions into a grammatical sketch of a language

It assumes that you have mastered the following material:

- ✓ basic linguistic writing skills (chapter 24 "Hints for Linguistic Writing")

Also, some of the examples here assume familiarity with material from various other chapters, but it is not necessary to understand the details in the examples to understand what they are illustrating about writing.

25.2. What is a grammar sketch?

A grammar sketch is a brief description of the grammar of a language. A useful grammar sketch is accurate, clear, and moderately comprehensive, even though it may not go into any one topic in much depth. It includes informal descriptions of the facts of the language with examples. It may also present a precise formal analysis of these facts in some theoretical framework. It should be informative and enjoyable to read for anyone interested in learning about the language. This chapter describes how to write such a sketch.

25.3. Remember your audience

In all writing it is important to have a clear picture of your audience. I have suggested that you write for students like yourself, who know the basics of grammatical theory, language typology, and analysis, but know nothing at all about the language you are writing about. Your job is to give them a short, effective introduction to the language.

Or, pretend that you have been working with some language group and have the opportunity to attend a grammar workshop or a university seminar. While there, you are asked to give a written description of the language, based on the data you have gathered. This is to be read by the other participants, including someone who will be beginning work on a language closely related to the one you are studying. You have the opportunity to introduce them to the basic facts of the language.

If you can think of specific individuals who will be reading your work, all the better. Write so that they will understand and appreciate it. Don't worry about impressing them; concentrate rather on communicating clearly.

25.4. Making your organization explicit

In writing about linguistics, there usually are numerous details to present. The big challenge is to do so carefully and thoroughly, while still keeping the big picture clear. Remind your readers frequently of the main topic under consideration, make the logic of your argument explicit, and summarize at key points. Give them a road map through all the details; the more details and the longer the paper, the more important it is to provide the reader with an orientation to the terrain before you charge into it.

For example, look at the next section of this chapter. The first paragraph gives a concise introduction and summary to the whole section, including an explicit statement of what topics will be covered. This orients you, the reader, about what to expect overall in the section, before plunging into the details.

25.5. Writing a section of a sketch

A grammar sketch is made up of several sections, each focusing on a different aspect of the grammar. Each section generally includes the following three types of information, arranged approximately in this order:

- informal description summarizing the facts that must be accounted for, with illustrative data
- a description of a formal analysis, with rules, lexical entries, trees or bracketed sentences, derivations, and diagrams as needed to help your reader understand your analysis
- (optional) problem data and why it's a problem

Let's take a look at these three types in more detail.

The INFORMAL DESCRIPTION of the facts and the ILLUSTRATIVE DATA should normally come first. This is the type of information that appears in the sample descriptions of other chapters. Informal description should avoid formal notation that not all linguists are familiar or comfortable with (like 'QP', 'Comp', 'PCC') and jargon (like PREDICATE ARGUMENT STRUCTURE) that is unique to particular theories. Instead, use terminology (like TRANSITIVE, NOUN PHRASE, POSITION CLASS, and REDUPLICATION) that most or all linguists will understand.

As for what facts to mention about a particular topic, a good guide is to consult the questions for analysis in the other chapters. Rely on these heavily, but remember that you may find other significant facts unique to your language that might not be mentioned in those questions.

Choose examples that illustrate your points about the structure of the language. Include morpheme-by-morpheme glosses and free translations for all examples. Examples should be numbered sequentially. In your discussion, you can refer to examples by number when necessary.

When the facts are complex, intersperse data with description. State one or two facts, then give an example or two. Then state more facts and give more examples. Don't give a reader too much data in one block without explanation.

After presenting the facts, explain how the facts can be accounted for in a FORMAL ANALYSIS. Don't just list the rules, lexical entries, etc., but introduce the reader to them individually. For example, try phrases like these:

(1)   In order to handle the above data, we need an NP rule such as the following...
        All this can be summarized in the following rule...
        Verbs will need to be subcategorized for transitivity in the lexicon...

Again, this is part of providing the reader with an explicit roadmap through the details of your analysis.

For more examples of how to discuss an analysis, just look through the chapters in this book. In general, follow the style that I have used, unless you can improve on it. (You undoubtedly can at many points; I welcome your suggestions on how to improve the sample descriptions or any other part of this book.) There is one major difference: you will be writing for people who already understand the content of this book, so you can often write more concisely than I have, with less explanation.

Finally, a section may occasionally include OTHER COMMENTS. For example, there might be a discussion of data that doesn't clearly fit your analysis. Keep such comments short in comparison to the rest of the section, and concentrate on what a reader needs to know about any inadequacies of your analysis. This is not the place for true confessions; your reader is interested in what you know, not what you don't know. You might also want to refer the reader to other sections that deal with related topics or other relevant published works.

25.6. Organizing a larger sketch about several topics in the same language

Here's one way you might go about organizing several sections, like those described above, into a larger grammar sketch.

A grammar sketch normally begins with a short introduction. It is usually sufficient just to present background information about the language, such as the language family it belongs to, the area where it is spoken, the number of speakers, the type of local society (agricultural, urban, or whatever). It's usually important to indicate the source of your data (your language consultant's name, approximate age, the place where he/she is from, and any other information that might help specify the dialect that you are describing). It is also often helpful to include a brief overview of the rest of the work, describing what each of the rest of the sections covers, even if this is obvious from their titles.

After this comes a series of sections, one for each topic, as described above. Keep these organized in some logical fashion. A table of contents at the beginning of a large sketch is a terrific help to your reader.

At the end, it may be useful to include an appendix which provides all the rules that you have proposed in various places of the sketch, sample lexical entries, etc. For each rule, include a cross-reference to one of the main sections telling the reader where he/she can find more information.

Of course, this is just one way to write a grammar sketch. I provide this to help you get started in writing, not to provide a recipe that must be followed with every language. As you think about your audience and what you have to tell them, as you gain experience in writing, and as you read other people's work, you will develop your own sense of what things to include and how to arrange them.

25.7. Citing other works

As you start writing larger sections, you may have occasion to refer to other published works. In linguistics, the most common way to do this is to include all bibliographic information in a reference list at the end of the paper. Then, when you cite the work in the paper, you do so by including the author's last name and year of publication in the main body of the text (not a footnote).

Exactly how you do this depends on how the sentence is worded. If you only cite the work without actually talking about it, then the author and year go inside parentheses.

(2)   Two previous studies (Gibson and Raposo 1986, Rosen 1989) claim that...

If you talk about the author, only the year goes in parentheses.

(3)   Gibson and Raposo (1986) and Rosen (1989) claim that…

If you talk about the work itself, then neither are in parentheses.

(4)   In Gibson and Raposo 1986 and Rosen 1989, one can read many claims that…

In all these cases, you can add specific page numbers after the year; this is generally a very considerate thing to do for harried readers and is normally considered essential for direct quotes.

(5)   Two previous studies (Gibson and Raposo 1986:27, Rosen 1989:294–295) claim that…
       Gibson and Raposo (1986:27) claim that…
       In Gibson and Raposo 1986 (p. 27), one can read many claims that…

Notice, too, that present tense is used when summarizing the content of other works. Though written in the past, they still exist in the present, and their content is regarded as being timeless.

25.8. Preparing manuscripts for others

When preparing a paper for use by others, be courteous and give them a manuscript that is easy to read (use pen or type). Write on only one side of the paper. If they will be reviewing or commenting on your work, leave adequate white space for their comments: use wide margins (minimum one inch) and double-space between lines.

If you are preparing final copy for archiving (long-term storage on microfilm or paper, such as a university thesis), there are extra things to pay attention to. Type generally must be at least 10 points and well-formed in order to microfilm well. Laser printers work best; but 24-pin dot matrix printers or inkjet printers are sometimes acceptable. (Dot matrix printer ink tends to bleed into the paper in just a few years and some inkjet ink smears when it gets wet, so archive a photocopy instead of the original.) Paper should be acid-free, such as 100% rag paper; otherwise it discolors and becomes brittle after a few decades.

When preparing a manuscript for publication, your publisher will generally have a set of specifications that you should follow.

25.9. Sample grammar sketches

Here are a couple of examples of grammar sketch sections.

Palauan Simple Active Declarative Clauses

Palauan exhibits two common word orders: SVO and VOS. SVO is more common in main clauses, but VOS also occurs.[1]

(1)   a. *A resechelim   a mla   mei.*
               your.friends   Perf come
       b. *Te   mla   me   a resechelim.*
               3pl Perf come   your.friends

           Your friends have come.

---

[1]Data from the two references cited at the end of the section. As is common in descriptive work, transcription here follows the practical orthography, which writes both /e/ and /ə/ with 'e'. Elsewhere in this book, I have distinguished these two phonemes in Palauan.

(2)   a. *A Droteo a milengelebed er a rebuik.*
           Droteo   was.hitting   boys
       b. *Ng milengelebed er a rebuik a Droteo.*
           3sg was.hitting   boys   Droteo

       Droteo was hitting the boys.

When a verb takes two objects, a recipient and a theme, the two may often occur in either order. However, when the recipient is plural it is awkward to have it after the theme. Note that the verb shows object agreement with the recipient, not the theme, in all cases.

(3)   a. *Ak milsa   a Helen a omiange.*
           1sg give/Past/3sgO   Helen   souvenir
       b. *Ak milsa   a omiange a Helen.*
           1sg give/Past/3sgO   souvenir   Helen

       I gave Helen a souvenir.

(4)   a. *Ak milsterir   a resechelik a hong.*
           1sg give/Past/3plO   my.friends   book
       b. *?Ak milsterir   a hong a resechelik.*
           1sg give/Past/3plO   book   my.friends

       I gave my friends a book.

(This description leaves open the question of which object, the recipient or theme, is the direct object, in sentences like (3) and (4).)
    Obliques occur after the object. They may occur on either side of a postverbal subject, the preferred order is subject before obliques.

(5)   a. *A rechad a killii   a ngikel er a kesus.*
           people   eat/Past   fish   on   last.night
       b. *Te killii   a ngikel a rechad er a kesus.*
           3pl eat/Past   fish   people on   last.night
       c. *Te killii   a ngikel er a kesus   a rechad.*
           3pl eat/Past   fish   on   last.night   people

       The people ate the fish last night.

    Josephs (1975) regards SVO order as basic and derives the VOS order from it by a transformation he calls SUBJECT SHIFTING. Waters (1979), on the other hand, provides a number of arguments that VOS is basic and that the apparent SVO order is the result of Topicalization (which can also front other constituents). Following Waters' hypothesis, then, we can posit the following rules:

(6)   S → VP NP[Su]

(7)   VP → V (NP[IO]) (NP[DO]) (PP)*

(8)   **Topicalization** (optional)
       Move NP or PP to the left of VP.

(9)   **Object Shift** (optional)
       Move NP[DO] to the left of NP[IO].

Although this analysis covers the basic facts, there are two details visible above that are not yet accounted for. (1) The direct object is apparently a PP (with the preposition *er*), not an NP, under some circumstances; the phrase structure rule for VP might need to be revised when a satisfactory analysis of this alternation is found. (2) When the subject is postverbal, it triggers subject agreement on the verb (realized with a prefix that is written separately in the practical orthography), but when it is preverbal, agreement is replaced by the word *a*, which may be the same as the invariant determiner that appears in most noun phrases.

References

Josephs, Lewis S. 1975. Palauan reference grammar. Honolulu: The University Press of Hawaii.
Waters, Richard C. 1979. Topicalization and passive in Palauan. ms.

English noun phrases

The phrase structure of English noun phrases is relatively complex. Articles, demonstratives, possessors, quantifiers, and adjectives precede the head noun, while prepositional phrases and relative clauses follow the head.

(1)   a. *the three old men [who stormed London Bridge]*
       b. *those idiots on the ladder*
       c. *the master's three sons*
       d. *my sticky molasses*
       e. *computers*
       f. *John*

Articles, demonstratives, and possessors do not co-occur, at least, not in modern speech.

(2)   a. **This your dog*
       b. **His this salamander*
       c. **That the book*
       d. **A my career*

This can be represented in the grammar by grouping demonstratives and articles in a category called D (determiner) and including D in the phrase structure rule for NP in opposition to a possessor NP and preceding the other constituents.

(3)
$$NP \rightarrow \left(\left\{ \begin{array}{l} NP[Poss] \\ D \end{array} \right\} \right) (QP)\,(AP)\,N\,(PP)\,(S')$$

Nouns differ in their ability to co-occur with various combinations of modifiers. Common singular count nouns normally require an article or quantifier, while proper, plural, and mass nouns do not.

(4)   a. *??Cat sees me.*
       b. *The cat sees me.*
       c. *One cat sees me.*

(5)   a. *John sees me.*
       b. *Cats see well.*
       c. *I see cabbage.*

A partial analysis of these distinctions can be made by using features like [±common] and [±count] to subcategorize nouns in the lexicon (following Chomsky 1965:107). In addition, rules (not worked out here) are needed which would account for the co-occurrence restrictions noted above.

A noun phrase can also consist of a demonstrative or pronoun by itself.

(6)   a. ***That*** *is hard to understand.*
        b. ***He*** *is cool!*

Pronouns can be handled by assigning them to the category NP in the lexicon, since they are mutually-substitutable for whole NPs, not individual nouns. Demonstratives can also be listed as NPs, in addition to their membership in the category D.

26
Grammar Filing

26.1. Goals and prerequisites

This chapter will help you do the following:

- ◎ extract relevant data from field notes into an organized grammar filing system
- ◎ use that system to develop an analysis
- ◎ keep your filing system organized and easy to read so you can find information later
- ◎ keep data distinct from analysis in your files
- ◎ file enough data to be useful, but not so much as to get in the way of analysis
- ◎ use your files to determine what additional data would be useful

There are no specific prerequisite readings, but I recommend that you not try filing until you have a large enough analytical problem, sufficiently disorganized and with enough diversity, to experience the benefits of a good filing system. Typically, this means waiting at least until after the first 10–15 chapters.[1] Some of the discussion makes reference to material in later chapters, but only briefly.

26.2. Filing

Analyzing a language is a large task. In order to complete it, you must have some way to focus your attention on one small part of the grammar at a time, ignoring all the other parts that are competing for your attention. This chapter discusses a filing system which will help you do that for your grammatical analysis, and chapter 27 "Lexical Filing" will help you do the same for the lexicon. Used properly, these systems do three things that any good linguistic filing system should do:

- store data and analysis in a way that allows you to find them again easily
- help you make progress in your analysis of the language
- serve as a basis for discussions with other people (colleagues and consultants)

---

[1]A filing and analysis exercise after completing chapter 14 "Nonactive Complements" makes for a good review about midway through the course.

Filing systems can be built around a variety of materials. Manual systems use file slips or ordinary pages. Computerized systems may either depend on specialized database programs, or they can simply imitate a manual system, using a word processor in place of a sheet of paper. Computer systems are fast, compact, and make it easy to revise, copy, rearrange, and find information. On the other hand, manual systems are more durable, can be used anywhere, and don't require the overhead (in equipment, software, special character support, and training) that is usually associated with a computer. Each medium has its own advantages, and you have to choose which one is most appropriate for your work situation.

Here, I describe a system that can be adapted for use either on paper or on a computer with a word processor. It is relatively easy to learn, flexible, requires a minimum of equipment, and illustrates the important principles of a good filing system.

Each section of this filing system consists of either a set of pages or a computer file focused on a single topic.[2] For instance, there may be separate sections on active clauses, different types of nonactive complements, possession, and different verbal affixes. Each of these sections can be called a GRAMMAR FILE.

If on paper, the files should be kept together, arranged in some logical fashion, and stored in a file folder or loose-leaf binder. If on a computer, keep the files together in one directory or folder, with names that make it clear what the contents are. (For more information on storage and protection, see chapter 27 "Lexical Filing.")

In each file, there are two types of information, DATA and ANALYSIS. By DATA, I mean all of the facts you need to account for, which may be isolated words, sentences, strings you know to be ungrammatical, or whole stories and other texts. Analysis may include charts, observations, guesses and formal hypotheses, ideas about further data to collect, and notes about what you don't understand. It is important to keep data and analysis distinct in your mind. Examples collected from native speakers are permanent, and you shouldn't change them once they are collected, unless you have clear indications from a native speaker that there is a mistake. The analysis, however, is your creation as you work with the data and may change frequently.

It helps to use visual aids and work habits to maintain this distinction. For example, data should be copied into a paper file in permanent pen. Copy it exactly, with no more editing except writing it more neatly than you may have when you first transcribed it. Analysis, however, may change frequently, so when you are making marks on top of the data, you should use pencil and avoid obscuring the data itself. Analysis that is written apart from the data should probably be in pen, for permanence. Even when you are quite certain that the analysis is correct, you should keep it visibly separate from the data, because you may still find out later that it needs revision. Keeping the two separate on paper will help you keep them distinct in your mind.

On a computer, you can use a different font or color to help distinguish the two types of information or put them in separate places. The ease with which you can change things on the computer can actually be a disadvantage here—you'll have to discipline yourself to leave data alone once it is copied into the file correctly.

26.3. How to make a file on a specific topic

Here's one way to go about creating a grammar file. These are suggestions, not hard-and-fast rules.

A. Decide what you are trying to learn with this file. What is its purpose? Put a brief title at the top, such as 'Simple active declarative clauses' or 'Noun phrases'. Think through the questions that you want to answer. (Refer to the questions for analysis in other chapters.)

---

[2]Some users may prefer to keep all the information together in one file which is subdivided into sections, each of which corresponds to what this chapter calls a "file".

B. Look through the data for examples that will help you meet your goal for this file. Copy them into the file. (On paper, use permanent ink.) Include a reference to your data source (e.g., a page number in your data notebook or a sentence number if they are provided for you). Be sure to include glosses with each example, exactly as they are given in the data source. Highlight the part of the sentence which is of interest, e.g., with brackets or a highlighting marker. (It is important to have the whole example, not just the part of interest, because the context may influence the internal structure of the item.) For example, if you were analyzing obliques in Choapan Zapotec, you might copy the following example into your file from page 23 of your data notebook (Alternately, you could cross-reference directly to the tape where the example is recorded; anything so that you can easily trace all data in your files back to its source.)

23.   *na?ra   ujo   ʒua   [tʃoapan   ] [nioge.   ]*
       well   went John   Choapan   yesterday.
       Well, John went to Choapan yesterday.

On paper, leave plenty of space between examples (2–3 lines) so you have room to write in comments later. On a computer, it is easier to align the interlinear data if you use a fixed-width (typewriter-style) font.

C. After you have found a few examples (usually 2–4), make some initial observations, and construct a first hypothesis using a formal rule. Make morpheme cuts as needed; on paper, use pencil, on a computer, use hyphens. Add other notes such as glosses and informal observations. It may be helpful to make a chart which rearranges or summarizes the data. Do whatever analytical activity moves you towards your goals; the important thing is doing it early. You may know that the analysis is inadequate, but getting something down on paper or in the file helps you focus your mind on how to improve it.

D. Don't worry if there are some facts that you can't account for. This will always be true. Just do the best you can in the rules, make a note of the facts that the rules don't account for, and go on to something else. Often, after you understand other parts of the grammar, you will come back to these examples, and their structure will be crystal clear.

E. Continue looking for data. If you find examples not covered by your hypothesis, copy them into the file and revise the hypothesis accordingly. If you find useful examples that don't change your hypothesis, either copy them into the file (if they are especially good) or simply include a page or sentence number so you can find them again easily.

F. In a manual system, as you gather more data, you will need more paper. Number each page in the file in order; start with page 1 at the beginning of each file, so that you can rearrange your different files and insert new ones easily. Write the file's name alongside the page number on each new sheet, in case pages in a file get separated by accident. Many people find it useful to write on only one side of the paper; this way, you can spread out the whole file on a table and see all the data at once.

G. Continue looking for data until you have found all the examples that relate to this file. Make a note in the file of how far you have searched through your source of data and when you did it. Then move on to another topic and another file.

H. Don't let yourself get hung up on one topic. If you are stumped, just jot down the problem, make a note of how much of the data you have searched through, and go on to some other topic. You may want to get help on this topic before attempting to pursue it further.

I. You may find it helpful to periodically summarize the data and analysis in each file. In a few brief sentences or notes, list what you have learned so far and (more importantly) what you want to look for next. Then, when you come back to this file later, you have a quick summary to remind you of all the important aspects of your analysis.

26.4. What data should you copy into each file?

To help decide what data should be included in each file, keep your goals clearly in mind. Look back at the questions for analysis in previous chapters; these will give you an idea of what to look for. Think, too, of what type of information you need to write formal rules; let your theoretical framework guide you.

You will want to be selective. Concentrate on getting *useful* examples rather than many of them. Having too many randomly-collected examples leads to a disorganized mess that is difficult to sort through when constructing an analysis. Be purposeful in the data you select. Quality is much more important than quantity; each example should ideally provide some new piece of information to move your analysis forward.

Two types of data are especially useful.

- Pairs or sets of examples that are virtually identical, but which differ in only one small detail. For example, examples that mean 'Tomorrow I will go to my sister's house,' and 'Yesterday I went to my sister's house' could provide helpful information about tense marking on the verb.
- Sets of examples that show the full range of variation possible for a particular construction. For example, if you're trying to write phrase structure rules for clauses, you'd want examples of intransitive, transitive, and ditransitive clauses, both with and without various combinations of obliques.

In most files that focus on the internal structure of some constituent, the primary goal is a phrase structure rule. Recall what types of subconstituents typically occur in constituents of this type, and look specifically for them. For example, in an analysis of noun phrases, look for ways of expressing definiteness, quantity, quality, etc. Look for maximal or near-maximal expansions (to find the relative order of elements) and minimal expansions (to find out which elements are optional).

For files that focus on closed classes, such as prepositions or tense affixes, try to compile a complete list of such elements. That is, you want at least one example of each different preposition (but not every example of every preposition that occurs in your data).

26.5. Organizing your filing system

Keep your files in some organized sequence, so you can find them easily. For example, you might adopt an overall organization similar to the following:

1. Sentence structure
   a. Commands
   b. Yes-no questions
   c. Content questions
   d. Focus
   e. Topicalization
2. Clause structure (in statements)
   a. Basic (active) clauses (subject, objects, obliques)
   b. Nonactive complements
      1. nominal complements
      2. adjectival complements
      3. locative complements
      4. existential clauses
   c. Variable orders of clausal constituents (other than what is covered under sentence structure)
   d. Relative clauses
   e. Complement clauses
   f. Oblique clauses

3. Phrase structure
   a. Noun phrases
   b. Verb phrases (if not handled under clause structure)
   c. Adjective phrases
   d. Quantifier phrases
   e. Adverb phrases
   f. Prepositional or postpositional phrases
4. Word-level categories and subcategories
   a. Verbs
   b. Noun
   c. Adjectives
   d. Numerals
   e. Other quantifiers
   f. Determiners
   g. Pronouns
   h. Prepositions or postpositions
   i. Adverbs
   j. Unmodifiable single-word obliques
   k. Interrogative (WH) words
   l. Conjunctions
   m. Others, especially closed classes, i.e., particles
5. Clitics (one file for each suspected clitic or each class of similar clitics, including reasons for considering it an ordinary word, bound word, phrasal affix, or ordinary affix)
6. Inflectional morphology (one file for each category of word or each position class, including paradigms, position class charts, complete lists of affixes and their glosses, formal analysis, etc.)
7. Derivational morphology (one file for each derivational affix or set of related affixes)

Alternately, you can use the table of contents from a published grammar in a related language. Whatever model you follow, don't follow it slavishly; adapt it to the structure of the language, your analysis, and your own personal needs. As you work, add new files and rearrange them as your understanding of the language grows. At any one time, though, you should keep things in some logical sequence. It helps to make a 'table of contents' similar to the list above for your filing system and to keep things arranged in that order.

On a computer, it can be helpful to include numbers or letters at the beginning of the file name so the files will be displayed in order. If necessary, use leading zeros so all the numbers have the same number of digits. So, for example, the above outline might be packaged into computer files with names like the following:

(1)   01a commands
        01b yes-no questions
        01c content questions
        01d focus
        01e topicalization
        02a active clauses
        02b1 nominal complements
        02b2 adjectival complements
        (etc.)

(On some operating systems, you'll have to abbreviate the file names to 8 characters and omit spaces.)

In a manual system, by all means, *keep all the pages of the same file together and in order!* (I wish I didn't have to mention that; my apologies to those who wouldn't dream of doing otherwise.)

26.6. Making the system work for you (and not vice versa)

There are two opposite but equally dangerous traps that people fall into with regards to filing. The usual mistake is to file too little and do most of the analysis on the original copy of the data. This places a tremendous burden on your memory, as you try to remember where all the relevant facts are for a particular topic, what hypotheses you have considered so far, etc. This leads to inefficiency at best and incomplete or incorrect understanding of the language at worst. Do enough filing to move your analysis along towards your goals.

The other trap is to file aimlessly and tediously, without a clear idea of what you are trying to do. You must keep your goals clearly in mind and stay aware of whether you are making any concrete progress towards achieving them. Don't just pile up mountains of data. Often, people do this out of confusion and anxiety; they keep themselves busy for hours, but don't make any progress. If you tend towards doing this, make a point of stepping away from your work every hour, quieting your mind, and putting things back in perspective. Establish habits now that will serve you well both at home and on the field.

26.7. Characteristics of a good grammar filing system

Good grammar files have the following characteristics:

- They help you make progress in your analysis.
- They are neat enough that you and your close colleagues (e.g., teachers) can read them without being distracted by their appearance.
- They have adequate organization:
    They are arranged in some logical order, so you can find information quickly.
    They are divided into small enough sections so that each section provides a focused and
        thorough treatment of just one topic.
    They are easy to expand and modify.
- They treat data with respect:
    Data and analysis are clearly separated.
    Each example can be traced back to its source (where it was first transcribed or recorded).
- The analysis includes informal observations, such as:
    brief descriptions of the data
    hypotheses about rules
    plans to obtain further data
    predictions made by your rules
    problems that you haven't covered
- The analysis includes elements of a formal analysis to make your hypotheses precise, plus explanations (when appropriate) about how this analysis works and why it is better than others:
    rules
    lexical entries
    trees
    etc.

26.8. For further reading

Healey (1975:427–51) and Samarin (1967:151–74) include information about various types of manual filing systems. Although such systems are gradually being replaced by computers, much of this information is still useful as it relates to principles applicable to any filing system. Further, some tasks (especially relatively small ones) will always be better suited to manual filing techniques than computerized ones, since there is usually considerable overhead involved in setting up a computerized filing system.

Although people have been using computers to file grammatical data for many years, systems that allow one to do so without much technical knowledge are fairly recent. In the Macintosh world, the program called HyperCard has proven itself quite useful, as Valentine (1990) demonstrates. For MS-DOS, Davis and Wimbish (1993) describe the Shoebox computer program and a grammar file outline that is packaged with it, which provides capabilities for grammar and lexical filing and interlinear text glossing. Shoebox is also available in a Windows/Macintosh version from the Summer Institute of Linguistics (http://www.sil.org on the Internet). For Windows (and eventually Macintosh), SIL has developed a software system called LinguaLinks which includes some grammar filing capabilities as well as lexical filing, interlinear text glossing, structured editors for producing grammar sketches, and ready access to a wealth of reference material.

Payne (1997) provides a great deal of helpful advice for preparing a grammar sketch, including information that would be useful in setting up a grammar filing system: an outline of topics to cover, questions to consider about each, and many examples from different languages illustrating the possible answers to those questions. For a much more detailed outline of the grammar of a language, see the Lingua Descripta questionnaire (Comrie and Smith 1977), which also provides a wealth of questions to consider, much like the questions for analysis in this book. Be warned, however, that it is very detailed (72 pages!), so you probably want to save it for use on the field, and even then be selective in your use of it.

27
Lexical Filing

27.1. Goals and prerequisites

This chapter will help you do the following:

- ◎ collect and file information about the vocabulary of a language
- ◎ alphabetize the information so you can find it quickly
- ◎ store your lexical and grammar files so that your data is safe

It assumes that you are familiar with the following material:

- ✓ the structure of the lexicon (chapter 6 "The Base")
- ✓ the basic concepts of filing (chapter 26 "Grammar Filing")

There are also a few references to other chapters, but nothing crucial.[1]

27.2. Lexicology

LEXICOLOGY (the study of the lexicon) is a basic part of any thorough description of a language. During the early part of a field linguistic program, your lexical file can serve as an organized system for keeping track of all the little bits of information that need to be known about each word in the language, particularly the information that you are not likely to remember well. As the program matures, the lexical file can be expanded and published as a dictionary, which is traditionally regarded as an essential part of a full description of a language, along with a grammar and a body of texts.

A lexical file is not the same thing as a lexicon. A LEXICON, as we have used the term, is a theoretical concept, referring either to a person's knowledge about the vocabulary of a language or to a formal analysis in some theoretical model of that knowledge (as described in chapter 6 "The Base," p. 50). A LEXICAL FILE, on the other hand, is an organized collection of information about the lexicon, which may be quite independent of a particular theoretical framework.

Lexical files traditionally have been kept on small slips of paper, like a card catalog at a library. Since computers are widely available, most lexical filing is computerized today. Computerized

---

[1] I wish to express my appreciation to Doris Bartholomew for many helpful comments on this chapter.

databases are more compact, easier to keep neat and organized, and faster than manual systems. Yet, the basic information that must be included is the same, regardless of the medium employed.

27.3. What information to include

The basic information to be included in a lexical file is discussed here. Of course, all of it will not be available when you first encounter a word. Include what you know at the time, then as you learn more, add to your file.

At a minimum, include entries for stems in all syntactic categories. Some people include entries for derivational affixes or even inflectional affixes (although these may better be handled in the grammar files). Names of people are usually omitted and there may be only limited coverage of animals and plants. Idiomatic phrases should also be included, usually listed under some key word that forms part of the idiom.

At a minimum each entry in the file contains basic information about the phonology, semantics, morphology, and syntax of an item and may include much more. Serious lexicographers sometimes collect dozens of bits of information about each word, but the basics consist of the following:

- transcription(s) of the word (phonology)
- definition and gloss (semantics)
- grammatical information (morphology and syntax)
- illustrative examples

Transcription(s) of the word (phonology)

Although you may start with a phonetic spelling, you should probably start omitting predictable phonetic detail as soon as possible (e.g., by using a practical orthography). It may be worthwhile to leave room for several different types of transcription; in particular, you may want to include an abstract (underlying) representation of the stem, when your phonological analysis progresses to the point that you can do so, or a transcription using standard phonetic symbols.

At first it may be hard to hear well enough to have a consistent transcription of the same item. One way to cope with this problem is to list all transcriptions, with references to where each is found in your data. When you decide later which is the best transcription, you can cross out the others.

For verbs, nouns, and other classes of words that may have a variety of inflected forms, there is always the question of which form to use in the entry. The stem form of the word should, of course, be included in the entry for your own reference. If the file will eventually be published as a dictionary for use by nonlinguists, it is often better to pick an inflected form that actually occurs in speech, rather than a linguist's abstraction like a stem, since native speakers may not recognize the stem without any affixes. Such a form is called a CITATION FORM. Exactly which form to use as a citation form requires some experimentation to see which form makes the most sense to native speakers. It may be

- a form that has a minimum amount of affixed material, for example, the third person singular form of verbs or the form used in singular commands
- a form with an abstract meaning, such as a nonfinite or irrealis form of verbs
- a generic form, such as the first person plural inclusive (at least for actions performed by humans)

When a word has some irregularly inflected forms (see chapter 12 "Suppletion and Morphophonemics"), you should list the irregular forms as part of the entry for that word. If the word is wildly irregular (like *go/went* in English), you may want to make a separate, secondary entry for each irregular form, with a cross-reference back to the main entry under the citation form.

Definition and gloss (semantics)

Include a definition of the word, either a translation or description of its meaning. If a word has more than one sense, identify them all. Be sure to distinguish multiple senses from homophones (distinct words that sound alike); each homophone should be listed in a *separate* entry. Generally you need both a full definition (which can sometimes be quite long) and a gloss (a short-hand way of referring to the meaning, e.g., for use in interlinear glossed text). In countries whose national language is not the same as your native language, you may want to include glosses and definitions both in the national language and your own. If neither of these languages is English, you may want to include a definition in English too, since including it will make your work available to a much broader range of linguists.

If your language consultants are bilingual, ask them to give you a gloss or definition for the word. Their intuitive perceptions of its meaning are some of the most important evidence you have about the meaning.

Be as precise and specific as you can. For example, be sure to state whether an item glossed as 'fish' is a generic term or indicates a particular variety of fish.[2]

Meanings can sometimes be difficult to pin down. It is especially important to include enough useful examples (see below) to illustrate each sense well.

Some lexical files also include information about a word's semantic class, synonyms, antonyms, etc.

Grammatical information (morphology and syntax)

Include both the syntactic category (N, V, A, etc.) of an item and the subcategories it belongs in (e.g., according to transitivity, gender, or inflectional class). Transitivity of verbs need not be spelled out with a SUBCAT list, but can be abbreviated (e.g., 'V [DO]' or just 'vt' for a transitive verb).

If you include affixes and clitics in the file, include other relevant grammatical information, such as:

- category of word it is attached to or is a part of
- its position class, if relevant
- any co-occurrence restrictions with other affixes
- whether it is a clitic and why you think so

Illustrative examples

Give examples in a sentence context, with word or morpheme glosses and a free translation. If possible, get a translation of the sentence from a native speaker. Though such translations may not be fully accurate (if they are not trained as translators), they still can contain many helpful clues as to the meaning of a word. If you feel you need to edit the translation in some way, distinguish your editing from the native speaker's original, which is really part of the data.

Bracket, underline, or otherwise highlight the word you are illustrating. Include references to a data source where the examples were obtained (unless they were transcribed directly into the file, in which case you should include the date and an indication of who gave you the example).

Examples are especially important to establish the meaning of a word. Try to get examples that vividly illustrate its meaning and use. Compare the following two attempts to illustrate the use of *metate* (a small stone table used for grinding corn in Mesoamerica); the second illustrates the meaning better.

---

[2]The question sometimes arises whether to include the Latin name for a species or genus as used by biologists. This gives a great deal of precision, but it is difficult for nonspecialists to identify plants and animals accurately. So, unless you have an expert who can do the identification for you, just include a description of the organism together with name(s) that it is called in the national language, leaving more precise identification up to others.

(1)   a. *There is a metate in the corner.*
       b. *We grind corn by crushing it with a mano on a metate made of granite.*

A body of texts with morphemes identified can be helpful as a source of examples. The texts can be searched to find instances of a word in a natural context, making it easier to identify its range of meaning and usage. However, isolated sentences taken from texts often do not provide enough information out of context to illustrate important aspects of the word's meaning or usage, so it may be necessary to work with a native speaker to develop illustrative sentences especially for the lexical file.

Other types of information

What is mentioned here is hardly a complete list. Some of the other types of information you may want to include are:

- Is the item derived from some other word? Unless this is obvious, give a cross-reference to the word that it is derived from.
- Is there important information on the item elsewhere, such as in a published source or your grammar files? Include a cross-reference to it.
- Is the item borrowed? If so, from what word in what language? Is the meaning or form different from the source word?
- Is the item only used/known by a particular subdialect (old people, men, a specific family or town)?
- Is it limited to certain social circumstances? Is it obscene, taboo, or otherwise inappropriate in certain social circumstances?

27.4. Sample entries in a lexical file

Here are examples of how you might arrange the above information on file slips or cards, with different types of information in different locations on the card.

tʃʰou	V trans.	1. see
	Class B	2. perceive

hu tʃʰou-na pa; kotu-na   (Hasim, 3/9/94)
I   see-past not dark-past
I (could) not see; (it was) dark.

pəkʰul	N	frog (large variety with
	anim.	black spots)

əni pəkʰul gələmp-na   (Abad, 4/10/93)
that frog   croak-past
That frog croaked

Here is how the same information might look if arranged in one type of computer database. The codes at the beginning of the line identify the type of information on that line.[3]

```
\lx   tʃʰou
\ps   V
\sc   trans., Class B
\sn   1
\ge   see
\rf   Hasim, 3/9/94
\xv   hu  [tʃʰou]-na  pa;   kotu-na
\me   I   see-past    not   dark-past
\xe   I (could) not see; (it was) dark.
\sn   2
\ge   perceive

\lx   pəkʰul
\ps   N
\sc   anim.
\ge   frog (large variety with black spots)
\rf   Abad, 4/10/93
\xv   əni  [pəkʰul]  gələmp-na
\me   that frog      croak-past
\xe   That frog croaked.
```

When data is entered on a computer, it is very important to make explicit what type of information each part of the entry represents, such as is done here with TAGS like '\lx'. (Different computer programs have different ways of tagging data, however, so things will probably look different in whatever system you use.) When a database is properly tagged, it allows the computer to reorganize the data for you in various ways, such as sorting all entries by the gloss or extracting a list of all example sentences from a particular person. It can be printed out to look like an ordinary dictionary, in a variety of different formats, without retyping or hand-editing.

> **tʃʰou** vt. 1. see *Hu tʃʰouna pa; kotuna.* I could not see; it was dark. 2. perceive

However, if data is typed initially in a word processor to look just like a printed dictionary, it is very difficult to sort, select, and transform it. All that you can do is print it out in one form. So, if you keep your dictionary on a computer, I strongly recommend that you do so as a database, not as a word-processing file.[4]

I don't recommend starting a lexical file on computer until after you have an analysis of surface phonological (phonemic) contrast and some system for representing the contrasts on the computer. Otherwise, handling all the special characters required for phonetic transcription becomes very

---

[3]This is an ASCII database appropriate for use with Shoebox (see Davis and Wimbish 1993), which uses markers based on those proposed by Coward and Grimes 1995. The abbreviations used in the field markers are: \lx lexeme (word in the vernacular), \ps 'part of speech' (syntactic category), \sc subcategory, \sn sense number, \ge gloss in English, \rf reference to source of example, \xv example in the vernacular, \me English morpheme glosses of the example, \xe English free translation of example.

[4]The importance of tagging also applies to grammar filing systems, particularly for the examples themselves (with separate fields for text, gloss, and translation) and other information that can be structured tightly into a database format. However, much information in grammar files, especially files of the sort described in chapter 26 "Grammar Filing," is not so easily classified into a small number of specific types of information, and this is why I have suggested using a word processor (p. 364) as one reasonable way to do grammar filing on the computer (at least, until specialized software for this purpose is developed). Even in a word processor, however, some system of tagging at least some of the information in the file can be very useful. Two ways to do this are to type standard format markers directly into the file as labels for various types of information and to make careful use of styles (in word processors that support them). However you do it, the most important thing is to use such tags consistently, so that you can rely on them later when using the computer to manipulate en masse the information that has been typed.

cumbersome, especially if (as is usually the case) there are a lot of mistranscriptions in early data that later need to be corrected. Similar considerations apply if you want to use a non-Roman orthography; make the basic decisions about the orthography and how it is to be represented in the computer before attempting to keyboard your data.[5] You may want to keep a small manual file on cards until you are ready to begin filing on the computer.

27.5. Alphabetizing

For large masses of data, you need some way of finding an entry quickly. The normal way to do this is to keep all entries in alphabetical order. This means you need an alphabetical order for the language being filed, which should be planned out carefully. (Computerized filing systems often alphabetize entries automatically, but you still have to tell them what the alphabetical order is.) You may be able to adapt the alphabetical order for a related language or the national language. If not, you will have to devise your own. Here are things that must be considered when designing alphabets.

You may need to find a place for symbols not in the English alphabet, especially if you are alphabetizing a technical orthography. New symbols are usually alphabetized just after a similar symbol in the English alphabet. Glottal stop (ʔ) often goes at the end; but some people prefer it just after *h*.

(2)   *a b d e ə ... m n ŋ o ... w y z ʔ*

There may also be digraphs in the orthography, two letters that represent one segment. Digraphs are sometimes alphabetized as if they are a separate letter. For example, Spanish traditionally alphabetizes 'ch' (which represents [tʃ] in the practical orthography) between 'c' and 'd', *not* between 'ce' and 'ci'. In contrast, some Spanish-speaking countries are now alphabetizing 'ch' as two letters.

(3)   Traditional   Innovative

c	*asa*		*c*	*a*	*sa*
c	*osa*		*c*	*h*	*amaco*
ch	*amaco*		*c*	*h*	*ispe*
ch	*ispe*		*c*	*o*	*sa*
d	*ar*		*d*	*a*	*r*

Diacritics on vowels are usually ignored except when they are the only difference between two entries, in which case they too must have some standard order (e.g., unmarked vowels before those with an acute accent).

(4)

When base letters are identical, diacritic determines the order

cóccix } Diacritic is ignored; base letters
como } are used to determine the order
cómo
contar } Diacritic is ignored

Vowel length may be treated the same way as a diacritic, whether it is written with double vowels (digraphs), a macron, or a separate length mark. That is, vowel length is typically ignored, except when two words differ only in the length of a vowel, in which case the word with the short vowel usually comes first.

---

[5]This is not to say that you can't change the analysis or orthography later, but most of the decisions you make early on will not change. Once the basic decisions are made, keyboarding is much easier, and if the data is keyboarded consistently from the beginning in accordance with just one analysis and orthography, it is much easier to change later.

(5) Length written as   Length written   Length written with
     double vowel   with macron   separate length mark

     bar   *bar*   *bar*
     bas   *bas*   *bas*
     baas   *bās*   *ba·s*
     bat   *bat*   *bat*
     baav   *bāv*   *ba·v*
     baw   *baw*   *baw*

Finally, certain characters may need to be ignored completely. For example, if you include hyphens in derived words to show where the morpheme breaks are, you probably want to have hyphens ignored completely for the sake of alphabetization.

(6) *compass*
     coop
     co-operate
     cop

Besides the main file that is alphabetized by the language, it may be useful to have a reversed index that is alphabetized by the definitions or glosses, so it is easier to find a word when you know only its meaning. This is especially helpful in a published dictionary and can be constructed very easily by most computerized filing systems.

27.6. Storage and protection

On the field, be sure to store your grammar and lexical files where they are safe, where they can't be damaged by rain, mildew, or rats! You have to be alert to risks and protect against them.

Larger sheets of paper are best kept in file folders, or better yet, in loose-leaf binders, so they don't get scattered inadvertently by the wind (or kids or chickens). For smaller slips, a shoebox or other cardboard container is not good enough. Wood or metal file boxes provide good protection from rodents and to a limited extent from fire and rain, but not from mold or insects. Large plastic food storage boxes protect from insects and moisture, but not from rodents or fire. To protect from mold in humid environments you may have to have a closet or box with a small constantly burning light bulb inside or make liberal use of desiccant packets like those packed with cameras and film.

Since there is no foolproof protection against all hazards, it is important to keep more than one copy of all important work. For manual systems, this can be done easily with photocopying machines (available in most countries). The extra copies should be stored in different locations, perhaps even in different cities or countries, in case a quick evacuation is necessary from your place of work. (This is necessary more often than we would like, and sometimes occurs quite unexpectedly.) One fieldworker in Vietnam in the 1960s used to make five copies of everything, four of which were mailed to various locations outside the war zone.

Computer files are more delicate than paper. They are subject to all the hazards of manual systems, plus damage from magnetic fields (from motors, telephones, speakers, magnets, etc.), mechanical failures, and accidental or malicious erasure (especially viruses). If you use a computer, sooner or later you will lose data. The only reasonable protection is to make spare copies of all important files on a regular basis. I recommend you copy changed files to some separate medium (floppy disk, backup tape, etc.) *every day*. A backup tape drive (or other high-capacity removable medium) pays for itself quickly in the time you save recovering a lost file.

Files that are archived on magnetic media like floppy disks or tape should be recopied every five years, since the magnetic image tends to fade with time. (Archiving on CD-ROM is more permanent.) Finally, you may want to make paper copies periodically too; if bad comes to worst, the material can be retyped or scanned in.

27.7. Keeping the job to a manageable size

The lexicon of a language can be quite large, even without all the technical terminology that swells dictionaries to huge proportions in languages like English and French. As a practical matter when preparing a dictionary for publication, you have to decide when to stop adding words to it or it may take forty years to get it finished. Setting an arbitrary limit on the number of entries, like 1,000 or 1,500, may work as long as you have some way of insuring that you've included all the most basic vocabulary in the language. A more ambitious goal is to stop when the dictionary is large enough that 90% of the words in the example sentences (or a comparable corpus of text material) are included in the dictionary; this often results in dictionaries with 6,000 or more entries which can take several years to polish for publication. You can also limit the size of the task by limiting the amount of information in each entry—omitting example sentences, including only the most basic senses of each word, etc.

27.8. Review of key terms

LEXICOLOGY is the study of the LEXICON of a language, which is the collection of idiosyncratic information about the language's words and idiomatic expressions. To study the lexicon, linguists compile a LEXICAL FILE, typically with one entry for each word (i.e., stem) in the language. When a lexical file is kept on a computer, it is important to identify the different parts of the entry with TAGS that identify the word itself, the gloss, the part of speech, etc. Often the form of the word is given in the entry not only as a bare stem, but also in some standard minimally-inflected form, called its CITATION FORM.

27.9. For further reading

If you are interested in reading more about lexicology, try starting with Bartholomew and Schoenhals 1983 or the works they describe in their "Annotated Bibliography of Reference Materials," such as Al-Kasimi 1977, Hartmann 1983, and Zgusta 1971.

If you ever need a good manual filing system for lexical research, see Healey (1975:427–51) and Samarin (1967:151–74) for many practical suggestions.[6]

For computerized filing systems, I currently recommend Shoebox (for Windows, Macintosh, and DOS; the DOS version 2.0 is described in Davis and Wimbish 1993; the Windows and Macintosh versions 3.0 are available online from http://www.sil.org) and HyperCard (Macintosh). Another alternative is LinguaLinks (available from LinguaLinks, Summer Institute of Linguistics, 7500 W. Camp Wisdom, Dallas TX 75236; description and ordering information also available at http://www.sil.org). LinguaLinks also provides tools for interlinear text production and a variety of useful reference materials.

The tagging system illustrated earlier is based on one proposed by Coward and Grimes (1995) for use with Shoebox; files tagged with this system can also be imported into LinguaLinks. This type of tagging is great for preparing and manipulating the data, but for long-term archiving, it should probably be converted into the tagging system proposed by the Text Encoding Initiative (Sperberg-McQueen and Burnard 1994:321–68). The Text Encoding Initiative (TEI) is a widely-available standard developed by a consortium of scholars in the humanities, has considerable software support (with more being developed each year), provides a richer set of tags, can represent the full hierarchical structure of an entry in a dictionary, and is part of a much broader system designed to tag a wide range of documents, not just dictionaries.

---

[6]For example, I used manual files for my dialect survey of Mexican Sign Language (J. Albert Bickford 1991), both so I could travel light and because there was no practical way to transcribe and file sign language data on the computer at that time.

Linguists who are studying a set of related languages often require large lexical databases showing sets of related words from different languages. For some general considerations in designing computerized databases for this purpose, see Anita Bickford 1989 and Johnson 1985.

Non-Roman orthographies still pose a significant challenge to computerized data processing. For an analysis of the complexities involved, see Simons 1989. Macintosh computers have the best support for such orthographies, since the Macintosh has ways of making the same orthography available with practically any Macintosh program. Shoebox version 2.0 provides limited support for non-Roman orthographies on MS-DOS computers; version 3.0 adds greater support on Windows/Macintosh.

Pullum and Ladusaw 1996 and Esling 1990 use an alphabetical order for phonetic symbols which is a good starting point for alphabetizing technical orthographies and which may also be useful for practical orthographies.

References

Aissen, Judith L. 1987. Tzotzil clause structure. Dordrecht: D. Reidel.

Akmajian, Adrian and Frank Heny. 1975. An introduction to the principles of transformational syntax. Cambridge: MIT Press.

————, Richard A. Demers, Ann K. Farmer, and Robert M. Harnish. 1990. Linguistics: An introduction to language and communication. Rev. 3rd ed. Cambridge: MIT Press.

Al-Kasimi, Ali M. 1977. Linguistics and bilingual dictionaries. Leiden: E. J. Brill.

Allen, Barbara J. and Donald G. Frantz. 1983. Advancements and verb agreement in Southern Tiwa. In Perlmutter 1983, 303–14.

Anderson, Stephen R. 1982. Where's morphology? Linguistic Inquiry 13:571–612.

————. 1985a. Inflectional morphology. In Shopen 1985, 3:150–201.

————. 1985b. Typological distinctions in word formation. In Shopen 1985, 3:3–56.

————. 1986. Disjunctive ordering in inflectional morphology. Natural Language and Linguistic Theory 4:1–31.

————. 1992. A-Morphous morphology. Cambridge Studies in Linguistics 62. Cambridge: Cambridge University Press.

———— and Edward L. Keenan. 1985. Deixis. In Shopen 1985, 3:259–308.

Andrews, Avery. 1985. The major functions of the noun phrase. In Shopen 1985, 1:62–154.

Aronoff, Mark. 1976. Word formation in generative grammar. Cambridge: MIT Press.

Baker, C. L. 1978. Introduction to Generative-Transformational Syntax. Englewood Cliffs, N.J.: Prentice-Hall.

Bartholomew, Doris A. and Louise C. Schoenhals. 1983. Bilingual dictionaries for indigenous languages. Mexico: Instituto Lingüístico de Verano.

Bickford, Anita C. 1989. Data base design for research in comparative Zapotec. M.A. thesis. University of North Dakota, Grand Forks.

Bickford, J. Albert. 1985. Spanish clitic doubling and levels of grammatical relations. Lingua 65:189–211.

————. 1987. Universal constraints on relationally complex clauses. Ph.D. dissertation. University of California, San Diego.

————. 1991. Lexical variation in Mexican Sign Language. Sign Language Studies 72.

Blake, Barry J. 1969. The Kalkatungu language: A brief description. Canberra: Australian Institute of Aboriginal Studies.

————. 1990. Relational grammar. New York: Routledge.

Blansitt, Edward L. 1986. SOVD languages. In Elson 1986, 29–38.

Borsley, Robert D. 1991. Syntactic theory: A unified approach. London: Edward Arnold.

Bresnan, Joan, ed. 1982. The mental representation of grammatical relations. Cambridge: MIT Press.

Bybee, Joan L. 1985. Morphology: A study of the relation between meaning and form. Amsterdam: John Benjamins.

Chomsky, Noam. 1965. Aspects of the theory of syntax. Cambridge: MIT Press.

———. 1970. Remarks on nominalization. In Roderick A. Jacobs and Peter S. Rosenbaum (eds.),
    Readings in English transformational grammar, 184–221. Waltham, Mass.: Ginn and Co.
    Reprinted in Noam Chomsky, 1972, Studies on semantics in generative grammar, 11–61. The
    Hague: Mouton. Also reprinted in Donna Jo Napoli and Emily Norwood Rando, 1979, Syntactic
    argumentation, 138–76. Washington, D.C.: Georgetown University Press.

———. 1977. Essays on form and interpretation. New York: North-Holland.

———. 1981. Lectures on government and binding: The Pisa lectures. Dordrecht: Foris Publications.

——— and Morris Halle. 1991. The sound pattern of English. Cambridge: MIT Press. (republication
    of the original 1968 edition)

Chung, Sandra. 1983. An object-creating rule in Bahasa Indonesia. In Perlmutter 1983, 219–71.
    Also Linguistic Inquiry 7:41–87 (1976).

——— and Alan Timberlake. 1985. Tense, aspect, and mood. In Shopen 1985, 3:202–58.

Clark, Eve V. 1978. Locationals: Existential, locative, and possessive constructions. In Greenberg
    1978, (Syntax) 4:85–126.

Comrie, Bernard. 1976. Aspect. Cambridge: Cambridge University Press.

———. 1981. Language universals and linguistic typology. Chicago: University of Chicago Press.

———. 1985a. Causative verb formation and other verb-deriving morphology. In Shopen 1985,
    3:309–48.

———. 1985b. Tense. Cambridge: Cambridge University Press.

———. 1989. Language universals and linguistic typology, 2nd ed. Oxford: Basil Blackwell.

——— and Norval Smith. 1977. Lingua descriptive studies: Questionnaire. Lingua 42:1–72.

——— and Sandra A. Thompson. 1985. Lexical nominalization. In Shopen 1985, 3:349–98.

Cook, Walter A. 1998. Case grammar applied. Summer Institute of Linguistics and the University of
    Texas at Arlington Publications in Linguistics 127. Dallas.

Corbett, Greville G. and Alfred D. Mtenje. 1987. Gender agreement in Chichewa. Studies in African
    Linguistics 18:1–38.

Coward, David F. and Charles E. Grimes. 1995. Making dictionaries: A guide to lexicography and
    the Multi-Dictionary Formatter (Version 1.0). Waxhaw, N.C.: Summer Institute of Linguistics.

Crofts, Marjorie. 1973. Gramática munduruku. Brazil: Summer Institute of Linguistics.

Crystal, David. 1991. A dictionary of linguistics and phonetics. 3rd ed. Oxford: Basil Blackwell.

Daly, John P. 1973. A generative syntax of Peñoles Mixtec. Summer Institute of Linguistics
    Publications in Linguistics and Related Fields 42. Norman: Summer Institute of Linguistics and
    the University of Oklahoma.

———. 1977. A problem in tone analysis. In William R. Merrifield (ed.), Studies in Otomanguean
    phonology, 3–20. Summer Institute of Linguistics and the University of Texas at Arlington
    Publications in Linguistics 54. Dallas.

———, Larry Lyman, and Mary Rhodes. 1981. A course in basic grammatical analysis. Workpapers
    of the Summer Institute of Linguistics, University of North Dakota Session 25 Supplement.
    Grand Forks, North Dakota.

Davis, Daniel W. and John S. Wimbish. 1993. The linguist's Shoebox. Version 2.0. Waxhaw, N.C.:
    Summer Institute of Linguistics.

De Guzman, V. P. 1986. Indirect objects in SiSwati. Second Biennial Conference on Relational
    Grammar and Grammatical Relations, Ohio State University, Columbus, May 2–4, 1986.

Derbyshire, Desmond C. and Geoffrey K. Pullum. 1981. Object-initial languages. IJAL 47:192–214.

Dryer, Matthew S. 1988. Object-verb order and adjective-noun order: Dispelling a myth. Lingua
    74:185–217.

———. 1989. Large linguistic areas and linguistic sampling. Studies in Language 13:257–99.

Elson, Benjamin F. 1960. Gramática del Popoluca de la Sierra. Xalapa, Mexico: Universidad
    Veracruzana.

———, ed. 1986. Language in global perspective. Dallas: Summer Institute of Linguistics.

——— and Velma Pickett. 1983. Beginning morphology and syntax. Dallas: Summer Institute of
    Linguistics.

Esling, John. 1990. Computer coding of the IPA: Supplementary report. Journal of the IPA 20:1.

Filbeck, David. 1972. The passive, an unpleasant experience. The Bible Translator 23:331–36.

Fischer, Susan D. and Patricia Siple. 1990. Linguistics: Theoretical issues in sign language research 1. Chicago: University of Chicago Press.

Fishman, Joshua A. 1977. Advances in the creation and revision of writing systems. The Hague: Mouton.

Foley, William A. and Robert D. van Valin. 1985. Information packaging in the clause. In Shopen 1985, 1:282–364.

Fromkin, Victoria and Robert Rodman. 1998. An introduction to language. 6th ed. Fort Worth: Harcourt Brace Jovanovich College Publishers.

Gazdar, Gerald, Ewan Klein, Geoffrey Pullum, and Ivan Sag. 1985. Generalized phrase structure grammar. Cambridge: Harvard University.

Gerdts, Donna B. 1990. Revaluation and inheritance in Korean causative union. In Postal and Joseph 1990, 203–46.

Gibson, Jeanne. 1980. Clause union in Chamorro and in universal grammar. Ph.D. dissertation. University of California, San Diego.

——— and Eduardo Raposo. 1986. Clause union, the stratal uniqueness law, and the chômeur relation. Natural Language and Linguistic Theory 4:295–332.

Gleason, Henry Allan. 1955. Workbook in descriptive linguistics. New York: Holt, Rinehart, and Winston.

Gonzalez, Nora Martinez. 1985. Object and raising in Spanish. Ph.D. dissertation. University of California, San Diego.

Greenberg, Joseph H. 1966. Some universals of grammar with particular reference to the order of meaningful elements. In Joseph H. Greenberg (ed.), Universals of language, 2nd ed., 73–113. Cambridge: MIT Press.

———, ed. 1978. Universals of human language, 4 volumes. Stanford: Stanford University.

Gregersen, Edgar A. 1967. Prefix and pronoun in Bantu. Indiana University Publications in Anthropology and Linguistics, Memoir 21 of the International Journal of American Linguistics (supplement to IJAL 33). Baltimore: Linguistic Society of America and American Anthropological Association.

Grimes, Barbara F., ed. 1996. Ethnologue: Languages of the world. 13th ed. Dallas: Summer Institute of Linguistics. [Also available online at http//www.sil.org.]

Grimes, Joseph. 1967. Positional analysis. Language 43:437–44.

———. 1983. Affix positions and cooccurrences: The Paradigm program. Summer Institute of Linguistics and the University of Texas at Arlington Publications in Linguistics 69. Dallas.

Grimshaw, Jane. 1982. On the lexical representation of Romance reflexive clitics. In Bresnan 1982, 87–148.

Gunn, Robert D. 1975. La oración sencilla en Bokotá. In S. H. Levinsohn (ed.), Observaciones preliminares sobre los sistemas gramaticales de las lenguas chibchas, Lenguas de Panamá, 2:83–135. Panama: Instituto Lingüístico de Verano e Instituto Nacional de Cultura.

Haegeman, Liliane. 1991. Introduction to Government and Binding Theory. Oxford: Basil Blackwell.

Haiman, John. 1980. Hua: A Papuan language of the eastern highlands of New Guinea. Studies in Language Companion Series 5. Amsterdam: John Benjamins.

Hammond, Michael and Michael Noonan, eds. 1988. Theoretical morphology: Approaches in modern linguistics. New York: Academic Press.

Harries-Delisle, Helga. 1978. Contrastive emphasis and cleft sentences. In Greenberg 1978, (Syntax) 4:419–86.

Hartmann, R. R. K., ed. 1983. Lexicography: Principles and practice. New York: Academic Press.

Healey, Alan, ed. 1975. Language learner's field guide. Ukarumpa, Papua New Guinea: Summer Institute of Linguistics.

Hines, Lilian M., Edward J. Welch, and Joseph W. Hopkinson. 1966. Our Latin heritage, book 2. New York: Harcourt, Brace, and World.

Hockett, Charles F. 1954. Two models of grammatical description. Word 10:210–31. Reprinted in: Martin Joos, ed., 1957, Readings in Linguistics, 386–99. Washington, D.C.: American Council of Learned Societies.

Hoogshagen, Searle and Doris Bartholomew. 1993. Gramática del Mixe de Coatlán. In Searle
    Hoogshagen and Hilda Hoogshagen (comp.), Diccionario Mixe de Coatlán, 335–410. Serie de
    Vocabularios y Diccionarios Indígenas "Mariano Silva y Aceves" 32. Mexico: Instituto
    Lingüístico de Verano.

Jackendoff, Ray. 1975. Morphological and semantic regularities in the lexicon. Language 51:639–
    71.

Jensen, John T. 1990. Morphology: Word structure in generative grammar. Amsterdam: John
    Benjamins.

Johnson, Mark. 1985. Computer aids for comparative dictionaries. Linguistics 23:285–302.

Josephs, Lewis S. 1975. Palauan reference grammar. Honolulu: University of Hawaii.

Kautzsch, E. and A. E. Cowley. 1910. Gesenius' Hebrew grammar. Second English edition. Oxford:
    Clarendon.

Keenan, Edward L. 1985a. Passive in the world's languages. In Shopen 1985, 1:243–81.

———. 1985b. Relative clauses. In Shopen 1985, 2:141–70.

——— and Bernard Comrie. 1977. Noun phrase accessibility and universal grammar. Linguistic
    Inquiry 8:63–101.

Kenstowicz, Michael and Charles Kisseberth. 1979. Generative phonology: Description and theory.
    New York: Academic Press.

Kimenyi, Alexandre. 1980. A relational grammar of Kinyarwanda. University of California
    Publications in Linguistics 91. Berkeley.

Klavens, Judith L. 1985. The independence of syntax and phonology in cliticization. Language
    61:95–120.

Klima, Edward S. and Ursula Bellugi. 1979. The signs of language. Cambridge: Harvard University.

Kornai, András and Geoffrey K. Pullum, 1990. The X-bar theory of phrase structure. Language
    66:24–50.

Krishnamurti, Bh. and J. P. L. Gwynn. 1985. A grammar of modern Telugu. Delhi: Oxford
    University.

Langacker, Ronald W. 1972. Fundamentals of linguistics analysis. New York: Harcourt, Brace,
    Jovanovich.

———. 1977. An overview of Uto-Aztecan grammar. Studies in Uto-Aztecan grammar 1. Summer
    Institute of Linguistics and the University of Texas at Arlington Publications in Linguistics 56.
    Dallas.

———. 1987. Theoretical prerequisites: Foundations of cognitive grammar 1. Stanford: Stanford
    University.

———. 1988. A usage-based model. In Brygida Rudzka-Ostyn (ed.), Topics in cognitive linguistics,
    127–161. Current Issues in Linguistic Theory 50. Amsterdam: John Benjamins.

———. 1990. Concept, image, and symbol: The cognitive basis of grammar. Berlin: Mouton de
    Gruyter.

Langendoen, D. Terence and Paul M. Postal. 1984. The vastness of natural languages. Oxford: Basil
    Blackwell.

Lazdina, T. 1966. Latvian. Teach Yourself Books. London: English Universities Press.

Lyons, John. 1967. A note on possessive, existential and locative sentences. Foundations of
    Language 3:390–96.

———. 1968. Introduction to theoretical linguistics. London: Cambridge University.

Marácz, László and Pieter Muysken, eds. 1989. Configurationality: The typology of asymmetries.
    Dordrecht: Foris Publications.

Matthews, Peter H. 1972a. Huave verb morphology: Some comments from a non-tagmemic
    viewpoint. International Journal of American Linguistics 38:96–118.

———. 1972b. Inflectional morphology. Cambridge: Cambridge University Press.

———. 1974. Morphology: An introduction to the theory of word-structure. Cambridge: Cambridge
    University Press.

McCarthy, John J. 1981. A prosodic theory of nonconcatenative morphology. Linguistic Inquiry
    12:373–418.

Merrifield, William R., Constance M. Naish, Calvin R. Rensch, and Gillian Story. 1987. Laboratory
    manual for morphology and syntax. Dallas: Summer Institute of Linguistics.

Miller, Carolyn P. 1964. The substantive phrase in Brôu. Mon-Khmer Studies 1:63–80.

Mohanan, K. P. 1982. Grammatical relations and clause structure in Malayalam. In Bresnan 1982, 504–89.

Nevis, Joel A. 1986. Finnish particle clitics and general clitic theory. Ohio State University Working Papers in Linguistics 33. Columbus.

Newmeyer, Frederick J. 1980. Linguistic theory in America: The first quarter-century of transformational generative grammar. New York: Academic Press.

———. 1986. Linguistic theory in America. 2nd ed. Orlando: Academic Press.

Nida, Eugene A. 1949. Morphology: The descriptive analysis of words. 2nd ed. Ann Arbor: University of Michigan.

Nunberg, Geoffrey, Ivan A. Sag, and Thomas Wasow. 1994. Idioms. Language 70:491–538.

Ohio State University Department of Linguistics. 1994. Language files: Materials for an introduction to language. 6th ed. Columbus: Ohio State University.

Padden, Carol and Brigitte Bendixen. 1980. An introduction to American Sign Language. University of California, San Diego. ms.

Palmer, F. R. 1986. Mood and modality. Cambridge: Cambridge University Press.

Payne, Thomas E. 1997. Describing morphosyntax: A guide for field linguists. Cambridge: Cambridge University Press.

Perlmutter, David M., ed. 1983. Studies in relational grammar 1. Chicago: University of Chicago Press.

——— and Paul M. Postal. 1983. Toward a universal characterization of passivization. In Perlmutter 1983, 3–29.

——— and ———. 1984. Impersonal passives and some relational laws. In Perlmutter and Rosen 1984.

——— and Carol G. Rosen, eds. 1984. Studies in relational grammar 2. Chicago: University of Chicago Press.

——— and Scott Soames. 1979. Syntactic argumentation and the structure of English. Berkeley: University of California.

Pollard, Carl and Ivan A. Sag. 1987. Fundamentals: Information-based syntax and semantics 1. Stanford: Center for the Study of Language and Information.

——— and ———. 1994. Head-driven Phrase Structure Grammar. Stanford: Center for the Study of Language and Information and Chicago: University of Chicago Press.

Postal, Paul M. 1986. Studies of passive clauses. Albany: State University of New York.

——— and Brian D. Joseph. 1990. Studies in relational grammar 3. Chicago: University of Chicago Press.

Pullum, Geoffrey K. 1985. Assuming some version of X-bar theory. In William H. Eilfort, Paul D. Kroeber, and Karen L Peterson (eds.), CLS 21 (Part 1): Papers from the general session at the twenty-first regional meeting, 323–53. Chicago: Chicago Linguistic Society.

——— and William A. Ladusaw. 1996. Phonetic symbol guide. 2nd ed. Chicago: University of Chicago Press.

Radford, Andrew. 1981. Transformational syntax. Cambridge: Cambridge University Press.

———. 1988. Transformational grammar: A first course. Cambridge: Cambridge University Press.

———. 1997. Syntactic theory and the structure of English: A minimalist approach. Cambridge: Cambridge University Press.

Rapaport, Tova R. 1985. Copular constructions in Hebrew. In William H. Eilfort, Paul D. Kroeber, and Karen L Peterson (eds.), CLS 21 (Part 1): Papers from the general session at the twenty-first regional meeting, 354–70. Chicago: Chicago Linguistic Society.

Robles Uribe, Carlos. 1962. Manual del Tzeltal (Gramatica Tzeltal de Bachajon). Mexico: Universidad Iberoamericana.

Rosen, Sara Thomas. 1989. Two types of noun incorporation: A lexical analysis. Language 65:294–317.

Ross, John Robert. 1973. The penthouse principle and the order of constituents. In Claudia Corum, T. Cedric Smith-Stark, and Ann Weiser (eds.), You take the high node and I'll take the low node: Papers from the comparative syntax festival, The differences between main and subordinate clauses, 397–422. April 12, 1973. Chicago: Chicago Linguistic Society.

Sadock, Jerrold M. and Arnold M. Zwicky. 1985. Speech act distinctions in syntax. In Shopen 1985, 1:155–96.

Samarin, William J. 1967. Field linguistics: A guide to linguistic field work. New York: Holt, Rinehart, and Winston.

Scalise, Sergio. 1984. Generative morphology. Dordrecht: Foris Publications.

Schachter, Paul. 1985. Parts-of-speech systems. In Shopen 1985, 1:3–61.

———— and Fe T. Otanes. 1972. Tagalog reference grammar. Berkeley: University of California.

Sells, Peter. 1985. Lectures on contemporary syntactic theories: An introduction to Government-binding Theory, Generalized Phrase Structure Grammar, and Lexical-functional Grammar. Stanford: Center for the Study of Language and Information.

Shopen, Timothy, ed. 1985. Language typology and syntactic description. 3 volumes. Cambridge: Cambridge University Press.

Simon, Ethelyn, Irene Resnikoff, and Linda Motzkin. 1992. The first Hebrew primer: The adult beginner's path to Biblical Hebrew. 3d ed. Oakland, Calif.: EKS Publishing Co.

Simons, Gary F. 1989. The computational complexity of writing systems. In Ruth M. Brend and David G. Lockwood (eds.), The Fifteenth LACUS Forum 1988, 538–53. Lake Bluff, Ill.: Linguistic Association of Canada and the United States.

———— and Larry Versaw. 1988. How to use IT: A guide to interlinear text processing. Dallas: Summer Institute of Linguistics.

Slocum, Marianna C. and Florencia L. Gerdel. 1965. Vocabulario Tzeltal de Bachajon: Castellano-Tzeltal, Tzeltal-Castellano. Mexico: Institute Lingüístico de Verano.

Smalley, William A. and others. 1963. Orthography studies: Articles on new writing systems. London: United Bible Societies, and Amsterdam: North-Holland Publishing Company.

Spencer, Andrew. 1991. Morphological theory: An introduction to word structure in generative grammar. Oxford: Basil Blackwell.

Sperberg-McQueen, C. M. and Lou Burnard. 1994. Guidelines for electronic text encoding and interchange. Chicago: Text Encoding Initiative. Current versions also available online http://www.uic.edu/orgs/tei.

Steele, Susan. 1978. Word order variation: A typological study. In Greenberg 1978, (Syntax) 4:585–623.

Strunk, William and E. B. White. 1979. The elements of style. 3d ed. New York: Macmillan.

Trask, R. L. 1993. A dictionary of grammatical terms in linguistics. London: Routledge.

Turabian, Kate L. 1996. A manual for writers of term papers, theses, and dissertations. 6th ed., revised by John Grossman and Alice Bennett. Chicago: University of Chicago Press.

Ultan, Russell. 1978a. Some general characteristics of interrogative systems. In Greenberg 1978, (Syntax) 4:211–48.

————. 1978b. Toward a typology of substantival possession. In Greenberg 1978, (Syntax) 4:11–49.

Underhill, Robert. 1976. Turkish grammar. Cambridge: MIT Press.

University of Chicago. 1993. The Chicago manual of style. 14th ed. Chicago: University of Chicago Press.

Valentine, Randy. 1990. My Ojibwe dialect survey. Notes on Computing 9(8):9–12. Waxhaw, N.C.: Summer Institute of Linguistics.

van den Berg, René. 1989. A grammar of the Muna language. Dordrecht: Foris Publications.

Van Haitsma, Julia Dieterman and Willard Van Haitsma. 1976. A hierarchical sketch of Mixe as spoken in San José El Paraíso. Summer Institute of Linguistics Publications in Linguistics and Related Fields 44. Norman: Summer Institute of Linguistics and the University of Oklahoma.

Venezky, Richard L. 1970. Principles for the design of practical writing systems. Anthropological Linguistics 12:256–70.

Vitale, Anthony J. 1981. Swahili syntax. Dordrecht: Foris Publications.

Walter, Stephen Leslie. 1980. Application of a cognitive model of linguistic structure to the analysis of selected problems in Tzeltal (Mayan) grammar. Ph.D. dissertation. University of Texas at Arlington.

Wasow, Thomas. 1985. Postscript. In Sells 1985, 193–205.

Waterhouse, Viola Grace. 1962. The grammatical structure of Oaxaca Chontal. Indiana University Research Center in Anthropology, Folklore, and Linguistics Memoir 19. Bloomington: Indiana University. Supplement to IJAL 28:2.

Waters, Richard C. 1979. Topicalization and Passive in Palauan. ms.

Weber, David J. 1993. Ortografía: Lecciones del quechua. Yarinacocha: Instituto Lingüístico de Verano.

Weber, David J. To appear. The dynamics of Quechua orthography. Los Angeles: Latin America Center, University of California.

Williams, Cindy S. 1993. A grammar sketch of Dǝmǝna. M.A. thesis. University of North Dakota, Grand Forks.

Williams, Larry P. 1995. Noun classification or spatial categorization: Damana orientation verbs. M.A. thesis. University of North Dakota, Grand Forks.

Wilson, Peter M. 1985. Simplified Swahili. Harlow, Essex, U. K.: Longman Group Ltd.

Wimbish, John S. 1990. Shoebox: A data management program for the field linguist. Dallas: Summer Institute of Linguistics and Ambon, Indonesia: Pattimura University.

Wise, Mary Ruth. 1971. Identification of participants in discourse: A study of aspects of form and meaning in Nomatsiguenga. Summer Institute of Linguistics Publications in Linguistics and Related Fields 28. Norman: Summer Institute of Linguistics and the University of Oklahoma.

Wolgemuth, Carl. 1981. Gramática Nahuatl de Mecayapan. Mexico: Instituto Lingüístico de Verano.

Zgusta, Ladislav. 1971. Manual of lexicography. The Hague: Mouton.

Zwicky, Arnold M. 1985. Clitics and particles. Language 61:283–305.

———. 1987. Suppressing the Zs. Journal of Linguistics 23:133–48.

——— and Geoffrey K. Pullum. 1983. Cliticization vs. inflection: English n't. Language 59:502–13.

Index

In this index, page numbers in italics indicate primary references to an item, such as when a concept is first explained or where there is an extended discussion of it.

389

F

M

main characters in a clause 93
main clause *10*
major category *68*, 109, 226
Malagasy 341
Malayalam 187
Mandarin Chinese 186
manner *94*
marker
    at beginning of relative clause 338
    ergative 282
    on locative oblique 98
    phrase (*see* tree diagram)
    plural 277
    subject/object marker, avoiding use
        of the terms 267
marking
    agreement (*see* agreement marking)
    case (*see* case marking)
    case/agreement, as grammatical tests
        294, 303, 304, 305
masculine *13, 21*
mass noun *8*
matrix clause *319, 323, 325, 358*
Matthews, Peter H. 118, 132, 136,
    149, 165, 179, 253, 290
maximal projection 84
meaning
    conventionalized 138
    lexical/grammatical 26, *40*
meaningful unit, minimal *19, 26*, 177,
    274
Mecayapan Nahuatl 21
Mesoamerica 373
Mesoamerican languages 98
Mexican Sign Language (MSL/LSM)
    141, 146, 149, 378
minimal
    meaningful unit *19, 25, 26*, 177,
        274
    utterance (word) 274
Minimalist program 60
minor category *68, 69*, 109
Mixe, Coatlán and Guichicovi 301
Mixtec
    Atatlahuca 170
    Peñoles 279, 280, 286, 322, 324,
        329
modifier agreement 266
modify 38
Mohawk 302
mood
    in syntax 236
    types of *15*, 28, *235*
morpheme *19–23*, 28, 274
    allomorphic variation *151–65*
    bound/free 29
    citing in running text 353
    ease of finding morpheme cuts 31
    in position classes 32–33
    number of morphemes per word 31
    problems with traditional definition
        25–27, 177, 179
    process *169*, 170, 171, 174, 175,
        177, 229
    subtractive *170*
    zero *27*
morphology *3*, 28
    A-morphous ix, 117, 121, 133, 144

basic questions when analyzing 30
derivation vs. inflection 113–16,
    135, *138–42*, 147, 149
derivational (*see* derivational
    morphology)
inflectional (*see* inflectional
    morphology)
irregular (*see* irregular inflection)
item and arrangement 117, 132
linear/nonlinear *167–79*
verbal 27
word and paradigm 117, 132
morphophonemics 151, *153–55*, 160,
    164, 281, 301
    analysis 160
mother (node) *41*
Move-α transformation (move
    anything anywhere) 218
movement (departure from basic word
    order) 206
movement (transformational) rules
    105, 203–5, 206, 208, 210, 211,
    214, 218, 225, 233, 344
    WH (*see* WH movement)
MSL (Mexican Sign Language) 141,
    146, 149, 378
multiple senses of lexical items 84,
    373
Muna 185, 188
Munduruku 90
mutation *169*, 171, 174, 175, 177
mutually exclusive *32*, 117
mutually substitutable *38*, 40, *54*, 62,
    75

N

N. *See* noun
Nahuatl, Mecayapan (Isthmus) 21
native speaker intuitions, reliability of
    336
naturalness *58*, 77, 285, 286
NC. *See* nonactive complement
Neg (negator) 99
negative command 236
neuter *13, 21*
new topic *213*
node, types of *41*
Nomatsiguenga 298
nominal complement *184, 187*, 192,
    195, 198, 212, 271
nominal morphology 133
nominalization 149, 178
nominative case *13, 253*
nominative-accusative pattern of
    case/agreement *269*
nonactive complement ix, *183–200*
    action vs. state *185*
    contrasted with direct object 184
    types of 184
nonactive verb *185*
nonconcatenative morphology. *See*
    nonlinear affixation
nonfinite verb/clause *324–25*
nonlinear affixation 117, *167–79*, 279.
    See also affix
nonovert. *See* silent (zero) elements
nonovert copula. *See* copula: lack of
    overt
nonpast tense *27*

nonrestrictive relative clause *331–33*
non-Roman orthographies 379
nonterminal node *41*
noun (N) *8*
    common/proper 8, 9, *53*
    count/mass 8
    having complements 320
    obligatory possession 29
    relational *98*
noun incorporation 277, *302*
noun phrase (NP) *11, 38*, 58, 61–66
    D as head of 68
    relative clause (*see* relative clause)
noun phrase accessibility hierarchy
    95, *340*
NP. *See* noun phrase
null-subject language *87*
number *13, 21*
    agreement in 262
numeral *9*

O

O (gap in relative clause) 342
Oaxaca Chontal 168
Obj2. *See* second object
object agreement. *See* agreement
    marking: with direct object
object incorporation 300, 302
object marker, avoiding use of the
    term 267
Object Shift transformation, in Palauan
    359
object, direct (DO) *11, 43*
    accessibility to relativization 341
    advancement to DO from oblique
        97, 300
    advancement to DO in dative shift
        82, 299–300
    advancement to subject in passive
        295, 298
    agreement 259, 261, 359
    as PP 95
    basic word order 106
    characteristics of 82
    contrasted with nonactive
        complement 184
    coreferential with subject 300
    defined in terms of dominance 55
    importance in Transformational
        Grammar 109
    incorporation 300, 302
    lack of overt 88, 215, 302
    marking strategies 90–91
    position with respect to obliques
        104
    prototypical semantic roles 81, 293
object, indirect (IO) *12, 76*
    accessibility to relativization 341
    advancement to direct object in
        dative shift 299–300
    advancement to IO from benefactive
        97, 300
    as PP 95
    basic word order 106
    characteristics of 82
    contrasted with benefactive oblique
        104
    marking strategies 90–91
    position with respect to obliques
        104